Challenges for the Indian Left

Edited by
Murzban Jal

Challenges for the Indian Left
Edited by Murzban Jal

ISBN 978-93-5002-477-5

First Published 2017
Reprinted 2018

Published by
AAKAR BOOKS
28 E Pocket IV, Mayur Vihar Phase I
Delhi 110 091 India
Email: aakarbooks@gmail.com

Laserset at
Arpit Printographers, Delhi 110 092

Printed at
Mudrak, 30A Patparganj, Delhi 110 091

Challenges for the Indian Left

Contents

Acknowledgments

I would like to thank everyone at the Indian Institute of Education, Pune—the legendary socialist humanist institute founded by the bohemian encyclopedic thinker J.P. Naik—who have been inspiring me to work on this volume. There are many people who have been inspiring me to work tirelessly. I would also like to thank Javeed Alam a beautiful comrade who was the first person to inspire to work on this volume. His words ring out loudly: "The Politburo has locked the brains of the comrades and have taken the keys away!" It is hoped that the locks are broken and after the long night of the Stalinist counterrevolution, the rise of fascism and Zionism, followed by the evangelic triumph of global capitalism; the dawn of critical and revolutionary thinking once again shines on Left politics. I would also like to thank many more beautiful comrades: Prabhat Patnaik, Paresh Chattopadhyay, Bernard D'Mello, Prasenjit Bose, Jairus Banaji, Kunal Chattopadhyay and Arun Patnaik and many other people for their scholarly essays. The volume would be most certainly be stillborn if not for K.K. Saxena of Aakar Books, and his labour of love for publishing Left books of the best quality.

Introduction:
In the Name of Marx

Murzban Jal

What avails lamentation in the face of historical necessity?

Karl Marx

When we are victorious on a world scale I think we shall use gold for the purpose of building lavatories in the streets of some of some of the largest cities of the world. This would be the most "just" and most educational way of utilising gold for the benefit of generations.

V.I. Lenin

In the USSR, violence and deception are official, and humanity is in daily life. In the democracies, on the other hand, the principles are humane, but deception and violence are found in practice. Beyond that, propaganda has a field day.

Maurice Merleau-Ponty

In short, what the sensitive liberals want is a decaffeinated revolution, a revolution which doesn't smell of a revolution. Francois Furet and others thus try to deprive the French Revolution of its status as the founding event of modern democracy, relegating it to a historical anomaly: there was a historical necessity to assert the modern principles of personal freedom, etc., but, as the English example demonstrates, the same could have been much more efficiently achieved in a more peaceful way. Radicals are, on the contrary, possessed by what Alain Badiou called the "passion of the Real": if you say A—equality, human rights and freedoms—you should not shirk from its consequences and gather the courage to say B—the terror needed to really defend and assert the A.

Slavoj Žižek

Prelude

From the above four quotes it is clear that there is a difference between Revolutionary Marxism and revisionism, between a Revolution with a Revolution and a Revolution without a Revolution. The decaffeinated revolution that Slavoj Žižek mentions is revolution, true, but a Revolution without a Revolution. One main reason for the crumbling of the Soviet Union is that it was built on the edifice of a decaffeinated revolution, a revolution that was perfected by Stalin, a perfection carried on from Khrushchev to Gorbachev.

Unfortunately despite tomes written on the Russian Revolution from John Reed's *Ten Days that Shook the World* to Isaac Deutscher's Trotsky trilogy and the biography of Stalin, Simone Pirani's *The Russian Revolution in Retreat: 1920-24. Soviet Workers and the New Communist Elite* and Alexander Rabinowitch's 1976 classic *The Bolsheviks Come to Power: The Revolution of 1917 in Petrograd* followed in 2007 by *The Bolsheviks in Power: The First Year of Soviet Rule in Petrograd*, the path taken by the 1917 Revolution from insurrection to collapse was not taken seriously from the epistemic vantage point that differentiates the two types of revolutions that I just mentioned.

If world history, as it seems, did not take this distinction between the two types of revolutions, in India it was only the ideology of the decaffeinated revolution that had gripped the minds of the party elites. And when in the late 1960s from pressure of the revolutionary cadre, the spark that was to start a prairie fire was ignited; it was once again the decaffeinated revolution that came on the scene of Indian history. For one, the courage to seize power was lacking by the party elites in the history of the communist movement in India. There has been from its inception the mortal fear of these party elites of a real revolution, or should one say in the language of Jacques Lacan and Slavoj Žižek the *Real Revolution* or the *Real of the Revolution*. In a way Žižek is correct when he says the following:

> Radicals are, on the contrary, possessed by what Alain Badiou called the "passion of the Real": if you say A—equality, human rights and freedoms—you should not shirk from its consequences

> and gather the courage to say B—the terror needed to really defend and assert the A.[1]

Unfortunately this courage to defend the revolution was always lacking by the Indian party elites. But then the courage to start the revolution has also been lacking. It was because of this lack of courage that propelled the Indian fascists to power in the 2014 National Elections. But it was not mere courage that the communist elites lacked. It was also a scientific understanding of Marxism which they lacked. It is thus to this scientific understanding that one turns attention to.

Asiatic Mode of Production and the Rethinking of the Indian Revolution

"The fundamental and most stable feature of Russian history", so Leon Trotsky says in his monumental *The History of the Russian Revolution*, "is the slow tempo of her development, with the economic backwardness, primitiveness of social forms and low level of culture resulting from it".[2] One could replace the words "Russian history" with "Indian history". The pictures of Russian and Indian histories would be uncannily alike. In India, however, on this very economic backwardness, rose the entire ideological superstructure whose ultimate goal, so we have been told, is Moksha. The formlessness of this cultural superstructure was a reflection of the formlessness of class relations. And behind this formlessness of class relations would stand the Asiatic mode of production and the Indian caste system.

In order to understand the formlessness of class relations within the Asiatic mode of production, it is necessary to look at this mode itself. For the time being I shall denote the Asiatic mode of production in the following simple points. It is important to understand that Indian liberal democracy and capitalism in India have grown from the edifice of the Asiatic mode of production. Not only have liberal democracy and capitalism emerged from the Asiatic mode of production, but also the decaffeinated revolution and fascism triumphant have roots in this mode of production.

In the context of the Indian mode of production—whether India is to be classified as capitalist ripe for the Communist

Revolution, or on the contrary whether India is semi-feudal, semi-colonial suited for the New Democratic Revolution or People's Democratic Revolution (the line held by the Indian Maoists, following Mao's idea of *Bloc of Four Social Classes* where the proletariat in alliance with the peasantry, middle class and the national bourgeoisie would lead the revolution)—it is necessary to have a short note on Marx's own ideas of class and class struggle. And since it is said that class struggle is the bearer of the Communist Revolution, it is important to understand what class struggle means in the Marxist repertoire. It is also important to understand what the character of class is in the Asiatic mode of production and why the formlessness of class and the domination of the caste system with its fetish for rank worship have led to the triumph of fascism in India. What is important to understand here is the nature of social formations in India and whether class relations are present in Indian history and what type of class relations are there, and when and how class relations have developed. Simply copying what Lenin and Mao said on class (the usual practice of the Indian comrades) will not do.

Remember that for Marx the single most important criteria for the understanding of class is that in the material production of life, people get into *relations* with one another and living as Marx says in "similar conditions", that "separate their mode of life, their interests and their culture from those of other classes, and put them in *hostile opposition* (my insertion, M.J.) to the latter".[3] It is then that "they form a class".[4] Living in isolation "without entering into manifold relations with one another" where "their mode of production isolates them from one another instead of bringing them into mutual intercourse"[5] does not lead to class formation. And if only "local interconnections" exist and "their interest begets no community, no national bond and no political organisation among them, they do not form a class".[6]

The question, then is, that would India dominated by caste (and its social organism of isolation and separation), be ripe for class struggle and the Communist Revolution? Or would the Communist Revolution in India be theorised from a perspective different from that already theorised? My argument is that the Asiatic mode of production offers another perspective on the nature of revolution in India, a revolution that cannot be predicated on the revolutions that took place in the 20th century.

It is with this noting of class and another perspective of revolution in India that I turn to the question of the Asiatic mode of production. I base my reading of the Asiatic mode of production on three grounds:

1. The state as sovereign. Here the state is understood as the sovereign and as the sovereign takes the form of what Marx calls the "absolute landlord".[7]
2. The caste mode of production, where the Caste Overlord is the sovereign. Here sovereignty lies with what Marx calls "village corporations" which are defined as "separate communities and republics" and realised as "idyllic republics" based on "slavery and the caste system".[8]
3. The emergence of feudo-capitalism with the advent of British colonialism.

It must be noted that the Asiatic mode of production, or should one say here the Indic-variation of the Asiatic mode, has all these three intrinsically woven both in its economic belly as well as etched in its ideological cranium. These three grounds stand even today. What I shall also say is that the faulty basis for analysing the mode of production—argued in the simple binary: "semi-feudalism or capitalism" (to borrow the repertoire of Alice Thorner[9])—lies in the inability to understand the Asiatic mode of production, especially the three grounds that I just outlined.

It is with the question of the state as sovereign and patron that controlled all land and labour activities that I begin the question of the Asiatic mode of production. This Asiatic state, or the Tributary State as Samir Amin calls it headed by a "despot", was involved in economic activity, albeit economic activity largely of an unproductive type in the capitalist sense of the term—*unproductive production*—where surplus was not reabsorbed in the production process (i.e. in the modern context:

in the circuit of capital).[10] This mode of production rendered "the expansion of production more or less impossible and reduced the direct produces to the physical minimum of means of subsistence".[11] What happened here is that restricted *productive consumption* took place, meaning that consumption of means of production by labour power and consumption of labour power by capital[12] was (and yet is) stunted. Here surplus produced was not absorbed in the circuit of capital. Instead it was unproductive consumption that took place where the parasitical classes consumed the surplus, stunted the production of surplus as well as repressed the emergence of the entrepreneurial bourgeoisie and the revolutionary proletariat. The formlessness of class relations is situated within this very context.

In the classical formulation of the Asiatic state, economic production was dependent on the state as sovereign. Surplus in the form of the political economy of the Asiatic mode took the form of tax-rent. The state as tax and rent collector was realised as an Oligarchic state under the guardianship of what Marx calls the "Oriental despot". In India this Oriental despot appears as the "Brahmanical Overlord". As patron it developed (and continuously develops to this day) a patron-client relation that is deeply institutionalised governing entire economic, political, ideological and cultural life-worlds. "Surplus labour", in this mode of production, to quote Marx, "belongs to the higher community (i.e. the Asiatic state, my insertion, M.J.), which exists ultimately as a person, and this surplus labour appears as tribute, etc....for the exaltation of the unity, partly of the real despots, partly of the imagined clan—being the god".[13]

The distinct feature of this Asiatic state is that besides it being a highly centralised state, is the tax-rent-receiving sovereign despot and as rent-receiving sovereign appears, as Marx says, as the "supreme lord".[14]

Next to this supreme lord stands the caste mode of production with the parasitical castes controlling the economic, social, cultural and political spaces. This is the second level of the Indian variant of the Asiatic mode of production. The labouring castes are seen as fragmented labour communities in opposition to the parasitical-exploiting castes. The state as

Brahmanical Overlord represses the subaltern castes and their life-worlds. Labour is seen as unclean as also the ideology of labour thus giving rise to the manufactured ideology of "spiritualism". This is the necessary part of the sedentary character of Indian history dominated by the caste system. Stagnancy and the ideology of stagnancy, along with the fetishism for hierarchical society based on status groupism and the ideology of rank society, dominate the Indian mode of production. The ideology of stagnancy and the dominance of the Brahmanical castes are expressed in the form of rituals and the suppression of rationality.

The post-colonial mode of production which I call "feudo-capitalism" or "Indian caste-capitalism" where generalised commodity production takes place, combined with the Oligarchic state, based on rank worship and the caste mode of production (albeit modernised in contemporary times). It is important to note that by "feudo-capitalism" one does not mean a European type of feudalism. Feudo-capitalism as a part of the Asiatic mode of production is not the same as R.S. Sharma's idea of "Indian feudalism". In feudo-capitalism, the bureaucracy of the modern nation state emerges as a caste group and thus as a political enclosed class dominating the subaltern classes in the forms of State Landlordism and State Monopoly Capitalism. The Managerial Corporate State that is now put in place after the triumph of the Indian fascists will be based on the edifice of the Oligarchic state.

These three points I shall reiterate as the leitmotiv of the Asiatic mode of production—or to be precise the Indic variation of the Asiatic mode. The scientific understanding of the labouring castes is seen within this new mode of production based essentially in the informal and unorganised sectors. These subaltern castes are also seen as the pool of surplus labour and parts of the surplus population. Whether this surplus population is also a part of what Marx calls the Industrial Reserve Army remains to be seen. But these subaltern labouring castes are most certainly like the "great refusal" (to borrow Herbert Marcuse's term), even like the existentialist "hellish other" (that Jean-Paul Sartre pointed out in his works).

To put it briefly and also to locate the subaltern castes within the ambit of the caste mode of production, I am recalling an earlier observation of mine:

> One will consequently have to look at the idea of the Asiatic mode of production from a perspective other than that of both Eurocentrism and the poststructuralist discourses influenced by Edward Said. The 'unchanging' character of pre-capitalist India that Marx talked of is to be seen in three perspectives: (1) that of the economic base where a form of sedentary type of culture arose based on a tributary mode of production, (2) where the Asiatic state because of its heavy investments in irrigation projects absorbed the surplus leaving little room for what Marx calls "productive consumption", thereby suppressing the emergence of a dynamic proto-bourgeois and the development of both cities and the sciences, thus leaving the caste-based agriculture economy and culture dominating the Indian life-world, and (3) the Brahmanical counterrevolution in the realm of ideology that synthesised the above two points in the realms of theology, rituals and ideology.[15]

What one needs to understand is that the Asiatic mode of production was not a mode that existed in some distant past. Instead one needs to see how capitalism grew from its edifice, while retaining the characteristics of the state as sovereign and Caste Overlordship. It is in this new perspective that we shall see the location of the modes of production debate, the relation between pre-capitalist social formations with capitalism, as also the relation between caste and class. It is also in this new perspective that we see how subaltern labouring caste groups become parts of surplus labour where the creation of "subsistence economy" and "informal sector" takes place within contemporary capital accumulation in India. By and large, almost all shades of the Indian Left have ignored this economic sector, just as they have ignored caste and the reproduction of caste in modern India.

Caste here is not understood merely as primitive division of labour, a view that was held by D.D. Kosambi'[16], but is something more complex", a complexity which continues to thrive in India. And it is this very overdetermined complexity that, by and large, the Indian Left missed out. The linking of caste with modern classes, thus the linking of caste with industrial capitalism and the global accumulation of capital remains the leitmotiv of understanding the nature of revolution in India.

Further the incorrect understanding of the Asiatic mode of production as a legacy of Eurocentric thinking, where an alleged superior Europe sought to theorise on a so-called inferior Asia, has led to disastrous effects. Yet it is important to point out that the Asiatic mode of production is indeed not only the most controversial topic in the social sciences, it is what Brendan O'Leary once called the "most controversial mode of production".[17] What needs to be done is to sort out this controversy. At the very beginning what I will claim is that it is imperative to understand that Marx's idea of the Asiatic mode of production has almost nothing to do with Eurocentric thinking, has nothing thus to do with the 13th century translation of Aristotle's *Politics*, nothing to do with the development of the so-called "science of politics" by Machiavelli. Thus it is imperative to understand that Marx's idea is not to be confused with either the Latin interpretations of Aristotle or with the works of Jean Bodin, Machiavelli and Montesquieu. Nor has one to confuse Marx's idea with that of Richard Jones' analysis of pre-capitalist Asia in his *Essay on the Distribution of Wealth*, though Marx did refer to Jones repeatedly. For Marx, the Asiatic mode of production is not a normative discourse. It is not like Karl Wittfogel's *Oriental Despotism* which drew a fictitious line of demarcation between apparent 'free' societies of the West and an alleged 'totalitarian' Eastern world. Instead the Asiatic mode of production is a specific and concrete mode of production, existing in its own right, following its own internal mechanism. It cannot be reduced to the same mechanisms of slave, feudal and capitalist societies of Western Europe as the Indian Left has wrongly being doing. As we shall see in the course of this introduction, there will be three different structures within the Asiatic mode of production: the centralised Oligarchic state, caste-stratified village communities and communities defying both the state and the caste system.

Remember that the idea that the Asiatic mode of production

is a product of the colonial mind is false where a supposed 'mystical and idealist East' stood in contrast to a 'rational and scientific West'. The Asiatic mode of production draws no "imaginary line" (to borrow Edward Said's term)[18]. It does not deal with "the romance, exotic locales, and mystery of 'the marvels of the East'".[19] If the poststructuralist Said was mistaken in his understanding of Marx, so is Irfan Habib mistaken. Because Habib—and remember that Habib is the finest Marxist historian on India—also puts (like Said, but without referring to Said's *Orientalism*) Marx as following Hegelian (thus European) "inherited generalisations"[20] on India, I am taking Habib as the epistemic point of departure to rethink the idea of the Asiatic mode of production as against Habib's observations on Marx.

It must be noted that Marx does not oppose "Oriental despotism" to British freedom, following the imperialist Macaulay, as Habib seems to imply.[21] Note Habib's observations:

> When Marx wrote in 1853 of Indian society before the British conquest, he seems to have taken as his starting point the descriptive elements in Hegel's interpretation of Indian civilisation. 'The Hindoos have no history', Hegel had said, 'no growth expanding into a veritable political condition.' The admitted diffusion of Indian culture had been 'a dumb, deedless expansion'. Thus, 'the people of India have achieved no foreign conquests, but have on every occasion been vanquished themselves.' It is essentially this judgment that is repeated by Marx in his well-known passage: 'Indian society has no history, at least no known history. What we call its history is but the history of the successive intruders who founded their empires on the passive basis of that unresisting and unchanging society.'[22]

Also according to Habib, Marx gave:

> ....identical descriptions of the village community for which he quotes *in extenso* from what was probably Hegel's authority as well as a passage from the celebrated Fifth Report of 1812.[23]

Habib's claim is that Hegel mentioning in his *Philosophy of History* of Caste Oligarchy as "the most degrading spiritual serfdom" and Marx's statement in his *British Rule in India* where

Hinduism "rendered murder itself a religious rite" were both aspects of Eurocentric imagination.[24] Habib continues: Marx was not "simply repeating Hegel".[25] Instead, according to Habib, "Marx had to begin from such assessments of Indian culture as happened to be the accepted one among the best bourgeois thinkers of his day."[26]

Habib seems to ignore Marx's multilinear theory of history. Subscribing to a great extent to the teleological-unilinear theory of history, the Asiatic mode of production is seen as a "lower position."[27] Habib's reading of Marx's 1859 'Preface' to *A Contribution to the Critique of Political Economy*, where the Asiatic mode of production is recognised, Marx is seen as appearing as "confident that the 'Asiatic' merited a separate place in the classification of the major 'modes of production' in human history."[28] But because of the teleological model of history that Habib seems to give consent to—i.e. history moving from 'low' to 'high'—typical of the 19th and 20th century evolution theory, the Asiatic mode of production is seen as a 'low' stage in human development.

There is without doubt no *absolute peculiarity* of the East. The East is no exotic or evil land of tales of either splendour or poverty. Nor is the East caught in an alleged 'low' mode of production. Instead, I will talk of "relative peculiarity"[29] based on a concrete analysis of modes of production, economic systems and social formations. Thus instead of the Orientalist thesis that a great abyss of the West that separates itself from the East, I shall mention in Trotsky's terminology as "combined and uneven development" of Europe and Asia.

Being careful about terminology is of great importance. A brief note on Marx's characterisation of the "Oriental despot" is thus necessary. Marx's idea of this "Oriental despot" is not anyway opposed to the free thinking liberal European. As we shall see, Oriental despotism—and here we are talking of the Indian variant of the Asiatic mode of production—is linked almost directly to the Indian caste system and the cunning hegemony of caste oligarchy. Hegel's "cunning of reason" can now be transcribed as the "cunning of the unreason of the Caste Oligarchs".

Consider this celebrated and much quoted passage from Marx where he talks of: "Idyllic village communities, inoffensive though they may appear, had always been the solid foundation of Oriental Despotism, that they had restrained the human mind within the smallest compass, making it the unresisting tool of superstition, enslaving it beneath traditional rules, depriving it of all grandeur and historical energies."[30] Marx also talks of the psychotic character of caste where what he calls "barbarian egotism" concentrates all its energies on "some miserable piece of land" while "quietly witnessing the ruin of empires, the perpetuation of unspeakable cruelties, the massacre of the population of large towns, with no other consideration bestowed upon them than on natural events...".[31] This caste mode of production or this form of the life-world of caste is "undignified, stagnatory, and vegetative".[32] It is realised as the "wild, aimless, unbounded forces of destruction" that "rendered murder itself a religious rite in Hindustan".[33]

And in the age of triumphant fascism where a large section of the Indian population is declared as traitors and terrorists who wage their imaginary and phantasmagorical bloody wars on the even more imagined poor Indian state and the even poorer holy land of India, but in contrast where cows are declared as first citizens; we find how revealing is Marx's 1853 statement where there is a *spectacle* of the fascist barbarians that exhibits human "degradation in the fact that humanity, the sovereign of nature, fell down on his knees in adoration of Hanuman the monkey, and Sabbala, the cow".[34] If in 1853 it was found that humanity was kneeling before monkeys and cows, after 2014 the Indian populace is made to kneel before the fascist barbarians.

Dialectical Reading of the Asiatic Mode of Production: The State and Communes

A further qualification of the Asiatic state is necessary so as not to confuse it with European feudalism. Consider Marx:

> Sovereignty here consists in the ownership of land concentrated on a national scale. But on the other hand, no private ownership

> of land exists, although there is both private and common possession and use of land.[35]

There is a parallel reading of Engels that we need to consider. The reading of Engels goes through a historical materialist reading. It ought not to be confused with a single-tiered reductionist understanding of this mode of production. As we shall see later, there will be a class of landlords (zamindars) developing as the third tier of Lordship, the first being the state, while the second tier will be Brahmanical Overlordship:

> The absence of landed property is indeed the key to the whole of the East. Therein lies its political and religious history. But how to explain the fact that Orientals never reached the stage of landed property, not even the feudal kind? This is, I think, largely due to the climate, combined with the nature of the land, more especially the great stretches of desert extending from the Sahara right across Arabia, Persia, India and Tartary to the highest of the Asiatic uplands. Here artificial irrigation is the first prerequisite for agriculture, and this is the responsibility either of the communes, the provinces or the central government. In the East, the government has always consisted of 3 departments only: Finance (pillage at home), War (pillage at home and abroad), and *travaux publics*, provision for reproduction. The British government in India has put a somewhat narrower interpretation on nos. 1 and 2 while completely neglecting no. 3, so that Indian agriculture is going to wrack and ruin. Free competition is proving an absolute fiasco there.[36]

The lack of property in land and the inability to create feudal landed property at least till the advent of British colonialism signifies two conflicting arguments. The first argument is that there were communes in Asia (alongside the state as despot and Brahmanical Overlordship), which opens the space of radical collectivity in non-Western societies based on a process of collectivisation and individuation within this collective. The second argument is that there had already developed social divisions based on caste and clans where there was lack of both collectivity and individuality with the dominance of caste, community and state over individuals and subaltern social groups. In the case of the dominance of the caste system, we get formlessness of class relations in Asia—what Marx calls in a different context: a "sack of potatoes"[37]—where a type of formlessness develops that has given rise to fascism. Individuality (not individualism, but individuality as critical subjectivity) here is also related to reason—reason that would be destroyed by the caste system. Marx's argument that the "positing of the individual as worker.....is itself a product of history" would take a different form in Asia [38]

Here it is important to ask: "Is capitalism a necessary stage in history and that communism could only come with the development of capitalism? Or would it be possible to skip the entire capitalist mode of production?" It is in this critique of the absolute necessity of capitalism that we see pre-capitalist communities, as Kevin Anderson says, "as building blocks for an alternative form of modernity".[39] And that is why I am saying that Marx's idea of the Asiatic mode of production should not be read as a static civilisation that has reached its dead end, where colonialism was needed for India to progress. Remember that in 1858, a year after the revolution against British rule in India, Marx writes to Engels, "India is our best ally".[40] In the same letter, Marx is talking of reading Hegel's *Science of Logic* and articulating the dialectical reading of capital accumulation. Marx's idea of the Asiatic mode of production is anti-elite, anti-colonial and anti-Eurocentric. Here I would agree with Anderson that Marx was

> ....suggesting that pre-capitalist Asian societies had been on a different historical trajectory. Moreover, although the Asiatic mode of production was said to be based on a rather static form of community property, Marx no longer saw it as necessarily "despotic" referring also to "democratic" forms of community governance in pre-colonial societies.[41]

"Despotic" and "democratic" governance in the Asiatic mode have to be seen in terms of conflicting social groups—the elites and the subalterns. In more than one sense of the term the stalwarts of the Indian Left (including D.D. Kosambi, R.S. Sharma and Irfan Habib) do not seem to have seen the Asiatic mode of production as an alternative mode of production that provides an alternative path to communism. The reason for this faulty reading in Indian history is that Marx's notes on non-Western societies have been completely ignored by the Indian Left. Anderson says that Marx's *Ethnological Notebooks* in the period 1879-82 comprise 90,000 words on the Indian subcontinent.[42] The Indian Left seems to have been oblivious to this section of Marx's repertoire. Anderson further says that a large part of these *Notebooks* for Marx "have yet to be published".[43]

What is clear from Marx's writings based on Maxim Kovalevsky's 1879 *Communal Landownership* and Robert Sewell's 1870 *Analytic History of India* that Indian society "from below"—i.e. the society of the artisans, craftsmen and peasants—was far from static. The idea of "stagnant Asia" is seen from the perspective of the critique of the ruling elite. It is not on stagnancy in economic production, but changes in forms of commune property relations—from "clan or kin-based communities to village communities not organised on kinship that periodically divided the common land on an equal basis"[44]—that Marx's subaltern historiography points out. One also finds in Marx's writings "social antagonisms...within the non-kinship based rural commune."[45] This dynamic of Indian history has to be noted. Unfortunately post-Kovalevsky and post-Marx, the history of communes in pre-capitalist India has yet to be written. The obsession with capitalist modernity and with European ideological thinking has made the ideas of private property and capitalism as timeless fetishes. For Marx, the capitalism which he analyses in *Capital* was the history of capitalism as it emerged in Western Europe. In "England alone", as Marx says, "which we take as our example has it the classical form."[46] Marx says that England serves as the "classical ground"[47] for the development of his ideas. But there are also other grounds, from the non-capitalist basis—a feature that he keeps central to his *Ethnological Notebooks*—which serves as an alternative path in historical studies. What happens is that these alternative paths meet. What is to be noted is the character of this meeting place. Would it be brutal capitalism being thrust on the non-capitalist world? Or would it imply that revolutions start not from the capitalist world, but from the margins of capitalism, revolutions that should ignite also revolutions in Europe and North America?

The point is to understand the nature of the revolutionary subject emerging in different cultures. What happens in India is that the caste system would crush all forms of rebellion, since it would also crush the ideas of individuality, collectivity and critical thinking. After all it is important to note that the "crisis of reason" to recall Max Horkheimer, "is manifested in the crisis of the individual".[48] It is in this context of alternative histories and alternatives forms of property—especially with the idea of no property of land in Asia—that I claim that since there are accusations against Marx that the idea of no property of land in Asia was false (thereby falsifying Marx's idea of the Asiatic mode of production and arguing for a unilinear theory of history combined with the idea of "Indian feudalism"), it is imperative to state that Marx made no generalised statements of "no property in land" in Asia. For instance in his 1853 letter to Engels, Marx talks of property in land in South India.[49] It is imperative to understand how private property developed in India, how Manu's laws and Brahmanism were instituionalised in the development of private property and how caste and caste alliances dominated the history of the development of private property. What is important to understand is that the state as sovereign with highly centralised powers differentiated state power in Asia from Medieval Europe. What is also important is to differentiate property relations and classes emanating thereon from the European model of class formation.

There are a number of points that one needs to note on the *specificity* of Indian history. For one, it has been noted that the Asiatic state did not emerge from class contradictions (a point that Irfan Habib critiques), but emerged as a bureaucratic elite which was itself part of an economic system.[50] Secondly concentration of power was *not merely* on economic differences, but *primarily* on social ones built on the principle of social stratification.[51] The absence of private property in the West European sense and the lack of individuation led to the *'civilisational' lethargy*, an *Asian Confucianism*, which impeded economic and political development.[52] But this does not mean that private property *as such* did not exist in India. Note what Marx once said about the emergence of private property with the dominance of the Brahmanical priest class:

> The priestly *pack* thus plays a *central* role in the process of individualisation of family property. The chief sign of undivided family property is its inalienability. In order to get this property, the legislation, which is developed under Brahman influence, must attack this bastion more and more...(What we find in India is, my insertion, M.J.) that gifts to the priest first, precede every other mode of alienation of immovable property. [53]

It is this character of the dominance of the priestly class as Brahmanical Overlords that is directly related to the second tier of the Asiatic mode of production, namely the emergence of Caste Overlordship. At this point it is important to note that the idea of Brahmanical Overlordship is not to be seen as existing in some remote past, or only with political reactionaries. It is something so deeply woven in Indian society that not only the liberal, but even the Indian communists were and are unfortunately yet seduced by it. Just look at the top brass of the Indian Left and you will find the Brahmanical Overlords—though dressed as one must confess in the uniform of Josef Stalin.

"Scratch a Russian Communist", so Lenin said in 1919 "and you will find a Great Russian Chauvinist". How true these words seem for India! The words however could be rewritten as: "Scratch an Indian party elite and you will find the soul of the Brahmanical Overlord residing in his unfortunate breast." To illustrate, note a recent textbook of the Communist Party of India (CPI) written by Anil Rajimwale. Note how this *A Brief History of the CPI: Through the Party Congresses* locates the legacy of the Indian communist movement in Swami Vivekananda, Bal Gangadhar Tilak and Lala Lajpat Rai.[54] This ideology of Brahmanical Overlordship is based on ritualistic and elitist ideology which promotes nothing but stagnancy. This is how I am reworking on Marx's idea of stagnancy.

To come to the main features of this stagnancy, let us reflect on "stagnant Asiatic despotism"[55] which is said to be based on:

> ...two circumstances which supplement each other: 1). The public works were the business of the central government, 2). besides, this the whole empire was divided into villages, each of which possessed a completely separate organisation and formed a little world in itself.[56]

What I am claiming is that this two-tiered structure is what Louis Althusser would call "structure in dominance" or the *structure of the dominant classes*. This structure of the dominant classes cannot be confused with a civilisational reading of Asia.

Further: village society dominated by the caste system was (and yet is) controlled "village corporations"[57]—the Panchayats—while the "zamindars and talukdars were nothing but officers of the government, appointed to look after, to collect, and to pay over the prince the assessment due from the village."[58] The zamindars were the "middlemen"[59] who took the form of "feudal landholders[60], while the state is seen as the "sole proprietor".[61] "Real communities" in this Asiatic mode are only "hereditary possessors".[62] This is what Irfan Habib calls, "State Landlordism".[63] After the 1793 permanent settlement of Lord Cornwallis a class of zamindars was created who would cease being sole tax collectors for the Mughal state. These zamindars would be the New Landlords. To quote Kevin Anderson:

> Cornwallis' "permanent settlement" of 1793, which made the *zamindars*, formerly hereditary tax farmers for the Mughal Empire, into landlords. The *zamindars* therefore gained unrestricted capitalist-style ownership over the areas they had formerly only taxed, including the right to evict those who were their tenants, the *ryots*, and the right to pass down these new acquisitions to their heirs.[64]

What happens here is that this legacy of State Landlordism, Caste Overlordship and New Landlordism is inherited by modern India. The subaltern labouring castes became clients of this State Landlordism, Caste Overlordship and New Landlordism. *They were left in the peripheries of village society in pre-capitalist India, and in contemporary times are left in the peripheries of both village society and civil society*. Here it is important to note what Ambedkar said about the village:

> I hold that these village republics have been the ruination of India. I am therefore surprised that those who condemn provincialism and communalism should come forward as champions of the village. What is the village but a sink of localism, a den of ignorance, narrow-mindedness and communalism? I am glad that the Draft Constitution has discarded the village and adopted the individual as its unit.[65]

In contemporary neoliberal times, the den of ignorance along with landlordism remains. What happens is that the character of the state takes the form of the Managerial Corporate State, but this form of Managerial Corporate State reiterates the totalitarian form of the classical Indian variant of the Asiatic state. Bureaucracy and rank worship, essential factors of the Asiatic state, also appear as the essences of the modern Indian state. Unlike feudalism in Europe that gave birth to a proto-bourgeois from the wombs of the artisan classes, the economic and cultural repression of the artisans (mainly classified as unclean-untouchables through the rituality of Brahmanical-Hindu religion as "religion from above"), did not give rise to the radical anti-feudal bourgeoisie.

Pre-capitalist Societies and the Question of "Direct Socialism"

In contrast to both the Orientalists who imagined India to be a part of the 'low' culture of development and also in contrast to the teleological theoreticians who worked with concocted ideas of evolution, I am talking of complex histories within the Asiatic mode of production and the possibilities of "direct socialism" for the Asiatic mode of production, i.e. a direct jump skipping the entire capitalist mode of production. What I am saying is that there is a genre called "Marx's late writings on non-Western societies" which have largely not been recognised by the Left in India. And this is despite Theodor Shanin's *Late Marx and the Russian Road* and Kevin Anderson's *Marx at the Margins.* What needs to be understood is that there are different perspectives argued for understanding social formations in non-European societies and these different perspectives are from a non-European viewpoint. And because of the lack of articulating this very important aspect of Marxism, the tendency to understand non-European societies came from the Mao-inspired articulation of agrarian societies which missed out Marx's important contributions as he had envisaged in his *Ethnological Notebooks,* a work that was published only partially and only for the first time in 1974 by Lawrence Krader. Even stalwarts of Indian history like Habib have said that these Notebooks are "not available to me".[66] The impression one got of Marx's understanding of India was only from his articles in the *New York Tribune* from 1853-1861 and the Marx-Engels correspondence (1852-62) and that too from the faulty thinking that I outlined in the previous section.

The result was that complex social formations and their internal dynamics were missed out. What was missed out was also the dynamics that could lead these societies directly to socialism without going through the process of capitalism. Not much has been said of this form of "direct socialism". A brief note on this is therefore extremely necessary. Writing in 1881, especially after the then Narodniki radical Vera Zasulich had written to Marx about the problems of socialist action in pre-capitalist Russia, Marx had claimed that Russia because of "unique combinations of circumstances" could compel the village commune to discard its primitive features and develop "collective production on a national scale", where one need not go through the "dreadful vicissitudes" of capitalism.[67]

What has been the tragic irony of history is that the very same "dreadful vicissitudes" of capitalism were carried through perfection by Stalin. What also needs being said that even today a large part of the Indian Left have not been able to understand these same "dreadful vicissitudes" of capitalism. In this very ironic situation and inspired by a form of Revolutionary Cynicism one chalks out a path of direct socialism that is able to skip the teleology of these very dreadful vicissitudes. What I am saying is that one should not be obsessed with a form of class-fetishism where only class in a West European type matters and nothing else. In this new reading one proceeds to a non-teleological understanding of history whereby one is able to articulate the idea of "subject positions" instead of the idea of the "vanguard classes". In this new perspective the historical conjuncture of class struggles in India from the perspective of South Asia is sought and thereby one finds both real social formations, as well as finds out how the unity of the Indian *popular classes* is possible.

And it is in this site that one claims that in more than one way the disconnect of the Mainstream Political Left from the labouring masses is based on a strange form of spurious theorisation of India, a theorisation that almost misses out Marx's original contributions to the study of non-Western societies. Despite Marx's warnings in 1877 that there could be "no general path of development prescribed for all nations"[68] and that historical materialism did not have a "master-key" to study each and every society,[69] what happened is that even the best scholars theorising on India worked with this general path of development prescribed for all nations governed by the phantasmagorical master-key. Consider the following from Marx's letter to Zasulich where the idea of the iron laws of history is placed in the hermeneutics of suspicion. And because a form of Marxism articulated a theory of the iron laws of history, all history was seen as necessarily going through the process from primitive communism via slave society, feudalism and capitalism to socialism. Note Marx's critique of this point of view:

> One should be on one's guard when reading the histories of primitive communities written by bourgeois historians. They do not stop at anything, even outright distortion. Sir Henry Maine, for example, who was an ardent active supporter of the British government in its policy of destroying Indian communes by force, tells us hypocritically that all noble efforts on the part of the government to support these communes were thwarted by the elementary force of these laws! [70]

and

> In my analysis of the origin of capitalist production I stated that its secret lies in the fact that it is based on 'divorcing the producer from the means of production' and that 'the *expropriation of the agricultural producer, of the peasant,* from the soil, is the basis of the whole process. The history of this expropriation, in different countries, assumes different accepts....In England, alone, which

> we take as our example, has it the classical form.' In so doing I *expressly* limited the 'historical inevitability' of this process to the *countries of Western Europe*.[71]

What happened is that the Left in India could not understand what capitalism in its classical form meant. They also could not understand that Marx implies a limit to the reading of the development of capitalism in Europe, a limit that has to be transcended. Instead the Indian Left has by and large mechanically applied what they thought Marx said in their study of the Indian mode of production. What needs being done is arguing for a new reading of Marx's study of India.

Consider the class-fetishism that the Indian Left suffers from. I shall once again turn to Habib. Habib notes that for Eric Hobsbawn, "the Asiatic system is not yet a class society, or if it is a class society, then it is a primitive form of it."[72] Habib further says, "If no classes then no class struggle."[73] In opposition to this form of class-fetishism I am recalling Engels 1888 note the lead sentence from the *Manifesto of the Communist Party*: "The history of all hitherto existing society is the history of class struggles"[74]:

> That is, all *written* history. In 1847, the pre-history of society, the social organisation existing previous to recorded history, was all but unknown. Since then Hauxthausen discovered common ownership of land in Russia, Maurer proved it to be the social formation from which all Teutonic races started in history, and by and by village communities were found from India to Ireland. The inner organisation of this primitive communist society was laid bare, in its typical form by Morgan's crowning discovery of the true nature of the *gens* and its relation to the *tribe*. With the dissolution of these primeval communities, society begins to be differentiated into separate and finally antagonist classes.[75]

What needs being recognised is that besides classes there are also other non-class formations which need critical and scientific exploration. What happens with this new reading of Marx is that not only is the idea of iron laws of history questioned, but also the necessity and inevitability of capitalism is critiqued. Because what happened in the old reading of iron laws of history, is that one had a dislocation of real history from the imagination of the hitherto known Left scholars, such that the most important "moment" (to borrow a term from Hegel) is missed out, namely the moment of class conjunctions and their relation to the Indian caste system. This dislocation would not allow the following: (1) the study of the emergence of the revolutionary proletariat in India, (2) what caste means even today, and (3) what the radical anti-caste thinkers from Jyotiba Phule to Ambedkar meant. This dislocation would not allow a Radical Left imagination of the understanding of the programme of the annihilation of caste and its relation to *direct socialism.*

In this site of direct socialism one says that the stages theory that the Indian Left believes in: namely that a bourgeois democratic revolution has to precede a socialist revolution is as false as the belief that history is an automaton governed by a puppet master. One knows that Walter Benjamin had critiqued this type of mechanical reasoning. Consider Benjamin:

> The story is told of an automaton constructed in such a way that it could play a winning game of chess, answering each move of an opponent with a countermove. A puppet in Turkish attire and with a hookah in its mouth sat before a chessboard placed on a large table. A system of mirrors created the illusion that this table was transparent from all sides. Actually, a little hunchback who was an expert chess player sat inside and guided the puppet's hand by means of strings. One can imagine a philosophical counterpart to this device. The puppet called 'historical materialism' is to win all the time. It can easily be a match for anyone if it enlists the services of theology, which today, as we know, is wizened and has to keep out of sight.[76]

Since we all know that there is no expert chess player guiding the puppet and since we know that history is no automaton, but comprises of real people with real needs, one would have to re-think the idea of Indian history from a Radical Left perspective.

Class Formlessness and Fascism as Political Moksha

Classes, class struggle and class solidarity are, as we all well know, the basis of Marxist science of historical materialism. The formation of proletarian class formation and class solidarity would need what Marx calls "common existence" and "common interest".[77] In India, this commonness would manifest itself not so much as in proletarian class solidarity, as in the brutal antagonism of caste groups built on monopolistic power, rank worship, the upper caste ideology of "labour as outcaste" and a parasitical-authoritarian bureaucracy completely alienated from the masses. Coupled with this caste-bureaucratic system, would be finance capitalism which would now model this Oligarchic state as the Managerial Corporate State.

"An oppressed class", so Marx continues, "is the vital condition for every society founded on the antagonism of classes".[78] But in India this formlessness of class that we are mentioning and the domination of the caste system would propel an uncanny economic system along with the even more uncanny cultural and ideological superstructure the world has ever known.

Moksha, so we know from this uncanny course of events, has been reached. That is after the 2014 National Elections when the prince of the lumpen-bourgeoisie found a crown of the Prime Minister on his not so prime head. What is Moksha? Moksha is not merely the release from the cycle of birth and death which the priests, sages and professors of philosophy had taught us. It is not a form of spiritual emancipation. It is going beyond good and evil, a going beyond that seek the status of the fascist superman. It is also a form of nihilism that Friedrich Nietzsche had recognised as the sickness of contemporary times. Modern India (i.e. after these very strange elections) has achieved this cynical Moksha. The fascist supermen have stormed the parliament. According to Hegel, history was to realise itself in the kingdom of reason. In India it would realise itself in fascism. 2014 would be like 1933 in Germany. Behind the posters announcing the era of development would be the fascist swastika.

Why did this happen? Why did the Indian elites have to be obsessed with Moksha and not with reason? It is not merely because the Indian elites built an entire edifice of political manipulation, economic depravity and cultural cynicism. It is because those who thought that Moksha is not only a joke but some form of tragicomedy, those who thought that revolution is an answer to manipulation, depravity and cynicism, would want a decaffeinated revolution, a revolution which does not smell of revolution. But then decaffeinated revolutions could also be forms of counterrevolution. The ugliest face of counterrevolution would manifest itself in the middle of 2014.

Why is this so? It is because instead of revolutionary zeal of internationalism and concrete analysis of concrete conditions (methodological themes that were central to Revolutionary Marxism, themes that made the 1917 Bolshevik Revolution), one had the zeal of revolution dampened with the decaffeinated revolution—the revolution that would only be an imagined revolution. This is despite the heroic struggles that the cadres of the various Communist Parties unleashed and despite their presence in large parts of the country especially in the states of Tripura, West Bengal and Kerala, not to forget the Red Corridor that brings in shivers to the Indian bourgeoisie. .

To counter both fascism and the dictatorship of finance capitalism one needs to start from revolutionary grounds that involve the masses at large. And in order to involve the masses at large, one needs the revolutionary humanist method that Marx insisted on especially in his *Economic and Philosophic Manuscripts of 1844*.

Methodologically, thus, one starts, as the authors of *The German Ideology* had said, with real individuals.[79] Combined with these real individuals is the activity and the material conditions of the lives of these individuals.[80] What one calls "concrete analysis" is what comprises this three layer structure of real individuals, their activity and material conditions of life. It is this combine that we would soon know as the mode of production from whence classes and political struggles would emerge. By and large because the Indian comrades could not fuse Marx's philosophy of revolution and humanism with actual practice, they got involved in economic reductionism and went searching for "basic classes", classes that would never appear on the scene of history, or when they were made to appear would go missing like the legendary Missing Imams found in the tales of messianic theology. It is this fact that alienated the

Left from the masses. And in this state of *alienated vacuum* created by the Left, the fascist forces entered and occupied this space of *alienated vacuum*. The fascists were all too happy to go to the masses and mould them in the image of the fascist superman. The masses wanted emancipation. The fascists gave them the superman.

The triumph of the fascists in India was because the intellectual legacy of Marxism came to be borrowed from sources where, for historical reasons, many of Marx's original works like the *Economic and Philosophic Manuscripts of 1844*, the *Grundrisse* and the *Ethnological Notebooks* would not be available to both the communist ideologues and the cadres. And when these texts became available to the world at large, these never became part of the political repertoire of the Indian Left. In this context the serious analysis of Marxist philosophy, caste and the Asiatic mode of production combined with the idea of multilinear historicism—the alternative subaltern humanist understanding of non-European history—could not be a part of its programme and methodology. This is also because the Indian Left movement from the 1920s was influenced by the Comintern which by 1928 was in total control of Stalin. The theoretical points of references were Stalin's *Dialectical and Historical Materialism*, *Problems of Leninism* and later *Economic Problems of Socialism in the USSR*. It was this Stalinist ideological problematic—half baked positivism and half crypto-theology—that would be the master-texts for the early communist movement.[81]

If Marx was referred and used, this was subservient to Stalin's manipulation of Marxism. The idea of the Asiatic mode of production was almost not known to the early comrades. It was only E.M.S. Namboodiripad who once used this, only to have this left in the chambers of forgotten reason. Stalin, it must be noted, had literally banned the debate on the Asiatic mode of production. The reason was that it was thought that the Soviet Union under Stalin had nothing to do with socialism and everything to do with this Asiatic mode. Marx's "Oriental despot" (one essential part of this mode of production) would be found in the character of Stalin. The unfortunate fact is that the Indian Left has not yet recognised this. Marx's *Ethnological Notebooks* (first published in 1974) by Lawrence Krader would till date be unread by almost all Marxists. As I said earlier, Habib quite recently said that this text is not available to him.[82] In this sense, it seems to be strange that one wants to theorise on the Marxist idea of Indian history when a substantial text of Marx is unread.

In this sense, the understandings of the contemporary mode of production and the revolutionary classes along with the complex-intermixture of modern classes and the caste system was left almost untouched despite the mode of production debate that emerged in the late 1960s. There are many reasons for this. One is the reliance on the Third International which got totally controlled by the Stalinist bureaucrats who wanted to manipulate world revolutions for their own cunning goals. But the main reason for all these anomalies is that after Lenin's death in 1924 a type of theoretical crisis set into the world communist movement whereby Marxist revolutionary repertoire was replaced by what one can call a duplicate Marxism in the form of Stalinism, where the science of revolution was displaced at best for ideologies of managing and manipulating revolution.

What needs being done in India is creating an alternative understanding of the Indian revolution, where the formlessness of classes is transformed into the formation of a class that is both "in-itself" and "for-itself"—the class that takes on the responsibilities of the revolution. Caste, it is important to note here, is the main reason for the formlessness of socialised proletarian formation. While the Left, by and large, ignored caste, it then started understanding the caste system (informed not so much by Marxism, but by NGO type of libertarianism) as a form of *différance* (to borrow the language of the postmodernists and deconstructionists), or even as represented as the "poorest of the poor" (to recall Arunndhati Roy)[83], or even as a form of ethnicity working under the rubric of identity politics. Right from its inception the Communist Party of India or the CPI (then undivided) under the leadership of S.A. Dange, Gangadhar Adhikari or B.T. Ranadive never brought the caste system embedded in the Asiatic mode of production in their understanding of Indian economics and politics.

One cannot put the understanding of caste and class in a formal Aristotelian either/or binary. One cannot say: "only class", as the way, by and large the Parliamentary Left has been doing. But one also cannot say: "only caste" as parties based on identity politics do. One has to understand class and caste, as "next door neighbours, and it is only a span that separates the two."[84] The radical difference is that modern classes are fluid and mobile, while the caste system is ossified. India has both these two locked in its unfortunate breast.

It is important to understand that Indian society is a society based on "gradation of castes forming an ascending scale of reverence and a descending scale of contempt"[85], a gradation that has helped the fascists to power. In this case, Indian capitalism has this hierarchical system of lordship and bondage, along with the scale of reverence and contempt, deeply etched in its economic, cultural and ideological cranium. The form of class relations that emerged in India would appear as an "enclosed class" system[86], even as a "gang or clique"[87]. Appearing as "warring groups"[88] and "close corporations"[89], the caste system prevented proletarian class politics to bloom. As "caste-clan system" and as *clannishness that pervades the dominant economic and political orders*, what bloomed was the not so flowery flower of fascism. In India the flower of fascism would appear in the form of the lotus.

Fascism as Brahmanical Overlordship

While the caste-clan system is generally located as a necessary part of pre-capitalist India, it is also to be understood as a necessary part of capitalist India. The fact that caste also serves as the social, political and ideological forms for fascism in India has to be mentioned.

Modern India could never annihilate the caste system, but re-order it for the purpose of capital accumulation. The idea that capitalism would by its alleged law of history annihilate caste is totally false. Marx's statement that "the country that is more developed industrially only shows, to the less developed, the image of its own future"[90], cannot be interpreted as pre-capitalist social formations disappearing, just as they are said to have disappeared in advanced capitalist countries.

Recall here Rosa Luxemburg's argument that capitalism needs pre-capitalist and sectors in order to re-produce itself.[91] I am extending this argument and saying that Indian capitalism did not and can never annihilate caste. Instead what we say is that capitalism in India (as capitalism of the periphery) reproduces caste. And in turn caste reproduces capitalism in India. But it not only reproduces capitalism, it also reproduces the forms of proto-fascistic and fascistic consciousness. In this sense, the communist revolution and the anti-caste revolutions would have to be *simultaneous* revolutions. All references to the stages theory where a New Democratic Revolution is said to precede a Communist Revolution is totally alien to India.

It is here that the scientific understanding of Brahmanical Overlordship comes in. Brahmanical Overlordship has two historical forms:

1. The per-colonial Overlordship that emerged with Shankara's counterrevolution against Buddhism where the ideology of social apartheid and the metaphysics of rituality with the dominance of the Vedic life-world was institutionalised, and
2. The colonial form where the Brahmans along with the Orientalists created the fictions of "Hinduism" and the "Aryan race" along with the British attack on the Mughal state, the annexation of Oudh and the creation of an anti-Dalit, anti-Muslim and anti-Persian class of ideological comprador created for the service to the British empire. The present Overlords are this class created by colonialism in the service to capitalism and imperialism.

At this juncture it must be noted that the Indic variation of the Asiatic mode of production is distinct from other Asiatic states, especially the Persian one headed by the centralised Oriental despot. Indian history has witnessed two forms of the Asiatic state: the state model which was taken by the Mughals—i.e. the classical Persian one modelled after the state of the

Achaemenian Empire that ruled Iran from 550 BCE to 330 BCE headed by the Oriental despotic "king of kings (*Shāhān Shāh-ī-Erān*)— and the Indic form of Brahmanical Overlordship with its political economy and ideology of stagnancy. Fascism in India appearing as Brahmanical Overlordship erases all traces of its Persian past. It takes the form of brutal Brahmanism and State Landlordism.

While it is well known that liberal secularism has been oblivious to the questions of fascism and caste, and along with it oblivious to the question to the ideas of graded inequality and division of labourers; there is also an alternative understanding of democracy and revolution, ideas that were introduced by B.R. Ambedkar, the great revolutionary, radical democrat and master par excellence of the critique of both caste and capitalism whom both the Indian liberals and the Indian Marxists inspired by Stalinism (and their reductionist and Eurocentric fetishism of 'class' devoid of concrete analysis) never bothered to understand. This, in a way, would be the biggest challenge for the Indian Left. And since the Indian Left ignored the caste question, their theory of fascism was nothing but the blind mimicking of the Comintern's definition of fascism as the "most terroristic dictatorship of finance capital". Finance capitalism would not be without its brain, soul and flesh. In India all three—the brain, soul and flesh—would be of caste and the fetish of rank worship. What European fascism did was that it attacked not only communism, but also attacked the entire tradition of the European Renaissance and the Enlightenment.

One could say that European Revolutions (especially the French Revolution) could take place only after the Renaissance and the Enlightenment. Likewise one is demanding an Indian Renaissance and Enlightenment. This Renaissance and Enlightenment would have to construct the idea of Marxist humanism, where the demand for a full human life is made the demand of communism. In contrast to this humanism, note the essential anti-humanism in the split personality and culture that Brahmanical Overlordship creates. Note the hierarchical system which is inherent in the Indian social structure. This is what the foundational myth of the so-called great and hoary Indian civilisation that fascism boasts of says:

> The Brahman was his (God's, my insertion, M.J.) mouth,
> of both his arms was the Rājanya made.
> His thighs became the Vaiśya, from his
> feet the Śūdra was produced.[92]

The tragedy is that political democracy in India has not been able to eradicate this anti-democratic mythical culture even in the popular masses despite the great revolutionary movements unleashed since the last few centuries. Instead this anti-democratic character appearing as myth, also appears, to borrow the terminology of Walter Benjamin, as *Trauerspiel* or simply "mourning play". In India this form of mourning appears as a false sense of happiness and as I have said in *Why We Are Not Hindus* also appears in the terminology of Fredric Jameson as the "hysterical sublime". I call this anti-democratic mythical culture that transfigures the sense of mourning into the feeling of false happiness and hysterical sublimity as "fundamental ontology" (following Martin Heidegger's *Being and Time*), where myth replaces scientific reasoning and authoritarianism replaces democracy. The tragedy is that this essential ontological division that the fundamental ontology of Indian civilisation offers is incorporated into the daily life-world. The fascists have been triumphant in the 2014 polls because of this anti-democratic ontological culture. And it is through the use of ritual (as Walter Benjamin reminds us in *The Work of Art in the Age of Mechanical Reproduction*) that this anti-democratic culture is able to reproduce itself, not only as a dominant ideology of the ruling classes, but also as an ideology that the masses have given consent to.

In order to understand this anti-democratic mythical culture, let us look at the deep structures of this foundational myth that the Indian fascists boast of. Note that it is one class of people who wield the Ideological State Apparatus. The upper caste elites—the Brahmans—have total monopoly of speaking. The proletarianised Śūdra can only be the feet. What is important to note, that even in modern India, this foundational myth is reflected. The Brahmans who comprise probably 3.5 percentage of the population of India, control the ideological and political apparatus like the bureaucracy, media, educational institutes, etc., along with the merchant class (the Vaiśya) who fund amply this form of Indian capitalism. One should however point out that the dominant mode of production in India is capitalist of the underdeveloped type that Paul Baran, Andre Gunder Frank and Arghiri Emmanuel reminded us of. It is futile to talk of semi-feudalism and link it to the caste question.

A certain methodological remark is necessary here that locates the political economy of underdevelopment and the culture emanating thereon. India has never had feudalism. Most certainly it did not have a European kind of feudalism. One cannot thrust feudalism as a "universal" category that is applicable to all societies in the world. Instead it is with this Asiatic concept of caste-clan with its ideology of rank worship and bureaucratic overdetermination of the economy that attention must now turn. While Marxist thinkers like Sharad Patil in Maharashtra took a serious study of caste in India, followed by Gail Omvedt, the idea of the Asiatic mode of production that has produced rank worship and the parasitical bureaucracy (which are yet present) was apparently missing from their studies. Patil talked of feudalism, albeit in the modified forms of "feudalism from above" and "feudalism from below". The same error was made earlier by the great historian D.D. Kosambi.

It is in these perspectives of the Asiatic mode of production with its oversize bureaucracy and the political economy of underdevelopment and dependency to capitalism of the "centre" of global capital accumulation that we shall be able to contextualise Indian capitalism and the caste question. *Caste must not be understood as a mere pre-capitalist remnant, but an active part of capital accumulation in India.* It is in this context of the global capital accumulation between the centre (West Europe, North America, Japan, etc.) and the periphery (Africa, large parts of Asia and Latin America) that reproduces caste whereby we understand the extremely important and scientific statement that the Indian working classes have two enemies: the culture and ideology of Brahmanical Overlordship (that is realised as the divided self manifested as cultural schizophrenia which produces economic and cultural stagnation) and capitalism.[93] Indian capitalism is not without its ritualistic, hierarchical and bureaucratic flesh that is rotting with its caste-based odour. Note from the quote from the *Rg Veda* how the upper-caste elites—the Brahman Overlords as the producers of ideology—constitute the "hereditary ruling class".[94] The Brahmans are thus literally the "mouth" of Indian politics and the ideologues of neoliberal capitalism. Since the ideology of Brahmanical Overlordhip stays dominant even today in the era of 21st century late capitalism, it is important to have a look at this very strange ideology. By Brahmanical Overlordship as the fetish for ranking, hierarchy and bureaucratic stagnation, so one means, is "the negation of the spirit of liberty, equality and fraternity. In that sense it is rampant in all classes and is not confined to the Brahmans alone though they have been the originators of it."[95]

A scientific understanding of the Indic variation of the Asiatic mode of production is necessary. For this we turn to Prabhat Patnaik who located the historical materialist understanding of the weaving of caste and rank worship with the downgrading of both labour and the sciences:

> The ideological hegemony of Brahmanism contributed to the stagnation of Indian society, not just by preventing a revolt of the exploited classes; it did so in another way as well, which E.M.S. Namboodiripad elaborated somehow later, basing himself on the work of the Marxist philosopher, Debiprasad Chattopadhyay. And it was by arresting the growth of science and technology, and hence of the productive forces beyond a point. Chattopadhyay had argued that the triumph of Brahmanism under Adi Shankara represented not only a reinforcement of the caste-system in the country, but a demise of science and hence of advances in technology. Paradoxically according to Chattopadhyay, the much celebrated triumph of Adi Shankara was the harbinger of a dark age when India lost the edge it had in scientific advances in mathematics, astronomy and other branches of learning, because of both the ideological and social implications of the triumph of idealism over materialism; and since, as Lenin said in *Materialism and Empirio-Criticism*, a scientist must be a materialist in practice, this represented a setback to science, and hence to technological advance. Socially, since the practitioners of technology, the artisans

> and craftsmen, were those who typically belonged to the "lower castes", the counterrevolution ushered by Adi Shankara means a social downgrading, and hence implicit devaluing, of technological advances.[96]

Brahmanism as the pyramidal model and ruling ideology of India is based on the downgrading of the artisans who were (and yet are) the practitioners of technology along with the downgrading of their scientific practice. Brahmanical Overlordship which defeated the oppressed people and constituted a victory of idealism over materialism laid the fertile ground for the lethargy and sluggishness of Indian civilisation. As a schizophrenic Frankenstein-like fetish that has now been given life of its own, it is ruling over people. We find this schizophrenic character when we understand that Brahmanical Overlordship "pervades everywhere and...regulates the thoughts and deeds of all classes..."[97] It becomes (to borrow Trotsky's term from a different context) "messianism of backwardness".[98]

What happened in these circumstances is that the emergence of a radical bourgeois was suppressed that would challenge the Asiatic caste-clan system. Along with the Asiatic caste-clan system, the dominance of the mercantile and usurious capitalist class also stunted the growth of industrial capitalism, along with the stunting of the growth of the socialised proletariat. What happened in South Asia is the emergence of a very different kind of bourgeoisie from that of the emergence of the West European bourgeoisie. In Europe, liberalism and the spirit of Protestant ethics, as the guiding doctrine of the bourgeoisie, emerged as a new ideology to meet the needs of a new world of rising capitalism. Here privilege and status were replaced by the celebrated theory of social contract which served as the judicial foundation of society. Science not only replaced religion as the dominant factor in giving shape to social ideas, but also delegitimised religion. In the Indian subcontinent the new order even post-1947 could not get rid of the old order, where caste as *status groupism* stunted economic and cultural growth.

If one puts the caste system in the Marxist perspective, the first three castes comprise various sections of the bourgeoisie, while the last is the Indian working class. Capital, landed property and the wages system, along with state power would be ordered according to caste hierarchy and caste alliances. But a simple reduction of the caste system into the modern class one may not exactly be a scientific idea. The relation is mediated by a very complex dialectic. What happens in India is that not only is the upper-caste elite struck by this uncanny caste-clan system, but also the modern proletariat is afflicted by this system which inhibits the formation of a vanguard proletariat (the celebrated *"for itself" proletariat* that Marx talks of in *The Poverty of Philosophy* in his typical Hegelese) that becomes a revolutionary force. And because of the principle of graded inequality, the various sub-castes in the last caste also fight amongst themselves for a superior status, instead of battling directly with the ruling elite. Caste also inculcates a sense of neurosis-psychosis. It is the Indian fascists who recognise caste as neurosis-psychosis and mobilise this for their violent politics. The radical idea of the *annihilation of caste* was turned by them in the ideology of the *perfection of caste.* These issues neither liberal secularism nor the dominant trend in the Indian Left that has been seduced by Stalinism has ever recognised.

In order to understand the nuances of caste we claim that the system of caste is to be understood as:

1. Enclosed, ossified and petrified class that is reified as a closed clan system with its parasitical bureaucratic system. As "semi-barbarian, semi-civilised communities"[99] they manifest themselves as a clan system, creating the structures of extreme hierarchy and the ideology of rank worship. The totem of purity and the taboo of pollution rule its ideological guidelines, while economic and cultural stagnation are its two main pillars. The principles of graded inequality (where various labouring-subaltern castes are unable to recognize their exploiter, but are themselves graded within themselves unequally) and division of labourers (where within the proletariat class there is a marked internal division based on the ideology of caste-hierarchy)—which are recognised as the main markers of caste society—now

are mobilised by fascism. Fascist politics perfects these principles of graded inequality and division of labourers.

2. As racism, albeit of the South Asian variety, where the upper castes are understood as being of higher biological stock and the lower ones considered as inferior. For the Rashtriya Swayamsevak Sangh (RSS), this idea of caste as race forms the leitmotiv of its fascist politics. Both V.D. Savarkar and M.S. Golwalkar leaders of the Hindu Mahasabha and the RSS respectively based their right-wing politics on the idea of race and racial superiority.
3. Of neurosis-psychosis which creates cultural and political schizophrenia and the creation of the ideology of neurosis-psychosis and cultural and political schizophrenia. This form of cultural illness and the ideological superstructure which caste creates is unable to generate critical thinking and a democratic culture. The main thing that this new form of cultural illness does is that it breeds the contempt of other social groups. The creation of authoritarian fascist politics is an essential part of neurosis-psychosis.

I am here bringing in the psychoanalytic concepts of neurosis and psychosis and then I am claiming that in late capitalism, neurosis (as the eternal recurrence of the self-same trauma) and psychosis (as the complete withdrawal from reality) reaches a new stage that I call "neurosis-psychosis". In early capitalism neurosis and psychosis were separate phenomena. In late capitalism dictated by finance capitalism, we see a new stage of mental illness called "neurosis-psychosis". Caste in this age of late capitalism perfects this strange phenomena called "neurosis-psychosis". Like the neurotic return of the self-same trauma, caste is negated only to return once again. Marx's celebrated statement that the Indian "self-sufficient communities that constantly reproduce themselves in the same form, and when accidentally destroyed, spring up again on the spot and with the same name"[100] is understood in this neurotic understanding of caste.

That is why I have insisted in my *The New Militants* and *Why We Are Not Hindus* that R.D. Laing's idea of the "divided self" and Theodor Adorno's "general regression of thinking" fits in best in the understanding of caste as "neurosis-psychosis" along with Marx's theory of alienation. The idea of the caste system as "a sort of equilibrium, resulting from a general repulsion and constitutional exclusiveness, resulting between all its members"[101] fits in Marx's theory of alienation, while the idea of the "wild aimless, unbounded forces of destruction"[102], fits in the theory of "neurosis-psychosis".

I shall come to this rather strange combination of class, racism and neurosis-psychosis that has given rise to fascism. What I am saying is that caste combines both the sites of the economic base and the political and ideological superstructure. But along with this theme, I have brought in Marx's problematic of alienation, reification and fetishism that deals with this peculiar form of capitalism in India where caste is not only preserved, but actively reproduced, albeit in modern, capitalistic forms.

What needs being said is that the fascism in India emerged from the cranium of the caste mode of production (with the fetishism of ranking) along with the crisis of capital accumulation. What the caste system does is that as warring gangs it produces the ideology of riots and wars thus creating fascist mass consciousness. In this sense one cannot stick to the old understanding of fascism as merely the "terroristic dictatorship of finance capital" devoid of concrete historical context. One has to understand what this form of terrorism is and how it takes state power. What needs being said is that fascism in India has been triumphant in the matrix of the crisis of capitalism and from the caste-class dialectic where the ideologies and politics of the warrior-priest caste not only is made to rule the roost, but is made literally to grip the masses. The Indian fascists have been able to mobilise the hierarchical caste system where the four enclosed classes: priests (*Brahmans*), warriors (*Kshatriyas*), merchants (*Vaiśyas*) and peasants (*Śūdras*), are joined by the *Ati-Śūdras* (those who are condemned to be outside the caste system). Note the pyramidal model where the workers and the peasants are made to stand at the bottom of this anti-democratic pyramid. If one cannot understand this pyramidal model of Indian society, one cannot understand the location and functioning of the dominant castes, the emergence of capitalism and the dictatorship of finance capitalism.

It must be noted that the Indian fascists place at the centre of their violent ideology, the figure of the warrior-priest. One must also note that this caste-based idea of the warrior-priest ideology evoked by the Indian fascists and their contempt for the Indian liberals, especially secular democracy in general and Jawaharlal Nehru and M.K. Gandhi in particular, is because the latter did not believe in this warrior-priest ideology. It must also be noted that it is not merely the case that the Indian fascists borrowed (and continue borrowing) from the Nazis. What is interesting to note is that the Nazis were avid readers of the *Vedas* and the *Gita*. And considering that the *Gita*, as the so-called 'Holy Book' of Hinduism, is being propelled by the RSS to be the National Book, it also implies that the Democratic Constitution is also in the process of being sidelined. It must be noted that Heinrich Himmler imagined that he was the mythical Hindu 'hero' Arjun and Hitler was Krishna, the ideologist par excellence of the caste system. For Himmler deeds of the most violent type do not harm the inner self. This he learnt from the *Gita*.

Note also how Mathias Tietke the German author of *Yoga in the Third Reich: Concepts, Contrasts, Consequences* talks of how Himmler lectured on reaching the status of "Kshatriyakaste" (the military and ruling elite of ancient India) where salvation (Moksha) is realised through bloody wars. Note also that for Walter Wust—German Orientalist and Nazi ideologue who from 1937 was the President of the Research Institute of the Ahnenerbe (literally "inherited from the forefathers") —Hitler was a "Chakravartin" (Indo-Aryan world emperor). In his speech of Posener, Himmler—influenced by the spirit of the *Gita* where Krishna the hero of the Hindu religion instructs Arjuna to attack his kin and kill them—said that it was the duty of every associate of the SS to carry out action without pity and without considering any human relationships. In this age of mass yoga, which the contemporary Indian fascist government is promoting, it is important to note how yoga enthusiasts like the German Indologist and SS Capt. Jakob Wilhelm Hauer influenced the Nazis on the Aryan theory of racial superiority. The Nazi order according to Himmler was conceived as a spiritual order—a spirituality that led to the consciousness of the superman—willing to kill without looking at the consequences, killing of relatives and family members not excluded. He demanded that one has to detach oneself from such concepts as "good" and "evil." Moksha is this fascist going beyond good and evil.

Without this understanding, it is impossible to understand the rise of Indian fascism. Why do we say this? We say this because the Indian bourgeois democratic revolution has not been accomplished and can never be accomplished. In this sense the very idea of the bourgeois democratic revolution could be a myth. This is because the bourgeoisie was incapable of being revolutionary any more. In India the bourgeoisie (especially the bania capitalists, the Kshatriya kulaks and upper caste ideologues, along with the political kulaks and the bureaucracy) carried caste within its economic base and ideological cranium. Let us see the picturisation of the haunting ghost and its embedment in the economic structure of society:

> Alongside of modern evils, a whole series of inherited evils oppress us, arising from the passive survival of antiquated modes of production, with their inevitable train of social and political anachronisms. We suffer not only from the living, but from the dead. *Le mort saist le vif!* We are seized by the dead![103]

Look at this ghost of the past that seizes us. This ghost is also a casteist ghost. It is of the Brahmanical Overlord dressed in democratic attire. But beneath all this clothing, the fascist body and mind are found. Of course the liberals could never do anything about this ghost and the return of the Overlord. But the Left was expected to do something. But it was also left dumb to the teeth. What they did was only create ideologies, sometimes also producing ideologies of revolution, just as the utopians always promised heaven on earth. And what did these ideologies of revolution (that are not only indifferent to the science of revolution, but which actively repress this science) do? These ideologies created the framework of an alienated and alien discourse—a form of reified consciousness—whereby the social framework of Indian society and history was actively veiled. And in India the crux of the problem was not able to identify the nature of the dominant mode of production which itself is based on the inability to understand the mechanism and dynamics of Indian history. What the Indian Left did was that it borrowed the unilinear and mechanist idea of history—where history was said to be a march-past from primitive communism via slave society, feudalism and capitalism, finally destined to culminate in communism. R.S. Sharma's theory of "Indian feudalism" and the Indian Left's idea of the New Democratic Revolution are examples of this mechanistic and unilinear theory of history. That this mechanical understanding governed by what Stalin thought to be "iron laws" reminiscent of theology was something that the Indian Left never bothered to ponder about. And since iron laws of history have never made real political revolutions, and since events are always made by real humans, the Communist Party imagined that it would appear as the messianic representation of these laws of history. Stalin (literally meaning the "man of steel") became the messianic representation of the iron laws of history. History would soon be replaced with messianic tendencies, on the one hand, and contemplation, on the other hand. In the contemporary Left movement, the Maoists represent the messianic tendency, while the Parliamentary Left (that went as the "Left Front") became the contemplative part.

What the dominant trend of the Indian Left did not understand is that Stalin left the legacy of the decaffeinated revolution, a revolution which does not smell of a revolution.

The Triumph of the Indian Fascists

The intensification of the juggernaut of global finance capital and the explosion of global capitalist contradictions in the form of the most recent economic crisis, while bringing the Islamic State in Syria and other parts of West Asia, also brought the Bharatiya Janata Party (BJP) the conservative political arm of the RSS led by the Indian Bonaparte Narendra Modi, to power in the 2014 National Elections. This victory of the RSS model of the Corporate Managerial State is to be seen in the light of not only anti-secular and anti-democratic politics of the RSS, but also the pro-imperialist leaning of this communal-fascist organisation. The RSS now in power wants to create what they call the "Hindu Rashtra" or the Hindu nation modelled after the Nazi Third Reich. This is an open threat to Constitutional Democracy in India and the single biggest challenge to the Indian Left.

This creation of a political phantasmagoria of the Hindu Rashtra, first exemplified in V.D. Savarkar's *Essentials of Hindutva*, while anticipating European fascism (it was written in the early 1920s when Mussolini had grabbed power in Italy), was based on feudal Europe's idea of Christendom. What Savarkar thought of creating, what he called "Hindudom", was modelled after this feudal European theological idea. The RSS created in 1925 had this model of nationhood right from its inception. If Savarkar was trained with European sensibilities, the RSS's version of the Hindu nation has always been nativist. Their models of governance have been the Peshwas in Maharashtra (1749-1818)—Brahmanical rulers where casteist authoritarianism was both their ideology and social and political practice. The RSS model of society and governance is based on the racist supremacist ideology of German Nazism, along with their Brahmanical supremacist tendency. Now with the rule of Zionist Israel, Zionism (one nation, one people, one language, along with the policy and practice of eliminating minorities) has also crept into its political baggage. Its authoritarian, racist and militarist tendencies have always been at the core of its theory and practice. It has three main opponents: Muslims, Nehruvian secularism and communism.

But the triumph of the fascists has also brought in the importance of Revolutionary Marxism. To deal with global capitalism in crisis and the emergence of fascism, Marxism which was declared dead by the Indian liberals and conservatives (much after Francis Fukuyama's messianic "end of history" thesis) after the collapse of the Soviet Union, suddenly found that this death was a false one and that Marxism was, as if, resurrected. This volume is on this death and resurrection of Marxism. It is also about the problems that the Indian Left have been facing, especially after the retreat in the 2009 National Elections, followed by the loss of the 2011 State Elections in the state of West Bengal and the consequent decimation in the 2014 National Elections. A short note on this decimation and the victory of the fascists is necessary.

The BJP won with 282 seats in these elections (31 per cent of the voters gave them the mandate), while the Congress Party which has ruled India for 52 out of the 67 years after independence got only 44 seats. Other parties which include regional parties got 148 seats. The Left Parties led by the Communist Party of India (Marxist) or the CPI(M) which had a large presence in the states of West Bengal (where they ruled uninterrupted for 34 years from 1977 to 2011) and Kerala got a dismal 10 seats. One of the Left Front parties, the Revolutionary Socialist Party (RSP,) broke from the Left Front to join the Congress led United Democratic Front where it won 1 seat. Only in the state of Tripura did the CPI(M) show its presence where it got 64 per cent of the votes. Of the total 10 seats the Left won, nine were of CPI(M) one of CPI. Six of the seats came from Kerala and two each from Tripura and West Bengal. Thus the total number of seats for the Parliamentary Left which had peaked at 59 in 2004 and came down sharply to 24 in 2009, sank to a mere and extremely insignificant 10 in 2014. Both the liberal democratic Congress Party and the Parliamentary Left got a thorough beating.

But this defeat was constituted in a specific logic where the leaders of the Parliamentary Left have been playing Sancho Panza to the Congress's Don Quixote since independence. A new script of this tragicomedy was written. To defeat the BJP which won in the 1999 National Elections, the Parliamentary Left and the Congress got together as the United Progressive Alliance (UPA). In the period 2004-9 the good Sancho thought that he could influence the even better Don. Conjured programmes were drafted and new methods for the transition to socialism germinated in the minds of the speculative Stalinists. But Don Quixote besides being a liberal democrat whose vision was set on the horizons of the American Empire needed the Left to be thrown off their magnificent liberal ship. Don Quixote signed the forbidden Nuclear Deal with the Yanks and the Left instead of being thrown out of the Yankee ship, themselves jumped into the choppy waters of the imperialist ocean.

A Note on this Volume

This volume begins with the CPI(M)'s backing the candidature of Pranab Mukherjee's candidature for the post of the President of India in 2013 and what the authors Soma Marik and Kunal Chattopadhyay claim as betraying the principles of democratic centralism. Here a clear-cut epistemic distinction is drawn in the revolutionary philosophies of Revolutionary Marxism and what the Parliamentary Left has been propagating and practising. Built on this difference between theory and practice, the volume moves into the issues of the contemporary character of imperialism and the socialist alternative (by Prasenjit Bose: see Chapter 2). One thing is clear in this volume—it is Marxism that can provide the alternative to capitalism and the growing inequalities embodied in its very cranium and belly. What Bose claims is that one needs to envisage socialism for the 21st century. After all, it is well known that the worst of socialism is better than the best of capitalism.

But there are larger epistemological issues involving the characterisation of socialism. After all one can validly ask: "What is the character of this socialism?", "Was the Soviet Union at any time socialist?" and "Can the same not also be asked about China?" Paresh Chattopadhyay in the third chapter talks about the "illusions" of conceiving China as socialist. But Chattopadhyay puts the blame not merely on Mao for the false understanding of socialism, but primarily on Lenin—or should one say a "double blame"—in the sense of constructing state capitalism in the name of socialism. The double blame is constructing a state (by replacing the Soviets) and constructing commodity production in the name of socialism. This issue, one must stress, is probably one of the biggest challenges for the Left. One cannot reduce the understandings of Lenin, Stalin and Mao to polemics. Strict scientific explanation must replace rhetoric.

While this volume takes the contemporary understanding of the Left in India as its leitmotiv, it is based on the scientific understanding of Marxism with the rich debates that have taken place within Marxism for over a century. Both empirical and theoretical issues are covered in this volume. The debate between Bernard D'Mello and Paresh Chattopadhyay (while focusing on Mao, and 20th century Marxists from the *Monthly Review* like Paul Sweezy) forms an essential part of this work. There are also chapters on the idea of the Communist Party (see Anup Patnaik's Chapter 4 'Communist Parties in India: Lessons from Gramsci's *Modern Prince*', and Chapter 6 'Gramsci's Critique of Civil Society: Its Contemporary Significance') as also the issues of democracy in communism (see Javeed Alam's 'Can Democratic Centralism be Conducive to Democracy?'—Chapter 20). While Lenin and Leninism are critiqued by Paresh Chattopadhyay and Alam, the importance of Leninism (see Chapter 22 'In Defence of Leninism') is included, an importance that is located within a philosophical reading of Leninism, especially the understanding of the dialectical method of Hegel. We also have a chapter on the need to transcend the old discipline of ideology for a New Materialist idea of what I call "desireology" (see Chapter 25 'Leninism as Radical Desireology'). This new discipline of desireology not only transcends the old discipline of ideology—I relate ideology not only to a form of false consciousness, as Engels did, but also to a form of repressed unconsciousness that is predicated on the fetishism of commodities—but creates what I call a "New Materialism". It is to this New Materialism known as the philosophy of praxis that attention must now turn.

This New Materialism deals with the general crisis and the decline of the Left which Prabhat Patnaik, Arup Baisya and Kripa Shankar (Chapters 11, 30 and 34) talk of, while Pranab Bardhan talks of the "avoidable tragedy of the Left" (Chapter 32). These are followed from Markar Melkonian's reading of the collapse of the Soviet Union (Chapter 7) followed by critiques by Paresh Chattopadhyay (Chapter 8), Cem Somel (Chapter 9) and then by a response by Markar Melkonian (Chapter 10). Achin Vanaik talks of "future perspectives" for the Maintream

Left (Chapter 13) while Dipankar Bhattacharya argues for a Left resurgence (Chapter 31). This volume ends with Jairus Banaji's reading of fascism (Chapter 37).

Locked Brains or the Prohibition Against Thinking

Actually it was a few years ago that two articles appeared in the *Economic & Political Weekly* penned by Prahbat Patnaik and Javeed Alam on the crisis of Marxism in India. To these two articles Prakash Karat, the then General Secretary of the CPI(M), replied back in the party journal *The Marxist*. It is important to understand that this debate of democratic centralism which emerged in the first years of the 20th century in the Russian Social Democratic Party (RSDLP) and which found a theoretical form in Lenin's *What is to be Done?* is an issue which is a burning one even today. One critique of democratic centralism is the liberal type that relates the Leninist idea of so-called "democratic centralism" with a conspiratorial almost Jacobin type of politics. There were also other critiques based on readings in 20th century Marxism. These critiques evoke Rosa Luxemburg and Trotsky, in their alleged critiques of Leninism. And then there is the Stalinist answer that borders on mere rhetoric. According to this type of rhetoric, initially the petty bourgeois intellectuals criticised democratic centralism. Now it is the party comrades who are in the process of criticising this idea of democratic centralism. Recently Paul Le Blanc in his *Lenin and the Revolutionary Party* brought up the important understanding of democratic centralism. According to Le Banc, "few terms have been so endowed with almost magical connotations, and have been so grotesquely distorted by commentators from almost all points of the political spectrum, as the term is sometimes said to be the essence of Leninism—democratic centralism".[104]

In a telephonic talk with Javeed, I pressed the need for a seminar on the debates surrounding the Left in India. Javeed immediately agreed. But he cautioned me that the party comrades have ceased thinking, in fact locked their process of thinking and given the key to the Politburo. This unfortunate process, that is not to be expected from comrades, has taken place and yet does take place.

In this background one can state that the rigorous scientific method that Marx had outlined in *Capital* where science was to strip the mystical veil and discover (*entdecken*) the rationality of society and history[105] would take a backseat in the Indian Left movement. The reason of this is not because the Left in India did not have intellectuals and communist militants in their ranks. Instead the reason is that the shadow of Stalinism and the ghost of a duplicate Marxism would haunt the Left in India, just as it would haunt the world communist movement.

And yet anyone who would be a passionate reader of the Marxist classics would know that labour would serve the makings of humanity—to borrow Engels' term: the "part played by labour in the transition of ape to human"—and that intellectual labour (or to use a term of Louis Althusser "theoretical practice") would serve the makings of the world communist revolution. However for the Left in India, the world would always be a small place, dictated by Stalin's notorious "socialism in one country". There are two problems, as we shall see, the generic question of "socialism in one country" and the specific one of "country" or the "national question", that would bring in the question of the nation state.

The issues that would emerge would be: (1) the impossibility of socialism in one country that Marx and Engels recognised and (2) the national question that cannot be reduced only to the history of West Europe and the formation of nation states with their respective bourgeois revolutions. Nation states, after all, do not have to be celebrated. They are made on the spilling of blood. Nation states of course are not natural phenomena. Instead one has to understand that nation states are predicated on the emergence and development of capitalism. This however does not mean that they are predicted on the transcendence of feudalism (to be understood in the dialectic of the transition of feudalism to capitalism) and thus declared progressive. Since there has been no "Indian feudalism", its transcendence is simply a chimera.

One cannot romanticise nation states. In fact the recognition of the subaltern histories of non-Western societies-spanning from West Asia to South Asia which have a common binding far transcends national boundaries constructed by colonialism. It is this alternative history that we need to bring out, this alternative that binds the subaltern people of Asia.

Besides the challenge of recognising the caste-Asiatic mode of production, one has the challenge of breaking out from the chains of the politics of the nation state for the creation of a genuine internationalism. This genuineness of internationalism is predicated on the formation of the Asian Soviets. This form necessarily involves the breakdown of the colonially constructed borders of India-Pakistan-Bangladesh-Iran-Afghanistan-Iraq-Nepal-Sri Lanka, etc.

The fact that the Parliamentary Left is nationalist (in the very bourgeois sense) one knows for sure. And any discerning reader of Marxism would know that National Socialism was a myth and that there was no possibility of this notorious "socialism in one country" that Stalin advocated since the mid-1920s. The fact that the Indian Left by and large yet believes to this date in this myth is shocking. And in order to understand that there can be no socialism in one country, let us take Engels' 'Principles of Communism', where to the question: "Will it be possible for the revolution to take place in one country alone?", one understands why Engels answers in one word is: "No".[106] One wonders why the Parliamentary Left has not understood this simple fact:

> Large-scale industry has already brought all the peoples of the earth, and especially the civilised peoples, into such close relations with one another that none is independent of what happens to the others. Further, it has coordinated the social development of all civilised countries to such an extent that in all of them bourgeoisie and proletariat have become the two decisive classes of society and the struggle between them the main struggle of the day. The communist revolution, therefore, will be not merely a national one; it will take place in all civilised countries simultaneously, that is to say, at least in England, America, France and Germany. It will in each of these countries develop more quickly or more slowly according as one country or the other has a more developed industry, greater wealth, a more significant mass of productive forces. Hence it will go most slowly and will meet most obstacles in Germany; most rapidly and easily in

> England. It will have a powerful impact on the other countries of the world and will radically alter and accelerate their course of development up to now. It is a universal revolution and so will have universal range.[107]

Somewhat later, in *The Class Struggle in France,* Marx chided the French proletariat for imagining that they would be able to "consummate a proletariat revolution within the national walls of France".[108] But this form of internationalism has been alien for the Indian Established Left, just as Marx's slogan "their battle cry must be the Revolution in Permanence"[109] is alien to them. For these revisionists, following the master revisionist Stalin, the idea of the Permanent Revolution was an illusion created by his phantasised enemy Trotsky. Just as Trotsky would become the phantasised and "hated-hellish other" for Stalin, internationalism would become this hellish other for the global Stalinists. The Indian Left would not be left out from this fantasy.

In this sense, internationalism was always removed from the genre of the Indian Left. On issues of foreign policy for example, (take the case of the relations between Pakistan and India), there is no difference between the policies of the liberal Congress and the Established Left, forget the very burning questions of the right of people to self-determination whether it is in Kurdistan, Baluchistan, or Kashmir. It is the same nation state that governs the politics and ideology of the bourgeoisie that governs the politics of the Indian Left. In this sense it was the map carved by British colonialism with the Indian nation state forming its contours that would serve as the political cartography of the Indian Left. For the Indian Left it was the Indian nation with its colonial constructed bureaucratic system and the parliamentary state that was to be protected and nurtured, as if, naturally evolving into socialism. Nothing could be more removed from Marx's revolutionary repertoire than this form of petty bourgeois nationalism.

Now consider Stalin's response to Marx's internationalism. For Stalin, contra-Engels: "We have in the main already accomplished such a revolution in one separate country, in our country".[110] Consider Stalin's nationalist rhetoric: "Of course, if Engels were alive, he would not cling to old formula. On the contrary, he would heartily welcome our revolution, and would say: "To the devil with old formulas! Long live the victorious revolution in the USSR".[111] One only wished that the "stubborn empiric" (to borrow Trotsky's term)—Stalin and the global Stalinists—had understood that revolutions are "world-historical"[112], and that revolutions have to be "simultaneous" and "all at once".[113] And if only the stubborn empirics had understood that if revolutions are merely nationalistic, merely local, then "want is made general, and with want the struggle for necessities would begin again, and the old filthy business (of class exploitation, my insertion, M.J.) would be necessarily restored".[114] It is important to note that Marx said this in the mid and late 1840s. What he said then happened in the Soviet Union in 1991. The "filthy business" was necessarily restored. But the Stalinists never understood this in 1991, nor would they ever understand it. In fact what Stalin did not understand, in fact began his school of falsification of Marxism, the Established Left took his myths lock stock and barrel. Marx's revolutionary repertoire would be left completely un-understood, if not totally misunderstood.

It is necessary to understand this Stalinist myth of National Socialism with another myth, namely the myth of socialist commodity production. Since it is this double myth combine which dominates, by and large, the workings of Left parties in India, one needs to understand these myths. And in order to look at the devastation that commodity production creates and how money, capital and exploitation are inherent in commodity production let us look at what Engels once said:

> Once the commodity-producing society has further developed the value form, which is inherent in commodities as such, to the money form, various germs still hidden in value break through to the light of day. The first and most essential effect is the generalisation of the commodity form. Money forces the commodity form even on the objects which have hitherto been produced directly for self-consumption; it drags them into exchange. Thereby the commodity form and money penetrate the internal husbandry of the communities directly associated for production; they break one tie of communion after another, and dissolve the community into a mass of private producers. At first,

> as can be seen in India, money replaces joint tillage of the soil by individual tillage; at a later stage it puts an end to the common ownership of the tillage area, which still manifests itself in periodical redistribution, by a final division (for example in the village communities on the Mosel; and it is now beginning also in the Russian village communes); finally, it forces the dividing-up of whatever woodland and pasturage is still owned in common. Whatever other causes arising in the development of production are also operating here, money always remains the most powerful means through which their influence is exerted on the communities. And, despite all "laws and administrative regulations", money would with the same natural necessity inevitably break up the Dühring economic commune, if it ever came into existence.[115]

When one understands that "the commodity-form and money penetrate the internal husbandry of the communities directly associated for production; they break one tie of communion after another, and dissolve the community into a mass of private producers", one also understands that the narrative of the collapse of the Soviet Union with its experiments of National Socialism and commodity-socialism was inscribed on its forehead right from the beginning. This is because the Soviet bureaucrats and oligarchs spoke in the language that the utopian socialists spoke in the 19th century. Utopian socialism (whether the type of Pierre Proudhon or Eugene Dühring) want *merely* the just distribution of capitalist wealth. The capitalist mode of production and the inherent contradictions and inequalities would never be examined. Stalin and Mao did exactly that. Look at Stalin's *Economic Problems of Socialism in the USSR* and Mao's *Critique of Soviet Economics* and one will easily decipher the essential revisionist and state capitalist characteristics of both Stalin and Mao. For the Parliamentary Left, it is the political economy of Stalin and Mao that serve as the models for their so-called socialist experiments.

It must be noted that Stalin's *Economic Problems of Socialism in the USSR* of so-called socialist economics institionalised this myth of commodity-socialism. The biggest challenge for the Indian Left is to critique this myth if it needs having a scientific basis. Take Stalin's own question: "Is commodity production a good thing?" Stalin answers: "It is not a bad thing".[116] One needs to combine the myths of National Socialism (of Stalin and Mao) and socialist production (again of Stalin and Mao). But it must be recognised that the theme of commodity-based socialism was not only an error, which though institutionalised by Stalin, also had a voice in his bête noire Trotsky.[117] Mao thought that value is not a relation of production (this is Marx's position,) but a thing. For Mao, value is a thing and a technique and "commodity production will serve socialism quite tamely".[118] Once this confusion is clear—of transforming the idea of value as a relations of production (Marx) to that of technique (Stalin and Mao)—one will be able to recognise the difference between the socialism of Marx and that of Stalin and Mao.

What we saw in 1991 is the spectacle that commodity would not serve socialism. Contra Mao, it would not serve socialism tamely. The taming of the commodity is like Shakespeare's *Taming of the Shrew*. What the tamers of the commodity forget is that commodity production is directly related to class formations, human alienation, the accumulation of capital and the crisis emerging thereon. What one has to remember is that commodity production is related not only to exploitative property relations but also related to the estranged mind and the politics of the repressed unconscious. Like the return of the repressed and "the traditions of all dead generations it weighs like a nightmare on the brains of the living."[119] Stalin had not only forgotten Engels, but Marx too. In contrast to the good commodity of Stalin and Mao, look at the commodity which is represented as the awful magician, theologian and necromantic artist:

> A commodity appears, at first sight, a very trivial thing, and easily understood. Its analysis shows that it is, in reality, a very queer thing, abounding in metaphysical subtleties and theological niceties. So far as it is the value in use, there is nothing mysterious about it, whether we consider it from the point of view that by its properties it is capable of satisfying human wants, or from the point that these properties are the products of human labour. It is clear as noon-day, that man, by his industry, changes the forms of the materials furnished by Nature, in such a way as to make

> them useful to him. The form of wood, for instance, is altered, by making a table out of it. Yet, for all that, the table continues to be that common, every-day thing, wood. But, so soon as it steps forth as a commodity, it is changed into something transcendent. It not only stands with its feet on the ground, but, in relation to other commodities, it stands on its head, and evolves out of its wooden brain (*Holzkopf*) grotesque ideas, far more wonderful than "table turning ever was" (*viel wunderlicher, als wenn er aus freien Stücken zu tanzen begänne. Man erinnert sich, dass China und die Tische zu tanzen anfingen, als alle übrige Welt still zu stehn schein—pour encourager les autres*)...... In order, therefore, to find an analogy, we must have recourse to the mist-enveloped regions of the religious world. In that world the productions of the human brain appear as independent beings endowed with life and entering into relations both with one another and the human race. So it is in the world of commodities with the production of men's hands. This I call the Fetishism which attaches itself to the products of labour, so soon as they are produced as commodities, and which is therefore inseparable from the production of commodities.[120]

Look at Marx's reference at "table turning", where tables begin to dance (*die Tische zu tanzen anfingen*), or where heads dance (*als wenn er aus freien Stücken zu tanzen begänne*). It must be noted that this dancing of heads and tables is related to the game of evoking of the spirits of the dead. The metaphor of this "table turning" where heads seem to dance was part of the 19th century fad of the European elites who were being involved in occultism, especially by playing with planchets. That is why Marx says that commodity production involves not only theology and metaphysics, but also magic and necromancy.[121] So to the question: "Is commodity production a bad thing?" one but has to disagree with Stalin. For commodities involve not only economics, but historical constellations which bind the base and the intellectual superstructure where not only classes and capital are produced and reproduced, but also the fetishism of consciousness and the regression of critical thinking. When one has entered the brave new world of commodity production, then one has also entered the world of the dancing tables and the wooden head (*Holzkopf*) possessed by the spirits of the netherworld.

But there is another part to this narrative of the fetishism of commodities and the dancing tables. In *Why We Are Not Hindus* I had said that in this idea of fetishism and being possessed by alien and dreadful spirits which rule us, one needs to replace the word "commodity" with "Hindu Rashtra". This is what we get after replacing the words:

> The "Hindu Rashtra" appears as, at first sight, a very trivial thing, and easily understood. Its analysis shows that it is in reality, a very queer thing, abounding in metaphysical subtleties and theological niceties. So far as it is value in use, there is nothing mysterious about it.....But so soon as the "Hindu Rashtra" steps forth as a commodity, it is changed into something transcendent. This "Hindu Rashtra" not only stands with its feet on the ground, but, in relation to all other commodities, it stands on its head, and evolves out of its wooden brain grotesque ideas, far more wonderful than "table-turning" ever was.[122]

The triumph of the fascists in the 2014 National Elections was a sign of the return of the dancing tables and wooden heads, dancing tables and wooden heads which have now become totally authoritarian. It was also a sign that the bourgeoisie with their wooden heads and the political elites with their dancing tables no longer need the Established Indian Left to play their role of the welfare commodity producers. After all, the commodities and dancing tables of the bourgeoisie would be more interesting and saleable than the commodities of the Stalin and Mao-inspired Established Left. Bourgeois commodities can dance better than the commodities of the Left.

The destruction of this Parliamentary Left could be said to be grafted in its very beginning, since this logic of 'good' commodity production along with their regular doses of Stalinist authoritarian politics would never leave their ideological parameters. Locked brains can, after all, never think. If Žižek said that liberal democracy perfected the technique of the *Denkverbot* or the "prohibition against thinking", then the Established Left would also fall in this liberal democratic genre. The trap for the Parliamentary Left—Stalinism authoritarianism and liberalism—would sink them into the marketplace where the fascists would be able to get a better price for their wares.

If M.N. Roy, Sultan Ahmed Khan Tarin, Ahmed Husan, Mohammad Shafiq Siddiqui, Rafiq Ahmed, M. Acharya, Evelyn Trent Roy and Rosa Fitingof, as the first fighters of the communist movement in the 1920s, created the possibilities of a vision that went much beyond the ruins of capitalism, the present Established Left could only keep the memories of these leaders as museum pieces. Even S.A. Dange, B.T. Ranadive, P.C. Joshi, E.M.S. Namboodiripad, C. Rajaweshara Rao, P. Sundarayya, Jyoti Basu and Harkishan Surjeet would be converted to memoirs. Locked brains can, after all, have only distant memories and that too frozen memories.

But history does find its dialectical modes of moving forwards. Indian fascism would find opposition clearly from the student movement which would now not be dependent on old modes of thinking. This movement would not bow to old ideas, to old modes of articulating emancipatory politics. They would also not bow down to the party leadership. Indian capitalism needed its gravediggers and the celebrators of revolution. It finally found this new light.

The Biggest Challenge: Understanding the Myth of Socialist Commodity Production

But quite often light is replaced with darkness. And in this era of triumphant fascism one cannot afford to get lost in darkness once again. The New Movement will have to recognise this fact. After all, utopias emerge when clear thinking is replaced with good wishes. If, however, strict scientific explanation needs to replace polemics in political economy, the same must be said about strict scientific explanation of the dynamics governing capitalism in particular and history in general.

Let us begin with the main myth—that of socialist commodity production, the myth that tore the Soviet Union into infinite pieces. For Marx, socialism (even in its alleged first stage), as he says in the *Critique of the Gotha Programme*, is not built on commodity production. This for certain reasons is not brought into the centre of Marxist reasoning. Note what Marx said in 1875:

> Within the co-operative society based on common ownership of

> the means of production, the producers do not exchange their products; just as little does the labour employed on the products appear here *as the value* of these products, as a material quality possessed by them, since now, in contrast to capitalist society, individual labour no longer exists in an indirect fashion but directly as a component part of total labour. The phrase "proceeds of labour", objectionable also today on account of its ambiguity, thus loses all meaning. What we have to deal with here is a communist society, not as it has developed on its own foundations, but, on the contrary, just as it emerges from capitalist society; which is thus in every respect, economically, morally, and intellectually, still stamped with the birthmarks of the old society from whose womb it emerges. Accordingly, the individual producer receives back from society—after the deductions have been made—exactly what he gives to it. What he has given to it is his individual quantum of labour. For example, the social working day consists of the sum of the individual hours of work; the individual labour time of the individual producer is the part of the social working day contributed by him, his share in it. He receives a certificate from society that he has furnished such-and-such an amount of labour (after deducting his labour for the common funds); and with this certificate, he draws from the social stock of means of consumption as much as the same amount of labour cost. The same amount of labour which he has given to society in one form, he receives back in another.[123]

The same is said by Engels in his *Anti-Dühring*. Note Engels:

> From the moment when society enters into possession of the means of production and uses them in direct association for production, the labour of each individual, however varied its specifically useful character may be, becomes at the start and directly social labour. The quantity of social labour contained in a product need not then be established in a *roundabout way* (my emphasis, M.J.); daily experience shows in a direct way how much of it is required on the average. Society can simply calculate how many hours of labour are contained in a steam-engine, a bushel of wheat of the last harvest, or a hundred square yards of cloth of a certain quality. It could therefore never occur to it still to express the quantities of labour put into the products, quantities which it will then know directly and in their absolute amounts, in a third product, in a measure which, besides, is only relative, fluctuating, inadequate, though formerly unavoidable for lack of a better one,

> rather than express them in their natural, adequate and absolute measure, *time.* Just as little as it would occur to chemical science still to express atomic weight in a roundabout way, relatively, by means of the hydrogen atom, if it were able to express them absolutely, in their adequate measure, namely in actual weights, in billionths or quadrillionths of a gramme. Hence, on the assumptions we made above, society will not assign values to products. It will not express the simple fact that the hundred square yards of cloth have required for their production, say, a thousand hours of labour in the oblique and meaningless way, stating that they have the *value* of a thousand hours of labour. It is true that even then it will still be necessary for society to know how much labour each article of consumption requires for its production. It will have to arrange its plan of production in accordance with its means of production, which include, in particular, its labour-powers. The useful effects of the various articles of consumption, compared with one another and with the quantities of labour required for their production, will in the end determine the plan. People will be able to manage everything very simply, without the intervention of much-vaunted "value".[124]

Note one does not need this much vaunted "value" in socialism. There is one more very important paragraph of Engels that one needs to note and understand:

> The concept of value is the most general and therefore the most comprehensive expression of the economic conditions of commodity production. Consequently, this concept contains the germ, not only of money, but also of all the more developed forms of the production and exchange of commodities. The fact that value is the expression of the social labour contained in the privately produced products itself creates the possibility of a difference arising between this social labour and the private labour contained in these same products. If therefore a private producer continues to produce in the old way, while the social mode of production develops this difference will become palpably evident to him. The same result follows when the aggregate of private producers of a particular class of goods produces a quantity of them which exceeds the requirements of society. The fact that the value of a commodity is expressed only in terms of another commodity, and can only be realised in exchange for it, admits of the possibility that the exchange may never take place altogether, or at least may not realise the correct value. Finally, when the

> specific commodity labour-power appears on the market, its value is determined, like that of any other commodity, by the labour-time socially necessary for its production. The value form of products therefore already contains in embryo the whole capitalist form of production, the antagonism between capitalists and wage-workers, the industrial reserve army, crises. To seek to abolish the capitalist form of production by establishing "true value" is therefore tantamount to attempting to abolish Catholicism by establishing the "true" Pope, or to set up a society in which at last the producers control their product, by consistently carrying into life an economic category which is the most comprehensive expression of the enslavement of the producers by their own product.[125]

Note the last eight words of Engels' sentence: "enslavement of the producers by their own product". This idea of the fetish character of commodity production, where commodities (realised as the value-form, exchange value, money and capital) control people, was totally alien to Stalin and Mao. For how could messiahs be controlled by anyone and anything? Note that for Marx, the commodity besides being a necromantic artist and metaphysician[126] is also a "born leveller and cynic" (*Geborner Leveller und Zyniker*)[127]. In contrast to Marx and Engels, look at what Mao said. According to Mao (and note his extremely unscientific observations):

> There are those who fear commodities. Without exception they fear capitalism, not realising that with the elimination of capitalists it is allowable to expand commodity production vastly. We are still backward in commodity production, behind Brazil and India. Commodity production is not an isolated thing. Look at the context: capitalism or socialism. In a capitalist context it is capitalist commodity production. In a socialist context it is socialist commodity production.[128]

And since the Indian Left stubbornly reads only this form of revisionism and since the Indian Left is predicated on the revisionism of socialist commodity production and refuses to look into the deeper structures that Marx and Engels had critiqued, their politics can only be reformist (reforming capitalism by transforming capitalist commodity to so-called socialist commodity production).

This act of completely transcending commodity production, one must note, remains the crux of the problem for Marxists to solve. When one talks of Marxist socialism, one essentially means non-commodity socialism. Ignoring this very important part of Marxism (critique of commodity production and the value-form) and then merely talking of collective and public ownership of means of production merely replaces the Marxist language of the critique of political economy with legalist concepts. The Indian Left not only duplicates the false language of Stalin and Mao. They actually go back to Proudhon and Dühring, forgetting that Marx in *The Poverty of Philosophy* and Engels in *Anti-Dühring* had critiqued both Proudhon and Dühring. What was critiqued by Marx and Engels was taken as the essential repertoire by the Stalinists and Maoists. Note Marx here who says how for Proudhon and the John Gray school of utopian socialism:

> *Goods are to be produced as commodities but not exchanged as commodities.* Gray entrusts the realisation of this pious wish to a national bank. On the one hand, society in the shape of the bank makes the individuals independent of the conditions of private exchange, and, on the other hand, it causes them to continue to produce on the basis of private exchange. Although Gray merely wants "to reform" the money evolved by commodity exchange, he is compelled by the intrinsic logic of the subject-matter to repudiate one condition of bourgeois production after another. Thus he turns capital into national capital, and land into national property and if his bank is examined carefully it will be seen that it not only receives commodities with one hand and issues certificates for labour supplied with the other, but that it directs production itself.[129]

What then is this revisionism based on? It is based on the idea of "the degradation of money and the exaltation of commodities" which is expressed as "the essence of socialism".[130] Note also the utopian socialists who have the pious wish for the national bank to oversee how commodity production takes place. If Gray had this fantasy of the national-utopian bank, Stalin and Mao transformed this utopian bank into the even more utopian state which would work as the socialist bank. This I call the essence of utopian revisionism which went from Proudhon and Gray to Stalin and Mao. The Indian Left took over these utopian fantasies. Science, or to be precise Marxist science, would be far away from their utopian minds.

Let us note another structure of this revisionist fantasy. Note what Stalin says in his *Economic Problems of Socialism in the USSR*:

> Our commodity production is not of the ordinary type, but a special kind of commodity production. Commodity production without capitalists....[131]

Note two things: (1) Stalin's idea of commodity production without the capitalists which has now become the signature of the Indian Parliamentary Left: *capitalism without the capitalists*, and (2) how Stalin's revisionism (where he decides to abolish Marx's essential ideas) becomes firstly totally absurd and then absolutely authoritarian:

> More, I think that we must also discard certain other concepts taken from Marx's *Capital*—where Marx was concerned with an analysis of capitalism—and artificially applied to our socialist relations. I am referring to such concepts, among others, as "necessary" and "surplus" labour, "necessary" and "surplus" product, "necessary" and "surplus" time. Marx analysed capitalism in order to elucidate the source of exploitation of the working class—surplus value—and to arm the working class, which was bereft of means of production, with an intellectual weapon for the overthrow of capitalism. It is natural that Marx used concepts (categories) which fully corresponded to capitalist relations. But it is strange, to say the least, to use these concepts now, when the working class is not only not bereft of power and means of production, but, on the contrary, is in possession of the power and controls the means of production. Talk of labour power being a commodity, and of "hiring" of workers sounds rather absurd now, under our system: as though the working class, which possesses means of production, hires itself and sells its labour power to itself. It is just as strange to speak now of "necessary" and "surplus" labour: as though, under our conditions, the labour contributed by the workers to society for the extension of production, the promotion of education and public health, the organisation of defence, etc., is not just as necessary to the working

> class, now in power, as the labour expended to supply the personal needs of the worker and his family...... I think that our economists should put an end to this in-congruity between the old concepts and the new state of affairs in our socialist country, by replacing the old concepts with new ones that correspond to the new situation. We could tolerate this incongruity for a certain period, but the time has come to put an end to it.[132]

If it becomes clear that Stalin and Mao did indeed tamper and manipulate Marx's essential ideas by replacing Marx's "old concepts" with Stalin's "new ones" which correspond to a "new state of affairs", then it becomes clear that the Marxism that we have inherited is a tampered and manipulated form of Marxism.

Very recently Peter Hudis has made the idea of post-commodity production socialism a central problem of his work.[133] "Envisioning socialism" as Prasenjit Bose calls it in this volume, has necessarily to deal with the following questions: "What is socialism?", "Would socialism have commodity production, value, money and consequently the wages system?" For post-Marx socialism, these very important questions remained not merely unanswered, but unasked.

For Marx, there can be no commodity production in socialism. Yet for certain reasons the Indian Left has never bothered to even raise this issue. For them (which includes even the Trotskyites) the Soviet Union was socialist (even "degenerated form" as Trotsky thought it to be). If then these state capitalist models of Stalin and Mao are the models of socialism, then the Left would very strangely be arguing only for a different model of capitalism. For the Stalinists and Maoists, it is the Yankee model which they find distasteful. So they create their own almost Platonic version (or neo-Platonic version, if you will) of state capitalism and pose it as socialist. At least for the CPI(M) it is the capitalists who are bad (or certain versions of capitalists—crony capitalists). Capitalism is in itself never seriously critiqued. The Stalinist and Maoist versions of capitalism would, of course, be far removed from their thinking radar. In fact these would be the models to be seriously studied and implemented. *Marxism would then become not merely revisionist through and through. It would become counterrevolutionary*. What has not been recognised is that the counterrevolution against socialism will not be raised as much by the White Armies as by the army of cheap commodities.

When Marx says that the same crap occurs once again in *The German Ideology* and the old filth is restored, he implies that the shit of capitalism occurs once again. One would have to begin once again. But for this one does not only have to wade through Auschwitz and Guantanamo Bay. One has to wade through the lavatories of capitalist unreason.

"The Truth is Out There" or The Lavatory Mode of Production

Sometimes, so Marx once said, one "makes even the lavatory an object of divine law".[134] And it is with this new finding that we make new beginnings. Beginnings are always hard to find. Hegel said so in his *Phenomenology of Mind*. And Marx in the *Grundrisse* said that one necessarily has to begin with solid foundations. One then has to begin with the question of the mode of production in India. For the time being one will skip the debate that began in the 1960s with Utsa Patnaik, Ashok Rudra, Paresh Chattopadhyay, Amit Bhaduri, Jairus Banaji and Gail Omvedt. Instead one will need to reflect on a different type of philosophising that Žižek reminded us of. According to Žižek, there are three types of toilets—the German, French and the Anglo-Saxon.[135] Note how this reminds us in an exactly opposite way of the three sources and components of Marxism: German classical philosophy, French socialism and English political economy.[136] What needs being said is that besides the flush of reason that is contained in dialectical materialism (found in the triad of German classical philosophy, French socialism and English political economy), there is another flush where what Žižek calls "excremental function" and ""excremental excess" are found.[137]

One may however ask: "What does this excrete have to do with the mode of production and how is this type of almost cynical philosophising have to do with understanding the dominant classes and the Left movement in India?" The answer is simple: "Excrete is intrinsically related to commodity production. But it is also related to human alienation". To understand this very fundamental and materialist understanding, let us recall the very first page of *Capital*, Vol. I where Marx uses three German words—*Ding, Sache* and *Gegenstand* all three words indicating the English word "thing"[138]. The commodity is a thing, so Marx says that "satisfies human wants of some sort of another".[139] What one needs to say is that the act of commodity production is an act of alienation. But it is also a type of excreting. Just as humans shit, so they are involved in the production of commodities. Commodities are literally not merely "things", they are shit. And just as in Žižek's readings of the three toilets, the shit shows itself and then disappears. So too in Marx: "Its existence as a material thing is put out of sight"[140]. It is in this sense that we call the capitalist mode of perfection the "lavatory mode of production". This idea of the lavatory mode of production is unleashed on not only the Indian economic and political elites, but also on the foundational myth of Indian caste-civilisation that we highlighted earlier. The foundational myth talks of mouth, arms, belly and feet. Since a number of anatomical parts are silenced, we like Phule's invoking of the creation myth of the caste system in *Slavery* bring in the silenced anatomical parts.

But there is something more in this new mode of production and that is the understanding that in the network of capital flows, capital flowing from North America and West Europe to Asia, Latin America and Africa, capital in being exported is literally shit in the peripheries of capital accumulation. Let us recall Žižek once again:

> In a traditional German lavatory, the hole into which shit disappears after we flush is right at the front, so that shit is first laid out for us to sniff and inspect for traces of illness; in the typical French lavatory, on the contrary, the hole is at the back—that is, shit is supposed to disappear as soon as possible; finally, the Anglo-Saxon (English or American) lavatory presents a synthesis, a kind of mediation between these opposite—the basin is full of water, so that the shit floats in it—visible, but not to be inspected. No wonder that in the famous discussion of European lavatories at the beginning of her half-forgotten *Fear of Flying*, Erica Jong mockingly claims that 'German toilets are really the key to the horrors of the Third Reich. People who can build toilets like this

> are capable of anything.' It is clear that none of these versions can be accounted for in purely utilitarian terms: each involves a certain ideological perception of how the subject should relate to unpleasant excrement which comes from within our body is clearly discernible—again, for the third time, "the truth is out there".[141]

It is this simple method of anthropological observation: "the truth is out there" which provides us a clue to popularising the question of capitalism and the mode of production in India. What needs to be said is that the accumulation of capital is actually an accumulation of shit. We have now what Žižek calls "the rise of 'dead nature'".[142]

So what is this truth which is "out there" and how does one understand the mode of production and the dominant classes in India? For this let us turn to Trotsky. Trotsky writing in his magnum opus *1905* said the following about Russia:

> In Europe 5.4 million square kilometres, in Asia 17.5 million, and a population of 150 million. In this enormous area, all stages of human development: from the primitive savagery of the northern forests, where men eat raw fish and worship trees, to the most modern social relations of the capitalist city, where the Socialist worker regards himself as an active participant in world politics......The most concentrated industry in Europe, based on the most backward agriculture in Europe. The most colossal government in the world, using all the achievements of technical progress of its own country. This is the soil on which social classes, grow, live and fight.[143]

In this context the mode of production debate in India about whether India is semi-feudal, capitalist, colonial, etc. ("where men eat raw fish and worship trees", to recall Trotsky once again, "having the most concentrated industry in Europe, based on the most backward agriculture") has truths in every layer of the argument. India, as the elites have said, incorporates everything that the world offers. No wonder what looks like semi-feudalism, semi-capitalism and the colonial mode of production, along with extreme high-tech finance capitalism is found in India.

Lenin (as we noted earlier) wanted to use gold for

constructing lavatories.[144] In a sense Lenin's use of gold was to put an end to gold as fetish. But then the German Revolution was defeated. Trotsky's "war communism" gave way to pure survival for the Bolsheviks. The New Economic Policy (NEP) came to replace Trotsky's war communism and the NEP bureaucrats came to replace the Bolsheviks. Gold and all the fetishism attached to it lived on and two notorious characters that Marx had warned in *Capital*, Monsieur Capital and Madame Rent, along with gold too did their "ghost walk as social characters and at the same time as mere things".[145]

Historical Materialism and the Ape with the Skull

"Gold? Yellow, glittering, precious gold?" so Marx said quoting Shakespeare's *Timon of Athens*.[146] Gold is what makes "black white, foul fair, wrong right, base noble, old young, coward valiant."[147] Gold is also what "makes the hoar leprosy adored, place thieves and give them title, knee and approbation, with senators on the bench".[148] For Marx the realisation and perfection of this logic of gold is capitalism and generalised commodity production. Lenin's idea of gold to be used for lavatories is a marker for the brutal barbarism of capitalism and imperialism. Yet it is this magical logic of gold that prevailed, the magical logic that turned the Bolshevik Revolution into the counterrevolution. That a counterrevolution did happen in the Soviet Union one generally recognises. The problem (as we have already stated) is that usually the time of the counterrevolution is situated in 1991. This is wrong. 1991 is only the time for the full manifestation of the counterrevolution. In actuality the counterrevolution took place in 1928. Its effect was lethal. As counterrevolution from "within" (as against a counterevolution "from the outside"), it disguised itself as the authentic workers' movement. What was born was a duplicate Marxism.

And because of this duplicate Marxism which speaks the voices of nationalism, abstraction and Revolution without a Revolution, one is left with a very ironic image of the revolutionary condition produced. The image is derived from a little statuette titled *Affe mit Schädel* ("Ape with Skull") sculpted by Hugo Rheinhold and gifted by Armand Hammer to Lenin which Lenin kept at his desk at the Kremlin. Not much has been said about this statuette, even less said about its relation with historical materialism. One needs to have a philosophical look at this picture. Let us thus have a look at it.

This little statuette is of an ape, posed in the style of Auguste Rodin's celebrated sculpture "The Thinker". The ape, like Rodin's humanist thinker, is deep in thought. He is sitting on books. Calipers meant for scientific measurement are held with his feet. But this figure is the exact reverse of Rodin's figure. The ape evokes the figure of Shakespeare's Hamlet who mourns the death of his court jester, Yorick. In his hands is a human skull. Amongst the books that he is sitting on, the most visible one is the *Bible* which has *eritis sicut dues* ("ye shall be as gods") written on it. *Eritis sicut dues,* one must note, is from the chapter Genesis in the *Bible,* recalling the temptation of Eve to eat the forbidden fruit from the tree of the knowledge of good and evil, by the snake, the devil himself. Darwin's magnum opus is also seen next to the *Bible*. The narrative of science and theology are intertwined in this statuette.

Now any reader of Marx will recognise that there is some sort of tragicomic dramaturgy found in this rendering. But why did Lenin keep this statuette on his study desk? Did he anticipate the counterrevolution and the complete collapse of the Soviet Union? Does the figure of the contemplating ape signify evolution in the reverse? Or are there other philosophical questions of knowledge, emancipation and power that had also fascinated besides Rheinhold and Goethe, also fascinate Lenin? Was then this ape with the skull nothing but another tragic rendering of European aesthetics akin to Goethe's *Faust*? A historical materialist answer is that Lenin was reminding himself that counterrevolution marches alongside the forces of revolution and history does not move, as if, according to some miraculous law of development.[149]

But this figure of the ape with the skull is not only about tragicomic dramaturgy. It is about the pursuit of knowledge, in fact, about what one may call after Friedrich Nietzsche as the "will to power" or in contrast to Nietzsche, as what Jürgen Habermas calls "knowledge and human interests". In *What is to be Done?*, Lenin had said that "without revolutionary theory there can be not revolutionary movement".[150] But we have a seeming contrasting narrative. In Goethe's magnum opus *Faust* the devil, Mephistopheles seems to be saying that one can have spontaneous revolution without theoretical intervention. Consider Mephistopheles:

All theory, my friend, is grey,
But green is life's golden tree.[151]

Now relate this couplet with Rheinhold's statuette and the concealed image of the Biblical tree of knowledge with its forbidden fruits. Goethe's tree (unlike Rheinhold's absent-present tree) is both green and golden. Yet the gold is not that of Lenin that is to be used for constructing lavatories. What Goethe is decrying (as Marx would do later) is the scholastic part of human knowledge (all theory is grey) claiming that scholasticism is basically nothing but pure sterility, and it is better to be tempted by the devil and taste the fruit of the knowledge of good and evil. Mephistopheles, in this sense, is the rebel, unlike Rheinhold's pondering ape who in pure contemplation refuses to partake in the class struggle, or if one remains with the Biblical narrative, then refusing to participate in the struggle between good and evil. Mephistopheles, in this sense, is the philosopher par excellence of the philosophy of praxis. But why did Lenin think it necessary to remind himself of this blundering ape? Why was there no Mephistopheles on his study desk?

This volume on the challenges for the Indian Left is on the struggle between Mephistopheles and the ape, praxis and contemplation, internationalism and nationalism, concreteness and abstractions and Revolution with a Revolution vs. Revolution without a Revolution. History knows Lenin, Trotsky, Rosa Luxemburg, et al. as, the Revolutionaries with a Revolution as against the other greats in revolutionary history—Georgi Plekhanov, Eduard Bernstein, Karl Kautsky, Zinoviev all who were without doubt great revolutionaries, but tragically Revolutionaries without the Revolution. They were thus duplicate revolutionaries, revolutionaries that ultimately feared the Revolution. The Established Left has perfected this rather bizarre Revolution without a Revolution.

But there is more to this Revolution without the Revolution, and that is the counterrevolution against the Leninist theory and praxis of the party (that he had first outlined in his *What is to be Done?* and reaching its climax in *State and Revolution*), a counterrevolution perfected by Stalin, speaking however in the name of Lenin. We noted that a counterrevolution took place against Marx. Now we shall see a counterrevolution against Lenin that speaks in his name. The Indian comrades would, by and large, follow the path given by Stalin. Lenin's revolutionary theme of the dialectics of spontaneity and intellectual work in the masses in his *What is to be Done?* would be totally absent from the understanding of the Indian Left. But there is more to the Stalin question than those of philosophical importance.

On December 24, 1922, an ailing Lenin (he was shot in the head by Dora Kaplan) dictated notes that go as the 'Letter to the Congress' where he says:

> Comrade Stalin, having become Secretary-General, has unlimited authority concentrated in his hands, and I am not sure whether he will always be capable of using that authority with sufficient caution. Comrade Trotsky, on the other hand, as his struggles against the C.C. on the question of the People's Commissariat for Communications has already proved, is distinguished not only by outstanding ability. He is personally perhaps the most capable man in the present C.C., but he has displayed excessive self-assurance and shown excessive preoccupation with the purely administrative side of the work.[152]

Lenin was talking of the dangers of split in the party. But the dangers of a split were not related only to the perception of Stalin as having an authoritarian personality, but related to the understanding of the relation of authoritarianism to the class structure of society. But there is another important question when one is reading this famous 'Letter to the Congress', namely, the question of dialectics. Consider Lenin:

> Speaking of the young C.C. members, I wish to say a few words about Bukharin and Pyatakov. They are, in my opinion, the most outstanding figures (among the younger ones), and the following

> must be borne in mind about them: Bukharin is not only a most valuable and major theorist of the Party; he is also rightly considered the favorite of the whole Party, but his theoretical views can be classified as fully Marxist only with the great reserve, for there is something scholastic about him (he has never made a study of dialectics, and, I think, never fully appreciated it).[153]

There are two conclusions that one derives from the above quotes, one that Stalin represented authoritarianism of the worst kind (all the comrades that Lenin mentions in the letter were killed by Stalin), and the other concern is the question of dialectics, especially that of Hegelian dialectics and its relation to Marxism that concerned Lenin at least since 1914. But why does one, so the reader may ask, talk of dialectics and Stalin after talking of dramaturgy, when one is talking of the question of Left politics in India? We are mentioning this because it is Stalinism (or if it is not the brutal kind of Stalinism, then it is the marriage of liberalism with Stalinism) and the lack of the understanding of dialectics that remain the core of Established Left politics in India till date. I am using the term "Established Left", as one will note in my chapters on Leninism in this volume.

But one may ask: "What about the Maoists who have been declared as the single biggest security threat by the previous Indian government? Would they also be Stalinists, *or would one have to understand them as Stalinists in rebellion against Stalinism?"* What I shall be doing here in the introduction is drawing the typology of the Indian Stalinists (the Established Left) and the Maoists in the philosophical background of *history that has turned against itself*.

And this revenge of history—history turning itself—is best represented by the triumph of the fascist BJP which won the 2014 National Elections with 282 seats led by its genocidal ideology of Hindu supremacy. This revenge of history would begin with the end of the rule of the Left Front where their uninterrupted rule for 34 years from 1977 to 2011 would end. The narrative of the collapse in West Bengal, and now down to minuscule numbers in parliament, could be said to be the finale of this tragicomedy. This volume locates the challenges for the Indian Left in this political background.

If Rheinhold's ape is pondering over a human skull sitting on books of theology and science, the question that one can pose is: "Who is the ape and whose skull is in the hands of the ape?" "Is the ape the Indian fascist and the skull that of the Indian Stalinist?" "Or is the ape a Stalinist and the skull that of the toiling masses?" "Or is the ape both a fascist and a Stalinist?"

Stalinism and Indian Stalinism

At this moment it is important to note what Stalinism in the Soviet Union represented and what the Indian Left movement became because of its ideological unclarity that succumbed to the Stalinist ideological prison house.

By Stalinism one means the following:

1. Counterrevolution in the Soviet Union where the New Economic Policy (NEP) bureaucrats replaced the grassroots communists followed by the massacre of the Old Bolsheviks.
2. Fear of World Revolution and the active attempt to sabotage World Revolution. The massacre of the Shanghai communists by Chiang Kai-shek in 1927 is an example of the fear of the World Revolution. Stalin knew that any revolution would displace the bureaucratic Thermidor. Stalin's role has been infamous in the alliance with the Kuomintang led by Chiang Kai-shek and the consequent suppression of the Chinese Soviets. This is what Stalin in his typical rhetoric way said. Note for him any autonomous action of the Chinese proletariat was foolish and the Chinese communists had to be appendages of the Kuomintang. Note this Stalinist rhetoric:

   > Chiang Kai-shek is submitting to discipline. The Kuomintang is a bloc, a sort of revolutionary parliament, with the Right, the Left, and the Communists. Why make a coup d'etat? Why drive away the Right when we have the majority and when the Right listens to us? ... At present, we need the Right. It has capable people, who still direct the army and lead it against the imperialists. Chiang Kai-shek has perhaps no sympathy for the revolution but he is leading the army and cannot do otherwise than lead it against the

> imperialists. Beside this, the people of the Right have relations with the General Chang Tso-lin [the Manchurian warlord] and understand very well how to demoralise them and to induce them to pass over to the side of the revolution, bag and baggage, without striking a blow. Also, they have connections with the rich merchants and can raise money from them. So they have to be utilised to the end, squeezed out like a lemon, and then flung away.[154]

Note the absurdity of using the rightists and then imaging that the right-wing can be "utilised to the end, squeezed out like a lemon, and then flung away". The next week (April 12, 1927) after Stalin's infamous speech, Chiang Kai-shek ordered his troops on the communists where thousands of the vanguard fighters of the Chinese Revolution were brutally massacred. Stalinism always meant that the proletariat was not yet conscious of its mission, that the time for revolution was "not ripe" and that every revolution was to be predicated on its national bourgeoisie. This effectually meant that every revolution has necessarily to be a decaffeinated revolution, an imagined revolution that never happens.

If the massacre of Chiang Kai-shek in 1927 had a Stalinist hand, the rise of the Nazis in Germany in 1933 was not, as if, Stalin was invisible from the scene. It is not merely the case that the Molotov-Ribbentrop deal (August 23, 1939) was an opportunist deal, or even a brilliant deal (as imagined by the Stalinists). It was sign of the simultaneity of two counterrevolutions—the fascist one and the Bonapartist-Stalinist one. In 1931 under the influence of Stalin the German Communist Party (KPD) called the Nazis "working people's comrades". It was also not the case that Stalin was a blundering idiot who shifted from the position that social democrats were social fascists (in fact worse that the fascists themselves), to the position of the united front where at the Seventh Congress of the Comintern in 1935, Georgi Dimitrov outlined the new policy of the "popular front".

3. Theological interpretation of Marxism where Marxism was declared a "science" which studies "laws" which "take place independently of the will of man. Man may discover these laws, get to know them, study them, reckon with them in his activities and utilise them in the interest of society, but he cannot change or abolish them".[155] Nothing more absurd could be formulated. Note how this contemplative attitude which Stalin keeps at the basis of his understanding of Marxism is completely in antithesis to Marx's dictum where the point is *to change the world*.[156]
4. Authoritarian state, socialist commodity production and nationalism in antithesis to Marx's stateless society that has necessarily transcended commodity production and national boundaries.

While a large part of the Indian Left inherited the above stated Stalinist baggage, what marks them off is their fetish for bureaucratic empiricism that may not be *actively* counterrevolutionary, but because of its unconscious and unwitting *Stalinist goal of capitalism without the capitalists*, post-Stalin Stalinism (which includes the Parliamentary Left) would be essentially pro-capitalist, nationalist and consequently against internationalism and the praxis of the international proletariat.

To conclude it is necessary to state that the Indian Left has also been married to Nehruvian liberalism. It is these two souls—of Stalin and Nehru—that are locked in the unfortunate breast of the Parliamentary Left. And like Faust they would inevitably be hurled to their capitalist hell.

Method

In the third volume of *Capital*, Marx says that the stripping of the "estranged outward appearance of economic relationships" forms the basis of the dialectical materialist method.[157] Marx says further: "All science would be superfluous if the outward appearance and the essence of things directly coincided"[158] and that the "force of abstraction" would serve as the microscope that would be able to discover the "economic-cell form" of society.[159] What is thus needed is the "microscopic anatomy" of society.[160] And in the Afterword of the first volume of *Capital* Marx says:

> My dialectic method is not only different from the Hegelian, but is its direct opposite. To Hegel, the life process of the human brain, i.e. the process of thinking, which, under the name of "the Idea," he even transforms into an independent subject, is the demiurgos of the real world, and the real world is only the external, phenomenal form of "the Idea." With me, on the contrary, the ideal is nothing else than the material world reflected by the human mind, and translated into forms of thought.
>
> The mystifying side of Hegelian dialectic I criticised nearly thirty years ago, at a time when it was still the fashion. But just as I was working at the first volume of *Das Kapital*, it was the good pleasure of the peevish, arrogant, mediocre Epigonoi who now talk large in cultured Germany, to treat Hegel in same way as the brave Moses Mendelssohn in Lessing's time treated Spinoza, i.e. as a "dead dog." I therefore openly avowed myself the pupil of that mighty thinker, and even here and there, in the chapter on the theory of value, coquetted with the modes of expression peculiar to him. The mystification which dialectic suffers in Hegel's hands, by no means prevents him from being the first to present its general form of working in a comprehensive and conscious manner. With him it is standing on its head. It must be turned right side up again (*umstulpen*), if you would discover (*entdecken*) the rational kernel within the mystical shell.
>
> In its mystified form, dialectic became the fashion in Germany, because it seemed to transfigure and to glorify the existing state of things. In its rational form it is a scandal and abomination to bourgeoisdom and its doctrinaire professors, because it includes in its comprehension and affirmative recognition of the existing state of things, at the same time also, the recognition of the negation of that state, of its inevitable breaking up; because it regards every historically developed social form as in fluid movement, and therefore takes into account its transient nature not less than its momentary existence; because it lets nothing impose upon it, and is in its essence critical and revolutionary.
>
> The contradictions inherent in the movement of capitalist society impress themselves upon the practical bourgeois most strikingly in the changes of the periodic cycle, through which modern industry runs, and whose crowning point is the universal

> crisis. That crisis is once again approaching, although as yet but in its preliminary stage; and by the universality of its theatre and the intensity of its action it will drum dialectics even into the heads of the mushroom-upstarts of the new, holy Prusso-German empire.[161]

But courtesy Stalin and the ape with the skull, the crisis of capitalism led to the decaffeinated revolutions. It is here that we need to understand that "the betrayal of socialism", as Raya Dunayevskaya once said, "came from within the socialist movement."[162] In this case of betrayal, what one needs is a reemergence of Revolutionary Marxism, that itself needs a creative and activist reimagining of Marxism. Revolutionary Marxism is not reactive like the political practice of our contemporary parliamentary comrades trained in both Brahmanical Overlordship and Eurocentrism.

It was Alvin Gouldner who once said that Marxism has two distinct strains—one is the critical one (following the line of reasoning started by Georg Lukács, Antonio Gramsci and Karl Korsch) and the other the scientific one (namely that of the structuralist school of Louis Althusser)[163]. However in contrast to Gouldner, it needs to be said that Marxist *critique* is not alienated from the realm of *science*, just as *human freedom* is not estranged from *necessity*. Yet what one finds is that the dominant trend in the Indian Left worked on the dualistic space of bourgeois positivism, where science and critique, necessity and freedom are broken as the two unfortunate parts of the Faustean soul.

In contrast to this split between humanism and science that has completed trapped and decimated the Old Left in India, we have Marx's reflections where his 1865 letter to J.B.S. Schweitzer defines science as the "critical knowledge of the historical movement which itself produces the material conditions of emancipation".[164] And in the *Economic and Philosophic Manuscripts of 1844* and in *The German Ideology* Marx talks of understanding the idea of a unified science, the science of history that has two sides: that of nature and that of humanity.[165] Science, in this sense, is always critical and humanistic.

It is this critical and humanist side of science that we must turn to. One then must close the chapter of what may be called "Old Socialism" in all its revisionist and corrupted forms that haunted the stage of 20th century world history. One can do this when one can drum dialectics not only "into the heads of the mushroom-upstarts of the new, holy Prusso-German empire", but primarily drum dialectics into the heads of the Hindu empire. It is only then can one herald a New Socialism. New Socialism recognises that communism is both humanism and naturalism.[166] It also recognises that communism is essentially humanistic and about the "appropriation of the human essence".[167]

Humanity, in this sense, and nothing but humanity, stands at the base of New Socialism. And in the epoch of global economic and environment disaster of apocalyptic proportions, humanity will have to think about its existence as *collective existence*. In this sense it will have to shed its caste, class and and national characteristics.

In this sense of belonging to a large collective, one recalls a philosophical statement that Spinoza espoused: "Neither to weep nor to laugh but to understand". But to understand one has to read, read every text, every sentence, word and letter.

And in this revolutionary sense, one needs to recall a messianic tradition, and tell the comrades:

Read,

Read,

In the name of Marx,

Read.......

NOTES

1. Slavoj Žižek, 'Introduction. Robespierre, or the 'Divine Violence' of Terror', in Maximilen Robespierre, *Virtue and Terror* (London: Verso, 2007), p. VII.
2. Leon Trotsky, *The History of the Russian Revolution*, trans. Max Eastman (London: Victor Gollancz Ltd., 1934), p. 25.
3. Karl Marx, 'The Eighteenth Brumaire of Louis Bonaparte', in *Marx. Engels. Selected Works* (Moscow: Progress Publishers, 1975), pp. 170-1.
4. Ibid., p. 171.

5. Ibid., p. 170.
6. Ibid., p. 171.
7. Karl Marx, 'To Frederick Engels, in London, Manchester, June 6, 1853', in *Marx. Engels. Selected Correspondence* (Moscow: Progress Publishers, 1975), p. 80.
8. Ibid.
9. See Alice Thorner, 'Semi-feudalism or Capitalism? Contemporary Debates on Classes and Modes of Production in India', in *Economic & Political Weekly*, December 4, 1982.
10. Remember that when the neoliberals after 1991 called the Indian Nehruvian state a 'socialist' state, it was a misnomer. The Nehruvian state (with its industrial licensing regime) in a certain sense was a continuation of the classical Asian state as sovereign and patron.
11. Karl Marx, *Capital*, Vol. III (Moscow: Progress Publishers, 1986), p. 796.
12. See Karl Marx, *Capital*, Vol. I, trans. Samuel Moore and Eduard Aveling (Moscow: Progress Publishers, 1983), pp. 178-9.
13. Karl Marx, *Grundrisse* trans. Martin Nicolas (London: Penguin, 1974), p. 473.
14. Karl Marx, *Capital*, Vol. III, p. 791
15. See my 'Asiatic Mode of Production, Caste and the Indian Left', in *Economic & Political Weekly*, Vol. XLIX, No. 19, May 10, 2014, p. 44.
16. See D.D. Kosambi, *The Culture and Civilisation of Ancient India in Historical Outline* (New Delhi: Vikas Publishing House, 2000), p. 50.
17. Brendan O'Leary, *The Asiatic Mode of Production. Oriental Despotism, Historical Materialism and Indian History* (Oxford: Basil Blackwell, 1989), pp. 7-39.
18. See Edward Said, *The Question of Palestine* (New York: Vintage Books, 1992), p. 3.
19. Ibid.
20. Irfan Habib, 'Marx's Perception of India', in *Karl Marx. On India*, ed. Iqbal Husain (New Delhi: Tulika Books, 2006), pp. XX-XXII.
21. Ibid., p. XXVII, n. 46.
22. Ibid., p. XX.
23. Ibid., p. XXI.
24. Ibid.
25. Ibid.
26. Ibid., pp. XXI-XXII.
27. Ibid., p. XXXIII.

28. Ibid., p. XXI.
29. See Marian Sawer, *Marxism and the Question of the Asiatic Mode of Production* (The Hague: Martinus Nijhoff, 1977), p. 159.
30. Karl Marx, 'The British Rule in India', in *On Colonialism* (Moscow: Progress Publishers, 1976), p. 40.
31. Ibid.
32. Ibid.
33. Ibid.
34. Ibid., pp. 40-41.
35. Ibid.
36. Frederick Engels, 'To Karl Marx in London, Manchester, June 6, 1853', in *Marx. Engels. Collected Works*, Vol. 39 (Moscow: Progress Publishers, 1983), pp. 335-6.
37. Karl Marx, 'The Eighteenth Brumaire of Louis Bonaparte', p. 170.
38. Karl Marx, *Grundrisse*, p. 472.
39. Kevin Anderson, *Not Just Capital and Class: Marx on Non-western Societies, Nationalism and Ethnicity*, (2010), http/// www.internationalmarxisthumanist.org/articles.
40. Karl Marx, 'To Frederick Engels in Manchester, London, 16 January, 1858', *Marx. Engels. Collected Works*, Vol. 40 (London: Lawrence and Wishart, 2010), p. 249. See also Kevin Anderson, op. cit.
41. Kevin Anderson, op. cit. Anderson uses the terms "communal property" and "communal governance" which in the Indian context has a reverse meaning. I have replaced the word "communal" with the term "community"
42. Ibid.
43. Ibid.
44. Ibid.
45. Ibid.
46. Karl Marx, *Capital*, Vol. I, p. 670. See also Karl Marx, 'First Draft of the Reply to V.I. Zasulich's Letter', in *Marx. Engels. Selected Works in Three Volumes*, Volume Three (Moscow: Progress Publishers, 1977), p. 152.
47. Karl Marx, 'Preface to the German Edition', *Capital*, Vol. I, p. 19.
48. Max Horkheimer, *Eclipse of Reason* (London: Continuum, 2004), p. 87.
49. Karl Marx, 'To Frederick Engels, in London, Manchester, June 14, 1853', in *Marx. Engels. Selected Correspondence* (Moscow: Progress Publishers, 1975), p. 80.
50. See Marian Sawer, *Marxism and the Question of the Asiatic Mode of Production* (The Hague: Martinus Nijhoff, 1977), p. 101

51. Ibid.
52. Ibid., p. 102.
53. Karl Marx, 'Excerpts from M.M. Kovalevsky', in *The Asiatic Mode of Production: Sources, Development and Critique in the Writings of Karl Marx*, trans. Lawrence Krader (Assen: Van Gorcum, 1975), pp. 366-67. Also see Kevin Anderson, *Marx at the Margins. On Nationalism, Ethnicity, and Non-Western Societies* (Chicago and London: The University of Chicago Press, 2010), p. 210.
54. Anil Rajimwale. *A Brief History of the CPI: Through the Party Congresses* (New Delhi: People's Publishing House Pvt. Ltd., 2012), pp. 3, 5.
55. Karl Marx, 'To Frederick Engels, in London, Manchester, June 14, 1853', in *Marx. Engels. Selected Correspondence* (Moscow: Progress Publishers, 1975), pp. 79-80.
56. Ibid., p. 79.
57. Karl Marx, 'Lord Canning's Proclamation and Land Tenure in India', in *On Colonialism*, p. 192.
58. Ibid.
59. Ibid.
60. Ibid., p. 193.
61. Karl Marx, *Grundrisse*, p. 472.
62. Ibid., p. 473.
63. Irfan Habib, 'Marx's Perception of India', in *Karl Marx. On India*, ed. Iqbal Husain, p. XXVIII.
64. Kevin Anderson, *Marx at the Margins. On Nationalism, Ethnicity, and Non-western Societies*, p. 211.
65. B.R. Ambedkar, 'On the Draft Constitution', in *Thus Spoke Ambedkar. Vol. I. A Stake in the Nation*, ed. Bhagwan Das (New Delhi: Navayana, 2010), p. 176.
66. Irfan Habib, op. cit., XXXIV, n. 84.
67. Karl Marx, 'First Draft of the Reply to V.I. Zasulich's Letter', p. 153.
68. Karl Marx, 'Letter to the Editorial Board of *Otechestvenniye Zapiski*, London, November, 1877', in *Marx. Engels. Selected Correspondence* (Moscow: Progress Publishers, 1975), p. 293.
69. Ibid.
70. Karl Marx, 'First Draft of the Reply to V.I. Zasulich's Letter', p. 154.
71. Ibid., p. 152.
72. Irfan Habib, op. cit., p. XXXI.
73. Ibid., p. XXXI, n. 69.
74. Karl Marx and Frederick Engels, 'Manifesto of the Communist

Party', in *Marx. Engels. Selected Works* (Moscow: Progress Publishers, 1975), pp. 35-6, n.

75. Ibid., n, pp. 35-6.
76. Walter Benjamin, 'Theses on the Philosophy of History', in *Illuminations,* trans. Harry Zohn (Glasgow: Fontana/Collins, 1979), p. 255.
77. Karl Marx, *The Poverty of Philosophy* (Moscow: Progress Publishers, 1978), pp. 159-60.
78. Ibid.
79. Karl Marx and Frederick Engels, *The German Ideology* (Moscow: Progress Publishers, 1976), p. 36.
80. Ibid., p. 37.
81. Communism in India, as general history, is divided in two forms—"communism from below" and "communism from above". That is why I am saying that there are two strands that influenced the early communist movement in India. One was the internal struggles for democracy in the Indian subcontinent, combined with the heroic struggles of the working classes in Europe, especially the Bolshevik Revolution. But there was another strand, namely what Trotsky called the "Stalin school of falsification". The non-Stalin political strand within the working class movement was almost unknown to the early communists. And when the critique of Stalinism arose, it took the form of a critique of Marxism. M.N. Roy is one such example. In the Stalinist school of falsification the old mythical and theological stories of the conflict of the gods and the devils were rewritten by Stalin as the story of the conflict between the Bolsheviks and the Mensheviks, where the "Party of Lenin" led by the saintly Stalin destroyed the devilish Trotskyites. See J.V. Stalin, G.E. Zinoviev, L. Kamenev, *Leninism or Trotskyism* (Chicago: Daily Worker Publishing Co., 1925). Zinoviev and Kamenev would later be classified as Trotskyites and enemies of the Soviet Union and executed in the infamous Moscow Trials of 1936. The Moscow Trials (1936-38) has been the greatest frame-up known in history. The entire Central Committee of the Bolsheviks at the time of the 1917 Revolution was executed by Stalin. Stalin was not only the only member left. He was also the main member who opposed the 1917 Revolution. While Zinoviev and Kamenev's opposition to the 1917 insurrection is known and documented, Stalin's fear of not only the 1917 Revolution, but fear of all revolutions is not yet studied. Stalin killed probably more communists than the fascists. That is why it is important

to note the essential features of "counterrevolution from outside" and the "counterrevolution from within".

82. Irfan Habib, 'Marx's Perception of India', p. XXXIV, n. 84
83. Arundhati Roy, 'Foreword' to Anuradha Ghandhy, *Script the Change. Selected Writings of Anuradha Ghandhy*, ed. Anand Teltumbde and Shoma Sen (Delhi: Daanish Books, 2011), p. XII.
84. B.R. Ambedkar, 'Annihilation of Caste', in *The Essential Writings of B.R. Ambedkar*, ed. Valerian Rodrigues (New Delhi: Oxford University Press, 2008), p. 268.
85. See B.R. Ambedkar, 'The Political Rights of the Depressed Classes', in *Thus Spoke Ambedkar. Vol. I. A Stake in the Nation*, p. 21.
86. B.R. Ambedkar, 'Castes in India', in *The Essential Writings of B.R. Ambedkar*, ed. Valerian Rodrigues (New Delhi: Oxford University Press, 2008), p. 253.
87. B.R. Ambedkar, 'Annihilation of Caste', in *The Essential Writings of B.R. Ambedkar*, p. 269.
88. Ibid.
89. Ibid., p. 272.
90. Karl Marx, *Capital*, Vol. I, trans. Samuel Moore and Edward Aveling (Moscow: Progress Publishers, 1983), p. 19
91. Rosa Luxemburg, 'The Accumulation of Capital—An Anti-Critique', in Rosa Luxemburg and Nicolai Bukharin, *Imperialism and the Accumulation of Capital*, trans. Rudolf Wichmann (London: Allen Lane, The Penguin Press, 1972), pp. 61-2, 77
92. See *Sacred Writings. Vol. 5. Hinduism. The Rg Veda*, trans. Ralf T. F. Griffith (New York: Quality Paperback Books, 1992), p. 603
93. See B.R. Ambedkar, 'Capitalism, Labour and Brahmanism', in *Thus Spoke Ambedkar*, ed. Bhagwan Das, p. 50.
94. See Ambedkar, 'The Failures of Parliamentary Democracy', in Ibid., p. 48.
95. B.R. Ambedkar, 'Capitalism, Labour and Brahmanism', p. 51.
96. Patnaik, Prabhat 'E.M.S. Namboodiripad's Perception of History', in *The Marxist*, XXV, 3-4 July-September 2009, pp. 5-6. See this volume Chapter 15.
97. B.R. Ambedkar, op. cit., 51.
98. Leon Trotsky, op. cit., p. 28.
99. Karl Marx, 'The British Rule in India', p. 40.
100. Karl Marx *Capital*, Vol. I, pp. 338-9.
101. Karl Marx, 'The Future Results of the British Rule in India', in *On Colonialism* (Moscow: Progress Publishers, 1976), p. 81.
102. Karl Marx, 'The British Rule in India', p. 41.

103. Karl Marx, 'Preface to the First German Edition', *Capital*, Vol. I, p. 20.
104. Paul Le Blanc, *Lenin and the Revolutionary Party* (Delhi: Aakar Books, 2016), p. 115.
105. Karl Marx, 'Afterword to the Second German Edition', *Capital*, Vol. I, p. 29.
106. Frederick Engels, 'Principles of Communism', in *Marx. Engels. Collected Works*, Vol. 6 (Moscow: Progress Publishers, 1977).
107. Ibid.
108. Karl Marx, 'The Class Struggle in France', in *Marx. Engels. Selected Works in Three Volumes*, Volume One (Moscow: Progress Publishers, 1977), p. 213.
109. Karl Marx, 'Address of the Central Committee to the Communist League', in *Marx. Engels. Selected Works in Three Volumes*, Volume One (Moscow: Progress Publishers, 1977), p. 185.
110. Josef Stalin, 'Reply to the Discussion on the Report of "The Social Democratic Deviation in Our Country"', in *On the Opposition* (Peking: Foreign Language Press, 1975), p. 447.
111. Ibid., pp. 448-9.
112. Karl Marx and Frederick Engels, *The German Ideology* (Moscow: Progress Publishers, 1976), pp. 54-5.
113. Ibid., p. 57.
114. Ibid., p. 54. It is important to note that Marx said this in the mid and late 1840s. What he said then happened in the Soviet Union in 1991. The "filthy business" was necessarily restored. But the Stalinist school never understood this.
115. Frederick Engels, *Anti-Dühring. Herr Dühring's Revolution in Science*, pp. 376-7.
116. J.V. Stalin, 'Economic Problems of Socialism in the USSR', in *J.V. Stalin. Selected Writings*, Vol. II (Calcutta: National Book Agency, 1976), p. 301.
117. See Leon Trotsky, *The Revolution Betrayed* (Delhi: Aakar Books, 2006), p. 78.
118. Mao-Tse-Tung, *A Critique of Soviet Economics* (New York & London: Monthly Review Press, 1977), p. 144.
119. Karl Marx, 'Eighteenth Brumaire of Louis Bonaparte', in *Marx. Engels. Selected Works*, p. 96.
120. Karl Marx, *Capital*, Vol. I, pp. 76-7; *Das Kapital*, Erster Band, (Berlin: Dietz Verlag, 1981), pp. 85-6.
121. Karl Marx, *Capital*, Vol. I, pp. 76, 80.
122. See *Why We Are Not Hindus* (Delhi: Aakar Books, 2015), p. 26.
123. Karl Marx, 'Critique of the Gotha Programme', in *Marx. Engels.*

Selected Works (Moscow: Progress Publishers, 1975), p. 319.
124. Frederick Engels, *Anti-Dühring. Herr Dühring's Revolution in Science* (Moscow: Progress Publishers, 1975), pp. 374-5.
125. Ibid., p. 376.
126. Karl Marx, *Capital*, Vol. I, pp. 76, 80.
127. Ibid., 89; *Das Kapital*, Ertser Band, p. 100.
128. Mao-Tse-Tung, *A Critique of Soviet Economics* (London: Monthly Review Press, 1977), p. 144.
129. Karl Marx, *A Contribution to the Critique of Political Economy* (Moscow: Progress Publishers, 1978), p. 85.
130. Ibid., p. 86.
131. J.V. Stalin, 'Economic Problems of Socialism in the USSR', in *J.V. Stalin. Selected Writings*, Vol. II (Calcutta: National Book Agency, 1976), p. 299.
132. Ibid., p. 300.
133. See Peter Hudis, *Marx's Concept of the Alternative to Capitalism* (Leiden: Brill, 2012).
134. Karl Marx, 'On the Jewish Question', in *Marx. Engels. Collected Works*, Vol. 3 (Moscow: Progress Publishers, 1975), p. 172.
135. Slavoj Žižek, *The Plague of Fantasies* (London: Verso, 1997), pp. 4-5.
136. V.I. Lenin, 'Three Sources and Three Components of Marxism', in *Marx. Engels. Selected Works* (Moscow: Progress Publishers), p. 23.
137. Slavoj Žižek, op. cit.
138. Karl Marx, *Das Kapital*, Erster Band, p. 49.
139. Karl Marx, *Capital* Vol. I, p. 43.
140. Ibid., p. 45.
141. Slavoj Žižek, op. cit., pp. 4-5.
142. Slavoj Žižek, *The Sublime Object of Ideology* (London: Verso, 1989), p. XIII.
143. Leon Trotsky, *1905*, https://www.marxists.org/archive/trotsky/1907/1905/ accessed May 25, 2016.
144. V.I. Lenin, 'The Importance of Gold Now and After the Complete Victory of Socialism', in *V.I. Lenin. Selected Works* (Moscow: Progress Publishers, 1977), p. 649.
145. Karl Marx, *Capital*, Vol. III , p. 830.
146. Karl Marx, *Economic and Philosophic Manuscripts of 1844* (Moscow: Progress Publishers, 1982), p. 121.
147. Ibid.
148. Ibid.
149. According to a Soviet version of this figure of the ape with the

skull was a warning "to mankind that it might degenerate into the primordial state if people did not put an end to wars and learn to live at peace with one another." See Y. Kashlev. *Cultural Contacts Promote Peaceful Coexistence* (Moscow: Novosti Press Publishing House, 1974), pp. 5-6.

150. V.I. Lenin, *What is to be Done?* (Moscow: Progress Publishers, 1975), p. 25.
151. Johann Wolfgang Von Goethe, *Faust*, Part One (London: Penguin, 1949), p. 98.
152. V.I. Lenin, 'Letter to the Congress, December 23, 1922', in *V.I. Lenin. Selected Works* (Moscow: Progress Publishers, 1977), p. 675.
153. Ibid., p. 676.
154. See Harold R. Isaacs, *The Tragedy of the Chinese Revolution* (Stanford University Press, 1961), p. 162.
155. J.V. Stalin, 'Economic Problems of Socialism in the USSR', pp. 288-89.
156. Karl Marx, 'These on Feuerbach', in *Marx. Engels. Selected Works*, p. 30.
157. Karl Marx, *Capital*, Vol. III, p. 817.
158. Ibid.
159. Karl Marx, *Capital*, Vol. I, p. 19.
160. Ibid.
161. Karl Marx, *Capital*, Vol. I, p. 29.
162. Raya Dunayevskaya, *Philosophy and Revolution—From Hegel to Sartre, and from Marx to Mao* (New Jersey: Humanities Press, 1982), p. 106.
163. See Kevin Anderson, *Lenin, Hegel, and Western Marxism* (Urbana and Chicago: University of Illinois Press, 1995), p. IX.
164. Karl Marx, 'To J.B.S. Schweitzer', London, January 24, 1865, in *Marx. Engels. Selected Correspondence* (Moscow: Progress Publishers, 1975), p. 145.
165. Karl Marx, *Economic and Philosophic Manuscripts of 1844*, p. 98; Karl Marx and Frederick Engels, *The German Ideology*, p. 34, n.
166. Karl Marx, *Economic and Philosophic Manuscripts of 1844*, p. 90.
167. Ibid., pp. 94, 109.

1

CPI(M) Support for Pranab Mukherjee, Dissidence, and the Marxist Idea of Working Class Democracy

Soma Marik and Kunal Chattopadhyay

The crisis and restructuring of international communism has finally caught up with sections of the Indian Left, even if in a limited form. The CPI(M)'s decision to support Pranab Mukherjee's candidature for the post of President of India in 2013 resulted in a greatly erroneous version of democratic centralism to be flouted, and in political debates of a principled nature being raised. Regardless of specific areas of agreement with Prasenjit Bose, the Jawaharlal Nehru University Students' Federation of India (JNU SFI) leadership, and others, including Dr. Ashok Mitra, these are fundamental points that need to be underscored. And we propose to not merely underscore but to elaborate on these.

When Prasenjit Bose's comments were posted in *Pragoti*, a website formerly pro-CPI(M) but now clearly supportive of the internal critics, they drew a huge amount of discussion, some of which was abusive and tended towards posing ad hominems in the direction of Bose. The nub of the accusations was that by making his criticisms public he had betrayed the party (and by implication the class). We want to discuss, in the light of the history of Classical Marxism, the question of principles and party disciplines, and the notion of democratic centralism. We will next discuss the political-programmatic issues involved—both the CPI(M) leadership's position and the position of its critics within the party. We begin with the political views of Marx and Engels on democracy.

Marx, Engels and Inner-Party Discipline vs. Democracy

For Marx and Engels, the idea of building a revolutionary party was linked to the precise nature of their political project. They were not communists advocating a revolutionary party. Rather, they were democrats who came to the conclusion that a struggle for consistent democracy would mean communism, and that only the proletariat could act as the universal class capable of leading that struggle. This had major implications for organisational structure and the nature of democracy both within revolutionary parties and within the class as a whole

Marx and Engels insisted, many times in their lives, that the fundamental political principle which was the minimum acceptable to them, was that of the self-emancipation of the working class. On several occasions, they wrote about this phrase in unambigouous terms. Perhaps two instances will suffice. In 1864, when drafting the preamble to the Rules of the International Working Men's Association (First International), Marx wrote,

> Considering, that the emancipation of the working classes must be conquered by the working classes themselves.[1]

And again, in 1878, Marx reacted to three German Social Democrats who had written that German socialism was, in a too one-sided manner, a working class movement. According to the German Social Democrats, the party needed an influx of educated and propertied supporters who alone were fit to represent the party in the Reichstag.[2] Taking up this claim and their further comment about the need to altogether avoid revolution in favour of reform, Marx and Engels criticised these authors as successors of the petty-bourgeois democrats of the 1848 revolution, who had no place in a workers' party and concluded:

> At the founding of the International we expressedly formulated

> the battle cry: The emancipation of the working class must be achieved by the working class itself. Hence we cannot cooperate with men who say openly that the workers are too uneducated to emancipate themselves, and must first be emancipated from above by philanthropic members of the upper and lower middle classes.[3]

So at different points of their careers they were willing to be in the same party with various kinds of people, but not with those who rejected the politics of working class self-emancipation.

Marx's party building ideas were founded on this basic political principle.

The League of the Just was the proletarian offshoot of an earlier republican organisation, the Outlaws' League. Both in ideology and in organisational concept, the new league, formed in 1836, could be called Babouvist.[4] Under the influence of Parisian secret societies the League of the Just participated in the insurrection of May 12, 1839. After its defeat, some of the leaders like Karl Schapper, Heinrich Bauer and Joseph Moll set up a unit in London. But while the London group soon renounced conspiracy and insurrection, Wilhelm Weitling in the continent developed a communist theory which still emphasised putsches and dictatorships. In 1845, this led to a sharp clash between Weitling and his former followers. The London leaders emphasised internationalism, the unity of communists and democrats, and strict non-violence.[5] The first two points brought them and Marx close. The idea of pure non-violence divided them. By the end of 1846 or early 1847, the London-based leaders of the League of the Just had rejected not only Weitling's outlook but also the French Utopian Communist Eteinne Cabet's plan for founding a Communist colony[6]. Cabet's rejection brought the League closer to Marx and Engels. In January 1847, Moll was sent to Brussels to invite Marx, Engels, Wolff and others to join the League. This group had, throughout 1846, "published a series of pamphlets, partly printed, partly lithographed, in which we mercilessly criticised the hotchpotch of the Franco-English socialism or communism and German philosophy, which formed the secret doctrine of the 'League' at the time."[7] Marx was hesitant about joining the League because of his reservations about its politics, but Moll made him overcome these hesitations, by arguing that Marx could expect to best influence the League members if he was a member himself.[8] In the summer of 1847, the first League Congress took place in London. Here it changed its name to Communist League.

The history of the League of the Just shows that the artisan communists like Schapper and Moll, having abandoned ultra-leftism, had adopted a more purely propagandistic approach than Marx ever did.[9] Throughout 1847, there was an intensive discussion on the programme and organisational perspectives of the League. Two Congresses were held and at least four draft programmes were written, two by Engels, one by Moses Hess, and one possibly by Schapper.[10] The Second Congress of the League, held in late 1847, endorsed the standpoint of Marx and Engels and authorized Marx to write the final text in the name of the League. This indicates, on one hand, that genuinely democratic consultations went on, and on the other hand, eventually Marx had certainly established his ideological domination, for he would hardly have been given a *carte blanche* to write what otherwise would have been a compromise requiring scrutiny by a committee. At the same time, a formal organisational control was maintained, as existing documents show.[11] The League itself had a definite organisational structure, and certain norms regarding practice. In August, sometime after joining the League, Marx and his friends launched a Workers' Educational Society in Brussels. This structure was used everywhere by the League to organise the broad masses of non-communist workers. The Rules of the League, the Address of the First Congress and the single issue of the journal, *Kommunistische Zeitschrift* show the general acceptance of proletarian democracy in party building theory.[12]

In 1864, after a gap of some twelve years, Marx joined a political party—or a united front of sorts. This was the International Working Men's Association or (as later known) the First International. In a letter to Engels, he stated point blank that he was opposed to a hyper-centralised body. He wrote to Engels that he had managed to persuade the majority to throw out the super-centralism and put in much more simple rules. He also wrote that:

> It was very difficult to frame the thing so that our view [Engels and Marx] should appear in a form acceptable from the present standpoint of the workers' movement. In a few weeks the same people will be holding meetings for the franchise with Bright and Cobden. It will take time before the re-awakened movement allows the old boldness of speech. It will be necessary to be *fortiter in re, suaviter in modo [bold in matter, mild in manner]*.[13]

In other words, while this was not the full communist programme of 1848 this was the minimum they could agree with. This has both organisational and political implications. Politically, we see that the minimum Marx would accept was the following:

Considering:

> That the emancipation of the working classes must be conquered by the working classes themselves, that the struggle for the emancipation of the working classes means not a struggle for class privileges and monopolies, but for equal rights and duties, and the abolition of all class rule;
>
> That the economical subjection of the man of labour to the monopoliser of the means of labour—that is, the source of life—lies at the bottom of servitude in all its forms, of all social misery, mental degradation, and political dependence;
>
> That the economic emancipation of the working classes is therefore the great end to which every political movement ought to be subordinate as a means;
>
> That all efforts aiming at the great end hitherto failed from the want of solidarity between the manifold divisions of labour in each country, and from the absence of a fraternal bond of union between the working classes of different countries;
>
> That the emancipation of labour is neither a local nor a national, but a social problem, embracing all countries in which modern society exists, and depending for its solution on the concurrence, practical and theoretical, of the most advanced countries;
>
> That the present revival of the working classes in the most industrious countries of Europe, while it raises a new hope, gives solemn warning against a relapse into the old errors, and calls for the immediate combination of the still disconnected movements;
>
> For these reasons —
>
> The International Working Men's Association has been founded.[14]

Throughout the history of the International, the free interplay of many views was common. Since it is only the final conflict with Bakunin that is brought out, and that in a distorted manner, let us note a couple of points briefly. Bakunin had created his personally controlled international body, and wanted to infiltrate the loosely organised International. When his proposal was turned down, he pretended to dissolve the International Alliance that he had created, and sought admission locally. The General Council, including Marx, fell into this simple trap, and allowed the Trojan horse in.[15] That Bakunin had never dissolved the secret organisation was a major charge against him in 1872 at the Hague Congress of the International. That the charge was true can be proved by acknowledgements from his own partisans, like Charles Perron or James Guillaume.[16] By infiltrating and by creating a parallel and secret body within an independent and democratic International, he was undermining the organisation. By recruiting into the Alliance while using the International as a front, he was violating the democratic rights of the International and its members. What is equally important is that Bakunin's own organisation was to be an "invisible dictatorship"—as dictatorial as he wanted organisations that he was infiltrating to be loose and chaotic. Arthur Mendel says, "One could not imagine a more rigidly centralised, authoritarian revolutionary organisation than the one Bakunin proposed." [17]

Inside the IWA, when Bakunin came into conflict with the members of the Romance Federation (French-speaking Switzerland), it was he who proposed, at the Basel Congress, that the General Council should have the right to suspend existing sections, and that it should be more authoritative.[18] This shows that it was Bakunin who was clashing with all sorts of members of the International, rather than Marx violating democracy, and further that it was at Bakunin's proposal that the powers of the General Council were extended in the way that the majority would ultimately use against Bakunin.

Another related issue is Marx's opposition to anarchism. A scrutiny of the documents leading up to the split show that anarchism was never the real political issue. When Bakunin did create an "anarchist" programme, Marx opposed it politically.[19] But he was not opposed to anarchists remaining inside the IWA. He was opposed to any one political-ideological current being proclaimed as the official ideology of the International. He was equally opposed to the transformation of the International into a specifically "Marxist" organisation, as he wrote in his letter to his supporter, Paul Lafargue on April 18, 1870.[20] He believed that theoretical clarification should keep pace with political experience.

The major conflict at the Hague Congress was over "political action". For the anarchists, building proletarian parties and fighting politically was taboo. It had to be an immediate revolutionary (insurrectionary) struggle. And Bakunin was fighting also to prevent the organisation from having any central leadership. Total centralism for his group. Total chaos for mass organisations. This was his goal, so that it would be possible to infiltrate and take over. At the Hague Congress, the Bakuninists did not debate the specifics of the Council's powers. They did not point out which aspects were undemocratic. They called simply for the abolition of the Council, so that no binding decisions could be taken or implemented, however democratically. By this time, Bakunin had shifted from a strategy of conquest from within to a strategy of split at any cost. Till mid-July 1872, Bakunin was trying for a takeover. The first version of the new plan was to boycott the Hague Congress. This was what his Italian adherents then did. But eventually realising that more supporters might be picked up by going to The Hague and precipitating a split there, such a line was adopted. On 14th August, Bakunin drafted a programme for a Slavic section that he founded, which stated that it was anarchist, and implied that the International had to be made an anarchist organisation. This was of course contrary to the rules, and it implies that in his mind, if not in actuality, Bakunin had already split. By 31st August, Bakunin even wrote a letter where the post split task was defined—to hold a rival Congress at Saint-Imier.[21]

At the Hague Congress, Bakunin and Guillaume were expelled for belonging to the Alliance in violation of the rules of the International. This expulsion proves, not Marx's authoritarianism, but the necessity of discipline as a component part of democracy in any working class organisation even at the international level.

But how tight should discipline be? Marx and Engels did not interpret workers' democracy to mean all-inclusive blocs. In 1882, the reformists and the revolutionaries in the French Parti Ouvrier split. Writing to Bernstein (1882), Engels welcomed the split, agreeing with Lafargue that the reformist majority was not a party because it had no actual programme. Generalising from this split he even wrote that every workers' party of a big country could develop only through internal struggle. He considered the split to be inevitable and good.[22]

The insistence on programmatic clarity, once class independence, and a general spread of socialist ideas had been achieved, was even more pronounced in the German case. In Germany two working class parties had been formed by the late 1860s. The ADAV had survived the death of Lassalle and the initial crisis after it. Meanwhile Johann Philipp Becker had organised branches of the International which later joined hands with dissident Lassalleans and the *Arebeiterbildungsvereine* (Workers' Educational Association) led by August Bebel and Wilhelm Liebknecht to establish the Social Democratic Workers' Party (SDAP) in 1869 (often called the Eisenachers). Marx and Engels supported this party despite their frequent criticism of Liebknecht. However, they reacted sharply when a merger of the Social Democratic Labour Party was proposed with the ADAV—they felt that united action could have been achieved without a party unity that made a great many ideological compromises with Lassalleanism. When this unity was accomplished at the Gotha Unity Congress (1875), Marx wrote, that if it was impossible to advance beyond the Eisenach programme they should have simply made an agreement about common action.[23] Though the idea of the dictatorship of an individual within the party was dropped, the domination of the parliamentary representatives was still there partly as a strategy to cope with the anti-socialist law. A historian of this party has shown that this model was chosen consciously in opposition to any attempt to build an underground party structure.[24] If this enabled the party to avoid prosecution and the secret society mentality, it was at the cost of party democracy.

Engels in his letter to Bebel wrote even more sharply that a new programme was a public banner by which the world judges a party and hence the retreat was harmful.[25] During the twelve-year period of the anti-socialist law, they were unable to develop this criticism further till 1890. But in 1891 at the time of programme revision, Engels published Marx's *Critique of the Gotha Programme* and got Bernstein to write a sharp critique of Lassalle's politics. Once the socialist outlook had spread within the class vanguard they considered it retrograde to dilute it in the name of proletarian democracy.

On the question of inner party democracy, the standpoint of Marx and Engels can be explained in the following terms: they supported the broadest democracy within the party, but also called for discipline. Their attitude to various events in the history of the German Party shows this. In 1879, the Reichstag (Parliamentary) fraction of the party permitted one of the deputies, Max Kayser, to vote for a tax proposal made by Bismarck. Marx and Engels condemned this as a betrayal of party discipline as well as socialist principle. They considered that the programme of the party was binding on parliamentary representatives. In the Circular Letter (written to Bebel, Liebknecht, Bracke and others) they also supported Hirsch, a party journalist, who had criticised Kayser and opposed the attempt of the Reichstag fraction to control the new party journal, *Socialdemokrat*, through an editorial commission which they called a censorship commission. The letter leaves one in no doubt about their hostility to what they considered an attempt by the leadership to escape rank and file control. Finally in the same letter, having criticised Hochberg, Bernstein and Schramm, for putting forward a petty bourgeois line reminiscent of 'True' Socialism they wrote: "In a country as petty bourgeois as Germany, there is certainly some justification for such ideas. But only outside the Social Democratic Workers' Party."[26]

Finally, in 1890-91, Engels made a number of comments regarding inner party democracy. In an oft-quoted letter to Sorge

(August 9, 1890) he said: "the party is so big that absolute freedom of debate inside it is a necessity... The greatest party in the realm cannot exist without all shades of opinion in it making themselves fully felt."[27] Shortly after this, Engels had Marx's *Critique of the Gotha Programme* published. An irate party leadership wanted to impose a censorship on *Neue Zeit*, their theoretical paper, edited by Kautsky. This shocked Engels who wrote to Kautsky that such a proposal whether in memory of the fraction's dictatorship during the anti-socialist law or in imitation of the kind of organisation that Schweitzer had built was unacceptable.[28]

Concerning mass organisations, their position was even more blunt. In a letter to the Lassallean leader, J.B. Von Schweitzer, Marx wrote that :

> a *centralist* organisation, suitable as it is for secret societies and sect movements, contradicts the nature of the trade unions... (in Germany) where the worker is regulated bureaucratically... the main thing is *to teach him to walk by himself.*[29]

In the International, Marx and Engels wanted to push the working class movement in a communist direction, but only to the extent that the workers could relate to communist theory, developed out of the political practice of earlier generations of workers, on the basis of their actual experience of struggle. For this, they considered it necessary to develop a radicalised trade union movement, which should pass from purely bread and butter issues to political action.[30]

However, this did not imply that the task of the Communists was to present trade unions with an ultimatum of accepting a communist programme or face sectarian denunciations. The IWA showed how Marx was prepared to move step by step to combine trade unions with political organisations. Indeed the Reform League, and the political activism of the English unions in general resulted substantially from Marx's endeavours.[31] In the long run, Marx saw his task as promoting the activist elements in the trade union wing to build a political party. Regarding the relationship between the Communist Party and the trade union their idea was quite consistent with the principle of proletarian democracy. The task was neither just to win votes nor to get some recruits. Marx and Engels emphasised on bringing as many unionists as possible close to the general political standpoint of the party. Engels specified the dialectics of the union-party relationship in an article praising the German SPD. "A great advantage to the German movement is that the trades organisation works hand in hand with the political organisation. The immediate advantage offered by the trades organisation draw many an otherwise indifferent man into the political movement, while the community of political action holds together, and assures mutual support to the otherwise isolated Trades Unions".[32] So the leading role of the political wing depended on its ability to provide the guidance to the trade unions. This is a difficult political task, steering between Scylla of party-controlled unionism (forerunner to the Stalinist Red Unionism), and the Charybdis of "trade union neutrality", by which reformist unionists in the next generation meant the withdrawal of support to socialists.[33]

In 1891, about 20,000 miners in the Ruhr area came out on strike, against the opinion of the SPD leadership, which felt that the government might use this as a plea to reintroduce some kind of Anti-Socialist Law. The party press criticised the miners publicly, at a time when they were subjected to massive repression including the use of the army. Engels felt that even if the assessment of the party was correct, it had no right to dictate the course of a class movement by "a rigid discipline of a sect". To Kautsky, he wrote that "every new group of workers *will be driven towards* us in the course of unwise, necessarily unsuccessful but, under the circumstance inevitable strikes of angry passion ...."[34]

Lenin and Party Democracy and Discipline

Stalinists and Cold War rightists have united in presenting Lenin as an ultra-disciplinarian and Stalin's forerunner. The Russian Revolution of 1917 posed the most serious challenge till now to international capitalism. The rise of the Soviets and factory committees put forward the possibility of a democratic system that far surpassed anything that existed in most capitalist countries then, or later.[35] Studies of the Bolshevik Party in 1917, likewise, have suggested that it was an extraordinary party, with tremendous levels of rank and file initiative and internal democracy combined with a deep revolutionary commitment.[36] This has however not deterred self-styled Sovietologists and Marxologists from saying that Bolshevism was fundamentally authoritarian, and that it led ineluctably to Stalinism. The flip side of the coin of course is the existence, even now, in India, of self-proclaimed communists or Leninists who claim that despite some petty mistakes here and there, Stalin was not one of history's major tyrants and a counter-revolutionary who destroyed the revolution, but a continuator of Leninism. Since both Stalinists and anti-communists often draw a straight line from Lenin's *What Is To Be done?* to the coming of the one-party state, three moments need to be discussed when such claims are made. One is of course the coming of the one-party state. Did it happen because of a pre-existing Bolshevik ideology and commitment? Leonard Schapiro, for example, in his *The Origins of Communist Autocracy*, wrote that he was writing the "story of how a group of determined men seized power for themselves in Russia in 1917, and kept others from sharing it."[37] Even leftists in times of retreat accept variants of this. Though attempts have been repeatedly made to present the picture of October as a democratic revolution, and also a picture of the civil war and imperialist intervention that forced the regime into a siege mentality, preconceived hostility has resulted in a textbook approach that denies the role of the civil war, or of White Terror. A second moment, indeed, the "original sin" of Leninism, is presented by numerous authorities. This is the very foundation of Leninism. According to what Lars Lih calls the textbook version, this version sees *What Is To Be Done* (hereafter WITBD) as the central Bolshevik text, and reads the message of the book as one according to which Lenin was suspicious about working class movements (identified with "spontaneity") and wanted to impose tight party control on the movement. The academic backing is provided by the following pieces of evidence: the contemporary criticisms of Rosa Luxemburg and Leon Trotsky, the critical comments by Vladimir Akimov, a delegate to the Second Party Congress who wrote an obscure piece revived in the late 1960s, and certain passages of WITBD. The third moment is a totally distorted picture of 1917 itself. Here, I call as my witness Charles Bettelheim, one time darling of Maoists, in his major work on Soviet history he emphatically rejects class dictatorship. He is willing to have the party feel the pulse of the class. But the party cannot submit its policies to democratic control by the class. That we are not exaggerating will be clear from the statement quoted below: "The establishment of the dictatorship of the proletariat means that the proletariat sets itself up as the ruling class and this cannot be done through organs of the Soviet type, which are mass organisations, or through state organs exclusively derived from these. The constitution of the proletariat as ruling class is necessarily effected through an apparatus that is specifically proletariat in ideology and aims, and in the role of leadership and unification that it plays in relation to the masses. In other words, through a proletarian party that plays this leading role, politically and ideologically, and plays it, too, in relation to the machinery of state issuing from the mass organisation."[38]

Had Bettelheim stopped even at this point, a tortuous explanation of the passage might have been made out to bolster a claim that he was not really opposed to workers' democracy, but merely emphasized the need for a vanguard party, though the idea of an "apparatus that is specifically proletarian in ideology and aims" without reference to actual social composition is bad enough. But later in the same book, Bettelheim grasps the nettle firmly by both hands: "The definition of the proletarian revolutionary line cannot be left to a mere 'majority vote' whether in a popular or workers' assembly, in a party congress, or in a meeting of the party's Central Committee. Experience shows that, faced with a profoundly new situation, it is usually only a minority that finds the correct path, even in an experienced proletarian party."[39]

The implications of these arguments are devastating. Had there been any truth in them one would have to conclude that humankind faces only a bleak future—between the horrors of late capitalism and the perpetual terrorism of Stalin and his heirs, including Pol Pot. Correct line by a minority is to be imposed if need be!! And the class itself will forever remain putty in the hands of party leaders—bureaucrats, self-proclaimed professional revolutionaries, people mostly originating outside the working class, sometimes with a leavening of a few workers successfully corrupted by the bosses.

But let us go back to Lenin.

Since two passages in WITBD are taken as the core of his centralism, it is necessary to understand the entire book in its proper context. Lenin would write later that it was a polemical book. Karl Radek, a communist leader important in the Russian Party after 1917, though originally a Polish Marxist, wrote after Lenin's death that in 1921, when a proposal had been made to translate and republish the book *Chto Delat?* (WITBD), Lenin objected, urging at least good commentaries "in order to avoid false application".[40] Yet bourgeois scholarship has repeatedly failed to do this. A text, it seems, is a text that requires no context. Who was Lenin polemicising against? What had they written? What, for example, was the difference between "the straightforward R.M." and the "weathercock Krichevskiis and Martynovs"? Why worry about such minute details, when one simply needs to know that Lenin had an "unspoken assumption" that the "majority of the population is actually or potentially reactionary", and an unspoken conclusion, "that democracy leads to reaction".[41] Or, as Leopold Haimson, a scholar closely connected to the documentation of Menshevik sources located in the USA, was to write, implicit in WITBD "was not merely a lack of faith in the capacity of the labour movement to grow to consciousness by its own resources, but also a basic distrust in the ability of any man to outgrow his 'spontaneous' elemental impulses, and to act in accord with the dictates of his 'consciousness' without the guidance, and the restraint, of the party and its organisations."[42] With our divine knowledge of Lenin's implicit ideas and psychoanalytic instruments that lay bare his inside, why do we need to bother examining the precise arguments to which he was responding, or to relate WITBD with his writings just before and just after it? Such examinations may confuse the reader by making her or him think that Lenin might (shudder) have held democratic views.

What did it mean, for Lenin to proclaim that he was a Marxist? It was not enough to declare adherence to Marx. Even Russian populists did that. It meant an allegiance to what was seen as the Marxist revolutionary politics of his era—the politics of Kautsky and the Erfurt programme, and a resolute opposition to Bernsteinian revisionism... In the 20th century, after the Russian Revolution, the idea of what Bolshevism was (though the idea may have been distorted in subsequent decades) inspired countless communists across the world. In the same way, in the late 19th and early 20th centuries, the SPD was the principal inspiration for revolutionary socialists across the world. Today, authors often quote approvingly the letter of a right-wing socialist, Ignaz Auer, to Bernstein: "My Dear Ede, one doesn't formally decide to do what you ask... one does it. Our whole activity... was the activity of a Social Democratic reforming party."[43] No doubt, there is good reason today, after the betrayal of 1914, after the supine surrender to Hitler in 1933, and after the total integration in bourgeois politics after World War II, to look at even the earlier history of the SPD with a degree of scepticism. But if we look at it from the standpoint of Russian radicals of the period under discussions, they could see the vicious efforts being made, even after the collapse of Bismarck's Anti-Socialist laws, to silence the SPD. Or, they could see how the vast masses of workers actually did treat the SPD as their party.

Lars Lih in his *Lenin Rediscovered*, argues that Kautsky's commentary on the Erfurt programme, and his book *Parliamentarism*, were profoundly influential, and the latter work brought together the logic behind what the Russians called the strategy of hegemony of the proletariat in the democratic revolution. Kautsky argued that while the working class would arrive at socialism through its own experience, left to itself, it could take a long time. Social Democracy, that is, a political strategy based on the ideas of Marx and Engels, had to merge with the working class movement. Social Democracy was needed, and would be heeded. It would be heeded because it was bringing, in Lih's formulation, good news for the proletariat. Kautsky's argument was that originally, socialism and the workers' movement were separate, but the birth of revolutionary socialism or Marxism changed that. Lih argues that the Erfurtian socialists displayed a set of features: an explicit acknowledgement of three sources of authority—the party, the programme, and Kautsky's writings; a commitment to the concept of merger mentioned previously; a definition of Social Democracy's mission as spreading the good news of the world-historical mission of the proletariat; an ambition of building a class-based political party, which would be disciplined, yet democratic, organized on a national plane, an insistence on the priority of achieving political freedoms, an expectation that the party would eventually lead the entire people (i.e. a commitment to a strategy of achieving proletarian hegemony). Finally, Erfurtianism, meant a commitment to internationalism. Lih then proceeds, in a meticulously written chapter, to use this checklist and examine Lenin's early writings.

What Lih does, and this is something done independently, in different forms, by Paul Le Blanc (in his book *Lenin and the Revolutionary Party* as well as in his anthology of Lenin's writings) and by Soma Marik, is to establish that in the entire period leading up to 1901-2, Lenin consistently expressed what Lih calls Erfurtian views (Marik and Le Blanc do not use the term).

There are distinct stages in the history of the growth of the Social Democratic movement in Russia and its transformation into a well-knit party. In the early 1890s, the handful of Social Democrats had focused on recruiting individual workers into study circles. The movement was by necessity underground because of the repressive nature of the autocracy. When the class struggle began to intensify in the mid-1890s, social democrats, including Lenin, made a turn—generalised throughout the movement by the publication of the widely circulated tract *On Agitation*, written by Arkady Kremer and with a foreword by Julius Martov—towards agitation around workers' immediate economic demands. At this stage, the circles remained entirely local in orientation, organised independently of each other, with no national organisation or publications. Some of the younger social democrats in this period began to overestimate the importance of the economic struggle and to downplay the importance of organising the working class for a political struggle against the autocracy. Eventually, a trend developed that tried to systematically theorise this limitation itself as the right strategy. In 1899, a tract called the *Credo* was circulated in social-democratic circles. Written by E.D. Kuskova, the document expressed sympathy with the reformist gradualism of Eduard Bernstein in Germany and argued that instead of fighting for revolution, Russian socialists should have a much more modest goal. As she wrote:

> Any talk about an independent worker political party is in essence nothing more than the product of the transfer of alien tasks, alien results, onto our soil. ...For the Russian Marxist there is only one conclusion: participation by helping the economic struggle of the proletariat, and participation in liberal oppositional activity.[44]

This argument, that the economic struggle was the only one worth waging for the workers, and that at most they should provide the economic struggle itself a political colour (i.e. pressure group politics, as opposed to revolutionary politics) was what the orthodox Marxists termed 'Economism', or in Lenin's hands at least, *tred-iunionism* (I follow Lih here). By this was meant, not doing trade union work, but seeking to restrict politics to the politics of trade unions. Accusing anyone of seeking to implement the programme of the Credo was about the most serious accusation Lenin could make, against anyone.

A classic statement of the economists' view was expressed in the newspaper *Rabochaia Mysl:* "What sort of struggle is it desirable for the workers to conduct? Isn't the desirable struggle the only one which they are able to conduct in present circumstances?"[45] This statement was nothing if not reminiscent of Bernstein's statement that the movement was "everything" and the final goal "nothing." No wonder Lenin and his co-thinkers considered economism the Russian variant of Bernstein's revisionism.

Lenin's response to the publication of the *Credo,* which he wrote while he was in Siberian exile (he had been arrested in 1895 and was released in the summer of 1900), was swift. His article, signed by seventeen other exiled socialists, argued, that the assertion about the Russian working class not having put forward political aims revealed ignorance about the Russian revolutionary movement. Lenin was particularly incensed, because populists criticised the Marxists for ignoring the political struggle, and the orthodox Marxists always rejected this populist charge. Now here were people claiming to be Social Democrats and putting forward just the kind of non-revolutionary programme the populists accused Marxists of having. Lenin argued that accepting the programme of the Credo would be tantamount to the political suicide of Russian Social Democracy. A point to remember, when reading those articles of Lenin, is that at that stage, for all its hesitations and nebulous formulations, Russian Liberalism still seemed a revolutionary force. So if the working class struggle was restricted to economic issues, it would become the tail of Liberals or populists, and lose the independent and potentially leading role in the struggle against the autocracy.

Not long after the emergence of economism, social struggles began to take on a more political character, which gave urgency to the ideological conflict over economic versus political struggle. The student movement picked up steam, as did government repression against it. Workers joined some of the student demonstrations. They also began organising May Day protests, including one that led to a general strike in Kharkov in 1900. In Petersburg in May 1901, workers of the Obukhov defence works engaged in running street battles with the police and Cossacks, then barricaded themselves inside the plant. Thirty thousand students participated in the general strike in the winter of 1901–02. In Moscow, a demonstration called to commemorate the fortieth anniversary of the ending of serfdom brought out thousands of workers who clashed with Cossacks. A November 1902 railway strike in Rostov on Don turned into a citywide general strike.[46] It was in this atmosphere that *Iskra* was launched. Two groups came together in the project—the founders of Russian Social Democracy, led by Georgi Plekhanov, Pavel Akselrod and Vera Zasulich, and a younger group, recently arrived in emigration, represented by Lenin, Martov, and Aleksander Potresov.

In political battles where a number of groups, whether claiming to be factions of the same party (as in Russia in the period under discussion) or to be rival parties (as in India within the far left today) fight for hegemony, very often, groups who are close, but have separate existence because of secondary differences, can have extremely sharp polemics. In many such cases, attempts are made to establish that the rival group's seemingly slight difference is actually the beginning of a massive slide into opportunism, sectarianism, or some other error. Lenin emerges, from Lih's account, as a very able polemicist in this tradition. This is not something very new. He has always been treated as a polemical author, constantly firing off shots at opponents. It is possible to look at other phases of party and Russian history to see him doing similar things. Thus, when the struggle was to save the underground party (and with it, the revolutionary programme) in opposition to the proposals of currents in the party who wanted to accept the police-controlled "legality" after 1907, Lenin can be found engaged in the same kind of polemics. There too, he attacked not just the liquidators, as those who proposed a legal party were called, but also the "conciliators", i.e. those who stressed the need for an underground party, but had a somewhat different attitude about the legal structures, including the trade unions. The so-called conciliators included Trotsky, as well as a large number of Bolshevik activists who at times (e.g. the 1910 Central Committee Plenum) sided with Trotsky. And so, Lenin often hurled thunderbolts at Trotsky far stronger than those he was directing towards the liquidators, who were being in any case massively defeated among the practical workers.[47] So, there exists a need to study each case, not as a general Leninist political strategy, but as a specific reaction by Lenin to a specific conflict.

Along with the myth of Lenin's scepticism about the revolutionary potential of the working class, there had grown up, of necessity, a myth about the "worker-phile" attitude of the "Economists". Lih brings to light the exact articles in dispute, and shows that the economists wanted to avoid the struggle for democracy, and in some cases firmly rejected the Erfurtian model. Lih provides a translation of an editorial from the

"Economist" paper *Rabochaia Mysl*, No. 1, October 1897, so that readers can read it for themselves. The editorial rejects the view that the working class struggle has any historic mission, of bringing socialism, not within a few days or years, but for the future. Instead, it asserts: "Let the workers conduct their struggle, knowing that they are not fighting for just some kind of future generation but for themselves and their children—let them remember that every victory, every foot of ground taken from the enemy, is one more step in the ladder leading to their personal well-being."[48] Evidently, the author of the editorial was clearly opposing the line stretching from Marx to Kautsky to Lenin, about the task of the working class being to become the "national class" (Marx's formulation in the *Communist Manifesto*), about the fusion of communist theory with the working class, and about the historic mission of the working class. The editorial, as Lih shows, was actually written by an intellectual, and does not reflect any "authentic" working class voice as against intelligentsia impositions by orthodox Marxists. And so, we are led to the conclusion, that the author of the editorial was advising workers—do not bother yourselves about profound missions, about a socialist future that only later generations will see, but try and get a few concessions. Combatting this attitude, not controlling workers, was what Lenin was concerned about.

Because *Rabochee dyelo* was Erfurtian, so the dispute between *Iskra* and this paper was not over fundamental principles, but tactics. It was in the course of this tactical dispute that Boris Krichevskii wrote an article in *Rabochee dyelo* where he introduced the concept of *stikhiinost*. I follow Lih in retaining the Russian original. It is forever claimed, if never proved, that Lenin was violently opposed to spontaneity, and condemned it for its bourgeois tendencies, demanding control from above through a tight, disciplined, small organisation. *Stikhiinost* is the word usually translated as spontaneity. So what was Krichevskii talking about and what was Lenin responding to? Krichevskii was writing about political explosions such as the worker demonstrations in 1901 in support of the students, attacking *Iskra* from the Left, claiming that *Rabochee dyelo* had a better response to the movement under discussion. Krichevskii had seized on an earlier article by Lenin, where Lenin talked about a *stikhiinyi* explosion, that is, an elemental, unplanned, sudden and powerful event. Indeed, this is a passage to which very few authors have paid attention (for obvious reasons), since Lenin wrote that "it is fully possible and historically much more likely that the autocracy will fall under the pressure of one of those *stikhiinyi* explosions.... But no political party, unless it falls into adventurism, can base its activity solely in the expectation of such explosions....".[49] Lenin argued that *Iskra* had been working according to a plan, while *Rabochee dyelo* tended to jump from event to event, banking on elemental upsurges. The dispute was not one over whether the working class should be controlled, but whether party building should base itself on hopes for sudden explosions. Krichevskii accused *Iskra* of overestimating a large, purposive, aware, well-organized proletariat. In that case, of course, it is difficult to understand why Krichevskii also accused *Iskra* of being a conspirator.

When Lenin wrote WITBD, therefore, issues like *stikhiinost*, and *konspiratsiia*, were forced on him, rather than his having chosen these issues as a matter of core values. *Rabochee dyelo* had an agreement with *Iskra*, which it was violating. Lenin was using the existing *Rabochee dyelo* articles to prove his point. So he had to follow Krichevksii's usage. He argued that if Krichevskii's proposal was taken seriously it would lead to denying any need for active Social Democratic leadership. Lenin's aim, in putting forward these arguments, was not to present a novel proposition, but to argue that his opponents were rejecting a widely accepted Social Democratic position. Nowhere in WITBD does Lenin express a worry that spontaneous working class struggles would lead to bourgeois politics, and therefore the working class must be bound tightly to party dictation. Instead, what we find, if we read WITBD as a whole, instead of zooming in on a couple of passages quoted around a thousand times, is Lenin assuming that the working class is rational, and arguing that the task of Social Democracy is to put across the socialist message to the working class movement, because if it is done properly, they will accept it, and will fuse with the socialist theory.

Lih makes a strong case for treating "conspiracy" and "professional revolutionary" also in a different way. The Russian word *konspiratsiia*, translated baldly into English as conspiracy, has a major problem. *Konspiratsiia* involved successful underground work. People living in democratic countries where they can have the luxury of a party office with a Red Flag fluttering boldly often do not realize what basic principles of party work in Tsarist Russia, or in Bismarckian Germany, could be like. Lack of skill in *konspiratsiia* would result in disaster for the party organisation, with its members arrested and links with the workers broken. Obviously, success in *konspiratsiia* meant keeping secrecy from the police, and to this extent it overlapped with conspiracy. But the RSDLP defined itself from the outset against the *Narodnaia Volia* strategy of conspiracy against the Tsar. Not secret plots against hated rulers, but awareness-raising and formation of purposivenes among the working class were the Social Democratic strategy. Lenin is presenting a case, in WITBD, of how to combine *konspiratsiia* with the expansion of participation. Regardless of the efficacy of his proposal, it is clear that he was trying to work out the tactics that would make possible a mass movement even under Tsarist autocracy.

The professional revolutionary, likewise appears not as the intelligentsia activist cut off from the workers, but someone who is not an amateur. In Lih's translation, it is a revolutionary by trade, that is, someone who treats it seriously, as full-time work. The shift by Lih is a legitimate one, yet one which even scholars with a knowledge of Russian had not thought of. Even in WITBD, Lenin talks about *professiia*, *professional'nye soiuzy* (trade unions) and so on quite often. Looking at the underground work metaphorically as a trade, he implies that the revolutionary needs a set of skills. While a professional revolutionary could at times be thought of as something akin to a professional soldier, the term revolutionary by trade does not carry the same connotation. In addition, Lenin nowhere implies that non-workers cannot be revolutionaries by trade. Indeed, his whole point was that workers must be made revolutionaries by trade. The revolutionary by trade was one who knew *konspiratsiia*, and one who knew the value of division of labour. However, Lih treats the term as one almost accidentally used by Lenin, as a result of reading a passage in an opponent's writing. Even if this was indeed the origin of the term, Lenin had more serious aims. As Marik has argued, he wanted to ensure that workers could become full-time revolutionaries.[50]

Lih traces the *Iskra* ideas about organisation (indeed the norms developing within Russian Social Democrats generally), including centralism, discipline, development of political skills, opposition to conspiratorialism cut off from worker milieus, *konspiratsiia*, division of labour, and the inapplicability of real democracy and transparency in the underground conditions. He argues that the ideal organisation presented by Lenin in WITBD (not the real *Iskra* organisation) was a summing up of the logical culminations of those norms. But these norms were seen as a specifically Russian application, in underground conditions, of the SPD norms, and not any "party of a new type". It is here that one could argue with Lih. He is correct, if he is talking about the *Iskra* period. But the revolution of 1905, the next period of underground, all led to the Bolsheviks developing ideas about a revolutionary party somewhat different from what the SPD had been even as a normative role model.

But Lih is certainly correct in arguing that WITBD shows a working class desiring better socialist propaganda, and an organisation being needed so that the revolutionaries on the ground could achieve their desired goal of taking to the masses the good news of socialism. Also, WITBD emerges as a much more limited purpose text than is often imagined, or pretended, by many critics for whom it is the core of the myth of Lenin's anti-democratic attitude. Perhaps the best revelation is the one where Lih shows Rosa Luxemburg excoriating Lenin for ignoring mass struggles, based on unsigned articles in the *Iskra* written, unbeknownst to her, by Lenin.

Bringing Consciousness from Outside

This has often been a major issue in storms over *Chto Delat?* The working class can, Lenin is supposed to have said, arrive only at trade union consciousness. The socialist consciousness was developed by the intelligentsia, and has to be injected into the working class from outside. Practically every historian who has tilted at the windmill of Lenin's elitism has cited the concerned passage. Few have bothered to examine the fact that Lenin was actually quoting Karl Kautsky, who, according to their myth, was a democratic socialist very different from Lenin. Kautsky, moreover, was presenting his explanation of the programme of the Austrian Social Democratic Party. Of course, this does not solve the problem. Perhaps Kautsky too was elitist. I suggest that Lenin was less elitist than Kautsky's formulation implies. A careful reading of *Chto Delat?*, even in existing translations, rather than the new one prepared with explanations by Lih, will show several elements. First, the use of the inside-outside counterposition in Lenin's hand means something different. He argues that the worker, to become revolutionary, cannot see everything purely from inside the factory and immediate surroundings. Second, Lenin, in his own discussion following the Kautsky quotation, injects an important qualification. Certainly, Lenin did write that:

> The doctrine of socialism grew out of those philosophical, historical, and economic theories that were worked out by the educated representatives of the propertied classes, the intelligentsia.[51]

Despite Lih's admiration for Lenin, in the chapter entitled "Scandalous Passages", he is compelled to admit that taken by itself the passage does show a move away from Lenin's Erfurtianism. This leads to a view that socialist doctrines grew up separately from the working class, that is, only non-workers could develop socialism, when we combine this with the other assertion that:

> The history of all countries bears witness that exclusively with its own forces the worker class is in a condition to work out only a trade-unionist awareness, that is, a conviction of the need to unite

> in unions, to carry on a struggle with the owners, to strive for the promulgation by the government of this or that law that is necessary for the workers and so on.[52]

However, Lenin moved away from this, a few pages later, when he said that workers such as Proudhon and Weitling participated in the development of socialist ideology. He remarked that they did so not as workers but as theoreticians. If this distinction means anything at all, it means that Lenin is actually contradicting the view that the intelligentsia is representative of the propertied class. There can be worker intelligentsia as well. And it is as theoreticians of socialism that we need to see any one of them, whether Marx or Kautsky, or Proudhon and Weitling. Moreover, Lenin's comment, "the doctrine... grew out of", suggests he was talking about those who have been called Utopian Socialists. In this sense, of course, the comment can be made to fit what Lih calls the merger narrative (the Marxist argument that theoretical socialism and the living working class movements merged with the rise of revolutionary, proletarian socialism or Marxism).

Lenin's whole thrust is to argue that the working class is *ready* to absorb socialist theory enthusiastically, and is only prevented by intellectuals who wish to restrict the working class to purely economic issues. Later in the same book, Lenin qualifies the point still further, arguing that in fact the working class *does indeed* gravitate towards socialist consciousness, but that it does not do so in an ideological vacuum. Bourgeois ideology, older, more prepared, with an ample supply of writers as well as funds, is able to spread confusion, and that is why it is essential to organize for revolutionary socialist propaganda. Those sections of the class that do spontaneously gravitate towards socialist politics before others must be organised together to exercise more influence over their fellow workers who are still influenced more by bourgeois ideology.

If we have spent such an amount of space for WITBD, that is because it is so systematically misread. For all Stalinist Party leaders, it is the idea of socialist consciousness coming from outside that matters, so that the history of class struggle is turned to wise decisions by the Party (or errors by "renegades") .

Democratic Centralism Under Lenin

The most interesting fact about democratic centralism is that the term was coined by Mensheviks, who opposed it to Lenin's so-called ruthless centralism. But Lenin did not only accept it but explained what he understood by it.

In WITBD already he stresses that a real democratic working class party had to be open unless it functioned under absolutist conditions.

> The political struggle of Social-Democracy is far more extensive and complex than the economic struggle of the workers against the employers and the government. Similarly (indeed for that reason), the organisation of the revolutionary Social-Democratic Party must inevitably be of *a kind different* from the organisation of the workers designed for this struggle. The workers' organisation must in the first place be a trade union organisation; secondly, it must be as broad as possible; and thirdly, it must be as public as conditions will allow (here, and further on, of course, I refer only to absolutist Russia). On the other hand, the organisation of the revolutionaries must consist first and foremost of people who make revolutionary activity their profession (for which reason I speak of the organisation of *revolutionaries*, meaning revolutionary Social-Democrats). In view of this common characteristic of the members of such an organisation, *all distinctions as between workers and intellectuals*, not to speak of distinctions of trade and profession, in both categories, *must be effaced*. Such an organisation must perforce not be very extensive and must be as secret as possible. [53]

Be it noted, he stresses that his prescriptions for underground functioning are for Russia— not even for Germany which had only fragmented democracy.

By 1905-7 the situation had changed. There had emerged a mass organisation of a unique type. Out of a general strike and the need to coordinate work while keeping the class enemy paralysed, workers elected the St. Petersburg Soviet of Workers Deputies. On 15th October, 226 representatives from 96 factories and workshops and 5 trade unions were present. On 17th October, the body named itself the *Soviet Rabochikh Deputatov* (Council of Workers' Deputies).[54] It was this example that inspired the setting up of Soviets elsewhere, in Moscow, Odessa, Novorossiisk, Donets, etc. There were also a few instances of Soldiers' Councils and Peasants' Councils.

The Soviet emerged in fulfilment of an objective need for an organisation that would represent people's authority, an organisation that would be flexible enough to encompass hundreds of thousands of workers of various factories, varying age-groups, diverse viewpoints, different level of skills and earnings, without imposing on them so much organisational restraint that this newly won cohesion would break down. The powers of the Soviets lay in the fact that the deputies were elected and that they could function publicly without gaining legal sanction from the state. This set them off from the parties, despite the fact that party activists could be, and usually were, workers or professional revolutionaries dedicated to workers' struggles. As Trotsky, at the age of twenty-six the great mass leader of the 1905 revolution, put it on the basis of his own experience:

> Prior to the Soviet we find among the industrial workers a multitude of organisations... But these were organisations within the proletariat, and their immediate aim was to achieve influence over the masses. The Soviet was, from the start, the organisation of the proletariat, and its aim was the struggle for revolutionary power.[55]

A section of the Bolsheviks were sceptical about the Soviets. Lenin's close activist Krassikov called it a non-party Zubatovite committee.[56] Lenin opposed this stance. He also opposed the position of those Bolsheviks at the Bolshevik Congress who called for tight organisations. Even the sympathetic Krupskaya recorded in her memoirs that the committee men were conservative, opposed to inner party democracy and undesirous of changes.[57] Lenin, from abroad, could see the need to change party tactics[58], to become more flexible, and get rid of the prerogatives of the committee men and induct more youth, and more workers in the committees.[59] The period when a pre-revolutionary crisis opens up is the period when a revolutionary party has the opportunity to become a mass party. Failure to ensure this transformation is as serious as any attempt to build a mass party when conditions do not permit it. At the Third Congress, Lenin and Bogdanov proposed that workers should be taken into the party at all levels in large numbers.[60] The delegate Gradov (Kamenev) accused Lenin of demagogically raising the question of the relationship between workers and intelligentsia.[61] Reports by Leskov, Filippov and Krassikov made it obvious that workers were not being drawn into the party. One delegate, Mikhailov, even accused in disgust that "the requirements for the intelligentsia are very low, and for the workers they are extremely high".[62]

Significantly, Mensheviks, no less than the Bolsheviks, were dependent on the work of the professional revolutionaries. But the Mensheviks saw no special role for them. Lenin, by contrast, viewed the professional revolutionaries and the party machine as a means of increasing the activity of the class vanguard. But their work could succeed only if the gates of the party were opened in revolutionary times. Once a programme and basic tactics were worked out, and an organisational structure set up, mass recruitment was deemed necessary, especially during a rising tide of class struggles.[63] Lenin urged repeatedly in favour of this transition. Events pressed in the same direction. As a result, party cells grew rapidly in factories.[64] Bolshevik recruitment grew at about the same pace as the Menshevik recruitment, and with, on average, a more proletarian and younger composition. Between early 1906 and 1907, both factions had grown massively.[65]

Inner party democracy was an area where Lenin learnt from experience. The Mensheviks, having ousted the Bolsheviks from the leading structures, had been ignoring calls for a fresh party congress.

The Third (purely Bolshevik) Congress had already adopted the stance that elections, and autonomy of local committees vis-a-vis the Central Committee, should be the norm. The new rules adopted at the Congress gave local organisations autonomy in matters relating to their area of activity (Article 6) and the right to issue party literature in their own names (Article 7).[66] In St. Petersburg, the new structure was that of an elected conference, due to meet at least twice a month. It was to be elected twice a year, and in turn it was to elect the party committee. Large numbers of members were drawn in the decision-making process. For example, the St. Petersburg Party decided to boycott the First Duma by 1168 to 926 votes.[67] Lenin even recommended referenda in case of important political questions.[68] The Bolshevik activist Pyatnitsky recollected a similar widespread application of democracy in Moscow.[69] On the question of the party press, Lenin stressed that here there could be no question of a mechanical "rule of the majority over the minority...."[70]

In November 1905, the Mensheviks held a conference. This was followed by a Bolshevik Conference (December 12-17). The two groups then set up a United Central Committee, with three Bolsheviks and three Mensheviks. Both groups, as well as the new Central Committee, now called for the reorganisation of the party on the principle of democratic centralism.[71] At the Fourth (Unity) Congress of the RSDRP, the Menshevik majority brought in a set of resolutions constituting the democratic centralist principles, viewed as a democratic norm of functioning.[72]

The stress is heavily on the rights of minorities, but with an important proviso, that the opposition must be a loyal opposition. The concept of a 'loyal' opposition was, however, carefully defined to avoid abuse of power. The ideological disputes had to go along with organisational unity, that is, the opposition could not hinder the work of the party. This was further clarified on one occasion, when the Central Committee sent a circular laying down the limits of public criticism. Lenin objected to the circular, saying that it had defined unity of action too broadly, but freedom of criticism too narrowly. He argued that the principles to be adhered were autonomy for local organisations, as well as democratic centralism. This implied "universal and full freedom to criticise, so long as this does not disturb the unity of a definite action".[73] In other words, even after a decision was taken, there could be criticism, but no obstruction to the carrying out of the decision, unless the decision itself was changed. Apart from Lenin's broad definition of the freedom to criticise, the kind of broadening of the rights of members that he was urging could be understood by looking at this act itself. He was publicly challenging the Central Committee. He wrote that before adopting such a resolution, the C.C. should have discussed the matter in the party.[74] Subsequently, he was to put forward the view that if a real mass party had to be built, rather than a sect, then different lines had to exist, and their open clash had to be viewed as normal.[75] From this conception, he also concluded that like-minded groups had the right to form factions.[76]

Lenin also emphasised that a party wishing to be the class vanguard had to inform the whole class about its activities, about inner party debates. Responding to the charge of factionalism brought by the Socialist Revolutionaries, he said that a mass party had to inform the masses "as to which leaders and which organisations of the party are pursuing this or that line".[77] He also pointed out in an essay of 1907, defending the development of the professional revolutionaries, that due to the development of their network, between 1903 and 1907 the RSDRP had been able to give the public information about the inner party situation, and to build a democratic legal organisation with the representative Congress when the situation permitted.[78]

During the ebb of the revolution, Lenin still countenanced differences of view in the party even as he excoritated wrong views politically. Thus, the expulsion of Bogdanov from the Bolshevik faction was effected as a necessary internal matter of the faction. A meeting of the "Extended Editorial Board of Proletariat" was called in June 1909. *The Proletariat* was the factional paper of the Bolsheviks, and a meeting of the extended editorial board meant in reality a camouflaged meeting of the Bolshevik central leadership. This meeting dissociated Bolshevism from Bogdanov's political line, and expelled Bogdanov from the Bolshevik faction. It is useful to look at Lenin's justification of this action.

> In our Party Bolshevism is represented by Bolshevik section [meaning faction]. But a section is not a party. A party can contain a whole gamut of opinions ...the extremes of which may be sharply contradictory...that is not the case within a section. A section in a party is a group of like-minded persons formed for the purpose

> primarily of influencing the party acceptance for their principles in the purest possible form. For this, real unanimity of opinion is necessary. The different standards we set for party unity and sectional unity must be grasped by everyone ....[79]

Bolshevism in 1917

We propose to restrict our examples here to two or three cases, in place of the far greater number that can be adduced, since this chapter is becoming unduly elongated. At the time of the March Conference, a three-way struggle ensued. The right-wing, led by Voitinsky, wanted unconditional unity with the Mensheviks. The centre, led by Stalin, wanted unification based on the political standpoint of Zimmerwald and Kienthal (i.e. a compromise anti-war stand that had temporarily united a revolutionary minority and a Kautskyite majority, but that had been criticised as inadequate by Lenin and the other émigré Bolsheviks, who along with Polish left-wingers like Karl Radek and others had formed a separate Zimmerwald Left). Finally, the Left, led by people like Molotov and Zalutsky opposed such attempts at unification. Lenin's arrival, while the March-April conference was still continuing, had the effect of dropping a bombshell on the party. He even felt that a clean break required breaking with "Old Bolshevism", and creating "a proletarian Communist Party" whose "elements have already been created by the best adherents of Bolshevism"[80] At this time, within the leadership (broadly defined) Lenin had only a few supporters. Alexandra Kollontai was his firmest supporter, while Nikolai Bukharin, when he returned to Russia a little later, would also support Lenin. In the Central Committee, and in the Petersburg Committee, Lenin found few supporters.[81]

Lenin's response was swift. He was aware that a leadership couldn't be built up overnight. So he had no aim of rejecting the Bolshevik party. But he recognised that a conservative inertia had set in in its upper layers, and decided to overcome that by appealing to the party ranks. Beginning with the publication of the *April Theses*, he launched an open campaign. He could do this with some confidence because while the official programme of the party called for a democratic revolution, Bolsheviks' tactics had highlighted class independence. His action showed that Lenin's conception of democratic centralism did not involve any consideration of subservience to the hierarchy, or any "central committee solidarity", when fundamental issues were involved. It also showed that there existed several trends within Bolshevism. As it has been argued, "Against the old Bolsheviks Lenin found support in.... the workers— Bolsheviks.... [who were revolutionary but] lacked the theoretical resources to defend their position."[82]

At the 7th All Russian Conference (April 24-29), while a sizeable block, led by Kamenev and Rykov, fought for Old Bolshevism,[83] the crucial resolution 'On the Current Moment' won with 71 votes for 39 against and 8 abstentions.[84] But on the question of splitting from the Zimmerwald movement Lenin stood isolated.[85] The critical attitude that he had taken to Old Bolshevism had to be toned down. Finally, in the nine-member Central Committee elected by the Conference, there were three firm Leninists (Lenin, Sverdlov and Smilga), two supporters of Lenin with qualifications (Stalin and Zinoviev) and four forming the right-wing (Kamemev, Nogin, Miliutin and Fedorov).[86]

Unless we are prepared to degenerate to utter cultism, we must admit that if Lenin had such rights, other members must have had, or should have had, such rights.

That they enjoyed such rights is seen clearly in the incidents of June. In June, when a debate took place over whether to organise a public demonstration calling for an end to the Provisional Government, the decision was not taken by the Central Committee alone, which would have been technically legitimate, but by a large gathering which included members of the Central Committee, the Petersburg Committee, the Military Organisation, representatives from the trade union and factory committee level party cells. It was this meeting that noted the mood of the masses in favour of a demonstration by a vote of 58 for, 37 against and 52 abstention, and declared that a demonstration would take place, if necessary defying the Soviet (47 for, 42 against, 80 abstention).[87] Facing a ban on the demonstration by the All-Russian Congress of Soviets, five members of the Central Committee had to meet on an emergency basis and call off the demonstration with Zinoviev, Kamenev and Nogin voting for calling off and Lenin and Sverdlov abstaining.[88] The party ranks responded by adopting resolutions condemning the Central Committee.[89] Lenin, in a speech before the Petersburg Committee, June 11, 1917, which had become radical due to recomposition in April, said:

> The Central Committee does not want to force your decision. Your right, the right to protest against the actions of the Central Committee, is a legitimate one, and your decision must be a free one.[90]

The right of the minority was not a mere formal right. A series of events highlight the effective nature of this right. A few cases can be mentioned. At the April Conference, Lenin and Kamenev were co-reporters in the discussion on general policy (reporters get an extended time and the right to speak a second time at the summing up). The personnel composition of party organs included diverse trends. Thus, the new Central Committee, elected by the 6th Congress, created a new editorial board for *Pravda*, the members being Stalin, Sokolnikov and Miliutin.[91] And when, at a critical moment, the Central Committee called on party members to stop collaborating with Maxim Gorky's paper, *Novaia Zhizn*, six party members who did collaborate with it wrote to the Central Committee:

> We consider it inappropriate that the CC should take decisions determining the political conduct of this or that group of party members in matters directly concerning them and on which they are better informed without consulting such party members in advance.[92]

Similarly, when a pseudo-democratic body, known as the Council of the Republic, was created through assigning blocs of seats to different kinds of organisations, the decision on whether to boycott it or not was not taken by the Central Committee alone. Trotsky, for the boycott, had a majority of one in the Central Committee. But a meeting of the party group at the Democratic Conference (called to create an institutional basis for the Kerensky regime), decided in favour of entering the Council by 77 votes to 50. The Central Committee accepted this verdict.[93]

So, right up to the eve of the October uprising, there remained a substantial minority that had a radically different conception of the tasks of the party, and this minority was associated with the highest party bodies. It was never excluded from the executive organs in the name of centralism. At the 6th Congress of the party, out of twenty-one members elected to the Central Committee, the current associated with Kamenev had several members—Kamenev, Zinoviev, Rykov, Nogin and Miliutin.[94] Several days before the insurrection, a Political Bureau was elected (for the first time) to carry out day-to-day leadership tasks. It included Lenin, Trotsky, Stalin, Sokolnikov, Bubnov, Kamenev and Zinoviev.[95] The last two were determined opponents of the insurrection, and even Stalin felt that Lenin's and Kamenev's lines could be reconciled.[96]

The collapse of inner party democracy—how logical a consequence of Leninism?

But, we will be told at this point, Lenin changed his position later. We want to present the situation below. Throughout 1918-1921, the Bolsheviks and the new born Soviet power faced an intolerable situation. There was civil war, backed by imperialism. And apart from small sections of the Mensheviks and Anarchists, all political parties clearly refused to accept Soviet power and took up arms. The Socialist Revolutionaries, who had found many passionate sympathisers, were notorious for both terrorist activities and cooperation with the right-wing —not just after but before October 1917.

Lenin, in his theoretical writings, was still insisting on the need to widen democracy. Thus,

> Kautsky has not understood at all the difference between bourgeois parliamentarism, which combines democracy *(not for the people)* with bureaucracy *(against the people)*, and proletarian democracy, which will take immediate steps to cut bureaucracy down to the roots, and which will be able to carry these measures through to the end, to the complete abolition of bureaucracy, to the introduction of complete democracy for the people.[97]

At worst, one can argue that there was a flaw of omission in the *State and Revolution*. Lenin's account of representative democracy can be criticised for being silent on the question of plurality, rival programmes within the workers' state, and on the distinction between counter-revolution and opposition.

Another criticism of Lenin that can be made is that in the article 'Can the Bolsheviks Retain State Power?' (October 1917), he said that since the Revolution of 1905:

> Russia has been governed by 130,000 landowners [opposing 150,000,000 people] .... yet we are told that the 240,000 members of the Bolshevik Party will not be able to govern Russia....(though, together with the supporters) we....already have a "state apparatus" of one million people....[98]

Here, the talk was chiefly of how the Bolsheviks could govern. By talking only of the Bolsheviks and their supporters, the role of the Soviet, and its relationship with parties, was obscured.

Overall, the Bolsheviks and the Soviet government they headed, had inherited a major economic crisis. Moreover, this crisis, accentuating sharply even before October 1917, had so intensified the class struggles that the struggle between revolution and counter-revolution did not have to await October. Bourgeois counter-revolution began from the moment the February Revolution started consolidating gains of soldiers and workers. Bolsheviks, left Mensheviks, other internationalist Social Democrats, left and centrist SRs, etc., were denied a passage to Russia. Many, like Lenin, had to return through Germany, taking advantage of Ludendorff's hopes of peace in the East through a left-wing victory in Russia. Others, like Trotsky, were arrested by the "allies" as they tried to make their way back to Russia via allied countries.[99] From the beginning, this was an international class war. Lenin and Trotsky both made this point. Thus, Trotsky wrote: "The workers' government will from the start be faced with the task of uniting its forces with those of the socialist proletariat".[100] The imperialist powers were not slow in replying to the Bolsheviks. Paleologue and Buchanan, the French and English ambassadors respectively, made repeated demands to the liberals for the suppression of the Bolsheviks. Buchanan was one of the major props behind Kornilov.[101] The Allied military missions also tried to treat the Russian army separately from the unreliable government.[102] The allies put pressure not only on the right-wing parties, but also on the Mensheviks and SRs, whose rejection of a government of all the socialist parties, based on the Soviets, stemmed in part from this pressure.[103]

It is clearly beyond the scope of the present study to offer a detailed summary of the civil war.[104] But it is important to keep the chronology of the civil war in mind. Within three days of the October Insurrection, right-wing forces were being assisted by moderate Socialists in an attempted coup d'etat having far less democratic basis than the Soviet insurrection. Within six weeks, White forces were being organised in South Eastern Russia.[105] Both the Entente and the Germans egged on the Ukraine against the Soviet regime.[106] In Georgia, a Menshevik regime was formed, and it got Entente support.[107] In February 1918, the Volunteer Army left the Don to move on the Kuban. After the Treaty of Brest-Litovsk, the Germans imposed a puppet ruler in the Ukraine, the Hetman Skoropadsky. They also occupied Latvia and Estonia. Finnish independence, confirmed by the Bolsheviks, was followed by a bloody civil war waged by the Whites.

The Finnish civil war gave a lesson in democracy to the Bolsheviks. When the Finnish socialists won a majority (103 out of 200) seats to the Sejm, Kerensky had dissolved it. Following October, a Council of People's Delegates had been proclaimed in Finland. This revolution was smashed by right-wing armed forces, led by Mannerheim, and militarily under the guidance of Germans led by General Von der Goltz. The defeat of the revolution was followed by mass murder. Some 23,000 Reds were killed.[108] In Helsinki, the Whites made workers' wives and children walk in front of their troops as they recaptured the city street by street. One hundred of them died. In Tavastehus 10,000 prisoners were interned and many subsequently massacred. In Kummen 500 were shot after the battle.[109] "In Lahti in one day some 200 women were shot with explosive bullets."[110] In Viipuri 600 Red Guards were lined up in three rows and machine-gunned to death.[111] It is estimated that 8380 captured Reds were killed illegally.[112] About 265 'legal executions' were based on 'illegal charges' [113] and 11,783 prisoners out of the 80,000 or so, died due to lack of food, sanitation, living space, etc.[114]

As in Finland, so in Russia, too, the counter-revolution was actively aided by both imperialist camps. The German ambassador, Count Mirbach, on arriving in Moscow, met a number of members of the Imperial Family.[115] Bruce Lockhart, a British officer, was in contact with Alexiev, Kornilov and Denikin. By April 1918, the Entente had come to the conclusion that they would have to invade Russia and overthrow the Bolsheviks.[116] In April 1918, the British and the Japanese seized Vladivostok. By the end of 1918, there were 73,000 Japanese troops in Siberia.[117] In all, in course of the civil war the Soviet regime faced the armies of 14 countries, who at different points supported Kolchak in the East, Yudenich's thrust for Petrograd in the North, and Denikin and the Cossacks' drive to Moscow from the South. By 1919, over 200,000 Allied troops were ranged against the Red forces.[118]

White Terror was a brutal anti-poor peasant, anti-worker, and anti-communist policy. The aim of the officers was not to establish parliamentary democracy, but a dictatorship. White-ruled territories were either run as military despotisms, or were given in charge of discredited bureaucrats of the Tsarist era. White Terror was massive; half of an entire captured regiment was shot dead, after being forced to dig their own graves, for being communists.[119] Two orders of Karsnov and Kaledin showed the class nature of White Terror:

Order No. 2428: It is forbidden to arrest workers. The orders are to hang or shoot them.

Order No. 2431: The orders are to hang all arrested workers in the street. The bodies are to be exhibited for three days.[120]

Under these strains, Bolshevik commitment to democracy creaked, bent, and ultimately broke. There was no doubt whatsoever among the Bolsheviks that survival of a workers' government in Russia depended on the spread of the revolution. Even Stalin could summarise the difference between Lenin on one hand and Zinoviev and Kamenev on the other over the October Revolution in these words: "There are two lines here: one steers for the victory of the revolution and relies on Europe, the second has no faith in the revolution and reckons on being only an opposition."[121] E.H. Carr concludes that the European revolution's proximity was the factor "on which the confident calculations....of every Bolshevik of any account, had been based."[122]

European Revolution was no chimera in this period. It began with the Easter Rising in Ireland in 1916. It continued with the fall of Tsarism. A naval revolt and a general strike in November 1918 overthrew the German Kaiser. Prince Max of Baden tried to assume a regency. But workers and soldiers set up Councils. Revolution had already descended on the streets of Vienna, Budapest and Prague. In Bulgaria, Tsar Ferdinand abdicated, and Stamboulisky, the peasant leader who had just been liberated from jail, got control over the government. Victor Serge writes: "From the Scheldt to the Volga the councils of workers' and soldiers' deputies—the Soviets—are the real masters of the hour."[123] In March, 1919, a Soviet government took power in Hungary. In the same year, massive labour unrest shook Britain. For two years massive class struggles convulsed Italy, until a fascist counter-revolution brought Mussolini to power.[124]It was on the basis of these struggles, unprecedented in scope, that the attempts were launched to build a Soviet Europe. By 1920, the Communist International counted in its ranks powerful parties in Italy, Czechoslovakia, France, Bulgaria, Sweden, Germany, Norway and Yugoslavia.

In January 1919, provocations had resulted in an untimely rising and the beheading of the KPD leadership. But the revolutionary wave was still very strong. "All power to the Councils", and "Dictatorship of the proletariat" became watch words of the European working class—for the first and last time in history. As Otto Bauer, an Austrian Social Democratic leader who worked hard to prevent the socialist revolution, explained, the Austrian proletariat (to give one example), "considered the establishment of the dictatorship of the proletariat to be possible."[125] An eyewitness wrote that "An ever widening circle saw in the workers' and soldiers' councils, based on the Russian Soviet model, the future structure of representation in Germany."[126]

Eventually, this world revolution was defeated. In 1921, Soviet Russia stood as the isolated, solitary, advanced outpost of a failed revolutionary wave. Counter-revolution was unable to conquer it. But its crisis became acute. The fate of Soviet democracy in Russia was settled as much in Berlin, Vienna, Budapest or Turin, as in Russia. But Soviet democracy was not murdered by Leninism. Robert Abrams' study of the local Soviets shows that in the period 1918-1921, local Soviets were able to displace the old political elite, and create a new political culture with a high degree of input from the lower classes.[127]

In the local Soviets, as late as 1921, the communists were not mostly predominant. In Volost executive committees, non-party members predominated. In district city executives, communists were in a slight majority. The advantage of being an organised party was that at the upper level, in the provincial city and congress executive committees, the communists had superiority. However, it has also been noted that the party grew from 24,000 in early 1917 to over ten times by July-August. So even the induction of communists in the Soviets shows the rise of a new layer of administrators. In 1919, the only year for which such statistics are available, only 12.5% of the district city executive committees could be considered Old Bolsheviks. In the provincial city executive committees in the same years, about 50% were Old Bolsheviks.[128] The proportion of Old Bolsheviks in the uezd congress executive committees, in fact, declined from 12.2% in 1919 to 7.6% in 1921.[129]

But as Soviets collapsed due to civil war and the dispersal of the proletariat, non-elected 'revolutionary committees' or expanded party committees, replaced them in many places.[130] Thus, non-elected, unrepresentative bodies began to be set up. With the elected, militant workers being replaced, functionaries now became more important. By the end of 1920, there were 5,880,000 such functionaries, and less than 2 million industrial workers.[131] In Vyatka, Stalin found that out of 4,766 members of the staff of the Soviet authorities, 4,467 were former Tsarist officials.[132]

Victor Serge spelled out the change with precision and clarity:

> With the disappearance of political debates between parties representing different social interests through the various shades

> of their opinion, Soviet institutions, beginning with the local Soviets and ending with the Vee-Tsik and the Council of People's Commissars, manned solely by communists, now function in a vacuum: since all the decisions are taken by the party, all they can do is give them the official rubber stamp.[133]

The last bastion of workers' democracy had been the Bolshevik party itself. After October, the pre-October divisions continued to exist, with Zinoviev, Kamenev, Ryazanov, Lunacharsky and others opposing Lenin, Trotsky and Sverdlov. There was no talk of imposing a unity by fiat. Kamenev's group insisted on defying the CC resolution and tried to put together an alliance with the socialist parties. They opposed the hard line advocated by Lenin, Sverdlov and Trotsky. At this, ten members of the CC demanded that the minority must abide by the accepted line and support a Soviet government. The CC minority thereupon offered to resign from the CC in order to retain their right to go to the people with their own views.[134] However, they did not have to resign in the end. This shows that the CC discipline was not unnecessarily rigid.

Several People's Commissars also resigned, and the Commissar for Labour, A.G. Shlyapnikov expressed his support for those commissars.[135] Ryazanov, Kamenev and Larin, in a letter to the CC, said that "we do not consider our disagreements with the CC to be a breach of the party rules... we consider that it is totally inadmissible to create a special regime for particular party members....[136] Another leading activist, S.A. Lozovsky, objecting strongly to the insistence on retaining Lenin and Trotsky in the Sovnarkom, wrote:

> I cannot, in the name of the party discipline, submit to the cult of personal worship and stale political conciliation with all socialist parties who agree to our basic demands, upon the inclusion of this or that individual in the ministry....[137]

The conflict that arose over the Brest-Litovsk Treaty is another well-known case.[138] On January 8, 1918, at a meeting of the Central Committee members with other leading activists, three lines were put forward. Lenin urged that peace terms be accepted. Trotsky called for disbanding the army, proclaiming the end of the war, but not signing such an insulting peace.

Finally, Bukharin called for a revolutionary war. Bukharin's position received 32 votes, Trotsky got 16 votes and Lenin 15 votes.[139]

A Special Conference, which met on 21st January, failed to take any clear stand. In the CC, Lenin aligned with Trotsky to block Bukharin. On 29th January, Trotsky broke off negotiations, declaring that Russia would not sign the annexationist peace, but was terminating the war.[140]

The Germans responded by ending the armistice and invading Russia.[141] Inside the party, the result was a crisis with the Central Committee first approving the action of the delegation at Brest Litovsk,[142] and then defeating both a call for revolutionary war[143] and a proposal for signing the peace.[144] Ultimately, on 18th February, Trotsky and his supporters partially sided with Lenin, arguing that if revolutionary war was launched, it would lead to a split in the party, which they could not risk under the circumstances. The proposal for immediate acceptance of German terms was adopted with 7 votes in favour, 4 against, and 4 abstentions.[145]

The CC minutes reveal a tremendous tension. The prospect of a split was freely discussed. Yet, it is worth noting how the party acted to heal the wounds. Party unity was indeed considered a vital necessity. But that was not interpreted to mean that disputes should be condemned. Such an issue, as war and peace (and the very existence, possibly, of the revolution) was debated with considerable publicity, including a Special Conference. Trotsky, who had some degree of agreement with the war faction, ultimately ensured their defeat, because he knew that if revolutionary war was waged, the party would split immediately, and Lenin's faction might even have to be arrested if they opposed a revolutionary war while war was actually being fought.[146]

Once Lenin's line was assured a victory, his most irreconcilable opponents tendered their resignations from the CC and from Sovnarkom. The response of Lenin and Trotsky was to propose forms of collaboration that allowed maximum flexibility to the minority while retaining them within the party. Lenin called for a guarantee that statements would be published in *Pravda* reflecting the standpoint of the minority. Trotsky's resolution, adopted unanimously, asked the members to "remain members of the leading party body, retaining the right to campaign freely against the decision adopted by the CC." This meant that the CC members were given the right to publicly differentiate themselves from the official stand of the party on this contentious issue. Similarly, Krestinsky's resolution on the six People's Commissars who submitted resignations asked them to carry on other work, without feeling bound by cabinet solidarity on the question of the Brest-Litovsk Peace. This was adopted unanimously.[147]

It is by obscuring these details that later Stalinist historiography presented a fiction about Trotskyite-Bukharinist counter-revolutionary activity stretching back to Brest Litovsk.

The Eighth Party Conference of December 2-4, 1919, held at the height of the civil war tightened party discipline. One of the conference resolutions dealt with discipline. Resolutions of party centres were to be "implemented rapidly and accurately", while failure to do so was to be counted as a "party crime."[148] Party fractions in non-party institutions were declared entirely subordinated to the party. Fraction members had to vote unanimously at meetings of the non-party organisations.[149] This meant that whereas in the past, party fractions had debated issues and even changed positions, now only smaller, official bodies, like the CC would direct them.

Until 1923, attempts were made to seriously ensure the authority of the Party Congress. Congresses were held annually from 1917 to 1923. Delegates were more or less freely elected before 1923. There was open discussion and free criticism of the party leadership. Commissions of various kinds were set up, with representation from different trends. In each Congress, standing rules enabled any group of a stipulated minimum (usually 40) number of delegates to present counter reports.[150] Final resolutions showed the result of tough bargaining. In short, the Congress reflected the normal cut and thrust of democratic party functioning..

Throughout the period between October 1917 and 1921, the party had different factions. The usual "right" and "left" terms are somewhat inadequate. The factions included those who stressed institutions of popular, participatory democracy (often called the "left"), those who stressed traditional civil liberties and democratic rights (often identified as the "right") and those who turned expediency into theory. The composition of the different trends changed from time to time, though some people, like Kollontai, Osinskii, Preobrazhenskii, etc. remained "left" consistently, while Zinoviev, Stalin, Molotov remained equally consistently among those who stood for political manipulations (Zinoviev would become left only in 1925-6, partly under pressure of the Leningrad proletariat), and Ryazanov was a more or less consistent "right"-ist and Lenin and Trotsky, in important respects, had identifications with the "left".[151] But Lenin was also capable of stiff action against oppositions, especially in 1921-22, while Trotsky in the same period emerged as a major theorist of the domination of the party, and of the CC.[152]

At the 9th Congress Lenin was accused of "vertical centralism", and a faction came into existence, calling for Democratic Centralism. Among its chief spokespersons were Osinskii. Bubnov, Sapronov and V.M. Smirnov. The Workers' Opposition came into existence in 1919. It was formed round an opposition to the party line on the trade union question. At the November 1920 conference of the Moscow Party organisation, 124 out of the 278 delegates expressed support for the thesis of the workers' opposition.[153] Lenin's prestige and organisational manipulations by Zinoviev and Stalin, were major factors in the ultimate defeat of this opposition. But meanwhile, this opposition was able to publicly air its view in various ways. Alexander Shlyapnikov's 'theses' were published in the party's organ.[154] Alexandra Kollontai wrote a more elaborate and extremely powerful pamphlet, *The Workers' Opposition*. It was published in an edition of 250,000 copies.[155] At the 9th Party Conference, the left-wing demanded, and got, more inner party democratic rights.[156] The party zealously sought to keep intact its rights. This went on till 1920-21. The 9th Congress had seen Trotsky presenting theses for the militarisation of labour. There was a growing challenge to this, resulting, eventually, in several platforms being presented. Alexandra Kollontai drew applause at the 9th Conference, when she asked Zinoviev what sort of freedom of criticism would be allowed and that party comrades must know whether criticism of party policies would result in their being sent off to a warm climate to eat peaches.[157] The dig was about an attempt by Zinoviev to get rid of Angelica Balabanoff from Moscow, to Central Asia for her critical stand.[158]

It was in 1921, at the 10th Party Congress, held amidst the tragic Kronstadt revolt, which combined worker-peasant anger with white guard manipulation, that the final blow fell. All opposition was banned. And inner party factions were banned.

A resolution was adopted 'On Party Unity'. It denounced factions and factionalism. It went on to say that "The Congress orders the immediate dissolution ... of all groups that have been formed on the basis of some platform or other ...."[159] The final clause of this resolution, kept hidden from the party, empowered the CC to expel even CC members from the party,[160] thereby violating utterly the sovereignty of the Party Congress. The decisions thus taken in haste, and in fear of counter-revolution, were to be of tremendous significance. The conjunctural issues were uppermost in Lenin's mind.[161] But the resultant decisions were not conjunctural. Lenin's definition of 'factionalism' as 'the formation of groups with separate platforms striving to a certain degree to segregate and create their own group discipline"[162] raised an important question. Had he himself not sought to do the same, off and on since 1903? In 1908-9, he had even expelled Bogdanov from the Bolshevik faction, arguing that a party could be a broader organisation, but a faction had to be restrictive, because it implied a specific platform. In a mass party, with hundreds of thousands of members, sharp differences could be properly articulated only if factions were permitted. The very premise of banning opposition parties who recognised Soviet power, and of factions in the communist party itself, was substitutionism. The party's line decided by the CC and approved the Congress, was deemed to be the proletarian line. The vast masses outside the party were by definition, prone to petty-bourgeois wavering.

In the name of a hierarchy of knowledge, the self-activity of the working class was reined in. The proletariat itself was viewed as never conscious enough (unless it agreed with the party line) to rule a country or progress to a classless society.

This was done, as we said, under exceptional circumstances. We say this, not to argue that Lenin was right, but to argue that one must keep in mind the specific circumstances. Even in 1921, Lenin was unwilling to take the position that this should be the rule for all time to come. Commenting on the formation of factions in the course of internal debates, Lenin said, "It is, of course, quite permissible (specially before a congress) for various groups to form blocs (and also go vote-chasing)."[163] And even after proposing a restriction on factions, Lenin tried to draw a line. When one delegate proposed an amendment which would have turned this into a permanent ban on factions, Lenin criticised the proposed amendment as "excessive" and "impracticable". He argued that if there were "fundamental disagreements" when the delegates were elected to the next congress, "the elections may have to be based on platforms".[164]

With all his caveats, Lenin was still wrong, as was Trotsky, who took several years to acknowledge that the decisions of 1921 had been positively bad. But why did Lenin take this position? It is usually argued that Lenin's main target was Shlyapnikov. The Left were certainly a part of his target. But he was more concerned about capitalist restoration. It should be noted that Lenin did not call for such ban on factions in the Communist International, which was considered a single world party divided into national sections. Indeed, the Workers' Opposition appealed against the Soviet Party to the Communist International. The ban on factions was meant to address a danger specific to the Bolsheviks being a ruling party under certain extremely negative conditions, and it was inextricably tied to the contemporaneous implementation of the New Economic Policy. More than the Left, the ban targeted the Right, that is, the forces connected to the old state apparatus of Tsarist Russia and of capitalism, which were coming back to try and swamp the politics of revolution. So, the ban on factions was a self-consciously limited and specifically local compromise to Lenin's mind, and not at all the expression of any kind of principle. It is a serious mistake to regard it otherwise. The fact that the ban on factions helped lead to Stalinism does not make it into an "original sin" by Lenin. And as for those who today try to use that "ban" to talk about bans on factions in communist parties as a matter of principle, they represent bureaucratic powers, forces originating in a petty bourgeois milieu that try to control working class organisations in their narrow interests, not the interests of the working class and its historic mission of proletarian socialist revolution.

Inner Party Democracy Today

Most of what we have related is easily available, as we have tried to show, by looking at the writings of Marx, Engels and Lenin. Once we are able to get rid of the historical errors, the appeals to authority based on distorted history, the issues become simpler. It is no longer a case of slapping down 50 volumes of Marx-Engels or 45 volumes of Lenin. It is a matter of using basic Marxist ideas about a proletarian revolution and a revolutionary party, and putting it in today's context. In a bourgeois democracy, however truncated, the revolutionary working class party has to be a democratic party. This means many things. In the first place this means that working within bourgeois democracy, the revolutionary working class party has to be more democratic than the bourgeois parties, not less. The relationship between the party, which incorporates only a small section of the working class under non-revolutionary circumstances, and a minority even in revolutionary times, and the class as a whole, through its many organisations, has to be democratically structured. In India, even if we accept the claims of the CPI(M) that it is a revolutionary party (and to be blunt, we do not do so) we would have to note the existence of a wide range of left parties—Stalinist, non-Stalinist, Maoist, and so on. There also exist a large number of trade unions, incorporating large masses of workers, ranging from radical but non-party, such as the NTUI, or on a small scale like the Jyoti Karamchari Mandal of Vadodara, to unions more or less closely attached to various left parties—CITU, AITUC, UTUC, AICCTU, etc. as well as unions close to bourgeois parties, beginning with the INTUC.

The practice of the CPI(M) has historically been one of building a tight party. Members have been told that bourgeois media always lies. So members are to read only party papers (nowadays also see TV channels that support the party) and believe them. This is in the long run untenable, since party members and members of mass organisations do live in the real world. The burden has fallen especially on party members, who are de facto asked to behave, even though we live in a bourgeois democracy where the media openly discuss all kinds of issues, as though it is still the deepest underground.

In a big party, whether one considers it revolutionary or not, there are bound to be different trends, different approaches to the changing reality. If this party claims to be a working class party, it has the obligation to explain to workers what these differences are. The argument that openly discussing these will also inform the bourgeoisie is not a serious objection. Clearly, one is not talking here of setting the date for the insurrection. The bourgeoisie has numerous ways of being informed about debates in workers parties, in any case. There had never been a revolutionary movement not infiltrated by the ruling class. Secrecy in the end helps only to keep the working class in the dark. Unless of course one goes back to the days of absolute secrecy, oath taking, execution of those who violate the oath, and so on. All that would have no space in a bourgeois democracy, and the more extreme forms should have no space in working class politics under any circumstances.

In the present case, the debate was whether or not to support Pranab Mukherjee, the Finance Minister in UPA-II, when he stood for the post of President of India. Nobody disputed that the post of president is a relatively unimportant one in India. However with the triumph of the BJP in the 2014 National Elections and with the decline of the dominance of secular and democratic forces, the President of India might play an important role in this era of emerging fascism. So should the left parties have voted for Mukherjee or not? This was a real debate over tactics. But the debate itself should have been conducted openly. The working class constituency of the CPI(M) had the right to be informed about the different opinions, the lines of argument, and the party, if it claimed to be a proletarian revolutionary party, had the duty, of ensuring that the working class was so informed. If this is not done, then we end up assuming that the mass of workers are forever ignorant louts, who, if they know what is good for them, should unquestioningly follow the revolutionary party. The only way out of this is the development and extension of working class democracy. In the given case, this means, if the CPI(M) was serious about being a revolutionary working class party, it should stop driving out those of its comrades who disagreed with the party decision, and instead open a real, comradely debate over the dispute, and do so in the open party press, not some closed door meetings.

APPENDIX

Extract from the Resolution of the Fourth International *The Dictatorship of the Proletariat and Socialist Democracy*[165]

In Response to Dogmas of Stalinist Origin

The ideology of the ruling bureaucracy has been and remains essentially pragmatic. But a certain number of theories and dogmas underpin this ideology and they have an internal coherence which is contradictory with revolutionary Marxist theory. This ideology of the bureaucracy—of which the key idea is the rule of the single party acting in the name of the working class—although not always explicitly formulated can be synthesised as follows:

a) That the "leading party" or even its "leading nucleus" (the "Leninist Central Committee") has a monopoly of political consciousness at the highest level, if not a monopoly of knowledge at least at the level of the social sciences, and is therefore guaranteed political infallibility ("the party is always right").

b) That the working class, and even more the toiling masses in general, are too backward politically, too much under the influence of bourgeois and petty-bourgeois ideology and "imperialist propaganda," too much inclined to prefer immediate material advantages as against long-term historical interests, for any direct exercise of state power by democratically elected workers' councils to be tolerable from the point of view of "the interests of socialism." Genuine workers' democracy would entail the risk of an increasing series of, harmful, "objectively counter-revolutionary" decisions, which would open the road to the restoration of capitalism or at the very least gravely damage and retard the process of building socialism.

c) That therefore the dictatorship of the proletariat can be exercised only by the "leading party of the proletariat," i.e. that the dictatorship of the proletariat is the dictatorship of the party, either representing an essentially passive working class, or actively basing itself on the "class struggle of the masses," who are nevertheless considered unworthy, unwilling, or incapable of directly exercising state power through institutionalised organs of power.

d) That since the party, and that party alone, represents the interests of the working class, which are considered homogeneous in all situations and on all issues, the "leading party" itself must be essentially monolithic. Any opposition tendency necessarily reflects alien class pressures and alien class interests in one form or another (the struggle between "two lines" is always a "struggle between the proletariat and the bourgeoisie inside the party," the Maoists conclude). Monolithic control of all spheres of social life by the single party is the logical outcome of these concepts. Direct party control must be established overall sectors of "civil society."

e) A further underlying assumption is that of an intensification of the class struggle in the period of building socialism (although this assumption alone does not necessarily lead to the same conclusion, if it is not combined with the previous ones). From that assumption is deduced the increasing danger of restoration of bourgeois power even long after private property in the means of production has been abolished, and irrespective of the level of development of the productive forces. The threat of bourgeois restoration is often portrayed as a mechanical outcome of the victory of bourgeois ideology in this or that social, political, cultural, or even scientific field. In view of the extreme power thereby attributed to bourgeois ideas, the use of repression against those who are said to objectively represent these ideas becomes a corollary of the argument.

All these assumptions and dogmas are unscientific from a general Marxist point of view and are untenable in the light of real historical experience of the class struggle during and after the overthrow of capitalist rule in the USSR and other countries. Repeatedly, they have shown themselves to be harmful to the defence of the proletariat's class interests and an obstacle to a successful struggle against the remnants of the bourgeoisie and of bourgeois ideology.

But inasmuch as they had become nearly universally

accepted dogmas by the CPs in Stalin's time and undoubtedly have an inner consistency—reflecting the material interests of the bureaucracy as a social layer and an apology for its dictatorial rule—they have never been explicitly and thoroughly criticised and rejected by a CP since then. These concepts continue to linger on, at least partially, in the ideology of many leaders and cadres of the CPs and SPs, i.e. of the bureaucracies of the labour movement. They continue to constitute a conceptual source for justification of various forms of curtailment of democratic rights of the toiling masses.

It should be noted that organisations other than those inspired by Stalinism put forward similar conceptions in this regard, justifying at least partially similar practices in their own ranks. This makes it all the more necessary to stress that all this is absolutely contrary to the teachings of Lenin and Trotsky, not to mention Marx and Engels, and of our historical movement. A clear and coherent refutation of these conceptions and of the practices which they motivate, is therefore indispensable to the defence of our programme of socialist democracy.

First: the idea of a homogeneous working class exclusively represented by a single party is contradicted by all historical experience and by any Marxist analysis of the concrete growth and development of the contemporary proletariat, both under capitalism and after the overthrow of capitalism. At most, one could defend the thesis that the revolutionary vanguard party alone programmatically defends the long-term historical interests of the proletariat, and its immediate overall class interests as opposed to sectoral interests of national, regional, local, special sectors or skill, over-privileged, etc., interests. But even in that case, a dialectical-materialist approach, as opposed to a mechanical-idealist one, would immediately add that only insofar as the party actually conquers political leadership over the majority of the workers can one speak of a real, as opposed to a simply ideal (literary) integration of immediate and long-term, of sectoral and class interests having been achieved in practice, with the possibilities for errors much reduced. Furthermore, this in no way excludes that on particular questions this party can be wrong.

In fact, there is a definite, objectively determined stratification of the working class and of the development of working class consciousness. There is likewise at the very least a tension between the struggle for immediate interests and the historical goals of the labour movement (for example the contradiction between immediate consumption and long-term investment in a workers' state). Precisely these contradictions, rooted in the legacy of uneven development of bourgeois society, are among the main theoretical justifications for the need of a revolutionary vanguard workers' party, as opposed to a simple "all-inclusive" union of all wage-earners in a single organisation. But this again implies that one cannot deny that different parties, with different orientations and different ways of approaching the class struggle between capital and labour and the relations between capital and labour and the relations between immediate demands and historical goals, can arise and have arisen within the working class and do genuinely represent sectors of the working class (be it purely sectoral interests, privileged sectors, results of ideological pressures of alien class forces, etc.).

Nor can it be excluded that several revolutionary parties might arise in a single country, whose differences might not be settled by a fusion before the revolution, a situation which would lead to the need to seek to form a more or less tightly knit front of these parties that would try to determine their political action in common.

Second: a revolutionary party with a democratic internal life does have a tremendous advantage in the field of correct analysis of socio-economic and political developments and of correct elaboration of tactical and strategic answers to such developments, for it can base itself on the body of scientific socialism, Marxism, which synthesises and generalises all past experiences of the class struggle as a whole. This programmatic framework for its current political elaboration makes it much less likely than any other tendency of the labour movement, or any unorganised sector of the working class, to reach wrong conclusions, premature generalisations, and one-sided and impressionistic reactions to unforeseen developments, to make concessions to ideological and political pressures of alien class forces, to engage in unprincipled political compromises, etc.

However there are no infallible parties. There are no infallible party leaderships, or individual party leaders, party majorities, "Leninist central committees," etc. The Marxist programme is never a definitely achieved one. No new situation can be comprehensively analysed with reference to historical precedents. Social reality is constantly undergoing changes. New and unforeseen developments regularly occur at historical turning points. The phenomenon of imperialism after Engels's death was not analysed by Marx and Engels. The delay of the proletarian revolution in the advanced imperialist countries was not foreseen by the Bolsheviks. The bureaucratic degeneration of the first workers state was not incorporated in Lenin's theory of the dictatorship of the proletariat. The emergence after World War II of many workers' states (albeit with bureaucratic deformations from the start) following revolutionary mass struggles not led by revolutionary Marxist leaderships (Yugoslavia, China, Vietnam) was not foreseen by Trotsky, etc. No complete, ready-made answer for new phenomena can be found in the works of the classics or in the existing programme.

Furthermore, new problems will arise in the course of the building of socialism, problems for which the revolutionary Marxist programme provides only a general framework of reference but no automatic source of correct answers. The struggle for correct answers to such new problems implies a constant interaction between theoretical-political analysis and discussions and revolutionary class practice, the final word being spoken by practical experience. Under such circumstances, any restriction of free political and theoretical debate spilling over to a restriction of free political mass activity of the proletariat, i.e. any restriction of socialist democracy, will constitute an obstacle to the revolutionary party itself arriving at correct policies. It is therefore not only theoretically wrong but practically ineffective and harmful from the point of view of successfully advancing on the road of building socialism.

One of the gravest consequences of a monolithic one-party system, of the absence of a plurality of political groups, tendencies, and parties, and of administrative restrictions being imposed on free political and ideological debate, is the impediments such a system erects on the road to rapidly correcting mistakes which can be committed by the government of a workers' state. Mistakes committed by such a government, like mistakes committed by the majority of the working class, its various layers, and different political groupings, are by and large unavoidable in the process of building a classless, socialist society. A rapid correction of these mistakes, however, is possible in a climate of free political debate, free access of opposition groupings to mass media, large-scale political awareness and involvement in political life by the masses, and control by the masses over government and state activity at all levels.

The absence of all these correctives under a system of monolithic one-party government makes the rectification of grave mistakes all the more difficult. The very dogma of party infallibility on which the Stalinist system rests puts a heavy premium both on the denial of mistakes in party policies (search for self-justification and for scapegoats) and on the attempt to postpone even implicit corrections as long as possible. The objective costs of such a system in terms of economic losses, of unnecessary, i.e. objectively avoidable sacrifices imposed upon the toiling masses, of political defeats in relation to class enemies, and of political disorientation and demoralisation of the proletariat, are indeed staggering, as is shown by the history of the Soviet Union since 1928. To give just one example: the obstinate clinging to erroneous agricultural policies even on detailed questions such as purchasing prices for certain agricultural products by Stalin and his henchmen after the catastrophe caused by the forced collectivisation of agriculture—which can of course be explained in terms of the specific social interests of the Soviet bureaucracy at that time—has wreaked havoc with the food supply of the Soviet people for more than a generation. Its negative consequences have not been eliminated to this day, nearly fifty years later. Such a catastrophe would have been impossible had there been free political debate over alternative economic and agricultural policies in the USSR.

Third: the idea that restricting the democratic rights of the proletariat is in any way conducive to a gradual "education" of an allegedly "backward" mass of toilers is blatantly absurd. One cannot learn to swim except by going into the water. There is no way masses can learn to raise the level of their political awareness other than by engaging in political activity and learning from the experience of such activity. There is no way they can learn from mistakes other than by having the right to commit them. Paternalistic prejudices about the alleged "backwardness" of the masses generally hide a conservative petty-bourgeois fear of mass activity, which has nothing in common with revolutionary Marxism. The bureaucracy is in deadly fear of socialist democracy, not for "programmatic" reasons, but because that form of government is incompatible with its material privileges, not to mention its power. Marxists favour the fullest possible flowering of socialist democracy because they are convinced that any restriction of political mass activity, on the pretext that the masses would make too many mistakes, can only lead to increasing political apathy among the workers, i.e. to paradoxically reinforcing the very situation which is said to be the problem.

Fourth: under conditions of full-scale socialisation of the means of production and the social surplus product, any long-term monopoly of the exercise of political power in the hands of a minority—even if it is a revolutionary party beginning with the purest of revolutionary motivations—runs a strong risk of stimulating objective tendencies towards bureaucratisation. Under such socio-economic conditions whoever controls the state administration thereby controls the social surplus product and its distribution. Given the fact that economic inequalities will still exist at the outset, particularly but not only in the economically backward workers' states, this can become a source of corruption and of the growth of material privileges and social differentiation. "The conquest of power changes not only the relations of the proletariat to other classes, but also its own inner structure. The wielding of power becomes the speciality of a definite social group, which is the more impatient to solve its own 'social problem' the higher its opinion of its own mission." (Leon Trotsky, *The Revolution Betrayed*, p. 102.)

Thus, there is an objective need for real control over decision-making to rest in the hands of the proletariat as a class, with unlimited possibilities to denounce pilferage, waste, and illegal appropriation and misuse of resources at all levels, including the highest ones. No such democratic mass control is possible without opposition tendencies, groups, and parties having full freedom of action, propaganda, and agitation, as well as full access to the mass media, as long as they are not engaged in armed struggle to overthrow workers' power.

Likewise, during the transition period between capitalism and socialism, and even in the first phase of communism, it is unavoidable that forms of social division of labour will survive, as well as forms of labour organisation and labour processes totally or partially inherited from capitalism, that do not enable a full development of all the creative talents of the producers. These handicaps cannot be neutralised by indoctrination, moral exhortation, or periodic "mass criticism campaigns" as the Maoists contend, and still less by mystifying expedients like having cadres or leaders work a few days a month or a week as manual labourers. These objective obstacles on the road to the gradual emergence of truly socialist relations of production can be prevented from becoming powerful sources of material privileges only if the mass of the producers (in the first place those likely to be the most exploited, the manual workers) are placed in conditions such that they can exercise real political and social power over any functionally privileged layer. The radical reduction of the work day, the fullest Soviet democracy, and full educational opportunities for rapidly raising the cultural level of all workers are the key conditions for attaining this goal.

To protect itself against the professional risks of power, the revolutionary party will have to reject its members accumulating positions in the state apparatus and positions in the leadership of the party.

The present conditions in the bureaucratised workers' states, which make the problem of advancing proletarian democracy difficult, would of course be altered qualitatively if (or when) either of the two following developments occur, or even more if they occur together: (1) A socialist revolution in one or more industrially advanced capitalist countries. Such a revolution would itself give enormous impulsion to the struggle for democratic rights throughout the world and would immediately open the possibility of increasing productivity on an immense scale, eliminating the scarcities that are the root cause of the entrenchment of a parasitic bureaucracy, as explained above. (2) A political revolution in the bureaucratically deformed or degenerated workers' states, particularly in the Soviet Union or the People's Republic of China. This would likewise signify an upsurge of proletarian democracy with colossal repercussions internationally, besides putting an end to the bureaucratic caste and its concept of building "socialism in one country".

Following a political revolution, common economic planning among all the workers' states would become realisable, thus assuring a leap forward in productivity that would help remove the economic basis of parasitic bureaucratism.

Finally, it is true that there is no automatic correlation or simultaneity between the abolition of capitalist state power and private property in the means of production and the disappearance of privileges in the field of personal wealth, cultural heritage, and ideological influence, not to speak of the disappearance of all elements of commodity production. Long after bourgeois state power has been overthrown and capitalist property abolished, remnants of petty commodity production and the survival of elements of a money economy will continue to create a framework in which primitive accumulation of capital can still reappear, especially if the level of development of the productive forces is still insufficient to guarantee the automatic appearance and consolidation of genuine socialist relations of production. Likewise, elements of social and economic inequality survive under such circumstances long after the bourgeoisie has lost its positions as a ruling class politically and economically; the influence of bourgeois and petty bourgeois ideologies, customs, habits, cultural values, etc., will linger on in relatively large spheres of social life and broad layers of society.

But it is completely wrong to draw from this undeniable

fact (which is, incidentally, one of the main reasons why state power of the working class is indispensable in order to prevent these "islands of bourgeois influence" from becoming bases for the restoration of capitalism) the conclusion that administrative repression of bourgeois ideology is a necessary condition for the building of a socialist society. On the contrary, historical experience confirms the total ineffectiveness of administrative struggles against reactionary and petty bourgeois ideologies. In fact, in the long run, such methods even strengthen the hold of these ideologies and place the great mass of the proletariat in the position of being ideologically disarmed before them, because of lack of experience with genuine political struggles and ideological debates and the lack of credibility of official "state doctrines".

The only effective way to eliminate the influence of these ideologies upon the mass of the toilers lies in:

a) The expropriation, along with all major means of production, of printing shops, radios, television channels, that is, the liberation of the media that is capable of massively spreading ideas from the material grip of big business.

b) The creation of objective conditions under which these ideologies lose the material roots of their reproduction.

c) The waging of a relentless struggle against these ideologies in the field of ideology and politics itself, which can however attain its full success only under conditions of open debate and open confrontation, i.e. freedom for the defenders of reactionary ideologies to defend their ideas, freedom of ideological and cultural pluralism, as long as they do not go over to acts of violence against workers' power.

Only those who have neither confidence in the superiority of Marxist and materialist ideas nor confidence in the proletariat and the toiling masses, can shrink from open ideological confrontation with bourgeois and petty bourgeois ideologies under the dictatorship of the proletariat. Once the capitalist class is disarmed and expropriated, once their members have access to the mass media only in relation to their numbers, there is no reason to fear a constant, free and frank exchange of ideas. This confrontation is the only means through which the working class can educate itself ideologically and successfully free itself from the influence of bourgeois and petty bourgeois ideas. The validity of Marxism will fully assert itself.

Any monopoly position accorded to Marxism (not to speak of a particular interpretation of Marxism) in the ideological-cultural field through administrative and repressive measures by the state can lead only to debasing Marxism itself from a critical and revolutionary science, as a weapon for the emancipation of the proletariat and the building of a classless society, into a sterile and repulsive state doctrine or state religion, with a constantly declining attractive power among the toiling masses and especially the youth. This was apparent in the USSR, where the monopoly position accorded to "official Marxism" masked a real poverty of creative Marxist thought in all areas. Marxism, which is critical thought par excellence, can flourish only in an atmosphere of full freedom of discussion and constant confrontation with other currents of thought, i.e. in an atmosphere of full ideological and cultural pluralism.

REFERENCES

1. Karl Marx: 'General Rules of the International Working Men's Association', in *Marx. Engels. Selected Works* (Moscow: Progress Publishers, 1977), p. 19.
2. Quoted in K. Marx and F. Engels, 'Circular Letter to August Bebel, Wilhelm Liebknecht, Wilhelm Bracke and Others' in *Marx. Engels. Collected Works*, Moscow [hereafter cited as *MECW*], Vol. 24, p. 264.
3. Ibid., p. 269.
4. This organisational concept has also been called Jacobin, or Jacobin-Blanquist. In the 1830s it could not be called Blanquist.
5. Minutes of the dispute between Weitling and Kriege on one side, and Schapper and others on the other, have been published in H. Forder, M. Hundt, J. Kandel and S. Lewiowa (eds.), *Der Bunde der Kommunisten: Dokumente und Materialien, 1836-49*, Berlin, 1970. There is no complete English translation but relevant extracts are cited in B. Nicolaievsky and O. Maenchen-Helfen, *Karl Marx: Man and Fighter* (Harmondsworth, 1976), pp. 119-21, and A. Gilbert, *Marx's Politics*, Oxford, 1981, pp. 67-73.
6. P. Annenkov, *Reminiscences of Marx and Engels* (Moscow, 1956), p. 152.

7. See *MECW*: 17, p. 79.
8. Ibid., p. 80.
9. At the time of his debate with Weitling, Schapper argued that society was not yet ripe for communism, so a whole period of education was necessary. "Kriege's talk is a mirror for me. That is just how I talked ten or eight years ago, yes, even six years ago (i.e. at the time of the May 1839 uprising – S.M./K.C.). But now.... I must entirely agree with what the reactionaries say: "People are not yet ripe".... A truth is never knocked into heads with rifle butts." *Bund der Kommunisten*, Bd. 1, p. 220.
10. F. Engels, 'Draft of Communist Confession of Faith', *MECW*: 6, pp. 96-103; and 'Principles of Communism', ibid., pp. 341-57. For the draft by Hess see A. Cornu and W. Monke (eds.) *Moses Hess, Philosophische und Sozialistische Schriften 1837-1850*, Berlin, 1961, pp. 336-66. The draft attributed to Schapper was an unsigned leading article in *Kommunistische Zeitschrift*, reproduced in D.B. Ryazanoff, ed., *The Communist Manifesto* (Calcutta, 1972), pp. 290-96.
11. See the letter from the members of the Central Authority quoted in Ryazanoff, p. 21.
12. See *MECW*: 6, pp. 589-600 for the Address, especially p. 598 for its repudiation of "barrack-room communism." For the Rules, see ibid., pp. 585-8. The whole issue of the journal is reproduced in D.B. Ryazanoff, ed., *Communist Manifesto.*
13. To Frederick Engels in Manchester, November 4, 1864, http://www.marxists.org/archive/marx/works/1864/letters/64_11_04-abs.htm
14. General Rules, October 1864, Written: between October 21 and 27, 1864; First published: in *The Bee-Hive Newspaper*, November 12, 1864, and in the pamphlet *Address and Provisional Rules of the Working Men's International Association ...*, London, November 1864. http://www.marxists.org/archive/marx/iwma/documents/1864/rules.htm
15. Arthur Lehning presents Bakunin's self-image as absolutely true. A. Lehning (ed.); *Archives Bakounine*, Vol. 1, Leiden, 1961. Paul Thomas, *Karl Marx and the Anarchists* (London, 1980), p. 318, recognises that the Bakuninsts were continuing the work of creating a parallel organisation inside the International, but claims that this was legitimate because the Alliance itself had always so claimed (pp. 304, 307-14). This is to say that the resolution of the General Council, rejecting dual membership, (*Documents of the First International: The General Council of the First*

International, Minutes, Vol. III, 1868-1870 (Moscow, 1964), p. 54, and K. Marx, 'The International Working Men's Association and the International Alliance of Socialist Democracy' in *MECW*: 21, pp. 34-6) was invalid, while the claims of an organisation that was at that time outside the International, and that got in by a fraud, was democratic and legitimate.

16. For Perron's testimony see E.H. Carr, *Michael Bakunin* (New York, 1975), p. 365. For that of Guillaume, see, H. Draper, *Karl Marx's Theory of Revolution* – IV (New York, 1990), pp. 281-2.
17. The quotation is from A.P. Mendel, *Michael Bakunin: Roots of Apocalypse* (New York, 1981), p. 306. For his authoritarian organisations, see also A. Kelly, *Mikhail Bakunin* (Oxford, 1982), pp. 243-5, and passim.
18. Quoted in H. Draper, *KMTR* – IV, p. 277 for the proposal. See also pp. 293-4 for a very revealing letter to Herzen.
19. For an instance of his attempt to create an anarchist organisation inside the International, see the programme of the Slavic section, cited in H. Draper *KMTR* – IV, pp. 286-7. For Marx and Engels on the right of ideological anarchists to remain within the International, see *MECW*: 44 (Moscow, 1989), pp. 309-10, 346.
20. *MECW*: 43, p. 485.
21. H. Draper, *KMTR* – IV, pp. 286-91.
22. Karl Marx and Frederick Engels, *Selected Correspondence*, [hereafter cited as *MESC*], pp. 352-3. See also *Engels-Lafargue Correspondence*, Vol. 1 (Moscow, 1959), Ibid., pp. 108-9.
23. K. Marx, 'Letter to Wilhelm Bracke', in *MECW*: 24, p. 78.
24. For the foregoing see R. Morgan, *The German Social Democrats and the First International* (Cambridge, 1965), A. Bebel, *My Life* (Westport, Connecticut, 1983), V.L. Lidtke, *The Outlawed Party* (Princeton, 1966), especially pp. 97-9, and F.L. Carsten, 'The Arbeiterbildungsvereine and the Foundation of the Social-Democratic Workers' Party in 1869', *English Historical Review*, April 1992, pp. 361-77.
25. *MECW*: 24 p. 72.
26. *MECW*: 24, pp. 259-62, 268.
27. Marx Engels, *Werke* [German Works, hereafter cited as *MEW*]: Bd, 37, Berlin, 1967, p. 440.
28. Ibid., Bd., 38, Berlin 1968, p. 41.
29. Ibid., Vol. 43, p. 134.
30. F. Engels, 'Trades Unions', in ibid., 24, pp. 385-6.
31. H. Collins and C. Abramsky, *Karl Marx and the British Labour Movement* (London, 1965), Chapter 5. See further V.L. Allen, 'The

Centenary of the British Trade Union Congress, 1868-1968, in *Socialist Register 1968*, http://socialistregister.com/socialistregister.com/files/SR_1968_Allen.pdf, accessed on October 8, 2006. The National Reform League was set up in 1865 largely at the initiative of the General Council of the International, and there was a considerable overlap in the leadership.

The period between the formation of the National Reform League in February, 1865 and the passing of the Reform Act in the summer of 1867 was characterized by organised agitations and mass demonstrations with undertones of class disaffection. An address issued by the League in May 1865 stated that "The Working Classes in our Country, the producers of its wealth, are in a degraded and humiliating position ... the men who have fought her battles, manned her ships, tilled her soil, built up her manufactures, trade and commerce ... are denied the most essential privileges of citizens...." At one conference jointly sponsored by the League and trade unions, it was resolved that unless the working class was enfranchised it would be necessary to consider calling a general strike. This was the high point of class radicalisation under the inspiration of the International.

32. F. Engels, 'The Workingmen of Europe in 1877', in *MECW*: 24, pp. 210-11.
33. However, Marx's belief in the need for political action and the politicisation of the trade unions did not lead him to propose that "the political party of the proletariat must define the economic tasks and lead the trade union organisation itself", A. Lozovsky, *Marx and the Trade Unions* (Calcutta, 1975), p. 25. Such a definition would concede too much power to the party, power which it need not actually gain through democratic processes, and to retain which it must become authoritarian. Indeed, Lozovsky's definition, originally written in 1933, reads more like a defence of contemporary Stalinist practice. For the attitude of post-Marx social democrats and trade unionists, see C.E. Schorske, *German Social Democracy, 1905-17: The Development of the Great Schism* (Cambridge, Mass, 1955), p. 11.
34. *MEW*, Bd., 38. p. 87. See also his letter to Bebel in ibid., p. 95.
35. There exist a mass of studies. The interested reader can see David Mandel, *The Petrograd Workers and the Fall of the Old Regime* (London: Macmillan, 1983), David Mandel, *The Petrograd Workers and the Soviet Seizure of Power* (London: Macmillan, 1984); R.G. Suny, 'Toward a Social History of the October Revolution', in *American Historical Review*, Vol. 88, No. 1, pp. 31-52, 1983.

36. See, for example, Paul Le Blanc, *Lenin and the Revolutionary Party* (Atlantic Highlands, New Jersey: Humanities Press, 1989). For a very recent study, see Soma Marik, *Reinterrogating the Classical Marxist Discourses of Revolutionary Democracy* (Delhi: Aakar Books, 2008).
37. L. Schapiro, *The Origins of the Communist Autocracy* (London: Bell and Sons, 1956), p. v.
38. C. Bettelheim, *Class Struggle in the USSR, First Period 1917-1923* (Hassocks, 1977), p. 109.
39. Ibid., p. 414.
40. K. Radek, 'On Lenin', *International Socialist Review*, Vol. 34, No. 10, November 1973, p. 29.
41. Richard Pipes, 'The Origins of Bolshevism' , in R. Pipes (ed.), *Revolutionary Russia* (Cambridge MA: Harvard University Press, 1968), p. 49.
42. Leopold H. Haimson, *The Russian Marxists and the Origins of Bolshevism* (Boston: Beacon Press, 1966), pp. 138–9. (First published 1955 by Harvard University Press).
43. E. Bernstein, 'Ignaz Auer, der Fuhrer, Freund und berater', in *Sozialistiche Monatshefte*, 1907, I, pp. 845-6.
44. Kuskova cited in Lars T. Lih, *Lenin Rediscovered: What Is to Be Done? in Context* (Brill, 2005), pp. 235-6. For English translation of the Credo, see Neil Harding (ed.), *Marxism in Russia: Key Documents 1879-1906* (Cambridge: Cambridge University Press), pp. 250-3, and V.I. Lenin, *Collected Works* [hereafter *LCW*], Vol. 4, (Moscow, 1977), pp. 171-4.
45. Quoted in N. Harding, *Lenin's Political Thought: Theory and Practice in the Democratic and Socialist Revolutions* (New York: Humanities Press, 1983), p. 150.
46. See on this Tony Cliff, *Lenin: Building the Party* (Chicago: Haymarket Books, 2005), pp. 82-4.
47. See Kunal Chattopadhyay, *The Marxism of Leon Trotsky* (Calcutta: Progressive Publishers, 2006).
48. Lih, *Lenin Rediscovered*, p. 278.
49. V.I. Lenin, *Polnoe sobranie sochinenii*, 5th edition, Vol. 5, p. 13.
50. See S. Marik, *Reinterrogating the Classical Marxist Discourses of Revolutionary Democracy* (Delhi: Aakar Books, 2008), pp. 239-41.
51. Lih, *Lenin Rediscovered*, p. 652.
52. Ibid., p. 650.
53. http://www.marxists.org/archive/lenin/works/1901/witbd/iv.htm.
54. O. Anweiler, *The Soviets* (New York, 1974), p. 46.

55. L. Trotsky, 1905 (Harmondsworth, 1971), p. 266.
56. V.S. Voitinskii, *Godu pobedi porazhenii*, Moscow, 1923, quoted in J.L.H. Keep, *The Rise of Social Democracy in Russia* (London, 1963), p. 230.
57. N.K. Krupskaia, *Memories of Lenin* (Moscow, 1959), pp. 124-6.
58. *LCW*: 34, p. 296; V.I.Lenin, 'New Tasks and New Forces' in *LCW*: 8, pp. 146, 218-9.
59. Ibid., 10, pp. 29, 32-3; ibid., 8, pp. 145-6; V.I. Lenin, 'Eleventh Congress of the R.C.P.(B.) in ibid., 33 (Moscow, 1980), p. 307.
60. V.I. Lenin, 'Draft Resolution on the Relations between Workers and the Intellectuals within the Social-Democratic Organisations' in ibid., 8, pp. 409-10.
61. Tretii s"ezd RSDRP (Moscow, 1959), p. 255.
62. Ibid., pp. 265, 267, 335, 362.
63. *LCW*: 10, p. 31.
64. Tretii s"ezd RSDRP, pp. 547-53.
65. At the 4th Party Congress in April 1906 it was, Bolsheviks 13,000, Mensheviks—18,000, according to D. Lane, *The Roots of Russian Communism*, pp. 12-3. Another estimate was that for 1907, which gave the Bolsheviks 46, 143 and the Mensheviks 38, 174 members, according to P. Broue, *Le Parti Bolchevique* (Paris 1963), p. 36. Ernest Mandel questions this set of figures, as well as other similar high figures, suggesting that they included members of party-dominated trade unions, sickness benefit associations etc. see his letter to P. Le Blanc, in P. Le Blanc, *Lenin and the Revolutionary Party*, p. 126. However, such workers did consider themselves to be Social Democrats, as it was shown by their role in the period of reaction from the second half of 1907.
66. R.C. Elwood (ed.) *The Russian Social Democratic Labour Party 1898-October, 1917* (Toronto, 1974). (This is Vol. 1, of R.H. McNeal, General Editor, Resolutions and Decisions of the Communist Party of the Soviet Union), p. 57.
67. V.I. Lenin, 'Reorganisation and the End of the Split in St. Petersburg', in *LCW*: 12 (Moscow, 1977), p. 396; V.I. Lenin, 'To All Working Men and Women of the City of St. Petersburg and Vicinity' in ibid., 10, p. 127.
68. V.I. Lenin, 'The Social Democrats and the Elections in St. Petersburg', in ibid., 11, Moscow , 1978, p. 434.
69. O. Pyatnitsky, *Memoirs of a Bolshevik* (Allahabad , n.d.), pp. 91-2.
70. V.I. Lenin, 'Party Organisation and Party Literature', in *LCW*: 10, p. 46.
71. R.C. Elwood , ed., *The RSDLP*, pp. 83, 87, 91.

72. See for a Stalinist transformation of this concept into a dictatorial monolithism, J. Peters, *The Communist Party: A Manual on Organisation*, New York, 1935, p. 23. see R.C. Elwood, ed., *The RSDRP*, p. 94 for the unity congress resolution.
73. V.I. Lenin, 'Freedom to Criticise and Unity of Action' in ibid., pp. 442-3.
74. Ibid., p. 443.
75. V.I. Lenin, 'But who are the Judges?' in ibid., 13, p. 159.
76. Ibid., p. 323. See also G. Zinoviev, *History of the Bolshevik Party* (London, 1983), pp. 143, 148-51. For an account of the Bolshevik faction after unification.
77. *LCW*: 13, p. 159.
78. Ibid., p. 103.
79. *LCW*: 15, p. 430. For a Bogdanovist statement of principle, see R.V. Daniels, *A Documentary History Of Communism*, Vol. 1 (New York, 1962), pp. 62-3. It should be noted that while for polemical purposes (to discredit the Marxist credentials of Bogdanov) Lenin went to great lengths to prove that these philosophical "errors" were major issues, he was not expelled from the faction for his philosophy, but his politics.
80. *LCW*: 24, pp. 40, 45, 50.
81. See A.L. Sidorov et al. (eds.), *Velikaia Oktiabrskaya Sotsialisticheskaya Revolyutsiia: Dokumenty i materialy* (Moscow, 1957), Vol. 2, pp. 15-6.
82. L. Trotsky, *History of the Russian Revolution* (London, 1966), Vol. 1, p. 306.
83. *Sed'*maia (Aprel'skaia) *Vserossiskaia Konferentsiia RSDRP* (Bolshevikov) (Moscow, 1958), pp. 50, 106.
84. Ibid., p. 373.
85. Ibid, p. 372.
86. Ibid., p. 228.
87. P.F. Kudelli, ed., *Pervyi Legalnyi Peterburgskii komitet Bolshevikov v 1917g* (Moscow, 1927), p. 157.
88. Ibid., p. 158, See Pravda, 10th June, for the Central Committee statement.
89. A. Rabinowitch, *Prelude to Revolution* (Indianapolis, 1968), passim.
90. *LCW*: 25, p. 81.
91. *The Bolsheviks and the October Revolution*, Minutes of the Central Committee of the Russia Social Democratic Labour Party (Bolsheviks), August 1917-February 1918 (London, 1974), translated by Anne Bone, with additional notes by T. Cliff, p. 10.

92. Ibid., p. 41, For the CC's revised decision, see p. 38.
93. Ibid., p. 67.
94. M. Liebman, *Leninism Under Lenin* (London, 1980), p. 153. Zinoviev had by then clearly come down on Kamenev's side.
95. *The Bolsheviks and the October Revolution*, pp. 88-9, Incidentally, this body, like the Military Centre created on October 16, did not provide any real leadership. That was done by those who led openly, in the Soviet.
96. See ibid., p. 112. See also Rabochii Put (the name under which Pravda was then being published) October 20, 1917.
97. *LCW*: 25, p. 486.
98. *LCW*: 26, p. 111.
99. For Lenin's return to Russia, see LCW 24, pp. 27-9. For Trotsky's internment, see L.Trotsky, *My Life* (Harmondsworth 1975), pp. 29–94. See A. F. Kerensky, *The Crucifixion of Liberty* (London 1934), pp. 235-94, for an attempt, as late as 1934, to portray Lenin as a German agent. See further Sir G. Buchanan, *My Mission to Russia* (London, 1923), Vol. 2, p. 121 for the complicity of Miliukov and Buchanan himself in Trotsky's internment.
100. L. Trotsky, 1905, p. 333.
101. Buchanan, *My Mission to Russia*, especially Vol. 2, pp. 159-63, and pp. 11, 119.
102. Sir Alfred Knox, *With the Russian Army 1914-1917* (London, 1921), Vol. 2, for his ties with Kornilov.
103. Cf I. Deutscher, *The Prophet Armed* (Oxford, 1976), pp. 347-8.
104. For a short summary, see D. Footman, *Civil War in Russia* (London, 1961).
105. On the Volunteer Army, see G.A. Brinkley, *The Volunteer Army and Allied Intervention in South Russia, 1917-1921*, South Bend, Indiana, 1966; P. Kenez, *Civil War in South Russia*, 1918 (Berkeley, 1971).
106. See T. Hunczak (ed.), *The Ukraine, 1917-1921: A Study in Revolution* (Cambridge, Mass., 1977).
107. See F. Kazemzadeh, *Struggle for the Transcaucasus, 1917-1922* (New York, 1951).
108. A.F. Upton, *The Finnish Revolution 1917-1918* (Minneapolis, 1980), p. 522.
109. V. Serge, *Year One of the Russian Revolution* (London, 1992), p. 187.
110. Ibid.
111. Ibid.
112. A.F. Upton, *The Finnish Revolution 1917-1918*, p. 519.
113. Ibid., p. 521.

114. Ibid., Serge, *Year One*, p. 187 writes that there were 70,000 soldiers.
115. E. Mandel, *October 1917, Coup d'etat or Social Revolution?* (Montreil, 1992), p. 22.
116. R.H. Bruce Lockhart, *Memoirs of a British Agent* (London, and New York, 1933), pp. 253-4, 265, 273, 283-5.
117. W. Bruce Lincoln, *Red Victory* (New York, 1989), p. 99.
118. Ibid., p. 198.
119. A Whiteguard report, quoted by E. Mandel, *October 1917: Coup d' etat or Social Revolution?*, p. 23.
120. V. Serge, *Year One...* p. 331.
121. *The Bolsheviks and the October Revolution*, p. 104.
122. E.H. Carr, *The Bolshevik Revolution*, Vol. 3 (Harmondsworth, 1966), p. 69. These were not, as Robin Blackburn, '*Fin de Siecle: Socialism* after the Crash', *New Left Review*, 185, January -February 1991, p. 24, claims, later justifications of the original, Bolshevik seizure of power.
123. V. Serge, *Year One* ...p. 319.
124. For Germany, see C. Harman, *Germany: The Lost Revolution* (London, 1982). For the rise of councils in Germany, Italy, and Britain, see D. Gluckstein, *The Western Soviets*. For a general survey, see T. Cliff, *Lenin*, Vol. 3, and Vol. 4, London, 1978 and 1979 respectively.
125. O. Bauer, *The Austrian Revolution* (London, 1925), p. 9.
126. H.N. Brailsford, *Across the Blockade* (New York, 1991), p. 140.
127. R. Abrams, 'Political Recruitment and Local Government: The Local Soviets of the RSFSR: 1918- 21, *Soviet Studies*, Vol. 19, No. 4, April, 1968.
128. M. Vladimirsky, *Sovety ispolkomy i s'ezdy Sovetov: Materialy k izucheniiu srtoeniya i devatelrosti organov mestriogo upravleniya*, Vol. 1 (Moscow, 1920), p. 7.
129. Ibid., and R. Abrams, *Political Recruitment and Local Government*, p. 576, citing other surveys.
130. Out of a total of 6000,000 workers who joined the Red Army, 180,000 were killed. Three million workers lost their jobs. M. Lewin, *The Making of the Soviet System* (London, 1985), p. 212.
131. T. Cliff, *Lenin*, Vol. 3, p. 158.
132. J. Stalin, *Works*, Vol. 4 (Moscow, 1953), p. 220.
133. V. Serge, *Year One...*, pp. 265-6.
134. See, *The Bolsheviks and the October Revolution*, pp. 129, 138-41.
135. Ibid., pp. 141-2.
136. Ibid., p. 147.

137. Quoted in N. Allen (ed.), *Leon Trotsky: The Challenge of the Left Opposition (1923-25)* (New York, 1975), p. 236.
138. For a detailed history of the Brest-Litovsk negotiation, see J.W. Wheeler-Bennet, *Brest-Litovsk:The Forgotten Peace* (London, 1939).
139. *The Bolsheviks and the October Revolution*, p. 173.
140. J. W. Wheeler-Bennett, *Brest-Litovsk*, pp. 227-8.
141. I. Deutscher, *The Prophet Armed*, pp. 382-3.
142. J.W. Wheeler-Bennett, *Brest-Litovsk*, p. 237.
143. *The Bolsheviks and the October Revolution*, p. 202.
144. Ibid., pp. 204-5.
145. Ibid., pp. 218-9, 223.
146. See, e.g. I . Deutscher, *The Prophet Armed*, pp. 389-92. Deutscher suggests that fears of a repetition of the internal blood-letting of the French Revolution that had taken place during the revolutionary wars guided Trotsky.
147. The Bolsheviks and the October Revolution, pp. 236-7, for Lenin's and Trotsky's statements and resolution, p. 232 for Krestinsky's resolution, and p. 236 for the unanimous adoption of the resolution.
148. Ibid., p. 96.
149. Ibid., pp. 47-8.
150. Ibid., p. 8. The exceptions were the 7th Congress and the 9th Conference, at which it was decided that any ten delegates could do so. See Deviataia Konferentsia RKP (b) Sentiabr' 1920 goda, Protokoly, Moscow, 1972, p. 3.
151. At the 11th Congress, which Lenin was too ill to attend regularly he called for a slogan that was in tune with the concerns of the Workers' Opposition, while Stalin and Zinoviev favoured a greater turn to the peasants. See e.g. Odinnadtsatii S'ezd RKP (b), pp. 380-410, for the speech of Zinoviev.
152. See his speech to the 10th Congress, in Desyatii S'ezd RKP (b) Mart, 1921, goda, Stenograficheskii Otchet (Moscow, 1963). pp. 350-1 (full text, 349-59).
153. R.V. Daniels, *The Conscience of the Revolution: Communist Opposition in Soviet Russia* (Cambridge, Mass., 1960), p. 138.
154. *Pravda*, January, 1921.
155. *LCW*: 32, p. 256, However, Kollontai, speaking to the 10th Congress said that in fact only 1500 copies had been printed and that with difficulty, Desyatii S'ezd RKP (b) p. 103. Anti-communist historians systematically ignore the civil war conditions. Thus D.W. Lovell, *From Marx to Lenin*, pp. 185-6 ridicules "defenders of the Soviet regime" for their defence of

communist violence or their attempts to explain that violence. But he has not a sentence on the tremendous level of right-wing violence. He hides these forces under the softer term 'opposition'. L. Schapiro, *The Origin* is likewise remarkable for the absence of any systematic account of the civil war.

156. R.V. Daniels, *The Conscience of the Revolution*, p. 117.
157. Deviataia Konferentsiia RKP (b), p. 188.
158. A. Balabanoff, *My Life as a Rebel* (New York, 1968), p. 238-9. On Kollontai and the Workers Opposition, see B. Farnsworth, *Alexandra Kollontai: Socialism, Feminism and the Bolshevik Revolution* (Stanford, 1980).
159. Ibid., p. 121.
160. Ibid.
161. *LCW*: 32, pp. 168-95, see also, ibid., pp. 241, 254.
162. Ibid., pp. 248.
163. Ibid., p. 52.
164. Ibid., p. 261.
165. http://www.internationalviewpoint.org/spip.php?article921.

2

Contemporary Imperialism and the Socialist Alternative

Prasenjit Bose

The anti-people character of the neoliberal regime and the bankruptcy of its free market ideology are getting thoroughly exposed with the deepening economic crisis and the irrational, vested-interest-driven actions of the bourgeois governments. With the weakening hegemony of neoliberal ideas, debates over alternatives to globalised capitalism are emerging, along with a revival of interest in Marxism and socialist ideas across the world. Attempts are also underway to better understand and analyse the contemporary world from a Marxist standpoint. This is important because the global realities have changed considerably since the days of Marx and Lenin.

Introduction

Financial and economic crises have always accompanied neoliberal capitalism over the past four decades from Latin America and Eastern Europe to South East Asia. The difference this time is that the metropolitan centres of capitalism in the US and Europe have themselves been hit by the crisis in a manner not witnessed since the Great Depression of the 1930s. Four years since the financial meltdown of 2008, over 50 million people are currently unemployed in the OECD countries (group of 34 developed countries) and the numbers of unemployed and poverty-stricken families are still rising. The imposition of austerity measures and cuts in welfare benefits by the neoliberal governments of the West even in the face of growing misery of the people have created mass discontent and triggered popular movements, particularly in the countries of the European "periphery" like Greece and Spain.

The developing economies, including the BRICS (Brazil, Russia, India, China and South Africa), are also being affected by the crisis. The confidence of the international financial institutions regarding economic growth in the developing countries becoming "decoupled" from that of the recession-hit advanced economies is fast evaporating. The impending recession in Europe, in the absence of any significant economic recovery in the US, is likely to have serious adverse impact on economic activity in the developing countries too, putting the livelihoods of millions of working people at risk.

The anti-people character of the neoliberal regime and the bankruptcy of its free market ideology are getting thoroughly exposed with the deepening economic crisis and the irrational, vested-interest-driven actions of the bourgeois governments. With neoliberal ideology in crisis, there is a parallel growing interest in Marxism. While the classics are being rediscovered and reread, attempts are also underway to better understand and analyse the contemporary world from a Marxist standpoint. This is important because the global realities have changed considerably since the days of Marx and Lenin.

Contemporary Imperialism

To argue that the world has changed, however, does not mean that the theoretical core of Marx's political economy analysis of capitalism has become invalid. Rather, as Marx had argued, capitalism remains to be a system based on class exploitation, which creates increasing wealth for the capitalists on the one hand and poverty for the workers on the other. The fact that inequalities of income and assets have risen over the past four decades both within the developed as well as the developing countries shows the prescience of Marxian analysis. The ongoing recession also validates Marx's characterisation of capitalism as a system ridden by periodic crisis, which destroys wealth and swells the ranks of the "reserve army" of the unemployed.

Taking forward Marx's analysis of accumulation and concentration of capital creating gigantic blocs of monopoly capital, Lenin had drawn attention towards the emergence of finance capital at the beginning of the 20th century, through the fusion of banking and industrial capital. The tendency of finance capital backed by the nation-states of industrialised capitalist countries, to expand across geographical boundaries seeking control over markets, resources and profitable investment avenues, giving rise to the phenomenon of imperialism, lay at the core of Lenin's analysis.

The accuracy of Lenin's analysis of inter-imperialist contradictions, based on national blocs of finance capital competing with each other, could be seen in the two world wars of the 20th century, which were fought between the imperialist powers to divide and re-divide the world in order to establish their own "spheres of influence". The Bolshevik Revolution was successfully led by Lenin in the backdrop of tsarist Russia's participation in the First World War, which heaped enormous miseries on the Russian people. Analysing global politics and major world events within the framework of imperialism and its dynamics and devising revolutionary strategies from an anti-imperialist standpoint thus became the cornerstone of Marxism-Leninism in the 20th century.[1]

International Finance and Inter-Imperialist Rivalry

While the imperialist imperatives identified by Lenin remain valid in the 21st century, major changes have come about in the dynamics of imperialism. The "unipolar world" that came into being following the collapse of the USSR in 1991 has also seen a muting of inter-imperialist rivalry. Conflicts of interest between the traditional imperialist powers do remain, but military confrontations and wars between them have become a thing of the past.

The way things have changed since Lenin's time can be seen in the emergence of international finance capital, which while originating in the advanced capitalist nations is no longer national in its form. The transnational banks and financial corporations today have global operations and move around large volumes of capital across national boundaries on a daily basis in search of quick speculative gains. Since international finance capital is globally mobile and fluid and it is not tied to specific industries, it does not serve its interest to divide the world market into rival national blocs. What it rather wants is a globally integrated and inter-connected market where it has unfettered freedom of movement and operations. In a world where international finance is fluid and mobile, stability of the value of the dollar vis-à-vis primary commodities like oil is a prerequisite for the stability of the international financial system.[2] This stability of the dollar is underwritten by the military power of the US state. No imperialist power today is interested in challenging this hegemony of the dollar.

Rivalries between imperialist nation states have therefore subsided under the hegemony of international finance capital. The major imperialist powers—the US, EU and Japan—function as a bloc under the leadership of the US, which ensures that any challenge to neoliberal globalisation and the hegemony of international finance capital is eliminated. This does not imply, however, that imperialist wars have stopped occurring. In fact, the post-cold war period has witnessed an even more aggressive imperialist militarism. But in all the wars of imperialist aggression in the past two decades, from Yugoslavia to Afghanistan, Iraq, Libya and the ongoing conflicts with Syria and Iran, the major imperialist powers have moved together under NATO. There may have been criticisms of "US unilateralism" by some of the US' allies from time to time, but the NATO has not only remained intact but is undergoing expansion both in its composition as well as its theatre of operations. Anti-imperialist forces today have to reckon with such unity of the major imperialist powers.

Changing Nature of Social Contradictions

Besides the muting of the rivalry between the major imperialist powers, there are other developments, which call for a rethink on the four major "world social contradictions" identified by the international Communist movement in the 20th century.[3]

With the collapse of the USSR and restoration of capitalism in Russia and Eastern Europe, socialism has considerably weakened as a force at the international level. Moreover, the trajectory of "market socialism" adopted by China and its gradual integration into the global economy has further complicated matters, making it difficult to fit the complex realities of a globalised world into the straightjacket of the "four major contradictions".

What has intensified under globalisation is the contradiction between imperialism and the peoples of the developing countries. This is manifested in the neoliberal policies adopted by the developing countries at the behest of their domestic capitalist classes in collaboration with international finance capital. In the bigger developing countries, which are fashionably termed "emerging economies" (the BRICS for instance), the domestic capitalist classes have significantly grown in size and strength and have emerged as global players. They have developed a *strategic junior partnership* with international finance capital, whereby they can jointly exploit the labour, the markets and the resources within their own countries as well as overseas.[4]

Sections of the urban middle classes and the rural elites, who benefit from the neoliberal policies, are allies of the big capitalist classes in the developing countries. In contrast, the basic classes of these developing countries—the organised working class, small peasants, informal workers in urban and rural areas, petty producers, etc.—bear the brunt of intensified exploitation and dispossession. The agrarian classes are particularly hit because of the crisis that neoliberalism precipitates in agriculture and the rural economy. This is not only intensifying the contradiction between imperialism and the basic classes in the developing world, but is also pitting the basic classes against their domestic capitalist classes giving rise to social and political conflicts over "development".[5] The struggles waged by the peoples of the developing countries against the neoliberal regime have become the decisive factor in shaping the future of globalised capitalism.

While the capitalist classes of the developing countries

largely collaborate with imperialist finance capital, contradictions between them have not disappeared. With the growth in the size and strength of the capitalist classes of the developing countries, their economic interests also collide with that of the traditional imperialist powers. This is seen most acutely in the scramble for natural resources, like oil, minerals, land, water and forests across the continents of Africa, Asia and Latin America. This contradiction also manifests itself on issues like trade liberalisation, agriculture subsidies, international migration, climate change or even on geo-strategic issues like Iran, Syria or South China Sea. Groupings like the BRICS, Shanghai Cooperation Organisation (SCO), etc. have come into being in order to promote "multipolarity" in world affairs.

Latin American countries are also making efforts to further regional cooperation independent of the US as reflected in the formation of the Community of the Latin American and Caribbean States (CELAC). This trend towards multipolarity is likely to get strengthened with the ongoing global economic crisis, which is reducing the weight of the advanced capitalist countries in the world economy. The Latin American experience over the past decade shows that increasing pressure of popular movements can force the domestic capitalist classes and social-democratic governments of the developing countries to resist imperialist dictates and pursue autonomous policies, at least in a limited manner.

The process of "financialisation" of various sectors of the economy under neoliberalism, through derivative instruments —like primary commodities through commodity futures; real estate through mortgages and CDOs; exports and imports through exchange rate derivatives, etc.—has led to a redistribution of the social surplus towards finance capital, leading to its unprecedented concentration as well as its cross-border mobility and speculative character. International finance capital has emerged as a parasitic class, which moves around the world—at times enmeshed and at times independent of industrial capital—sucking up the surplus that is being generated in various centres of production.

The net result of this process of financialisation has been a phenomenal rise in income and asset inequalities, even within the advanced capitalist countries, where real wages have either stagnated or fallen over the past three decades. Economic growth has also been driven by asset price bubbles and debt-induced hyper-consumerism, which has met its inevitable fate in a financial meltdown and recession. The bailout packages handed over to the culpable financial giants funded by the taxpayer's money, even as millions of ordinary people have lost their jobs and homes and sunk into poverty, have accentuated class contradictions within the metropolitan centres. The "occupy" movements and anti-austerity protests in the US and Europe signify this trend. This opens up fresh possibilities for the anti-capitalist movements in the developed world and anti-imperialist movements in the developing world to make common cause against neoliberal globalisation.

Rebuilding the Socialist Alternative

The basic problem confronting the anti-imperialist forces today is the weakening of the socialist forces at the global level. Even though exploitation, oppression, crisis and misery are inherent to the functioning of globalised capitalism, it endures in the absence of a powerful socialist challenge. The collapse of the USSR remains to be the main factor behind the lack of confidence in socialism, which many suffer from, even within the Left. Despite its many successes in meeting the basic needs of the people, raising their living standards and providing social security; remarkable achievements in the fields of industry, science and culture and the heroic resistance and victory in the war against fascism; the first socialist state in history could not eventually sustain.

The reasons behind the decay and downfall of the USSR have been widely debated for long. Controversies continue to remain over the course adopted by the USSR in different historical conjunctures: What if Lenin's NEP had not been reversed and the forced collectivisation undertaken under Stalin avoided? What if the transition had been managed better without the purges of the other revolutionary leaders from the communist party, starting from Trotsky and Bukharin? What if

Khruschev had not denounced Stalin's legacy? What if Gorbachev's reforms were differently envisioned? While these historical questions do not have easy answers, what is noteworthy is that each of these consequential changes in the course of socialist construction was imposed from above, without any meaningful participation or acceptance by the people.

That itself was the biggest problem with the USSR and all the other countries which followed its model. The structure of the single party state established after the revolution pre-empted the possibilities of democratic debates, discussions and mandates involving the people over important questions of development and state policy. Rather, ideological-political debates were sought to be resolved through distorted factional struggles and backroom intrigues within the higher echelons of the CPSU, leading to purges, imprisonments and even executions.

The argument that socialist construction was being carried out under imperialist encirclement, which necessitated such an approach, is unconvincing, since it is difficult to believe how revolutionaries of yesteryears debating over contending positions could turn into imperialist agents overnight. In any case, if socialism is meant to be a superior social system compared to capitalism, the people in socialist societies should be empowered to have more say in determining policies. What happened in the USSR, in contrast, was that socialist construction increasingly became a top-down bureaucratic exercise, with state policies swinging between extremes depending on who occupied the topmost chair. The people also got increasingly alienated from the socialist state in the absence of substantive democratic rights and freedoms.

Socialism with Chinese Characteristics

The Chinese revolution under Mao's leadership was a national liberation movement and an anti-feudal/anti-capitalist revolution gelled into one. Here too, socialist construction and planning were carried out under a single party state in a top-down manner. With the enormous progressive transformation brought in by the socialist construction in China, distortions similar to those witnessed in the USSR also reappeared. Matters precipitated after the Sino-Soviet split in the early 1960s, with a full-scale campaign launched within the party against "capitalist-roaders", which led to purges and imprisonment during the chaotic period of the cultural revolution. Even a revolutionary leader like Liu Shaoqi was not spared.

While seeking to restore normalcy and stability after the turbulent years of the cultural revolution, however, Deng Xiaoping never even attempted to undertake any democratic restructuring of the state apparatus. He was convinced about the negatives of the rigid and over-centralised planning model of the USSR, but saw no problems in its political system. Under such a set up, the market-oriented reforms initiated by China in the 1980s ultimately led to the adoption of an export-dependent growth trajectory since the 1990s. Much like the neoliberal trajectories adopted elsewhere in the developing world, China attained high GDP growth rates but at the cost of sharply rising socio-economic inequalities, a declining share of workers' income in the GDP and a massive increase in high-level corruption, land grabbing and environmental damage.

China today has the largest number of dollar billionaires in the world after the US and Russia. Not only has a strong capitalist class emerged in China, but this capitalist class is venturing into other countries of Asia, Africa and Latin America in search of resources and profitable investment avenues. The CPC has also cleared the way for the entry of big capitalists into the party. The Constitution of the CPC which was amended in November 2002 now starts with the following formulation:

> The Communist Party of China is the vanguard both of the Chinese working class and of the Chinese people and the Chinese nation. It is the core of leadership for the cause of socialism with Chinese characteristics and represents the development trend of China's advanced productive forces, the orientation of China's advanced culture and the fundamental interests of the overwhelming majority of the Chinese people. The realisation of communism is the highest ideal and ultimate goal of the Party. The Communist Party of China takes Marxism-Leninism, Mao Zedong Thought,

Deng Xiaoping Theory and the important thought of Three Represents as its guide to action.

The CPC now explicitly recognises that it represents the "development trend of China's advanced productive forces" which is a euphemism for capitalists and "the overwhelming majority of the Chinese people", not only the Chinese working class. This shift from "Deng Xiaoping Theory" to "Three Represents" marks a clear step towards the legitimisation of capitalism in China. Thus, market-oriented reforms under the "dictatorship of the proletariat" and the "leadership of the Communist Party" have not been able to guarantee that China keeps to the "socialist road".[6]

This is not to argue that capitalism has been fully restored in China. Given the history of the CPC and the nature of contradictions apparent in China today, it is evident that anti-capitalist forces are still at play. The process of transition in China today, however, is certainly not in the direction of socialism—which not only entails the development of productive forces but also a progressive socialisation of wealth and resources, the reverse of which is happening currently. This is further confirmed by the re-orientation of China's foreign policy, with anti-imperialism and socialist internationalism being abandoned in favour of an increasingly aggressive pursuit of nationalist self-interest. Unless progressive social and political forces in China are able to reverse these retrograde trends, "socialism with Chinese characteristics" will be reduced to a mere slogan.

Envisioning Socialism in the 21st Century

The short point that follows from the critical discussion on USSR and China is that in order to revive confidence in the socialist ideology and rebuilding the socialist alternative, the question of democracy needs to be squarely addressed. The single biggest failure of the socialist experiments of the 20th century has been in institutionalising democratic forms and practices in the course of social transformations. It is because of this failure that mistakes once made could not be corrected till irreversible damage was done.

Rather than becoming shining examples of liberated societies where people could enjoy more freedom, dignity and rights, the socialist regimes eventually got identified with deviations, factional intrigues, purges and individualist cults. A caricature of all these errors combined together can be seen in the shape of North Korea's Democratic People's Republic of Korea (DPRK) today, where a military dictatorship headed by a dynasty rules over the people masquerading as a socialist regime. This legacy needs to be forsaken by the anti-imperialist forces for good.

A socialist state in the 21st century needs to be envisaged as one, which not only guarantees all the civil rights and political freedoms available under bourgeois democracies, including the right to form political parties, free and fair elections, free media etc. but also goes further in people's empowerment and participation in decision-making through democratic decentralisation and institutionalised forms of direct democracy like referendums, people's assemblies, right to recall elected representatives, etc.[7] The proletarian character of the socialist state must be protected through constitutional provisions, prohibiting the concentration of private wealth and resources.

In other words instead of a "dictatorship of the proletariat", the socialist state should be a "proletarian democracy". This proletarian democracy should also champion the cause of social justice, by promoting gender equality and initiating affirmative action to bring to an end all forms of oppression and discrimination based on religion, race, caste, language and nationality, etc.

The economic programme of socialism in the 21st century should be primarily geared towards guaranteeing basic universal rights to food, housing, education, healthcare and social security through public provisioning and ensuring full employment. The experience of neoliberal capitalism shows that these social goals cannot be attained under the spontaneous operations of a free market economy dominated by international finance capital and private monopolies. Therefore, economic planning needs to be adopted alongside nationalisation of strategic sectors like finance, natural resources and core industries, in order to mobilise and channelize resources to meet the social goals. Besides the public sector, which should dominate in the large-scale industries, other forms of social ownership like workers' or collective ownerships and small private ownership should also be allowed to exist and compete with the public sector.

The market structure under socialism should be different from the capitalist markets, which are distorted by cartelisation and speculation. The socialist state should play a role in promoting cooperative enterprises by small producers, especially in sectors where technological innovations lead to de-scaling.[8] The rents accruing to the giant oligopolies on the basis of Intellectual Property Rights especially in sectors like software, medicine, media and entertainment, should be prevented by promoting alternative structures of creating knowledge and innovations, like free and open source movements in software, biology, drug discovery, etc., where new technologies are developed by cooperative communities ("creative commons").[9]

Surplus land should be confiscated from the landlords and redistributed among the landless under a socialist regime. Peasant agriculture should be encouraged in the developing countries through state support alongside promotion of voluntary cooperation among the peasantry. Forcible acquisition of land and other common resources should be prohibited. All land acquisition should be based on prior informed consent of the landlosers, fair compensation and proper rehabilitation. Industrialisation and changes in land use should be undertaken in a planned manner, through democratic consultations and making displaced persons direct beneficiaries of the process.

Socialism in the 21st century has to address the crucial issue of environmental degradation and ecological sustainability. The issue is not confined to global warming and climate change. The basic question is that since natural resources are finite, what should be the appropriate manner of using such resources. The global "commons" like atmospheric space, water, forests, minerals, etc. are increasingly being usurped by big corporate capital for profits and the consumption needs of the affluent elite. If all developing countries follow the same trajectory of wasteful capitalist development like the advanced capitalist countries, can it be ecologically sustainable? The socialist state should adopt an alternative ecologically sustainable and socially equitable development trajectory.

Transformative Coalitions

While envisaging such a socialist transformation in the 21st century, it is important to ensure that the anti-imperialist forces fighting for such a socialism also organise themselves on the basis of democratic principles. This is not only because the traditional organisational form of the Communist Parties across the world—"democratic centralism"—has almost without exception led to lesser democracy and more centralism in practice. The very notion of "a" vanguard party of the working class has become problematic in a context where the working class itself has undergone a process of severe fragmentation under the impact of globalisation.

Working class unity and resistance in a setting characterised by increasing contractualisation and informalisation of the workforce can be more effectively built through coalitions of various forces representing different sections of the labouring classes. For the developing countries, where the peasantry and rural labourers comprise the majority of the population, building the worker-peasant alliance remains the key task for any revolutionary transformation. This is also more realistically achievable in today's context through alliances and coalitions of radical political forces and social movements rather than a monolithic party attempting to mobilise an entire class on its own. Openness towards democratic debates and discussions is a prerequisite of such coalition-building.

As the global economic crisis deepens, such broad-based and transformative coalitions against neoliberal capitalism need to be formed in order to usher in revolutionary change and move towards socialism in the 21st century.

REFERENCES

1. In the Preface to the French and German editions of *Imperialism, the Highest Stage of Capitalism* (1920) Lenin said that the purpose of the book was to present a "a composite picture of the world capitalist system in its international relationships at the beginning of the 20th century—on the eve of the first world imperialist war". In the Preface to the initial edition he wrote: "I trust that this pamphlet will help the reader to understand the fundamental economic question, that of the economic essence of imperialism, for unless this is studied, it will be impossible to understand and appraise modern war and modern politics."
2. See Prabhat Patnaik's *The Value of Money* (New Delhi: Tulika Books, 2008).
3. The four major "world social contradictions" were (a) contradiction between socialism and imperialism (b) inter-imperialist contradiction (c) contradiction between imperialism and the third world and (d) contradiction between capital and labour within the advanced capitalist countries.
4. This relation of strategic junior partnership, which the big capitalist classes of the developing countries have developed with imperialist finance capital, is a new phenomenon. According to the 2012 Forbes list of the world's richest, the countries with the highest number of dollar billionaires after the US (425) are Russia (96), China (95) and India (48). This is quite different from the "comprador" character of the capitalist class in some third world countries in the 20th century, who were mere commission agents. Nor is the characterisation of a "nationalist bourgeoisie" appropriate any longer because of the predominantly collaborationist nature of the big capitalist class vis-à-vis imperialist finance capital.
5. An example of such conflicts is the current political battle in India over allowing FDI in retail trade, where a majority of the people is pitted against the MNCs and Indian corporates, with the Indian government siding with the latter. The protests against large-scale land grab in China or corruption and cronyism in Russia also reflect such conflicts.
6. Elucidation upon the 'Four Cardinal Principles' in March 1979, Deng Xiaoping had said: "The Central Committee maintains that, to carry out China's four modernisations, we must uphold the Four Cardinal Principles ideologically and politically. This is the basic prerequisite for achieving modernisation. The four

principles are: 1. We must keep to the socialist road. 2. We must uphold the dictatorship of the proletariat. 3. We must uphold the leadership of the Communist Party. 4. We must uphold Marxism-Leninism and Mao Zedong Thought."

7. For a discussion on the radical democratic reforms initiated by the progressive regimes of Venezuela, Bolivia and Ecuador in recent times, see Steve Ellner, 'Distinguishing Features of the Latin American New Left: The Chavez, Morales and Correa Governments', *The Marxist*, XXVII, October-December, 2011.
8. Jayati Ghosh writes: "It is also true that material conditions have changed to make largeness less desirable or necessary in some respects...technology—especially the convergence of ICT and energy technologies—is opening up new possibilities of productivity growth in decentralised settings, which increase the possibilities for a locally managed, decentralised, but globally connected post-carbon economy...Where economies of scale are known to be significant, there is renewed exploration within the Left of forms like cooperatives and other combinations in different manifestations. The aim is to find a balance between large and small, which will obviously differ according to context." *The Emerging Left in the "Emerging" World, Ralph Miliband Lecture on the Future of the Left* (London, 2012).
9. See Prabir Purkayastha's 'The Need for a New Socialist Vision', (ZNet, 2009).

3

'Illusion of the Epoch' On the Question of Socialism in Mao's China

Paresh Chattopadhyay

An important section of the Left, opposed to what they consider to be the capitalist path followed by China after 1978, seems to believe that China had evolved into socialism after the victory of the Communist Party of China (CPC) under Mao in 1949. Needless to add, this was also claimed by the rulers of China (who of course continue to assert that China has remained socialist ever since). Let us discuss the issue.

According to China's spokespersons, the CPC's victory meant the triumph of the "new democratic revolution" accomplishing the "anti-feudal, anti-imperialist" tasks. The subsequent period till the end of the First Five Year Plan was a "transitional period" of "socialist construction". Beginning with 1956-57, China entered socialism.

One could on the whole possibly agree with the assertion about the "new democratic" (essentially bourgeois) character of the Chinese revolution at its initial stage continuing for about a decade. However, the claim that China subsequently became socialist is highly problematic, to say the least, if socialism is understood, following Marx, as a classless "society of free and associated producers" with no state, no commodity production and no wage labour (even when one accepts Lenin's misleading version of socialism as the 'lower phase of communism'). As we know from Marx, before the lower phase of communism arrives there is a whole "revolutionary transformation period" during which the proletariat excercises its 'dictatorship' (the "rule of the immense majority in the interest of the immense majority") precisely in order to eliminate all classes including itself and its class rule (Marx makes no distinction between communism and socialism. It is Lenin's 'contribution' which became very useful to the new rulers of Russia after October 1917 as well as to all the rulers of 'really (non) existing socialist' societies later to follow).

Mao's position, concerning the character of the Chinese society for the period beginning in the late 1950s is ambiguous. On the one hand, he speaks in terms of an already existing "socialist regime" in China. On the other hand, he stresses the existence of the "proletarian dictatorship" during the same period. He refers to the "socialist relations of production" while at the same time draws attention to the existence of commodity production and wage labour in China. It is not difficult to see that these inconsistencies arise from Mao's sense of reality of China's social relations of production as well as his inability to transcend the theoretical limits set by the ideology of "Marxism-Leninism".

While Mao's practice differed considerably from Stalin's, the same could not be said of Mao's ideological framework. He completely accepted Stalin's un-Marxian position that "the system of ownership is the basis of production relations". Marx in fact stressed the opposite.

Stalin declared the then Russia to be "socialist" on the basis of the juridical elimination of individual private ownership of the means of production, thereby standing Marx on his head.

Mao too proclaimed the establishment of China's "socialist system" on the basis of the juridical change in the form of the ownership of the means of production. Thereby Mao made complete abstraction from the real relations of production or, rather, he assumed an equivalence between a juridical change in the ownership and a change in the real relations of production.

Marx would call this a "juridical illusion". Mao was fully aware of the real existence of wage labour and commodity relations in China which have no place in socialism as envisaged by Marx.

The contradiction is clear in Mao's statement:"China is a socialist country... At present our country practises the commodity system, an eight grade wage system, and wage system is uneqal, and in all this scarcely differs from the old society; the difference is that the system of ownership has changed". This goes well with Stalin's concept of socialism, certainly not Marx's. In Marx's own texts such a statement would hold perfectly for a capitalist society {particularly if one remembers Marx's statement in the manuscripts of *Capital* III about the "abolition of capital as private ownership *within* the limits of the capitalist mode of production itself"(emphasis in Ms.): (The meaning of 'private property' [in capitalism] as 'class private property', this fundamental meaning of private property [as opposed to its usually accepted meaning as individual private property] in Marx's texts seems to have escaped most of the Marx readers).

Mao's assertion of the existence of classes in socialism is a revision even of Lenin who, following Marx, underlined that "socialism means abolition of classes". Increasingly after the 1950s classes were conceived by Mao not in terms of social relations of production but in terms of ideology. This position of Mao, again, is understandable.

On the one hand, Mao had to assert, following 'Marxist-Leninist' ideology that China was a socialist society on the basis of the juridical elimination of individual private property in the means of production. On the other hand, he confronted, along with commodity production and wage labour—the hall mark of capitalism—country's continuing pre-capitalist-capitalist cultural framework. This meant, among other things, bureaucracy in the Party as well as in the state and different kinds of corruption, unacceptable in a society supposed to have succeeded capitalism through revolution.

Thus according to him, though China was already socialist, classes and class struggle continued to exist in the Chinese society. In order to prevent a 'Soviet' type (the word is put by us within inverted commas simply because Soviets in the original revolutionary sense of workers' and peasants' self-governing organs ceased to exist in Russia beginning around mid-1918 thanks to the Bolshevik seizure independently of the Soviets and monopolisation of power) "restoration of capitalism", the "capitalist roaders" in China had to be eliminated through a series of "cultural revolutions"(We have no knowledge of the reply of the accused to this serious charge. As far as we know there was never an open debate on this issue so that people at large could know exactly what was happening and {in the case of the masses of Chinese toilers supposed to be the masters of society} participate with their absolutely free opinion).

In Marx "cultural revolution" as an independent category does not exist (as far as our knowledge goes). And this is as it should be. A socialist revolution is an all-embracing self emancipatory project undertaken by the immediate producers which contiues over an entire epoch (the formation of the proletarian power is simply the "first step" in this revolution as the *Manifesto*, 1848, underlines). (Hence, for example, there is little sense in the Left's much used expression 'victory 'of the October Revolution, {abstracting from the unpleasant fact that October, 1917 did not represent a proletarian victory. The Bolsheviks seized power not from Kerensky but from the Soviets.}). There is no need for a separate cultural revolution after society has entered humanity's history leaving its pre-history behind, as Marx had characterised human society after capitalism. For the period intervening between the establishment of the proletarian rule and the advent of socialism is precisely the period when, in the words of Marx, "the working class passes through long struggles, through a series of historic processes transforming circumstances and individuals". That is why Marx calls the period immediately preceding socialism (after the establishment of the proletarian rule) the "revolutionary transformation period". The necessity of cultural revolution in socialism, that is, after the transformation period is over, is indeed a contradiction in terms.

Even assuming Mao meant '"proletarian dictatorship" when he spoke of socialism (never mind the contradiction!) in China, it would be hard to prove that the post-1949 China lived under such a dictatorship in the sense of Marx. To start with, the CPC under Mao, with all its undoubtedly innovative practices, remained well within the bounds of a Leninist 'vanguard' party (which goes directly against the self-emancipatory principle of the proletarian rule). The CPC's victory in 1949 could hardly be called a self-emancipatory act of the Chinese toilers themselves (abstracting from the fact of the proletariat forming an infinitely small fraction of the Chinese toilers) based on the principle: "the emancipation of the working classes is the task of the workers themselves".

The CPC was, at best, and so it undoubtedly thought itself to be, a party for the toilers but could not really be called a party of and by the toilers themselves. Remaining outside the toilers' effective control and, completely unaccountable to them, and, to all intents and purposes, claiming to know the toilers' interests better than the toilers themselves, the CPC, like the Bolsheviks, considered leading and directing the toiling masses as its 'duty'. Similarly, post-1949 China lacked the basic characteristics of a proletarian dictatorship in the emancipatory sense of Marx. Armed workers did not replace the inherent instruments of repression such as the standing army and the police, nor was the bureaucracy replaced by the functionaries freely elected and subject to recall by the immediate producers. On the contrary, the Chinese regime, like its Russian prototype, confirmed what Marx had written about the earlier forms of political power, that the Revolution had "transferred the direction of the state machinery from one set of the ruling classes to another" instead of "smashing it" (It might fruitfully be recalled that shortly before his death Lenin himself had admitted this much for his "proletarian regime" calling it a "misfortune").

The fundamental decisions which affected the masses of labourers in China were, in fact, made and enforced (again as in the Russian prototype) by the party leadership unaccountable to and over the heads of the immediate producers of China who were simply exhorted to participate in executing those decisions. The general body of Chinese labourers had little to do with central questions concerning what, how and for whom to produce. Planning for economic development, the collectivisation (communisation) of agriculture (its basic rationale and strategy), the division of the total national product between consumption and accumulation, the distribution of investment among different branches of the economy as well as the mode of distribution of products for personal consumption were well beyond the control of the immediate producers. For example, the regime prided itself on emphasising that "Chaiman Mao personally directed and fixed the resolution on the edification of the people's communes."

The initiative to launch the 'Great Proletarian Cultural Revolution' (GPCR) came not from the country's labouring masses but from the "Chairman in person". He on his own set the criteria for characterising which "person(s) in authority "was (were) "taking the capitalist road." The rhetoric of the 16-point "decision" on the GPCR about the need "for the masses to liberate themselves" is immediately contradicted by the statement that "Mao Zedong's thought is the guide to action" as well as by the assertion that people opposing this thought were "ultra-reactionary bourgeois rightists and counter-revolutionary revisionists" (As if these statements represented the freely expressed, unconstrained, views of the labouring masses themselves).

In a society supposed to be marching towards the second stage of communism every move was centred on following Chairman Mao's "latest instructions". Indeed, the continuing emphasis on Mao being the "great teacher (cf. Rosa Luxemburg: the working class does not require a school master), great leader, great supreme commander, great helmsman" directly contradicts, besides the regime's rhetoric, Marx's self-emancipatory perspective of the "proletariat organised as the ruling class" mediated by the "conquest of democracy" ultimately ushering in a "union of free individuals". As the *Internationale* intones, "there is no supreme saviour, no god, no Caesar, no tribune. Workers! We are our own saviours".[1]

Let us note that even in what is usually considered as the most libertarian work in the (post-Marx) 'communist' tradition—*the State and Revolution* by V.I. Lenin—both state and wage labour are present—"all citizens" are the "hired employees of the state" enjoying "equality of labour and wages" in the 'first phase of communism'. His reading of Marx on the Paris Commune is also strange to say the least. Marx had praised the Paris Commune for its "Revolution against the state itself" not against "this or that form of state power".

In one of his early works Marx had already emphasized that "State and slavery are indissociable". For Lenin, on the contrary, the Soviets in Russia would constitute a "commune state...a state of which the Paris Commune was the prototype" (*The Tasks of the Proletariat in the Present Revolution*); and he sees in the Soviets "a state of the type of the Paris Commune" (*Dual Power*). Unbelievable reading! Needless to add, "a society of free and associated producers" or "a union of free individuals" is totally incompatible with state and wage labour (including commodity form of the products of labour).

As regards private property in the means of production under capitalism, I would now add that Lenin and those who followed him, had a pre-Marxian idea of private property which bourgeois jurisprudence has taken over from the Roman law—that is, 'property of separate individuals' (see *State and Revolution*). For Marx it is private property of a part of society-class private property basically of the minority of society, while the great majority is separated (alienated) from the means of production, depending for its survival uniquely on the only property it possesses—its labour power (physical and intellectual) as a commodity. In his 1860s manuscripts Marx calls the latter 'pauper' irrespective of how much of wage/salary it earns . Hence my proposition: The existence of wage/salaried labour is a necessary and sufficient condition of the existence of private property in the means of production. Hence it is false to claim on the basis of state ownership in the means of production that private property has been abolished. In Vol. 2 of *Capital,* Marx refers to the 'state as capitalist' when there is wage labour in its productive enterprises. As regards the alleged claim of a section of the Left, you do not change the essence of a thing by simply giving it a different name, and secondly, it is wrong to claim that there was no commodity production in the Soviet Union.

Lenin uncritically took over, it seems, from the Second

International (like a number of other things), the distinction between a socialist society and communist society. There is no textual evidence in Marx and Engels for this distinction, as far as their extant works (till now) are concerned. This is no innocent looking minor philological point. By making socialism the transition to communism, Lenin (unintentionally I imagine) paved the way for his Russian and international followers) to turn socialism into a society where every hideous act of the rulers was permitted in the name of fighting the 'counter-revolutionaries'. (In this 'socialism' classes and class struggles continue to exist). As regards wage labour it exists in Lenin's 'socialism' (see *State and Revolution*). One problem—among others—most of the leftists pay scant attention to the question of *social relations of production* while speaking—favourably or unfavourably—on the character of the 20th century regimes which claimed to be socialist. All their attention is on politics. This cannot be called a materialist outlook. By the way, when I mentioned *State and Revolution* taken as a libertarian book I already indicated those whom I meant 'communists', that is, in the Leninist tradition.

As regards the seizure of power by the Bolsheviks, at the moment when they were seizing power the "provisional government" had power only nominally, and the Soviets were rapidly gaining strength. This was vividly illustrated by the quick defeat of the counter-revolutionary generals by the Soviets, I mean by the coalition and combined strength of of the socialist forces in the Soviets. Kerensky was about to compromise with the generals That is one of the reasons why the much maligned Kamenev was against the seizure of power by the Bolsheviks independently of the Soviets. Kamenev had thought that by a simple democratic process the Bolsheviks would gain majority in the Soviets, and he did not share Lenin's illusion of the European revolutions breaking out and saving the Russian revolution. And he—not Lenin—proved correct. As a matter of fact, Lenin had no trust in the normal democratic process. (See his derogatory remarks on the Soviets in his confidential correspondence with the members of the Bolshevik leadership, while mouthing "all power to the Soviets" outside).

Another important point which shows considerable opposition to the Bolshevik monopoly of power even inside the party. On the eve of the second Congress of Soviets the delegates from all over Russia, arrived in Petrograd, were given a questionnaire to fill up, where one question was about what type of government they wanted. Most of the delegates, where the Bolsheviks were a majority answered "all power to the Soviets", that is, as the authoritative historian Rabinowitch has shown (in the book *The Bolsheviks Come to Power)*, a coalition of all the socialist forces in the Soviets, excluding the Right. By this single act—the seizure of power—the Bolsheviks succeeded in putting a brake on the great revolutionary movement of Russia's working people based on their genuinely self-governing organs (Soviets and the factory committees), which had arisen spontaneously all over the vast country. By blocking the vast democratic movement from going forward and later maturing into a genuine socialist revolution (in Marx's emancipatory sense) the Bolsheviks literally had turned counter-revolutionary, against their will, one could add.

Now the question whether the 1871 Commune was a state. I do not think it was. This was of course the view of Marx and Engels. It could not have been a state simply because it had no "apparatus" (much to the regret of Lenin). Engels in his letter to Bebel (1875) also cited by Lenin in his *State and Revolution*—justly emphasised that (in this connection) "the whole talk of state should be dropped" and he proposed to substitute for state the term "Commune". The Paris commune could also not be considered a proletarian dictatorship in Marx's strict sense of the term (as the political rule of the working people during the revolutionary transformation period between capitalism and communism. Still a relatively backward capitalist country France was far from having attained the objective conditions for a socialist revolution. In this regard, Marx's 1881 letter to Domela-Nieuwenhuis is revealing.

Finally, the dictatorship of the proletariat is of course a state ruled by the working people (not substituted by a party), but is supposed to be the least repressive of all states appearing earlier in social evolution. Given Marx's supposition that the working people (wage and salary earners) constitute the great majority (in the context of advanced capitalism), it requires only minimum force to neutralize the attempts of the (old) slave holders to restore the ancient régime. Secondly this rule is only provisional, not lasting, continuing till the old relations of production disappear.

REFERENCES

1. It should be clear that we have not raised here the highly controversial issues such as number of famine deaths, existence and number of labour camps or the violence applied on the dissidents particularly during the GPCR. In other words, even assuming the total absence of these debatable issues, the uncontroverted fact that the labouring masses of China only followed the directives for executing the 'tasks 'laid down from 'above' by the CCP leadership uncontrolled by and unaccountable to the mass of the immediate producers, including the existence of the 'wage slaves' is enough to show the absolutely unfree character of the post-1949 regime in China, even leaving the question of the existence of the first phase of communism.

4

Communist Parties in India: Lessons from Gramsci's *Modern Prince*

Arun Patnaik

The present chapter proposes to examine Gramsci's concept of the modern prince, mythical prince, the Communist Party. It seeks to re-examine a proposition in Gramsci—"the party tends to become universal and total"—in the light of history of Communist Parties in India. Gramsci reminds us that the CP must primarily draw its world-view in and through its own history rather than look outside or outwards for building itself. One is reminded of D.D. Kosambi's criticism of the (united) Communist Party of India's ideology as Official Marxism (= OM, a powerful Hindu mantra): the united CPI fought many heroic battles but its worldview was ill-informed being derived from outside or from parallel movements in Russia/China/Europe rather than national-popular history in India. It substituted an immanent critique of history with borrowed models of class struggle and recited these models as mere mantra(s) or formulae. The CPI imitated European models of class struggle as Dange, Damodaran and many others (from the CPI) imitated Engels' model in the 1950s. The CPI oscillated between the Soviet model of class struggle (insurrections) and the Chinese path of partial armed struggle (guerilla warfare) during the heyday of the Communist-led Telangana movement in the 1950s. Years later, they imitated the Chinese model of struggle in the CPI (ML) movement in the 1960s as the CPI (ML) parties lately admitted at an international conference in 1995: 'Communists missed specificities in India's history'.

The Communist Parties (henceforth CPs) in India today symbolise certain rigidities like mass isolationism, domineering attitude towards alliance partners or non-party intellectuals or non-party people—what Gramsci calls Piedmontese tendencies or sectarianism. Where do such rigidities come from within the party? The CPs also appear to be dogmatic in the face of new social movements and have a tendency to parrot their party principles, in a doctrinaire fashion, against these new forms of political movements. What is this inexplicable dogmatism in the party? When did dogmatism begin to grip the CPs? Why and how are such dogmas sustained within the party? How does the party, for example, explain the loss of support from a small mass of people who ultimately go on to constitute part of "oceanic communities"? Does the party, for example, have regrets about losing the support of the Gorkha voters for sometime to come? Is this phenomenon global or local? Why do CPs take a nosedive: it demanded a small state for the tribals in 1956 and took quite the opposite position in 1987 when it opposed the same demand of the Gorkhas, thus leaving the field wide open for the BJP to appropriate the CP's original position on the small state in the 1990s? If we follow dialectics in our analysis, it also demands an exploration of the opposite tendencies within the party. Do you witness any critical reflections of such dogmatic positions within the party? Do we have a history of critical traditions within the Communist Parties? Are these tendencies able to survive within the party? Who are these activists? What are their contributions? Or, are these critical tendencies ultimately purged by the party over a period of time?

Marx, Lenin and Gramsci

Before I start with Gramsci's party building, let me issue a caution in the beginning.[1] We must conceptualise Gramsci's concept in relation to not merely his socio-intellectual context (that means in relation to Marx, Lenin and European history) but also try to see how far they are relevant in Indian history, in relation to the Indian Communist Party history and so on. While doing so, we will be failing in our intellectual duty if we do not follow dialectics as well as historical materialism. That means we should be following the same kind of principles that Gramsci advises all Marxists everywhere to follow: certain universal principles of Marxist method. Second, we should be aware that all principles of Marxist method are not universal. For the simple reason that Marx was good because he was a good historian. He was always willing to learn from history and revise his own principles. That this attitude—all principles must be derived from history—is central in Marx's thought. Like Marx, Gramsci is acutely aware of supra-historical ideals getting popular in the communist camp, holding back its further progress and thus remains a keen student of Marx's historical sensitivity.[2]

I wish India's Communist Parties had learned very important ideological and political lessons from this significant historical and methodological truth in Marx. The CPI factions refused to learn this point from Marx; that is to say, they refused to learn from India's history, by repeatedly falling back on European labour standards now, or by following the Soviet model or by using the Chinese model of feudalism or anti-feudal struggles. Despite the towering figure of Indian history D.D. Kosambi passing several strictures against the then undivided CPI's reflection of Indian history, the party refused to debate with his historiography. That this story in the history of the CPI is a very important account in this presentation, we shall return to this point a short while from now.

But Gramsci's "eagle's eyes" (that is actually Lenin's obituary phrase for Rosa Luxemburg) did not fail to notice this very sharp methodological turn in Marx towards an immanent view of history. Summarising Marx, Gramsci writes: "Two points must orient the discussion: (1) that no society sets itself tasks for whose accomplishment the necessary and sufficient conditions do not either already exist or not at least beginning to emerge and develop; (2) that no society breaks down and can be replaced until it has developed all the forms of life which are implicit in its internal relations".[3] There is still a third dimension in Gramsci's theory. He goes on: "From a reflection on these two principles, one can move on to develop a whole series of further principles of historical methodology. Meanwhile, while studying structure, it is necessary to distinguish organic movements (relatively permanent) from movements which may be termed "conjectural" (which appear as occasional, immediate, and almost accidental)".[3]

The first and the foremost lesson from the above discussions is as follows. All principles of Marxism so far including that of Gramsci or Lenin or Marx must be derived from and assessed in relation to the actual and living history. They are great minds. But these minds put together appear even subordinate and secondary before historical truths. As historical discoveries are made from time to time, theirs as well as our theories, depending on the historical periods under discussion, will have to be relooked, rethought, revised and made up-to-date. *Not a single principle should be imposed from above by the Communist Party just as Marx refused to impose his own principles on the world.*[4] That the Party's truth(s) must keep pace with history and historical truth(s). Otherwise, the Party would be sooner or later outdated and outmoded by history. To do so, the Party must continuously learn from history. To do so, the Party must continuously listen. Listen to whom? Remember Lenin's advice scattered over here and there.

Lenin himself was a very intent listener. His ideas can be summarised as follows. The Party must listen to a plural group of people: (1) listen to inner-party democracy; (2) attentive to all non-party left intellectuals; (3) listen to common people outside the Party fold; (4) the last but not the least, the Party must learn from advances made by science and by the liberal or even right-wing philosophers or scientists (e.g. learn work discipline from Taylorism; learn many empirical truths from positivism and so on). The Party should evolve its principles of organisation only after summing up all these experiences. The Party should not forget any of these four groups and exclude any of them from this process of dialogue with some while engaged in a confrontation with others. The Party must not collapse into Bakunin-type voluntarism; that is to say, it must not evolve Party principles purely out of its own will. Also, the Party must not fall back upon sectarianism; that is to say, it must not derive Party principles from one of the above sections excluding the other groups and then impose these principles on the whole society. It would be a travesty of truth to forget Lenin when we are talking about Party building. Gramsci comes back to some of these points of Lenin repeatedly or sometimes on his own without knowing Lenin's similar positions in his reflections in *Prison Notebooks*.

Gramsci's Uniform Methodology to Understand Politics of the CP and the Ruling Classes

Gramsci argues that passive revolution is a very harmful strategy, if the CP should follow it. Passive revolution is essentially a process whereby the ruling classes aim to capture the minds of the masses—a process where war of position is present but war of movement or war of manoeuvre or frontal attack is somewhat missing in this long and protracted war against European feudalism for the birth of a new nation state founded upon liberal democratic principles. This process began after 1848 and lasted up to the time of the rise of fascism. What is the significance of 1848 for Antonio Gramsci? The birth of the *Communist Manifesto*? The authors of the *Manifesto* at the same time and at once summed up the spirit of that time: the spectre of communism had begun to haunt the whole of Europe. How true and up-to-date Marx and Engels were in their understanding of contemporary Europe! Since the birth of communism rather than its *Manifesto*, to put it more accurately, the European bourgeoisie had adopted a war against feudalism through passive revolution rather than active revolution as in the cases of France or England. They were anxious to avoid the anti-feudal struggle of the Cromwellian or Jacobin type. The spectre of communism—not even real communism but, I repeat, a mere spectre of it—was haunting them for creating a society better than capitalist society which they themselves were striving to achieve—a task not even half completed by the European bourgeoisie by 1848.

In this long period of passive revolutionary strategy, there were various tendencies predominant and Gramsci comes out with a long chain of concepts sometimes with Italian names and sometimes with European names to understand this process: Caesarism (precarious balance) or stable coalition of compromise or unstable equilibrium, Piedmontese tendency (trying to dominate an alliance), the Napoleonic export of nation state or civil codes, molecular transformism, appropriation, hegemonic or hegemony, presence/absence of war of position (intellectual and moral critiques)/war of movement (political movement)/war of manoeuvre (military attack), economism, corporatism, educator state, bureaucratic centralism, nation state without popular will, the leading role of traditional intellectuals, and many more. More important for us is to understand that all these concepts can be applied to not merely understand the nature of ruling class coalitions but also the nature of popular coalitions of which Gramsci's CP is a central pillar. That is how Gramsci understands the role of the CP by following certain uniform standards. He does not follow one set of criteria for assessing the role of the ruling classes and another set for the CP or popular alliances. The fact that Gramsci gave forewarning to the CP to desist from following a passive revolution strategy, which is very harmful for the popular elements speaks volumes of sincerity, frankness and independent thinking associated with him. He saw, anticipated and understood the need to correct these mistakes in the CP. That is why the early warning, from one of its founders, for the CP or the party of "the future state". The CP is variously described by Gramsci as "the embryonic state", "integral state", "ethical state", "the party of democratic centralism", "the party of organic intellectuals", "the party of cultural and political leadership, and intellectual and moral leadership", "the party as the unity of theory and praxis", "the party as unity of common sense, religion and philosophy", "the party that should unite state with factory councils" and "the party of philosophy of praxis" and so on. To repeat my point regarding the uniform methodology followed by Gramsci, I would say that passive revolution is defined as a process of absences of these elements of the future state that must evolve in the present party. This should conclusively prove that Gramsci shows contempt for double standards in methodology that are being followed by contemporary Marxist or post-Marxist intellectuals caught up with the mentality of political correctness.[5]

I have just begun to say something of Gramsci's concept of Party. These, as above, are various descriptions of the party. But I have so far talked about at length so many important clues or outlines that we must keep in mind to understand the CP and to understand all these dimensions of the Party. These methodological guidelines are to be kept in mind to avoid many slippery or opportunistic reflections on the CP or on the nature of the ruling classes. We must be sincere to the body of arguments or even hints that are offered by Gramsci.

These various descriptions of the Party should be seen as "categorical imperatives" that need to be done rather than "empirical imperatives" that are already done. Strictly speaking, the Party should be derived from a dialectical mix of both these imperatives: Partly positive empirical imperatives or partly many good things of today but it should be based on an unfolding reality. That means, factually, the Party might seem something different but must try to base on many good things that are already happening within the Party today and yet must try to be different from what it is today and become something else: the Party of the future state, integral state; the Party of a historical bloc; the Party of a bloc dialectic; the Party of dual perspectives or two-line struggles; the Party of organic intellectuals; the Party of philosophy of praxis and many more. Now let us discuss these various descriptions of the CP in some details. These imperatives should be seen as part of a process of becoming that includes being rather than being that excludes becoming of the CP.

To put it in simple terms, the Party should not only be engaged in transforming an unequal society but also aim at transforming its very being—a kind of dual transformation—so that both society and the Party should become something else as expected or planned. The Party must follow a dual struggle—one against society on the basis of society and the other against itself on the basis of itself. What are these plans for the CP? What are these expectations of the CP from none other than one of its founders and a critical, a very independent minded activist intellectual?

The Communist Party and Universals

First, let us begin with the Party's universals. Gramsci says that the Party is a universal or totalising category and it has also universal principles. The Party is a "collective will tending to become universal and total."[6] Recollect whatever I said about Lenin. The Party or the modern prince or mythical prince must pick itself up as a collective entity rather than as an individual. This individual probably is not a person. What Gramsci probably means is what Lenin says. The Party should not derive principles from the individual experiences, from experience of one of the four individual sections as described above. It is a collective entity. It must, without fail, derive principles from a summary of individual experiences of all the relevant sections as already outlined by Lenin. We have seen this aspect before. So I need not elaborate repeatedly. That is how the CP can aspire to be truly "universal and total". People—all these four sections (try to add to Lenin's individual sections if you can but I could not)—constitute the whole of society. When each section sees some of its own principles in the whole of the CP, they would feel elated, recognised and absorbed. Every section will start telling another section: "Lo and behold! The CP's principles are our own" but they will also find that the Party says much more. Then each individual section will start wondering where these extra principles of the Party come from. Then they will discover that all the Party's own principles are derived and summarised from the entire society in a dialectical way as stated before. That is how the Party becomes "universal and total". Having seen their own sectional principles in the whole Party, having realised that the Party has borrowed, summarised and synthesised all its principles from different sections of society, each section will start to learn from the Party and know about the extra principles of the Party and then will become less sectarian and more broad minded as the Party is. The Party which is initially a good listener or learner now becomes, on public demand, good educator.

The CPs world over have become very sectarian and narrow-minded. Let alone owning some universal truth, they are now afraid of even partial truths. They are the harbingers of political correctness which has now spread tentacles within new social movements for most of the leaders of new social movements are actually ex-comrades of the CPs. They have nurtured identities, class labels, party labels and negative mind sets, rejectionist outlook so much so that Ramachandraiah calls this entire process "siege mentalities" of the CPs.[7] That is to say, the parties tend to think that if they say something positive of contemporary bourgeois science or philosophy and something positive of new social movements or postmodernism or something positive of globalisation or contemporary capitalism, the CPs would be further split up and fragmented and their cadres might join these 'enemy' forces. Thus, the CPs might ultimately cease to be communist parties. Why this fear? Why this alarmist trend or siege mentality in the CPs?

In their joint work, *Monopoly Capital,* Paul Baran and Paul Sweezy argued how with the birth of communism in 1848, Western capitalism lost its world outlook to communism. While that is true for the 19th century, they forgot to add that by the time of their write-up in the late 1960s, Western capitalism regained its world outlook from the Communist Parties by ideologically encircling them. To draw an analogy from Fidel Castro, infiltrate the enemy camps with comrades and weaken from inside and help them disintegrate. What Castro did to his enemies in a small island, the much more wily and intelligent rulers of Europe have now done the same thing by encircling and then forcing the CPs to fall in love with its worldview and thereby failing to appeal to new and newer universals. Since then the CPs are caught up with siege mentalities and are behaving now like encircled tigers fretting and fuming inside their cages or now looking down on other social movements with utter contempt from their self-imposed cocoons or now behaving with a frog-in-the-well syndrome.

Look at the dynamism of capital after the 1950s and compare that with those of the CPs the world over. What lessons has capitalism learned from the birth of the October Revolution onwards or its own failings in the subsequent decades following 1917? What lessons have the CPs learned from the collapse of socialism in 1989? Commenting on the former tendency in Western capitalism, Gramsci makes a few brilliant observations. This new tendency was just beginning in Western capital when Gramsci observed but, I dare say, this conjectural moment has grown into an "organic trend" in the movements of contemporary capital. After every seizure of state power by communism since 1917 or the failure of capitalism to counter communist influences over the 20th century, the capitalist class has learned every bit of positive things from communist history. I think this is one of the most original points made by Gramsci.[8]

Gramsci argues that since the success of the October Revolution in 1917, the European ruling classes have started to listen to Marx very seriously and started isolating essential features from non-essential aspects in Marx—a procedure Paul Sweezy, a long-standing Marxist economist, invites and advises non-Marxists to follow and test Marxian ideas many years later. One very important lesson the European rulers have learned is from the following maxim of Marx: so long as there is room for productive forces to grow under the existing production relations, people would not prefer revolutionary tasks. This historical principle that Marx discovered has become an essential lesson for European ruling classes despite two imperialist wars between 1917 to 1950 and fascist assaults on democracy. During the post-war period, the Western capitalist classes have achieved a kind of social and political equilibrium all over. This could happen due to the fact that the ruling classes learned objective lessons Marx's doctrines. I am referring to the experiments carried out in the field of productive forces especially technological, scientific revolutions and the consequent rise of scientific manpower. These experiments in productive forces have thwarted the possibility of political revolution in the West and have also thwarted the possibility of a genuine globalisation.

In the absence of political revolution, a new wave of social movements and their NGOs pressing for a series of reforms have caught the minds of common people. There are therefore non-revolutionary conditions created by an organic contradiction between productive forces and the production relations. When there are no organic contradictions in society, society is not willing to undertake revolutionary tasks. What should the Communist Parties do? Are they redundant now? Who is responsible for this fate? They themselves. Their old agenda of revolution is postponed for a long time to come. Also, the associated concepts like the dictatorship of the proletariat, the seizure of the state power, the destruction of the old state machinery and so on are kept inside the trouser pockets of CP workers just as Nehru said that the CPI was inside his trouser pocket!

And I dare say that the World Bank has not given up the famous slogan of CPs since Marx's times: the dictatorship of the proletariat. Making further inroads into the frontier areas of the CPs, the Bank argues, very selectively though but significant enough, for a policy of 'empowerment' of the Dalits, Blacks, Women, following the pressures from these new movements. I propose that the Bank's policy of empowerment is similar to Marx's concept of the dictatorship of the proletariat provided we all agree with my other submission that new social movements are on the "frontier areas" of CPs. In my defence, I submit the following.

I have borrowed this term "frontier area" from Pierre Bourdieu, a very influential French thinker. But its effective use here is somewhat different from what Bourdieu intends in the cultural field. A frontier area is not a main area. It is essentially a border area with immense possibilities which are not available in the mainland. The main site of the CPs is the working class and its struggle. Dalits, women and adivasis are in its border areas of struggle. Just as people in the frontier areas are interconnected with the mainlanders in the cultural field, so also these new subaltern groups are interlocked with the working class. Eighty per cent of Dalits constitute the rural working class in India. What about women? Women's oppression is more universal than class oppression at least in time and space. As Marx says in *The German Ideology,* women do suffer from the most "original" form of oppression: sexual division of labour in family and field. And Marx continues, sexual division of labour is "the first stage" in the social division of labour. So in terms of time, women's oppression precedes class exploitation. Yet, in terms of space too its presence is felt in more areas than class exploitation. At least, in many tribal areas where classes are not formed yet or in the process of formation, women's oppression is felt due to elaborate norms of sexual division of labour.

What is the attitude of the CPs towards non-class categories? Especially gender which is more universal than class? The parties are following the policy of frog-in-the-well syndrome. It has looked down upon the new social movements. With a mindset of a mainlander's prejudice, the CPs look down upon the frontier areas of struggle where there are many areas of interests which are common between the working class, Dalits, and women. For all these new social movements, on the other hand, due to humiliations meted out by the mainlander's prejudice, frog-like arrogance heaped on them by the CPs, Gramsci's CPs today will not be considered as "tending towards universal and total". Thus, Gramsci's party is probably one of the many universals today but it does not represent "total society" any more. In order to be "tending to total", as Gramsci argues, the CPs must shed their intemperate language towards each other, towards new social movements, carry on dialogue rather than try to dominate them. To do so, they must carry out the class struggle but come out of its cocoons. Without class struggle, the CPs will cease to be a Communist Party but with class struggle alone, they will be forced by their own agenda to retreat into cocoons.

To aid and abet this process of retreat by the CPs and more and more retreat into cocoons of class struggle, so that the alliances of working class-Dalit-women would not materalise to challenge capitalism, the World Bank has now taken up the policy of empowerment of Dalits, Women and Adivasis. I submit that the Bank has learned this new policy from the weak, fragmented, severally split, and thereby encircled, outdated and discredited Communist Parties. After years of research, they have found a new mantra for the ever persisting and ever demanding new social movements. What proof we have to say?

Now let us now turn our attention towards this point.

The Bank's concept of empowerment is deeply linked with two or three arguments in Marx which have been aptly highlighted by many liberal democratic thinkers who are sympathetic to Marx sans his political commitment. There are people like Amartya Sen and his research team; there are people like Gabriel Almond and his research team and so on. They are the 20th century followers of Descartes who give 'enlightenment advice' to anybody and everybody for a hefty fee. They have also worked very closely with the Bank. These people are so well-read about Marx that many Marxists in the Third World will feel ashamed to talk to them as we are without their creative imagination. I will reflect on this body of literature which has probably gone into the Bank's policy making. This body of literature has learned two most important things from Marx which are actually closely associated with the policy of empowerment: capacity building and people's aspirations to govern themselves. But the Bank's policy of empowerment is limited and restricted to local governance or micro processes and not beyond them in relation to national or even regional political economy.

Needless to say that Marx's concept of the dictatorship of the proletariat represents both these tendencies: the working class must develop its own capacity as this is the most under-capacitated class among all modern classes and it can do so only by a process of self-governance. These are two most positive points in Marx for liberal democratic thinkers like Sen and Almond and everything else associated with the said concept is non-essential: like transformation of the state machinery at national level and international level or equitable distribution of property.

What are the important lessons that the Communist Parties have learned from the collapse of socialism in 1989? They have retreated more and more into cocoons and cages. Some of them are afraid of calling themselves Communist Parties and are now busy in frequently renaming themselves. They have learned nothing from anybody living or dead except defending the same old socialist system, opposing globalisation for conspiring the collapse of socialism or blaming the reformers for conspiracy. If they had learned any important lesson, then they should have reformed themselves first. Since that has not happened, any other change may be minor. Who then is afraid of the spectre of communism? Who has kept Marxian concepts in their trouser pockets? Who is caught up with a siege mentality? While the World Bank has come up with a policy of co-option for the new social movements, the CPs are blaming everybody including new social movements for playing into the hands of the Bank or foreign funds, thus leading to the collapse of socialism or resulting in the weakening of socialist forces. Notice that cause is blaming effect. This siege mentality is so much so that both party and non-party intellectuals are afraid of talking about the Party critically. Blame globalisation and the Bank for every other problem faced by the CP?

The Communist Party and Indian History

There are specific historical problems that are associated with the CPs in India. We shall now return our attention to this borrowing mentality of the CPs in India which we have already hinted in this text in relation to Kosambi's polemics with the official Marxism or what he calls as 'OM'. Kosambi argues that the undivided CPI had a bankrupt understanding of Indian history. Kosambi took exception to comrade Dange's approach to our history published by People's Publishing House (PPH) then. By comparing Dange's book *From Primitive Communism to Slavery in Ancient India* with Nehru's *Discovery of India*, Kosambi argues that his admiration of Dange's political cause is undying. Dange had stood by the working class in Mumbai; Dange had suffered 'police hospitality' (Kosambi's euphemism for police brutality) under Nehru's government. Dange was the leader of the undivided CPI with unflinching loyalty to the Indian working class. But the immaturity Dange had displayed in simply following Engels' book *The Origin of Family, Private Property and the State*, superimposing that model of history of Europe on Indian history, Dange had committed a huge inexcusable crime on India's heritage. Now, compare Dange's book with that of Nehru. We will realise how Gramsci is correct in saying that after 1917, the mature ruling classes fall back on Marx wherever possible. Nehru did exactly that.

Nehru, now the leader of the Indian bourgeoisie, was absolutely correct in saying that Marx's method of history is superior to anybody else. While the leader of the Indian ruling classes did follow Marx the historian, the CP leaders here spoiled our understanding Indian history by certain blind imitations of everything European or Russian or Chinese, being enamoured by the successful parallel experiments in these countries.

I would like to add one more point raised by Kosambi: with Nehru's book. The Indian bourgoisie had outgrown its childhood and become more mature, whereas in Dange's history, Marx's method of inquiry has been substituted for a shoddy and blind imitation of Engels' model of class analysis. Kosambi argues, "The outstanding characteristic of a backward bourgeoisie, the desire to profit without labour or grasp of technique (read R&D), is reflected in the superficial 'research' so common in India; it would be pathetic to find it also in the writings of one who has suffered for his belief in Marxism".[9] Dange's official Marxism (OM) is so 'anxious to identify' in Indian history with the general stages of family and classes set out by Engels that one can find atrocious statements made by Dange on almost every page. Broadly speaking, Dange tried to identify chattel slavery in India by equating with the formation of Dasa (in English slaves). But what is known as the Sudra caste, Dasyus, formed by the aid of the state, actually prevented real slavery in India. Lower castes cannot be equated with slaves as Dange does. Thus, Dange's very title is wrong, for his sources contain neither primitive communism nor slavery. As Kosambi argues, Marxism is not a 'substitute for thinking'. It is rather a guide for new thinking and action. Dange's OM, however, is not a troubled to read his own sources and proper materials on the history of India as he tends to superimpose Engels' class analysis on our history. Kosambi said but for the fact that Dange was a key leader of the undivided CPI, he would not have cared to comment on his book.[10]

I do not want to say anything about how the communist movement led by the CPI, immediately after independence, followed the Soviet model of class struggle under B.T.

Ranadive's leadership at the national level which was at variance with the call by the Andhra Committee for the Chinese path of struggle under C. Rajewara Rao's leadership especially at the height of the Telangana armed struggle.[11]

I would like to add how the communists followed the Chinese model of struggle, misread Indian feudalism in terms of Chinese feudalism, followed and still follow especially within CPI (ML) factions and the CPI(M), the method of partial strategic warfare (in parliamentary mode) or the Yenan model of armed struggle. In 1995 in an international workshop held in Hyderabad on 'The Specificities of Indian Revolution', all the ML groups confessed that they have not so far understood the specificity of Indian feudalism or put it more sharply, the specificities of Indian history. They argued, for the first time, how they did not understand Indian feudalism and were misled to think that Indian feudalism was like Chinese feudalism and asked the Indian masses to follow the Chinese path of class struggle. And what are then the specificities of Indian Revolution? According to the document prepared by one comrade Appa Rao of the People's War Group (PWG) from jail, the following are specifities of Indian feudalism ignored by the CP. The party ignored that Indian feudalism is built from above. There is centralised state machinery in India unlike in China. The centralised state unites and defends the ruling classes through politico-military strategy. It also disorganises the toiling masses. In China, however, the state was 'decentred'. The Chinese rulers were factions of landlords who were disorganised rather than united. They were defending themselves by their respective armies. So the CPC adopted partial strategic warfare and liberated one zone after another, and this too after fully studying the preparedness of the local mass movements against the decentred landlords and their history of armed conflict with the common people. Thus, Appa Rao goes on.

How are these a few remarkable advances made in the Party's understanding or probably turning points in its ideological positions? What the PWG in 1995, just as the undivided CPI, however, missed is that these aspects were also part of Kosambi's understanding in the 1940s and 1950s.

Therefore, there is nothing new about them. If the CPI had debated with Kosambi, the undivided CP would have probably learned all these things in the 1950s itself.

These ideological positions are now very comforting. That was in 1995. And what is still disturbing for me is that the PWG is saying only 10 per cent of what Kosambi says. Kosambi argues that there is a Chanakya tendency and there is a Manu tendency in Indian feudalism. These were great institutional builders of Ancient India. What the PWG in the above document referred to was to the Chanakya tendency—feudalism from above, though in a very incipient way. What it missed however was the so-called Manu tendency—feudalism from below. That means feudalism was well organised from below through the caste system built by Manu and so many traditional intellectuals later on. By doing so the Indian rulers avoided the need to build chattel slavery as in Europe or even the need to frequently rely on the local or national army to suppress the aspirations of common people, unlike the ruling classes in China. This point was missed by the PWG in 1995. Moreover, the Appa Rao document hesitates to draw all necessary political inferences from certain ideological advances that the same document achieves. This is another form of the siege mentality of the Group. As a result, the Group is still engaged in many adventure dramas inspired by the Chinese model of partial strategic warfare in Indian conditions, instead of discarding it as the said document politically anticipates but refuses to say so.[12]

And, to repeat, what the undivided CPI missed in 1948, the PWG missed in 1995—all these points and many more insights from Kosambi by excommunicating his historiography. So, it was falling back on Engels' model of class analysis now or on a Soviet model of class struggle now or years later, after splits in 1967, on a CPC's model of class struggle now. In all these tendencies there lies a feverish zeal to blindly borrow successful models from abroad and a stubborn refusal to learn from Indian history. That provoked D.D. Kosambi to criticise the CPI for substituting historical truth with the received wisdom of Marxism. This would have provoked Marx to say the same thing to his Indian followers what he told his Russian admirer in 1878:

"He absolutely insists on transforming my historical sketch of the genesis of the capitalism in Western Europe into a historico-philosophical theory of the general course fatally imposed on all peoples, whatever the historical circumstances in which they find themselves placed, ...I beg his pardon. (It does me both too much honour and too much discredit.)"[13] Superimposing external historical models on India's history is indeed a major failing in the history of CPs in India. Should I dare say that when you borrow models from abroad and superimpose on a people, you tend to quarrel more which might have been a very important reason for several splits in CPs in India and has also probably prevented the CPs uniting together even now? Only further research can tell us more and show the conditions that divide the CPs then and now, and also show new conditions for their unity.

Conclusion

In conclusion, I must confess how inadequate and limited my account of Gramsci's concept of Party is. I have spoken about two aspects of the Party in Gramsci in some details: the Party as a universal category, "tending to be total"; and the Party as an immanent critique of history. There are many more aspects of Gramsci's theory of Party: the Party of organic intellectuals, the Party of war of position/war of movement/war of frontal attack, the party as historic bloc, the Party as union of the state and factory councils, the Party as union of common sense, religion and philosophy, the Party as unity of theory and practice, and so on. As I said, there are however too many aspects of the Party to be covered in any paper.

Finally, I would like to avoid possible misunderstandings of my essay. First, a likely criticism may arise: it is an academic or intellectual criticism of the CPs, that the present critic has no grass-roots knowledge of the parties, implying thus this critic is not to be taken note of having any worth. I dismiss this off-hand as a party apologia, for the very same people are likely to sing its praises if I do not criticise the Party at all and work within the Party's premises as a "tailist intellectual" (to borrow this expression from Mao). Second, it is possible that some people are likely to criticise it on the ground that it is a cynical account of the Communist Parties and there is no solid concrete appreciation of the parties and that many good things they have contributed in past and present, despite many repressions. I take this criticism seriously. Third, on a higher plane, a few comrades may still criticise that the essay proposes a dialectical analysis of the parties but moves in a very one-sided way to criticize the movement. It proposes an immanent critique of the movement but to fails to live up to it. Thus, the author's position is a paradoxical one. I take this criticism even more seriously. But I have two options in my reply. Either I adopt the same position as that of the Communist Parties: adopt "blame it on Rio" syndrome or follow the "frog-in-the-well syndrome". Then, I lose moral rights to criticise the movements just as many CPs have lost moral high grounds to criticise globalisation. I cannot criticise with the same seized mentalities of the CPs, yet remain fair in my assessment of them. The CPs fail more often to note many strengths of contemporary capitalism—its resilience; its ability to co-opt the exploited and resistance alike; its ability to innovate new science; new technology; its gospel of hard work and work discipline etc; the positive tendencies within finance capital (remember Marx's definition of financial capital: "it is capital without private property"); its ability to learn from Marx, Gramsci and the CP history to manage its recurrent crises faced by globalisation; its ability to encircle communist movements—its principal enemy—for a long time to come; its ability to stomach contradictions without resolving them for a longer period like a python devouring its preys; and so on and so forth.

I will be failing in my duty, if I argue here with a siege mentality. I will be adopting the attitude of Bakunin, if I denounce Communist Parties and capitalism in the same way Bakunin did denounce capitalism and Marx or I will be adopting the same Bakunin-like attitude of the CPs today if I denounce globalisation or CPs with much more fury and fretting. Any sober analysis demands dialectical or immanent critique. If I have not been able to identify the positives or strengths in the CPs and its movements in India from its past or present and that too in any elaborate fashion, it is only due to constraints of space and time in this essay. That demands probably a much longer work.

I dedicate this essay in the memory of comrade Prananath Patnaik, one of the founding fathers of the CPI (Odisha unit). Many of his Communist comrades would have forgotten his words today. But a socialist leader of Rourkela recounted them in 1990, many years after he had died, "If Prananathbabu were alive I would have probably joined the CPI, because he was a good listener and used to insist that all his comrades should learn from non-party people—both intellectuals and commoners. This capacity vanished in the CPI in Orissa after his death."

REFERENCES

1. That is the way suggested to me to read Gramsci by Y.V. Krishna Rao but that is also a correct way everybody in India should look at Gramsci or Marx or Lenin: the question of relevance of models/concepts borrowed from these thinkers must be critically discussed in relation to India and cannot be simply assumed away as demonstrative truth or worse still, self-evident truths.
2. Marx's warning to Vera Zasulich on her attempt to create a supra-historical scientific model of capitalism in his theory that can be followed anywhere in the globe. As against this effort by his Russian followers, Marx argues that his analysis of capitalism is valid for Western Europe only as of now. Karl Marx, 'Pathways of Social Development: A Brief Against Supra-historical Theory', in Hamza Alvi and T. Shanin (ed.), *Introduction to the Sociology of 'Developing Societies'* (London: Macmillan, 1982), pp. 109-110.
3. A. Gramsci, *Prison Notebooks* (New York: International Publishers, 1971), p. 177.
3. Ibid.
4. See an interpretation of Marx as provided in my essay on 'Theological Marxism' (in the present volume).
5. A few very influential essays have been written about 'Nehru and Passive Revolution' by Partha Chatterjee, 'A Critique of Passive Revolution' by S. Kaviraj, 'Gramsci in Hindutva Times' by Aijaj Ahmed and so on. But the authors have shown exemplary opportunism in following Gramsci's concepts. Both Chatterjee and Kaviraj define passive revolution as a sign of precarious class coalitions, which is actually a part of the

Gramscian concept. Both of them are silent on the birth of socialism, at least its spectre, at the moment of genesis of passive revolution. I do not intend to probe into the authors' silence but I have difficulties in accepting an inadequate definition attributed to Gramsci. Similarly, Ahmed's otherwise very eloquent essay on Hindutva does not try to say anything on the political and ideological weaknesses of the Left secularists, e.g. its electoral compromises with the Jana Sangh, its refusal to articulate cultural principles of syncretism, its proclivities to economic reductionism and so on, which went a long way in facilitating the rise of Hindutva forces. Such opportunistic interpretations clearly go against Gramsci's attempt to evolve uniform methodology to scrutinise the politics of the ruling class or the Communist Party. However, a recent genuine application of the Gramscian concept is to be found in *A Biography of the Indian Nation* by Ranabir Samaddar (Sage, 2002), who argues how passive revolution, apart from a strategy of precarious class coalition, is actually a counter to various forms of class struggle waged by subaltern classes.

6. Gramsci, op. cit., p. 129.
7. C. Ramachandraiah (CESS, Hyderabad) in a personal conversation with the author.
8. Gramsci cites a liberal journalist's views: "....it would be interesting to know whether in their heart of hearts the more intelligent industrialists were not convinced that 'critical economy' (Marx's *Capital*) contained very good insights into their affairs, and whether they do not take advantage of the lessons thus acquired." See, Gramsci, op. cit., 391-92. In fact, recently at a ministerial conference held in Davos to promote globalisation, a Korean industrialist said that he learned a lot from a frequent reading of Marx's work, 'Profits, Wages and Capital'.
9. See D.D. Kosambi, 'Marxism and Ancient Indian Culture' (1948) in *History and Society: Problems of Interpretation* (Bombay: University of Bombay, 1989), pp. 73-4.
10. Kosambi, op. cit., p. 78, and also his major book, *An Introduction to the Study of Indian History* (Bombay: Popular Prakashan, 1975), (especially the last two chapters).
11. Refer to Y.V. Krishna Rao's biography in this connection in I Mallikarjuna Sarma (ed.), *In Retrospect*, Vol. 5, Part II, Ravi Enterprises, 2003; See also Javeed Alam's essay, 'Communist Politics in Search of Hegemony', in Partha Chatterjee (ed.), *Wages of Freedom* (New Delhi: Oxford, 1995), pp. 188-90.

12. I asked Vara Vara Rao what are the political inferences of this remarkable ideological shift of the PWG? And why is the CP silent about drawing political conclusions from these significant ideological shifts? Why are these political inferences missing in this document and so on? VV replied that the Party should ponder over and come to definite political conclusions soon. How soon since 1995 as the CP has moved ahead with more insurrection after renaming itself as the Maoist party? Meanwhile, the CP faction has set up caste-based mass organisations, it is wary of recognising 'autonomy'-seeking anti-caste groups. That is true for all CP factions in India today.
13. K. Marx, op. cit., in Hamza Alvi and T. Shanin (eds.), *Introduction to the Sociology of 'Developing Societies'* (London: Macmillan, 1982), pp. 109-10.

5

Fifteenth Parliamentary Elections 2009 and Left-Wing Politics in India

Soma Marik and Kunal Chattopadhyay[1]

The elections of 2009 to the Indian Parliament had resulted in a revived United Progressive Alliance Government, tilted even more to the Right than in the five years from 2004 to 2009. The bourgeois media has given it an exuberant thumbs up, while the stock market has been steadily moving up since the complexion of the new government became clear, crossing the 15,000 mark. On the other hand, a series of commentators on the secular, democratic and left parts of the spectrum have put forward analyses that try to come to terms with the huge decline of the Left between 2004 and 2009. This is certainly an important dimension, and though we will briefly consider the other actors, our chief aim will be to look at the questions of how and why the Left had such a bruising electoral fortune, and what rebuilding a revolutionary Left should mean in India. But even that calls for looking at the class aims of the bourgeoisie and the contradictions of bourgeois democracy, the roles and the gains and losses of the UPA and NDA, before we focus on the mainstream Left.

The 2009 Congress Victory: Verdict in Favour of "Reforms"?

The first thing the election results reveal is that there was no great wave in favour of the Congress in 2009. The wave existed in the imaginations of media barons and their paid journalists, who argue that this wave means an end to communalism, caste-based politics, as well as the Left's attempts to pull India back from advancing triumphantly along the path of reforms. The imagined wave has also been accepted by those Left leaders like Biman Bose, the State Secretary, who wish to deny or minimise the swing in favour of the Trinamool Congress (TMC) and its allies (Congress, SUCI) and the responsibility of the CPI(M)'s policies in West Bengal for its radical decline.

True, the Congress significantly increased its tally by 61 seats. But that was from an extremely low figure of 145 (seats won in 2004). Even now, it is a minority party (206 MPs in a Lok Sabha [Legislature] of 543 seats), and the pre-poll UPA got less than the required 272 seats, though it now has enough assurances from others (Samajwadi Party, Rashtriya Janata Dal, Bahujan Samaj Party, etc) who were not its pre-poll allies to ensure the survival of its government.[2] Among these, the Samajwadi Party (SP) and the Rashtriya Janata Dal (RJD) are splinters of the Janata Dal, the most ambitious attempt at creating a national "third party". Both are based on particular caste-community alliances, and while both speak some kind of populist rhetoric, they are best seen as smaller bourgeois formations. The Bahujan Samaj Party (BSP) is the most ambitious attempt so far to forge a Dalit (former "untouchable") party, but vitiated by the fact that its main leader, Mayawati, has a totally autocratic style, and thrives more on symbolic gestures like putting up statues of Dalit heroes than practical work. Secondly, the Congress did not fight the elections on a programme of "reforms". It fought the elections by talking about the "*aam admi*" (ordinary person) and what it had done for them. It targeted the rural poor, the urban poor, as well as the salaried (government employees and government-aided) in a number of ways. It ensured that the success of the NREGP (National Rural Employment Guarantee Programme) was attributed to the Congress. It implemented the recommendations of the Sixth Pay Commission (March, 2008) unusually quickly. It cancelled a series of peasants' debts. Some of these can be written off as populist gimmicks. But the NREGP has certainly been a significant gain for the worst hit rural poor. In effect, NREGP claimed to have given an average 48 days' employment to 44.6 million workers. In other words, it was less than half successful, but even that did mean a degree of employment for the rural poor. Of the total 2.16 billion days of employment generated, women got 47 per cent, a high enough proportion to enthuse, one would suggest, many poor rural women, who often might not find it worth their while to vote, to have done it this time. Of the 2.7 million projects, 1.2 million were completed.[3] In other words, while this was merely bourgeois reformism, for once, this reformism did deliver, and that after one and a half decades when state support to the poor was being systematically tapering off in the name of "reforms". In addition, we can say, that if the Congress today is projecting Rahul Gandhi's campaigns as one of the major factors in its turn around, then that campaign focused clearly on the poor.

This does not mean that the Congress is a party of Social Democratic reform. This is actually a contradiction of bourgeois democracy in a country like India.[4] Periodically, the parties have to go to the common people for votes. The elections of 2004 showed dramatically that class does matter, even if in an extremely limited and distorted way. The BJP had gone in with its "India Shining" campaign, stressing high technology and economic growth. It and the National Democratic Alliance (NDA), lost, contrary to not only its own expectations but the hopes of Indian big capital and the bulk of the pollsters. At the same time, other votaries of globalisation, of cyber-development, whether Chandrababu Naidu (Telugu Desam Party, Andhra Pradesh) or Digvijay Singh (Congress, Madhya Pradesh), also lost. The Left won its highest ever seats in the Indian Parliament in the history of the country, not for what it had done, but for what it promised to do, i.e. fight globalisation, or neoliberalism, which does exist, contrary to those who try to argue that it is an invention of the Left. The urban workers and the rural poor, in so far as possible, voted against their most determined enemies. In that sense, the mandate of 2004 was for a halt to privatisation and for restoration of state intervention in the economy, and for some redistributive justice. Once the elections were over, however, a different kind of pressure came into play. Big capital does not operate by the "one person one vote" principle. It operates by the force of its wealth. With Manmohan Singh, the original Finance Minister who had opened the doors to foreign (imperialist) capital as well as Indian big capital through his policies of 1991-6, and P. Chidambaram, the creator of the United Front government's (1996-98) "dream budget" in charge, reforms went forward. For the first four years, most of the economic policies of the government simply ignored popular needs. Even the growing incidence of farmers' suicides did not lead to any major measures till quite late, when the next round of elections were already casting their shadows ahead. Thus, in 2004 as in 2009, the idea that the Congress was a party of pro-market reforms was based on the links between the Congress and the ruling class, not because of the election campaigns of the Congress. The debacle of the BJP in 2004 suggested that in India, the time had not come for a party to project itself openly as a party championing the economic policy of the big bourgeoisie. The one exception to this is the ability of the BJP to project itself as both the party of monopoly capital and the party of the people in Gujarat.

The NDA and the BJP

In general, however, the NDA, and particularly the BJP, had received important electoral blows. Between 1989 and 1999, it had been riding an ascending curve. In 1989 it won 88 seats. In 1991 it got 120, in 1996 its seats rose to 161. In 1998 it had 179 seats to start with, and by the time parliament was dissolved its seats rose to 182. In 1999, it got 182 seats again. This came down in 2004 to 138 and to 116 in 2009. The "secular" bourgeois media and official ideologues and hack-writers are happy, seeing in this proof that communalism is steadily declining after the high water-mark of 1998-99.

The reality is far more complex. The fountainhead of communalism is the RSS. It has a plethora of frontal organisations. The BJP is its electoral arm. It is true that that electoral arm has suffered a setback. But the period since 1989-92 (the Ram Janambhoomi campaign[5]) has seen the RSS extend its tentacles in civil society, through a variety of organisations.

Moreover, it has been successful in redefining the terms of debate. Thus, under its years of attack, "secularism" has been substantially redefined. India's nuclear policy, though it had shifted much, from a pledge not to build weapons to the first Pokhran test under Indira Gandhi and the refusal to sign the CTBT later, was pushed into an open building of N-weapons by the NDA government. The defeat of the BJP in 2009 therefore exists along with a considerable success of the RSS in spreading its views. Since all parties took an authoritarian stance after the Mumbai attack by terrorists, and Parliament passed draconian laws unanimously, the BJP did not gain by its "national security" posturings. But it cannot be doubted that the turn by all, including the Left, to such a position represents a victory of those who most strongly fought for an authoritarian turn in the polity, i.e. the RSS. In that sense, to see the decline in the BJP seats as a collapse or rout of the RSS is to be blind to realities. In addition, it must be recognised that none of the secular parties, including the mainstream Stalinist Left, have been willing to fight the RSS and its affiliates by confronting them on the streets or by sustained political-ideological battles, making electoral defeat of the BJP their sole tactical line. This means that the RSS penetration of civil society is challenged only by relatively small radical and committed groups.

The Rout of the Left

Of great importance is the need to analyse why the Stalinist Left parties' votes declined. In this discussion, most of our emphasis will be on West Bengal. This is not due to some Bengali provincialism on our part. Rather, for over three decades, West Bengal has been the staunchest supporter of the mainstream Left. Even during the genuine pro-Congress wave of 1984, it was in West Bengal that the Left vote held reasonably steady. And of course, the West Bengal model has been projected by the CPI(M), not only all over India, but even abroad, as a genuine alternative path of development. That makes an in-depth assessment of what happened in West Bengal the key to understanding the prospects before the Left. Apologists for the Left parties, whether Vijay Prashad in *Counterpunch*[6] or others in India, have tried to put forward a series of half truths and inanities. First, there is the story of the Congress wave, a fable we have already disposed of. Second, there is the advocacy of a political line of crass class collaborationism. From the (correct) observation that the RSS is a fascist force, even serious Marxist commentators like Sobhanlal Dutta Gupta have fallen into the error of arguing that advocating a third alternative between the BJP and the Congress was similar to the sectarianism of the Communist International and the German communists between 1929 and 1933, an error that allowed the Nazi rise to power.[7] This is to make the mistake of thinking that the electoral face of the Congress, its *aam admi* rhetoric, as well as its token genuflections to secularism, are serious and confer on it the credentials of an Indian equivalent of a Social Democracy. A third argument is to recognise that there has been a sharp drop in seats, only to cover it up, as the CPI(M) Political Bureau has done, by talking about a marginal reduction in votes. As the Politburo says: "The serious reverses suffered by the CPI(M) and the Left parties in West Bengal and Kerala are of deep concern. The CPI(M) has lost 25 sitting seats from these two states. The CPI(M) has won 16 seats with a vote share of 5.33 per cent which is marginally less than the 5.66 per cent it got in the 2004 Lok Sabha elections."[8] This fudges some other figures. Thus, it conceals the fact that the CPI(M) contested many more seats in 2009 (82) than in 2004 (69) so that total votes cast for its candidates went up for that reason. It conceals the fact, that in West Bengal, its vote share went down from 38.57 per cent in 2004 to 33.1 per cent in 2009, with the same number of seats being contested (32 seats). In Kerala, it contested 14 seats this time in opposition to 13 in 2004, yet its vote share went down from 31.52 per cent to 30.48 per cent. Even in its most successful base, Tripura, its vote share has gone down from 68.8 per cent to 61.9 per cent (2 seats).[9]

Prakash Karat, the CPI(M) General Secretary, has written an article that makes curious reading.[10] Karat rightly writes that there was no Congress wave in 2009. However, by lumping the votes at the all India level, Karat makes it appear that the Congress gain has been at the cost entirely of the BJP. But the significant factor is, while Karat can pretend to give a full explanation for why the Congress victory is not a victory, whereas the BJP defeat is a massive defeat, when it comes to explaining his own party's strategy and its collapse, he is silent. He has to record the number of seats, of course. But interestingly, he does not record the 5 per cent drop in votes in West Bengal. More important, he does not look at what the elections show about his brand of building a "Third Front". This was a hastily cobbled, utterly unprincipled alliance. One partner, the Biju Janata Dal of Orissa, had been a member of the BJP-led NDA for a long time. It broke only during the elections of 2009, with Patnaik calculating shrewdly that in the aftermath of the anti-Christian communal violence at Kandhamal, the BJP was an electoral burden. That this had nothing to do with principled secularism can be seen from his long tolerance of Narendra Modi and the other BJP luminaries (and his silence over the 2002 pogroms in Gujarat), or for that matter the growth of the Bajrang Dal and VHP in Orissa during his government, till electoral compulsions suggested a rupture. Another ally was the Telugu Desam Party in Andhra. In 2004, the CPI and the CPI(M) had denounced the TDP for its support to the NDA as well as for its role in Andhra. So even by the logic formally put forward, this was not a very principled formation. Its equidistance from the Congress and the BJP was based on electoral calculations, not secularism. And this is of course not the end of the story. As we propose to discuss later, Karat's model does not break from popular frontism and class collaboration.

More subtle are those like Vijay Prashad. But they trip themselves up every so often. Prashad, for example, observes that good governance has allowed the Biju Janata Dal in Orissa or the Janata Dal(U) in Bihar to do well on a regional basis. Leaving aside the question of whether Kandhamal is an instance of good governance by the BJD, this is in fact a damning indictment of the CPI(M) led government in West Bengal. In West Bengal, the Left citadel for the past three decades, the elections were fought almost entirely on local issues as if it was a state assembly election rather than Parliamentary election. The Left did try to inject some national policy issues in the campaigns (e.g. the Indo-US nuclear deal), but was repeatedly forced to confront the almost entirely localist campaigns of a united opposition. As a result, it ended up responding about the relationship between industrialisation and agriculture (and the rights of peasants), in a defensive vein. Leading the charge was of course Ms. Mamata Banerjee of the Trinamool Congress. She had developed, over the past couple of decades, a finely honed one-point agenda—remove the CPI(M) from power. For this she has swung from one ally to another, from one slogan to another. But this time in 2009, she had not only the Congress as ally, but also a large number of Leftists—both dissidents from the Left Front and far Left parties, along with Left and liberal intellectuals who broke with the CPI(M). This last force, not an inconsiderable one, was turned into a consolidated force and projected as the sole voice of civil society, partly due to the brutal land grab and state and party violence unleashed over the last few years, and partly by effective media projection. This force was possibly also responsible for the nearly ninety-page manifesto of the TMC, with its populist rhetoric ranging from jobs for all to land for the landless and gender justice.

The Stalinism of the CPI(M) and the Eventual Backlash

In the end, this was a feat achieved by the CPI(M). Its 32 years of continuous rule in West Bengal has seen a development of what can be best called Stalinism in One Province. What distinguished the rule of the CPI(M) in West Bengal from the rule of bourgeois parties in other provinces, or rule by Social Democratic reformists anywhere, was the retention of most of the Stalinist political culture. As in East Europe in the past, the first targets of Left Front rule were actual or potential left-wing challengers. Any time "Naxalites" have raised their heads; there has been repression, documented year after year by the Association for Protection of Democratic Rights (APDR) and others. Repeatedly, the state under CPI(M) rule, as under rule by other parties, has arrested political activists from the Left, launched false cases, and unleashed massive state and party-cadre violence. In recent years, this has increased in a big way.[11] The "Maoist threat" has been one of the standard pleas (the other is "secessionism") used in order to unleash massive repression. Thus, popular resistance to the building of an SEZ and state repression in Lalgarh has been termed Maoist, and efforts are under way to destroy the movement.[12]

From the village to the capital, real power lay with the "party machinery" in general and "party office" in particular, backed up by an increasingly tight grip over the police, including the political surveillance of all Left opponents. This has been construed by the CPI(M), as well as by its opponents, as "vanguardism" in operation. Though this is an election analysis, we feel there is a necessity of discussing this misconception in some detail. The Leninist concept of the vanguard party had nothing to do with imposing party control and silencing the masses. In *What is to be Done?*, the book for which he is most often attacked, Lenin argued that the revolutionary party could be built only by drawing together the most conscious working class elements and fusing them with the revolutionary socialist intelligentsia. His talk about the vanguard was not based on any idea that a party only had to proclaim itself to be the vanguard. His thrust was to proletarianise and democratise the socialist organisation. Moreover, Lenin talked about the working class being the vanguard of the revolutionary struggles.[13]

Sobhanlal Datta Gupta, in his important essay, while exploring the possible reasons for the alienation of the CPI(M) in West Bengal, has argued: "What needs to be recognised today is that in a liberal democratic and plural polity like India the theory of vanguardism has lost much of its relevance."[14] We would have no dispute with this comment, if two corrections were inserted. The first is, this "vanguardism" was never Leninism but a debasement and distortion of Leninism imposed by Stalin, and that it had never been a revolutionary strategy. It was a useful strategy for bureaucratic control over the mass movements by a substitutionist force, in India chiefly a Stalinist force with heavy petty bourgeois intelligentsia domination. In a liberal democratic set up, Leninism would have taken on a somewhat different outlook than in Russia, the kind of strategic development being discussed in the Communist International in its early years (the working class united front, less stress on the underground, more stress on elections as mobilisation strategy, systematic work in trade unions and other mass organisations, and so on).

A Leninist party is built as a revolutionary party. When Lenin talked about the vanguard, he stressed the need to unite the most militant and politically alert workers in the party. The concept of professional revolutionary meant a serious attempt to create working class leadership within the party, formed of working-class militants so as to centralize and coordinate their efforts against the system. The idea was to give these activist-workers a respite from daily wage-work enabling the vanguard to be active on a more permanent basis. A study of Lenin's tactics show that he was actually quite flexible. During the *Iskra* period he was urging the unity of revolutionary intellectuals with worker-militants. During the revolution of 1905 he wanted to open wide the doors of the party for militant workers. During the dispute over liquidationism he wanted to ensure the unity of the underground with the open movement, without letting go the gains of the past.[15] He rejected both minority revolutionism and any idea of parliamentary socialism to be accomplished on behalf of the working class. The revolutionary organisation has to help the working class understand collectively the need for a socialist transformation of society, for the socialist revolution. That is the dialectical relationship between the vanguard party and the mass self-organisation of the working class. The Stalinist vanguardism, as we see practised in India, asserts that the party has all the wisdom, and its task is to correctly transmit its ideas to the masses. And in bourgeois countries, whether in the developed or in the underdeveloped ones, the Stalinist parties have ceased to be revolutionary parties a very long time ago. In the case of West Bengal, what we saw since 1977 (we could argue the same for earlier years too, but leave them out here) was the Stalinist model, where the party organisation controls the state, the mass organisations are mere transmission belts, and the party does not learn from the masses but merely seeks to direct them.

Some economic concessions did come to workers and

peasants, especially in the early years of the Left Front regime. This was not a by-product of revolutionary struggles, but the need to cater to one's constituency in order to ensure the votes keep on flowing. These included land distribution, though that had been more widespread during the short-lived United Front regimes, or Operation Barga, or the registration of share-croppers so that eviction became more difficult.[16] At the same time, decisions about who would be the beneficiaries of policies, from land distribution or the recording of names under Operation Barga, to more recent actions like listing of names under the BPL scheme have been used as a weapon to force toiling people to line up with the CPI(M). The state bureaucracy was also pressed into the service of the party.

A systematic attempt was made to capture the bastions of civil society. There had always been a powerful Left presence among West Bengal's intellectuals. But in power, the CPI(M) used institutional bases in a ruthless way. Beginning with its assault on Calcutta University, sub-standard party hacks and lackeys willing to toe the party line, were selected into academic positions across the province. The College Service Commission, and then the School Service Commission, ostensibly set up to ensure fair selections, became weapons to control the intellectual element at lower levels. Dissident intellectuals found every avenue blocked. Between 2007 and early 2009, those intellectuals, theatre personalities and other artistes who opposed the CPI(M), found all their programmes being cancelled under pressure of local party committees. On the other hand, tame "progressives" received much patronage, including state level funding, Rabindra Puraskars (awards) were handed out to the "deserving" (few are those, like Sumit and Tanika Sarkar, who donated the money towards the relief measures necessary for the victims of violence in Nandigram) as were the party level Muzaffar Ahmed awards (reminiscent of the Stalin Prizes). The result of this bureaucratic control was the transformation of Marxism, that most critical instrument, into a debased and establishment doctrine.

As time passed, even the older generation Stalinists, who had fought trade union or agrarian battles, dwindled. The overwhelming majority of CPI(M) members in West Bengal today are muscle-flexing elements who have joined the party after 1977 (i.e. they are people who never fought against ruling class oppression or state violence), and see the party as the road to self-aggrandisement. The party provides them with jobs, income, power and so on. Even in the trade union field, where a basic working class organisation is involved, tremendous corruption has set in. However, we have no wish to use this corruption to debunk the trade unions, as the bourgeois media and wide sections of middle class "civil society" forces do.

Ultimately, it was this politics, this arrogance, intolerance and violence, this attempt to capture all levels of society, that led to massive popular rejection of the CPI(M) in West Bengal. The popular anger boiled over when peasants felt that their land was being taken over by the state against their will, to be handed over to Indian or foreign big business for the profit of those handful of people. Singur, Nandigram and Lalgarh were the flashpoints of these struggles between 2006 and 2009.

To sum up those issues, the CPI(M) has been pushing arrogantly a neoliberal agenda without taking the people into confidence. West Bengal has been among the forerunners in enacting legislation on SEZ, even before the Central SEZ Act.[17] In Singur, land was acquired, not for an SEZ, but for the Tata Motors, but using the same Land Acquisition Act, 1894, that would be used if land was targeted for SEZs. The Singur announcement came on May 18, 2006, when the Tata group chairman Ratan Tata announced a small car project at Singur, 40 km from Kolkata, on the same day when Buddhadeb Bhattacharya was sworn in as the state's chief minister after the massive electoral victory of the Left Front. They wanted to take over peasants' land to build industries, granting land at throwaway prices to Indian and international big capital (the Tatas in Singur, the Salim group in Nandigram, the Jindals in West Midnapur). And they flatly ignored peasant protest, which began in Singur from 25th May, just a week later. When unprecedented popular resistance forced the Tatas out of Singur, the government refused to accept defeat and return the land to the peasants. In Nandigram, peasants retained their land, but at a high blood price. In Lalgarh, the battle was still on. Singur and Nandigram are better known, partly because of the TMC connection. Since the Lalgarh struggle (which began in November 2008) is waged by mainly "tribals", and without connections with mainstream parties, it is least reported outside West Bengal, and when it is, the West Bengal government's claim that it is all the handiwork of the CPI(Maoist) is often accepted. In reality, in all these struggles, the starting point was the decision of the government to impose its fiat. In each case, land takeover was decided without any democratic consultation, and with paltry compensations being offered. A British colonial law was used to take over the land. An ostensibly left-wing government had at least the duty of holding consultations, taking popular opinion, before going in for land takeover. Instead, the government in fact used typical liberal-democratic methods. It claimed that since it had been elected by the people (with 235 MLAs in a House of 294), it had the right to decide what the people needed. That local people could have their own ideas of what constituted development, and what kind of development they really needed was simply ignored, and opponents of the land-grab labelled "anti-development".[18] It is only now, after the total rout, that the West Bengal CM is reported to have said that in no development project would land be taken unless there was local acceptance.[19] Yet even now there is no reference to returning the land forcibly taken from peasants in Singur.

After the elections, a number of CPI(M) leaders have noted that there was a significant swing of the Muslim vote away from the CPI(M). It is not known whether the CPI(M) has carried out a careful scrutiny of whether there was also a significant swing of women's votes away from the left. But gender and community issues are not unimportant for the CPI(M).

Bengal politics, as we noted earlier, has a strong left ambience. The Left has had a long history of mobilising women, since the days of the Mahila Atma Raksha Samiti (Women's Self-Defence League) in 1942-43. But in recent times, the role of the CPI(M), in connection with "development" and land grab, in connection with repression of dissidents ("Maoists", "separatists", etc), and even in connection with protecting "its own" police when the police commits atrocities on women, have led to a image of the CPI(M) as a party that is unconcerned about women's rights. The elections saw the CPI(M) issue a series of sector-specific slogans. The one on women began by charging, quite correctly: "There was no effort on the part of the [UPA] government to prioritise social mobilisations against continuing retrograde practices such as sex-determination tests, dowry demands, child marriages and violence against women"[20]. It also went on to condemn the central government for not being serious about passing the Women's Reservation Bill, for having retrograde economic policies, and for not doing anything to change the educationally marginalized condition of women. The charges are quite legitimate. No bourgeois party does anything more than pay lip service to gender justice.

But when we look at the practice of the CPI(M) and the Left Front in West Bengal, do we really see anything different? In West Bengal, violence on women has been widespread. The APDR, Nari Nirjatan Pratirodh Mancha (NNPM—Forum Against Women's Oppression), Ahalya, Sachetana and Pragatisheel Mahila Samiti (Progressive Women's Association) listed in a leaflet 42 cases of custodial rapes between 1982 and 1992.[21] Government and party leaders repeatedly used patriarchal discourses in talking about rapes.[22] Indeed, this general patriarchy comes out when we look at the Left Front women's wings' call to women in the 2009 elections. The appeal calls on "mothers and sisters" to vote for the Left and the anti-Congress and anti-BJP Third Front. And while the Left stressed reservation of seats for women, it had such a dismal record in West Bengal, that even Mamata Banerjee, who has never been famous for any feminist sensibilities, trumped them. Out of the 42 Left candidates, only two were women (Susmita Bauri and Jyotirmoyee Sikdar, both of the CPI(M)). The TMC had 27 candidates in West Bengal, of whom five were women. The demand for reservation sounds hollow, because there is inadequate gendering of the party structures. Few women are put up as candidates, because calculations suggest there are few women capable of winning the elections. As for alternative economic policies, the support for SEZs of course affected women as badly in West Bengal, as elsewhere in the country. And the terrible violence, including on women, is on record. This includes the gruesome murder of Tapasi Malik in Singur.[23] Malik is indeed an example. Women in Singur related to members of the NNPM (including one of the present authors) that supporters of the ruling party had threatened them with utterances like "we will turn you into another Tapasi Malik". So women who dare to protest will be threatened in such a manner by activists of the ruling party. Finally, in an agitation at Lalgarh, on the night of November 6, 2008, the police, led by the superintendent of police of West Midnapore district, went on a rampage, arresting and attacking tribals in retaliation to the Maoist attempt at attacking the West Bengal Chief Minister in Shalboni on November 2, 2008. Women were brutally kicked and beaten up with batons and butts of guns. Chitamani Murmu was hit on an eye and eventually lost that eye. Panamani Hansda was kicked on her chest and suffered multiple fractures, and had to hospitalised. Eight other women were badly wounded. These police brutalities sparked off the now months long revolt.[24]

The swing of the Muslims as voters away from the Left Front also requires deeper discussions. We would argue that in place of seriously looking at the interests of Muslims, who, as the Sachar Committee report shows, are placed economically and educationally in very backward conditions in West Bengal, the Left Front in recent times has been indulging in tokenism and the occasional liaising with minority communalism, just the same as their opponents, the TMC. With a 25.2 per cent Muslim population, the Left Front government over 32 years had provided just 2.1 per cent of government jobs to Muslims. West Bengal had the worst record of all Indian states in this respect. By comparison, with 9.1 per cent Muslims Gujarat's government employees include 5.4 per cent Muslims. This is the worst indictment on the secularist mantle of the West Bengal Left Front. And since West Bengal is the flagship of the Left, this has all-India implications. Mohammad Salim, the CPI(M)'s deputy leader in the Lok Sabha, lost from Calcutta North. Salim was banking on Muslim votes. The results indicated that Muslims, a traditional support base for the Left, had shifted loyalties to the opposition. Apart from the long years of neglect, glaringly pointed out by the Sachar Report, this constituency saw the direct impact of the CPI(M)'s shameless handling of the Rizwanur Rehman case (late August 2007), where the party colluded with some of Calcutta's top police officers, trying to protect them after they had violated laws and seemed to be those responsible, at least, for the suicide of Rehman, following their collusion with well-known industrialist Ashok Todi to force his daughter, an adult woman who had married Rehman, to abandon him and return to her father, including by repeatedly calling the duo to police offices and threatening them. Three of the policemen have subsequently been indicted by court. That Rehman was a middle class Muslim boy and his wife the daughter of a rich Hindu was what gave this, not just a class, but also a communal angle. In rural areas too, the impact of the land grab effort was serious. A large number of Nandigram peasants are Muslims. And when the CPI(M) woke up to the threat that Muslims might vote against it, their reaction was to try to cultivate Muslim communalism, rather than look after genuine socio-economic needs of this single largest minority. A small communalist organisation held Calcutta to ransom on November 21, 2007, (a few days after party cadres and police had "liberated" Nandigram from its rebel peasants), demanding the ouster of Taslima Nasreen from West Bengal, allegedly because she was anti-Islam. The government responded with alacrity, forcing her out of West Bengal, and putting pressure on the central government, so that when her visa ran out, she was pushed out of India altogether. Of course, Taslima Nasreen, born a Muslim and a woman, did not have any votes, even if she campaigned for women's rights. So deporting her was seen as an easy way to gain support from (or stop losing the support of) the Muslim community. Sadly for the CPI(M), the Muslim community did not rally behind the communalists, so driving out Nasreen did not fetch it great gains, while tarring it with an anti-woman stance.

So, in the first place, the vote in West Bengal was a rejection of the rule of the CPI(M), and its combination of Stalinism and aggressive neoliberalism. And the main force tapping into this rejection was the TMC. This had to do with Ms. Banerjee's excellent malleability to ally with anyone from the BJP to the small Maoist groups if it brought down the CPI(M). When people got fed up with the CPI(M), her party seemed the obvious one to turn to, since the TMC alone has never supported the CPI(M), and because building left wing alternatives seemed a hard and long-term task, while people wanted short cuts and quick success. Secondly, of course, she did position herself with the popular mood in 2006-09, opposing the taking over of peasants' land and condemning violence on protesters.

The CPI(M) thought it could respond by arguing before the middle class that the TMC was anti-development, highlighting the departure of the Nano from West Bengal. In the urban seats, they made this a major campaign plank. But clearly, this did not cut much ice. Calcutta North, Calcutta South, Dum Dum, Barrackpur, Barasat, Jadavpur, and Howrah, all urban seats, saw a total rout of the CPI(M). In the two Calcutta seats, they lost every assembly segment. One explanation for this is, while the rich may have been angry with the TMC, the ordinary middle class, forced to pay donations to the "party funds", forced to vote in mass organisations the way the party wants, forced to buy the *Ganashakti* (the CPI-M daily) in many localities under compulsion, did not see the air conditioned shopping malls and the Nano as reasons to vote CPI(M). In the home of Nano itself, Singur, the CPI(M) had campaigned that the departure of Tata meant a huge loss of jobs. Singur falls under the Hooghly parliamentary constituency. Eight times winner Rupchand Pal of CPI(M) lost. Dr. Ratna De (Nag) of the TMC received 5,74,022 votes, against Pal's 4,92,499.

In Kerala, the CPI(M) vote declined by over 1 per cent. There, the Congress share went up 8 per cent, while the BJP share went down about 4 per cent. In 2004, the Left Democratic Front, led by the CPI(M) got 19 seats. Since then, factional conflicts in the CPI(M) have come out in the open, discrediting the party. Party Secretary Vijayan has been accused of corruption, and that too has tarnished the party's image. In a bid to cut into the Muslim

League votes, the CPI(M) this time decided to form an alliance with a rank Muslim communal organisation, the People's Democratic Party, something that did not go down well with the voters. On top of that, the huge mandate of 2004 clearly went to the head of the party, and it started ignoring its partners and taking decisions on its own, with the result that the cohesion of the Front was far less evident in 2009.

Apart from party level issues, the changes in Kerala also have to be noted. The vaunted "Kerala model" has been steadily eroded, as the left-led government opted, even if on a lower key than West Bengal, for shopping malls, IT parks, private higher educational institutions, and so forth. Kerala is a small province. As land began to go out of peasants' hands, often legally as they sold it, the expectations the toilers had from the left government gave way to disillusionment.These were the factors that led to the Kerala debacle.[25]

The electoral victory of the CPI(M) in Tripura is significant. There, the NREGP was well-implemented. Nor was there any attempt to forcibly take away land from peasants in order to gift it to rich industrialists. This shows that if reformism is practised then some votes do hold, particularly considering the terrible attacks on the livelihood of workers, peasants and the urban poor carried out since 1991 all over India.

There have been several commentators both within the Left and among mainstream journalists, for whom Prakash Karat's decision to break with the UPA was the key factor in the collapse of the Left. This has a partial truth. Karat chose to break, not on economic issues (the Left had been propping up the UPA for over four years despite its anti-people policies, and West Bengal had followed those same policies) but over the nuclear deal. And then, the CPI(M) or the Left Front as a whole, hardly made the nuclear deal the central plank of their electoral campaign, or even their hastily cobbled Third Front's politics. The debate between Karat and his opponents within the mainstream Stalinist left is purely tactical. Both sides agree that they need to form an alliance with progressive bourgeois forces. For Karat, those progressive bourgeois forces exist outside the Congress. His opponents within the Stalinist left fall into two groups. One group are simply opportunistic, arguing that if the Left had been supporters of the UPA at the Centre, TMC would have been unable to forge an alliance with the Congress in West Bengal. The other group take a position going back to P.C. Joshi, arguing that the progressive forces are in the Congress, and therefore the Left must forge alliances with such forces.[26] The dispute is ultimately a tactical one. Neither side has any strategy that calls for building an independent working class pole in Indian politics. Given the historic role of the Congress as the major party of the Indian big bourgeoisie, to call for an alliance with the Congress is to perpetuate the subordination of labour to capital. But to equate an alliance with a group of regional parties of dubious antecedent and linkages with local as well as big capital, does not provide any break with the core of this class collaborationism. The CPI(M), as we saw, hailed Navin Patnaik as one of the new stars of its alliance. But Patnaik's government in Orissa was responsible for the Kalinganagar massacre, where tribals were gunned down to take over land for Tata Motors. [27]

The bourgeois journalists who are expressing their glee at the Left's discomfitures are of a different type. For them, the Indo-US nuclear deal is a matter of "national pride". Now "we" are beloved of the Empire. Moreover, it enables "us" to not have signed the NPT, to have scuttled the CTBT, to have tested nuclear bombs, and then to have gained "status" as a member of the nuclear club. However, what is important is to note that during the elections, the nuclear deal did not figure prominently as a campaign issue.

The break with the UPA was not on key principled grounds. The CPI(M) election manifesto talked critically about the economic policies of the UPA. Yet those policies had been "tolerated" by the CPI(M). And opponents of Karat are in an even more unenviable position, for they are therefore suggesting that those policies should have been tolerated all the way to the elections. It is therefore our submission that no revival of the Left as a principled force is possible, as long as the debates remain stuck within these polarities.

The Issues of the Indian People

As we commented earlier, parliamentary elections in bourgeois democracies distort the picture. Yet in a country where the democratic system exists, the call for boycott and insurrection is not a very realistic one, and it is moreover one that reveals more about the potential authoritarianism of the so-called vanguards who would have nothing to do with multi-party democracy as such. So how are the real aspirations of the people to be reflected? No short cuts exist, though one is perpetually trotted out—this is the advocacy of some kind of alliance with bourgeois parties who appear as the lesser evil. From expanding the NREGP, to fighting to reopen closed mills and factories, to increasing wages in the unorganized sector, to fighting for land rights and the right not to be displaced for "development" that benefits only the ruling class and the circles around it, real demands of people can be supported not by alliances with bourgeois parties, but by mass movements. Failure to recognize this and a belief that the CPI(M) is such an evil incarnate that one can ally with any force to get rid of it, led a large number of non-mainstream Stalinist and Maoist parties and groups to line up behind the TMC-Congress alliance. They seek to replace Stalinist control by right-wing populism. What is the TMC? It originated from the Congress, and its politics was the typical West Bengal Congress politics reminiscent of the 1970s—including hooliganism and right-wing violence. It has always been a very authoritarian party, where one leader takes all decisions, and any disagreement with her expressed in public will get the member tossed out of the party before you can say Trinamool Congress. How can a party that is internally authoritarian be a real upholder of democracy? By its side, the CPI(M) with its regular Party Congresses, State Conferences, Central and State Committee meetings, appears a model of democracy, despite all we have said about it.

Perhaps even more important is the fact that despite its huge rightward shift, the mainstream Left in India has not cut off all links with the working class. Ultraleftists and apologists for the line of alliance with the TMC will argue that in India all political parties have trade union wings. While this is true, it is also true that left-led trade unions, whether blue-collar (the CITU, the AITUC, the UTUC), or white collar (the AIBEA, the BEFI, the Government Employees unions, and so on), have played a militant role. Throughout the previous two decades, the bank and finance sector privatisation has been resisted by these unions. It is not just by the number of Left MPs that aggressive capitalist attacks have been resisted. As late as September 2008, a united movement of bank employees shut down most nationalised banks, with over 9,00,000 employees taking part in the strike. Opposition to privatisation, outsourcing of jobs, and merger of banks were part of their demands. It is by such specific struggles, rather than by beginning with an abstract call for opposition to globalisation, that working class resistance can be built up. Just as peasant resistance was about land, not primarily throwing the CPI(M) out of power, so the trade union struggles are primarily about saving jobs, wages, and pensions. But a clear asymmetry can be seen here between the most reformist and most Stalinist left on one hand, and its opponents, on this issue. The chief media patron of the TMC, the Ananda Bazar group, has been extremely vocal in campaigning for privatisation. The supporters of globalisation have been long demanding 'reforms' of trade union laws, i.e. making it even more difficult to form trade unions and even easier for bosses to ignore them even when they exist. Attacks on the Contract Labour Act and the Industrial Disputes Act have been repeatedly mounted from the capitalist class.[28] The Left-led trade unions, including those led by the Stalinist and reformist Left, are parts of the struggle to defend labour rights. There are two ways one can criticise these unions. A revolutionary Marxist would argue that these unions are often bureaucratic, that rank and file democracy is particularly absent in many blue collar unions, that sensitivity about gender, or other forms of special oppression (e.g. about Dalits or low caste people, Adivasis or 'tribals' and minorities, especially Muslims) is often very low. Thus, it has often happened that union leaders have struck a deal, and the full text has not even been translated into all the languages known to the workers of that particular mill or factory. It has often happened, that 'general class goals' have been essentially male-defined discourses, while 'women's issues' have been relegated to the fringes as considerably unimportant (though there have also been efforts to organise women workers separately, or to create women's cells, in some cases). One example, from an area both authors, as teachers, are familiar with, is the rule for college teachers even in West Bengal, that maternity leave with pay is not given unless the teacher concerned was in employment for at least nine months. Despite women activists (including on one occasion one of the present authors) moving resolutions in the teachers' union, this has never figured as an important issue to be resolved through serious discussion and agitation. But when the bourgeois press talks about unions and corruption, that is a joke. Who corrupts the union leaders? Is it not the ruling class? The demand for getting rid of unions, for getting rid of "outsiders" (i.e. organisers who are not employed by the factory), all these are aimed at further intensifying exploitation. The judiciary has likewise been attacking general strikes. In India, historically, general strikes have gone beyond the working class, turning into *'bandhs'* or closures of entire cities or even attempts to shut down the entire country. The declaration that this is illegal, is a clear indication that this attack is not one merely ideological in nature, or that only sections of the rulers are involved. Using the relatively "clean" image of the judiciary (in contrast to the corrupt image of bourgeois parliamentarians and the executive) it has been used as the instrument to try and ban the more militant, and more political forms of strikes. This has to be seen as one more of a series of attacks. And in this struggle, whatever their shortcomings, the trade union leaders have an interest in opposing the state. The task of the revolutionary left has to be one of participating in every such struggle, and within the struggles, to push for greater trade union democracy, greater accountability of union leaders to the rank and file, struggles for real attention to all special oppression, and struggles to unionise the unorganised. Of course in these areas the mainstream Stalinist left is bad. One example is bureaucratic unions and their attitude to women workers and their simplest of demands, such as toilets for women, or ensuring that rules regarding equal pay for equal work are strictly implemented, instead of women being shunted into poor paying jobs or their jobs being reclassified. But for example, if we want to fight for women's rights in the workplace, if we want to resist using women as sex objects, we cannot rely on the representatives of the ruling class as better supporters than the unions. The revolutionary left cannot assume the posture that in the battle between unions and the bosses and their state, they are neutral.

The politics of the TMC is a simple one—anti-communism. Leftists who side with it are deluding themselves if they think it is only an opponent of the CPI(M). The one-point agenda led Ms. Banerjee to line up behind the BJP, and to keep silent during the Gujarat pogroms of 2002. As a then partner of the NDA, the TMC has to take responsibility for the SEZ policy pushed by the NDA. Given this, its anti-SEZ rhetoric for West Bengal should be viewed with deep scepticism, as a ploy to win votes. And if we wish to ignore the past, her present is simple—in order to overthrow the CPI(M) she wanted to replace it as the ally of the Congress. In that case, she is committing herself to the economic policies of the Congress, since Finance and Commerce, will be retained by the Congress.

An additional dimension must be stated unambiguously. We have no expectations from the TMC. But there are plenty of leftists, from organisations to independent intellectuals, who have voted for the TMC in the hope that there will be a positive development. They have a grave responsibility. Already, the TMC-Congress bloc has begun showing it has its own brand of politics of violence. The leftists who support the TMC cannot take the position that they condemn the murder of Tapasi Malik, activist of the Singur peasants' movement, but support, at least by remaining mute spectators, when Sumana Mandi, the minor daughter of a local level CPI(M) leader Loncho Mandi, is murdered by being set on fire.[29] Nor can they claim the high moral ground if they remain silent when an agricultural labourer, Bhagan Mahato, is brutally beaten up for the crime of being a member of the CPI(M), and his daughter is compelled to write posters announcing his resignation from the CPI(M) to save his life.[30] Once before in West Bengal's history, the Right had come to power by combining middle class hostility to the CPI(M) with huge violence. This time, revanchisme is widely heard in popular discourse among the urban middle class, the traditional base of the TMC.

Can the mainstream Stalinist Left revive? Of course they can revive electorally. If the Congress-TMC alliance falters at the centre, the Left votes can increase. But should such electoral ups and downs be taken as the main marker of a left revival? The answer is an unequivocal no. Building a genuine revolutionary left alternative has to start by returning to the politics of class independence and self-emancipation. The Stalinist Left and its allies (the former anti-Stalinists like RSP and RCPI who have now succumbed to the charms of parliamentary cretinism) have long forgotten the meaning of that politics. Returning to such politics means fighting to reverse the ruling class policies, fighting to restore and expand democratic rights, and forging an alliance of the oppressed. It means, in the field of elections, fighting for working class united fronts and a complete break with all bourgeois parties and popular frontist alliances. And it also calls for building a revolutionary party that draws into it the best, the most militant elements of the toiling masses, and develops its programme by looking at the real struggles of the people for survival and for ending exploitation.

REFERENCES

2. In an attempt to make the public forget this reality, bourgeois journalists, whether or not they support the Congress, have adopted a systematically false manner of presentation. Few care to mention the actual seats tally. Instead, it is carelessly tossed, that the Congress has a majority. Thus, the *Ananda Bazar Patrika*, on May 29, 2009 in its editorial, said that "the Congress party has obtained a good majority in Parliament". Swapan Dasgupta, a pro-BJP author, writes about the "awesome advance" of the Congress in *The Telegraph*, May 29, 2009.
3. The data is taken from Ashok V. Desai, 'Beginning of Change – Success After Some Near-failures is Appreciated All the More', *The Telegraph*, May 19, 2009.

4. The English language media in India functions virtually as the voice of the ruling class, given the essentially elite readership of these papers. So it is not surprising to read in an editorial of *The Telegraph*, that: "It is striking how much of the Congress's manifesto is missing from the programme... all the populist promises that found a prominent place in the manifesto, such as empowerment of the weaker sections, welfare of farmers' families and health security for all, have been put on the back burner. If, therefore, a sceptic were to conclude that the Congress's populism was just a way of selling itself to voters, he would be justified. This may upset someone who believes that parties should keep their word; but it would come as no surprise to those who understand the difference between politics and policy." *The Telegraph*, May 27, 2009. Interestingly, even bourgeois journalists are arguing, at times, that the decline of the Left vote is due to its moving away from its historic promises. This suggests the bourgeois media is actually paying a compliment to communism, arguing that while bourgeois parties are under no compulsion to keep their promises or to be honest, people claiming to be communists should be more accountable.
5. The Ram Janmabhoomi campaign began when the Congress under Rajiv Gandhi tried a game of balancing Hindu and Muslim communalisms. The Hindu communalist side of its equation was to allow the revival of a dormant communalist claim, about how an alleged temple honouring the mythical Hindu hero Ram had been destroyed to build a mosque. The RSS seized on this with glee, and built a massive mobilisation campaign. For general discussions on the Ram Janmabhoomi campaign, see Sarvepalli Gopal (ed.), *Anatomy of a Confrontation: The Babri Masjid-Ram Janmabhumi Issue* (New Delhi: Penguin Books, 1991). For assessments about its role in the development of the BJP's politics see some of the essays in Kunal Chattopadhyay (ed.), *The Genocidal Pogroms in Gujarat: Anatomy of Indian Fascism* (Vadodara: Inquilabi Communist Sangathan, 2002).
6. Vijay Prashad, 'One Step Forward, One Step Back: The Indian Elections: A Game Changer?', May 19, 2009, http://www.counterpunch.org/prashad05192009.html (accessed on 25.5.2009).
7. Sobhanlal Datta Gupta, 'Left's Exit: Notes for Consideration of All', *Mainstream*, Vol XLVII, No 23, May 23, 2009, put up in the internet in http://www.alterinter.org/auteur2467.html?lang=fr (accessed on May 25, 2009). The history of the struggle against

fascism shows that Stalinist sectarianism of the "Third Period" variety was damaging, but further study also shows that class collaborationism in the name of Popular Fronts, where bourgeois parties were brought in as allies, as opposed to the working class united front, was equally damaging, as in the defeat of the Spanish Revolution, or the collapse of the radical wave in France after the general strike of 1936. For this, see Pierre Broue and Emile Temime, *The Revolution and Civil War in Spain*, London: Faber and Faber, 1972. For a discussion on contemporary (1930s) Marxist critique of Popular Frontism, see Kunal Chattopadhyay, *The Marxism of Leon Trotsky* (Calcutta: Progressive Publishers, 2006), Chapter IX.

8. CPI(M) Press Statement, in http://cpim.org/ (accessed on May 25, 2009).
9. *The Telegraph*, May 20, 2009.
10. Prakash Karat, 'Those Writing the Epitaph of the CPI (M) Will be Proved Wrong', http://vote.cpim.org/node/2054 (accessed on May 28, 2009).
11. For the early years of the present decade, there is a large Bengali collection, Amit Bhattacharya, Parimal Ghosh, Mihir Chakaborty, Subhendu Dasgupta and Madhubanti Maitro (eds.), (2003), *Rashtro, Shantras, Protibaad* (State, Terror and Protest), Calcutta: Association for the Protection of Democratic Rights.
12. On Lalgarh, one of the best resources is the website Sanhati, which has a whole section on Lalgarh. See http://sanhati.com/front-page/1083/#19 (accessed on 25.05.2009).
13. For discussions on Lenin, see the following: Soma Marik, *Reinterrogating the Classical Marxist Discourses of Revolutionary Democracy*, (Delhi: Aakar, 2008), Chapter VI; Lars T. Lih, *Lenin Rediscovered: What Is to Be Done? In context* (Leiden and Boston: Historical Materialism Book Series, Brill, 2008) and Paul Le Blanc (ed.), *Revolution, Democracy, Socialism. Selected Writings, V.I. Lenin* (London: Pluto Press, 2008).
14. Sobhanlal Datta Gupta, 'Left's Exit: Notes for Consideration of All'.
15. See Soma Marik. See also Paul Le Blanc (1993). *Lenin and the Revolutionary Party* (New Jersey: Humanity Books, 2008).
16. For our assessment of the Left Front's reforms and limitations, see Soma Marik and Kunal Chattopadhyay, 'The Left Front and the United Progressive Alliance', (2005), in http://www.europe-solidaire.org/spip.php?article1037
17. See Shalti Research Group (2008). SEZ In West Bengal. Kolkata,

Shalti Samiti, for a detailed study of the Left Front's SEZ policies.

18. We had gone to Nandigram, along with others, after the first round of party-state violence in March 2007. We met a number of women, who asserted that they were not anti-development, but wanted the kind of development that would improve the conditions of peasants (e.g. better roads, better terms for agriculture, etc). Debasish Sen, Kunal Chattopadhyay, Kuntal Ghosh, Maroona Murmu, Safiul Mollick, and Soma Marik, 'A Brief Report on Nandigram', May 25 (posted on the internet May 27), 2007. See http://kunal-radicalblogger.blogspot.com/. Similarly, when the members of the Nari Nirjatan Pratirodh Mancha (Forum Against Women's Oppression) went along with other Calcutta-based women to meet militant women of Singur, in course of their interviews these women told us that they did not want cash compensation, but land for land. They stressed that being uprooted is something that cannot be met by compensations. Nari Nirjatan Pratirodh Mancha (2007). Capturing the Voices of the Women of Singur: Before and After Land Acquisition. Calcutta, p. i.
19. *The Telegraph*, May 25, 2009.
20. CPI(M) Lok Sabha Elections 2009, Aam Admi Suffers in 'High Growth' India Women A Litany of Broken Promises. http://vote.cpim.org/sites/default/files/Women_1.pdf (accessed on 25.05.2009)
21. NNPM, APDR, Ahalya, Sachetana and Pragatisheel Mahila Samity, Mathura theke Neharbanu – Hefajate Dharshan Bandho Hok, Calcutta, 1.10.1993.
22. On this see Mira Roy and Soma Marik, *Women Under the Left Front Rule: Expectations Betrayed* (Vadodara, Documentation and Study Centre for Action, Revised Edition, February 2007), pp. 13-15.
23. Sudhanva Deshpande and Vijay Prashad in 'The Political Economy of a Crisis', *Counterpunch*, May 23, 2007, wrote that: "The most sensational was the murder of a young woman, Tapasi Malik, who had been a leader in the Singur struggle against the land acquisition. The blogs and the capitalist media blamed this death on the CPM. The Central Bureau of Investigation is now of the view that she was killed by her father and brother. Whatever the outcome, this is a criminal matter that was cavalierly taken as evidence of the decadence of the Left". Now of course two CPI(M) activists have been convicted in a trial court (they have appealed in the High Court and are out on bail).

But this is not noted in Prashad's analysis of the CPI(M)'s electoral debacle, let alone Prashad or Deshpande tendering an apology.

24. Partho Sarathi Ray, 'November 13, 2008: Background of the movement', in http://sanhati.com/front-page/1083/ (accessed on May 25, 2009).
25. See K. Saradamoni, 'Communist Parties Have Let Down the People of Kerala', *Mainstream*, Vol. XLVII, No. 23, May 23, 2009.
26. P.C. Joshi was one of the most successful General Secretaries of the undivided CPI. While the political line the CPI pursued under his leadership was certainly popular frontist, and while it also included the opposition to the Quit India movement, the CPI grew rapidly and was able to make inroads into a number of areas, including the peasant movement, among intellectuals, among women, students, under his leadership. After independence, there were major differences within the CPI over the line to be taken (though Moscow's interventions had a major role to play in that, too). Joshi argued that Indian independence was a living reality, and the task of the communists was to build a National Front comprising the Congress, the Communists and other democrats to defend national independence, safeguard the country's integrity and protect and further the interests of the toiling masses. For a detailed discussion see Gargi Chakravartty, *P.C. Joshi: A Biography* (New Delhi: National Book Trust, 2007).
27. See Pramodini Pradhan, Secretary, PUCL Bhubaneswar Branch, 'Police firing at Kalinagar', http://www.pucl.org/Topics/Dalit-tribal/2006/kalinganagar.htm (accessed on May 29, 2009).
28. See on this Rohini Hensman, 'The Impact of Globalisation on Employment in India and Responses from the Formal and Informal Sectors', *CLARA Working Paper*, No. 15, http://www.iisg.nl/clara/publicat/clara15.pdf p.13 (accessed on 6. 3. 2009).
29. *The Hindu*, February 24, 2009. Online edition, http://www.hindu.com/2009/02/24/stories/2009022457930100.htm accessed on May 26, 2009.
30. *Ananda Bazar Patrika*, April 24, 2009.

6

Gramsci's Critique of Civil Society: Its Contemporary Significance

Arun Patnaik

In the era of neoliberal capitalist globalisation, two contradictory discourses are clearly noticeable in the civil society movement. On the one hand, there are votaries of civil society, who offer a militant view of the state and argue that the state must be challenged on the grounds of transparency, accountability, downsizing and so on. Such a view was long ago articulated by John Locke. According to this view, civil society is the bearer of rights and could be a source of resistance to the state, in case the state violates human rights. This view, as also Locke's, does not seek to problematize civil society. On the contrary, civil society, in this view, is the principal organiser of human life. Such a view is usually found in the neoliberal critiques of the state today. On the other hand, the various sections of the Left, using a productivist model of politics or a feminist model or environmentalism, wonder how civil society could be seen as a source of resistance to the state power as civil society legitimises capitalism and the coercive state power. Both these pro-civil society stances and anti-civil society stances form a dichotomy in the era of globalisation today.

Aspects of the above dichotomy were perceived for the first time by Gramsci during the inter-war period, while some other aspects are products of our time. Due to various reasons, as stated below, Gramsci's original position on the subject is little known. However, Gramsci modifies both pro-civil society stances of liberalism (originally Locke's) and anti-civil society stances of the Left (originally Marx's). It would be pertinent to recollect certain original positions articulated on these issues by Gramsci long ago. The present chapter proposes certain middle grounds, recovered from Gramsci, as a way out of the above dualism.

Gramsci's Problematic

Gramsci launches a sceptical (=liberal) view of power in civil society on the foundations provided by Marx, but on the basis of a revised understanding of Marx via a critical reading of liberalism. For him, it is now necessary to be sceptical of powers in civil society, without giving up a liberal belief in the intrinsic merits of civil society. Only Hegel before Gramsci is sceptical of powers of civil society but his scepticism is expressed in terms of state power rather than civil society's norms. Hegel considers civil society as a complex set of institutions that believe in particularities, whereas the state promotes universalities.[1] His definition of civil society is construed from the point of view of the state. In contrast to Hegel, Gramsci shows clearly how it is possible to criticise civil society on the basis of civil society's own norms rather than the state power as shown below. He is sensitive to a liberal sceptical view of power: an institution of power, to start with, must be examined critically from inside rather than from outside its domain. Gramsci, for the first time, applies scepticism to reflect on powers of civil society within Marxist tradition, even though he fails to apply the same yardstick to state power.[2] But where he does succeed, as shown below, he exposes the liberal apologia for civil society vividly as never before.

Gramsci scholars notice that Gramsci does not share with Marx's vision of abolishing civil society. For Marx and Engels, there is no distinction between civil society and class relations: "civil society as such only develops with the bourgeoisie".[3] When classes including bourgeoisie are abolished, civil society also withers away. Gramsci scholarship is confused, partly due to ambivalences in Gramsci's own conceptualisations. Recently,

Femia argues that Gramsci's `revisionist turn' moves away from "Marx's open hostility of liberal values" and is also the basis of post-Marxian turns in Europe.[4] Femia is sceptical of Gramsci's attempts to take liberal turns and also assumes a dichotomy between liberalism and Marxism. Buttegieg claims that for Gramsci civil society is "integral part of the state..."[5]

This is as good as saying that civil society means 'the ideological state apparatus', whereas the state's political society is represented by its coercive wing.[6] Similarly, Chantal Mouffe, another Gramsci scholar, confesses that she was oblivious of the significance of liberalism in socialist strategy including Gramsci's.[7] Therefore, an attempt is made below to show how Gramsci turns liberal within the socialist camp. There are two crucial strengths of liberalism recognized by Gramsci.

Liberal and Socialist Views of Man: A Dichotomy

First, Gramsci is very sceptical of both liberal and socialist conception of 'man' (feminists, excuse Gramsci!). He expresses dissatisfaction with regard to liberal/catholic view of man defined through the individual only. He also argues that a socialist view of man defined through social units like productive forces and production relations is not very satisfactory. Gramsci tries to break free from this dualistic conception of man. He argues: "....it is necessary to reform the concept of man. One must conceive of human beings as a series of active relationships (a process) in which individuality is perhaps the most important element among other elements to be taken into account. The humanity which is reflected in each individuality is composed of various elements: 1. the individual; 2. other men; 3. the natural world."[8] It is a mere Aristotelian rhetoric to claim that "man is a political animal". He argues, "...not all necessary consequences have been drawn from this, even on an individual level."[9] Why is each person a philosopher, while each is a scientist too? Why, for example, are all his contemporary communists not like Karl Marx with the similar level of productive forces and class relations as Marx's? Here, he anticipated Sartre's revolt against Marxism. Decades later, Sartre asked a similar question: if class determines the nature of each individual, why then are the contributions of all his contemporary petty bourgeois romantics not as memorable as Valerie's?[10] One may ask, following Gramsci or Sartre, a similar question: why are all contemporary 'petty bourgeois' humanist poets/essayists not as memorable figures as Rabindranath Tagore? Therefore, there is something unique in each individual or even a small group. What are these unique aspects of each individual or each sub-strata of a class? How does one understand each person's creativity or stagnation or decay within the same class ideology? So, he pleads for a revision of the dichotomous conceptions of man subscribed by individualism and socialism.

Civil Society's Positive and Negative Functions

Second, despite many ambiguities in his definition of civil society, Gramsci makes a very important distinction between civil society and classes on the one hand, and civil society and state power on the other hand. Borrowing an economic analogy, it may be said that for Gramsci civil society provides 'backward linkages' (inputs) for the state while it receives 'forward linkages' (outputs) from classes. Therefore, civil society occupies a space between class and the state.[11] Bobbio argues that superstructure has two elements: civil society and the state.[12] For Bobbio, civil society articulates consent and moral/intellectual leadership (positive elements), whereas the state represents coercion and ideological/political leadership (negative elements). This chapter uses Bobbio's language and offers a different interpretation of Gramsci's civil society. On Bobbio's interpretation of Gramsci, civil society is a positive phenomenon, whereas the state is a negative phenomenon. Contra Bobbio, Gramsci suggests that both positive (like moral/intellectual) and negative functions (like ideological/political) coexist within the domain of civil society. Texier emphasises the opposite side neglected by Bobbio that civil society serves moral and intellectual functions of ruling classes, providing for rationalisation of hegemony and does not say anything on the need for civil society in future as proposed by Gramsci himself. Gramsci however emphasises that civil society provides 'rationalisation' (intellectual or moral elaboration) of class-state (negative element) on the one hand and ethical state (positive element) on the other hand.[13]

For Gramsci, civil society is not simply a positive political phenomenon as claimed by Bobbio.[14] It receives class instincts, class interests, and class struggle and tries to normalise them through family, religious associations, cultural groups, and networks of social capital. For example, not merely neoliberal thinkers but also the poor feel that they are poor as they have not availed opportunities due to their moral inferiority and so on.[15] Such moral beliefs are cultivated in and through many networks like family, secular religion, educational institutions and so on. White racism claims that there exists a great inherited difference between whites and Negroes as groups, preventing solidarities on common issues.[16] The subaltern classes tend to live in a world of ambivalent consciousness of their own selves, property, education, job, and so on due to 'normalizing' functions of civil society.[17]

Foucault's theory does talk about limits to power but in a voluntaristic manner. A typical Gramscian account of power would not allow for any voluntaristic assertion, while admitting limits to power. See, Arun K. Patnaik, 'Gramscian Concept of Commonsense', *Economic & Political Weekly*. More often, their claims against private property or unemployment or for substantial wages or for education, houses and so on, are delegitimised by civil society institutions. It produces a condition of "moral and political passivity".[18]

The subaltern classes sometimes feel that they deserve what they should get. They deserve 'this fate'. A kind of fatalism sets in due to their weak position in civil society.[19] Thus civil society prepares its members ideologically to justify economic exploitation by private property. Civil society receives economic outcomes but manufactures these outputs as ideologies that give credence to economy under capitalism. It prevents economic crisis from snowballing into political instability. It is through civil society, class life looks 'normal'. By using an economic analogy, it may be said that economic outcomes are like 'forward linkages' (outputs) of civil society. Civil society organs, through ideologies, receive economic outcomes like crises or depression and prevent them for becoming major class conflicts.[20] Gramsci calls for "in-depth study" of how civil society normalises the "fighting spirit" of the subaltern by organizing its "defensive systems" in a war of position (like economic depressions, etc.) to support a class-state.[21]

Civil society organisations also have primary functions with regard to the state power. Continuing with the same economic analogy, it may be said that these institutions supply political/ ideological 'inputs' (backward linkages) to the state power. It supplies political and ideological leaders or norms to state power. Civil society is a source of strength of state power. The state is represented by political or ideological leadership that complements economic-corporate leadership of capitalism. Both these kinds of leadership—ideological and political—are prepared by civil society networks.

First, it legitimises coercive functions of state power. Everybody in civil society feels that everybody else may encroach into each other's privacy, property, employment and so on. So, a neutral ground is created by civil society so as to justify the need of the state. Members of civil society feel that as they have no time to look after security interests of each other, they need a special organ with special powers. Also, the state functionaries are trained by civil society networks to remain neutral to purely economic-corporate interests.

Second, as Anne S. Sassoon argues, the state adopts certain principles of civil society and emerges as 'ethical educator' or ethical state.[22] It educates not merely rulers but also the common public. It manufactures public opinion in economic matters. In turn, the concept of law that belongs to the state can be extended to civil society networks as, through customs and conventions, the public can be brought under a collective pressure—a sort of tacit coercion. Thus, civil society supplies the state power with many 'inputs' or 'backward linkages' (raw materials). It supplies different kinds of leadership to manage class-state. Its puritan ideologies organise 'support' (to use a behavioural concept) for a coercive class-state.[23] Gramsci rejects any dichotomy between consent and coercion and argues how civil society networks, especially puritan ideologies, try to offer rationalisation of coercion in economic base as well as political society. Moreover, customary pressure or tacit coercion operates within the sphere of civil society as a sort of parallel moment of legal coercion of the state power.

In the above discussions, we have seen a sample of ideological/political functions internal to civil society. These functions may be called negative functions. Let us now examine intellectual/moral functions or what Bobbio calls 'positive' functions of civil society. Civil society follows one very crucial moral principle: manufacturing consent of its members. Though it tries to win over the consent of the subaltern classes, it does more than that. It trains members in citizenship. It educates people in the values of privacy, individual freedom, and in leadership and so on. It trains people in respecting each other's privacy. It trains people to become intellectuals of some substance. It imparts rational and social thinking over time. Each member now feels: 'where there is will, there is a way'. Not simply Bentham but also ordinary citizens believe that they live in a world of equality of opportunities, though ordinary perceptions are very ambivalent. These functions are positive as they are mainly based on the principle of consent (moral). Second, civil society also performs what Gramsci calls 'cultural functions' as distinct from economic functions.[24] It builds upon ability or capacity (intellectual) of its members through education imparted by civil society networks. It is in civil society that the child is educated to be 'social and rational' in his/her life-cycles. The child becomes intellectual, a philosopher and scientist in and through civil society networks. But these positive functions (moral/intellectual) coexist with negative functions (ideological/political) in civil society. The negative functions are justified through the ideology of persuasion. Members must be mutually persuaded to argue for coercive powers of the state. As a result, the positive functions are not universalized as civil society provides a basis for class-state.

While Gramsci shares Marx's vision that socialism must abolish class exploitation, and state violence, he also thinks that socialism means re-establishment of civil society's positive plurality. Socialism, for Gramsci, means reconstruction rather than disappearance of civil society. Gramsci revises Marx's assumption that associational life is only economic-corporate and that politics is politics of production.[25] Though, he along with Marx believes in "the disappearance of the state", he broadens Marx's view of politics by both separating civil society from economy and by offering a broader understanding of it. Gramsci argues: "It is only possible to create a system of principles asserting that the state's goal is its own end, its own disappearance, in other words the re-absorption of political society into civil society."[26] For him, the plural functions of the present civil society would have to be redefined rather than be abolished as claimed by Marx. It may still perform moral functions and intellectual functions (like education or care) rather than ideological and political functions (like training to dominate or coerce) in future. The principles of consent are universalised by a 'regulated society' that must shed off principles of violence or domination. The present civil society has put its own ethical or consent principles at the altar of capital and the state. Hence, it cannot be taken for granted with regard to the human rights question. For it may normalise exploitation (in economy) or coercion (within the state or family). It has no ability to push its own positive principles (consent) to prevail in the entire society, as it is also geared to draw subaltern's consent to class outcomes (backward linkage) and state coercion (forward linkage). Moreover, the claims against economic exploitation, familial or political violence may be de-legitimised or brushed aside by a self-seeking civil society. As a result, it may restrict the growth of human rights issues.

Bobbio rightly reminds us of Gramsci's insights into the need for a future 'regulated society'.[27] Bobbio then tries to shows how, according to Gramsci, civil society withers away as the state disappears.[28] Nowhere, Gramsci says so. Gramsci, on the contrary, argues that the future civil society would reabsorb the state and would have to address a very significant 'cultural function'. Gramsci assumes that socialist society will have to face a foundational question that Aristotle and Hobbes (for Gramsci: Catholics) asked: 'how to make man'? Gramsci draws an insight from the Catholic religion which believes that a human being is born alone and is solely responsible for his or her crimes.[29] As a result, Catholics believe that each human being needs the moral order of a society so that each becomes 'rational' and 'social'.[30] Gramsci argues that there is some truth in Catholic claims. He also suggests that liberal individualism draws very important philosophical insights from Catholicism and builds its own ideology. Therefore, he states clearly that a number of special institutions should be there under socialism to transform every child into a rational human being in several stages through moral and intellectual functions.[31] The future civil society must renew the twin tasks: economic functions and cultural functions—being performed by the present civil society.[32] Thus, Gramsci argues that new society must have a variety of special institutions ranging from family, educational, cultural organisations and so on that must cumulatively undertake the tasks of human civilisation: how to 'make man'? His project echoes the idea of institutional pluralism of liberalism set up since Hobbes and pleads for its recognition in the socialist camp. It is incorrect to claim that he advocates the disappearance of civil society by means of civil society, as claimed by Keane against Gramsci.[33] He would have rather agreed with John Keane that a socialist project must be concerned with a transformation of civil society by means of civil society rather than abolish altogether and thus would pave the way for a creation of socialist civil society.[34]

Contemporary Significance for a Humans Rights Discourse: Certain Implications

It may be interesting to recall here that Gramsci began his political career in the Socialist Party of Italy (PSI) as a member activist in its Human Rights Cell. I would like to claim that economic-civilisation functions of a human rights movement, which he learned from his activist days in this cell remained close to his passions, to which he returned in his defence of what Bobbio calls civil society's 'positive functions'. Gramsci opens up frontiers of human rights on the basis of and beyond production-centred politics ("a politics grafted directly on to the economy"[35]) of socialist predecessors of the 19th century. Human rights activists, following Gramsci's plea, need to be vigilant of rationalisation of exploitation or violence by civil society institutions ranging from the family onwards. Similarly, Gramsci is sensitive to politics performing 'cultural' tasks and it opens up new rights/duties. As civil society performs dual tasks, both positive and negative functions, new rights open up on the foundations of civil society. Henceforth, human rights activists would realise the need to be critical of negative functions of civil society, while they would also re-affirm positive functions in the rights discourse. A significant inference is now possible to draw from the above: human rights activism should not be seen merely opposing negative functions of civil society but also must concentrate on the construction of positive functions, and work towards its 'universalisation'. The human rights movement needs a dual perspective of civil society: politics of opposition/construction. As Gramsci reminds us that the positive functions of civil society are not universalised as yet which should be a goal of human rights discourse. While human rights activism must participate in civil society that aims at the transformation of each human child into a rational and social being and so on (a construction activity), human rights activists must at once be vigilant of politics of discrimination that may impose fetters on human rights (an oppositional activity). For example, where families may practise discrimination against the girl child or woman, human rights activism must sensitise members to respect non-discriminatory practices that promote gender rights like education, sharing care and upbringing of children, equal share of domestic work and so on, thus reducing the drudgery of women's work. Gramsci's self-critical perspective of civil society should be seen as an evolutionary process, a process that must look beyond Gramsci's time. However, what remains important for human rights activism is his self-critical perspective rather than a liberal complacent/opportunist view of civil society.

Gramsci's Theory and Its Implications for New Foundations of Rights

First, for Gramsci a human rights discourse must begin with

the very location of being of the individual. He argues that this is a very important lesson from Catholicism. Therefore, like Hobbes and Locke, Gramsci also argues that the individual is the primary unit of the human rights axis, a point not very well recognised by the Gramsci scholars.

Second, a radical human rights discourse must recognise ontological/natural rights. Whereas for Gramsci, following Marx, a key foundation of rights is to be located in human praxis (praxis includes rationality): the ability to reshape nature while constructing society. Social construction follows our interaction with nature. Society may facilitate or fetter human praxis. When society/civil society may fetter human praxis or human interaction with nature or restrict a human being's access to nature as "a persona" (to borrow from Rousseau) or its "resources" (to borrow from the Enlightenment) or both, then claims for or against arise. Such claims are human rights or ontological rights. Thus, not just rationality but praxis constitutes a very important basis (of human rights), a point discovered by Marx and reaffirmed by Gramsci, even though it must be admitted that Marx's theory is inattentive to a human rights theory.

Third, our interaction with each other or social interaction constitutes another foundation of human rights. Gramsci argues that society may practise different kinds of inequalities which may give rise to claims for or against inequalities. Such inequalities must be challenged by human rights activism on the grounds of human rights axis. Thus, unlike liberals or neoliberals, Gramsci opens up human rights issues in civil society too. In a society of inequalities, practised by economy, civil society and political institutions, human rights activism must challenge all these institutions that may hinder each human being from accessing nature's resources/production or ethical/civilisation resources or both and thus may prevent each from capacity-building in different directions.

Fourth, Gramsci modifies Marx's proposal that identifies civil society with economic/production relations. By separating civil society from class and from the state, Gramsci opens up new possibilities in the socialist camp. A new civil society that would not advocate class inequalities or state coercion must provide each person with rights to access two distinct resources: economic (production) entitlements and (civilisational) cultural entitlements. Marx notices the need for the first aspect very well under capitalism and argues for its universalisation under socialism as capitalism denies economic entitlements to everybody. But Marx fails to notice the need for cultural entitlements in bourgeois society. Certain special institutions in civil society are required to promote cultural entitlements, a point Gramsci learns for liberalism and Catholicism rather than from Marxism. On this issue, he stands in unison with a liberal claim: civil society imparts a new sense of civilisation in each person. Under capitalism, civil society is not able to universalize such cultural entitlements by not being in a position to offer such entitlements to everybody. Socialists must fight for equal/universal access to such civilisational entitlements and not just fight for universal access to economic (production) entitlements for each person. Thus, Gramsci pleads with socialists to recognise the need for a new socialist civil society rather than argue for the abolition of civil society. Gramsci makes a breakthrough in a liberal theory by challenging liberal complacency about civil society since Locke's time. He also invests a new meaning in political society since Marx's time and thus defends Marx's withering away of the state in a distinctive way. But this is a different subject matter of a future investigation.[36] So long as civil society remains an ideal of human civilisations, Gramsci's critique will be remembered for ever.[37]

REFERENCES

1. C. Taylor argues that for Hegel civil society "is the sphere of the individual in which universality is only abstract". See, Charles Taylor, *Hegel.* (Cambridge: CUP, 1975), 433. This obviously implies that the state is the sphere in which universality is concrete. Civil society is thus defined in terms of its teleological other.
2. Two years since the paper was written, it may now be stated that Gramsci succeeds in offering an "expansive view of state" within the Left wing tradition as never before. Taking a cue from pre-1921 Lenin, he offers a new interpretation of the withering away

of the state. But it may be explored separately in a different paper.

3. Marx and Engels, *The German Ideology* (1847) (Moscow: Progress Publishers, 1976), 98. However, credit must go to them for saying that civil society is a social form of interaction between human society and nature in all histories: "The form of intercourse determined by the existing productive forces at all previous historical stages, and in its turn determining these, is civil society." Ibid., 57. Gramsci was unaware that he shared this view of Marx and Engels and developed their views even further.
4. Joseph Femia, 'Civil Society and the Marxist Tradition', in S. Kaviraj and S. Khilnani (eds.), *Civil Society: History and Possibilities*, (Delhi: CUP, 2002), 146. In the Gramscian sense, civil society is not the same as political society (the state). It is one thing to say it is an 'integral state' but it is altogether a different thing to claim that it is an integral part of the state, as Buttigieg claims. See, Marcus Green, 'Gramsci Cannot Speak: Presentation and Interpretations of Gramsci's Concept of the Subaltern'. *Rethinking Marxism* (14:3, 2002), 6.
5. J.A. Buttigieg, "Gramsci on Civil Society", Boundary 2, 22: 3 (1995), 4. Marcus Green, however, does not share such a view of Gramsci's position. He argues clearly that though civil society, for Gramsci, is super structural, it is not part of the state.
6. J.A. Buttigieg, "Power, Consent and Gramsci." Streaming MP3, International Gramsci Society, 2004, (http: / / www.italnet.nd.edu/ gramsci/audio-video/). Buttigieg, op. cit., 26. For a contrasting interpretation, see Joseph Femia cited above. Femia argues that when Gramsci uses the term to distinguish Western European societies from that of Russia, he comes out very clearly that civil society is a distinct space located between class relations and the state power. See, Femia, op. cit., 139-140.
7. Chantal Mouffe and Ernesto Laclau, "In Interview." Ed. Ian Angus. Institute of Humanities, Simon Fraser University, 1999. (http: / / www.knowtv.com / primetime / conflicting / mouffe.html) She argues, "Well, I should point out that, at the moment when we began to develop that, we were not thinking so much, in terms of the relation with the liberal view." By 'that', she means their joint book, *Hegemony and Socialist Strategy: Towards a Radical Democratic Politics* (London: Verso, 1985).
8. See, Antonio Gramsci, *The Selections from Prison Notebooks* (New York: International Publishers, 1971), 352.
9. A Gramsci, op. cit., 353.
10. Sartre, J.P. *Search for a Method* (New York: Vintage Books, 1963), 53-58.

11. Femia, op. cit., 139-140; Also, N. Bobbio, 'Gramsci and the Concept of Civil Society', in John Keane (ed.), *Civil Society and the State* (London: Verso, 1988b), p. 90.
12. Bobbio, N., Ibid.
13. Bobbio and Texier posit opposite arguments, both having evidences for their arguments in Gramsci. See Jacques Texier, 'Gramsci, Theoretician of the Superstructure', in C Mouffe (ed.), *Gramsci and Marxist Theory* (London: RKP, 1979), 70-71. The point however is Gramsci holds a middle position on civil society. Gramsci argues that civil society provides for 'cultural' resources for both class-state (Texier: Ibid) and ethical-state (or 'state without a state') (Bobbio: 94). For a distinction between class-state and ethical-state, however, see Gramsci, op. cit., 262-263.
14. Bobbio identifies civil society with "a factor of hegemony" but locates civil society in the realm of consent and the state with force. See Bobbio, op. cit., 95. Bobbio forgets to tell us that consent to force, or to exploitation is not at all a positive element for Gramsci.
15. For this sort of social Darwinism as relay of popular beliefs and stereotypes, see Gunnar Myrdal, *Objectivity in Social Research.* (London: Gerald Duckworth & Co, 1969), 98. As a result, the poor live with 'intellectual and moral inferiority', Ibid.
16. Ibid., 22. *Political Weekly*, 23: 5, (1988): PE 2 – PE 10. (http://www.jstor.org/stable/4378042)
17. Here, normalizing function is used in a Gramscian sense. As in Foucault, power is seen as a benign process by the subaltern classes but, unlike in Foucault, power has inherent limitations from the point of view of their 'common sense', another Gramscian term.
18. Gramsci, op. cit., 333.
19. Ibid., 337.
20. Ibid., 235. Gramsci argues, "....civil society has become a very complex structure and one which is resistant to the catastrophic 'incursions' of the immediate economic element (crises, depressions), etc."
21. Ibid.
22. Anne S. Sassoon, "Civil Society", in Tom Bottomore and others (eds.), *A Dictionary of Marxist Thought* (Oxford: Blackwell, 1983), 74.
23. Gramsci, op. cit., 299.
24. See, Gramsci, op. cit., 242, argues, "Educative and formative role of the state. Its aim is always that of creating new and higher types of civilisation; of adapting 'civilisation' and the morality of the broadest popular masses to the necessities of the continuous

development of the economic apparatus of production; hence of evolving even physically new types of humanity". Gramsci here alludes to a distinction between civilisational/moral function and economic/production function of the state. After the state disappears, these functions need to be delivered by civil society. Also, see his explicit reference to these twin functions already performed by civil society, not simply bý the state, op. cit., 258-59.

25. Gramsci, op. cit., 259, argues, "Marx's was not able to have historical experiences superior (or at least much superior to) to those of Hegel; but, as a result of his journalistic and agitational activities, he had a sense for the masses. Marx's concept of organisation remains entangled amid the following elements: craft organisation; Jacobin clubs; secret ... groups; journalistic organisation". According to Gramsci, Marx could not grasp the dynamics of civil society organisations.
26. Ibid., 253.
27. Bobbio, op. cit., 94.
28. Ibid., 95.
29. Gramsci, op. cit., 351-52, "... there does not exist, historically, a way of seeing things and of acting which is equal for all men, no more no less". Gramsci learned this principle from Christianity. Referring to Catholic individualism, he argues, "...it insists on putting the cause of evil in the individual man himself, or in other words, it conceives of man as defined and limited individual". Ibid., 352.
30. Ibid., 337.
31. See his notes on education in new a society, Ibid., 40-41.
32. By economic/production functions Gramsci refers to (a) "interaction with nature" or productive forces. By civilisational/ moral functions Gramsci refers to society's civilisation tasks of "making man" through a continuous re-invention of a range of institutions that lay down norms for what Gramsci calls the growth of (b) "the individual" as also his interaction (c) "with the other men", as cited above. The former may be called economic entitlement and the latter cultural entitlement. By culture, Gramsci refers to moral and intellectual resources in a wide sense of the term. For culture in Gramscian sense, Bobbio, op. cit., 94.
33. John Keane argues, "Gramsci's interest in civil society is wholly opportunistic as he is driven by the reverie of abolishing civil society by means of civil society. Civil society is temporary and dispensable arrangement." Author (ed.) op. cit., 25.

34. John Keane, *Democracy and Civil Society* (London: Verso, 1988a), 64.
35. Gramsci's reference to Hegel and Marx on civil society, op. cit., p. 259.
36. Taking a cue from Lenin's praxis rather than Engels, Gramsci's concept of political society offers a new possibility of politics of the state, while defending "the withering away of the state". For problems in Engels' interpretation of withering away of the state, see R. Miliband, "STATE", in T Bottomore, et. al., op. cit., 467. However, this is a matter of separate investigation. Yet, it must be confessed that Gramsci's polemic against 'man in general' suggests a celebratory view of human praxis, human history, etc. He errs in denying limits set by nature on praxis/history and fails to recognize what Hobbes calls 'animalism' in each human being. His deficient view poses a few problems for a socialist theory. See the Italian Marxist S. Timpanaro, *On Materialism* (London: Verso, 1980), 45 and 236-37. An instrumental approach to the state, however, may not necessarily imply an instrumental approach to nature or civil society. For example, Marx's approach to nature/animals is free from instrumentalism. John Bellamy Foster, "Marx and the Environment", in E.M. Wood and J.B. Foster (eds.) *In Defence of History* (New York: M R Press, 1997 and Delhi: Aaakar Books, 2006). Lawrence Wilde, "The creatures, too, must become free: Marx and the Animal/Human Distinction", *Capital & Class*, 72 (2000), 37-53. Texier, J. 1979. "Gramsci, Theoretician of the Superstructure": Gramsci and Marxist Theory, ed. Chantal Mouffe, 48-79. London: RKP. Timpanaro, S. 1980. *On Materialism*. London: Verso. Wilde, L. 2000. "The creatures, too, must become free: Marx and the Animal/Human Distinction", *Capital & Class*, 72: 37-53.
37. Gramsci intends his *Prison Notebooks* as a reflection of his commitment for issues that may last for ever. See, for a war of position for ever—a typical Gramscian theme more applicable in the context of civil society, Joseph Francese, 'Thoughts on Gramsci's Need "To Do Something 'Für ewig'"'. *Rethinking Marxism*, 21:1, 2009: 54 – 66.

7

A Marxist Post-mortem of Soviet Socialism

Markar Melkonian

The question at hand is: What is the significance of Marxism since the fall of the Berlin Wall? It is a big question, pointing in more than one direction. One could, for instance, discuss Karl Marx's impact on present-day mainstream social sciences, historiography, and other cultural fields, high and low. This impact is often unacknowledged or ungratefully denied, but it is no less deep and enduring for all that. Or one could discuss the whys and wherefores of resurgent Marxism in Latin America and elsewhere, or even the spectre of Marx, recently sighted, ambling the halls of President Obama's White House. But I do not want to take this discussion in these directions. Instead, I want to consider the question: Can Marxism account for the defeat of 20th century socialism? If Marxism cannot do this and do it well, then it seems to me that, in the present tense, it should have little "significance" to speak of. The authors of the *Communist Manifesto*, after all, were supposed to be students of "actual relations springing from an existing class struggle, from a historical movement going on under our very eyes."

Reviewing recent arguments for and against Marxism, one gets the feeling that few of them are new. Cold war triumphalists have echoed earlier views of the Austrian School and its continuators, while other ideological victors have had little to add to the earlier views of philosophers like Karl Popper, Leszek

Kolakowski, and Robert Nozick, or Sovietologists in the Robert Conquest mould, or the God-that-Failed type of confessional literature.

Leaving aside Francis Fukayama's darkly comic prognostications, the nearest thing to a new critique, as far as I am aware, has been launched by some of the more politically committed proponents of socio-biology and its successors, notably Wilson and Pinker.[1]

As others have reminded us, though, much of what the champions of the "new sciences of human nature" have had to say can be traced back 100 years, to Herbert Spencer and his followers.[2] Of course, this is not to say that Pinker, Wilson, or any of the other recent critics are mistaken; the fact that a criticism is not novel does not mean that it has missed its target or that it is irrelevant. It merely denies these critics the advantage of novelty.

Many sundry objections to Marxism have been instances of the straw man argument. Others applied to one or another unwieldy version of Marxism, but not to the "lean, mean" version that I described in a primer that first appeared in the mid-1990s.[3] Still other objections have applied to this or that view that Marx and Engels might have held at one time or another, but not to Marxism as developed by their legatees. We are not here interested in what Marx or Engels happened to have said at this or that time in their careers; after all, Marx had not always been a Marxist. Rather, we are interested in a Marxist perspective on events of the last century, a perspective informed by a long line of thinkers since Marx and Engels. We are interested here in *historical materialism—Marxism,* not *Marxology.*

These observations notwithstanding, some criticisms remain compelling, and of course the jury is still out on others. Whatever the strengths of the objections and responses though, the fact remains that *there is no argument like failure.* Rightly or wrongly, the prestige of Marxism has been tied up with "really existing socialism" in Soviet Russia and its satellites. *Marxism has failed the test of prediction,* it seems, and it has failed to meet its own criterion of adequacy, describing "a historical movement going on under our very eyes". It would be surprising then, if so many erstwhile Marxists had *not* abandoned it as what the philosopher of science Imre Lakatos called a "progressive research programme."[4]

It is not entirely true, though, that Marxism or Marxists failed the test of prediction when it came to the demise of Soviet socialism. One of the most astute previews of the demise of the Soviet Union was also one of the earliest sustained arguments to this effect, namely, Leon Trotsky's book, *The Revolution Betrayed*, first published in 1936. More than 50 years before the fall of the Wall, Trotsky argued that a privileged and despotic bureaucracy had taken control of the state machinery of the Soviet Union, thereby controlling the productive resources of the country. The Soviet Union was still a workers' state, Trotsky wrote, because the bureaucracy constituted a *stratum* rather than a *class* properly speaking. But if eventually it succeeded in institutionalising its position, establishing special forms of private property and legitimising them in law, then the gains of the October Revolution would be reversed.

Trotsky's degraded-workers'-state approach is just one of many left-wing characterisations of the Soviet Union, each with its corresponding account of the demise. Because literature on this topic is vast and my space is limited, I do not propose here to survey competing accounts. Suffice it to note, however, that other Marxists have made poignant predictions too, including Milovan Djilas, in a book published in the 1950s.[5] So without conceding the point that Marxists across-the-board have failed the best of prediction, I want to bring Marxism itself to bear on the demise of "really existing socialism" in the 20th century, and to compare my preferred Marxist account with the most plausible non-Marxist accounts.

I will begin by describing three of the strongest prevailing non-Marxist explanations of the demise and indicate why I think they are one-sided at best. I will then proceed to introduce my preferred view, which highlights the formation within the Soviet Union of the class that would dig the grave of the first workers' state. One of the things that make this an identifiably *Marxist* view is precisely that it emphasises the role of *classs* in social processes such as the one under discussion. By way of conclusion, I will consider whether Marxism can account for the fact that the full ascension to power of a capitalist class in post-Soviet Russia did not unleash productivity, as the cold war victors had promised and as was the case in the wake of the modern bourgeois revolutions.

If my preferred Marxist view can account for this fact in a satisfactory way, then this would mitigate a common criticism of Marxism, namely that in the last years of the last century it was blindsided by historical processes that it cannot well explain. This all has an obvious bearing on prospects for socialism in the 21st century and beyond. Aside from a couple of very gestural remarks towards the end of the discussion, though, I will not attempt to address this urgent topic here.

I make no apologies for the very general character of this discussion. Hardt and Negri are right at least in their contention that it is both appropriate and crucial to discuss such topics at a high level of generalisation. Twenty years have passed since the fall of the Berlin Wall; returning capitalism now has a track record, and summarisation is in order.

A Couple of Definitions

Before proceeding, though, let us agree on a couple of definitions. In this discussion the term *Marxism* refers to an intellectual tradition and a research programme, not to what academics sometimes call a "political ideology". We are here concerned with Marxism as a conceptual vocabulary and a way of describing the passing scene; we are not concerned with Marxism as a repertoire of rhetorical devices or as apologetics for this or that party. The term *historical materialism* is synonymous with *Marxism.* Historical materialism may be viewed as an interdisciplinary social science framework unifying in one way or another the fields of anthropology; political economy, political science, sociology, and historiography, as well as social and political philosophy and perhaps philosophy of science. Either that or it is an alternative discipline, a science of history and society that could eclipse these conventional social sciences and philosophical fields. *Socialism* I take to be *workers' power*, the state power of workers as a class.

As I use the word, then, *socialism* is synonymous with the term *dictatorship of the proletariat.* It is the name of a *political* state of affairs, not an economic system —let alone a mode of production with its own distinctive "spontaneously" reproducing social relations. Central planning and state ownership of the means of production are neither sufficient nor necessary conditions for socialism.

Prevailing Post-mortems

Cold war victors have propagated three explanations of the demise of the Soviet Union:

(a) The huddled masses of Russia and the Captive Nations yearned to be *free* in Milton Friedman's sense of the word, namely, to be abie to engage in a wider range of voluntary exchanges with other individuals. Eventually they raised their heads to demand a much wider range of freedom than the socialist system or any command economy could perrnit.

(b) Soviet socialism lost the economic competition with free-market capitalism. It failed to meet rising demands for high-quality consumer goods and services, including entertainment, international travel, and *les chases les plus fines de la vie.*

(c) Soviet socialism conflicted with human nature. It was just a matter of time before the population of the Soviet Union threw off the last untenable prevalence of generalised altruism, in favour of kin selection and the reciprocal altruism that characterises market relations.

Other prefered explanations focus on the escalating conflicts among nationalities within the USSR, or on large-scale betrayal by leaders of the CPSU, or on exogenous factors such as imperialist machinations and military encirclement. Some or all of these factors have contributed to the demise of the Soviet Union; however, in my view even the most consequential of them did not constitute *determining* factors, and some were instances or effects of more general processes at work in the three explanations listed above. (It will be noticed that the Party betrayal scenario, shorn of conspiratorial overtones, is compatible with the more comprehensive view that I will present.)

Let us take a closer look at these inter-related explanations, starting with the masses-yearning-to-be-free account.

Writing in 1989, shortly before the fall of the Berlin Wall, Zbigniew Brzezinski, National Security Advisor to US President Jimmy Carter, wrote that the Soviet order "failed to take into account the basic human craving for individual freedom". This was a common theme of Sovietologists, celebrity dissidents, and cold war commentators, and it is perfectly captured by the televised images of youths swinging sledge hammers against the Wall. The Soviet Union collapsed, it is said, under the weight of its own unfreedom; it collapsed because the population, and ultimately even the Soviet elite, experienced "totalitarianism" as intolerable. This picture, at first sight so incontrovertible, begins to buckle under the weight of sceptical scrutiny. For one thing, by the time the young men reached the Wall with their sledge hammers, the contest for power had already been decided. For another thing, if it really were the case that Soviet "totalitarianism" imploded because it withheld freedom from its people, then why haven't more rigid regimes, in say Egypt, or Saudi Arabia, similarly collapsed? Clearly, the familiar picture of oppressive regimes collapsing under the weight of popular opposition captures something important about the demise of the Soviet bloc. But I wonder if that opposition was as direct and unproblematic as this metaphor would have it. Without rejecting the familiar picture, I wonder if it would not be more productive to try to describe how it happened that regimes in Central and Eastern Europe, unlike regimes in, say, Sudan, Malaysia, or Equatorial Guinea— produced subjects that urgently *needed* a certain kind of freedom. Possible reasons for this discrepancy immediately present themselves, including the relative prosperity of the East European Soviet bloc countries, the fact that conspicuously many of the longest lived repressive regimes have survived in predominantly rural and non-industrial settings, and the legitimising role of religious ideologies within certain neocolonial or postcolonial contexts.

In any case, here it would seem we have a task not so much

for Steven Pinker's "new sciences of human nature" as for a Marxist theory of ideology, a materialist and *historically specific* theme of the constitution of subjectivity. Debates continue to rage over the meaning of *human nature* and the usefulness of the term for biologists and practitioners of the social and behavioural sciences whatever the consequences of the debates. Though, no consistent historical materialist is going to deny that humanity is a product of natural selection and that the human brain is largely a result of adaptations that have taken place over the course of hundreds of millennia. But a Marxist theory of ideology, unlike Pinker's brand of evolutionary psychology, will at least set itself the task of explaining why it is that different sets of social relations at different times and places have reproduced such strikingly different sorts of *people,* people with very different values, interests, and needs.

What about the claim that socialism failed to deliver the goods? As early as 1968, Egon Neuberger of the Rand Corporation predicted that the centrally planned economy of the Union of Soviet Socialist Republics (USSR) eventually would meet its demise, because of its "demonstrably growing ineffectiveness as a system for managing a modernising economy in a rapidly changing world". Twenty-one momentous years later, in 1989, economic historian Hobert Heilbroner explained the facts of life to readers of *The New Yorker* magazine: "Less than 75 years after it officially began, the contest between capitalism and socialism is over: capitalism has won. Capitalism organises the material affairs of humankind more satisfactorily than socialism."[6]

Economic Explanations

Here too of course there is more than a grain of truth. It is an understatement to say that the Soviet economy had been underpeforming for many decades, as we know, the rate of economic growth had been falling. Let us remind ourselves, however, that even during the infamous "period of stagnation", when patronage, corruption, and inefficiency infused the Soviet economy from top to bottom, it was still delivering bread, jobs, pensions, and basic medical attention to the larger part of the population. By contrast, 20 years of capitalism in Russia have denied these things to millions of Russians. A generation has passed with decades of transcontinental impoverishment, falling life expectancies and birth rates, soaring unemployment and infant mortality, a near-catastrophic fall in population, and a raging epidemic of self-administered alcohol poisoning. The gap between rich and poor has become even wider, and the billionaires have grown ever more imperious. And yet the Russian people's cup of wrath does not appear to be overflowing, at least not in any discernibly organised way. If Heilbroner's categorical version of the economic-failure explanation were sufficient, then why have Russians remained so quiescent in the post-Soviet era, after 20 years of much worse failure on the part of Russia's new autocrats?

I do not have a plausible answer to that question. One possible response might be that Russians have not yet lost the habit of passivity that they had acquired during the Soviet decades, even as they have acquired the habit of rejecting anything smacking of collectivism. But this response raises obvious objections and leads to even stickier questions. With reference to Russian passivity for instance, how did it happen that a generation lost it temporarily, just in time to overthrow a supposedly totalitarian regime—and then promptly slumped back into it? The passivity is selective, and we want to know why. In any case, there you have it: thanks to a universal and unchanging human nature (rooted perhaps in biology), the victory of capitalism in the 20th century is the final victory. Socialism, capitalism's only rival in the 20th century, was incurably inefficient, and because it flouted the natural craving for individual freedom, it pitched itself, moment-to-moment, against intractable human nature. The history of 20th century socialism demonstrates, as clearly as could be demanded, that as long as humankind persists, capitalism may be the best alternative.

The 40th President of the United States brought together all three of these themes. In his June 8, 1982 address to a joint session of British Parliament, Ronald Reagan declared: "It is the Soviet Union that runs against the tide of history by denying human freedom and human dignity to its citizens". He then added:

> It also is deep economic difficultly. Over-centralised, with little or no incentives, year after year the Soviet system pours its best resources into the making of instruments of destruction. The constant shrinkage of economic growth combined with the growth of military production is putting a heavy strain on the Soviet people.

When it came to the growth of military production in the Soviet Union, of course, Reagan himself could take some credit, since his administration escalated the arms race and stroked a proxy war on Russia's south-eastern border. Increased defence spending further weakened the Soviet economy, shunting resources from production of consumer goods to the military. What is of more interest here, however, are the words that follow Reagan's previous passage: "What we see here is a political structure that no longer corresponds to its economic base, a society where productive forces are hampered by political ones." Facing a British Parliament composed in part of a deeply divided Labour Party in a country with over three million unemployed workers, the Great Communicator abruptly dropped his Morning-in-American lyricism in favour of a *Marxissant* phraseology in which "political forces" that "hamper" "economic bases" "run against the tide of history".

This caricature comes close *in certain respects* to summarising what did in fact take place in the last decades of the existence of the first workers' state, culminating in Yeltsin's counter-coup of August 1991. Since the 1970s, more and more Soviet citizens in positions of power had come to view the property relations characteristic of the old order as fetters on the further development of the productive forces. These fetters included such things as legal limits on ownership of land and other means of production, a constitutionally guaranteed right to a job, "artificial" price controls, insufficient economic incentives, restrictions on the proliferation of the new information technologies, and isolation from global markets and financial institutions. As a result of this perceived conflict between incumbent social relations and ascendant productive forces, the integument burst. A new leadership rose to power and set about to transform "the entire immense superstructure" in its own image.

The Soviet System's Gravediggers

As we have seen, Reagan's speechwriters resorted to Marxist-sounding phraseology to convince an astute audience of the impending demise of what he would later (and in the presence of a very different audience) dub "the Evil Empire". Despite the accuracy of the prediction itself, though, Reagan's speechwriters depicted the gravediggers of the Soviet Union implausibly, as a formless mass of freedom-lovers, united by little more than opposition to conservative "political forces". Reagan has presented us with a picture of apolitical or anti-political masses, composed of individuals imbued by nature with the profit motive and a yearning for negative freedoms, squaring off against big government. As I will argue in the next section, however, it seems more accurate to say that the gravediggers—or at least many of the most active of them in Russia—comprised an increasingly compact and self-consciously politicised elite that owed its privileges and thus its existence to the very Soviet system that it had to dismantle in order to remake the country in its image. In order to complete its historical task, though, the gravediggers had to come together as a proper class in and for itself.

As we have seen, the problem with prevailing non-Marxist explanations of the demise of the Soviet Union is not that their claims are all false or useless. Each of the three explanations in the previous section captures something right, but each is partial or one-sided. The demise of Soviet socialism was a complex process, and so it would not be surprising if the explanation were complex. How then do the three common non-Marxist explanations fare when taken jointly? We have already noted that they are closely related doctrinally. We might combine them and summarise the result as follows: Because a socialist system or any command economy must curtail individual freedom, and because it will fail to satisfy universal needs as well as the rival capitalist system, socialism cannot long endure, at least on a large scale. This is a more-than-familiar story, repeated by everyone from classical-liberal economist Ludwig von Mises to the latest evolutionary economist. As I have suggested, however, it fails to account for "actual relations springing from an existing class struggle", at least when we take into account the longevity of a wide variety of repressive capitalist regimes, present and past.

It bears emphasising that the development of productive forces during the period of stagnation was hampered not so much by Reagan's unspecified "political forces" as by a legally and constitutionally sanctioned system of property relations that enjoyed the support of a significant part of the population of the Soviet Union right down to the bitter end. The supporters were to be found within the lower—and mid-levels of the Party, within the official unions, the KGB and the military, and in many other walks of life. The most strident opposition, by contrast, was composed, at least till late in the day, of Party apparatchiks and insiders, managers of large state enterprises, and a range of professional intellectuals, celebrities, and other notables. By that time, it had become obvious to many of the most powerful and well-connected elites that private ownership in the means of production would permit them to amass fortunes and to secure the smooth, systematic transmission of wealth and privilege to their sons. Trotsky called these rising forces "the bureaucracy"; Milan Djilas called it the "new class", and latter-day writers have dubbed it "the power-wielding class of the nomenklatura."[7]

Trotsky did not describe the bureaucracy as a *class*, since the bureaucrats did not own productive property. Djilas, by contrast, claimed that the privileged elite in the Soviet Union was in fact a new class with a distinct relationship to the means of production; however, he did not claim that this new class was associated with a self-sustaining mode of production. If Marxist theory is correct, Djilas wrote, then Soviet- type societies must eventually either relapse into capitalism or undergo social revolution leading towards genuine socialism. It should be noted, however, that although the elite had long occupied positions of control over major means of production, relations of ownership and inheritance prevented this group from systematically appropriating the surplus product, at least on a large scale. For this reason, Trotsky's account seems more compelling than accounts that characterise this elite or bureaucracy as an already-constituted capitalist class. As a member of the Politburo of the Central Committee of the CPSU (1980-91), and then as General Secretary of the Party (1985-91), Mikhail Gorbachev drew early support from this constituency in Russia. By the late 1980s, even the remnants of Soviet power in the lower echelons of the Party and public organisations had lost faith in the Party and the state, while at the same time the nomenklatura (or at least its non-military constituents) and its intellectual allies tacitly agreed that the Soviet system must be brought down. Nothing in the way of conspiracy was required; the consensus developed spontaneously, from thousands of points across the Union, from the Kremlin to the Republican and regional levels, right down to the capillary level of firms and individual lives.

Of course, other Marxist interpretations have achieved prominence, too. Economist Paul Sweezy, for example, held that the Soviet bureaucracy had replaced the dictatorship of the proletariat with "the dictatorship of the bureaucracy". According to this "bureaucratic-exploitative" interpretation, the usurpation of state power by the bureaucracy had resulted in a "new form" of post-capitalist society—a hybrid somewhere between capitalism and socialism, in which the bureaucracy had the power to exploit the workers through the extraction of surplus value. Compare this to Hardt and Negri's view that "The Soviet Union was better understood not as a totalitarian society but rather as a bureaucratic dictatorship."

Perestroika partially opened the flood-gates to extra-legal capitalist enterprise on a larger scale, and privatisation enabled upstart magnates to grab the productive assets and the natural resources of the state and cooperative enterprises. These magnates or so-called oligarchs comprised the "New Russians" (and their Ukrainian counterparts) and their republican and regional franchises, and many hailed from outside the ranks of the old nomenklaturas. The years that followed saw a tortured, conflict-ridden process of competition and partial amalgamation of these two overlapping groups of aspiring capitalists, the upstart magnates and the scions of the old nomenklaturas.

The largely non-Party pedigree of the oligarchs is a matter of controversy; accounts differ in, for example, Hoffman, Satter and Eyal, Szelényi and Townsley. In post-Putin Russia, the political fortunes of the magnates have waned, but in other former Soviet Republics they have transformed themselves into genuine oligarchs. The case of the former Soviet Socialist Republic of Armenia is instructive. Many of the most notable oligarchs and high-ranking officials in Armenia today (as in several other non-Russian former Soviet Republics) do not appear to be scions of the nomenklatura.

As we know, Gorbachev's erstwhile supporters dropped him like a hot potato as soon as Boris Yeltsin's fortunes rose. The "oligarchs", including expat billionaires (and $40 billion from the IMF, plus a bevy of foreign public relations experts), plumbed the depths of depravity to buy the 1996 Russian presidential election for Yeltsin. Newly unfettered from Soviet constraints on property relations, and having vanquished all conservative contenders, the fractious capitalist class-in-formation commandeered the old centre, replaced the constitutional, legal, and governing superstructure of the old order with new institutions consonant with full-blown capitalism, and came into its own as a ruling class. Similar processes on a smaller scale took place in the regions and in the former Soviet Republics, the still-designated "newly independent states", and the former "Captive Nations". Patronage, privatisation, new tax regimes, and the embrace of multilateral lending institutions—these were all ad hoc developments, and the results were unpremeditated; nevertheless, they were causes and consequences of the formation of new capitalist classes shattering old state structures. At many levels and in several locales, then, the processes that produced new ruling classes were *political* processes at least as much as they were *economic* processes.

A dozen years after the final demise of the Soviet Union, 11 out of 20 presidents of eastern European nations (excluding the former Yugoslavia) and former Soviet Republics were former party insiders, the local nomenklaturas. We should note at least parenthetically, however, that the non-Russian republics were not simply miniature replicas of Russia. In the Baltic Republics, in Ukraine, in the Caucasus and Central Asia, capitalist restoration proceeded at different tempos and according to the respective logics of the locales. In the course of the years, the Russian nomenklatura and many of its local franchises discovered a confluence of interests with the non-Russian nationalists. But this was not a smooth or unilateral process of consensus-building. During Gorbachev's tenure, for example, the local nationalists were the bane of some of the most visible representatives of the All-Union nomenklatura, notably the General Secretary himself.

According to Kaviraj, for example, the economic reforms associated with perestroika had an overriding political character. With reference to the process of privatisation, the case of the post-Soviet Republic of Armenia is instructive once again. While privatisation was in full swing, editors of a Yerevan newspaper repeated common observations: "Seen more as a political than an economic process, privatisation has been used to manipulate the character of the emerging Armenian industrial class. With the president and his allies monitoring the process case by case, some enterprises have been sold to high-ranking officials, while others went cheap to their kin and close friends. Many others were granted to political allies" (*Hayastani Hanrapetoutioun*, Yerevan, May 13, 1996, p. 83). "The tax regime also offered profits to political elites and their supporters. Most estimates found that less than 10 per cent of formally collected taxes ended up in government coffers." "Patronage politics was essential to the development of a tightly interwoven political-economic system, but the arrangements that emerged were ad hoc, not predesigned."

It is tempting to say that the Soviet Union in its final years was as hollow as the dummy missiles that trundled past Lenin's Tomb on Victory Day. But if the account that I have described is correct—if an ascendant capitalist class had been forming within the body politic of the USSR long before the August 1991 coup attempt—then the ubiquitous metaphor of a *collapse* is misleading: the Soviet Union did not *collapse*, at least not politically. Rather, what took place in 1991 or 1989 or some time earlier, was the bursting of an integument of one kind or another. The integument, however, was as much *political* as it was *economic*: a new class-in-formation captured strategic locations in the Soviet state and the All-Union economy and stood poised, however unwittingly, to play its historical role, to complete the process of remaking the old order in its image.

What took place in 1989 or 1991, then, was very different from the prevailing pictures. We should register in passing that this account conflicts with the *capitalist restoration thesis*, associated with Mao Tse Tung, and the related thesis of "state capitalism", which according to Charles Bettelheim, involves state ownership of the economy, with the extraction of surplus value through wage labour. If the capitalist restoration thesis were the case, then why the need for a Gorbachev or for *Perestroika*? Why the need for a Yeltsin? Why the personnel change, the counter-coup, and the scrapping of the old constitution? And why the massive, enormously costly, counter-revolutionary upheaval in Russia and other parts of the former Soviet Union, the massive destruction of capital, the massive stripping and restructuring of the economy, including the loss of markets, both domestically and internationally? And what are we to make of the rocket ascension of the "New Russians" in the 1990s?

As we will see in the next section, it was also very different from the picture of the great bourgeois revolutions of the modern period.

After the Fall

Reagan had famously predicted the demise of what he referred to as the "bizarre" social experiment of "communism". What he failed to predict, however, was that 20 years after the fall of the Berlin Wall a large part of the population of Russia and even of some of the former "Captive Nations" would come to rue the passing of the Soviet period. The subsequent years have not born out the triumphalist hype about a new dawn of freedom and prosperity.

A capitalist class-in-formation rose to power, but Russia's

return to capitalism differed in many respects from the bourgeois revolutions of the early modern period. For one thing, the French bourgeoisie had already constituted a class in-and-for- itself long before 1789; by contrast, it does not appear that the nomenklatura had yet constituted itself as a class until years after Yeltsin's 1991 counter-coup. Even more significantly, in the case of the early modern revolutions, the rise to power of a capitalist class resulted in the dramatic expansion of productivity that Marx and Engels celebrated in the *Communist Manifesto* and subsequent works. In post-Soviet Russia and much of the Soviet bloc, by contrast, productivity has plummeted far below its dismally low levels during the period of stagnation. This consideration is enough to cast doubt on the claim that Russia's return to capitalism was a *revolution*.

The capitalist class-in-formation in Russia has come into its own as a ruling class within the context of globalised markets, a global division of labour, and multilateral arrangements over which the United States held undisputed sway. Since then, Russia's rulers have functioned as regional brokers for international capital, within the framework of a reinvigorated imperialist system and an unyielding global hierarchy of power. Under these circumstances, Russia's new rulers could not play the role of a modern national class, of establishing national markets, presiding over capital expansion, and revolutionising productive forces. In these respects, too, the post-Soviet rulers of Russia differed sharply from the ascendant bourgeoisies of the modern revolutions in Europe.

If the end of the Soviet order had opened the door to freedom and prosperity as advertised, or if Russia's former cold war adversaries had not distinguished themselves over the course of the past 20 years as unreconstructed imperialists, then my preferred Marxist explanation of the demise would come off as considerably less plausible than alternative explanations. But this is not what happened. Instead, falling productivity has plunged millions of working-class households into poverty; prisons are filled to overflowing; ethnic cleansing has taken its predictable toll, and Russian voters have been subjected to extreme forms of political manipulation, exemplified by the 1996

Russian presidential campaign. In the course of the last 20 years, fallout on the diplomatic front has included NATO expansion into Eastern Europe and former Soviet Republics, a protracted US bombing campaign against Russia's historical allies in Serbia, two US wars in Iraq, new US military bases in Central Asia; foreign-subsidised "colour revolutions" in Ukraine and Georgia, and of course the US invasion and occupation of Afghanistan. Yeltsin and his successors have presided over the precipitous demotion of Russia as a global power, even as the US and other former cold war adversaries have projected their state power far and wide, across borders and into the Russian Federation itself.

These consequences do not square well with the assumptions and expectations that accompany the non-Marxist accounts of the demise of the Soviet Union. They are, however, entirely compatible with the Marxist account that I have just sketched in gestural strokes. This Marxist account, moreover, makes it possible to combine the best insights of the non-Marxist views within a coherent, overarching theoretical framework that is both materialist and historically specific.

Ironically, then, one of the reasons why Marxism is significant today is because it provides the best available explanation for the demise of the Soviet Union and the defeat of socialism in the 20th century. G.A. Cohen, a key figure in analytic Marxism, drove the irony home: "...the Soviet failure can be regarded as a triumph for Marxism: a Soviet success might have embarrassed key propositions of historical materialism, which is the Marxist theory of history".[8]

This, it seems to me, is one measure of the significance of Marxism in the 21st century.

REFERENCES

1. Edward O. Wilson, *On Human Nature* (Cambridge, MA and London: Harvard University Press, 2004); Stevan Pinker, *The Blank Slate: The Modern Denial of Human Nature* (New York: Penguin, 2002).
2. Richard Hofstadter, *Social Darwanism in American Thought* (Boston: The Beacon Press, 1955); Merk Curti, *Human Nature in American Thought: A History* (Madison: University of Wisconsin Press, 1980); Stephen Gould, *The Mismeasure of Man* (New York:

W.W. Norton, 1996).

3. Markar Melkonian, *Marxism: A Post-Cold War Primer* (Boulder: Westview, 1996).
4. Imre Lakatos, *The Methodology of Scientific Research Programmes: Philosophical Papers*, Vol. I (Cambridge: Cambridge University Press, 1978).
5. Milovan Djilas, *The New Class: An Analysis of the Communist System* (London: Thames & Hudson, 1957).
6. Robert Heilbroner. 'The Triumph of Capitalism', in *The New Yorker*, January 23, 1989, pp. 98-99.
7. Leon Trotsky, *The Revolution Betrayed: What is the Soviet Union and Where Is It Going?* (New York: Pathfinder Press, 1972); Milovan Djilas, op. cit., Robert Daniels, 'Political Processes and Generation Change', in Archie Brown (ed.), *Political Leadership in the Soviet Union* (London: The Macmiilan Press, 1989).
8. G.A. Cohen, 'Marxism after the Collapse of the Soviet Union', in *Journal of Ethics*, 3: 99-104, (1999).

8

On a Strange Misreading of Marx: A Note

Paresh Chattopadhyay

The remarks below concern certain selected points in the earlier interesting and scholarly chapter by Markar Melkonian (MM hereafter) entitled 'A Marxist Post-mortem of Soviet Socialism'. However it is important to point out that MM's ideas of socialism and dictatorship of the proletariat do not correspond to those of Marx. Further "Soviet Socialism" was neither Soviet nor Socialist, even in Lenin's time.

MM's first salvo is "Can Marxism account for the *defeat* of the 20th century *socialism?*" (our emphasis). Also towards the end of his piece he speaks again of the "*defeat* of *socialism* in the 20th century" (our emphasis). MM writes: "As I use the word, then, Socialism, is synonymous with the term dictatorship of the proletariat", then adds that "this is also the sense in which Marx used the term" and refers to the *Critique of the Gotha Programme* as the text where this is claimed to occur. Again, MM opines that "socialism" is "workers' power, the state power of the workers as a class", and that "socialism is the name of a political state of affairs, not an economic system, let alone a mode of production". Again, the very title of the chapter in question carries the leading term "Soviet socialism", and this term is also used more than once in the body of the text. Similarly, the Soviet state is called (by MM) a "workers' state". We propose, in what follows, to discuss first the author's idea of socialism and then his idea of the proletarian dictatorship in the light of Marx's own position on these subjects. We then take up the question of "Soviet socialism".

Socialism in Marx

For Marx, socialism is conceived as the society succeeding capital(ism). Contrary to a widespread, but wrong idea, socialism is not a transitional society preparatory to communism. Socialism for Marx *is* communism (including the two stages). That socialism is a society *distinct from and transitional* to communism has no textual basis in Marx. Lenin, without himself originating this distinction, made it famous. For Marx, communism, socialism, Republic of Labour, society of free and associated producers or simply Association, Cooperative Society, (Re)union of free individuals, are all equivalent terms for the same society.

The victorious outcome of the workers' *self-emancipatory revolution* is the socialist society, an "association of free individuals"—individuals neither personally dependent as in pre-capitalism nor objectively or materially dependent as in capitalism—which is a *classless* society. With the disappearance of classes, there is also no political power, no state, and so no "workers' state" either in the new society.[1] Indeed, *The German Ideology* emphasises that the "organisation" of the new society is "essentially economic".

What about the idea of the "dictatorship of the proletariat" which MM says is "synonymous with socialism", and claims that this is also found in Marx's *Gotha Critique?* Now, the conquest of political power by the proletariat is not the end of the proletarian revolution, it constitutes, in fact, only the "first step *(erste Shritt)* in the revolution" *(Manifesto)* which continues through a prolonged period till the capitalist mode of production is replaced by the "associated mode of production", the basis of socialism. This is the "revolutionary transformation period *between* capitalist and communist society" during which the proletariat exercises its dictatorship *(Gotha Critique,* our emphasis). Marx reminded Bakunin (1874-75) that during this period capital as a relation (hence the proletariat) is still not eliminated. Hence, by definition, proletarian dictatorship cannot be "synonymous" with socialism.

A 'Workers' State'?

Let us now examine the author's affirmation of the existence of "Soviet socialism", of the "defeat of (this) socialism", and his view that the Soviet Union was a "workers' state". Now, the so-called "Soviet socialism" was neither Soviet nor socialism. It was not "Soviet" simply because the Soviets in the original sense of independent organs of the labouring people's self-rule went out of existence within a few months of the Bolshevik victory. And it would be impossible to demonstrate that there was at any time "socialism" in Marx's *(self) emancipatory* sense—an association of free individuals—in that country. On the contrary, it was a regime where—to invert Tagore's expression—the "mind was full of fear and the head held low". This "socialism" contained the central pillars of the old society—not only state, but also commodity production and wage labour—the direct opposite of the "(Re)union of free individuals". So, if there was no socialism, there could also not be any question of the "defeat" of socialism.

In fact, there is no evidence that even the accession to political power by the Bolsheviks signified a proletarian or socialist revolution (or at least its beginning) in Russia in the sense of Marx, that is, a revolution which is the outcome of the "autonomous movement of the immense majority in the interest of the immense majority." The so-called October Revolution was neither initiated nor led by the labouring people of Russia. Their role was simply to follow the "leaders". In October 1917, the fate of over 170 million people was decided by a handful of non-proletarian radicalised intelligentsia—far removed from the site of the real process of production and exploitation, unelected and unrevocably and totally unaccountable to the labouring people at large.' Through the substitution of a whole class by a single party, power was seized under the slogan "all power to the soviets" not from the Provisional government but really *from the soviets themselves*, the authentic organs of labouring people's self-rule created by the *self-emancipatory* countrywide spontaneous popular uprising in February 1917.

This pre-emptive strike was perpetrated independently of and behind the back of the Congress of Soviets depriving it of the right of maternity/paternity regarding the founding act of the new order. Not only did the Soviets ceased to exist (by the summer of 1918), but also another set of workers' self-governing organs created in workplaces by the factory workers before October—the factory committees—lost their autonomy and were simply annexed by the trade unions dominated by the Bolsheviks. The destruction of the labouring people's self-governing organs by the (single) Party power settled once and for all the question of the existence of a "workers' state" in Russia, as affirmed by MM uncritically following the claim of the regime's rulers.

Completely contradicting Lenin's pre-October promise of destroying the old state machine and introducing a "Commune-state" in Russia with election and recall of all position holders, there was "organised introduction of party members at all levels into every branch of the administrative apparatus, and the key positions in the administration were filled by party nominations". The new power "instead of smashing the old (tsarist-bourgeois) state machine", had simply taken it over intact and "perfected it". How strange on the part of Lenin to have regretted this fact later, having himself presided over the complete liquidation of the self-governing organs of the labouring people and the consequent birth of bureaucracy right at the start of the regime.

A Socialist Regime?

One wonders how the regime is compatible with "socialism" in Marx's sense. We should stress that bureaucracy was further strengthened by the total absence of free elections after the last and freest countrywide election to the constituent assembly in early 1918 and the "denial of the right to exist to all the dissidents of the revolution beginning 1919". Working in the same direction was the introduction of press censorship and prohibition of newspapers and periodicals critical of the regime. What a contrast with the 1871 Commune! "The Commune had been an entirely democratic regime, based on universal suffrage, a variety of parties, the liberty of press and association, even of the adversaries of the Commune". Indeed, soon began the mass disenchantment and unrest among the workers. After the initial feeling of triumph, mass dissatisfaction of the working people was followed by open conflict, repression of the mass protests, and at an "extraordinary" meeting of the delegates from 15 major metal working plants of Petrograd at the beginning of April 1918, the Bolsheviks were denounced for "assaulting the workers' movement with the tsarist methods". This trend continued throughout 1918 finally reaching the Baltic fleet.

Much of the mass unrest and opposition to the regime arose out of the very difficult economic situation of the workers faced with extreme hunger and cold. There was, however, one place —Kronstadt—whose working people understood better than elsewhere the nature of the new power which in their eyes had turned out to be a Party dictatorship going back on the Party's earlier October and pre-October promises. Thoroughly disillusioned, they rose against the Party power with the slogan "all power to the Soviets, not to parties", and "down with counter-revolution of the Right and the Left". "It was essential for the Communist Party", wrote, an eminent historian, "to suppress the idea of Kronstadt as a movement which defended the principles of the October Revolution against the Communists — the idea of a third revolution". And, on the completely false charge of collaboration with the Whites, the movement was bloodily suppressed. Thus ended "a bustling, self-governing Soviet democracy the like of which had not been seen in Europe since the Paris Commune" wrote the unmatched historian of Kronstadt, Israel Getzler. Such, then, was the "workers' state" in Russia even under Lenin, long before the "oriental despot" came to power.

REFERENCES

1. On Serge's testimony, on the eve of the October seizure of power, the membership of all the revolutionary parties of Russia taken together amounted to less than 1% of the total population and of this latter percentage the Bolsheviks constituted only a fraction. And, of course the decision to seize power was certainly not taken by the agreement of the party as a whole. It was the work of literally a handful of persons constituting party's "leadership".

9

On a 'Marxist' Post-mortem

Cem Somel

This chapter is with reference to Markar Melkonian's 'A Marxist Post-mortem of Soviet Socialism' which claims that a rigorous analysis of the Soviet transition to capitalism calls for a revision of the concept of class and necessitates a reassessment of the economism in Soviet Marxism.

Since the demise of the Union of Soviet Socialist Republics (USSR) and the restoration of capitalism in the former socialist countries, socialism has been reduced to a failed, discredited project. Since then, social movements have been struggling to stem the bourgeois "reforms" intensifying social oppression and expanding the exploitation of human beings and nature. Social movements resisting the onslaught are on the defensive and have been losing ground because they lack a common social project that would meet the demands for justice. The correct diagnosis of what went wrong with the socialist project in the 20th century is crucial for laying out a fresh undertaking that should prove more viable than the real socialism of the 20th century. The diagnosis is necessary for the new project to transcend the failures of the past. Any attempt at reviving the socialist ideal must confront the honest question: "Why did the Soviet working class not defend the Soviet Union?"

A historical-materialist account that explains the demise of the Soviet Union and the restoration of capitalism there should logically enhance and enrich the historical materialist understanding of history. Marxism was the official ideology of the USSR. How did historical materialism enable the ruling party (the Communist Party of the Soviet Union) to steer the country towards the restoration of capitalism? A Marxist post-mortem of Soviet socialism should explain what was wrong in the theory and in the implementation of Marxism in the USSR. It should suggest lessons for avoiding the historical errors of the past.

Historical materialism should incorporate in its corpus the socialist experience of the 20th century. Only then can Marxism become a political force again, and not dwindle to an academic peculiarity.

Why did the Soviet proletariat not resist and prevent the legal transition to capitalism in 1992? This is the question. Whether the people of the former USSR now rue this transition or not is beside the point, as are comparisons of productivity or social indicators before and after the legal transition. A post-mortem diagnoses the causes of death, not what happens to the corpse thereafter.

A rigorous analysis of the Soviet transition calls for a revision of the concept of class. Classes are not created by legislation; rather the obverse happens: ruling classes legislate. If we define class as "a social group, composed of members with a common position with respect to *the control of the distribution of the surplus,* and who pass on these positions to their offspring" we can see that the transition was carried out in the USSR by a class who already was wielding this kind of economic and political power. Legal ownership of means of production is only one of the institutions for controlling distribution. Control over access to education, control over taxation and public expenditure, control over social security policies are other effective instruments for distributing the surplus.

It is superfluous to quibble over whether there was a class ruling in the USSR in the 1980s, or whether there was a "class-in-the-making". Nepotism among the nomenklatura and their blatant economic privileges were the norm in the USSR already under Leonid Brezhnev. The ruling class in the USSR and the class social formation there may not have an established name in Marxist theory. This does not disprove that the USSR (under Brezhnev at the latest) had evolved into a class society; it only shows that Marxists still refuse to apply historical materialism to the study of the USSR.

The definition of social class by control over distribution also helps resolve another theoretical problem. Marxists have been unable to observe classes in non-European social formations (Indian, Ottoman, Chinese, etc.) because of the fixation on defining classes by the ownership of the means of production. Defining classes by their position in the control over the surplus is sufficient to recognise classes both in capitalist and non-capitalist class social formations.

To return to the issue: The proposition that classes are to be diagnosed by their position with respect to ownership of the means of production was the very tool used to blind the working people in the USSR to their subjugation and exploitation. The USSR officially held that it was a classless society, because there was no private property in the means of production.

But when did classes actually emerge in the USSR? This calls for a detailed study of diminishing social mobility, increasing control over higher education, increasing concentration of material privileges and power in families of the party elite in the USSR.

The analysis of the transition to capitalism in Russia also necessitates a reassessment of the economism in Soviet Marxism. It was held that with the alleged abolition of classes, problems of gender, environment, ethnic and religious identity had been solved or had become irrelevant. So the "dictatorship of the proletariat" became a repressive apparatus over any proletarian who might protest the destruction of the environment, who might take exception to manifestations of Russian "overlordship", who might protest religious persecution, who might inveigh against gendering or gender discrimination. Repression did not solve these problems. As the Soviet ruling class corrupted the state, these social grievances surfaced with a vengeance.

As long as Marxism is fixated on economic exploitation based on property relations, and ignores other forms of exploitation and the various forms of oppression in hierarchical social structures (whether it be in the family, in trade unions, in state bureaucracies or in communist parties) it cannot explain why working people in the USSR did not resist its dismantling.

Historical materialism has to incorporate the 20th century experiences of real socialism if it is to provide any guidance for socialist struggles in the future. This calls for concrete analyses of forms of exploitation and oppression in social formations where no private property exists in the means of production.

Melkonian identifies Marxism with historical materialism and describes the latter "as an interdisciplinary social science framework, unifying in one way or another fields of anthropology, political economy, political science, sociology, and historiography, as well as social and political philosophy and perhaps philosophy of science. Either that or it is an alternative discipline, a science of history and society that could eclipse these conventional social sciences and philosophical fields". If Marxism and historical materialism have become as disconnected from political action as the above conception—and the consequent post-mortem—implies, then they are doomed to insignificance in the real world of social struggles.

10

Post-'Post-mortem': A Response to Chattopadhyay and Somel

Markar Melkonian

Paresh Chattopadhyay in an earlier chapter 'On a Strange Misreading of Marx: A Note' has raised terminological objections and differences of historical interpretation. He believes that I have used the terms socialism, communism, and dictatorship of the proletariat in ways that Marx himself would not have endorsed. According to Chattopadhyay, my claim that socialism is a state of affairs distinct from and transitional to communism "has no textual basis in Marx". Socialism, he says, is the more encompassing term, and communism refers to a higher stage of socialism.

Without conceding that my use of these terms is at odds with Marx's frequent usage, I wish to point out that Marx and Engels did not use these terms in the same way throughout their careers and in all contexts. In one context, for example, Marx described communism as "the riddle of history solved", while in another context it designated a social order which, once achieved, would inaugurate the "real history" of our species. It is not at all surprising that these terms would have taken on different meanings throughout the four tumultuous decades of Marx's career as a thinking fighter. This is especially the case in view of the fact that Marx had remarkably little to say about the post-capitalist future. His 10,000 pages of unfolding theoretical work contain perhaps 100 pages of descriptive references to socialism or communism, and much of this takes the form of negative claims and warnings against concocting "recipe books for the cook shops of the future".

Chattopadhyay notes that subsequent figures who had been influenced by Marx, notably Lenin, typically (but not always, I would add) used the terms socialism, communism, and dictatorship of the proletariat as I have used them. What Chattopadhyay might call "the higher form of *socialism*", Lenin called "the higher form of *communism*", or simply "*communism*". A perusal of one or two high-traffic online dictionaries of Marxism might be enough to make the case that, if there is anything like a prevailing usage by Marxists near and far, then I come close to it. I see no advantage in adopting an uncustomary usage, for the sake of a *Marxological* point that, in any case, is disputable.

We do appear to agree, at least, that the "higher stage" of a post-capitalist order will be communism, with or without a preceding adjectival phrase.

When it comes to Chattopadhyay's discussion of the term dictatorship of the proletariat, there is more agreement. Chattopadhyay reminds us that, according to Marx, the conquest of political power by the proletariat is not the end of the proletarian revolution, but is rather the first step in the social revolution. The much longer revolutionary process, he notes, "continues through a prolonged period until the capitalist mode of production is replaced by the 'associated mode of production.'" This protracted "revolutionary transformation period between capitalist and communist society" is what Chattopadhyay identifies as the dictatorship of the proletariat.

Indeed, Chattopadhyay's remarks bolster my claim that the term dictatorship of the proletariat is synonymous with socialism. Chattopadhyay avoids this conclusion only because he ascribes a less-familiar meaning to the word socialism. Let us place the two alternative vocabularies side by side: according to Chattopadhyay, Marx is supposed to have held that political revolution will inaugurate (a) a more prolonged revolutionary phase of proletarian dictatorship[1], followed by (b) the lower stage of communism or socialism, and then, eventually, (c) the higher stage of communism. According to my preferred vocabulary, by contrast, political revolution will hopefully inaugurate (a) proletarian dictatorship or socialism, which then in the fullness of time will segue into (b) communism—that *is* to say, a social order in which classes and the workers' state have disappeared and the communist mode of production prevails.[2] The reader is free to decide for himself or herself which of these alternative vocabularies is preferable.

This sort of terminological disagreement is not unusual among Marxists and communists, and I suspect that it is a reflection of some deeper malaise. I suspect it is just one more signal (as if we needed any more) that, despite mounting inequalities, exploitation, disenfranchisement, warmongering, and despoliation of the planet, there is nothing today that one could properly call an International Left.

Historical Interpretation

This delivers us to the issue of historical interpretation. The Soviet Union, Chattopadhyay writes, was neither Soviet nor socialist. It was not Soviet because the Bolsheviks soon shut down the Soviets and factory committees, or transformed them into what Stalin later called "convey or belts" of the party and the state. Nor was it socialist, insofar as socialism is the self-emancipation of the working class, because the Bolsheviks substituted a single party for a whole class. I do not entirely disagree with these claims, but the interpretation strikes me as excessively one-sided. Here I wish only to register two observations:

> On the eve of the October Revolution, Lenin viewed Russia as the weak link in the chain of imperialism, a link which if shattered would set loose revolutionary forces in the industrialised West. Lenin explicitly connected prospects of socialism in Russia, prospects for building the dictatorship of the proletariat, to the success of the political revolutions in the West. As we know, Revolutions did indeed break out in Germany in 1919 and elsewhere, but unfortunately for a generation of Europeans, these revolutions were put down with truncheons and lead. After the defeat of the revolutions in the West, and finding themselves economically decimated, embargoed, besieged and invaded, dire

> circumstances forced Lenin and the Bolsheviks to hunker down, switch gears, and pivot, in an attempt to salvage something of the revolution.

Surely these considerations should inform our evaluation of Lenin and his comrades, just as similar considerations should inform our evaluations of, say, Spartacus, Mazdak, Thomas Muntzer, or Ambedkar.

With reference to the caricature of the ruthless and manipulative Leninists, Ronald Suny's book, *The Baku Commune*,[3] presents a fascinating and very different picture of Bolshevik power under the most desperate of circumstances. The brief, turbulent existence of the Bolshevik-led Baku Commune contrasts sharply—with Kronstadt when it comes to the democratic practices that Chattopadhyay endorses—universal suffrage, multiparty elections and governance, democratic accountability, and active Soviets and factory committees that drew their support from the militant, multinational oil indusuy workers. Beset by foreign intriguers, riven by bloody ethnic conflicts, surrounded, isolated, and ultimately doomed in the path of an advancing foreign army, Stepan Shahumyan, the "Lenin of the Caucasus", was able to somehow organise for the common defence and welfare of Baku, all the while keeping a tight lid on even the most defensive acts of revolutionary violence.

Class and Post-Soviet Russia

In his critical comments ('On a 'Marxist' Post-mortem', Cem Somel appears to believe that I hold that the Union of Soviet Socialist Republics (USSR) was at some point a classless society. On the basis of this assumption, *it* seems, he asks rhetorically, "But when did classes actually emerge in the USSR?" I hope I did not create the impression that the USSR was ever a classless society Stalin's preposterous announcements notwithstanding, the Soviet Union most certainly was a class-divided society, from the beginning to the end.

I probably contributed to the confusion by inadequately defining a class as a social group "composed of members with a common relationship to ownership and control of the means of production". Somel, by contrast, defines a class as "a social group composed of members with a common position with respect to the control of the distribution of the surplus, and who pass on these positions to their offspring". Somel's definition of "class" is closer to my definition in a primer that I wrote in the mid-1990s:

> Class. A large group that differs from other such groups in a society in the following four ways: (1) the place it occupies in a given mode of production; (2) its relationship to possession, legal ownership, or control of the means of production; (3) its ability or inability to appropriate a surplus product, in a manner determined by a given mode of production: and (4) the share of total social wealth its members have at their disposal.[4]

Somel's definition is more clear and concise than my formulation above, and it is more accurate than my definition in the post-mortem article. Moreover, his definition importantly includes the addendum that class membership involves the transmission of positions of control (or relative powerlessness) to progeny.[5]

Somel is on target, too, when he writes that a correct definition of a class will allow us to see that the transition to capitalism was carried out in the USSR by a social group that had already wielded economic and political power. This group included high party functionaries, high-ranking bureaucrats in all-union and republican ministries, and managers of large firms. Members of this group and their close kin made up part of the Russian, republican, and regional nomenklaturas. Later in the process, in one locale after another, the nomenklaturas joined in a tense, frequently adverse alliance with upstart New Russian "oligarchs". Russia's post-Soviet rulers and bosses, then, emerged from deep within the Soviet order, by way of complicated processes that historical materialists are especially well-equipped to describe.

Somel poses what he rightly considers to be a crucial question: Why did the Soviet proletariat not resist the transition to capitalism in the early 1990s? We will probably agree on elements of a partial explanation, including the role of the party in controlling, demoralising, and ideologically disarming generations of workers, and stripping them of the very institutions that were supposed to represent them and advance their interests. Because state security agencies, schools, and the state-run media were also under their control, any independent activity by workers was bound to be disorganised and easily routed. Defeat fed into popular disillusionment and passivity, even as the top bosses and bureaucrats were coming together rapidly as an incipient capitalist class.

Somel writes that whether or not the people of the former USSR now rue this transition is beside the point. "A post-mortem", he writes, "diagnoses the causes of death, not what happens to the corpse thereafter". But surely autopsies serve prospective purposes. What happens to the corpse—or what does not happen to it—is often a clue to both the immanent cause of death and the ultimate cause. In the case of the USSR, what did not happen to the corpse was the resurrection of Russia in a new body. In the past 20 years, Russian workers have seen their living standards and birth rates plummet, and "surplus deaths" skyrocket into the millions. And yet till just recently, Russian workers have remained quiescent. Surely these post-Soviet developments have a bearing on the common claim that the USSR fell because it had become clear to everyone that capitalism could do a better job of delivering the goods. It seems to me that this is an important insight, with obvious political significance for the medium-term future.

Theory and Practice

Somel poses the question: "How did historical materialism enable the ruling party (the Communist Party of the Soviet Union) to steer the country towards the restoration of capitalism?" My response—as automatic as it is perhaps too neat—is that what was wrong with the implementation of Marxism in the USSR was that it was not implemented, at least not since the first years after the October Revolution. If Soviet policy makers could for decades deny the class character of the USSR, then how could they be said to have implemented Marxism at all? Whatever one may wish to call the official ideology of the Soviet Union during Stalin's tenure, Marxism did not inform Soviet policy any more than John Locke and

Jeffersonian democracy inform United States policy today.

Of course, this raises more questions than it lays to rest, including the question: Why was socialism not implemented? And, the more ominous question: Is it even implementable? I suspect that the answer to the latter question might be: no, socialism could not have been implemented in 20th century Russia, even by the most principled and sagacious Marxists. We did not have a failure of Marxism here, or even primarily a failure of leadership; the disaster that was the leadership of the USSR after Lenin was more a result of much deeper failure than a cause of it. Comparing the state of the Russian Federation today to its immediate predecessor, it has become clear that the problem with Soviet Russia had much more to do with the fact that it was *Russia* than that *it* was *Soviet.* What Somel has called the "failed, discredited project" of 20th century socialism was the failure of attempts to build socialism on a non-capitalist foundation. On this point, too, Lenin's post-revolutionary fears have been realised, and Marx and Engels have been vindicated, unfortunately, for most of us.

Somel appears to hold the common view that Marxism per se is both a political commitment and a theory of society or history. So when I describe Marxism as a research programme, he concludes that, "If Marxism and historical materialism have become as disconnected from political action as [Melkonian] implies, then they are doomed to insignificance in the real world of social struggles".

Theory and class struggle are interconnected, of course. Perhaps they are even dialectically interrelated. Theory is itself a kind of productive practice, and the class struggle is inseparable from mental conceptions. Beyond these observations, though, I am not sure that there is much more that needs to be said under the heading of theory and practice. Marxists have spilled much ink expostulating on the subtleties of the unity of theory and practice, but here is still a distinction to be drawn between a class allegiance and a social science. In any case, to put it bluntly, I would rather run the risk of theoreticism than invite the vagaries, repressions, and disasters of a resurrected "proletarian science".

But perhaps Somel has posed the problem wrongly. Perhaps the problem is not so much that historical materialism is disconnected from social struggles, but rather the reverse. Marxists might take a brief recess from the hand-wringing and self-flagellation to reflect on the fact that when workers in Eastern Europe and Russia embraced the opponents of Marxism, they were the first and the worst to lose. Identity politics has been worse than a failure, and the massive movement with the revealingly un-Marxist title, the "anti-globalisation movement", has disappeared with hardly a trace.[6]

When workers have relinquished class analysis, they have lost benefits for which their predecessors had fought long and hard.

With due respect to Somel, what we have witnessed in recent decades is that when political action is disconnected from Marxism, the social struggles are doomed to failure, co-optation, or worse. In the welter of escalating social struggles today, from Tahrir Square to Red Square, and from Liberty Square to the Niger Delta, those with a stake in sweeping transformation need to accurately identify their enemies, to appraise their resources, and to formulate realistic goals. The most clear-sighted environmentalists, the most militant union activists, the most perseverant fighters for women's rights, the most determined enemies of imperialism— they all need fighting Marxists and thinking communists, in the most ecumenical sense of the word.

REFERENCES

1. I assure that we agree, too, that the term dictatorship of the proletariat has tyrannical implications. The relevant contrast-term is dictatorship of the bourgeoise, which describes a wide range of political orders, including the class dictatorships that obtain in even the most liberal capitalist democracies today. Since workers greatly outnumber capitalists, the prospect of socialism holds the hope for greater democracy.
2. I use the verb forms "will inaugurate" and "will segue", but of course there is nothing inevitable about any of this.
3. *The Baku Commune, 1917-18: Class and Nationality in the Russian Revolution* (Princeton, NJ: Princeton University Press, 1972).

4. Markar Melkonian, *Marxism: A Post-Cold War- Primer* (Boulder: Westview, 1996), p. 134.
5. Somel's definition would have better served my purposes of describing the gestation of the Nomenklatura within the USSR, and distinguishing between them and the upstart New Russians who comprised many of the most powered and visible members of the so-called "oligarchs".
6. A notable exception is the creation of alternative media outlets.

11

The Crisis of the Left

Prabhat Patnaik

The Indian Left is facing a crisis at present, of which the electoral reverse suffered by it in the 2009 and 2014 Lok Sabha elections is but a mundane expression. This crisis, in my view, is essentially a theoretical crisis, not just in the obvious sense that in a philosophy that sees theory and praxis as an integrated totality, every practical setback must ipso facto reflect some theoretical failure, but in the more basic sense of its having developed an implicit theoretical ambiguity at its core. Since this crisis can be overcome only by overcoming the lack of theoretical clarity that exists *practically* at the moment, I shall mainly deal here with certain theoretical issues. For doing so, however, I shall begin with some preliminary remarks on Marxist theory.

There is a theoretical ambiguity in the Left that underlies this crisis that the Indian Left now finds itself in. On the issue of industrialisation, the real issue is whether it occurs through subservience to the logic of capital or it occurs without compromising the dialectics of subversion of the logic of capital. Subscribing to the view that the only immediate choice is between "development" and an attempt to overthrow the system negates any scope for Left politics.

The scope for Left politics arises by rejecting this binary choice, by transcending the problematic that the only immediate choice is between subservience to the logic of capital and attempting to overthrow the system. Transcending this problematic is precisely the resolution of the theoretical crisis of the Left. And the possibility of politics that is created thereby will also resolve the practical crisis of the Left.

1

Capitalism according to Marx constitutes a "spontaneous" system (to use Oskar Lange's (1963) term), in the sense of being self-driven, in accordance with its own immanent tendencies. This view has profound implications for our perceptions of capitalism and socialism. For instance, the "individual" who is supposed to "arrive" under capitalism as a "free agent" turns out to be no more than a mere mediating agency through whom these immanent tendencies work themselves out. (Marx himself had seen the capitalist as "capital personified", i.e. the capitalists' actions did not reflect the exercise of "free choice", but were themselves "dictated" by the immanent tendencies of capital which trapped the capitalists into a Darwinian struggle that made them act in particular ways.) It would follow from this that even "individual freedom" was possible only under a system that overcame spontaneity, viz. socialism.

Likewise, if there are immanent tendencies arising from the economic functioning of capital, then it would follow that politics in a bourgeois society must be driven by economics, i.e. the political arrangement must be such that it does not thwart, but on the contrary carries forward or at least permits the realisation of the immanent tendencies of capital. From this it would again follow that authentic democracy, where people become subjects of their own history, is possible only under a system that overcomes spontaneity, viz. socialism, where the operation of the economy is shaped by people exercising political control over it, i.e. where politics drives economics. In short, the case for socialism arises from the fact that capitalism as a spontaneous system is incompatible with human freedom; freedom can be realised only in a system that overcomes this spontaneity, viz. socialism.

Of course, there may be historical conjunctures where the balance of class forces may be such that the proletariat and its allies acquire sufficient weight to exercise political power to thwart the realisation of capitalism's immanent tendencies, to "reform" capitalism to make it more humane. But such "reforms" make the system dysfunctional, necessitating either further "reforms" in the direction of further socialisation of the ownership of the means of production, or a slide-back to a situation where the immanent tendencies of capital get realised in an unconstrained manner. In short, every systemic intervention in the functioning of capitalism sets off either a dialectics of further intervention or a dialectics towards the negation of such intervention, or, as I would put it, either "a dialectics of subversion of the logic of capital" or "a dialectics of subservience to the logic of capital".

Two Kinds of Dialectics

I mentioned above that every systemic intervention sets up either of these two kinds of dialectics. But the systemic intervention itself, and the prevention of such intervention, are themselves part of these two alternative kinds of dialectics. We can therefore say that class struggle under capitalism takes the form of effecting either one of these dialectics—either the dialectics of subversion of the logic of capital or the dialectics of subservience to the logic of capital.

It follows that Marxism is not a "stage theory": it does not say that the dialectics of subversion of the logic of capital must begin only at a certain "stage", only when capitalism has reached a certain "stage", that there is some optimum time when the proletariat, and the party that brings theoretical comprehension to its ken, should "launch" this dialectics of subversion. On the contrary, this dialectics of subversion is inherent in class struggle; the proletariat's access to socialist theory, brought to it by the revolutionary intellectuals, only ensures that class struggle is conducted "scientifically", and hence *productively*, and leads to the overcoming of "spontaneity", i.e. to socialism. True, the *success* of the dialectics of subversion in going beyond the system would depend upon the conjuncture, but the unleashing of the dialectics of subversion is intrinsic to the system, is part of its existential reality. Every strike, every act of resistance, every protest against subservience to the logic of capital, is ipso facto a part of the dialectics of subversion, which therefore is organically linked to the system itself.

Dialectics of subversion

It follows, then, that any group of intellectuals, or any political formation, that advances a "stage theory" and advocates on its basis a postponement of, or a "temporary" withdrawal from, the dialectics of subversion of the logic of capital, necessarily gets detached from the proletariat and its allies, and willy-nilly becomes a part of the dialectics subservience to the logic of capital. Of course, to say that proletarian political formations must always be part of the dialectics of subversion of the logic of capital is not to say that they must always and immediately be engaged in attempting a revolutionary overthrow of the system. That is naive and ultra-Left. The dialectics of subversion is not synonymous with the immediate attempt at revolutionary overthrow; to argue otherwise is to assert, entirely erroneously, that being ultra-Left or accepting the dialectics of subservience to the logic of capital, are the only two alternative courses of action.

Remarkably, however, the spontaneity of capitalism extends even to a spontaneous tendency towards overcoming the dialectics of subversion. And this occurs through the process of centralisation of capital. Capital is always coming together in larger and larger blocks, but workers take time to overcome their fragmentation. Hence the process of centralisation of capital is simultaneously a process stealing a march on the workers, of overcoming the resistance of the workers. For instance, if 10 capitalists own 10 factories, then the workers in any one of them can strike for and even obtain a wage increase. But if all 10 factories are owned by one capitalist then he can always shift production from one particular factory to another, thereby defeating the striking workers in any one particular factory, *unless the workers in all 10 factories come together under one organisation and strike together.* Since the latter takes time, centralisation, which is part of the spontaneous tendency of capitalism, constitutes also a spontaneous mechanism for stealing a march on the workers, for overcoming the dialectics of subversion. In particular, when centralisation takes the form of globalisation of capital, where capital can move freely across nations but workers are organised at best within individual nations, the ability of capital to overcome the dialectics of subversion to its logic gets considerably strengthened.

Centralisation of capital, I just mentioned, constitutes an immanent tendency of capital. But one can go further. The downgrading or displacement, not just of small capitalists, which is what centralisation of capital refers to, but of peasants, petty producers, artisans, fisherfolk, small traders, retail shopkeepers, and independent craftsmen by big capital, which is under the command of the big bourgeoisie, is an inherent trait of capitalism, an immanent tendency that is of crucial importance in societies like ours.

2

The post-Second World War period was one historical conjuncture when the balance of class forces within capitalism in the metropolis, especially in Europe that had been ravaged by the war, favoured the proletariat. In France and Italy, the communists emerged as by far the most significant political force; in several other countries, the social democrats came to power on working class support, including in Britain, where Winston Churchill, the war-time prime minister, was defeated in the post-war elections despite having acquired a halo during the war. Though the introduction of Keynesian demand management, together with welfare state measures, within the capitalist system, meant defending capitalism immediately against the socialist threat, it also meant a systemic intervention in the functioning of capitalism.

In Third World countries, decolonisation brought, outside of the socialist countries, independent bourgeois-led states into existence, which, even while building capitalism in their respective countries, did so within a *dirigiste* regime. Third World *dirigisme,* even while building capitalism, entailed, in deference to the legacy of the anti-colonial struggle, a systemic intervention in capitalism, a fact that led even an astute observer like Michael Kalecki to categorise such regimes as "intermediate regimes" under the hegemony of the petty bourgeoisie. This categorisation was off the mark, since *dirigisme* was ushering in capitalism, and not some alternative system of "state capitalism" (the state capitalist sector, or the public sector, as it existed, helped the development of capitalism), and hence the state could be characterised only as a bourgeois-led state; but it recognised that there was something different about this capitalist development, that it was capitalist development marked by a systemic intervention in what capitalism normally looks like.

Check on Immanent Tendency

One aspect of this intervention in countries like India that concerns us here is that it kept in check the immanent tendency of capitalism to downgrade and displace petty producers, especially small traders, middle and rich peasants, and small capitalists. On the contrary, large segments of the peasantry were offered cheap credit from nationalised banks (which had to meet a target in this regard), subsidised inputs, assured prices backed up by a procurement mechanism set up by the state, extension services, protection from the world market, and insulation from the vicissitudes of the world price movements. The fact that the benefits of such measures were unevenly distributed across the peasantry, and that they ushered in a process of capitalist development in the countryside, based both on the erstwhile landlords and rich peasants (not to mention "gentlemen farmers" from urban areas), should not obscure the role they played in checking the immanent tendency of large capital to downgrade, destroy and dominate petty production.

The process of centralisation of capital, taking the form of globalisation of capital, especially of finance, and the formation on the basis of it of an "international finance capital", has played a crucial role in replacing these *dirigiste* regimes by neoliberal regimes, and in reimposing upon countries, both in the metropolis and in the Third World, the dialectics of subservience to the logic of capital. This change from *dirigisme* to neoliberalism in countries like India has been accompanied by a change in the position of the big bourgeoisie: from asserting its relative autonomy vis-a-vis imperialism, and hence, despite collaborating with imperialism, representing in a certain sense *national* interests and *national* aspirations with regard to imperialism, it has got closely integrated with international finance capital and seeks a strategic alliance with imperialism.

Crisis of Peasant Agriculture

But the neoliberal regime has once again brought in its wake the tendency towards the downgrading and decimation of petty production, exhibited above all in our country through a crisis of peasant agriculture that has led to 1,84,000 peasants committing suicide. But it is not only the peasantry and the petty producers who are the victims of neoliberalism. Large segments of the working population have seen an increase in their hunger and penury in the neoliberal period.

Just one bit of statistics will suffice to make the point. The proportion of the rural population having less than 2,400 calories per person per day, which is the official definition of "poverty" in India, has increased between 1993-94 and 2004-05 from 74.5% to 87%; and the proportion of the urban population with less than 2,100 calories per person per day has increased from 57% to 64.5% over the same period.[1] But the increase in distress caused by neoliberalism also makes it possible to build a united resistance against it. In particular, neoliberalism creates the historic possibility of forging a worker-peasant alliance.

The political survival of capitalism has hinged crucially upon the fact that it has been able historically to enlist the support of the peasantry against the proletariat, with the argument that an attack on capitalist property will be followed by an attack on peasants' property. It is this that caused the fall of the Paris Commune: the French peasants' support for Thiers rather than the Communards was crucial in the defeat of the Commune. On the other hand, the success of the Bolshevik Revolution and subsequent socialist revolutions was because of the ability of the working class to enlist the support of the peasantry.

Historic Opportunity

In countries like India where bourgeois leadership over the anti-colonial struggle could not be replaced by working class leadership, the reason for it lay in the bourgeoisie's continued sway over the peasantry (which is why the post-independence *dirigiste* regime took steps to thwart the immanent tendency of capital to downgrade and destroy petty production). Neoliberalism loosens this sway because it unleashes this immanent tendency which had been held in check during the period of *dirigisme.* This creates a historic opportunity for the success of the dialectics of subversion of the logic of capital. In short, the Left, far from facing a crisis, should, for this reason at least, be making great advances in the present conjuncture.

3

Needless to say, the task of carrying forward the dialectics of subversion of the logic of capital falls not just on the political formations and mass organisations of the Left, but also on the state governments run by them. The fact that the Left in India ran three state governments is indicative of its political importance and of the popular support it once enjoyed. It is an achievement that the Left could once take satisfaction from. But the significance of this achievement lies precisely in the fact that it is as much a *result* of the dialectics of subversion of the logic of capital, as a means of *carrying forward* that dialectics.

Two Constraints

There are however two obvious constraints that come in the way of the Left governments, and, by implication of Left mass organisations which cannot pursue a trajectory completely independent of the Left governments, in carrying forward the dialectics of subversion. One is the role of the urban middle class. As capitalism in India runs the risk of losing peasant support, it has succeeded in garnering to itself the support of the urban middle class, which has done well from globalisation and the neoliberal policies unleashed by it. Unlike in Latin America where financial crises, caused by the phenomenon of financial liberalisation, have given rise to deep real crises, having an adverse impact not only on the workers, peasants and agricultural labourers, but also on the urban middle class, in India no such deep crises have occurred in the neoliberal era that could make the urban middle class disillusioned with the system.

This new-found support base of the system is ironically a result of the Left's intervention itself (which does not of course mean that the Left should not have intervened the way it did). The Left's successful resistance to financial liberalisation and capital account convertibility has stood the economy in good stead, in warding off the sort of financial crises that have affected every other major region in the world apart from China. This has resulted in the maintenance, till now, of a high growth rate in the real economy, whose beneficiaries have been not the workers, peasants, petty producers and agricultural labourers, but, apart from the big bourgeoisie, the "financial class", the landlords and sizeable capitalists in both urban and rural India, the urban middle classes. They have developed a stake therefore in the neoliberal regime and have become a major new prop for the big bourgeoisie and a source of local support for imperialism.

Difference between India and Latin America

This is a major difference between India and Latin America and explains why the Latin American Left has been in the ascendancy while the Indian Left is facing a "crisis": the latter has not yet garnered the support of the peasantry which would be forthcoming in the new situation, even as it has lost ground among the urban middle classes, who have *as yet* been beneficiaries of the neoliberal dispensation.

The importance of the urban middle class however lies not just in its numbers. It is the class from which the literati, the media-persons, the academicians, and the "makers of opinion" are recruited. Just as it plays the historic role of producing the elements that act as the carrier of revolutionary ideology to the proletariat, likewise it can also play the role of producing the elements that act as the carrier of the ideology of subservience to the logic of capital to the same proletariat. Which elements come out predominantly from the urban middle class at any juncture depends inter alia upon the material experience of the urban middle class itself. The urban middle class therefore can play the role in certain conjunctures, such as the one that prevails in India today, of ideologically subverting the dialectics of subversion of the logic of capital, even by exerting influence on sections of the Left to proceed in directions that are contrary to its historical mission.

The second constraint arises from the enormous pressure on state governments exercised by the central government that is the main driving force behind neoliberalism. The fiscal squeeze on state governments is the chief instrument for exercising such pressure. Given this overall fiscal squeeze, the central government works relentlessly, through a variety of weapons, to impose upon state governments, including especially the governments led by the Left, the dialectics of subservience to the logic of capital. These weapons include: a host of centrally-sponsored schemes, designed by agencies like the World Bank, which the state governments have practically no option but to accept; a continuous pushing of the "Public-Private- Partnership" model for developing everything under the sun from infrastructure to higher education; an entrapping of states into a syndrome of competing against one another in offering concessions to capitalists for initiating "development"; and so on. Class struggle, in short, is refracted through centre-state relations, with the former being the agency for pushing upon the latter an agenda of subservience to the logic of capital.

4

These pressures, being exerted on the one hand by the urban middle class that wants "development" within the neoliberal regime so as to create even better opportunities for itself, and on the other hand by the central government that represents big bourgeoisie interests and hence presses for a strategic alliance with imperialism and closer integration with international finance capital, to the detriment of the mass of working people, become particularly powerful because they act in a certain theoretical-ideological context. This context consists in the prevalence within certain segments of the Left of two specific theoretical positions.

The first believes that globalisation is a "modernising" force and hence the Left should not turn its face against it. This is an old argument that has always enjoyed a certain currency in progressive-liberal circles. Its fallacy consists in the fact that, as in "dual economy" models in economics, it sees society as consisting of two *disjointed* segments, the modern and the traditional, without looking at the dialectical interrelationships between the two.[2] The fact that the so-called "modernity" engendered by the penetration of imperialism, much like the "modernity" introduced by colonialism, has the simultaneous effect of strengthening anti-modernity is missed by it.

Diverse Ways

This strengthening happens in diverse ways. Sometimes it is a direct fallout of imperialist strategy itself, such as in Iraq where US invasion has had the effect of exacerbating the Shia-Sunni divide and destroying the secular fabric of that society. Sometimes it is the unintended consequence of, or the response to, an imperialist-supported "modernity", such as in Iran, where imperialist greed for oil led to the installation of the Shah, whose systematic and brutal victimisation of the communists and progressive nationalists left the space open only for the Islamic clerics to emerge as the principal opposition.

Sometimes, as in Afghanistan, the "anti-modernity" used as part of imperialist strategy changes into an anti-imperialist movement and comes to haunt imperialism as a Frankenstein's monster.

In short, any acceptance by the Left of imperialism as a "modernising" force and hence a dilution of anti-imperialism for that reason will have the effect of permitting the anti-modern forces to don the mantle of anti-imperialism, and hence of actually thwarting "modernity". The only agency under whose aegis "modernity" can develop in societies like ours is the Left, for it alone combines a "modern" outlook with implacable opposition to imperialism that squeezes the people. Any compromise in this implacable opposition on the ground that imperialism too is after all a "modernising" force, only has the effect of weakening the Left and strengthening the "anti-modern" elements in society. But, as mentioned earlier, there are segments within the Left that get impressed by the so-called "modernity" of imperialist globalisation, and this creates conditions for the dialectics of subservience to the logic of capital to take root even within the Left.

The second position, related to the first, believes that India's integration into the world of globalised capital, and the associated set of neoliberal policies, is leading to the development of "productive forces" in the country (of which the high growth rate being experienced by the Indian economy is taken as evidence), and is therefore historically progressive. Since a mode of production becomes historically obsolete only when the relations of production underlying it become a fetter on the development of the productive forces, capitalism in our country has not yet fully run its course. The Left-ruled state governments, therefore, should use the as-yet-unexhausted potential of capitalism for developing the productive forces in their respective states.

Four Problems

There are four basic problems with this argument. First, it is a throwback to the "stage theory" discussed earlier, and is therefore methodologically erroneous. The question at any moment before the proletariat and the political formation that arms it with theory is not whether to accept or oppose capitalism, but how to carry forward "the dialectics of subversion of the logic of capital" *even while working towards the development of the productive forces within a bourgeois society*, a task that may have fallen upon the Left in a particular conjuncture. Not to recognise the centrality of this latter question, as mentioned earlier, will lead to an isolation of the Left from the proletariat and its allies, i.e. from the basic classes.

Second, this argument is methodologically wrong for another reason, namely, it restricts the immediate choice only to the binary opposites of accepting or opposing capitalism, which is analogous to the binary opposites mentioned earlier: subservience to the logic of capital, or attempt at an overthrow of the system. This is the immediate binary choice that both the ultra-Left and the neoliberals pose before us. Indeed the ultra-Left position and the neoliberal position are identical ("identity of opposites"), in that both believe that the only immediate choice before society is either subservience to the logic of capital or an attempt to overthrow the system. This problematic is wrong.

Third, the conception of the "development of the productive forces" it puts forward is extremely narrow. The development of productive forces refers neither merely to the level of technology[3] nor merely to the mass of "things" that the society can produce at any time. The concept includes the development of the "producers" themselves. As Marx had said in *The Poverty of Philosophy*:

> For the oppressed class to be able to emancipate itself, it is necessary that the productive powers already acquired and the existing social relations should no longer be capable of existing side by side. Of all the instruments of production, the greatest productive power is the revolutionary class itself. The organisation of revolutionary elements as a class supposes the existence of all the productive forces which could be engendered in the bosom of the old society.

It follows from this that the dialectics of subversion of the logic of capital, without which there can be no "organisation of revolutionary elements as a class", is itself a part of the process of development of productive forces under capitalism. To think of the development of the productive forces separately from carrying forward this dialectics of subversion is wrong.

And finally, even if we take the "development of productive forces" in the narrow sense as referring only to "things", subservience to the logic of capital is neither necessary nor sufficient for Left-led state governments, even within a bourgeois society, for ushering in such development. It is not sufficient because all states are vying for capital investment, and mere subservience to the logic of capital will not be enough to attract capital investment. It is not necessary because, notwithstanding all the hurdles placed by the central government, alternative means of undertaking investment, for example, through the public and cooperative sectors, do exist and can be used. Indeed, such alternatives can be used to put a ceiling to the level of accommodation that can be provided to the capitalists, to set, as it were, a "reservation price", that clearly indicates that the state government can go thus far and no further. Using these alternatives therefore is an important part of a strategy of carrying forward the dialectics of subversion of the logic of capital even while carrying out the task of "developing the productive forces" within a bourgeois society.

5

But, it may be asked, what concretely does "subversion of the logic of capital" mean? For the political formations and mass organisations of the Left it has a clear and well-known meaning. But what about the Left which has considerable presence in some states? There is no formula that the Left there has to follow, but subversion of the logic of capital must mean checking wherever possible the operation of the immanent tendencies of capital and insulating the "basic classes" in every possible manner from the consequences of these tendencies. Given the constitutional limitations on these governments and the enormous pressure exercised by the union government to make all state governments subservient to the logic of capital, this is not an easy task, but the nature of the task is clear.

It certainly means preventing all direct forms of primitive accumulation of capital, such as the forcible dispossession of the peasants from their land for "development", or the forcible curtailment of the activities of the fishermen (such as what a new central government legislation is threatening); but it also means preventing less directly visible forms of primitive accumulation, such as through turning the terms of trade against peasants and petty producers (which is what the Indo-ASEAN Free Trade Agreement will entail for large segments of Kerala's petty producers). The state government may not always *succeed* in preventing all these measures, but it has to struggle against them and also provide whatever succour it can within its limited means against the adversity they cause. It also means making full use of whatever residual welfare schemes exist within the central government's budget, struggling for more such schemes, struggling to rid them of their neoliberal integuments, and formulating schemes at the state level within the limited means at the disposal of the state governments to provide succour to the basic classes against distress, since every such succour strengthens the ability of the "basic classes" to struggle. And above all, as already mentioned, it must mean enforcing a "reservation price" vis-a-vis capital, by having alternative possibilities of effecting investment other than through the enticement of capital. To say all this is not to suggest that the Left-led governments are not doing these things, but they must be seen as part of an alternative *strategy*, a strategy of subversion of the logic of capital, rather than as a set of mere empirical measures. The acceptance of a theoretical perception with a conscious focus on such an alternative strategy alone will overcome the Left's current theoretical ambiguity.

Industrialisation

An example will illustrate the need for this perception. Much debate has taken place recently about the need for industrialisation in West Bengal. While many critics of the Left have argued against industrialisation, if not always explicitly then at least implicitly, they have been rightly criticised for taking a "Luddite stand". The capacity of modern large-scale industry to generate employment is limited, so that the hope that such industrialisation will absorb labour reserves to any significant extent is a far-fetched one (which indeed is an argument for exploring the possibilities of industrialisation in a more comprehensive sense, going beyond the mere implanting of modern large-scale industrial units). But, even if such industrialisation does not significantly absorb labour reserves, insofar as the products of such industry are used in the country, not having such industries would entail reliance on imports, on foreign loans, and hence eventually on imperialism, which must be avoided.

Hence opposition to industrialisation, even in the sense of implanting modern large-scale industrial units, lacks validity. But the real issue is not whether industrialisation occurs or not, but whether it occurs through subservience to the logic of capital or whether it occurs without compromising the dialectics of subversion of the logic of capital. The issue in short is not one of "use-values", i.e. what *thing* is produced, but of relations of production, i.e. whether the production of the *thing* jeopardises the Left's role in carrying forward the dialectics of subversion.

Subscribing to the view that such a dialectics of subversion is impossible for the Left if it leads state governments, that the only immediate choice is between "development", a euphemism for subservience to the logic of capital, and an attempt to overthrow the system, which is what both the "development advocates" and the ultra-Left would want us to believe, negates any scope for Left *politics*. The "development advocates" would conclude from this view that the Left must abandon its politics and become subservient to the logic of capital; the ultra-Left would conclude from this view that the Left should abandon its politics and join insurgency. Both are wrong. The scope for Left politics arises precisely by rejecting this binary choice, by transcending the problematic, common to both the ultra-Left and the neoliberals, that the only immediate choice is between subservience to the logic of capital or attempting to overthrow the system. Transcending this problematic is precisely the resolution of the theoretical crisis of the Left. And the scope for politics that is created thereby will also resolve the practical crisis of the Left.

REFERENCES

1. These figures are taken from Utsa Patnaik's 'Neo-Liberalism and Rural Poverty in India', *Economic & Political Weekly*, July 28, 2007.
2. I have developed this argument at greater length in a 2002 essay 'The Antinomies of Transnationalism'. See my *The Retreat to Unfreedom* (New Delhi: Tulika Books, 2002).
3. See in this connection Georg Lukacs' review of Nikolai Bukharin's book *Historical Materialism* (republished in 1966). In his 'Technology and Social Relations' In *New Left Review*, 1966.

12

West Bengal's Next Quinquennium, and the Future of the Indian Left

Sumanta Banerjee

In the aftermath of the defeat of the CPI(M)-led Left Front in West Bengal (in the 2009 15th Lok Sabha Elections, the 2011 15th Assembly Elections, and the recent 2014 16th Lok Sabha Elections) the popular mood hovers between hope and fear about the new Trinamool Congress-led government. The new government will not live up to the aspirations for *poribarton* (change), for it is closely bound to the neoliberal order. As far as the CPI(M) is concerned, Singur and Nandigram were the last straw on the camel's back that provided the trigger for the popular explosion of anger and frustration that had been gathering steam over the years. What does all this mean for the future of the party and the Indian Left?

By rejecting a thoroughly discredited CPI(M), and opting for a highly dubious Trinamool Congress (TMC), the West Bengal electorate have reversed and replaced the old dictum with a new one: "A half-known devil is better than a well-known one."

On the one hand, the CPI(M) has paid the price for its unpardonable crimes and misdeeds while heading a Left coalition government in that state during the past three decades. On the other hand, during the next five years, the electorate will curse themselves for bringing to power an equally unscrupulous—if not worse—Trinamool Congress-led coalition.

But at the moment, both the victors and their supporters are in high spirits. Mamata Banerjee's triumph can be attributed to her skill in tapping into (i) the reservoir of accumulated mass anger against the outrages committed by the CPI(M)'s arrogant leaders, cadres and panchayat heads in the vast countryside; (ii) the desperate need of the urban middle class to get out of the CPI (M)'s stranglehold on civil society, which determined every stage of their professional careers from appointments to promotions, and commandeered every step in their quotidian existence from buying a house to selling it; and (iii) in the absence of a better alternative, the ultimate choice for both these unhappy sections of the electorate to vote for the only available option— the Trinamool. But it is a Pyrrhic victory for the party— to which I shall return later.

Mamata Banerjee provided a platform for the coalescence of two tendencies among the voters—partly their visceral anti-CPI(M) attitude, and partly their hope for a *poribarton* or change in terms of better governance, education, health facilities and employment. Their choice was not political, but purely existential. It is this that differentiates the anti-incumbency verdict of 2011 from that in 1977.

Without Ideological Vision

In 1977, the West Bengal electorate were offered an alternative political package of socio-economic reforms and restoration of democratic rights that was presented by the CPI(M)-led Left Front (as opposed to the Emergency-tainted Congress). That it betrayed us in carrying out its promises is a different story into which I shall go in a while. But in contrast to the political ethos of the Left programme in those days—however deficient— today's Trinamool leadership lacks any ideological vision of change either in politics, economics or culture. Unlike the ideationally bound homogeneous multiparty Left Front of 1977, the Trinamool is a party based solely on the charisma of a single personality who has usurped some of the Leftist slogans, and drawn a heterogeneous medley of supporters ranging from ex-Congressmen, disgruntled Left intellectuals and opportunist Maoist cadres to retired senior police officials and right-wing representatives of big industrial interests. In fact, her election campaign represented an interesting unique selling proposition (USP) in the West Bengal electoral scene, marked by a deft mix of a populist image of a pro-poor leader (dressed in a crumpled sari and living in a humble house in a crowded middle class locality) and simultaneously of a media-savvy politician adept in the modern technological gimmicks of press-button solutions and instant recipes—like her slogans assuring ten lakh jobs (aimed at the skilled unemployed), and the reported promise to change Kolkata into London (to meet the tastes of the upwardly mobile upper middle class youth). Despite all her claims of loyalty to *Ma-maati-manush* (mother, the indigenous soil and their people), the colonial model of London still prevails over the mindset of the chief minister of West Bengal. That provides the key to the future contours of the state's economy under her rule.

The two electoral trends—the negative vote of a rejection of the Left Front, and the positive vote for the promise of a better governance under the Trinamool—coexist in an ephemeral zone where the popular mood however between hope and fear about the new government. This ambivalence has not escaped the notice of the corporate sector—the most important stakeholder in the coming economic fortunes of West Bengal. In the midst of the media hype in anticipation of Mamata Banerjee's victory, on the eve of the announcement of the results, it was a representative of this sector that hit the nail on the head, when he wrote:

> Very few people seem to want to vote for her—but everyone wants to vote against the CPM (sic), which means that ...Bengal hates the CPM more...which means that performance will be key to Mamata's survival...which means West Bengal will be wide open for political competition... (Surjit S. Bhalla, Chairman of Oxus Investments, *Indian Express*, May 13, 2011).

Mamata Banerjee's political survival for the next five years is ensured by the overwhelming majority which she enjoys in the legislature. But how will her performance during this period make any difference, in bread and butter terms, to those who voted her to power?

Poribarton or *Protyaborton?*

These were the two terms that were bandied about between the Trinamool and the CPI(M) during the election campaign—the former promising to bring about a "change" from the three-decade old failed Left Front monopoly of power, and the latter urging the voters to "return" it to power to enable it to fulfil its long-forgotten promises that were made in 1977. Now that the Trinamool has won on the platform of *poribarton*, the new government will have to live up to the aspirations for change inspired by Mamata Banerjee. The popular expectations can be summed up in the following order of priorities: (i) immediate restoration of the much-needed peace in the countryside—which had been ravaged by years of violent intimidation by power-hungry local CPI(M) leaders and cadres; (ii) end to the prevailing corruption in the operations of the public distribution system, the panchayati administration, and the centrally-sponsored schemes like the rural employment programmes; and (iii) a reconstruction of West Bengal's economy and society on the basis of provision of jobs, guarantee of social justice, and delivery of civic services.

But on all these hopes, there hangs a pall of uncertainty and fear. The hope for peace is clouded over by the vendetta mounted by the Trinamool cadrès—as evident in the recent killing of some CPI(M) followers and vandalising of its party offices in a few areas. If this trend increases, it will pose a challenge to democratic rights activists who till now had opposed such violations of human rights by the CPI(M) *harmads* (pirates) only, and joined the Trinamool in its electoral campaign to defeat the Left Front. The fear is further accentuated by the composition of the newly-elected 184 Trinamool MLAS—69 of whom are facing serious criminal cases (based on the declarations of these candidates themselves, as compiled by the Association for Democratic Reforms and New Elections Watch). West Bengal is on the way to joining the North Indian mainstream, where history-sheeters appear to be the favourites of the electorate. As for corruption, those who elected Trinamool party candidates to panchayats in the West Bengal countryside a year ago have already discovered to their chagrin that they are no better than their CPI(M) predecessors, and are following the same route of nepotism and siphoning off of public finds to their personal coffers, that had been earlier institutionalised in the rural areas by the Left Front. In fact, an MP from the Trinamool Congress itself, the poet Suman Kabir, soon after his party's candidates occupied the panchayats, came out openly against their looting spree, describing them as gluttons who scream: "Khao...khao..!" (eat...and eat more). Yet, the rural electorate voted for the same Trinamool in the assembly elections. It suggests their mood of utter helplessness and cynicism. They accept the reality that Trinamool, like any other party coming to power, will perpetuate the corrupt order, but hope that it may at least for the time being restore peace and ensure delivery of essential services.

Mamata and Corporate Interests

Coming to the larger issue of a long-term programme of rejuvenating West Bengal's economy, Mamata Banerjee is a babe in the woods, totally innocent of the challenges that she will be facing. They are more intractable than those she handled during her stint as the union railways minister—in the course of which she made a mess, what with her profligacy in inaugurating new high speed trains every now and then without any concern for financial viability or safety of passengers, leading to both loss of revenue and rising accidents. Judging by her record as a union minister, we are waiting in trepidation lo watch how she, as a chief minister drives the "Duronto" (the favourite term of hers—which in Bengali means both powerful and unmanageable—with which she has named her newly introduced trains!) administration of West Bengal.

To start with a few much-vaunted promises made by her: how is she going to return the 400 acres of land, which are still in the legal possession of the Tata-owned small car project in Singur to their original owners? Even if after those lands are restored to the farmers—may be through the government's enormous financial compensation to the Tatas, or a time-consuming judicial process—they cannot resume cultivation since the agricultural fields have been flattened into cemented roads. Does Mamata Banerjee have any programme to restore or rehabilitate the victims of her anti-Tata campaign in Singur? Or, how is she going to provide ten lakh jobs at the drop of a hat? The backlog of an industrial labour force that had been rendered jobless due to closures and lockouts (acquiesced in by a passive Left Front government all these years) await reemployment. Where are new factories going to come up? In the continuing contest over acquiring land for industrialisation, she will soon concede to the demands of the industrial tycoons whom she is wooing to invest in West Bengal.

It is no coincidence that she has appointed the FICCI head honcho Amit Mitra as a minister in her cabinet. But how is she going to put into order the financial mess of West Bengal—heavily burdened with a debt of about Rs two lakh crore (the legacy bequeathed to her by an overindulgent Left Front government which had wasted most of that amount in subsidising salaries of its idle employees in Writers' Building in Kolkata and district headquarters, of absent teachers in schools and colleges, and incompetent doctors in medical hospitals)? While a friendly centre can certainly bail her out with a favourable economic package, given the prevailing structure, such financial help is likely to be siphoned off again into fattening the same old corrupt and inefficient institutions, and a new group of politicians and their hangers-on, under the Trinamool regime—as already apparent from the experience with the panchayats ruled by that party.

It just takes one step backward for any newly elected ruling party to retreat from the electoral promise of *paribarton* for the masses, to the post-electoral comfortable cushion of *protyaborton* —or a return to the old habits of self-aggrandisement, use of the police to repress protests, and the restoration of the same inequitable and oppressive order. These habits acquire legitimisation under the neoliberal order of globalisation, where the individual pursuit of private profit is promoted as a sign of economic growth and as more important than the public need for healthcare, education, housing and other basic rights. Despite Mamata Banerjee's promise of meeting these public demands, her government, being bound to the neoliberal order, will have to make a right-about turn, and traverse the same trajectory that had been initiated by her predecessor—the Left Front. It is worthwhile therefore to briefly examine that itinerary. I shall be concentrating primarily on the CPI(M), as it is regarded as the main voice of the Parliamentary Left—both in its role as the leader of the erstwhile Left Front government in West Bengal for the last three decades, and its current position as a minor opposition party in the Lok Sabha and national politics.

Beginning of the Rot

Most of the commentators trace the defeat of the CPI(M) to its suicidal handling of the situation in Singur and Nandigram in 2006-07, and discern signs of the beginning of its fall, first in the routing of its candidates in the panchayat elections that followed it, and later in the 2009 Lok Sabha polls. In other words, they feel that it was only during the last phase of its rule (2006-11) that the CPI(M) made serious mistakes which alienated it from the people. My contention is that the roots of the disaster can be traced back much farther to its earlier phases—long before Buddhadeb Bhattacharya launched his disastrous mission of forcing multinational-sponsored industrialisation down the throats of suspicious farmers. Singur and Nandigram were the last straw on the camel's back. They provided the trigger for the popular explosion of anger and frustration that had gathered steam against the ruling CPI(M) all these years—on various counts.

In fact, rumblings of discontent against the Left Front had started reverberating within a few years of its assuming office, though less publicised and confined to a few areas of concern. One such issue was human rights. Although the CPI(M)-led government kept its electoral promise of releasing all political prisoners (the majority of them being its erstwhile enemies, the Naxalites), it failed to punish or remove the notorious police officials who were nailed for atrocities from 1970 till the Emergency period, by the two commissions set up by the government itself—the Sharma Sarkar Commission and the Haratosh Chakravarty Commission. Instead of following up their recommendations to reform the police administration, the

West Bengal state home ministry (which was under the charge of the veteran Chief Minister Jyoti Basu) reinforced the old system of using the same police force and its disreputable officers and minions to suppress demonstrations of popular protest.

Marichjhapi and After

One of the first such instances was the unleashing of the police in Marichjhapi in 1979—two years after the Left Front came to power. The Left had earlier promised to resettle the refugees from the erstwhile East Pakistan in West Bengal. Assured of that promise, a few thousand refugee families (who had earlier been relocated by the Congress government to Dandakaranya in the then Madhya Pradesh) arrived in the Sunderbans to settle down there. In a curious volte face, the CPI(M)-led Left government retaliated by arresting them and forcing them to return to Dandakaranya. But a large number of these families managed to slip through the police cordon and reach Marichjhapi in the dense forests of the Sunderbans, where they cleared the jungles and started cultivation. The Left Front government accused them of violating official laws like the Forest Act, and threatening the lives of the renowned Royal Bengal Tigers! It launched a police operation to forcibly remove these refugees in May 1979—which led to the killing of a large number of men, women and children, whose bodies were allegedly dumped into the river. (The long-suppressed history of this episode has been unravelled by Ross Mallick in his well-documented essay 'Refugee Resettlement in Forest Reserves: West Bengal Policy Reversal and the Marichjhapi Massacre' in *The Journal of Asian Studies*, Vol. 58, No. I, February 1999.) The years following Marichjhapi saw the re-emergence of the police as a trigger-happy force ready to suppress all manifestations of popular discontent. In the two-year period of 1980-81 alone, there were at least 248 cases of police firing killing 62 people, including women and children. During the same period, the number of killings of under-trial prisoners in police lock-ups and jails showed an alarming increase—recalling the days of the Emergency. It had reached such an extent by the end of the

Left government's third term in office, that in 1992 Justice D.K. Basu of the Calcutta High Court had to intervene, censure it and ask it to follow strict procedures to prevent torture and death in police custody. But, typical of the CPI(M)'s insensibility to human rights, its government preferred to defend its sadistic cops and went to the Supreme Court to challenge his recommendations. In 1996, the apex court issued its verdict in the *Basu vs State of West Bengal* case, which essentially upheld Justice Basu's opinions and laid down 11 requirements regarding the arrest, interrogation and investigation.

Agrarian Constituency

Despite its atrocious record on the issue of human rights, the CPI(M) however made impressive gains in the agrarian sector during its first five years of rule by distributing land to the peasantry, ensuring the rights of sharecroppers, raising the wages of daily labourers, and decentralising power through panchayats. But by the beginning of the 1980s, it had reached a dead end of sorts. Its failure to anticipate that the small size of holdings (available to the rural poor through land redistribution) would yield inadequate income; its indifference to the need for state investment in agricultural inputs and infrastructure to help these small farmers; its lack of a long-term plan of agro-industrial enterprises to provide jobs for the unemployed rural youth led to a stagnation in the rural economy. It was not as if the CPI(M) leadership was unaware of the signs of the impending crisis. Following its return to power for the second term in 1982, on 18th September of that year in the West Bengal assembly, Bhaktibhushan Mandal—an MLA of the Forward Bloc, a partner in the ruling Left Front—warned that the owners of small plots (beneficiaries of land redistribution) were facing crisis because of the mismatch between the expensive inputs that they had to use and the poor returns from their output. He felt that unless they could supplement their income with other jobs, it would be difficult for them to survive. The CPI(M) leadership turned a deaf ear to such warnings—at the cost of alienating, through the next two or three decades, these large sections of the rural populace who were getting increasingly impoverished.

The Panchayati System

As for its second achievement—the panchayati system—the CPI(M) did indeed gain popular support from villagers who for the first time were promised participation in policy decisions at the ground level and overcoming the rules and hurdles of a bureaucratic administration. But it soon degenerated into an institution dominated by local CPI(M) and other Left Front party leaders and apparatchiks who diverted the government funds from investment in social welfare for the villagers to build party offices and their own houses (which stuck out like sore thumbs from amidst the surrounding miserable conditions, and quite understandably became the main targets of popular anger during the anti-Left agitations on the eve of the elections). Again, these trends did not suddenly appear in the 2000-11 phase of Left Front rule. The roots of the corruption were embedded in the manner in which the panchayats were composed. In the first panchayat elections held under Left Front rule in June 1978, the majority of the candidates chosen by the CPI(M) and its allies who got elected, came from the better-off middle class farmers (50.7%) and school teachers (14%), while from among the rural poor (claimed to be the main base of the Left), the sharecroppers constituted only 1.8% and the agricultural labourers 4.8%. Given this inequitable class composition in the panchayats, it is no wonder that their *pradhans* soon turned them into dens for exploitation of the rural poor through intimidation and corruption. Again, the distortion in the functioning of the panchayati system was not unknown to the top leadership of the Left Front government. As far back as 1982, its then minister for panchayats, Debabrata Bandyopadhyay (belonging to the Revolutionary Socialist Party) made a statement from the state secretariat acknowledging that the majority of the panchayat members had been found to be corrupt, adding that out of the 3,242 panchayats only 1,160 had submitted audit reports (July 19, 1982). The years that followed were marked by further moral and political degeneration of the Left-run panchayats— the bulk of which were controlled by the CPI(M).

The Industrial Sector

Let us turn to the industrial sector. The industrial proletariat are designated by the CPI(M) in its programme as the leaders of its proposed people's democratic revolution. But during all these years, while factories closed down throwing thousands of workers on the streets, the Left Front government remained a passive spectator, refusing to lift its little finger to help even attempts by workers' unions to form cooperatives and run the factories. It is not surprising therefore that the CPI(M) lost in the working class belt. The workers have punished the party for its industrial policies that have paved the way for the closure of old factories and their retrenchment, and for the entry of both new Indian and multinational concerns in the industrial scene where these workers have no scope for re-employment.

To go back to the record of the Left Front government's treatment of industrial disputes—right from the 1980s, while the workers acceded to their chief minister Jyoti Basu's advice to refrain from lightning strikes, the factory owners were allowed by him to resort to closures and lockouts. The number of strikes came down from 43 in 1981 to 29 in 1982, while during the same period 54 factories imposed lock-outs affecting the livelihood of 53,000 workers, and industrial houses announced closures of 13 units throwing out 12,300 workers. (Debashish Bhattacharya, *Bampontheera-Mahakaraner-Montri-Hoye-Ja-Korechen,* Calcutta 1983). The trend remains the same today. According to figures collected by the Labour Bureau in 2005, the number of strikes in West Bengal was 26, while that of lockouts was 182—indicating the unequal level playing field of trade union negotiations under the CPI(M) regime. The CPI(M)'s present tilt towards the multinational Salim, or the Indian industrial tycoons like the Tatas and Jindals, can be traced back to the industrial policies it adopted in the 1980s.

Through all these years of growing disenchantment among the rural people, a sense of betrayal among the industrial working class, and increasing alienation among the urban poor and middle classes, a smug CPI(M) leadership at its headquarters in Alimuddin Street in Kolkata remained totally indifferent to the warnings emanating not only from newspaper reports, but also sounded by some of their old leaders, as well as by Leftist observers and economists (from outside the official CPI(M) circle) of the impending disaster (quite often in the pages of *Economic-&-Political-Weekly*). While in a cavalier fashion they dismissed the newspaper reports as "bourgeois propaganda", they should have at least paid heed to the admonition given by one of their veteran leaders—Benoy Chowdhury (who as a minister in the first Left Front government initiated the land reform programme). Before his death in the 1990s, he openly denounced his party organisation as dominated by leaders in cahoots with "contractors and (real estate) promoters". But, the party headquarters felt that it could afford to ignore the commissions obtained by its district level apparatchiks through dubious deals with these contractors and promoters, as long as they delivered the regular monthly quota to the party coffers. Ignoring popular discontent with such misdeeds in the urban areas, the party leaders at Alimuddin Street assumed that they could retain the allegiance of their largest constituency—the rural peasantry—as bonded followers for ever, by constantly reminding and demanding from them gratitude for the reforms that they initiated some 30 years ago. But, as explained earlier, those mechanisms of agrarian reforms had already turned out to be half-way measures by the 1980s, stagnated into economic inertia in the 1990s, and degenerated into tools of partisan aggrandisement in the hands of the CPI(M) in the 2000s. Given this history of a programme that began with land reforms which empowered one generation of the rural poor, but left the next generation without any viable means of further improvement of their socio-economic status, it is no wonder that the Bengali villagers today ridicule the CPI(M)'s habit of living off its past achievements, by quoting a popular Bengali saying—*Kobey-polao kheyechhilam, ekhono hatey tar gandho legey- achhey* (We ate pilau many years ago, but its aroma still lingers around our fingers)!

Muslim Constituency

The other traditional constituency of the CPI(M)—the minority Muslim community—also discarded it this time. Yet, the Left

Front-ruled West Bengal was always regarded as the safest citadel of the religious minorities, which provided refuge to a victim of the 2002 anti-Muslim carnage in Gujarat. West Bengal has been known as a state ruled by a Left government which had always prevented the outbreak of communal riots (barring a few instances following the 1992 Babri Masjid demolition). Yet, despite the memory of Mamata Banerjee's being a part of the NDA government which presided over the massacre of Muslims in Gujarat, the Muslims of West Bengal in general voted for her. Was it a gesture of protest against the Left Front's indifference to their basic requirements—a fact substantiated by the Sachar Committee Report? In their short-sighted tactics, the CPI(M) leaders had thought that they could woo the Muslim voters by acceding to the demand of their fundamentalist mullahs to ban Taslima Nasreen's book and banish her from West Bengal. At around the same time—in order to keep the North Indian Hindu business houses operating in their state in good humour and ensure the regular flow of funds from them to the CPI(M) coffers—they threw their administrative weight behind the industrialist Ashok Todi, when he opposed his daughter's choice to marry a Muslim commoner—Rizwanur Rehman. Kolkata's top police officials were alleged to have intimidated Rizwanur and forcibly separated him from his wife Priyanka. Soon after, Rizwanur was found dead on a railway track in 2007. Investigations indicated that he could have been driven to suicide by the police officers and the Todi family. The Left Front government's refusal to punish the guilty policemen antagonised not only Rizwanur's family (which suspected that he was murdered) but also large sections of the community which felt that the CPI(M) was protecting the Hindu industrialist Todi—a sentiment which was exploited by Mamata Banerjee, who set up Rizwanur's brother, Rukbanur as a Trinamul candidate against the CPI(M).

Party Takeover of Administration

Coming to the record of the Left Front's governance in West Bengal, one expected that the CPI(M)—as a typical social democratic party promising to create a welfare state—would at least follow two rules of the parliamentary system that it had chosen to join. But, in its narrow objective of clinging to office by any means, the party defaulted first by elevating its headquarters at Alimuddin Street in Kolkata, into an extra-constitutional centre, and encouraging its district and village level party bosses to virtually take over the reins of day-to-day administration, and replace the state institutions and their officials. (An excellent inside view of this steady and calculated debilitation of the administrative machinery is provided by Kalyani Chaudhuri—a senior bureaucrat who served under the Left regime—in her book: *When the Pendulum Stops: Death of Bengal Bureaucracy* (Kolkata: Nachiketa Publishers). In the process, the CPI(M) leaders and their minions destroyed the state's educational and health infrastructure, by usurping the administration of prestigious institutions like the Calcutta University, Calcutta Medical College, appointing their own protégés (who often turned out to be totally incompetent) and allowing their trade union activists in these institutions to run the daily administration. During my visit to Kolkata in the 1990s, I listened to complaints from patients waiting at the Calcutta Medical College, about their having to grease the palms of the CPI(M) run employees' union to gain admission for treatment. I alerted my friends in the CPI(M)—both in Kolkata and Delhi—about these alarming trends. But they dismissed them as isolated instances. The second obligation of a social-democratic party operating within a bourgeois parliamentary system is the toleration of political competition in a democratic space. But the CPI(M), during its rule, squeezed that space to serve its own partisan interests, by trying to eliminate its political competitors. During successive assembly elections right through the 1990-2000 period, there were allegations that the CPI(M) supplemented its fast dwindling number of votes (which it could anticipate from its eroding popularity) with rigging (with its musclemen preventing the genuine voters from casting their votes, and instead of them the party-appointed presiding officers stamping the ballot papers in favour of the ruling party candidates). While agreeing that such intimidation had taken place (my friends in Kolkata have narrated their own experiences of similar threats that prevented them from casting their votes in the last four assembly elections), I think that the CPI(M) did not win those elections by rigging alone. It could still depend on support from a loyal core of followers on the one hand, and manoeuvre the half-hearted sections of the rural electorate in its favour on the other, since they could not find any alternative party. The successive victories of the CPI(M) in West Bengal (even after the growing disenchantment with its performance in the 1990s) were due to the party's judicious mixture of coercion and persuasion. In the 2011 election, this twin strategy did not work because of two factors. First, the CPI(M)'s coercive apparatus was kept on leash by the Election Commission, aided by the central security forces to protect the voters. Second, the CPI(M)'s persuasive appeal could not convince its rural electorate, since they perceived the Trinamool as an alternative this time.

Future of the CPI(M)

Neither the CPI(M)'s central leadership, nor its state units have shown signs of any serious introspection over the causes of their elimination in West Bengal and of any intention to radically change the party's method of functioning. While in West Bengal, the erstwhile chief minister Buddhadeb Bhattacharya and the party's vociferous state secretary Biman Bose have retreated into a sulking silence, the CPI(M)'s general secretary Prakash Karat has refused to own responsibility for the acts of omission and commission that could have led to the defeat of his party both in the 2009 Lok Sabha poll and the 2011 assembly elections. It is clear that despite being utterly disgraced, the leadership is in no mood to step down. As for its cadre in West Bengal, the mercenaries (musclemen known as *harmads*) among them will seek patronage from the new rulers; the weathercocks among the middle class professionals are already making a beeline for the Trinamool office, and the handful of ideologically-motivated old activists both in the trade unions and peasants' organisations are too demoralised to revive the party.

The latter do not find any potential leaders in their organisation who can replace the mandarins who continue to run the party from New Delhi, and the 1960s batch of student leaders who have been thrown out of power in West Bengal after 30 years. Having watched the degeneration of their party —which began in 1964 with the promise of serving the workers and peasants and ended up by being a middle class *babu*-dominated organisation turning its guns against the same oppressed classes—these honest activists will soon retreat into a state of *boshey-jaoa*—the term used in Bengali for lapsing into political inaction. In other words, since the CPI(M) will remain saddled with its present leadership which stubbornly refuse to acknowledge past mistakes and purge the organisation of corrupt and criminal elements, it will be reduced to a nonentity in West Bengal politics in the coming years. The party's national leadership is also yet to take up the more fundamental challenges—how can it stem the erosion of moral principles brought about by its obsession with the electoral rat race of populism and opportunism? How can it reconcile its role as a social-democratic party (whether in power or outside) with its mode of anti-democratic functioning that harks back to Stalinist authoritarianism?

This brings us to the implications for the future of the Left in Indian politics in general. It is about time that one makes a sharp distinction between the CPI(M) and Left ideology. As apparent from the record of the CPI(M) in power in West Bengal, the party steadily departed from its earlier commitment to the protection of the rights of peasants and workers and ultimately sacrificed them at the altar of industrial tycoons and multinational companies; it turned its back on the promise to restore civil liberties by rejuvenating a notorious police force to use it against the poor. At the national level also, the party showed scant regard for ideological principles by seeking alliance with corrupt politicians on the plea of forming a futile Third Front. The CPI(M) therefore has forfeited the right to be called a Left party, and should be treated as any other opportunist political formation (like the caste-based, or regional parties that pursue their own narrow interests with the sole purpose of coming to power), devoid of a wider ideological commitment.

Implications for the Left

There is an urgent need for a realignment of forces within the Indian Left. It should start with the rejection of the hegemony of the CPI(M), and restoration of credibility among the masses by reestablishing the long-lost links with the peasantry, industrial workers and other dispossessed sections of our society. The New Indian Left—if one may designate it—can be a broad formation of both the Left parliamentary parties (e.g. the smaller partners in the present Left Front which had been critical of "big brother" CPI(M)) and the non-parliamentary movements. It should align with the various popular campaigns taking place outside the political mainstream (e.g. Narmada Bachao Andolan, anti-POSCO movement), extend support to the civil liberties and democratic rights groups, engage in a dialogue with the Maoists, and in collaboration with all these forces, work out an alternative strategy for socio-economic change. Will the intellectuals and economists who adorn the CPI(M) list of members and sympathisers and give credibility to it, stop identifying their party as the only custodian of the ideology that they believe in, and lend their talents instead to the campaign for this new Left movement?

13

Future Perspectives for the Mainstream Indian Left

Achin Vanaik

After the 2009 and 2014 Lok Sabha Elections, the Parliamentary Left has clearly suffered so serious a defeat that it would not be out of place to describe the current situation as one of crisis. The fact of the matter is that it is not just its poor electoral showing that constitutes a grave warning but that there is the widespread sense that even as a grass-roots mobilisational force it has reached a historical trough compared to its own past. How then does this Mainstream Left seek to revive itself? Can it become a significant political and social force with the capacity to help reshape Indian politics and society for the better and in ways that can move towards a capitalism transcending a socialist future? The views presented here are personal and pertain mainly to the mainstream Parliamentary Left of the Communist Party of India (Marxist)—CPI(M), Communist Party of India (CPI) (and perhaps at a stretch to the Communist Party of India (Marxist-Leninist)-Liberation—CPI(ML)-L) excluding the Communist Party of India (Maoist) which pursues a strategy aimed at armed overthrow of the Indian state, a strategy that creates its own problems of militarised authoritarianism internally but also, in this writer's view, has no chance of success.

Insofar as the Mainstream Communist Left defines itself in relation to capitalism, what the different parties, forces and intellectuals of this Left perceive is going to be the future trajectory of global and Indian capitalism will shape their own understandings of what should be the future trajectories of the Indian Left. In this respect the Right is right: meaning that the kind of capitalist reality currently available is the only form of capitalism now possible. This is a neoliberal form of capitalism that is irreversibly rapacious ecology-wise and which can adopt a more or less human face. That is to say, it can be what has been referred to as a "compensatory neoliberalism" with an array of targeted rather than universalist welfare schemes; or a much less welfarist-inclined "disciplinary neoliberalism". What this indicates is that even the pursuit of establishing a social democratic capitalism nationally or globally, i.e. the vision of a global cosmopolitan democracy that must necessarily rest on some form of global Keynesianism, is a chimera even as a transitional goal, perspective or state of affairs.

The Left must, of course, start with and propose various social democratic perspectives such as strong welfarism, full employment, green economics, greater social and cultural rights and more empowerment of ordinary people, not because it believes that these are fully or properly achievable within capitalism but precisely because they are not! Therefore, such demands and the struggle for their achievement can be the spur towards the creation of a much more radical understanding of the need to break with capitalism as soon as possible. In short, the Indian Left even as circumstances and its own failings have put it more on the defensive than in its past, it must now be more radical in its programme and practice than ever before. Strategically speaking, even allowing for the necessity of possible tactical compromises and retreats, offence is not just the best but the only realistic strategy for it to advance. What does this mean or imply? Where is the Indian Left now at? And where does it go from here?

The Left and Its Challenges

For some 20-odd years after the collapse of the communist bloc of the Soviet Union and Eastern Europe and the capitalist transformation of post-Mao China, India was the only country in the world that saw both communist parties that are the political legatees of the Stalinist Third International and of Maoism not just survive for so long but actually grow and become more influential. This is testimony surely to the Indian peculiarity—its distinctive combination of being at the macro-level a remarkably stable bourgeois democracy yet having extraordinary levels of economic impoverishment and multiple forms of social, cultural and political oppression, often of extreme brutality.

This has allowed Stalinist and Maoist conceptions of "national development" disguised as the "true socialist project" to maintain wide appeal, even as it has meant the absence of an adequate and effective strategy for successfully confronting and undermining a capitalism encased within its "best political shell" of a genuine and real even if limited and weak liberal democracy. The end result is that the main, i.e. the biggest organised currents of the Communist Left have failed to avoid the two dangers of overall subordination, or complete negation of parliamentary politics.

Both paths have and will continue to prove dead ends for those unwilling to change the course of their politics—their theories and programmes, their organisational structures and practices. The suggestions here, as mentioned above, are directed not at all communist forces but at those which at least formally acknowledge the necessity of combining parliamentary-electoral and extra-parliamentary politics and are also formally committed to anti-imperialism, socialist internationalism and the goal of transcending capitalism. There are, in this regard, certain key guiding principles for parties and organisations pursuing genuinely transformative politics even when operating within the framework of a capitalist liberal democracy.

For such forces it is the programme that should make the party, not the other way around. That is to say, there are strict limits to the dilution of their programme and even to parts of it and to the related demands of this programme, for the purposes of accommodating strategic or even tactical alliances with other forces or for the sake of achieving power or for expanding the party's social-electoral base. Furthermore, what follows from this principle is that even as one may strive to attain provincial power within an overarching bourgeois framework, the primary purpose is not to remain in power at all costs and therefore to make programmatic and policy adjustments accordingly but to remain true to, and consistent with, the programme and its related reform projects, even if this means having to step down from power or face defeat at the polls. Compromises are sometimes necessary but must be based on principle. Defeats do take place and must be acknowledged as such. Retreats should not be disguised as useful or desirable detours.

Another key principle is that anti-capitalist parties must be cadre-based and must resist at all costs the temptation to become loose, non-cadre based parties which prioritise above all, having the widest cross-class, cross-caste, cross-gender voter base and accordingly therefore must abjure the politics of polarisation via the practices of extra-parliamentary mobilisations on progressive rather than diversionary or jingoistic causes. In fact, the only way radical left political forces can steadily advance electorally is via the successes of their extra-parliamentary mobilisational politics on the widest possible range of issues reflecting the widest range of contemporary injustices. In short, the balance between parliamentary-electoral pursuits and extra-parliamentary mobilisational activity must always be titled strongly towards the latter. But this in turn imposes two crucial realities.

First, the fate of radical left parties and their political prospects is tied above all to the character of their cadre base, even more than to their social bases which will be more variable, uncertain and fluctuating in their loyalties as can be expected, given the operative framework of a multiparty competitive system. Securing, maintaining, expanding and deepening the political-ideological consciousness, commitment, morale and moral discipline of its cadre base is paramount. Without this there cannot be the kind of ongoing mobilisational politics that must lie at the very heart of Left party politics and that must incorporate the various kinds of just struggles whether waged in the name of the politics of redistribution or of recognition, for both the politics of life chances and of life choices, for livelihood concerns and identity concerns. Cadre discipline, enthusiasm and commitment are voluntary and cannot be institutionally imposed from the top. That voluntary commitment endures only if it (a) comes from a deep belief in the righteousness of the cause, in the integrity of the guiding ideological framework, in the validity of the party programme that concretely expresses the route to the achievement of final objectives. (b) It comes from being part of an organisation whose internal culture is strongly democratic and therefore capable of continuous self-correction. (c) It comes from constant involvement in the actual struggles of the oppressed masses. What all might follow from this? One makes bold to suggest the following:

(1) Theoretical-ideological revamping—the complete rejection of the whole Stalinist tradition of politics, programme, organisation. Only in this way can there be the kind of revitalisation of the socialist cause that is necessary.

(2) Programmatic revision rejecting the two-stage approach to bringing about revolutionary change and all that goes with this perspective by way of social compromises and class alliances with this or that section of the so-called progressive bourgeoisie.

(3) Programmatic clarification that socialist democracy will be deeper and wider than bourgeois democracy, providing for even greater civic, social, cultural, economic rights as well as for the participation of many parties including those which are avowedly bourgeois and capitalist with of course the proviso that violent overthrow of a post-capitalist order is constitutionally prohibited.

Internal Democracy and United Fronts

Organisationally, any Communist Party worth the name must be structured in such a way as to be sensitive to the context in which it operates and to maximise internal democracy. Although the Indian Mainstream Left has a more internally democratic structure than all other bourgeois, Dalit or ethnic-based parties in the country (something that is invariably ignored by critics) this is far from enough.

(1) What is required is not the rejection of the principle of

democratic centralism but a recognition that this is a fundamentally political, not an organisational, concept. Insofar as a party must seek to develop a totalising and overarching vision encompassing an understanding of all forms of oppression and exploitation and of how to struggle against them, this vision can never be the property of a few leaders or theorists or the monopoly of the central committee or the politburo. It can only be arrived at, maintained, corrected and advanced through maximum freedom of debate, discussion, dispute and argument tested through practice. As in the best periods of historical Bolshevism and as the practices of its most principled legatees have shown, there must exist full freedom for party members to connect horizontally with each other, to seek intra-party political support for views independent of control by higher leadership bodies. That is to say, there must be a structure of rules and norms that allows for tendency and faction formation rights, for proportionate representation for tendencies and factions at all levels in the pyramid of leadership bodies.

(2) Insofar as India has its specificities of oppression, recognition of the importance of this means there should be reserved representation proportionate to the changing membership weight in the party for Dalits/most backward classes, tribals and women at all levels in the pyramid of leadership bodies. The value of this in attracting militants from such oppressed groups and in advancing the party's capabilities and credibility in the waging of such sectoral struggles should be self-evident.

(3) One of the greatest failures in India has been the uneasy and mutually suspicious relationship between the Left parties and the social movements independent of them. Though the fault for this is shared, it is the parties, especially the Parliamentary Left that must take greater responsibility to rectify this state of affairs. Not only must it give committed support to such movements but must also often consciously adopt a determinedly low-profile back-seat role as well as not treating such movements as primarily recruiting grounds for enhanced membership. Moreover, in legislative assemblies at all levels,

such Left parties must act as the parliamentary tribunes of progressive movements with as much determination and commitment as would be the case if such movements had their own representative leaders in such assemblies.

(4) Forging greater Left unity is a must. The view that the CPI(M) and the CPI have fundamental programmatic differences preventing their merger is frankly utterly unconvincing to those outside and perhaps many within as well, thus raising suspicions that bureaucratic wrangles and controversies over the possible spoils of office after a merger have been the main obstacles to such a development. Furthermore, the pattern of United Front (UF) behaviour has also left much to be desired. Such fronts on specific issues or on agreed though limited programmes are not mechanisms where establishing a unity of action must presume that there be unity of analysis or argument. While what unites the constituent parts of the UF is always more important than what divides them, there must also be acceptance of full freedom of debate and dispute in which different organisations will seek to express their points of view and to win over adherents to their perspectives regarding tactics to be followed or programmatic adjustments to be made. UFs are most effective when they are democratic, when they combine commitment to overall unity precisely because they incorporate freedom to criticise. Such an approach to UFs has always been anathema to Stalinist approaches where the dominant partner has invariably sought to maximise allegiance to its perspectives not through maximum freedom for political debate and criticism but through other means.

Such suggestions as presented above are far from adequate in addressing today's "crisis of the Indian Left" but they would, in the view of this writer, constitute a modest step forward in the collective effort to rejuvenate the Indian Left.

14

Who is the Problem, the CPI(Maoist) or the Indian State?

Himanshu Kumar

The adivasis regard the Maoists as their friends for it is these rebels who have stood by them. All the normal channels of redress are closed for them. The police beat them. The political parties—be they the Congress or the Bharatiya Janata Party—are with the Salwa Judum. The courts do not give them a hearing. The media does not care. Where else will they go except to the Maoists? When the police attack them, it is the Maoists who save them. In these 17 years since I have been in Dantewada I have seen how the Naxalites have worked among the adivasis. This is the fight of the poor. If the centre thinks it can crush these people, it is mistaken. Sometimes extreme oppression can embolden those who are fighting.

Seventeen years ago I went to Dantewada following Gandhiji's belief that the real India lies in the villages, and young people must go there to rejuvenate them. The villagers gave me land to build my ashram. Under the Fifth Schedule, the gram sabha was empowered to do so. But the government demolished the ashram in 2009, sending a force of 1,000 policemen, anti-landmine vehicles... That is when the adivasis finally acknowledged that I was like them! My home could also be demolished.

In the forests of Dantewada, people live like aboriginals used to, in tune with nature. Natural justice prevails there. In the jungles, there is no police, no crime. I went to Dantewada a month after my marriage. My wife and I built a hut without any walls, just a roof. I would leave my wife to travel all over Madhya Pradesh, for five to six days at a time. She never felt afraid.

Forcibly Emptying the Villages

In 2005, the Chhattisgarh government began feeling the Maoists in Dantewada were a danger. It started the Salwa Judum, which means Collective Peace Campaign. They knew the Maoists had support among the adivasis, so they decided to empty the villages. They forced the villagers out of their villages and tried to shift them into camps near police stations, at the edge of the village road. They got together a force of goondas (anti-social elements) who along with the police, would pounce on the villagers and force them into camps.

But adivasis are used to living in the midst of nature, near a stream, on top of a mountain. Each adivasi house is far away from the other. Here, the government had built sheds; you step out of one and face the next; behind yours is another one. When the adivasis tried to run away from these sheds, this "patriotic" force would shoot on them, catch them and put them in jail, rape them.

At one point, there were 54,000 people in the camps, from 1,000 villages. The government claimed it had "sanitised" 644 villages. Fifty thousand adivasis had run away to the jungle. That is when the Chief Minister (CM) Raman Singh declared that those who have come to the camps are with us, and those who have run away are with the Naxalites.

I wrote an Open Letter to the CM—as the chief of the state, "you are saying that those citizens who choose to stay in their own homes are Naxalites! And will you give orders to shoot them?" That is exactly what he did. There would be attacks on the same village again and again. The adivasis would try to come back and cultivate their land; every time they would be caught and terrible atrocities inflicted on them. Their harvests would be burnt. In such a situation, it was the Naxalites who supported the adivasis. That is why they regard the Naxalites as their friends.

The Salwa Judum forces want liquor, chicken, mutton, women; and they want these every day. They take these from the adivasis. We are blind to that. But when the adivasi picks up a lathi to oppose the police, we cry foul.

The state talks of the violence of the Maoists, but it is the state which is violent. The home minister keeps talking about peace. But how can peace come when you are constantly attacking the adivasis? Then you expect me to tell the Maoists, stop your violence. The situation has now reached a point where every outsider is looked upon by the adivasis as an enemy. The state has created a situation in which the adivasi looks upon his own fellow countryman as an enemy.

State Opposition to Rehabilitation

The Supreme Court has ordered the government to rehabilitate the villagers, compensate them. Not one village was rehabilitated, nor one adivasi compensated. On June 10, 2008, the Supreme Court gave instructions that the National Human Rights Commission (NHRC) investigate the conditions in Dantewada in the wake of Salwa Judum. Our activists took tribals from Dantewada and some of those who had fled to Andhra Pradesh (AP) to meet the NHRC team. On 11th June, when the villagers of Nendra were returning, some Salwa Judum people stopped the jeep and beat up the tribals. We phoned the director general of police, asking if it was a crime to talk to the NHRC? Nothing happened. Those adivasis were made to sign a paper saying that they were forced to give statements to the NHRC.

As a Gandhian, I got furious. In front of me people are being assaulted, only for talking to an official fact-finding team. I decided we would not move from this village. If they want to burn the village, let them burn me first. We persuaded the villagers to come back. On 1st July, we formed a human shield around the village. We stayed in Nendra for six months. We sent volunteers to bring the villagers back from AP. To their credit, they came and stayed. For three years they had been unable to cultivate their land. They had no seeds; their cattle had run away; their village had been burnt repeatedly. We arranged for their rehabilitation. That is how the first village was settled. The villagers nearby gathered courage and approached us. Our activists began repeating the same experiment there.

When the collector came to know that adivasis, escorted by our activists, were on their way to Lingagiri village, he called me up. It was a Saturday, 4.30 pm. He knew the next day, Sunday, every government office would be closed. He said all the forces were busy with elections and would not be able to provide them with any security. I told him, "when did I ever ask for security? Under the Constitution, you cannot stop anyone from going home." But when they reached the bridge, the police stopped them. The police had not been able to cross that bridge for three years. I called up the collector and asked him: "Are you going to allow people to go back home? If not, we will have to take them to the Supreme Court and tell it that you were not allowing its orders to be implemented." Everyone crossed that bridge that evening.

But the administration did not give up. They confiscated my vehicle; we had to go to court to get it released. We found that the police had taken away half the rations meant for the villagers. Who can save a police force that acts like this?

The adivasis began cultivating their land again. But once more, the police started attacking the rehabilitated villages. Still we kept on trying. Now, peace reigns in these 30 villages. Anyone can go and visit them. We have told the government—use these as a model. The people are comfortable there, so they are not interested in fighting. But the government goes on attacking them with a single aim: they should run away and then the government can give their land to industrialists for mining.

The adivasis then decided that their youngsters would guard the village from the Salwa Judum forces. They started patrolling their villages with whatever they had—lathis, field implements. They began hiding their grain in the mountains. Now the Home Minister of the last UPA government started describing these youngsters as Naxalites, saying they have taken up arms against the government.

The government does not want peace; it wants land. It is so arrogant; it does not want to accept the crimes it has committed. We have tried to file 1,000 first information reports (FIRs)—all serious crimes such as rape, abduction, setting fire to homes. They were not registered. The superintendent of police (SP) said the police would not register them because they are false complaints. The Supreme Court said a police officer cannot decide if a complaint is true or false, especially if the complaint is against the police.

Administrative and Judicial Bias

A girl came to us saying she had been gang-raped for two days in the police station. The SP did not register our FIR. We went to the Supreme Court, which asked the state government to reply. The SP said in his reply: "We asked the accused, have you raped this girl? [The accused were Salwa Judum leaders] They said, "No. She's slandering us." So that is how our police investigate rape complaints—they now ask rapists if they have raped, and decide on the basis of their answers.

When we campaigned for the release of Binayak Sen, we also wanted an end to Salwa Judum, the release of all those in detention under the Chhattisgarh Special Public Security Act, and the scrapping of the Act. Nothing happened. Now, in fact, the Act is being used against all villagers. "You gave water to the Maoists, you showed them the way—you too are an accused", the authorities allege.

Your judiciary, your administration, your democracy—you yourselves are destroying them all. Then there is not much left for the Naxalites to do! Once writing and talking become crimes—Binayak Sen was only writing, I was only talking—what do you do? Can you blame the adivasis who pick up guns in sheer helplessness?

In January, 19 adivasis were killed. Four girls were raped. We went to court. The government pleader keeps taking adjournments. The judge keeps changing. The special police officers (SPOs) killed three adivasis, and their widows filed a writ in the high court. The government replied that they were killed by Naxalites, and the women were forced by the Naxalites to file a writ against the police. The judge swallowed this.

Ordinary villagers are killed and passed off as Naxalite commanders. All we have asked for is a Central Bureau of Investigation (CBI) inquiry and ex gratia compensation. But the judge tells the villagers—"choose which camp you want to stay in; the government will look after you."

Operation to 'Hunt' Adivasis

In the first phase of Operation Green Hunt held in September, the forces had attacked an entire family. First, they stabbed the father, then the mother, then the young daughter. With rifle butts, they broke the teeth of her two-year-old son and chopped off a part of his tongue. I wanted the press to hear their stories, so I decided to take them to Raipur. The Raipur Press Club asked me for proof that they were not Naxalites. I told them that even the government is not calling them Naxalites! They decided not to allow me the use of their premises. So now the adivasis cannot go even to the media. Who will they go to?

All roads are closed for them. The police beat them. The political leaders—be they Congress or the Bharatiya Janata Party (BJP)—are with the Salwa Judum. The courts do not give them a hearing. The media does not care. Where else will they go except to the Maoists? When the police attack them, it is the Naxalites who save them. If you really want peace, put an end to the root cause of the popularity of the Naxalites.

We have tried to create conditions in which violence comes to an end. But in an atmosphere where the police cut off breasts of old women and stab old men, and rape... You can imagine what would be the fate of any policeman who falls into the villagers' hands. The state should not create such conditions. The political leaders must ask why the Naxalites are popular. Why are our democratically elected governments not popular? If an adivasi goes to the police and says, "the *patwari* took away my money", will the police go and investigate?

The day your police's guns are raised to defend the rights of the poor, Naxalism will end. If my child is creating havoc, would I not try to find out why he is acting like that? Can't the prime minister ask the Maoists: why is there so much violence?

The Naxalites have been preparing the adivasis for decades, telling them there will be a big fight. The other day as I was walking, an old man lying under a tree called out to me and asked me, *"Ladaai hogi, na?"*

That is why I tell political leaders of the mainstream parties, do not enter this area. "The adivasis are waiting; you will be trapped", I have been telling them. These adivasis are not like people in Uttar Pradesh. They can jump on you and snatch your bodyguard's AK 47. In Operation Green Hunt the forces will be killed in greater numbers than they have in Jammu & Kashmir. In September, 2009, they began Operation Green Hunt. They could not kill a single Maoist. But six COBRA jawans got killed. All they could kill were old adivasis and children. A six-year-old was stabbed; an 85-year-old was bayoneted and killed in his bed. The police are committing cold-blooded murder. Then the government asks—are you with us or with the Naxalites? I can openly say—we are not with your police. We are with those adivasis who are being killed.

Digvijay Singh wrote an article on how development is the counter to the Naxalites' influence. I wrote to him, putting forward four demands. The first is—withdraw your forces. Seven hundred villages have been cordoned off. The villagers cannot go out; no outsider can enter. If the adivasi goes to the weekly bazaar five km away, she knows the SPOs will catch her. So she goes to a bazaar that is 85 km away. It takes two days to go and two days to come back. So four days of every week were spent walking. I asked her, "why do not you buy enough rice for a month?" She replied: "We can buy rice worth only as much as we get for our mahua. If our mahua sells for Rs 20, we can bring rice worth Rs 20."

This situation is because of the state, not because of the Naxalites. Characterising those areas as liberated zones is part of the state's strategy. They can then complain that the state is not allowed to function there. It is actually the Salwa Judum that has stopped the functioning of the state. No institution of the state functions there, nor does any law. Even Article 21—the right to life—does not exist there. The adivasis are being hunted. Sometimes violence grows out of fear and helplessness.

In these villages that are cordoned off, everything has been closed down by the government. There is nothing there—no schools, no doctors. The government told the high court these are all Naxalites. The police kept saying there is no point distributing rice through ration shops because the Naxalites will loot them. So for the last five years, there has been no distribution of rice. Has any Naxalite died of starvation? The medical officers tell me, if their doctors go to treat patients in the jungle, the CRPF beats them up. If teachers go, they beat them up. They are furious—they tell the teachers, "you do not get blown up when you go in, why do we? You must be in league with the Naxalites." I tell them, "teachers and doctors do not go in with weapons like you do!"

The Dantewada collector is merrily giving permission to non-tribals to take over tribal lands. The government itself is taking over the land and giving it away. But it is because of the presence of Maoists that these companies are not able to start their projects.

Driven to the Wall

The picture we constantly get is that the Naxalites are awful, but the state is good. Ask the adivasis of Dantewada. I told some politicians, "do not talk to the Maoists, talk to those you call their victims, to the adivasis. You are their democratically elected leaders. The public is supposed to love you; you are supposed to love the public. If the public has stopped loving you and started loving the Naxalites, you must find out why."

My personal practice is non-violence. My work in the last 17 years has been to strengthen democratic institutions, to create awareness among the villagers about the constitutional rights guaranteed to them; about welfare schemes, how to fight for their rights in a democratic way. Because the Naxalites had taken up guns, we went there to strengthen non-violence! But the government called us Maoists! That is how the state works—they drive you to the wall, they harass you, and then call you a Naxalite.

Vinoba Bhave used to say about the Naxalites: "These youth are motivated by compassion for the poor. I salute them." When he began his Bhoodan movement, he set back the Naxalites by 30 years. In these 17 years I have been in Dantewada I have seen how the Naxalites have worked among the adivasis. For carrying one bundle of firewood, the forest guards would punish an adivasi woman by raping her. If they did not pay a three-rupee fine, the guards would extort Rs 300.

Then in the 1980s, the Naxalites came there. They would capture a forest guard and tie him up and ask the adivasis to beat him. That was the first time the adivasi realised they too had some power. The state should have empowered them by punishing the guards! The state never fixed a minimum price for mahua; the Naxalites did.

The adivasis had never been violent. But whenever they tried to raise their voice, the state would send the police. Why is it that the Naxalites have never been violent against me? For me they bring out the cot and give me water and say "come, guruji, sit." In the beginning, the Maoists had declared that there would be no government programme in our zone. But we carried on with our work. Now they have sent a message—we will not interfere in Himanshu's work, because he has no political ambition. People talk about Maoist violence against the police, against innocent citizens. You must go to the depth of the violence to understand it. If an SPO is killed, the government declares that an innocent was killed and the media goes to town. If an old adivasi is killed, the police say a Maoist area commander was killed. The adivasis live in perpetual fear. If you are continuously hunted, made to flee your home, and you find a place to live away from the police, then someone comes who you suspect might inform the police about your whereabouts... It happened to me once. The government had requested me to help them trace the survivors of a helicopter that had crashed in the forest. They were too afraid to go in. The families of those on the helicopter were frantic. I negotiated and went in. But the police cheated me. They promised they would not follow us, but they did. And in their typical style, en route, they looted chickens, liquor. The Maoists thought I had brought the police. They tied me to a tree and would have finished me off had they not learnt the truth. They would finish off any of their own who betrayed them.

I stayed three days in that village. There was no one over 40 years old there—they just do not live longer than that. Children were typically malnourished. There was an eight-year-old guarding us. He had a cap and a whistle, both of which he was very proud of. I asked him, "when did the police last come to your village?" He said, "two years back." What did they do? They burnt 40 homes, killed three people, raped that woman standing there. This village was just behind Bailadila; it was covered with coal dust. There was no school there. This is the Indian model of development.

Only Justice can Bring Peace

The government tells democratic rights groups—you tell the Maoists to stop the violence. But we tell the government—you tell your forces to stop their violence. Just register the FIRs the human rights groups have filed against your police. You do not do even that much and you keep asking them to spell out their stand on violence. What do you want us to say? We live there; we know the situation. Some incidents look terrible when viewed from the outside. It has happened that a group of SPOs have gone around burning village upon village. And the villagers managed to surround this very group and killed them.

In the last five years, no leader has come to Dantewada to ask the adivasis what their problems are. So I thought I would take the adivasis to Delhi. I thought there would be a huge *hungama*. I took these wounded adivasis to the Constitution Club. Nothing happened. Such is the condition of city-dwellers today; they do not care what is happening in the villages. They are the ones who want peace, they who are living comfortable lives. They want peace so that their comfort can continue uninterrupted. But those who bear the attacks—their priority is justice. Vinoba Bhave had said: "Where there's in-justice there cannot be peace". But the government will not talk about justice.

Why have lakhs of citizens taken up arms? We middle class people find it inexplicable. We live in cities; the police are for us; the government is for us. We are on one side. On the other side are those for whom there is no police, no government. They have nothing to eat. They are the ones who have picked up arms. These people have been deprived for years. There is a structure. Those who are outside this structure—this is their fight. If you were to ask—whom does all the land on this earth belong to? The answer would be to all of us. Yet, the reality is that some have more land, some less. You live in the city, so you have more. You are a Brahman, so you have more. You are educated, so you have more. The child who is born in Marine Drive can demolish the home of the child born in Dharavi. Why not vice versa?

Inequality is inbuilt into the system. All these notions about who can command more resources have become part of our value system, and then our political system. Both are supported by our economic system. These constitute the basic structure of the society. It is this structure that keeps the poor poor and the rich rich. We are content with this structure. But what of those who bear its brunt? They want to break it. This fight is against structural violence. This would not end till the structure changes so that all become equal.

The man who is in distress will fight. This is the fight of the poor. The Naxalites have just tagged on. If there had been no Marx, no Gandhi, would not the poor have fought? They do not need the Naxalites or the Gandhians. But sometimes a Vinoba, a Gandhi, or the Maoists join them in their fight. If the centre thinks they can crush this fight of the poor with the army, they are mistaken. Sometimes extreme oppression can embolden those who are fighting.

If the centre really wants peace, it can be got in a week. They should go and spread happiness among the adivasis. Aanganwadis, health services, schools—open all these again. Instead, you think you can kill them slowly by inflicting suffering upon suffering on them. If you put a rug on fire, the rug gets burnt. You send your COBRA forces and they stab an old man in his bed. You are doing exactly as the Maoists predicted you would do. They have been telling the adivasis for years that the state is an oppressor.

Today, the world over, the poor are being looked upon as a burden who are depleting the resource base. They should now be finished once and for all, so that the rest of us can lord it over the earth. The adivasis are the most vulnerable. What our government is planning is genocide of the adivasis. This is the direction in which our modern civilisation is going. Will we support this? Will you be able to kill lakhs of people? You will try. But when they rise up and kill you, you would not be able to save yourselves.

There are three types of poor—(i) those who survive on your riches—the balloon-seller, the domestic servant, construction workers; (ii) those who feel they are unworthy of being rich; they feel they are low caste, uneducated; they can never be rich; and (iii) those like the adivasis who lived happily in the forests till you invaded their land to make yourself richer. That is why they have taken up arms. And you run to the state. Once the other two categories join the third, everything of yours will be destroyed. What is our stand in this? Vinoba used to say: "To accept injustice is wrong; I will instigate the poor against such acceptance". What is happening in Chhattisgarh is not without the middle class' consent.

You are sowing the seeds of violence and mayhem. Before Salwa Judum, Maoists numbered only 5,000. After Salwa Judum, the Maoist strength grew to 1,10,000—a 22-fold increase. After Operation Green Hunt, every surviving adivasi will become a Maoist full-timer. And when the Maoists increase in number, they expand their base. They will reach Mumbai, Delhi. I feel sorry for the young men in the forces too. They lose either way. If they do not join the paramilitary and police, they will die of hunger. And once they join, they will die too, for sure. Why are you sending these young men to their death so that the wealthy corporations will benefit? You are making young people fight other young people so that those corporations may accumulate more wealth.

I appeal to you, come to Bastar; stand with the adivasis.

15

E.M.S. Namboodiripad's Perception of History

Prabhat Patnaik

E.M.S. Namboodiripad would have described himself as being engaged in the "modest" task of applying Marxism-Leninism to the concrete conditions of Indian society. But this description needs to be amended for two reasons: first, any application of theory is itself a theoretical task. It represents simultaneously a development of theory, an enlargement of the corpus of Marxism-Leninism, and hence an expansion of its theoretical frontiers, which, since there is no hierarchy among theoretical endeavours, can by no means be described as "modest". Secondly, EMS did not just delve into Marxism-Leninism to find answers to the concrete problems confronting the Indian revolutionary movement, such as the agrarian question or the nationality question. His stand on all these questions was informed by an overall reading of Indian history, and this reading was arrived at through an application of Marxist analysis to the historical "facts" about Indian society as thrown up by researchers.[1] This overall reading, since it differs so fundamentally from the classical Marxist reading of European history, marks, in a specific sense, a major advance of the frontiers of Marxism.

To be sure, the basis for this reading had been laid by Marx himself, who had been so struck by the difference between the European and Asian histories that he had developed the concept of the "Asiatic Mode of Production" as a *sui generis* category. But EMS's perception of Indian history that I have just referred to does not relate only to some phase in the pre-colonial period of Indian history. And even though he subscribed for long to the concept of the Asiatic Mode, his general perception of Indian history remained unchanged even after Marxist scholarship had moved away from the Asiatic Mode and EMS himself, in deference to the trends in scholarly research, had appeared, as we shall see, to have diluted his allegiance to this concept. It is this perception of his, in the wider sense, about Indian history, with which the present article is concerned.

EMS is unique among Indian Communist thinkers in developing such an overall perception of Indian history, and in consciously locating analyses of specific issues that arose in the context of praxis, within such an overall perception. In this sense he bears a resemblance to Antonio Gramsci who had been seriously involved in studying Italian history; and it is not surprising that late in his life he had developed a deep interest in Gramsci's work. Undoubtedly there were other Communist thinkers in India, even excluding academic Marxist scholars like Kosambi and Habib, who also wrote on Indian history. But EMS was different. He wrote neither to defend "orthodoxy", i.e. to establish that Marx's description of the sequence of the modes of production, in the classical transition to capitalism, held in the case of India as well; nor on specific themes alone. He was unique in attempting to develop, on the basis of established research, an overall sense of Indian history from a Marxist perspective. His was an authentic theoretical quest into Indian history. True, any such characterisation of EMS's work entails *reading into* his published writings a pattern and a meaning, which has necessarily got to be an ascription; but this is unavoidable for the proper assessment of a major thinker.

The main feature of EMS's perception is a recognition of the remarkable continuity in Indian history, where what appear as "breaks" or "transitions" amount really to no more than "superimpositions". Indian history, he had said at the 1971 seminar of the Indian School of Social Sciences held at Chennai, is characterised by a series of "superimpositions" which nonetheless leave certain essential features at its core unchanged. Giving a facetious example of what he meant he had added: "If Indian scientists were to send a sputnik to the moon, then before doing so they would perform a 'puja' for the success of the mission."

Perhaps EMS's route to Communism is what accounts for this theoretical quest. He was born into an orthodox Brahman landlord family and came to Communism through the social reform movement, Gandhism, and Congress socialism. A deep engagement with issues of caste, religiosity and patriarchy always remained with him, and with it, naturally, the puzzle of why this society had not grown out of this caste-based feudal system over such a long history. He brought these questions to Marxism and sought to find answers to them through the application of Marxist analysis. The novelty of his theoretical quest arose from this.

I

EMS's interest in the Asiatic Mode of Production was quite natural in this context. Marx had developed the concept precisely to explain the relatively unchanging nature of the Indian and other Asiatic societies over long stretches of time, and to answer the question: why did these societies not develop capitalism despite the fact that they had generated enough surpluses to sustain mighty empires? Marx had visualised these societies, especially India on which he had access to a variety of material emanating from colonial sources, as consisting of a number of "cells" in the form of village communities over which the mighty empires rested. The rulers changed; empires arose and collapsed, to be followed by newer empires; but the system of village communities on which these empires rested continued in its old unchanging ways, with the peasant, cultivating his "miserable patch of land", being completely oblivious to the battle, raging nearby between two rival armies, whose outcome would determine the identity of the overlord to whom he would have to hand over his surplus.

While the analytical characteristic of the Asiatic Mode was clearly spelt out by Marx, namely that the "fundamental principle on which it is based" is "that the individual does not become independent of the community."[2] On the actual historical elements underlying this principle he had an open mind and kept refining and reshaping his views as new material came his way. Marx's views on the exact historical elements that went into the making of the Asiatic Mode therefore did not reach a final definitive form. The absence of private property in land (sometimes, following the lead of the French traveller and chronicler Bernier, identified as all land being the property of the King); the unity of agriculture and manufacturing (which in turn was sometimes thought of as unity within the household and sometimes as unity within the village community without the intervention of "commodity production"); the importance of irrigation works whose maintenance required a centralised state that absorbed the bulk of the surplus, leaving little room for the emergence of any significant class of proto-bourgeoisie: these were some of the elements that figured from time to time in the writings of Marx and Engels as defining the Asiatic Mode of Production.

Historians have explored at great length if these elements existed in India in the pre-British period; and the answer seems to be in the clear negative.[3] The widely prevalent system of hereditary land grants to private individuals would suggest the existence of property relations different from those visualised by Marx. And while it is true that the surplus was commoditised, which is quite different from and lacks the impact of commodity production *per se*, even the latter had made an appearance, with cash crop production not being uncommon. As a consequence, differentiation within the so-called village community, with trade being a two-way process between town and country, had also established its presence. Whether all this would have led to a development of capitalism, either spontaneously, or, as in Japan, in conscious response to the development of capitalism in Europe, if colonialism had not imposed an altogether different trajectory on this society, remains a moot question. But, the pre-colonial Indian society was not exactly an unchanging one *in the sense that the Asiatic Mode was supposed to be.*

EMS, as suggested earlier, diluted his allegiance to the

concept of the Asiatic Mode,[4] in the sense of relying on the specific elements emphasised by Marx in developing this concept, for explaining the continuity in Indian history. But he neither abandoned his perception of this continuity, central to which was the phenomenon of caste, nor his quest for an explanation of this continuity.

He provided a provisional explanation which figured in many of his writings. The following long extract culled from one of his writings summarises his position:

> The slave society of the type that emerged in ancient Europe did not take roots here. Not because, as our chauvinists would have us believe, the Indians are more humane than the ancient Greeks or Romans, but because the break up of the ancient-primitive communist or tribal-society took place here in a way different from that in Greece and Rome.[5]

The division of the society into the exploiters and the exploited assumed here a form which in a way covered up the reality of exploitation. It was not into the minority of the owners and the majority of slaves but into the three *varnas*—the *Kshatriya*, the *Brahmana* and the *Vis*—that society came to be divided first. It was the *Vis* that came to be divided into the *Vaisa* and the *Sudra*, the latter consisting of the mass of toilers. The three superior *varnas* constituted the exploiting sect while the *Sudras* were the exploited.

This division of society into *varnas* helped the dissolution of tribal society and the formation of a new order. Its development into the *jati* system with its division of labour helped the process of developing the mode of production. The proliferation of castes and sub-castes with a definite occupation or means of livelihood allotted to each is the form in which class division originated and developed in India.

This Indian edition of slavery provided the soil on which the 'glorious civilisation' of India was built. We may thus amend Engels to say: "without caste oppression and exploitation, no civilisation or culture of ancient India."

While the division of society into the exploiters and the exploited was thus common to the slavery of Greece and Rome on the one hand and to the *varna*-caste system of India, there is a major difference between the two: the exploitation and oppression was open, naked in the Greek and Roman slavery, while it was covered up in the *varna* caste system in India.

The revolts of the slaves against their masters was quite natural for the Greek and Roman society; the exploited and oppressed castes and sub-castes in India, on the other hand, reconciled themselves to their 'inferior' position in society which was sanctified by religious scriptures. This prevented a repetition of the revolts witnessed in ancient European society, revolts which led to the revolutionary replacement of slavery by a feudal society which was followed by the anti-feudal revolts out of which arose the modern bourgeois society.

As opposed to this two-stage transformation, slave to feudal and feudal to capitalist, in Europe; India remained tied to the same old order under which the overwhelming majority of the people belonged to the oppressed and backward castes. This is the essence of what Marx called India's "unchanging" society where the village was not touched by the wars and upheavals at the higher levels, the British conquest being the first revolution.

The ideological hegemony of Brahmanism contributed to the stagnation of Indian society, not just by preventing a revolt of the exploited classes; it did so in another way as well, which EMS elaborated somewhat later, basing himself on the work of the Marxist philosopher, Debiprasad Chattopadhyay. And that was by arresting the growth of science and technology, and hence of the productive forces beyond a point. Chattopadhyay had argued that the triumph of Brahmanism under Adi Shankara represented not only a reinforcement of the caste system in the country, but a demise of science and hence of advances in technology. Paradoxically according to Chattopadhyay, the much-celebrated philosophical triumph of Adi Shankara was the harbinger of a dark age when India lost the edge it had in scientific advances in mathematics, astronomy and other branches of learning, because of both the ideological and the social implications of the triumph. Ideologically it was a triumph of idealism over materialism; and since, as Lenin had said in *Materialism and Empirio-criticism*, a scientist must be a materialist in practice, this represented a setback to science, and hence to technological advance. Socially, since the practitioners of technology, the artisans and craftsmen, were those who typically belonged to the "lower castes", the counter-revolution ushered in by Adi Shankara meant a social downgrading, and hence implicit devaluing, of technological advances.

Chattopadhyay, on the basis of J.D. Bernal's work, had contrasted this with the case of Europe, a contrast that EMS accepted. Talking of the European Renaissance, Bernal had said: "What was really new was the respect given to the practical arts of spinning, weaving, pottery, glass-making and, most of all, arts that provided for the twin needs of wealth and war, those of the miners and the metal workers. The enhancement of the status of the craftsman made it possible to renew the link between his traditions and those of the scholars that had been broken almost since the beginning of the early civilisation."[6] EMS concluded that "the defeat of the oppressed castes at the hands of Brahmanic overlordship, of materialism by idealism, constituted the beginning of the fall of India's civilisation and culture, which in the end led to the loss of national independence."

EMS's explanation, somewhat different from the Asiatic Mode theory but proposing its own version of an unchanging village community, did not of course provide a *materialist* explanation for the phenomenon of continuity, and its underlying stagnation; but it did draw attention to the phenomena of continuity and stagnation and to the self-perpetuating character of the caste-based feudal society, which neither generated any internal dynamics by way of technological progress, nor faced any external disruption by way of major advances in trade (such as the external disruption in Europe caused according to Henri Pirenne by the opening of the Mediterranean trade) that could have subjected it to the "dissolving influence of commerce". (The progress of commodity production in late Medieval India, which was noted above, and which EMS also underscored when he drew attention to the growth of commercial and usurious capital[7], but not manufacturing capital, in the pre-colonial society, was obviously too feeble to break the back of the caste-based feudal society).

II

EMS's position on the nationality question is in conformity with this historical perspective of his. According to standard Marxist theory (articulated by Stalin in this instance) the coming into being of linguistic nationalities is associated with the formation of a unified market, since a common language facilitates such a formation. This in turn makes the emergence of linguistic nationalism a part of the process of the emergence of the bourgeoisie to a position of ascendancy. In the English context for instance, the Elizabethan era can be seen as the period of emergence of linguistic nationalism (Shakespeare being the prime product of this era), and simultaneously of a bourgeoisie to a position of ascendancy, from where it launches a bourgeois revolution in 1640 against the anti-bourgeois Stuart monarchy.

This perception however creates a conundrum in the Indian context: how does Marxist theory look at the Bhakti movement? If the Bhakti movement is seen as marking the formation of linguistic nationalities, then standard Marxist theory would suggest that this period must have been marked by the emergence of a bourgeoisie to a position of ascendancy. On the other hand if the formation of the modern bourgeoisie is seen to have occurred in the colonial period, then we cannot apply the term "linguistic nationalities" to the phenomenon that was emerging during the Bhakti movement, as EMS had done in his book *The National Question in Kerala*.

Hence if one based oneself on the classical Marxist perception, then either one would have to describe the process underlying the Bhakti movement differently, as Amalendu Guha has done by calling it the formation not of "linguistic nationalities" but of "regional communities of culture" which pre-date nationalism in any form; or one would have to trace the emergence of the bourgeoisie to a much earlier epoch, as some Soviet scholars had done who had referred to the period the Bhakti movement as characterising "India's bourgeois revolution". In short, EMS's position in *The National Question in*

Kerala was not in conformity with the standard Marxist position, for which he was criticised by Amalendu Guha.

EMS readily accepted the criticism but took the position that while the "regional community of culture" was not identical with the formation of a nationality, it was a precursor to the linguistic nationality; and it was based not on the manufacturing bourgeoisie but on the mercantile and usurious bourgeoisie which did develop under the old system. EMS's position, by seeing proto-linguistic nationalism (which is how he saw the "regional communities of culture") neither as a feature nor as an immediate precursor of any bourgeois revolution or even of any imminent bourgeois ascendancy, also argued against the view of there being any "breaks" or "discontinuities" in Indian history, of the sort that some Soviet writers had suggested.

EMS's view on the nationality question is in conformity therefore with his general perception of Indian history, namely that it was marked by a remarkable continuity rather than discontinuity, by changes that were too gradual to qualify as basic structural shifts, by stasis rather than any major dynamics with regard to the development of productive forces, and by superimpositions rather than any externally-stimulated revolutionary transformations. At the core of this continuity was the caste-based feudal system. This perception which had initially made him adopt the analytical category of the Asiatic Mode of Production remained intact even when in deference to historical research he diluted his adherence to the concept of the Asiatic Mode. But he remained committed to his general position on continuity, even though that might have been at variance with the work of several historians, like the Soviet school just mentioned, and many others who saw, in the replacement by the sultanate of the older feudalism, of the pre-Sultanate period, an important qualitative shift occurring in Indian society.

III

It was in keeping with his perception of Indian history as being marked by a strong continuity that EMS accepted the view of Marx, and Rajni Palme Dutt, about the complex impact of colonialism on Indian society. The proposition that even Third World societies could have developed capitalism independently, if not spontaneously then at least in response to the emergence of capitalism in Europe, had been advanced by Paul Baran (it had earlier also figured in the writings of Mao Zedong in the context of China). From this it followed that colonialism, *by thwarting possible independent capitalist development in Third World societies and imposing on them an exploitative relationship for the benefit of metropolitan capitalism,* played a largely negative historical role in these societies. On the other hand, if these societies were seen as being held in the grip of stagnation and stasis because of the nature of property relations prevalent in them, then the intrusion of colonialism, by breaking up the stability of the old order, could be seen as playing a certain positive role, even though the colonised people had to pay a heavy price for it. But a recognition of the destructive role of colonialism having a historically positive element, is not the same as welcoming colonialism, let alone approving of it. On the contrary there was no contradiction between accepting the classical Marxist analysis of the impact of colonialism and also accepting the nationalist critique of it; in fact the two could well go together, as they did in EMS's perception.

Marx had distinguished between the destructive and the regenerative roles of colonialism, and while the destructive role was there for all to see, even though it might have had a positive historical content, the regenerative role scarcely ever materialised during the colonial period. True, in talking of the regenerative role, Marx had been referring exclusively to the development of the material production, and not to the distribution of the fruits of progress to Indians, which, according to him, had to await either a revolution in Britain or till the Indians had shaken off the colonial yoke. But even the level of material production under colonialism did not develop to the extent anticipated by Marx. Even the spin-off by way of industrial development that he had visualised as a consequence of the introduction of the railway network, did not materialise.

This fact, together with the fact that colonialism sought to enlist the support of the landlord class, whose composition might have undergone a change without changing the basic exploitative relations of the caste-based feudal society, meant that its destructive role, though massive in one sense, was inadequate in another sense. Putting it differently, colonialism, notwithstanding its destructive impact, through "de-industrialisation", "drain of surplus out of the country", displacement of petty production and the break-up of the "self-sufficient village communities" (which were already disintegrating), and the introduction of modern private property, still represented a "superimposition" that did not deal the necessary smashing blows to the caste-based feudal society of the pre-colonial period.

EMS was particularly fond of quoting the paragraph from the Programme of the CPI(M) that made this point: "Neither the British colonialists whose rule continued for over a century, nor the Indian bourgeoisie into whose hands power passed in 1947, delivered those smashing blows against pre-capitalist society which are necessary for the free development of capitalist society and its replacement by socialist society." He had once remarked that critics did not appreciate the immense amount of effort that had gone into the formulation of this one paragraph. It represented the essence of his own thinking.

IV

Dealing those smashing blows to the caste-based feudal society was the task that had devolved upon the Indian bourgeoisie when it came to power at the time of independence. But the Indian bourgeoisie was singularly unequal to the task. In EMS's view, the Indian bourgeoisie came late on the historical scene and started building capitalism at a time when the world capitalist system itself was facing a general crisis. Unlike the bourgeoisie in the classical era of the emergence of capitalism which had dealt smashing blows to the old order, the Indian bourgeoisie compromised with feudalism, precisely because it was itself threatened by the world-wide awakening of the working class and needed the support of the feudal landlords to defend its property. The threat to bourgeois property could be warded off through an alliance between feudal and bourgeois property. To be sure, the requirement of building capitalism meant that the feudal landlords had to be persuaded to become capitalist landlords, i.e. on the basis of the existing land concentration, without breaking up large landed property, capitalist relations had to be introduced into Indian agriculture, so that it could meet the needs of capitalist industrialisation. But this amounted to another "superimposition", the "superimposition" of capitalism on the existing pre-capitalist relations, i.e. on the caste-based feudal society.

The bourgeoisie's historic incapacity to deal smashing blows to the old society entailed a betrayal. The pre-independence Congress Party had promised "land to the tiller", which could be achieved only on the basis of a break up of land concentration. But upon coming to power, the bourgeoisie compromised with the erstwhile feudal landlords and went back on its slogan. To be sure, some limited land reforms were enacted in Congress-ruled states, but they only gave ownership rights to the rich peasants allowing them to become capitalist farmers as well. Hence, the capitalist elements in the countryside were drawn from two major sources, and not just one: there were the erstwhile feudal landlords who in the new circumstances were turning towards capitalist landlordism; and there was a section of the rich peasants, who, having acquired ownership rights, were now willing to invest in agriculture and become capitalist farmers.

The conversion of feudal landlords into capitalist landlords meant a simultaneous conversion of erstwhile tenants of the feudal landlords into agricultural labourers. Implicit in the process of superimposition of capitalism therefore was a reduction in the rights over land of a section of tenants, their eviction from the land they had been cultivating for years and recruitment into the ranks of agricultural labourers. And since the capitalist landlords typically cultivate on the basis of modern labour-saving technology, the swelling of the ranks of agricultural labourers simultaneously meant a pauperisation of vast segments of the small and marginal peasantry evicted from land.

New landowners are rising by seizing land from those who

have been evicted from land as a prelude to the implementation of the land reform laws and from those who left their lands due to non-payment of dues, and cultivating land on capitalist basis. Many of them are the new form of the earlier feudal landlord. They have turned themselves into capitalist farmers by using the land seized from the tenants, making use of the provisions for "self-cultivation" in the laws as well as the money received as "compensation". Besides, there are former rich peasants-turned-capitalist farmers who could cultivate land more profitably by taking advantage of the concessions provided in the laws. The main difference between these capitalist farmers and the old feudal landlords is that the old feudal landlords gave land to tenants from whom they collected rent, while the capitalist farmers hire labour and conduct agricultural operations more profitably."[8]

From this it did not follow that Indian agriculture had become capitalist. There was a process of development of capitalism, but this was "superimposed" on a pre-capitalist setting (resulting in the development of what Lenin had called "semi-feudal capitalism"). EMS expressed the matter as follows: "In India many of the forms of exploitation of the pre-capitalist system are continuing, some in the original and some in changed forms. There exists along with these a new system of exploitation as a result of capitalist development."[9]

The "superimposition" of capitalism on the caste-based feudal society therefore meant on the one hand a superimposition of capitalist exploitation on the pre-existing forms of feudal exploitation; on the other hand by its very nature it meant a process of pauperisation as well. In short, land concentration remained; caste oppression together with patriarchy remained; the deadweight of oppressive feudal customs remained; and even as the technological basis of agriculture underwent some change and modernisation, the degree of pauperisation in the countryside intensified. The pauperisation of the peasantry which had been unleashed by the "superimposition" of colonial oppression was further compounded by the pauperisation caused by evictions on the road to capitalist agriculture.

Capitalist development under the aegis of a bourgeois-landlord state, where the bourgeoisie, having come late on the historical scene when the world capitalist system itself has entered into the period of general crisis, has to form an alliance with the landlord class, is both narrowly-based and crisis-prone. The absence of land re-distribution keeps the domestic market for industrial goods of mass consumption narrow, and arrests the development of productive forces in agriculture, which in turn acts as a constraint upon the pace of constant threat; bouts of inflation accompany the growth process; and in so far as such inflation shrinks the market for industrial goods, inflationary recessions become endemic. And since through these crises the pace and pattern of capitalist industrialisation is such that the capacity of the capitalist industrial sector to absorb labour from the overcrowded rural economy remains extremely limited, the deadweight of caste oppression and patriarchy, the mix of capitalist and pre-capitalist forms of exploitation, and the continuity of a state of pauperisation of the masses, remain undiminished.

As the state tries to get out of the inflationary situation, which calls forth mass resistance from the industrial workers, government employees and middle class salary earners, by turning the terms of trade against the peasantry, the locus of resistance shifts to the latter. Economic crisis leads to an enmeshing of the regime in political crisis, from which it seeks to extricate itself through recourse to semi-fascist methods, of which the imposition of the infamous Emergency was a typical example. In short, the contradictions of what Lenin had called "semi-feudal capitalism" or what EMS would have called the "superimposition" of capitalism on a caste-based feudal system, pose an ever present threat to the continuation of bourgeois democracy and the preservation of even such civil liberties and rights of resistance that the working people enjoy within the system.

V

EMS's political economy analysis of post-independence planning therefore was integrated with his overall reading both of Indian history and of the world situation, characterised by the general crisis of capitalism on the one hand and the emergence of a socialist camp on the other (notwithstanding the divisions that afflicted the latter). The conclusion he drew from this reading is that since the bourgeoisie was incapable of dealing those smashing blows to the old feudal order, of breaking land concentration which provided the basis for the continuation of caste oppression, social exclusion and patriarchy, it was the historic task of the proletariat, allying itself with the peasants and the other sections of the oppressed, to deal those smashing blows. And the proletariat having acquired state power will not stop at the stage of building capitalism but will move on to socialism. Hence, marching towards socialism was the means of breaking the stasis in societies like ours; marching towards socialism alone would entail a change that would be more than a mere "superimposition". The ultimate realisation of the dreams of the social reformers, and of the fighters against caste oppression, not to mention all those who were appalled by the misery and poverty of the masses, could come only with socialism.

But EMS, again rather like Antonio Gramsci, was acutely conscious of the arduousness of the task before the socialist forces. Precisely because the task was stupendous, involving nothing short of ushering in, through stages, a revolution that would cleanse the society of centuries of oppression and filth of the worst kind, it was extremely difficult. The system of caste oppression that could only end with socialism was itself a barrier in the path of progress towards socialism, as it divided the oppressed. The series of "superimpositions" that enmeshed different forms of exploitation made the task of combining the exploited even more difficult. It required patient, systematic effort.

EMS, in discussing the impossibility of having a centralised leadership of the world communist movement today, categorised countries on the basis of the role that communist parties played in them. And in doing so, he introduced an interesting term. Instead of simply talking of capitalist and socialist countries, he introduced the additional term: "countries" in which "revolutionary proletarian parties" exert "powerful influence on policy making".[10] And he categorised India among such countries. By refraining from drawing a mere binary distinction between "capitalist" and "socialist" countries, EMS was drawing attention to a significant phenomenon, namely that the revolution was not one single *event* but a *process*, and that the revolutionary party could "exert powerful influence on policy making" even when it did not have state power, which was itself a progress on the path of the revolution. Once again there is an echo here of Antonio Gramsci's concept of the "war of positions". Gramsci had argued that in countries of Western Europe the revolutionary struggle had to be a protracted one involving advances as in a "war of positions" rather than victory in one surgical strike. EMS appears to be arguing along similar lines.

EMS's deep sense of history and his understanding of the revolutionary process derived from this sense, deserve serious study by the Left, which has to carry forward his analysis to the neoliberal phase of India's capitalist development. A study of EMS's writings is especially necessary in the current conjuncture when some retreats have been forced on the Left in the "war of positions" that EMS would have seen as a hallmark of the Indian revolution.

REFERENCES

1. A very good example of this is his "Communication" to *Social Scientist*, December 1982, Issue number 115, where he puts forward his views on the Nationality Question, in the context of discussing Amalendu Guha's criticism of his 1952 formulations in *The National Question in Kerala*, through a process of locating these views within an overall reading of Indian history.
2. Karl Marx, *Pre-capitalist Economic Formations*, ed. with Introduction by E.J. Hobsbawn (London: Lawerence and Wishart, 1964), p. 83.
3. Irfan Habib, *The Agravian System of Mughal India* (Bombay: Oxford University Press, 1963).
4. While he uses the concept of the Asiatic Mode of Production in his 1952 book *The National Question in Kerala*, in his subsequent work *Kerala: Society and Politics* (1984) he says: "This formulation made by Marx has become a point of serious debate among scholars. Some of them make the term the basis of the study of every single

country in Asia, while others virtually deny the very concept, maintaining that Engels never used it, Marx too did so only once, etc." He goes on to add: "It should however be noted that for Marx the term 'Asiatic Society or mode of production' was not a substitute for a concrete analysis of society and its evolution in individual Asian countries", and lists some common features of historical development in "oriental countries", extending from "China in the east to Arabia and Egypt in the west".

5. E.M.S. Namboodripad, *Kerala: Society and Politics* (New Delhi: National Book Centre, 1984).
6. Quoted in E.M.S. Namboodripad, 'Adi-Shankara and His Philosophy: A Marxist View', in *Social Scientist,* January-February (1989), No. 188-189.
7. The growth of commercial capital of course can occur even in the absence of commodity production proper, simply on the basis of the commoditisation of the surplus alone.
8. E.M.S. Namboodripad, *Selected Writings,* Vol. 1 (Calcutta: National Book Trust, 1982), p. 291.
9. Ibid., p. 289.
10. E.M.S. Namboodripad, 'The Relevance of Lenin's 'Imperialism' to the Current World Situation', in Prabhat Patnaik (ed.) *Lenin and Imperialism* (Delhi: Orient Longman, 1986), pp. 241-2.

16

What is Maoism?

Bernard D'Mello

What is Maoism? What of its origins and development? What went before its advent? What are its flaws? Where is it going? Where should it be going, given its legacy? The questions are of great import, for Maoism has given birth to a movement which has taken root in India, survived for more than four decades in the country, and the state has now unleashed a massive counter-insurgency operation to crush it.

This chapter attempts a stepwise approach to finding first answers to the questions—What is Marxism? What is Leninism? What is Stalinism?—and thereby aims to understand what Maoism is all about.

Anuradha Ghandy (Anu as we knew her) was a member of the central committee of the Communist Party of India (Maoist) (CPI (Maoist)). Early on, she developed a sense of obligation to the poor; she joined them in their struggle for bread and roses, the fight for a richer and a fuller life for all. Tragically, cerebral malaria took her away in 2008. What is this spirit that made her selflessly adopt the cause of the damned of the Indian earth—the exploited, the oppressed, and the dominated—as her own? The risks of joining the Maoist long march seem far too dangerous to most people, but not for her—bold, courageous and decisive, yet kind, gentle and considerate. Perhaps her days were numbered, marked as she was on the dossiers of the Indian state's repressive apparatus as one of the most wanted "left-wing extremists". That oppressive, brutal structure has been executing a barbaric counter-insurgency strategy—designed to maintain the status quo—against the Maoist movement in India. What is it that is driving the Indian state, hell-bent as it is to cripple and maim the spirit that inspires people like Anu? Practically the whole Indian polity—from the semi-fascist Bharatiya Janata Party to the main affiliate of the Parliamentary Left, the Communist Party of India (Marxist)—have pitched in against the Maoists, backing a massive planned escalation of the deployment of paramilitary-cum-armed-police, this time with logistical support from the military, to crush the rebels. It seems that sections of monopoly capital—including Arcelor Mittal, the Essar Group, Vedanta Resources, Tata Steel, POSCO, and the Sajjan Jindal Group—have given an ultimatum to the state governments concerned and the union government that they will dump their proposed mining/industrial/SEZ projects if the local resistance to their business plans are not crippled once-and-for-all.

Righteous indignation against 'left-wing extremism' has reached a crescendo, buttressed as it is by sections of the commercial media, with images and profiles (dished out to the fourth estate by anti-terrorist squad officers) of apprehended revolutionists. A few years back, my son—lanky, unkempt, his hair dishevelled—came home from school one day to tell us that his teacher called him a Naxalite (what the Maoists are popularly called). I asked him, "How did you react?" He queried, "Daddy, who are these guys, these Naxalites?" I answered, "Well, they are rebels who resent the deep injustice meted out to the poor." He responded, "Well then, I feel proud to be called a Naxalite". The boy is still very young, but he will soon approach that wonderful time of his life when his urge to understand what is going on in the country and the world will be unquenchable. More recently, a malicious and vengeful advertisement by the Home Ministry in the newspapers painted the Maoists as "cold-blooded criminals". Maybe it is time for me to consider how I will answer his question: "What is Maoism?"

An answer to such a query requires a stepwise approach to

finding first answers to questions such as: "What is Marxism?" "What is Leninism?" "What is Stalinism?" Only then, can one get to understanding what Maoism is all about. For after all, Mao's Marxism undoubtedly stemmed from the Leninist school; he applied Marxism, Leninism (the latter, a school of Marxism in the age of imperialism) and Stalinism (a decomposed form of Leninism which he also struggled to overcome and go beyond), as a method of analysis of the social reality of China. But more, he intervened in that reality through conscious social-political action guided by Marxist theory and from the late 1920s to the end of the 1960s continuously learnt from events, thus making possible an enrichment of the original.

What has come to be known as Maoism had its material roots in China's underdevelopment, the failed practice of the Chinese Communist Party (CCP) in the urban areas in the 1920s, and its subsequent peasant-cum-guerrilla-based movement in the countryside. Theoretically, and in practice, Mao's Marxism was enriched by overcoming and going beyond Stalin's mechanical interpretation of Marx's theory of history. And, Mao constantly applied Marx's "materialist dialectics" in helping to understand and resolve multiple "contradictions"—internal conflicts tending to split what is functionally united—with the likely outcome following from the reciprocal actions of the opposing tendencies. It is the fusion of all of this with the original Marxism and Leninism that constitutes Maoism. Like Marxism, at its best, it is a comprehensive world view, a method of analysis and a guide to practice, not a set of dogmas. What then is meant by the Maoist dictum "learn truth from practice"? With this preview, we are now in a position to move on. At the outset itself, let me say that while I speak solely for myself, I make no claim whatsoever to originality. I wrote this piece as a self-clarifying exercise and submitted it for publication in the hope that it might help others like me, striving to be educated about matters that are not academic.

What is Marxism?

In searching for an answer to this question, I can do no better than what the *Monthly Review* has taught me. In one of the founder-editor's words:

> Marxism is above all, a comprehensive world view, what Germans call a *Weltanschauung*—a body of philosophical, economic, political, sociological, scientific ... principles, all interrelated and together forming an independent and largely self-sufficient intellectual structure. ...It is a guide to life and social practice, and in the long run its validity can only be judged by its fruits.[1]

In its view, prior to the development of capitalism, civilisation had been impossible without exploitation; the social surplus appropriated was:

> concentrated in the hands of a few, so that luxury, wealth, civilisation at one pole was necessarily matched by poverty, misery, and degradation at the other.
>
> It was into such a world that capitalism was born ...incomparably the most productive and in that sense progressive society the world had ever seen. ... indeed, for the first time ever it made possible a society in which exploitation and the concentration of the surplus in the hands of a few was no longer the *necessary* condition for civilisation.
>
> Now humanity faced ... a prospect without precedent. Would it go forward to a new and higher, non-exploitative form of civilisation ... or would the exploitation of the many by the few continue to be the way of human life? Marx believed that ... capitalism ... would never be able to make use of ... (society's productive forces) for the benefit of the workers who he thought were on their way to becoming the majority of the population.
>
> ... Sooner or later...the workers would become conscious of their real class interests, organise themselves into a powerful revolutionary force, seize power from the capitalists, and begin the transition to a communist society-from which exploitation and classes would finally be abolished.
>
> It hasn't worked out that way. Workers in the more developed capitalist countries were able to make enough gains by struggle within the system to forestall the emergence of a revolutionary consciousness. A significant part of these gains came at the expense of dependent and exploited countries of the Third World, which were thereby prevented from using their resources for their own independent development. As a result, the centre of revolutionary struggle shifted from the advanced to the retarded parts of the capitalist world.[2]

While Marxists share a conception of reality, they differ in many respects in explaining the world and in assessing it. Also, the intellectual structure created by the founders of Marxism—Marx and Engels—has been significantly modified and adapted, as it no doubt should, with advances in human knowledge and understanding, and with the development of capitalism into a global system. But, and of course, its scientific validity should be judged in the first instance by its contributions to the ability to explain reality.

However, there is something even more exacting—in the very long run, Marxism has to be judged by the fruits of its project of taking humanity along the road towards equality, cooperation, community, and solidarity. We should have done this earlier, but it is now apt to bring into focus the most crucial character of Marxism, something, following Sweezy, we alluded to at the beginning of this chapter. The whole purpose of constructing and reconstructing its distinctive intellectual structure to understand the world was and is so that this exercise may lay the basis of changing society for the better. This is stated most succinctly in Marx's 1845 *Theses on Feuerbach*: "The philosophers have only *interpreted* the world; the point however is to *change* it." But integrating theory and practice (developing a strategy and a set of tactics for changing the world for the better and implementing them) is far more difficult and messy a project.

Marx and Engels wrote *The Communist Manifesto* in December 1847 and January 1848, but they never even attempted to define, let alone provide any blueprint of the transitional society (their followers called it socialism) which would in time —that was the expectation—evolve asymptotically towards communism, never really reaching it. As Sweezy has it, in Marx and Engels' conception, the transitional stage/society ("socialism")[3] would begin its existence as "primarily a negation of capitalism which would develop its own positive identity (communism) through a revolutionary struggle in which the proletariat would remake society and in the process remake itself."[4]

But, frankly, the proletariat in the developed capitalist countries, for reasons already mentioned, was increasingly losing its quality as the source and carrier of revolutionary practice. The development of the working class, the advance of human capability—always at the very centre of the forces of production—was not perceived by the workers as being hindered by the relations of production; the latter was not discerned as intolerable by the workers as long as they were able to extract better terms from capital through their struggles (strikes, etc) within the confines of the system. Why should they then bear the risk of losing what they were gaining in the present when what they could gain by revolting against the system was highly uncertain and far away in the future? In other words, Marx and Engels did not blame the workers for the lack of a revolutionary consciousness; the objective conditions were not there for its germination.

What then of early Marxism (it was not called Marxism in Marx's time, but for convenience we are designating even that period within its scope) in its mistaken expectation, drawn mainly from its analysis of the living and working conditions of the working class (in Engels' *The Condition of the Working Class in England*, written in late 1844, early 1845 when he was 24) and the logic of Marx's the famous 1859 Preface to *A Contribution to the Critique of Political Economy* that class in the advanced capitalist countries would eventually, sooner or later, revolt and emancipate itself? The, at first spontaneous, and later on, organised struggles of the workers, led by the parties of the Left, were eventually able to force the ruling class and its political representatives to bring in the factory laws and various social legislations, and implement them, which convinced the workers that things could get better even within the confines of capitalism. In this, no doubt the surplus from the toilers in the colonies/ neo-colonies/semi-colonies/dependent countries (the "periphery"), shared not only between the local elites and the ruling classes in the "centre", but also to an extent, by the working classes there, helped provide part of the cushion. As a result capital at the "centre" got richer and stronger too.

Marx and Engels did not take all of these developments into account and so proved wrong in their expectations of a socialist Europe. But, to his great credit, Marx did brilliantly take account of—besides the massive expropriation in Britain through the enclosures—capitalism's pillage, in its mercantilist phase, of what later came to be called the "periphery" or the Third World, in Part VIII of *Capital*, Volume 1, entitled, 'The So-Called Primitive Accumulation'. He also did not ignore "unequal exchange"—through siphoning a part of the surplus created in production via funds used by a distinct class for trade in commodities (merchant capital)—with the periphery, in the competitive phase of capitalism. Basically, merchant capital played a crucial role in the periphery, albeit as an appendage of industrial capital at the centre.[5] Marx had not the opportunity to reorient his theory of accumulation to take account of what had begun to happen at the end of his life, the emergence of capitalism as a global system with the ushering in of monopoly capitalism. But, we have it from Sweezy that he was fully aware of the causal relationship between the development of capitalism at the "centre", in his day, in Europe and the development of underdevelopment in the "periphery".[6] Early Marxism however proved inadequate in elaborating a theory of accumulation on a world scale that would explain the functioning of capitalism as a global system. All the same, Marx suggested a way of analysing capitalism—how capital got its wealth from the pillage of the "periphery", from expropriation through the enclosures, from the surplus labour of workers in the past, and from the acquisition of smaller and weaker units of capital; how the superstructure (the state, the legal system, the dominant ideology and culture) was adapted and modified to facilitate all of this; and with what potentialities. That method was "materialist dialectics", which was applied by the best of his followers—two of whom were Lenin and Mao —to understand the ever-changing world and to intervene to change it for the better.

Meanwhile, the parties leading the various working class movements in Europe, members of the Second International, continued to pay lip service to the cause of proletarian revolution. But, soon they were exposed for what they really had become when in 1914 they supported their respective governments in the war, an act demonstrating nothing less than the self-destruction of internationalism, and the quashing of many a hope of proletarian revolution.

What is Leninism? What is Stalinism?

It was in these the worst of times that Lenin, a thoroughly orthodox Marxist, struck a momentous chord on the political stage with his pamphlet, *Imperialism: The Highest Stage of Capitalism* (1916), explaining the war then raging in terms of a division of the world into separate spheres of influence and the inter-capitalist struggles for its redivision. Lenin's purpose was limited mainly to explain the nature of the war then underway and what should be done by socialists leading the working class. Lenin urged that rather than fighting and killing each other in this imperialist war, the workers must be convinced to convert the imperialist war into a civil war to overthrow their respective bourgeoisie. The impact of accumulation on a world scale in shaping the nature of "underdevelopment" of the "periphery" and, in turn, on the accumulation of capital at the "centre"—and the consciousness of the working class there—were not the focus.

Instead, in Lenin's view, the super-profits of monopoly capital were, among other things, used to bribe an upper stratum of the working class—thereby creating an "aristocracy" of labour—and some leaders of the working class movements. Lenin thus blamed the political leaderships of the social-democratic parties leading the movements of their respective working classes and their betrayal of the majority of their respective proletariats. The fact that the objective conditions in Europe had changed, which thwarted the permeation of a revolutionary consciousness in the workers on the continent, eluded him. But it may be said—on the whole—of Lenin and the Bolsheviks that in the course of their practice they rescued Marxism from those of its adherents who mistakenly and mechanically interpreted Marx as a "historical determinist".

But let me explain the Marxist position. A "determinist" way of thinking argues that history and the given conditions existing on the ground uniquely determine what is likely to happen next. In pure contrast, a "voluntarist" point of view holds that almost anything can happen subject to the will and positive resolve of effective leaders and the resolute support they get from their followers. In my view, Marxism is neither "determinist" nor "voluntarist"—in its conception, at any given moment there are a range of possible outcomes, determined both by history and the existing conditions and context. The actual outcome from among this set will depend on social action. That is, which particular intermediate goal the leaders choose from the range of possibilities ("strategy") and whether they and their supporters go about trying to achieve that result with appropriate tactics, and respond "correctly" to the course of events that unfold. Clearly, Lenin—and Stalin, and Trotsky, we might add—put great weight on patterns of leadership—centralised direction by a revolutionary elite. Mao did not disagree with this, but from experience emphasised the necessity of honest and correct feedback from the party rank and file and the masses.

Stalin has called Leninism the Marxism of the era of "imperialism" and "proletarian dictatorship". But he is one who evokes deep anguish among many socialists. On the one hand, he was the only top leader among the Bolsheviks who came from the wretched of the earth (his father was a poor cobbler and his mother was of poor peasant-serf stock), fortunate to have been educated at a religious seminary; it was under his leadership that the Soviet Union and its Red Army vanquished the might of the German armed forces in the Second World War to safeguard humanity from fascism. And as long as he lived it was possible to believe (mistakenly, in the view of some) in the existence of a global coordinated movement in active revolutionary conflict with capitalism and imperialism. But, on the other hand, he consigned Leninism and socialism to the grave. Stalin had forgotten: that which is not democratic can never be socialist. Indeed, as Harry Braverman put it:

> The destruction of the old Bolshevik Party closed innumerable possibilities to the Soviet Union, and it is hard to envision them all. [And, in a footnote, he adds] Stalin did not stop with the annihilation of the left and the right oppositions, led respectively by Trotsky and Bukharin. He turned on his own faction, and, as

> Khrushchev told the Twentieth Congress, executed 98 of 139 (70%) of the Central Committee selected at the Seventeenth Congress in 1934.[7]

Paresh Chattopadhyay argues that the very notion of socialism in Lenin and the other early Bolsheviks (before Stalin's consolidation of power) was completely at odds with that of Marx.[8] The suggestion seems to be that, given this original flaw, and economic and social backwardness, it was only a matter of time before the ruling elite in the Soviet Union metamorphosed into a ruling class, legitimising its authoritarian (and, in this view, exploitative) rule in the name of Marxism. Certainly, as a result, Marxism and Leninism have been discredited in the eyes of many. After all, following the seizure of power in October 1917, did the means not begin to shape the very ends to eventually overwhelm the socialist aspiration? However, I think one should take account of what has come to be called "Lenin's last struggle"—warning of serious danger from the growth of a ruling bureaucracy and from the "crudity" of Stalin. Beyond this, it seems to me, and I have come to believe this, that given the existence of class, patriarchy, racism (and caste, one might add) over millennia, power and compulsion are deeply rooted in social reality; indeed, they have almost become part of the basic inherited (but not unchangeable) *human condition*, which leads one to make a very strong case for civil and democratic rights and liberties (these have been gained through historic struggles waged by the underdogs) that should not be allowed to be abrogated come what may.

For our purpose over here, however, it would be pertinent to briefly mention the way Lenin conceived of the revolution in "backward" capitalist Russia where, in his analysis, the bourgeoisie and its political representatives were incapable of bringing about the "bourgeois-democratic revolution"—overthrowing czarism and seizing and dismantling the feudal estates—making it imperative that the working class in alliance with the peasants take over that task, only to quickly move on to the next stage, that of socialist revolution. In all of this, the worker-peasant alliance was to be led by the vanguard party. Lenin's conception of such a party then becomes germane—its purpose was to politically organise and bring revolutionary ideas to the working class, more generally, the masses, and lead the revolution to establish a "dictatorship of the proletariat". Marx had conceptualised the latter as a system in which, following the seizure of power, this would be the *regime* in which the proletariat would "not only exercise the sort of hegemony hitherto exercised by the bourgeoisie", but a "form of *government*, with the working class actually governing, and fulfilling many of the tasks hitherto performed by the state", and Lenin fully endorsed this view.[9] Of course, in Lenin's way of thinking, the dictatorship of the proletariat was to be exercised by the workers under the guidance of the vanguard party.

The latter evolved over time—in the conditions imposed by illegality, inner-party organisation was different in 1902 from that following 1905, and then February 1917, when a mass-based party adhering to "democratic centralism" was seen to fit the bill. Democratic centralism was conceived as an inner-party organisational principle and practice where the various factions within the party strictly adhere to the guideline "freedom of discussion, unity of action."[10] Of course, what happened in practice was the stamping out of the democratic component; in 1921, factions were virtually outlawed, something Stalin is said to have taken advantage of to ultimately secure his domination of the party.[11] In parallel, the dictatorship of the proletariat—conceived as a dictatorship over the former ruling classes, but a democratic role model as far as the masses were concerned—came to be "widely associated with the dictatorship of the party and the state over the whole of society, including the proletariat"[12] which came to be associated with Stalinism.

Stalinism—a decomposed version of Leninism closely associated with the regime in the Soviet Union from the late 1920s to the time of Stalin's death in 1953—has to be seen, as Ralph Miliband rightly emphasised, in the context of Russian history.[13] However, given the constraint of brevity, we can, at most, only list its principal characteristics, drawing largely—but not uncritically—from Miliband[14]:

- the outlook that it is possible to build "socialism in one country";

- the opinion that under socialism there must be a very strong state;
- the view that class struggle intensifies with the advance of socialism;
- the cult of personality, with an obsessive focus on the supreme leader's will;
- forced collectivisation and rapid industrialisation;
- suppression of dissent, critical intelligence and free discussion within the party;
- the "political" trials and the purges, and elimination of most of the major figures of the Bolshevik Revolution;
- the forced labour camps where thousands of ordinary people suffered complete ruin (recalling this makes me cry);
- opposition to fascism and a decisive contribution to the Allied victory over it; and,
- the discrediting of Marxism-Leninism because of a mechanical interpretation of it, and its stamping as official state ideology to legitimise elite/ruling class power.

All the same, it seems that Lenin's aspiration and vision of the socialist state—as expressed in *State and Revolution*, written in the summer of 1917—after the seizure of power was inspired by Marx's lauding of the 1871 Paris Commune and drawing lessons from it about the future socialist "state". Marx was emphatic that the working class, after taking power, should not simply take control of the existing structure, institutions and machinery of the old state, all of which had to be "smashed" and replaced by a state of a radically new type. Consider Ralph Miliband[15] who sets forth Marx's depiction of the credo of the Commune, which Lenin seems to have accepted, and the role of the party envisaged by the latter in his tract, *The State and Revolution*:

> [All state officials] would be elected, be subject to recall at any time and their salary would be fixed at the level of workers' wages. Representative institutions would be retained, but the representatives would be closely and constantly controlled by their electors, and also subject to recall. In effect, the proletarian majority

> was intended not only to rule but actually to govern in a regime which amounted to the exercise of semi-direct popular power.
>
> A very remarkable feature of *State and Revolution*, given the importance Lenin always attributed to the role of the party, is the quite subsidiary role it is allotted in this instance.

But Lenin's vision of the socialist state "did not survive the Bolshevik seizure of power". Yet, he "never formally renounced the perspectives which had inspired *State and Revolution*". Can we thus conclude that Lenin wanted "the creation of a society in which the state would be strictly subordinated to the rule and self-government of the people?"[16] The contrast between theory and practice, in this respect, could not have been starker. Frankly, one has to clearly distinguish between what one says and what one does. After all, what happened to the Congress of Soviets—soviets which had the potential to be self-governing organs of the workers and the peasants—that had arisen almost spontaneously from the movement of February 1917? By the summer of 1918 the soviets had no more than a mere formal existence. The main institution of the dictatorship of the proletariat, the Soviets of Workers' and Soldiers' Deputies (independent of any one party), took the back seat, with the party leadership at the steering.[17] Indeed, the dictatorship of the proletariat was deemed impossible except through the leadership of the single party; socialist pluralism too got precluded. But, to be fair, it is important though to note that Lenin, in his last writings, expressed the need to create the basis for popular self-governance, for which, he felt, there must be a genuine revolution, where culture flowers among the people. Was he then calling for a "cultural revolution", something that Mao launched in China in 1966 with the aim of "preventing capitalist restoration?"[18]

Maoism: Evolution and Development

> Millennia are too long: Let us dispute over mornings and evenings.
>
> – Mao Zedong (1963)

The conventional wisdom of the day presents Mao as some kind of a "monster", for instance, in Jung Chang and Jon Halliday's

2005 book, *Mao: The Unknown Story*, which, in its obsessive intent to denigrate Mao, is least concerned with the known facts about the man.[19] It is evident that a "battle for China's past" is underway, with the elite intelligentsia leading the attack. The latter are Chinese, who were the victims, real or imagined, direct or indirect, of the Cultural Revolution (CR), and some leading lights in the "China Studies" field the world over, who have always been prone to somersaults depending on the direction of the political wind in Washington.

The credo of objectivity that is repeatedly claimed is a myth. It is not surprising that in a world where "the ideas of the ruling class are in every epoch the ruling ideas", the views of the beneficiaries of the CR, the peasants and the workers, who gained in terms of education, healthcare and other aspects of social welfare, as also, in the "voice" they got in the fields and the factories, and in the political arena, are not being heard.[20]

With this necessary communication of the side I lean on, let me then get to the origins of Maoism, which got its lease of life in the immediate aftermath of the eventual rejection of the disastrous line of "united front from within" (leading to restraints on organisational independence), which was virtually forced on the CCP by the Third International (the Comintern) in 1923. It was claimed by the latter that the Kuomintang (KMT), led by Chiang Kai-shek (after Sun Yat-sen died in March 1925), represented the "revolutionary national bourgeoisie" of China. This alliance was supposed to produce national liberation and the bourgeois-democratic revolution (revolution led by the bourgeoisie in alliance with the workers and peasants), but led only to the disastrous defeat of the communists at the hands of Chiang's counter-revolution in 1927, leading to the civil war (1928-35).

But even in defeat there was a silver lining: no doubt the Chang-led KMT control—led the bulk of the armed forces; but the Fourth Army deserted in August 1927 to join the communists, which led to the founding of the Red Army. A new leadership of the CCP gradually began to coalesce around Mao; however, it was only by around 1932 that this budding "Maoist" authority gained legitimacy and the CCP could forge, and refine over time, its own strategy and path to achieve the goals of the "New Democratic Revolution" (NDR).

It was the CCP under Mao that most effectively challenged the Comintern line by refusing to surrender control and leadership to those who could not be relied upon to carry through to the very end the struggle for genuine national independence or the fight against feudalism/semi-feudalism. The quality of the leadership was crucially important.[21] It adopted the strategy of Protracted People's War (PPW), which relied on the peasants, built rural base areas, carried out "land to the tiller" and other social policies (for instance, dealing with the gender question through the mobilisation of women in the countryside) in these areas (run democratically as miniature, self-reliant states) thereby building up a political mass base in the countryside to finally encircle and "capture" the cities.

Here it needs to be emphasised that it was only during the anti-Japanese resistance (1937-45), when the contradiction between Japanese imperialism and national independence became the principal one (playing the leading role), relegating the fight between feudalism and the masses to a secondary and subordinate position, that the CCP managed to shift nationalist opinion progressively in its favour.

At the core of the NDR was opposition to the transformation of the society under the leadership of the bourgeoisie and its political representatives. The NDR—unambiguously led by the Communist Party—suppressed the big bourgeoisie because, even as it retained private capitalist enterprise, it was primarily meant to create the prerequisites for socialism.

At the heart of the course of the NDR, from 1927 to 1949, was the building of base areas, involving the following:

(1) Achieving victory in the political struggle, thereby establishing the basis for running a miniature state in the base area; (2) winning the economic struggle—land to the tiller, land investigation, promotion of mutual aid and cooperation, and achieving the development of the productive forces (the material means of production and human capabilities) in agriculture and small industry; and, (3) carrying off the cultural and ideological struggle, with a great deal of overlapping among the three.

All of this—whether political, economic, or cultural and ideological—entailed following the "mass line", which is a distinctive feature of Maoism. This is a method of involving the masses in how, for instance, each of the above is to be done and then implementing what had been decided upon with their participation. The party leaders thereby correctly understand the opinions of the people, and so fashion the required policies in a manner the masses will support and actively implement. Mao summed this up pithily as: "from the masses, to the masses". Indeed, in the process of participating in the "land to the tiller", land investigation, and in the ideological struggles, the people understood the local class structure and the ideas and institutions bolstering the status quo.

This brings us to three crucial dimensions of Maoist theory and practice in trying to enrich the democratic process. These three dimensions are the Leninist vanguard party, the mass organisations, and society. In the Maoist conception of the vanguard party, just like in Lenin's centralised guidance by a revolutionary elite, this elite leadership is drawn from intellectuals, workers and peasants, with the difference that workers and peasants are sought to be represented, over time, in greater proportion. What is however distinctive in Mao is the conscious effort to fuse the inner-party organisational principle of democratic centralism ("freedom of discussion, unity of action") with the mass line ("from the masses, to the masses"), the mass organisations under party leadership providing the crucial link between the two. However, a word over here about the claim of the vanguard party being led by the proletariat might be in order. Here, as Benjamin Schwartz[22] explains, in Maoism, the term "proletarian" refers to a set of moral qualities—"self-abnegation, limitless sacrifice to the needs of the collectivity, guerrilla-like self-reliance, unflagging energy ... iron discipline, etc"—as the norm of true collectivist behaviour. Proletarian leadership then comes to be constituted by a set of intellectuals, workers and peasants who excel in these moral requirements.

We are thus beginning to grasp some distinctive features of Maoism—the conception of NDR as opposed to that of

Bourgeois Democratic Revolution; PPW; "base areas" and the way they are established; the principal contradiction (which may change over time) steering the course of the PPW; and, democratic centralism *plus* the mass line. It is then time to introduce what may indeed be the *differentia specifica* of Maoism, best done by illustration from Maoist practice in China. We have already alluded to the idea that the road to socialism was already entered upon and struggles to persist on that road were undertaken early on in the new democratic stage of the revolution itself. We said that the big bourgeoisie is suppressed during the NDR itself in order to lay the ground—create the preconditions—for socialism. Why?

Socialists, more than others, are well aware that there are definite limits to the compatibility of capitalism and democracy, that is, if the latter is understood as government in accordance with the will of the people.[23] But from a capitalist point of view, such democracy is acceptable and considered viable only if the majority continues to believe that the capitalist system is the best for them, or that there is no alternative but to live with it. The moment this belief erodes, democracy becomes a potential danger to capitalism, best illustrated in the case of Chile from 1970 following the coming into office of a party pledged to beginning the transition to socialism, where upon the big bourgeoisie collaborated with Washington and the military took over to save capitalism there.[24] To circumvent such a possibility, a new type of democracy ("New Democracy") has to be created which does not preclude the transition to socialism if the majority want it, for which, the big bourgeoisie has to be suppressed. In effect, the NDR does not do away with capitalism, but it confiscates the property of the imperialists and the big bourgeoisie—those at the apex of wealth, power and privilege—and hence stymies the anti- democratic opposition to socialism from their representatives and backers.

But let us elaborate upon the Maoist idea of steps within the new democratic stage, steps in the transition to socialism, and steps within the socialist stage itself, and the thought that the preconditions of a subsequent step/stage in the process of progressive change must be created within the step/stage that has to be transited from. The land reform programme leading on in steps to communes can be used as an apt illustration. It may be best to take William Hinton's books, *Fanshen: A Documentary of Revolution in a Chinese Village* (1966) and *Shenfan: The Continuing Revolution in a Chinese Village* (1983), which together provide a rich documentary account of the land reform in Long Bow village of Shanxi province during 1946-48, onward to the formation of mutual aid teams, and from 1953, the merging of those teams into "elementary cooperatives", and from there to advanced cooperatives and further on into communes, and tracing developments up to 1971. They tell a whole lot of facts, even those that contradict what the author is trying to argue, but it is difficult to even propose a framework to look at this whole social canvas. Subsequently Hinton has helped provide such an enabling structure,[25] though he also revised his assessment following the publication of *Shenfan*.

Perhaps it would be best to begin where *Fanshen* concludes:

> Land reform, by creating basic equality among rural producers, only presented the producers with a choice of roads: private enterprise on the land leading to capitalism, or collective enterprise on the land leading to socialism.[26]

In 1948 itself, the peasants had begun to form mutual aid teams where a small number of households pooled resources other than land (tools, implements, draft power, occasional labour) but still cultivated the land on an individual basis. Then in 1953 the formation of elementary cooperatives got underway, in which land as well as other resources were pooled, but individual ownership rights were maintained. Incomes were based partly on property ownership and partly on labour time committed to cooperative production in ratios set to garner majority local support. Here dividends had to be paid on the assets, including land, made available, but the complaint of the middle and rich peasants was that this was not as much as they would otherwise have got, that is, if they had cultivated individually by hiring in labour. But when crop yields began to increase because of more intensive use of labour in the cooperative mode, the conflict regarding how to divide the income as between the labour contributed and the assets pooled became sharper.[27] The resolution usually took the form of moving from something like a labour to capital share of 40:60 to 60:40, for, over time, it was living labour that had created the addition to assets. A time would then come when the new assets created by labour overwhelm the original assets pooled at the time of the formation of the cooperative, when it then became appropriate to abolish the capital share of the net output, that is, move to "advanced cooperatives".

The latter entailed a definite socialist advance, involving all peasant households being incorporated in such producer cooperatives, with common ownership of all productive resources. As Hinton puts it:

> When the new capital created by living labour surpasses and finally overwhelms the old capital with which the group started out, then rewarding old shareholders with disproportionate payments amounts to exploitation, a transfer of wealth from those who create it by hard labour to those who own the original shares and may, currently, not labour at all.[28]

Of course, with one more step on the collective ladder, the advanced cooperatives were turned into larger units of collective economy *and* government—the communes. The point however is that in each step of the ladder leading up to collectivisation, the preconditions of the next step were introduced, which helped resolve the old contradictions and smoothed the transition to the next step/stage.

But, it is alleged that the strategy of the Great Leap Forward (GLF) (1958-61) and the organisation of the People's Communes, and the left deviations of that period led to a massive famine in which up to 30 million people are said to have died.[29] Then, there have been the excessive violence and the personal tragedies of the CR. For both, the excesses of the GLF and the CR, Mao and Maoism have been held entirely responsible. Hinton however disagrees. To get to the truth, he explains the context —that of "protracted political warfare".[30] The NDR was a revolution of a new type, new in that it was meant to create the preconditions for the socialist road, unlike bourgeois-democratic revolutions that open the road to capitalism. Following 1949, however, the resolution of the contradictions with semi-feudalism and imperialism brought the contradiction between capitalism and the Chinese working people to the fore—the latter became the principal contradiction.

> Right from the time of the launch of the NDR, the CCP had been divided into two major factions—a "proletarian" one, headed by Mao, and a "bourgeois" one, headed by Liu Shaoqi and Deng Xiaoping; pre-liberation, the former was based in the liberated areas, while the latter was in the KMT-dominated cities. After liberation in 1949, the two factions "merged as one organisationally, but they never did merge ideologically".

This led to a fundamental split over development strategy and policy ever since Mao took China decisively on to the socialist road. It was on the eve of the GLF that Mao declared on February 27, 1957 (*On the Correction Handling of Contradictions among the People*): "...the question of which will win out, socialism or capitalism, is still not settled". As Hinton put it: "No policy, from either side, could be applied without contest", which meant extreme friction between the two factions.[31]

Basically, in order to resolve the contradiction between the "proletarian line" and the "bourgeois line" within the party in favour of the former, the Maoists, in the CR, tried to plant the seeds of a later stage of socialism in the earlier stage it—self, thus doing away with a mechanical separation of the two stages and concentrating instead on their interrelations. The two stages of socialism, supposed to follow chronologically, are the phase where distribution of the social product is according to the principle "from each according to her/his abilities, to each according to her/his work" followed by the phase where distribution is according to the norm "from each according to her/his abilities, to each according to her/his needs".

It is then clear that Maoists reject Stalin's mechanical interpretation of Marx's 1859 Preface to *A Contribution to the Critique of Political Economy* as a deterministic theory of history. Mao accused Stalin of emphasising only the forces of production (the means of production and human capability) to the neglect of the relations of production (relations at work, and ownership relations that bestow control over the forces of production and the product), and the superstructure (institutions such as the state, the family, religion, education, and the law, and culture and ideology). Even among the productive forces, Stalin—Mao alleges—in a relative sense, neglected the growth of human capability, which should have constituted the core of the forces of production. Again, Stalin essentially viewed the direction of causation as a one-way route from change in the forces of production to alteration in the relations of production, and thereon to revamp of the superstructure.[32] Mao instead argued that elements of the superstructure are transformed only with a considerable lag; the old culture hangs on long after the material base of the economy is radically altered. But, if a conscious effort is made to change the elements of the superstructure, this, in turn, affects the economic base (the productive forces and the relations of production). Hence, Mao was bent on ushering in the People's Communes even before the modernisation of agriculture, for the former, in his view, by changing the relations of production and elements of the superstructure, the latter with a lag, would, in turn, spur the productive forces. Hence, also the stress upon the stifling economic effects of the prevailing class structure of the factories during the CR, or of the domination of landlords and "comprador-bureaucrat" capitalists in the pre-liberation period, or on the liberating effects of smashing the superstructure (for example, Confucian culture).[33] How apparently open-ended the interrelations among and between the forces of production, the relations of production, and the superstructure are in Mao's conception of Marx's theory of history?

Marrying the Various Strands

We have seen in this chapter that, at its best, Marxism leads one to expect a close inter-relationship between theory and practice; where either is scarce the other will be acutely disadvantaged. Maoism, by and large, has privileged practice over theory—it views practice as the foundation of theory. But what does the Maoist dictum "seek truth from practice mean"? At its best, and if one reads Mao's July 1937 definitive *On Practice: On the Relation Between Knowledge and Practice, Between Knowing and Doing*, he takes on both, the dogmatists and the empiricists, the "right opportunists" and the "leftists". As he puts it: "Practice ['class struggle, political life, scientific and artistic pursuits'], knowledge, again practice, and again knowledge. This form repeats itself in endless cycles, and with each cycle the content of practice and knowledge rises to a higher level". And, in his outstanding August 1937 essay *On Contradiction* he holds that contradictions—the struggle between functionally united opposites—cause continual change. Development stems from the resolution of contradictions and strategy involves choice of the form of struggle most suited to resolve a contradiction. But the desired qualitative alteration can be brought only through a series of stages, where the existing stage is impregnated with the hybrid seeds of the subsequent one, thereby dissolving the salient contradictions of the former and ushering in the latter. Mao's Marxism was of the Leninist school, albeit tending closer to its Stalinist version (which, as we have seen, is a decomposed version of Leninism), but struggling to overcome and go beyond Stalinism.

We have traversed a wide canvas with some wild strokes, covering the ground from Marxism to Leninism, and from there to its Stalinist revision, and then to Maoism in terms of its evolution and development in China from the late 1920s to the late 1960s, focusing on its *differentiae specifica*. The latter, we have found, are:

- the poor peasantry of the interior of a backward capitalist/semi-feudal society rather than the urban proletariat constitute the mass support base of the movement;
- theory of revolution by stages as well as uninterrupted revolution, implying a close link between successive stages;
- the stage of NDR, which makes capitalism much more compatible with democracy, thereby aiding the transition to socialism;
- the path and strategy of PPW, which relies on the peasants, builds rural base areas, carries out "land to the tiller" and other social policies in these areas (run democratically as miniature, self-reliant states) thereby

building up a political mass base in the countryside to finally encircle and capture the cities;

- the conception of "base areas" and the way to establishing them;
- "capturing" (winning mass support in) the cities by demonstrating a brand of nationalism that is genuinely anti-imperialist, thereby re-orienting an existing mass nationalist upsurge (as during the anti-Japanese resistance, 1937-45 in China) in favour of the completion of the NDR;
- democratic centralism *plus* the "mass line", ensuring that "democracy" does not take a backseat to "centralism" and making sure the people are involved in policymaking and its implementation;
- the central idea that contradictions—the struggle between functionally united opposites—at each stage drive the process of development on the way to socialism, which is sought to be brought about in a series of stages, where the existing stage, at the right time, is impregnated with the hybrid seeds of the subsequent one, thereby dissolving the salient contradictions of the former and ushering in the latter;
- open-ended interrelations among and between the forces of production, the relations of production, and the superstructure; and
- the idea that political, managerial, and bureaucratic power-holders entrench themselves as a ruling elite and, over a period of time, assume the position of a new exploiting class, and that the people have to be constantly mobilised to struggle against this tendency.

"Materialist dialectics" as a way of thinking and a guide to doing was a powerful tool in Mao's hands, but its weaknesses were perhaps inherent in its very strengths; in the end, the very method led him to hugely overestimate the pace of change and vastly underestimate the obstacles to change. Marx too fell into the same trap when his very method of analysis led him to believe that revolution was around the corner, immensely underrating the huge barriers to progressive change. Does the very application of the method of materialist dialectics lead its practitioners to err on the side of "voluntarism" in their practice?

If one looks forward from the vantage point of 1969—the year marks the beginning of the end of the Maoist era—the great reversal from "socialism" to capitalism lay ahead.

Even in the mid-1960s the question of whether it will be capitalism or socialism in China was still unsettled. At the age of 72, the guerrilla in Mao stirred again—better to burn out than to hit the skids. As Jerome Ch'en, quoting Mao the poet put it:

> The Chinese revolution was at a cross-road. It could "look down the precipices" and beat a retreat or "reach the ninth heaven high ..." and then "return to merriment and triumphant songs". The choice, according to the poet, depended entirely upon one's "will to ascend".[34]

Four years later, all that remained were the embers—the time had come to just fade away. Not much later, his closest comrades, Zhou Enlai and Zhu De passed away. The Bard of Avon's idea that "all the world's a stage" has acquired the status of a cliché, but it must surely have been one of the great pleasures of Mao's life to have been on the same stage with the two of them. The time was now up for one of the greatest Marxist revolutionaries of all time to ascend to the stars to join them, and Marx, Engels, Lenin, Trotsky, Stalin, the 20 million soldiers of the Red Army who had died in the war against fascism, the many ordinary peasant-guerrillas of the PLA who sacrificed their lives in the long march to a better world.

Maoism, however, needs to be taken to task; one cannot but ask: Why did the peasants and workers not resist the great reversals to capitalism in China and the Soviet Union? Were these regimes, as long as Mao and Stalin were around, really socialist, as has constantly been the claim of latter-day Maoists? The truth could only be highly disappointing, that is, if one were to judge Maoism, as is only fair, by the fruits of its project of taking humanity along the road towards equality, cooperation, community, and solidarity. In China itself, Maoism did not succeed on this score—all the united actions of the workers and the poor peasants, all the mass education of the Maoist period did not seem to have brought about their intellectual development to a point where, when it came to taking on the "capitalist roaders" after 1978 to uphold the ideas of equality and cooperation as against hierarchy and competition, they did precious little. Maoism failed to provide a successful working model of socialism in the 20th century. What is worse, even as Mao was in his last years, China entered into an accommodation with US imperialism against the Soviet Union—Mao's *On Contradiction* was misapplied to justify the arrangement. In a blatant violation of an important Maoist tenet, nationalism got the better of anti-imperialism when in 1974 Deng Xiaoping used so-called "three worlds' theory" to rationalise the "right-wing" turn in China's foreign policy. But despite all these shortcomings, there can be little doubt that over the longer period, from the late 1920s to the late 1960s, Maoism did something unprecedented in human history—it brought about a drastic redistribution of income and wealth in China; it radically reordered the way Chinese society's economic surplus was generated and utilised, all for the better.

Mao's Legacy and the Future of Maoism

It is time then to talk of Mao's legacy. As we have seen, Maoism has a definite view about how to get to socialism, and about what needs to be done to meet the basic needs of everyone in a poor country. Development is to be on an egalitarian basis—we are all in it together and everyone rises together. What then of Mao's legacy, Maoism? Surely, this is open to all who share his *Weltanschauung*, his method of analysis—materialist dialectics—his values, his vision, and choose to embark together on the long march to socialism, knowing before hand, that the journey is fraught with considerable peril.

What then of the future of Maoism and the renewal of socialism that it promises? Frankly, "whatever chance there may have been that the revolutions of the 20th century could or would provide successful working models of socialism" have long since been extinguished; "socialism, we are told, has been tried and failed".[35] But, as Marx was the first to show, the obstacles to a better future cannot be meaningfully addressed within the framework of capitalism. The challenge then is to revive and renew the legacy of socialism. In this, can Maoism illuminate the way?

Maoism has its roots in Marx who was, above all, a *radical* democrat—he demanded the reincarnation of community and mass solidarity; he dreamed of the communion of human beings with nature; he stressed the dialectic of liberation; he looked forward to a just society alongside "rich individuality"; and, as Paresh Chattopadhyay reminds us, he insisted on the removal of commodity exchange, the division of labour, the state. But, then, Lenin too, in his *State and Revolution* appeared as a thoroughgoing democrat, though he introduced into his conception of socialism elements that are antithetical to the "association of free individuals"—wage labour and the state.[36]

Given the *radical* democratic streak running from Marx to Mao, the best thing that Maoism could do is to commit to the promise of *radical* democracy; after all, while it is true that there cannot be liberty in any meaningful sense without equality, for the rich will certainly be more "free" (have more options) than the poor; so there also cannot be equality without liberty, for then some may have more political power than others.

So far, all revolutions inspired by Marx have only enjoyed the support or participation of a significant minority. Can the commitment to *radical* democracy up the tide to get the help of the majority? Will the means then be carefully chosen so that they never come to overwhelm the socialist aspiration?

NOTES

1. Paul Sweezy, 'What is Marxism?' in *Monthly Review*, Vol. 36, No. 10, March, 1985, p. 2.
2. Ibid., pp. 3-4.
3. Paresh Chattopadhyay, in personal correspondence, draws my attention to the view that Marx spoke of a "political transition *period*" (not of constituting a distinct "society") from capitalism to communism under the rule of the proletariat; socialism and communism, for him, were simply the alternative names for the same classless society he looked forward to, after capitalism.
4. Paul Sweezy, 'Marxism and Revolution 100 Years after Marx', in *Monthly Review*, Vol. 34, No. 10, March 1983, pp. 2-3.
5. See Geoffrey Kay, *Development and Underdevelopment: A Marxist*

Analysis (London: Macmillan, 1975).
6. Paul Sweezy, 'Note on the Centennial of *Das Kapital*', in *Monthly Review*, Vol. 19, No. 7, December 1967, p. 16.
7. Harry Braverman, 'Lenin and Stalin', in *Monthly Review*, June 1969, p. 54.
8. Paresh Chattopadhyay, 'Worlds Apart: Socialism in Marx and in Early Bolshevism', in *Economic & Political Weekly*, Vol. 20, No. 53, December 31, 2005.
9. Ralph Miliband, 'Dictatorship of the Proletariat', in Tom Bottomore (ed.), *A Dictionary of Marxist Thought* (New Delhi: Maya Blackwell, 2000), p. 151.
10. Monty Johnstone, 'Democractic Centralism', in Ibid., p. 135.
11. Monty Johnstone, 'Party', in Ibid., pp. 408-9.
12. Ralph Miliband, 'Dictatorship of the Proletariat', in Ibid., p. 152.
13. Ralph Miliband, 'Stalinism', in Ibid., p. 517.
14. Ibid., pp. 517-9.
15. Ralph Miliband, 'State and Revolution', in Ibid., p. 524.
16. Ibid., p. 525.
17. Ralph Miliband, 'The State and Revolution', in Paul Sweezy and Harry Magdoff (ed.), *Lenin Today: Eight Essays on the Hundredth Anniversary of Lenin's Birth* (New York: Monthly Review Press, 1970).
18. George Thomson, 'From Lenin to Mao Tse-tung', in Paul Sweezy and Harry Magdoff, op.cit., p. 125.
19. Mobo Gao, *The Battle for China's Past: Mao and the Cultural Revolution* (London: Pluto Press, 2008), Chapters 4 and 5.
20. Ibid.
21. Paul Sweezy, 'Socialism in Poor Countries', in *Monthly Review*, Vol. 28, No. 5, October 1976, p. 10.
22. Benjamin Schwartz, 'The Philosopher', in Dick Wilson (ed.), *Mao Tse-tung in the Scales of History: A Preliminary Assessment Organised by the China Quarterly* (Cambridge: Cambridge University Press, 1977), p. 26.
23. Paul Sweezy, 'Capitalism and Democracy', in *Monthly Review*, Vol. 32, No. 2, June 1980.
24. Ibid.
25. William Hinton, 'Mao, Rural Development and Two-Line Struggle' in *Monthly Review*, Vol. 45, No. 9, February 1994; *China: An Unfinished Battle—Essays on Cultural Revolution and Further Developments in China* (Kharagpur: Cornerstone Publications, 2002); 'On the Role of Mas Zedong', in *Monthly Review*, Vol. 56, No. 4, September, 2004.

26. William Hinton, *Fanshen: A Documentary of Revolution in a Chinese Village* (New York: Monthly Review Press, 1966), p. 603.
27. William Hinton, *Shenfan: The Continuing Revolution in a Chinese Village* (New York: Vintage Books, 1983), pp. 142-3.
28. Willian Hinton, 'Mao, Rural Development and Two-Line Struggle', in *Monthly Review*, Vol. 45, No. 9, February 1994, pp. 6-7.
29. The figures have been disputed though, among others, by Utsa Patnaik (2004: 10-12) and Joseph Ball (2006).
30. Willian Hinton, 'On the Role of Mao Zedong', in *Monthly Review Press,* Vol. 56, No. 4, September 2004, p. 51.
31. Ibid, pp. 54, 55, 56-9.
32. Mao Tse-tung, *A Critique of Soviet Economics* (New York: Monthly Review Press, 1977).
33. Christopher Howe and Kenneth R. Walker, 'The Economist', in Dick Wilson (ed.), *Mao Tse-tung in the Scales of History: A Preliminary Assessment Organized by the China Quarterly* (Cambridge: Cambridge University Press, 1977), pp. 176-7.
34. Jerome Ch'en and Mao Tse-tung, 'An Unpublished Poem by Mao Tse-tung', in *The China Quarterly,* No. 34, April-June, 1968, p. 5.
35. Paul Sweezy, 'Socialism: Legacy and Renewal', in *Monthly Review*, Vol. 44, No. 8, January, 1993, p. 5.
36. Paresh Chattopadhyay, 'World Apart: Socialism in Marx and Early Bolshevism', in *Economic & Political Weekly*, Vol. 20. No. 53, December 31, 2005.

17

On 'What Is Maoism?': Some Comments

Paresh Chattopadhyay

This chapter is a rejoinder to Bernard D'Mello's 'What Is Maoism?' where one argues, among other things, that (1) the reader is not given the opportunity to verify whether the author's interpretations tally with the original texts of Marx, Lenin and Mao because he does not quote from the original texts; (2) the author and Paul Sweezy are wrong in particular interpretations of Marx and Engels; (3) Lenin misinterpreted Marx on socialism and was responsible for the degeneration of the Russian Revolution; (4) Mao was an ideological Stalinist; and (5) the category Cultural Revolution is alien to Marx.

The absolute necessity of the existence of the widest democracy for a socialist society runs like a red thread through D'Mello's essay, which is a rarity in the left thinking in India, and for this insistence, he deserves high praise indeed. The hard labour that he has put in this work is also very impressive and commendable. We have, however, a couple of comments to make on some of his positions, which, hopefully, he will take in the right spirit. One striking aspect of the essay is the almost complete absence of reference to works by Marx whose name is otherwise very often mentioned in developing the arguments of Lenin and Mao. In the same way, not much is seen of Lenin's own texts and only a few of Mao's. In contrast, we come across references to the works of a whole host of interpreters of the thoughts of Marx, Lenin and Mao. We submit that the readers should have been given a chance to verify from the texts of Marx (and Engels), Lenin and Mao how far the interpretations tally with the original texts. We have, for example, problems with the interpretations of Marx by Sweezy and Miliband read in the light of Marx's original texts. To paraphrase a Tagore song, "I understand what *you* say, *their* words puzzle me". Below we discuss a few points, which strike us as problematic.

Marx's Wrong Expectation

On the question of socialist revolution and socialism, what Marx had believed has been belied. The author holds, following Sweezy that things "have not worked that way". The author adds, "Marx and Engels proved wrong in their expectation of a socialist Europe" (By Europe, he presumably means the advanced capitalist countries). Why? Because they did not take into account the gains of the working class from the existing system itself. However, "Lenin and the Bolsheviks rescued Marxism from those who mechanically interpreted Marx as a historical determinist". Then he goes to the very root of the "mistaken expectation" of Marx and Engels (he speaks of the ideas of Marx and Engels as "Marxism" which is of course an ideologically loaded term) drawn mainly from Engels' *Condition of the Working Class in England* (1845) and Marx's Preface to the *Contribution to the Critique of Political Economy* (1859). Let us try to disentangle this very dense formulation. The opening statement, faithfully following Sweezy, is simply a faithful rehash of Lenin's position. We will take it up a little later. First, we deal with the cause of this wrong expectation. How this shortcoming is associated with the two texts remains not very clear, just as the question of any connection between these two texts themselves. A "reasonable" interpretation of the author's position would be that from Engels' 1845 work "Marxism" concluded that the European workers' increasing misery would lead them to revolution. As regards the 1859 text of Marx the idea here seems to be that this text could be made to mean a "deterministic" approach to revolution and thereby this would constitute an obstacle to revolution.

Unable or unwilling to confront Marx himself directly the proponents of this rather widespread idea among the Left squarely put the blame on the "revisionists" of the Second International for this deformation and the consequent absence of revolution in Europe. As to the first cause, the argument has an astonishing implication. It implies that Marx remained a permanent prisoner of Engels' ideas of 1845, whereas anyone with a modicum of knowledge of Marx's writings knows that nobody was more aware of the dynamics of capitalism, what revolutionary changes capitalism as a historical (and not natural) mode of production was going through as well as its inherent limitations. Similarly nobody was a keener observer of workers' daily struggles through their organisations to improve their lives compelling, from time to time, the governments to force the capitalists by legislation to limit their aggressions against the working class (like the factory acts in England).

Our author seems to accept the popular idea of Marx as a partisan of the thesis of continuous immiserisation of the working class. True, in Engels' book in question the idea of the workers earning just the minimum necessary for survival is there and for a time Marx shared this idea, but he rejected it in *Capital* (Engels no longer subscribed to it). Marx had a much richer position on the question. First of all, in the chapter on the "buying and selling of labour power" in *Capital I*, Marx noted that contrary to the case of other commodities there enters into the determination of the value of labour power "a historical and moral element". Quite naturally, in a sys*tem* where the "machine employs the workers, workers do not employ the machine" (Marx's paraphrase of Ricardo), workers' economic situation was indissolubly associated with the accumulation of capital. "Accumulation is the independent variable, wages are the dependent variable", as Marx wrote in the chapter on the "general law of capitalist accumulation". Here, he noted:

> Under more favourable conditions of accumulation a larger part of the workers' own surplus product, always increasing and continually transformed into additional capital, comes back to them in the shape of means of payment, so that they can extend the circle of their enjoyment; they can make some additions to their consumption fund of clothes, furniture, etc., and can lay by small reserve-fund of money.

Then Marx added:

> A rise in the price of labour, as a consequence of accumulation of capital, only means, in fact that the length and weight of the golden chain the wage-worker has already forged himself, allow of a relaxation of the tension of it.

A point not much discussed is that the system of wage labour itself—which comprises manual and intellectual labour under capital—Marx saw as dehumanising the individual, however elevated the remuneration is. Drawing on his earlier discussion (1844-46, 1857-58) Marx wrote in his very first notebook of 1861-63 "poverty signifies nothing but the fact that individual's labour power is the only commodity which s/he can dispose of" (Marx-Engels, *Complete Works in English* (*MEGA*) II/3.1:36). This Marx calls "absolute poverty of the worker". In his 1863-65 posthumously published text, *Results of the Immediate Process of Production*, Marx elaborates:

> The world of wealth develops as an alienating world dominating the worker and in the same proportion grows her (his) subjective poverty. *Fullness* on one side corresponds to the *emptiness* on the other side and they march together.

Therefore, when Marx spoke about socialist revolution at a particular stage of social development he had this "material dependence" of the worker (as he calls it in his 1857-58 manuscript) in mind irrespective of the level of remuneration and the accompanying material advantages of capital's "wage slaves".

Now we come to Marx's 1859 text. In order to link Marxism's failure of expectation regarding proletarian revolution in the advanced capitalist countries with this text, one would have to say (if one does not want to blame the text itself and thereby question Marx directly) that this text is ambiguous, giving scope to the "revisionists" to overemphasise the objective factor—the forces of production and neglect the subjective factor—the will and consciousness of the working class. This, we submit, is the subtext of what our author is affirming. And this is the usual argument of the revolutionaries against the "revisionists" who are seen as preventing the revolution from happening. We submit that the very idea that a handful of "revisionists" could prevent the working class from revolting, which act by definition is the crowning point of the "independent movement of the immense majority in the interest of the immense majority" (Marx and Engels, *Communist Manifesto*, 1848) is a reflection of the idea of a servile working class being led by a small group of illuminated individuals who alone know the truth. This is condemning the working class to a state of perpetual subordination.

Before we proceed further, let us remind the readers that 12 years earlier Marx had already designated the proletariat as the "greatest productive force". As regards the 1859 text itself, let us note that the part of the text dealing with Marx's materialism is basically a condensed version of his earlier two texts—*The German Ideology* (1845) and *Poverty of Philosophy* (1847). And, it is also important to emphasise that Marx makes *this* text later in *Capital* more than once the reference point of what he calls the "materialist basis of my method". Now what does this text say exactly? Here is the gist:

> No social formation ever disappears before all the productive forces for which there is room in it have developed, and new, higher relations make their appearance before the material conditions of their existence have matured in the womb of the old society itself. Therefore humanity always sets itself only such tasks as it can solve since the task itself arises only when the material conditions for its solution already exist or at least are in the process of becoming.

(The last four lines were paraphrased by Rosa Luxemburg in her critique of the Bolshevik leadership, for which she was vilely attacked by the Leninist George Lukács.)

Following this materialist conception of history, Marx argues that socialism is a product of history, not of nature or individuals' arbitrary will. As the 1848 *Manifesto* observes, the material conditions of the emancipation of the proletariat are the product of the bourgeois epoch. In his 1857-58 manuscript, Marx wrote:

> If in the society as it exists we did not already find the material

> conditions of production and the corresponding relations of circulation for a classless society in a latent form all attempts at exploding would be Don Quixotism.

And years later, a few years before his death, in his polemic with Bakunin, Marx stressed in his critical cospectus (1874-75) of Bakunin's book *Stateism and Anarchy* (1873):

> A radical social revolution is bound up with certain historical conditions of development. The latter are its preconditions. It is therefore only possible where, with capitalist development, the industrial proletariat occupies at least a significant position.

Then, he added:

> Bakunin understands absolutely nothing of social revolution excepting its political phrases. For him its economic conditions do not exist.

Lenin Overturned Marx

Flushed with victory of what he considered as socialist revolution, Lenin, in 1918, declared, clearly against Marx's materialist approach, that "things have worked differently than what Marx and Engels had expected". Sweezy's statement, cited above, is an uncritical, almost word for word repetition of Lenin's statement. In fact, under the "illusion of the epoch" as Marx would call it, such lucid scholars as Sweezy, Carr and Deutscher remarkably easily vindicated Lenin against Marx's materialist prognostic.

So far the "expectations" of Marx and Engels have not been refuted for the simple reason that there has been no socialist revolution or (naturally) socialism anywhere in the world in the Marxian meaning of these terms. Contrary to what Sweezy thought, socialism has not been tried and therefore socialism has not failed. Of course, one could always argue that this very fact of the absence of proletarian revolution until now is itself a refutation of Marx's prognostic. However, there is no evidence that Marx had fixed a calendar for the advent of the new society the way the pious Christians wait for the Second Coming of Jesus. But, a more important point, from the point of view of Marx's materialism, is that the objective situation in the capitalist countries in general has not yet reached the point where the "greatest productive force"—the wage and salary earning hired labourers in their great majority could no longer accept the existing society (that is, the complex of the social relations of production) and rise in revolt. After all, capitalism is only a few hundred years old.

The point is that Lenin, of course in the name of Marx, completely overturned— that is, *revised*—both the conditions of socialist revolution and the meaning of socialism itself as they were envisaged by Marx following the materialist conception of history. And history, the "best of all Marxists"[1] has already rendered its verdict on Lenin's position as we all know. Ultimately, the "rescuer of Marxism" could not himself be rescued.

Our author says that Lenin's aspirations and vision of the socialist state as expressed in *The State and Revolution*—after the seizure of power were inspired by Marx's lauding of the Paris Commune. He adds that "Marx was emphatic" that the working class after taking power should not simply take control of the existing structure, institutions of the old state all of which had to be smashed and *"replaced by a new state"* (our emphasis). Now this is a paraphrase of what Lenin had said on this question. In his article 'Can the Bolsheviks Retain State Power' (1917) Lenin wrote:

> Marx taught that the proletariat cannot simply lay hold of the readymade state machine and use it for its own purposes, that the proletariat must smash this machine and *substitute a* new one *for it* (emphasis ours).

Lenin here *revised* in a vital way what "Marx had taught". Let us read the teacher's own words. In his *Civil War in France* (1871, composed in English), Marx wrote, "The working class cannot simply lay hold of the readymade state machinery and wield it for its own purposes". At about the same time, in a letter to Kugelmann dated April 12, 1871, available in *On the Paris Commune*, Karl Marx and Frederick Engels, 1971 Progress Publishers, Moscow, Marx reminded his friend that already in *Eighteenth Brumaire*, he had declared that the:

> next attempt of the French Revolution will be no longer, as before, transfer of the bureaucratic military machine from one hand to the other, but to smash it, and this is the preliminary condition of every real people's revolution on the continent.

If we closely read the texts of these two individuals we see most of the things that Marx had written find their place in Lenin's text, but Marx nowhere says what we have underlined in Lenin's text or in our author's text, following Lenin. This is literally Lenin's *revision* of Marx's text, by Lenin's own definition of this dreaded term. In Lenin's hand, the full revolutionary meaning of the Marxian text is seriously watered down. Why? Because Marx always thought the state as an alien, repressive machinery for the individual, whatever be the type of the state. Already in the early 1840s, he had written "The existence of state and the existence of slavery are inseparable". In the same text, Marx precisely wrote:

> Even the radical and revolutionary politicians seek the cause of evil not in the essence of the state but in a specific form of the state which they want *to replace by another form of state* (our emphasis).

In the posthumously published 'First Outline' of *The Civil War in France* Marx counted as one of the achievements of the communards the:

> displacing of the state machinery—the government machinery of the ruling class—by a *government machinery of their own* (our emphasis).

The remarkable thing is that Marx does not see the replacement of the old state machinery by a new state machinery. It is the government, not the state that enters the scene. In the same text, Marx writes, "This was a Revolution not against this or that form of state power. It was a Revolution against the State itself", as if he saw the realisation of what he had expressed as a general statement about three decades earlier.

Lenin and Bureaucracy

Our author quite consistently with his stress on the

indispensability of democracy for socialism regrets the rise of bureaucracy in Russia not long after the Bolshevik victory. The principle of "democratic centralism" lost its democratic component in practice. He particularly mentions the virtual outlawing of factions within the party beginning with 1921 "something Stalin is said to have taken advantage of to secure his domination of the party". Blaming Stalin for "Soviet" bureaucracy is the easy pan. Our author seems to try to absolve Lenin from much (if not all) of the responsibility for the growing bureaucracy by recalling Lenin's "last struggle-warning of danger from the growth of a ruling bureaucracy".

The author's discussion of rise of bureaucracy in the 'Soviet' Union, we submit, is oversimplified. It is somewhat surprising that while our author is rightly concerned with democracy as a principle, when he comes to discuss the regression of democracy in the USSR, his focus is mainly on the loss of democracy *within* the Communist Party. The rapid loss of democracy within the society at large does not seem to bother him. Victor Serge, a great contemporary eyewitness, remarked in his *Memoires:* "Soviet democracy lasted from October 1917 to the summer of 1918. Afterwards the Communist Party began to suppress all the revolutionary groups and parties". Isaac Deutscher wrote in *The Prophet Armed* (1963), referring to the period 1921-22:

> For the first time since 1917 the bulk of the working class, not to speak of the peasantry, unmistakeably turned against the Bolsheviks... If the Bolsheviks had now permitted free elections to the Soviets, they would almost certainly have been swept away from power (p. 504).

As regards the role of Lenin personally in this regression of democracy, he cannot get away from it so easily. Stalin came only later and with a vengeance. Deutscher analyses with rare lucidity the rise of Stalin in his *Stalin: A Political Biography* (1949) on which we draw. Stalin's candidature as general secretary of the party was sponsored by Lenin. Stalin was voted into all his positions of power by his rivals.

> The General Secretary knew how to justify each act of repression against malcontent Bolsheviks in the light of the party statutes as they had, on *Lenin's initiative* and with Trotsky's support, been

> amended by the Tenth and Eleventh Congresses. He was careful to explain every step he made as an inevitable consequence of decisions previously adopted by common consent (our emphasis).

Within months of the October uprising, how the "revolution was in retreat from the aims of social liberation it had proclaimed" has been very well described in a recent publication based on the newly opened Russian archives by a young researcher, Simon Pirani.[2] This "retreat" did not have to wait for Stalin for its start. In fact, the resolution to ban the factions within the party was moved by Lenin in person at the Tenth Congress (1921) of the party, and the decision, as Pirani notes, was taken after the briefest discussions at a closed-door session, held after many delegates had already left. Much later Trotsky, through his own painful experience as an outcast from the system, wrote that the Tenth Congress "brought the heroic history of Bolshevism to an end and made way for its bureaucratic degeneration" (cited in Pirani).

But whatever might have been the contribution of the Tenth Congress to the strengthening of the bureaucratic process, its basic cause did not lie there. It has to be traced to October 1917 itself, to the starting point of the new regime—ignored by most of the observers and certainly by the dominant Left (including academics like Sweezy and Miliband). The surest antidote to bureaucracy was generated in the great council ("soviet") movement of the labouring people and soldiers arising spontaneously in early 1917 in Petrograd and spreading fairly rapidly all over the vast land, gaining increasing strength with a strong possibility of going over to the next stage of social evolution—socialism (communism)—if allowed unfettered freedom to go ahead. The councils as the self-governing organs of the labouring people, through the system of universal free election and recall by the electorate of *all* holders of administrative positions would make the rise of bureaucracy simply impossible.

This unique opportunity—the great chance of the century—was destroyed by the pre-emptive strike by the Bolsheviks who under the cover of the great popular slogan "All Power to the Soviets" seized power before the Second Congress of Soviets could meet, behind the back and over the head of the Congress of Soviets (the leader literally denigrating the Soviets in his private correspondence with his colleagues in the leadership) and paved the way for a single party rule. An important point should be noted here. Here we draw on the superb blow-by-blow account of the period July-October (1917) by the eminent historian Alexander Rabinowitch.[3] On the eve of the Second Congress the delegates assembled in Petrograd for the event were asked to fill out detailed personal questionnaires. Tabulation of these questionnaires reveals the striking fact that an overwhelming number of delegates (including, of course, the Bolshevik delegates who constituted the biggest single group), supported the transfer of "all power to the Soviets", that is, the "creation of a Soviet government presumably reflective of the party composition of the Congress".[4] Rabinowitch concludes his great book thus:

> It bears repeating that the Petrograd masses, to the extent that they supported the Bolsheviks, in the overthrow of the Provisional Government, did so not out of any sympathy for strictly Bolshevik rule but because they believed the revolution and the Congress to be in imminent danger. Only the creation of a broadly representative *socialist government* by the Congress of Soviets, *which is what they believed the Bolsheviks stood for*, appeared to offer hope of insuring that there would be no return to the hated ways of the old regime (p. 314; our emphasis).

It is indeed ironical that Lenin, after having presided over the liquidation of the workers' organs of self-government (the Soviets and the factory committees) could, "in his last writings", according to our author, "express the need for creating a basis for popular self-governance". Given this liquidation it is not surprising at all that within a very short period after the establishment of the Party-State there arose an administration with a body of unelected officials, hierarchically organised from top downwards. Similarly, within the newly created 'Red' Army, the principle of election of officers was abolished, the rights of soldiers' committees were clipped, and the erstwhile Tsarist officers—universally hated till now—were placed in responsible positions. Towards the end of his life, Lenin had to admit that the Bolsheviks "effectively took over the old state apparatus from the Tsar and the bourgeoisie".

Naturally, the regime felt threatened by the existence of the thoroughly democratic Soviet of Kronstadt, which defied it by demanding the implementation of all the democratic, libertarian promises that the Bolsheviks had made before coming to power and later did not deliver, and raised the slogan "all power to the Soviets, not to parties". Consequently, on the totally fabricated charge that the Kronstadt sailors and toilers were at the service of the Whites, the counter-revolutionaries, the regime massacred thousands of them (only Lenin had the honesty to deny the charge at the Tenth Congress of the party). Thus ended "a bustling, self-governing, egalitarian democracy, the like of which had not been seen in Europe since the days of the Paris Commune", writes the well- known historian, Israel Getzler, in perhaps the best documented book on the subject by an academic, *Kronstadt 1917-1921: The Fate of a Soviet Democracy.*

Mao's Bolshevik Connection

Our author offers a competent narrative of the development of the political dynamic of the post-1949 China dominated mostly by Mao. He quite correctly stresses the close connection of Mao's thought with the ideas of Lenin and Stalin and at the same time he shows Mao's critical attitude to them, to Stalin's ideas in particular. Though Mao's Marxism was closer to the Stalinist version of Lenin's Marxism, rather than Lenin's Marxism itself, Mao at the same time was "struggling to overcome and go beyond Stalinism". After arguing that Mao criticised Stalin's mechanical materialism, our author asks, "how apparently open ended the interrelations among and between the forces of production, relations of production and the superstructure are in Mao's conception of Marx's theory of history?" He says, "Marx (like Mao) fell into the (same) trap when his very method of analysis led him to believe that revolution was around the corner, immensely underrating the huge barriers to progressive change. Does the very application of the method of materialist dialectics lead its practitioners to err on the side of 'voluntarism' in practice?"

We submit that whenever Marx thought, "revolution was around the corner" he precisely did not follow his own "materialist method". This comes out in a remarkable self-critical letter that he wrote to Engels immediately after he had finished writing the first volume of *Capital* (7 December 1867). Not much attention has been given to this important letter. In this letter, he only refers to himself as the "author" of *Capital,* without mentioning his own name. Here is the most important part (given in our translation):

> One should distinguish between two things (in *Capital*): positive developments and tendentious conclusions. The developments constitute a direct enrichment of the science, since the real economic relations are treated here in an entirely new way, *following the materialist method.* As regards the tendency of the author, here also a distinction is in order. When the author demonstrates that the existing society, considered from the economic point of view, carries within itself the germs of a new form of higher society, he is only showing, on the social plane, the same process of transformation, which Darwin has established in the natural sciences. However, the merit of the author is to show progress hidden even there the modern economic relations are accompanied by consequences which are immediately disastrous. Thereby all utopia is destroyed. Contrariwise, the subjective tendency of the author—he was perhaps obliged to act this way bound by his party position and his past—that is, the manner in which he presents the result of the present day movement, of the present day social process has no relation with its real development. One could perhaps show that his 'objective' development refutes his own 'subjective' fancies' (our emphasis).

One aspect of Mao's Stalin connection is not found in our author's otherwise important narrative and has hardly been discussed in the literature. With all his otherwise significant differences with Stalin, Mao's ideological position in its fundamental aspects was Stalinist. He completely accepted Stalin's un-Marxian position that the system of ownership is the basis of the relations of production. In Marx, following the materialist conception of history, it is the exact opposite. For Marx, real relation of production forms the foundation on which arises the juridical relation of property. It is what Marx calls a "juridical edifice", arising from the production relation (see the

1859 Preface mentioned earlier). Stalin required this inversion in order to prove the socialist character of the society he was leading. He declared the 'Soviet' Union to be socialist on the basis of the juridical elimination of *individual* private ownership of the means of production, thereby standing Marx on his head. Mao too proclaimed the establishment of China's "socialist system" on the basis of the juridical change in the form of ownership of the means of production.

This was totally abstracted from the real relations of production, or rather Mao assumed an equivalence relation between a juridical change in ownership and a change in the real relation of production. Marx would call this a "juridical illusion". (This "juridical illusion" has engulfed the rulers of the Party-States and their international sympathisers and followers since Stalin.) Mao was of course fully aware of the existence of commodity production and wage labour in China, which have no place in Marxian socialism, and did not go to the absurd length of the Stalinist position that this wage in socialism is different from the capitalist wage (copying from Bukharin and Preobrazhensky without acknowledgement). The contradiction is clear in Mao's statement:

> China is a socialist country... At present our country practises the commodity system, an eighth grade wage system, and the wage system is unequal, and in all this scarcely different from the old society; the difference is that the system of ownership has changed.

This goes well with Stalin's concept of socialism and would correspond to what Marx would consider as (state) capitalism. Mao's assertion of the existence of classes in socialism—even when (wrongly) understood as the lower phase of communism, à la Lenin—is a complete revision even of Lenin who said that "socialism means the abolition of classes". But it goes well with Stalin's position. Increasingly, after the 1950s, classes were conceived by Mao not in terms of production relations but in terms of ideology and culture. According to him, though China was already socialist, classes and class struggle continued to exist. In order to eliminate "restoration of capitalism", the "capitalist roaders" had to be eliminated through a series of "cultural revolutions".

In Marx, cultural revolution as an independent category does not exist. A socialist revolution is an all-embracing self-emancipatory act undertaken by the working class which continues "in permanence" over an entire epoch. There is no need for a separate cultural revolution after society has become socialist. For the period intervening between the establishment of the proletarian rule and the advent of socialism is precisely the "period of revolutionary transformation" during which the "working class passes through long struggles, through a series of historic processes *transforming circumstances and individuals*" as Marx wrote in 1871 (which takes care of cultural transformations as well).

A final word. The Communist Party under Mao was at best a party for the labouring people but could not really be called a party of and by the labouring people. Remaining outside the labourers' effective control and claiming to know their interests better than the labourers themselves, the Chinese Communist Party, like the Communist Party of the USSR, considered leading and directing the labouring people as their "duty". The fundamental decisions concerning the fate of the labouring people were made and enforced by the party leadership unaccountable to, indeed, over the head of the general body of China's labouring people who were, as in the USSR, simply exhorted to participate in executing those decisions. Ultimately it was Mao on whose decisions depended the destiny of a whole people. The regime prided itself on stressing, "Chairman Mao personally directed and fixed the resolution on the edification of the people's communes". The initiative to launch the cultural revolution came, unsurprisingly, not from the labouring people themselves but from the "Chairman in person". In a society supposed to be marching to communism every move was centred on Mao's "latest instructions". The continuing emphasis was on Mao being "the great teacher, great leader, great supreme commander, great helmsman". There indeed is an unbridgeable gap between this society of *subordinated* labour and a society of "associated labour plying its toil with a willing hand, a ready mind and a joyous heart" (Marx, "Inaugural Address of the International Workingmen's Association", 1864).

NOTE

1. R. Hilferding, 'State Capitalism or Totalitarian State Economy' in Irving Howe (ed.), *A Handbook of Socialist Thought* (London: Victor Gollancz, 1972).
2. Simon Pirani, *The Russian Revolution in Retreat, 1920-1924* (London: Routledge, 2008).
3. Alexander Rabinowitch, *The Bolsheviks Come to Power* (London: Pluto Press, 1976).
4. Ibid., pp. 291-92.

18

Did Lenin and Mao Forsake Marx?

Bernard D'Mello

This chapter is in disagreement with some of the criticisms of the previous chapter 'What Is Maoism?' by Paresh Chattopadhyay which is related to ways of interpreting the Marxist classics and particular interpretations of Marx and Engels. One deals with Chattopadhyay's pronouncements that Lenin misinterpreted Marx on socialism and was responsible for the degeneration of the Russian Revolution. One also deals with Chattopadhyay's theses that Mao was an ideological Stalinist, and that Cultural Revolution is alien to Marx's thought.

Briefly, Chattopadhyay's (PC) remarks, observations, and criticisms are as follows:

(i) The reader is not given a chance to verify from the texts of Marx, Engels, Lenin, and Mao as to how far my interpretations tally with the originals because I do not engage in the usual practice of textual quotations;

(ii) There are a couple of problems with the interpretations of Marx by Sweezy and Miliband that I have relied upon, for instance, my mistaken reflection, following Sweezy, that Marx and Engels proved wrong in their expectation that the working class in the more developed capitalist countries would, sooner or later, bring about socialist revolution;

(iii) Lenin completely misinterpreted, indeed, "*revised*" Marx on the very "meaning of socialism", the "conditions of socialism", and so on, and was to blame for the degeneration of the Russian Revolution, but I try to absolve him of his responsibility;
(iv) Mao was essentially an ideological Stalinist; and
(v) "Cultural Revolution" (CR) is alien to Marx's thought.

Interpreting the Classical Marxist Texts

With regard to (i), I did not take recourse to textual quotations from Marx, Lenin, or Mao, or kept such references to a bare minimum, because I do not think that this is the only way to resolve debates. I am put off when Marxists, all too often, think that textual quotations from the "classics" are the last word on any and everything. I do not think that Marx, Lenin or Mao would ever have claimed that they said the last word on anything. Instead, Marxists should understand and deal with social phenomena by using Marx's method, "materialist dialectics", and in the spirit of Marx, rather than interpreting and explaining passages in Marx's, Lenin's, and/or Mao's writings and fitting them to unravel what happened or what is happening.

With regard to Marx and Engels, first, it is important that we take what they had written at particular times in the course of their lives, whether in the 1840s, or in the 1850s and 1860s, or later on, in the 1870s and 1880s, within the *specific context* in which they expressed themselves. Second, they did change their views with the passage of time, and third, like all human beings, they were fallible. For example, what Marx said in the preface to the first German edition of *Capital*, Volume I (1867) that the "country that is more developed industrially only shows, to the less developed, the image of its own future", he no longer stood by towards the end of his life. To him, in 1881, industrially advanced England no longer showed "backward" Russia what it was supposedly destined to be. Indeed, in the last phase of his life—in the 1870s and up to the time he died in 1883—he began to think differently about the prospects of socialism in the "centre" and "periphery" of the global capitalist system (characterised by "uneven development"). Take, for instance, his imagining the transfer of technology from a developed country to the Russian commune and its adoption under the control of the actual producers there after the revolution. Of course, there is continuity *and* discontinuity in his thought from the 1840s to the early 1880s, continuity, for instance, in his philosophy of the essence of being human, given his passion for social justice.

PC has quoted extensively from Marx to question some of (what he considers are) my (and Sweezy's) interpretations of Marx and Engels. I am now expected to, in turn, point to other quotations and further texts to contradict him, and then, the reader is supposed to be the arbiter among the competing interpretations, but I will not engage in any of this. Instead, the reader can go back to the relevant section of my essay 'What Is Maoism?' and read it along with what follows over here.

While we Marxists share a *Weltanschauung*, we do differ quite a bit in our interpretations and assessments of even the classical Marxist texts. Indeed, the School of Marxism that I come from considers Lenin's writings, along with those of Marx and Engels, as part of classical Marxism, but PC will probably differ on this. I think that a mere selective, literal reading of a part of the texts will not resolve the question of the validity of one interpretation over the other. It is necessary to state one's theoretical position first.

As readers of my essay 'What Is Maoism?' may have gathered, I am close to the *Monthly Review* School. At the core of my essay is the view, for reasons mentioned therein (which *seem* to have escaped PC's attention), that the centre of the revolutionary struggle for socialism had shifted from the "advanced" to the "backward" parts of the global capitalist system. One has only to look at the dispossessed masses of the "periphery" of the world capitalist system, their lived experience, which represents "the focal point of all inhuman conditions in contemporary society". It is in this mass of humanity that "the human being is lost", but "has won a theoretical consciousness of loss and is compelled by unavoidable and absolutely compulsory need...to revolt against this inhumanity". The young Marx and Engels in *The Holy Family* wrote what we have just paraphrased about the industrial proletariat of Western Europe in 1844. However, for reasons that we wrote about in our essay, within a few decades such a brilliant depiction no longer captured that proletariat's existential situation any more. Nevertheless, it applied/applies so well to the dispossessed masses of the "periphery" of the world capitalist system—to Russia when Lenin and his comrades were formulating their strategy and tactics of revolution in the second decade of the 20th century, to China when Mao and his comrades were doing the same in the 1930s, and to the dispossessed masses organised by the Communist Party of India (Maoist) in India today. In fact, Marx and Engels' depiction of the existential situation of the West European proletariat then, and its correspondence with the lived experience of the dispossessed masses of the "periphery" today or in Russia in 1917 or China in the 1930s is what provided me with one of the essential links connecting Marx to Lenin, and onward to Mao. I tried to follow Marx's method in dealing with the question of what Maoism was all about—its precursors, how it came into being and developed (practice-knowledge—practice), how it worked and how it is working, where it is likely leading (the forces promoting change in the doctrine's thought and practice, and those maintaining equilibrium).

Marx and Engels' Wrong Expectation

Let us then come to (ii). Frankly, though I may not agree on all that he wrote, I admire Paul Sweezy's writings. In my essay; which, as I stated, makes "no claim whatsoever to originality", and that I wrote "as a self-clarifying exercise", I found Sweezy and some of the other writers of the *Monthly Review* School, including Ralph Miliband, most enlightening. I have put these writings together in my book *What is Maoism and Other Essays*.[1] My purpose in writing the essay 'What Is Maoism?' was to get across to the young layperson, not so much to the scholar, so that she/he could help make up her/his mind about Maoism.

Regarding PC's objections to my (and Sweezy's) interpretations of Marx, I must state that I cannot even presume to speak on behalf of the late Paul Sweezy, but I will respond the way I have understood him. PC is mistaken if he thinks that my view (and Sweezy's) of Marx and Engels' wrong expectation of the working class in the more advanced of the capitalist countries, sooner or later, bringing about a socialist revolution came mainly from Engels' description of that class' inhuman living and working conditions in the first half of the 19th century and Marx's famous 1859 Preface to *A Contribution to the Critique of Political Economy*. Indeed, from the latter, I (or Sweezy) never concluded that Marx was an "economic or historical determinist". However, did Marx and Engels ever go on to rigidly use the famous formula of the Preface involving the forces of production, the relations of production, and the super-structure in any of their historical writings when they brought in the connection of political and social structures with the economic base? No.

I, in fact, following Sweezy, hinted at the improvement in the living and working conditions, as also, the political status of the working class in the second half of the 19th century— the rising trend in real wages, unionisation, political representation, the origins of the welfare state—due to rapid growth (and accumulation of capital) following the failure of the revolutions of 1848. However, and again, following Sweezy, I stressed the increasing exploitation of the "periphery" that was to come later on, in the last decades of the 19th century. As I put it:

> ...the surplus from the toilers in the colonies/neo-colonies/ semi-colonies/dependent countries (the "periphery"), shared not only between the local elites and the ruling classes at the "centre", but also, to an extent, by the working classes there, helped provide pan of the cushion.[2] As a result, capital at the "centre" got richer and stronger too.

PC seems to have totally missed this.

Blaming Lenin and His Comrades

Of course, Lenin "revised" Marx; so did Trotsky and Mao, for capitalism had changed from Marx's time. Surely, his theory needed to be supplemented and modified to account for the changing reality as well as the new advances in knowledge since then. I was referring to the "revisionism" of "Eduard Bernstein and others" in the sense of their emptying Marxism of its revolutionary content. Lenin never did that. Let us then come to (iii). Did Lenin completely misinterpret, indeed, *"revise"* Marx on the very meaning of socialism, the conditions of socialism, the socialist "state", and so on, in the sense of draining them of their revolutionary content? Was he really to blame for the degeneration of the Russian Revolution? Did I try to absolve him of his responsibility for what happened?

The industrial revolution came late to Russia, at the end of the 19th century, spawning an industrial proletariat. Its living and working conditions resembled those of the English workers in the first half of that century, which the 24-year-old Engels had so brilliantly depicted. The Russian proletariat was receptive to the Marxist ideas that Lenin and his comrades tried to impart to them. Indeed, the Bolsheviks successfully guided them to victory in the 1917 Revolution. In my essay, I made the criticism of Lenin and the other Bolsheviks that following the seizure of power, in the context of the bloody civil war over four years, the means began to shape the very ends to eventually overwhelm the socialist aspiration. I, however, commended the way the Bolsheviks conceived of the revolution in "backward" capitalist Russia, the worker-peasant alliance they helped forge, the vanguard party and its organisational principle of "democratic centralism", and so on. Given Russia's "backwardness", Lenin and his close comrades felt, not without any real basis, that the dictatorship of the proletariat could only be realistically brought about and exercised by the workers under the guidance of the vanguard party.

Tragically though, as I had written, following Miliband, the democratic component was stamped out of "democratic centralism" and the "dictatorship of the proletariat" degenerated into "the dictatorship of the party and the state over the whole of society, including the proletariat". Why and how did these come about? We have no reason to lay the blame on Lenin, as PC does.

The society brought into being after the revolution could not but have been ridden with deep contradictions and sharp conflicts, that is, if it was in transition between capitalism and socialism (communism). Would Marx and Engels have conceived of it any differently? We are talking of the period of revolutionary transformation of capitalism into socialism (communism), which, of course, cannot be conceptualised as a distinct society in its own right. In their *Critique of the Gotha Programme* (1875), the founders of Marxism talked of two phases of communism, and, later on, Lenin called the first phase "socialism" (this had by then become the common usage), one where the "bourgeois right" is not abolished in its entirety.[3] Now, Lenin was interpreting Marx the best he could; he did not designate the transition period as socialist. Does all of this imply, as PC would claim, that Lenin misinterpreted, indeed, *revised* Marx's meaning of socialism? I am afraid, I cannot agree with PC. Of course, I am not referring to the later proclamation of the Communist Party of the Soviet Union's allegiance to "Marxism-Leninism", and calling the Soviet Union "socialist". That usage was certainly not consistent with classical revolutionary Marxism as understood by Marx, Engels, and Lenin.

Was Lenin a 'Don Quixotist'?

Coming to the "conditions of socialism", was Lenin a "Don Quixotist", as PC seems to think, falsely imagining that the material conditions of the emancipation of the proletariat had emerged in "backward" Russia to the point where it was ripe for transformation into a classless society?[4]

Surely, the same question can be asked of Mao and China. PC's idea here, if I have understood him correctly, is that all societies have to pass through the stage of developed capitalism before they can aspire to make a transition to socialism. I am afraid I cannot agree with this. For, and it is of utmost importance to take into account that, from an early stage, the capitalist system has been composed of two poles, a self-directed "centre" and a dependent "periphery", the former, independent, developed, and dominant, the latter, dependent, underdeveloped, and subordinate. The process of accumulation of capital in the centre has driven the system; the periphery has been shaped by "coercion and market forces to conform to the requirements and serve the needs of the centre". The rate of exploitation "is and always has been vastly higher in the periphery than in the centre".[5] We might also add that the pillage of Mother Nature and the expropriation of social property are of a vastly higher order in the periphery than in the centre.

All this enables the dominant classes in the periphery to derive the privilege of consumption and levels of living corresponding to those of the dominant classes in the centre, at the same time making possible the required flow of surplus to the centre. However, what of their other—the workers, peasants, and the marginalised poor in the countryside and the urban slums? They are condemned to a life of poverty, misery, and degradation, often below the margins of what are, reasonably considered, subsistence levels of existence. The high rate of exploitation in the periphery, built into the very structure of the system, is the source of its failure to develop a mass market, and approach "developed" status. Indeed, the very high rate of exploitation requires a highly repressive political system; the constitutions and bourgeois democratic institutions copied from or modelled on the centre are empty facades.

Now, what is so "Don Quixotelike" if a revolutionary vanguard party of the Leninist variety, going by such a theoretical analysis and finding a broad correspondence with the historical and contemporary reality, sees a revolutionary break with the capitalist system as the way out for the vast majority of the people in its country of residence in the periphery, hoping that revolutions occurring elsewhere in the global system will mutually aid each other in their transition periods to socialism? The vision of socialism, which took shape at the "centre" and was best articulated by the founders of Marxism, Marx and Engels, was reincarnated in the "periphery", first, in Russia at the dawn of the 20th century, and then in the 1920s in China.

Marxism, as articulated (yes, *revised*, but not in the manner of Bernstein) by Lenin and his Bolshevik comrades, and later on, by Mao and his comrades in the Chinese Communist Party, offered a vision of the future and a conception of how to get there. Nevertheless, for Russia and for China, getting there appeared in a different light than it did to Marx in the middle of the 19th century. The proletariat was relatively small; moreover, in Russia, the Bolsheviks had very little influence in the countryside where the vast majority of the population lived. Yet, under the resolute leadership of the Bolsheviks, the proletariat overthrew the regime that had come to power in the February (old dates) Revolution of 1917. However, in what followed, four years of bloody civil war, massive US, British and French military aid to the White armies up to late 1919, lack of food, and complete disarray, the proletariat was practically broken up and decimated, and the Bolshevik government, losing mass active support, with its very survival in question, and the economy ruined, had no alternative but to rely heavily on the conservative bureaucracy and specialists of the discarded regime, and institute emergency measures that suppressed civil liberties.[6]

Any wonder then that with this economic and social catastrophe the Commune-state rapidly metamorphosed into the Party-state; the role of the Commune rather than that of the Party and the withering away of the state, both envisaged in *The State and Revolution*, just evaporated into thin air in no time. The archives of the former Soviet Union have now been open for almost 19 years, and there is certainly more to learn from, but, above all, one needs a political perspective,[7] and, I am afraid, I cannot identify with PC's. What PC is essentially implying is that Lenin began what Stalin completed, period.

Strangely, PC cites Alexander Rabinowitch's fine study *The Bolsheviks Come to Power: The Revolution of 1917 in Petrograd* (1976) to prove his thesis that Lenin presided over the liquidation of the Soviets! In fact, Rabinowitch shows, among other things, that the programme of Lenin and his associates corresponded with the aspirations of Petrograd's workers and soldiers; the October Revolution was an expression of what the genuine popular forces there really wanted. Is this not complimentary to Lenin and his comrades, coming as it does, from a first-rate historian? PC also refers to Victor Serge's *Memoirs of a Revolutionary* and to Isaac Deutscher's *The Prophet Armed* and

Stalin: A Political Biography in his support, but Serge and Deutscher never took the positions that PC takes on Lenin or Leninism.

PC brings up the 1921 insurrection of the sailors of Kronstadt and its brutal suppression, even when there was no evidence that the counter-revolutionary Whites had any role in instigating, organising, or directing the rebellion. It is with regard to state repression of the former exploited classes that our self-critical capacity should come to the fore, and, here, I am with PC.

Kronstadt evokes a deep sense of anguish in me. It makes me think as to how, with our limited capacities, but with Marx's method of analysis, we might help the socialist movement worldwide in understanding and learning from the Russian Revolution and the transition period that followed. What went wrong and why? PC's putting the blame on Lenin in explaining this part of the historical process is, I am afraid, both un-Marxist and unconvincing, for it relies largely on the subjective, and, indeed, the individual, in its argument.

More crucially, in practical terms, disputes over Lenin's understanding of a phrase in *Critique of the Gotha Programme* become significant only when the sectarian mind translates them into matters of fundamental importance, of the "which-side-are-you-on" variety. For example, at the very start of the civil war in Russia in the summer of 1918, when the revolution was faced with the first White armies, their terror and their pogroms, Lenin was shot in an assassination attempt by Fanya Kaplan, a left "Socialist-Revolutionary". She explained that she considered him a "traitor to the revolution" because she disagreed with the dissolution of the constituent assembly. Lenin recovered, but the bullet wounds contributed greatly to the decline in his health that led to his premature death in January 1924, before his opposition to Stalin could be given practical effect.

Clearly, in general, the transition period may lead to socialism after the revolution in a "backward" capitalist country if certain necessary conditions are fulfilled, which leads to the job of identifying the specific tasks of the transition period, as also the new institutions to be put in place. What needs to be done to avoid the great reversal to capitalism or the emergence of a new ruling class that seems to crystallise from the privileged stratum that has a tendency to surface early on in the aftermath of the revolution? Of course, with imperialism around, the danger of capitalist restoration would be omnipresent, and therefore, the state will have to continue to exist as a repressive apparatus against imperialist intervention.

Was Mao an Ideological Stalinist?

Mao seems to have understood the unfolding of the process of formation of a new ruling class during the transition period after the revolution better than most other Marxist-Leninists and did what he could, unsuccessfully though, to prevent it. Nevertheless, PC considers him an ideological Stalinist. He claims that Mao "completely accepted Stalin's un-Marxian position that the system of ownership is the basis of the relations of production". He also refers to Mao's Stalin-like "assertion of the existence of classes in socialism". He also refers to the personality cult. Let us deal with these in turn.

I, for one, will not separate ideology and practice. Also, and here I can straight-away agree with PC, I will not pretend that there were no ugly features in the Maoist period from 1949 to the late 1960s; for instance, the cult of "Mao's thought" during the CR was ridiculous and even harmful to scientific temper.

Now, if we believe that analysis and criticism of ideology cannot be separated from any consideration of actual practice, then PC's criticism of Mao's ideological Stalinism is incomplete. I emphasise this because I think that in the Maoist period, practice led the way to theory; indeed, the latter was often half-baked in its formulation. Let me first deal with what I think was at the core of my argument that Mao, in fact, struggled against Stalinism (a decomposed form of Leninism). Despite the two-line struggle within the Chinese Communist Party (CCP), he ensured that, following liberation, China avoided the Stalinist practice of "primitive socialist accumulation".[8] The latter was against the interests of the peasantry and, in fact, dealt a severe blow to the worker-peasant alliance in the Soviet Union, and led to the build-up of a many-times-more repressive state there. Mao wanted to avoid the repression that took place in the Soviet Union. Under his leadership, China in the late 1950s took a radically different path—the Great Leap Forward and the communes—that, though it faced severe setbacks[9] during 1959-61, did well with the subsequent launch of the Green Revolution, the surplus now coming from the increase in labour productivity in agriculture *and* industry.

The other major step was the CR. It is in the CR that Mao encouraged mass mobilisation and initiative on the part of students, workers and peasants in the major "class struggles":

(a) Against the old exploiting classes,
(b) In opposition to the ideologies, values and cultures of the old ruling classes which remained ingrained in the society of the transition period, and
(c) At odds with the powerful and privileged stratum that had emerged in the party, the government, the enterprises, the communes, the educational system, and so on, which developed a stake in maintaining its favoured position and passing it on to its progeny.

The latter were seen as an incipient new ruling (and hence, exploiting) class, which had to be nipped in the bud, and the workers and their allies (the students, peasants, and so on) were expected to mobilise themselves and take the initiative to suppress this class in the making. After all, how could a system claiming to be in transition to socialism allow this powerful and privileged stratum to capture and control the fruits of economic modernisation? I think what confounds PC is the use of the word "socialism" by Mao instead of the more accurate "political transition period". In addition, "class"[10] and "class struggle" had been used rather loosely by Mao, but this was in order to incorporate, under one social movement, all the three types of struggles mentioned above. However, theoretically, upon successful completion of the transition to socialism, in the socialist stage too, Mao correctly, I think, conceives of non-antagonistic contradictions, for instance, over the distribution of the product, especially in the transition from the distribution principle "from each according to his/her ability, to each according to his/her work" to the tenet "from each according to her work, to each according to his/her need". Mao's 'Reading Notes on the Soviet Union's Political Economics' of 1961 and his 'Speech on the Book, *Economic Problems of Socialism*' of 1959 perhaps suggest that PC ought to revise his view of Mao as an ideological Stalinist, for in these, one finds elements of an incisive critique of Stalin's philosophy, politics and economics. Moreover, coming to practice, if, like Stalin, Mao also believed that the system of ownership alone determined the relations of production, how could he have stressed the stifling economic effects of the prevailing class structure of the factories, even with nationalisation of the means of production complete, during the CR? Indeed, Mao was clear that nationalisation of the means of production was only the first step; according to him, "there is still a process to be gone through...there is work to do" in order to usher in and institutionalise genuine socialist relations of production.[11]

Cultural Revolution, *Uninterrupted* Revolution

This brings us to PC's pronouncements that "Cultural Revolution" is alien to Marx's thought and that the "Communist Party under Mao was at best a party for the labouring people but could not really be called a party of and by the labouring people". PC also draws attention to classes being conceived by Mao "not in terms of production relations but in terms of ideology and culture". Let us examine these contentions.

I too have not found any reference to "Cultural Revolution" in Marx's thought, but of course, unlike in Lenin's and Mao's lifetimes, a successful "proletarian" revolution ushering in the "political transition period" (the period of revolutionary transformation of capitalism to socialism) did not unfold before or in his lifetime, and so he did not have occasion to deal with it. Lenin and Mao analysed such situations the best they could, rightly or wrongly, and took measures (correct or mistaken) to bring about the desired transformation, but in the end, failed.

Mao's "last battle" to prevent "capitalist restoration" was the CR. In 1967, his "theory" of *uninterrupted* revolution, which we referred to in our 'What Is Maoism?' essay, was extended, in practice, to focus on the political, ideological and cultural superstructure—institutions that wield power and instil or alter the ideas and values held by individuals and classes in society. It involved extensions of Mao's thought on contradictions,[12] the determinants of class bias, which, besides one's economic position, include one's ideological, cultural and political locations,[13] and the conception of the possibility of "capitalist restoration".[14] With the emphases placed on the ideological and cultural determinants of class bias, which, I think, began to be practised after the Lushan Plenum of 1959, I am therefore not surprised that PC was incorrectly led to thinking that Mao now conceived of classes not in terms of the relations of production but based on ideology and culture.

More importantly though, is the CR's relation to Mao's "theory" of *uninterrupted* revolution, and the continuity of the latter with Marx's idea of *permanent* revolution.[15] In common, they share the primacy of process in the dialectic of event and process, part and whole. *Uninterrupted* revolution asserts that the political party and other organisations of the revolutionary class[es] must be free of all the debilitating influences coming from the exploiting class[es] and maintain their independence and uncompromising opposition to those classes if the revolution was to be taken to its logical end. In this, then, there seems to be a link with Marx. For the main aims of the CR, the fact that it is, indeed, a revolution, takes care to avoid Stalinist errors in the handling of contradictions, seeks to apply the democratic norms of the Paris Commune, and that the revolutionary classes know that it calls for uninterrupted struggle over the long haul, are all there in the famous 'Sixteen Points' of 8 August 1966.[16]

Of course, we know this did not reflect the full complexity of events, but as Marxists, surely we must get to the social basis of the then power struggle within the CCP and examine what the two main factions in the "two-line struggle" stood for. The Maoists in China were then at the helm of a revolution against a powerful and privileged stratum in the Party, the government, the enterprises, the communes, the educational system, and so on, whose power and privileges had to be severely curtailed, otherwise these would ultimately lead to "capitalist restoration". However, the CR failed and capitalism was restored in China; there were a whole lot of ugly features in practice during the CR, including the excesses, the cult of "Mao's thought", and so on, but we do need to learn from all of this. How do we do things, which need to be done, in the right ways, avoiding the wrong methods, conducts, manners, and routes?

Conclusion

The short 20th century ended with the defeat of the opposition to the rule of capital, whether in China or what was then the Soviet Union. That opposition had many weaknesses and was internally divided; moreover, capital was very strong. It has been a devastating defeat, but this is not the "end of history"; the conditions that gave rise to an opposition continue to exist, which guarantee that the opposition to capital will stage a comeback as newer generations of the dominated, exploited and oppressed, and intellectuals who cannot remain unmoved take their side, both taking the place of those who die or retire. Instead of blaming Lenin and Mao for the failure of the revolutions of the 20th century to provide successful working models of socialism, and, in an un-Marxist and unconvincing way, trying to explain major historical processes and events in terms of the subjective, and indeed, in terms of the roles of individual leaders like Lenin and Mao, surely we can do better.

I, for one, have no doubt that Lenin and Mao were Marxists committed to the overthrow of unjust and exploitative systems and replacing them with ones based on the principles of socialism as expounded by Marx and Engels. Nevertheless, after the revolutionary seizure of power, the struggles of the "political transition period" unfolded, when things went terribly wrong. The transition from a society in which the majority is deprived of the fruits of its collective labour, where acquisitive success is all that seems to matter, and where the individual's social consciousness is crippled, to a society in which "the free development of each is the condition for the free development of all"—as Marx and Engels, writing in late 1847, put it in *The Communist Manifesto*—though within the realm of the possible, was/is almost certain to witness a number of false starts. Nevertheless, *radical* democracy is not beyond the bounds of possibility. Marx once said that there would be many defeats before the working class learns how to be a ruling class. History comes with many setbacks, but, if we analyse these with the use of Marx's method, we can learn a great deal and do things the right way the next time around.

NOTES

1. See Bernard D'Mello, *What is Maoism and Other Essays* (Kharagpur: Cornerstone Publications, 2010).
2. A caveat is however due. In saying that the working class in Western Europe had become "reformist", we did not imply that it might never again acquire a revolutionary consciousness.
3. In Part I of Marx and Engels (1875) at http://www. marxists.org/ archive/marx/works/1875/gotha/ ch01.htm:

   But these defects are inevitable in the first phase of communist society as it is when it has just emerged after prolonged birth pangs from capitalist society. Right can never be higher than the economic structure of society and its cultural development conditioned thereby.

   In a higher phase of communist society, after the enslaving subordination of the individual to the division of labour, and therewith also the antithesis between mental and physical labour, has vanished; after labour has become not only a means of life but life's prime want; after the productive forces have also increased with the all-around development of the individual, and all the springs of cooperative wealth flow more abundantly—only then can the narrow horizon of bourgeois right be crossed in its entirety and society inscribe on its banners: From each according to his ability, to each according to his needs!
4. By the way, Lenin could then only envisage the prospect of socialism on a European scale, not in Russia on its own.
5. Of course, in the periphery, a large part of the workforce is "exploited directly and indirectly by landlords, traders, and usurers, primarily in the countryside but also in the cities and towns", but the surplus extorted is "commercialised and becomes indistinguishably mingled with capitalistically produced surplus value" (Sweezy, *Four Lectures on Marxism* (Kharagpur: Cornerstone Publications, 2008), p. 76.

6. In *The Russian Revolution*, written by Rosa Luxemburg in 1918, among other things, she protests the suspension of democratic rights for the opponents of the Bolsheviks, which, she felt, would isolate the party from the people and turn it into an authoritarian bureaucracy. As usual, like in her 1904 article "Organisational Questions of the Russian Social Democracy", she had the long-run implications and possibilities in mind, ignoring the exigencies and context of the present. Nevertheless, we need to revisit these insightful critiques that Rosa penned.
7. I have in mind here the perspective of the eminent historian Moshe Lewin who has consistently argued against attempts to backdate Stalinism to 1917. In *The Soviet Century* (2005), Lewin revisits his earlier works, now with the benefit of more primary sources and the work of contemporary Russian historians, to reaffirm his earlier thesis that Stalinism, which evolved in the period 1928-39, represented a sharp break from Leninism of the period up to 1924. In this, Lewin had access to documents, available in the wake of Gorbachev's "glasnost", about the clash between Lenin and Stalin. Readers will recall that in our "What Is Maoism?" essay, we had relied on a brilliant review by Harry Braverman of Lewin's *Lenin's Last Struggle* (1968), which is about the period from December 1921 to March 1923, when Lenin honestly tried to throw light on the negative aspects of the regime and courageously suggest what needed to be done.
8. Paul Sweezy, *Post-Revolutionary Society* (Kharagpur: Cornerstone Publications, 2000), p. 75.
9. At the time, Mao was self-critical of the adventurism he encouraged and his poor understanding of how to deal with economic problems.
10. Take, for instance, Mao's statement, "the officials of China are a class, and one whose interests are antagonistic to those of the workers and peasants".
11. Mao as quoted in Jack Gray's, 'Mao Zedong', *Oxford Concise Dictionary of Politics*, (Oxford: Oxford University, 2009), p. 330.
12. See 'On the Correct Handling of Contradictions among the People', 27 February 1957, at http:// www.marxists.org/reference/archive/mao/selected-works/volume-5/mswv5_58.htm. Mao refers to the contradictions in the transition period thus:

    ...At the present stage, the period of building socialism, the classes, strata and social groups which favour, support and work for the cause of socialist construction all come within the category of the people, while the social forces and groups which resist the socialist revolution and are hostile to or sabotage socialist construction are all enemies of the people.

The contradictions between ourselves and the enemy are antagonistic contradictions. Within the ranks of the people, the contradictions among the working people are non-antagonistic, while those between the exploited and the exploiting classes have a non-antagonistic as well as an antagonistic aspect. There have always been contradictions among the people, but they are different in content in each period of the revolution and in the period of building socialism.

13. See 'On the Correct Handling of Contradictions among the People', 27 February 1957, at http:// www.marxists.org/reference/archive/mao/selected-works/volume-5/mswv5_58.htm. With respect to the determinants of class bias:

    In socialist society, class contradictions still remain and class struggle does not die out after the socialist transformation of the ownership of the means of production. The struggle between the two roads of socialism and capitalism runs through the entire stage of socialism. To ensure the success of socialist construction and to prevent the restoration of capitalism, it is necessary to carry the socialist revolution through to the end on the political, economic, ideological and cultural fronts. The complete victory of socialism cannot be brought about in one or two generations; to resolve this question thoroughly requires five to ten generations or even longer.

14. See Mao in 'On Khrushchev's Phoney Communism and Its Historical Lessons for the World', July 1964, at http:// www.marxists.org/reference/archive/ mao/works/1964/phnycom.htm. Reference to the possibility of a reversal came in 1957 itself:

    ... Class struggle is by no means over. The class struggle between the proletariat and the bourgeoisie, the class struggle between the various political forces, and the class struggle between the proletariat and the bourgeoisie in the ideological field will still be protracted and tortuous and at times even very sharp. The proletariat seeks to transform the world according to its own world outlook, and so does the bourgeoisie. In this respect, the question of which will win out, socialism or capitalism, is not really settled yet. Marxists remain a minority among the entire population as well as among the intellectuals. Therefore, Marxism must continue to develop through struggle. Marxism can develop only through struggle, and this is not only true of the past and the present, it is necessarily true of the future as well. What is correct invariably develops in the course of struggle with what is wrong.

15. "...He [Napoleon] *perfected* the *Terror* by *substituting permanent war* for *permanent revolution*.... The history of the French Revolution, which dates from 1789, did not come to an end in 1830 with the victory of one of its components enriched by the consciousness of its own *social* importance" (Marx in *The Holy Family*, Chapter 6, Section 3, "Critical Battle against the French Revolution", at http://www.marxistsfr.org/archive/marx/works/1845/holy-family/ch06_3_c.htm.
16. "Decision of the Central Committee of the Chinese Communist Party Concerning the Great Proletarian Cultural Revolution", Adopted on 8 August 1966, and published in *Peking Review*, Vol. 9, No. 33, 12 August 1966, pp. 6-11, at http://www.marxists.org/subject/china/peking-review/1966/PR1966-33g.htm.

19

Re-Envisioning Socialism

Prabhat Patnaik

Central to the Marxist project is the quest for human freedom which requires a transcendence of capitalism. What is important, however, is the overall vision that we have of the socialism that will emerge, one which accords centrality to human freedom, which remains continuously "open" and untainted by ossification in any form, and which constitutes an unleashing of democracy and a perennial engagement of the people with politics.

Socialism, and economic liberalism, paradoxically share the same intellectual origin, namely Adam Smith's idea of bourgeois society as a self-acting, self-driven economic order.[1] Any restriction placed on the functioning of this order by meddlesome sovereigns or governments is at best futile and at worst pernicious since it destroys the coherence of its functioning. Adam Smith saw this order as being in conformity with the laws of nature, and, in its consequences, benign and productive of "progress", in the sense of an augmentation of the "wealth of nations". He and his followers therefore drew the implicit conclusion that nothing lay beyond capitalism, that we had come to the end of history. As Marx was to say of classical political economy: "...there has been history, but there is no longer any".[2]

The Case for Socialism

While accepting the fact however that bourgeois society constitutes a self-acting, self-driven order, if we see this order analytically not as being benign and productive of progress, but as being antagonistic and exploitative, giving rise to the growth of wealth at one pole and of misery at another, then the quest for human freedom, precisely because government intervention cannot mend it, must require a transcendence of this order. The same "spontaneity" (to use Oskar Lange's term) which underlies the bourgeois economic order and constitutes the case for economic liberalism if its consequences are seen to be benign, gives rise to the very opposite conclusion, of the need for a revolutionary overthrow of this order, if its consequences are seen as destructive and dehumanising.

This of course was Marx's argument. His case for socialism was "scientific" in the sense that it took classical political economy as its starting point but came to different conclusions precisely by re-examining classical questions at greater depth. It did not entail placing a capitalist and an imaginary socialist order side by side and establishing the comparative superiority of the latter; it did not entail asking questions like: "what is the justification for a separate group of persons, the capitalists, earning profits, when the society could function just as well if the means of production are collectively owned?".[3] In short, it did not make out an ethical case for socialism, a case based on an abstract extrinsic comparison between systems on ethical grounds. True, it took mankind's quest for freedom as given, but it showed that this quest necessarily entailed going beyond capitalism. This is also why Marxism must not be confused with a theory of the inevitability of socialism.[4] To say that the quest for freedom cannot be satisfied within capitalism is not the same as saying that socialism is inevitable. The matter in short is one of praxis, not of prediction.

Marx's argument however was not just this; it went deeper. Capitalism is inimical to human freedom not just because it spontaneously produces wealth at one pole and misery at another as a condition for its self-reproduction, and not just because inequality, insecurity, and the non-availability of the means to satisfy a certain minimum level of material needs (which may itself be changing over time), all of which are conditions for freedom in the sense of the realisation of one's creative potential, are incapable of being achieved under capitalism; it is inimical to human freedom precisely because within it mankind is trapped in a self-acting and self-driven order where individuals become the objects of external coercive forces. This is true not just of workers, but even of the capitalists whom Marx in *Capital* (Volume I), described as "capital personified", that is, as human agents through whom the immanent tendencies of capital are mediated.[5]

Not only is it the case that the outcome of the functioning of the system is different from the intentions of the individuals participating in it, but these intentions themselves are neither a matter of individual volition, nor autonomously sociologically caused (like the desire to "keep up with the Joneses", etc). The very logic of the functioning of the order imparts to the different individuals specific motivations which they can ignore at their own peril, the peril of getting displaced from their positions within the economic order. For instance, a capitalist who chooses to opt out of the Darwinian struggle of survival, in which all capitalists are caught, will get displaced as a capitalist; and so on.

In his discussion of commodity fetishism, Marx had talked of the fact that social relations within capitalism appeared as the relations between things, and that the outcome of social relations appeared as the inherent property of things (such as for instance the "fantastic" notion of latter-day bourgeois economics that profits arise because of the productivity of "capital", seen as a set of means of production detached from its relational aspect). In fact however his analysis went further: human beings under capitalism were actually indistinguishable from things; human beings under capitalism became "objectified". Apropos Ricardo, *Marx* says: in *Theories of Surplus Value*, Part II:

> In this conception, the workers themselves appear as that which they are in capitalist production—mere means of production, not an end in themselves and not the aim of production .... Ricardo expressed these tendencies consistently and ruthlessly. Hence

> much howling against him on the part of philanthropic philistines.[6]

This "objectification" is different from, though related to, "reification" and "alienation", both of which are phenomena characterising capitalism. "Objectification" refers neither to how things appear under capitalism, nor to the fact of the products of labour appearing in the alienated form of capital; it refers to the phenomenon of capitalism being a self-driven self-acting order, in which the immanent tendencies of capital are mediated through human beings, who therefore cease to be subjects and are reduced to the status of mere objects. This objectification is a denial of freedom: capitalism is incompatible with human freedom because it objectifies human beings. The case for socialism is that it alone creates the condition for human freedom by overcoming this objectification, for which a necessary condition is the social ownership of the means of production.

Ending Objectification

The above argument for socialism differs in a basic sense from the arguments usually advanced in favour of socialism. And it is important to emphasise this difference because from these different arguments different visions of socialism follow. The usual arguments are of two kinds: "productivist" arguments and "distributivist" arguments. Let us consider the former. A very common argument for socialism is that it carries forward the development of productive forces which at a certain stage gets arrested by the relations of production characterising capitalism. This "march-of-the-productive-forces" argument for socialism can at first sight derive sustenance from several of Marx's writings, notably his famous preface to *A Contribution to the Critique of Political Economy*; but it represents a superficial reading of Marx, especially when, as is usually the case, "productive forces" are defined exclusively in material terms. This superficial reading which informs a good deal of current official Chinese literature on socialism, was epitomised by the former Soviet prime minister Alexei Kosygin's remark that socialism was synonymous with a 7 per cent growth rate![7]

Marx did not see productive forces exclusively in material

terms. And his remark that a mode of production becomes obsolete when it has developed the productive forces to the highest level it is capable of, should not be given a crude and exclusively material interpretation. This is borne out by his own statement in *The Poverty of Philosophy*[8]: "Of all the instruments of production the greatest productive power is the revolutionary class itself. The organisation of revolutionary elements as a class supposes the existence of all the productive forces which could be engendered in the bosom of the old society." A "revolutionary proletariat" in short is not just a productive force, but represents the highest level of development of the productive forces in a bourgeois society.

This statement, however, is in keeping with Marx's perception of socialism as essential for human freedom. The break from the human condition of unfreedom under capitalism, starts with our knowledge of this unfreedom, i.e. starts with a scientific as opposed to an ideological understanding of the roots of this unfreedom. "Freedom", Engels had said in *Anti-Dühring* echoing Hegel, "is the recognition of necessity". The immanent laws of motion of the capitalist mode of production constitute, in this context, this realm of necessity. Freedom from these laws begins with the knowledge of these laws and culminates in the formation of a revolutionary proletariat in which this knowledge has developed to a point where it can break into revolutionary praxis.

In the process of the development of this knowledge, particular episodes in the development of capitalism, such as crises and stagnation, no doubt play an important role, in providing practical proof of the validity of this knowledge, but this is not the same as saying that the existence of crises and stagnation is what constitutes the case for socialism or that there is some final phase of stagnation which constitutes the denouement for capitalism (which is what Bernstein had interpreted Marx as saying and which Lenin had explicitly attacked by saying that "there is no such thing as an absolutely hopeless situation" for capitalism).

The same goes for the "distributivist" argument. While no doubt egalitarianism and "distributive justice" cannot be achieved under capitalism, and require socialism for their realisation, they are not synonymous with socialism, which, to repeat, seeks to end the objectification of human beings and constitutes a necessary condition for human freedom.

Denial of Democracy

The objectification of individuals in bourgeois society is not a matter relating exclusively to the esoteric realm of the political economy of such societies; it permeates their very being. The realm of the economic after all does not stand alone, in isolation from the other realms; it is embedded within the whole. The realisation of the immanent tendencies of capital requires therefore that the functioning of these other realms must also be in conformity with what is needed for such realisation. The state in a bourgeois society, for instance, must be such that it aids the realisation of its immanent tendencies. It may of course under certain exceptional circumstances, slow down such realisation in the interests of the system as a whole, by placing temporary restrictions upon it; but it cannot altogether prevent the realisation of the immanent tendencies of capital.

Anti-democratic

It is for this reason that bourgeois society is fundamentally anti-democratic. Human beings cannot be objects in the realm of the economy and subjects in the realm of the polity, save in very exceptional situations, which are invariably transitory, where there is a disjunction between the economy and the state.

To say that bourgeois society is fundamentally anti-democratic may appear odd at first sight, since its own claim has always been that it alone can guarantee democracy. But implicit in the notion of a self-acting and self-driven economic order functioning independently of human will and consciousness, is not just a denial of freedom but also a denial of democracy. This denial however is camouflaged in various ways. Formal bourgeois democracy invariably operates under layers and layers of insulation against the possibility of the people actually intervening actively in the political process as subjects.

The process of putting in place of these insulations becomes especially transparent in societies like ours for a specific reason.

Bourgeois democracy with universal adult franchise was introduced in our country shortly after independence itself, prior to the consolidation of bourgeois rule, unlike in countries like Britain and France where universal adult franchise came nearly three quarters of a century after the climacteric marking the start of the consolidation of bourgeois rule. The process of consolidation of bourgeois rule in countries like ours therefore requires, as it were, a "counterrevolution" against the existing democratic institutions and practices. This counterrevolution of course also entails inter alia a change in the relationship between the big bourgeoisie and imperialism, for without the latter's help the consolidation of bourgeois rule cannot be carried out (one of the visible symptoms of this change at present being the Indo-US Nuclear Agreement); but the counterrevolution in the realm of democracy, involving efforts to snuff out the political activism of the people, is quite evident (with the judiciary, which is neither directly nor indirectly accountable to the people, playing a leading role in it).

The means of attenuation of democracy in bourgeois society are several: the first, which Lenin had emphasised, is the ossification of the state where the bureaucracy and the standing army become the core of the state apparatus, and the elected governments become increasingly ornamental. The second is the fragmentation of the people into ethnic, linguistic, or even religious groups, or even into sheer atomised individuals incapable of collective praxis. (the invoking of Christian fundamentalism on issues like abortion and gay rights has been a potent weapon in recent years in the hands of the Republican Right in the United states for obtaining majorities which have then been used to serve corporate interests.) The third is the denial of meaningful choices to the electorate, since the agendas of the different political parties, each trying to appease a middle class constituency in thraldom to the bourgeois order, tend to converge (a fact used with great effect of late in India where the imperative of so-called "development" has made parties belonging to very different segments of the political spectrum adopt almost identical pro-capitalist policies).

Scant Respect

The very fact that despite the opposition to the Iraq war by the majority of people in each of the advanced capitalist countries engaged in the war, the war still drags on, shows the scant respect shown to popular opinion in capitalist democracies; and a major factor explaining this phenomenon is the absence of any significant difference among the political parties. The fourth is the inculcation of insecurity among the people, which encourages mutual distrust among them, prevents united action and creates a favourable ground for the maintenance of the status quo through violence. Given the fact that resistance, no matter in what form, is ever-present in any bourgeois society and its periphery, to capitalist and imperialist exploitation, the inculcation of such insecurity is by no means difficult. One segment of the people can always be made to feel insecure through demonising another segment which happens at the time to be engaged in such actions of resistance. The fifth is the deliberate promotion of mindlessness among the people by the media and the peddlers of popular culture. One can go on listing such factors and much has been written on this subject anyway. The basic point is the incompatibility of authentic democracy where the people are the political subjects with capitalism where they are the objects.

Socialism, it follows, constitutes a necessary condition for the authentic realisation of democracy. The proposition that socialism and democracy are incompatible is part of the propaganda of capitalism. On the contrary, socialism which aims to overcome the objectification of the people in bourgeois society, is alone compatible with democracy; it alone can create the conditions for the full flowering of democracy. But more than that, socialism is the full flowering of democracy, a proposition which we shall examine later. Since the claim that socialism and democracy are incompatible is usually supported with reference to the actual practice of former socialist countries, a brief discussion of that experience is in order here.

Actual Practice of Former

Old socialism came as a result of revolutionary expediency, through seizing an opportunity created by the war, in order to save mankind from the barbarism of that and other similar wars. It appeared in a relatively backward country; it appeared abruptly; it did not spread, as was originally expected, to other countries, especially to the relatively more advanced countries; and it was encircled, and isolated and had to fight for its very survival against vastly superior forces throughout its existence. As a communist character puts it apropos the Soviet Union in Graham Greene's last great novel *The Human Factor*: "My country has been at war since 1917". It is within this context of isolation, of desperate efforts to develop the productive forces to overcome the challenge of encirclement, including increasingly from Nazi Germany, and of the estrangement from the peasantry arising from this desperate bid for raising the productive capacity of the country, that the political institutions of the Soviet state were formed. And these institutionalised a dictatorship of the party in the name of the dictatorship of the proletariat.

True, this isolation of the Soviet Union was overcome in the post-Second World War years when the socialist camp became much larger, but the new entrants to this camp were also relatively backward countries, and in the case of many even the entry was a result of the Soviet Red Army's victorious march against Nazism. Far from providing succour to the Soviet Union they were often a source of strain on it; and far from contributing to a reconfiguring of Soviet political institutions, they themselves imported the Soviet political "model".

The fact that this "model" represented a far cry from the vision of the Soviet state which had informed the revolution is obvious. On the eve of the revolution itself Lenin had said: "We can at once set in motion a state apparatus consisting of ten if not twenty million people."[9] The vision clearly was of a state that had got dissolved into the class itself; a state that was an association of workers, vastly different from the bureaucratised, ossified bourgeois state, where a tiny coterie of persons takes crucial decisions behind closed doors affecting the lives of millions of people, without the people having any say in the matter; a state that unleashed the political praxis of the working class. But the actual political institution that came into being was a highly centralised dictatorship of the party, which eventually brought about a depoliticisation not only of the working class but also of the party itself (where, as we know in retrospect, a person could become the General Secretary of the Communist Party of the Soviet Union without believing in socialism).

Novel Objectification

To what extent this was the result of specific mistakes, or of "personality factors", whether, even within the constraints of the circumstances, a different course could have been taken, are matters that need not detain us here. The basic point is that old socialism, even while it overcame the "spontaneity" of capitalism, even while it got rid of the old problem of capitalist "objectification", ensured full employment, and set up the most gigantic welfare state the world had even seen, introduced a very different and altogether novel form of objectification itself. The substitution of private ownership of the means of production by state ownership (which is supposed to express social ownership) and the accompanying substitution of commodity production by national planning, may overcome bourgeois objectification, but the only way that the people can acquire the role of being subjects in a socialist society is through political praxis. (The old Yugoslav model, reminiscent of the syndicalist position, which believed that subjectivity can be restored to the people in the realm of the economy itself, by having worker-managed factories, did not overcome commodity production and hence bourgeois objectification.) The depoliticisation of the working class meant that this subject-role was never acquired by the people. They escaped bourgeois objectification, but got trapped into another kind of objectification in a society which also had its own form of fetishism. This latter objectification is lucidly captured by Jean Paul Sartre (1965) in his satirical remark: "Budapest's subway is in Rakosi's mind; if the subsoil does not allow it, then the sub-soil must be counter-revolutionary!"

The foregoing must not detract in any way from the enormous historic achievements of old socialism. Leaving aside what it achieved internally in those societies where it prevailed, it was responsible for the defeat of fascism, for making possible the entire process of decolonisation, and for putting a check on the depredations of imperialism for well over half a century. As Joan Robinson used to say in her Cambridge seminars, "we would not be sitting here today but for the Soviet Union". Nonetheless, the fact remains that old socialism was a product of its times. Apart from anything else, the times today are vastly different. For instance, inter-imperialist rivalries which played such an important role in Lenin's thinking, are far more muted today. The socialist project today must be based on very different foundations for this reason at least, if not for the more basic reason that the realisation of its vision of overcoming the objectification of human beings requires such a re-foundation.

Flowering of Democracy

Central to any such re-foundation must be the people's political praxis. Since authentic democracy consists in unleashing this praxis, socialism must be seen as the full flowering of democracy. An economistic perception of socialism as consisting essentially in state ownership of the means of production is not enough; socialism must mean the unleashing of authentic democracy in the sense of political praxis of the people. This praxis is limited at any time by lack of understanding of the conjuncture. The role of the revolutionary party is to provide this understanding. The revolutionary party locates and opens doors when no doors are visible. It points the way forward for people's political praxis at every stage, so that the process of unleashing of democracy, which constitutes the essence of socialism, does not get stymied. The role of the revolutionary party is not to substitute itself for the people, not to depoliticise them as a counterpart of the establishment of its own dictatorship; it is on the contrary to politicise them, to ensure that their political praxis is not thwarted, by pointing at every stage the way forward.

This however requires not just a right set of institutions through which the relations between the party and the people, the relations between the party and other parties, etc, are mediated, but also the right approach to Marxism. The old socialist view canonised Marxism, saw it as a closed and complete system, which only had to be grasped, like a religious text, through perseverance, and "applied" to specific contexts. According to old socialism there was a "thing" called Marxism (or rather Marxism-Leninism, since Lenin too was canonised in hyphenated splendour), and Mao "applied" it to China, and we have to apply it to India. This fundamentally erroneous attitude has been a predominant characteristic of a good deal of left thinking to this day.

It is erroneous because it arbitrarily separates "theory" from its "applications" and does not recognise that "application" too is theory. It is erroneous because via this separation it implicitly presents a religious attitude to Marxism, as a closed complete theory. It is erroneous because it refuses to recognise the progress of knowledge which mankind acquires and which should be a source of enrichment of Marxism; instead it arbitrarily and unjustifiably selects only those strands of the advance of knowledge which in its view support canonical Marxism, and treats the rest as inconsequential if not reactionary. And it is erroneous because in the process it devalues theoretical endeavour on the Left, and discourages creativity. The attitude becomes: "Since Marx has said everything of importance that there is to say, what more can I say except simply finding more evidence of his correctness?"

All this is usually sought to be justified by saying that if we abandon the "texts" then we will be in a world of theoretical free-for-all which would stand in the way of praxis. To believe this however is to believe that people cannot act except with reference to canonical texts, i.e. they cannot act except when inspired by a religion, which itself constitutes a fundamental epistemological negation of socialism. The people cannot acquire the role of subjects in social and political life, if they do not acquire the role of subjects in the theoretical domain. To say this is not to applaud half-educated cocky self-assurance; it is simply to break the religious approach to Marxism, to treat it as essentially an open system.

Understanding the Present

There is in other words at every moment an attempt to understand the present through a reconstruction of Marxism.[8] every attempt at understanding the present is a theoretical endeavour, based not on an "application" of a given closed set of doctrines, but a creative effort to reconstruct Marxism. Its validity has to be judged, as in all theoretical efforts, not with reference to whether or not it deviates from the "text", but whether or not it is correct, i.e. whether or not it enables us to understand the present. Every thinking person who wants to carry the cause of socialism forward, is thus engaged in reconstructing Marxism. Debates among such persons are inter alia debates among alternative reconstructions of Marxism, each seeking to make the present comprehensible through the use, in different ways, of concepts left to us by Marx, Lenin, and others, but not necessarily confined to these concepts alone (which is another way of saying that Marxism must be continuously nourished by advances in knowledge).

It is in this rich atmosphere of discussion that the revolutionary party must function, for this alone can provide a check against its going horribly wrong in its assessment of the present. Free scientific discussion is like oxygen for a revolutionary party; without such discussion it cannot survive. But such free discussion in turn requires not just complete intellectual freedom, but also the existence of a multiplicity of opinions (which in turn entails a multiplicity of political parties), and a redefinition of the concept of "democratic centralism" as the organising principle of a revolutionary party. It is not often appreciated that Bukharin and other "left-wing communists" who opposed the treaty of Brest-Litovsk were freely bringing out their own newspaper *Kommunist* even during the most difficult post-revolutionary times, which argued against the official position of the Bolshevik Party. And while Lenin, the strong advocate of "democratic centralism" as the organising principle of the Bolshevik Party, entered into fierce polemics with the left-wing communists, the question of silencing them through disciplinary action never arose. Such silencing of dissent was a later and altogether unwholesome development. The dictatorship of the party under old socialism was typically justified through a dichotomy between "science" or "theory" which was the preserve of the few, who happened to be in leading positions, and "politics", where the masses participated, increasingly without enthusiasm, in conformity with this "theory". The "theory" in this conception was necessarily a closed system. Once we see theory as open, once we eliminate the dichotomy between theory and "politics" or theory and "applications", or "theoreticians" and "activists", the intellectual ground for any dictatorship of the party would have been removed.

A basic question which has been raised in the context of socialism relates to the motivation for work in a socialist society.[10] In a feudal society, people work because of the pressure of customs and traditions, backed by force; if the serf does not put in his labour in the lord's field or does not hand over product rent (where labour rent has been so commuted), then he will be physically punished, and if he does not work in his own field sufficiently hard, then his income net of rent will force him to starve.

Reserve Army

In a capitalist society, people work because of the existence of the reserve army of labour, which acts as a coercive, disciplining device. If a worker is suspected to be a "laggard" or a "troublemaker", then he is dismissed and some one else takes his place, such substitutes being always available owing to the existence of the reserve army. But in a socialist society, where there is neither the fear of the Monseigneur's whip, nor the fear of being unemployed, since the economy is operating at full employment and in any case substantial welfare state measures are available to all, what will be the source of the motivation for work? Some would even suggest that political authoritarianism, as expressed through the dictatorship of the party, becomes indispensable for the functioning of a socialist society, precisely because it operates close to full employment and has an array of welfare state measures, i.e. the modus operandi of such a society must include an element of coercion.

Instruments of Discipline

The old Yugoslav answer to this, which paralleled something tried briefly in the Soviet Union during the Gorbachev era, was to make peer pressure an instrument for work discipline. In worker-managed factories, the workers' collective itself would take on the role of pulling up laggard workers, and this social pressure from one's own fellow workers would be sufficient to inculcate work motivation among workers. In Gorbachev's time when contracts were signed between the state and workers' collectives, again the question of imparting work motivation was relegated from the domain of the state to that of the workers' collectives which could bring peer pressure to bear on workers. But Yugoslav socialism was afflicted with substantial unemployment even in the heyday of self-management, so that while peer pressure was dubious, the fear of the "sack" was very real. And the Soviet experiment did not last long, quite apart from the fact that had it continued, it might have reproduced features of the Yugoslav system, based as it was on similar syndicalist perceptions.

The Yugoslav leadership always said that workers' management did not negate social property, that it was workers' management of social property; it simply entrusted the management of social property to individual factory-based workers' groups. The system does nevertheless mean a fragmentation of the working class, not into atomised individuals but into atomised groups of factory workers. Since the relations between the different worker-groups managing different factories are mediated through the market, "market socialism" is a form of commodity production which reproduces the well known features of commodity-producing bourgeois societies, such as inflation, unemployment, and huge inequalities. "Market socialism" of this sort is a contradiction in terms, a negation of socialism (from which it follows that the concept of "socialist commodity production" which China has been talking about of late is equally untenable, though the idea of using markets for certain specific purposes in socialist societies is not).

A socialist society clearly needs social commitment as the

basis of work motivation (apart from the fact that work must itself become a source of joy). All the solutions to the problem of work motivation discussed so far take it for granted that the workers are motivated exclusively by individual self-interest, and then examine how to coerce them into work despite this. This may have been an accurate reflection of the reality of old socialism, especially in its later years, but it cannot form the basis of a socialist society. Such a society clearly needs social commitment and an overcoming of the exclusive preoccupation with individual self-interest which bourgeois society tries to inculcate. Indeed the overcoming of such exclusive preoccupation with individual self-interest is what underlies combinations among workers[11] within bourgeois society itself, and hence constitutes the starting point of the journey to socialism. And the journey to socialism which begins with the overcoming of the exclusive preoccupation with individual self-interest among workers, culminates in the formation of a revolutionary proletariat.

Marx clearly therefore saw in politics, in the fact of struggle of which politics is the expression, a means of overcoming the individual self-interest that characterises bourgeois society. Old socialism depoliticised the workers. Our vision of the socialism of the future must entail a resurrection of politics, a perennial engagement with politics on the part of the working class, which will also provide the answer to the problem of work motivation in socialist societies.

Relevance of Socialist Agenda

The two and a half decades after the Second World War witnessed the most ambitious effort to "reform" capitalism that has ever been undertaken. Keynesian demand management by capitalist states brought down unemployment rates to unprecedented low levels. The boost to demand created a strong inducement to invest and hence rates of growth unprecedented in the history of capitalism. These were accompanied by high rates of labour productivity growth, because of which, in the context of near-full employment conditions, the workers succeeded in obtaining high rates of growth of real wages. These, together with social security measures introduced by social democratic governments, made capitalism appear as a humane system. On the other side, decolonisation rid capitalism of the stigma of keeping the majority of the world's people under its oppressive political yoke. It seemed for a while that capitalism had indeed changed, and made the case for socialism redundant, exactly as Keynes had wanted, predicted and theorised about: "A somewhat comprehensive socialisation of investment will prove the only means of securing an approximation to full employment... It is not the ownership of the instruments of production which it is important for the state to assume."[12]

The end of this long boom, which has been called the "Golden Age of capitalism", constitutes proof that the "spontaneity" of the system cannot be overcome, save temporarily and that too under exceptional circumstances. The hegemony of capital over labour gets undermined by the near full employment conditions that prevail: the "sack" loses its power, and inflation gathers momentum over time as workers feel emboldened to press higher wage claims,[13] which in turn creates pressures from capital for the restoration of a substantial reserve army of labour. Adding to these pressures is another fact, namely, the capacity of the state, which naturally, is a nation state, to carry out Keynesian demand management, gets undermined as the immanent tendency towards centralisation of capital gives rise to globalisation of finance and hence an international finance capital. Since ignoring the caprices of this international finance capital, including its preference for government—expenditure deflation, entails the risk of capital flight, the nation states willy-nilly have to fall in line and eschew Keynesian demand management.

Transient Keynesianism

Keynesianism in retrospect therefore must be seen as a transient phenomenon, based on an exceptional post-war conjuncture. As the conjuncture passed, undermined inter alia by the immanent tendencies of capital, the programme of "reformed capitalism" was given a quiet burial. Not only did growth rates in world capitalism plummet, not only did unemployment in the advanced capitalist countries approach double-digit figures and remain stuck there, not only did the absolute real wage rate of the workers show a virtual stagnation in the post-"Golden Age" period, but even the tendency towards decolonisation got reversed, with imperialism making a determined attempt to reappropriate the world's natural resources, especially oil, for itself.

In this recolonisation attempt it enjoys the backing of the Third World big bourgeoisie, which has done a volte face, from leading the people against imperialism, to collaborating with imperialism against the people's interests. And the people are back to a situation reminiscent of the pre-decolonisation experience of an acute agrarian crisis, of secularly adverse movements in the terms of trade against primary commodity producers, of expropriation of peasants' land by corporate interests, of the grinding down of petty production, and in general of an unleashing of primitive accumulation of capital, or what I would prefer to call "accumulation through encroachment" in the periphery. Since all this is not accompanied by any significant increases in employment in the modern capitalist sector within the periphery, the outcome is growing unemployment, destitution, hunger, poverty, and insecurity. In short, all talk about the "reform" of capitalism has come to nought.

The socialist agenda therefore remains as relevant today as ever. And unless the socialist movement gathers momentum, the anger against imperialism will continue to take the most violent, destructive, inhuman and unproductive forms, like terrorism. The choice before us today, as it was at the time of Lenin and Luxemburg, is between socialism and barbarism, between a situation where a predatory imperialism remains locked in perennial combat with equally ruthless groups of terrorists, thus threatening the very survival of our civilisation, and one where the very system that produces both imperialism and its terrorist "other", is overthrown.

This revival of socialism of course will take time. The old Comintern perception of a "general crisis of capitalism" giving rise, within a comparatively short period of time, to the overthrow of the system, lacks relevance in today's context, where, apart from any thing else, the inter-imperialist rivalries that had produced such a prognosis, are far more muted. Georg Lukács' view, expressed in an interview in the *New Left Review*, that just as the transition from feudalism to capitalism was a long drawn-out one, spanning almost 300 years, likewise the transition from capitalism to socialism is likely to be a long drawn-out one, appears more plausible at this moment. If this perspective is accepted, then the collapse of the Soviet Union or the recent distortions in China would appear simply as episodes in this long transition. But anyone who has faith in the future of mankind, cannot remain sceptical about the occurrence of this transition.

The precise mode of this transition, and the precise problems that would arise in the course of this transition are issues whose discussion must await another occasion. What is important however is the overall vision that we have of the socialism that will emerge. That can only be of a socialism which accords centrality to human freedom, which remains continuously "open" and untainted by ossification in any form, and which constitutes an unleashing of democracy and a perennial engagement of the people with politics.

REFERENCES

1. On this Smithian conception see Maurice Dobb's *Theories of Value and Distribution Since Adam Smith* (Cambridge: Cambridge University Press,1973).
2. Marx was to add, by way of explanation: "There has been history, since there were the institutions of feudalism, and in these institutions of feudalism we find quite different relations of production from those of bourgeois society which the economists try to pass off as natural and as such, eternal."
3. This is how "Ricardian socialists" like Hodgskin and Bray argued for socialism.
4. The notion of the "inevitability" of socialism has been criticised strongly by Althusser. See his *The Humanist Controversy and Other Writings* (London:Verso, 2003).
5. Karl Marx, *Capital*, Vol. I (Moscow: Progress Publishers, 1986), p. 555.

6. Karl Marx, *Theories of Surplus Value*, Part II (Moscow:Progress Publishers, 1975), p. 548.
7. Quoted in Mao Zedong in an interview published in Schram.
8. Karl Marx, 'The Poverty of Philosophy' in *Marx. Engels. Collected Works*, Vol. 6 (Moscow: Progress Publishers, 1976), p. 211.
9. Quoted in the introduction to Slavoj Žižek's *Revolution at the Gates. Lenin's Writings in 1917* (London: Verson, 2006).
10. A full discussion of this can be found in my *Economics and Egalitarianism* (Delhi: Oxford University Press, 1990).
11. See Marx's discussion in *Marx. Engels. Collected Works*, Vol. 6 (Moscow: Progress Publishers, 1976, pp. 206-11) on this subject.
12. J.M. Keynes, *The General Theory of Employment, Interest and Money* (London: Macmillan, 1949), p. 378.
13. This is lucidly discussed in a prescient essay by Kalecki. See his 'Political Aspects for Full Employment', in *Selected Essays on the Dynamics of Capitalist Economics, 1933-1972* (Cambridge: Cambridge University Press, 1971).

20

Can Democratic Centralism Be Conducive to Democracy?

Javeed Alam

Democratic centralism has generally been accepted as the principle for building communist organisations, whereas it was only meant to address the organisational demands of a particular historical context in Tsarist Russia. By institutionalising centralism and leaving democracy undefined, this organisational form has fostered authoritarian tendencies and undermined the growth of new ideas in the working class movement. This is seen in India where the engagement of the communist parties with democracy has remained ad hoc and untheorised. This chapter argues that democratic centralism has been an obstacle for the communist parties to be able to creatively respond to new situations and conditions.

Insofar as the absence of democracy—seen minimally as civil and political rights and unhindered freedom of speech and their institutional buttressing—in the erstwhile socialist states is more or less recognised by all, it is important to try and locate the ground, or the prior condition, that may have allowed authoritarian practices to gain roots. When a phenomenon is not simply a distortion, now and then or here and there, but assumes a universal shape over time, then it is likely to be a pointer to internal features of a structural nature within the Communist Parties (CPs). Democratic centralism (DC) being the generally accepted principle of the internal organisation of the CPS needs to be singled out for a critical look. By now it seems to me quite clear, that DC, in the way it stands, provides one such structural condition for the throttling of democracy inside the CPs. In itself there may not be anything necessarily wrong with the principle—its working remains corrigible and can still be the basis for organising revolutionary activities in society—but the way it has come down historically, there is a serious imbalance in its internal features. Let me look at some of these features in an ascending order of importance.

Parcelling Out Truth

Of the two components that go to make up democratic centralism, democracy and centralism, it was only the concept of centralism that was broken down into its constituent elements and given a concrete form. It was concretised in a way where relations between the higher and lower bodies of the party in terms of power and authority, responsibility and discipline, decision-making and accountability and related activities around these were given precise weightages and a definitional content. These were clearly visible to all in the CPs. The component of democracy was never, and has not been yet, systematically concretised, nor has it been given a clear definitional sense. It has operated only as a generalised assertion within the conceptual totality that is made up of these contrary pulls. What are the inalienable claims or rights of the lower bodies vis-à-vis the higher bodies except to appeal. The only concretised feature of democracy—elections from the lower to the higher bodies—has always been vitiated by the system where panels of names are proposed by the higher bodies to the lower ones. The elections too are conducted under the supervision of representatives of a higher body and that too by a simple yes-no show of hands. This makes for a situation in which power and authority constituted themselves, and were not derived in a bona fide manner from below. What became intrinsic, as a result, within the CPs has been an overwhelming privilege for centralised authority over democracy.

This distorted functioning of DC can also be seen in the way information and understanding has been handled within the CPs. Only what is deemed necessary is reported from the politburo (PB) to the central committee (CC) and from the CC to the state secretariat so on downwards to still lower bodies, with information and understanding shrinking like in a funnel as one reaches the lowest bodies. This makes the lowest bodies incapable of any independent decision-making, opinion formation or proper assessments and judgments and raises a fundamental question about the claims of Marxism-Leninism to be a science, or, as I would put it, capable of being a science. It is, in effect, being said that only a selected few in the CP can do science and the blind have to be led.

Is understanding or, let us say, "truth" divisible and thus legible to be parcelled as found necessary by the leadership? Given this, the easy reduction in practice, across the world, of class into party and the party into leadership should not therefore be an enigma. Nor should the fact be surprising that very often the party-leader could so easily assign to himself the role of History by virtue of possessing the Truth.

The issues centred around DC need to be carefully re-examined for two more reasons. First, a certain historical necessity may justify degrees of centralisation and secrecy during periods of revolutionary struggle for capture of state power. But justification under necessity cannot be a ground once revolutionary power is stabilised nor can it be extended indefinitely. In other words, a socialist state or movement must be careful of the point at which certain principles start becoming ineligible within a larger programmatic frame of reference. For example, when it moves from making the revolution to the construction of a socialist society or, alternatively, in conditions of democratic contestations where organised political forces enjoy freedom of unhindered competition for power to control the state. To justify, in the name of revolutionary imperatives, a permanently centralised, authoritarian power structure seems merely an alibi for authoritarian and responsible use of power or the permanence of dictatorship.

As an aside, it should be remembered that the idea of DC was worked out as the organisational structure for the Social Democratic Party in the Tsarist empire which was an extreme case of despotic rule through a repressive police state. It was primarily to guard against such a state and political context that specific precautions were required. I do not know if Lenin did or would have recommended DC as a necessary and universal principle. What we do, however, know is that Lenin was perfectly at ease with other organisational forms which existed in other social democratic parties, like those in Germany or Hungary.

It is important that no organisational form be treated as a principle and therefore be considered as immune from re-inspection.

The Question of Principle

This therefore raises, secondly, a question of fundamental importance about the very nature of different aspects that make up a revolutionary project. Is DC an independent principle under all conditions within a Marxian revolutionary programme in the way building and sustaining an exploitation-less society is? Or, is it valid only under certain stipulated conditions, like those where the ruling classes systematically use state power to repress and destroy the working class movement? Making this distinction between an *independent principle* and a *contingent organisational form* under stipulated conditions allows its own elaborations. So I see no more need to go into further details, except to say that DC is not and cannot be constitutive of Marxism-Leninism in the way concepts like classless society, non-exploitative mode of production, inalienability of human attributes, etc are. Its essence can only be a derivative necessity for the making and consolidation of revolution under stipulated conditions.

Elevating an organisational form to being constitutive of revolutionary projects gave rise to a problem which has acquired a character typical of a paradox. To get to the root of this paradox let us ask a question. Who is the CP answerable to? The answer, in face of the actual practice, boils down to saying that the CP is answerable, and therefore accountable, only to its own theory. It is true that all positions relating to *human praxis* justify themselves on grounds of their theoretical understanding; in other words, intellectual positions, or knowledge claims based on praxis, both generate and evaluate actions introspectively all along. But in view of the practice in CPs, as argued above, theory did not remain an open search for scientific validation, as in the hands of Marx, Luxemburg or Lenin, but became a restrictive and restricted activity. The "truth" of the theory came to be defined and handed down from above. The higher one was located in the party, the stronger became the claim to hand down theoretical truths. The key feature of Marxism, which calls for constant self-critical evaluations of truth-claims, got frozen in 'Socialist' societies and communist thinking. It needs to be stressed that in any kind of critical re-evaluation the politburo or any other body of the party cannot have a privileged position, however much its authority to decide the *programme* or the *line* may be justified. Anyone who is intellectually equipped with the body of Marxist knowledge is potentially as capable of critique and re-evaluations as anybody else in positions of authority or power.

The Self-Fulfilling Prophecy

As for accountability, or the mode of justifications of practice, this led to something akin to a paradox because the CP first *defines* what is constitutive of its theory and from the angle of justifications *reads* its own self-defined theory. The paradox was never understood for what it meant for revolutionary projects because the problems created in practice were always seen in terms of 'deviations'. Deviation may be a useful concept to review and correct practice. But a dialectical way of viewing the social reality will show that all problems are neither capable of being understood, nor resolved, in terms of deviations since this implies infallibility of theory as defined and embodied in the CP. Theory itself, if it is to continue to function in tandem with science and not decline into routine ideological practice, needs constant renewal. Renewal needs debunking and possible invalidations. This requires multiple sources of debate and investigations. The practice of the CPs foreclosed these possibilities and the repercussions have been many. Let us explore two of them here.

For the CPs, whether they were in power or not, it led to a relative drying up of new sources of ideas. New ideas—as expressions of independently carried out concrete investigations of specific situations which then grow into knowledge—is something the CPs get deprived off. Moreover, it also resulted in a straitjacketing of the relationship of the leadership, both with the cadre and the class and mass organisations and of all of these with the people at large. The consequence of this for the growth of CPs and their evolution into a creative fountain of emancipatory ideas and solutions specific to varied societies is before us today. From the advantageous position hindsight it is possible to say that the repercussions for the CPs in power, including in India, have been quite devastating. The established practice created far too difficult a relationship between the CP and the non-party "masses" and, in day-to-day matters, between the cadre and the people in general. The cadre tended to act, on the one hand, as a brake and gatekeepers in checking the articulation and flow of ideas inconvenient to the CP and, on the other, drilled into the people what was thought of as correct by the CP. They should rather have been, if they were to be the link in the democratic chain, acting as the gathering points for the divergent views, dissensions, private dissents, disappointments, anger, etc among the people.

It appears that communist thinking became suspicious of multiple sources of debate, opinion and independent investigations, based on a wrong analogical reading of the prevailing practice in liberal-democratic societies. It saw, I believe, the multiple sources as necessarily dependent on antagonistic class interests and their organisational expressions. This need not necessarily be so. The CPs in general, and in the post-revolutionary situation more so where big capital and landlord interests are destroyed even if their thinking modes survive, can so work that these multiple sources are treated as so many points of social discourse; that is, discursive intersections.

Constant critical self-evaluation of theory, being a major requirement, needs pluralism. Pluralism of what kind is something that requires systematic experimentation within socialist practice and a priori answers will be futile. The CPs altogether rejected these questions as counter-revolutionary bourgeois clap-trap. In the period of post-revolutionary reconstruction, the continued recourse to Lenin's use of polemical debunking, not only of hostile ideas from those opposed to revolution but also 'erroneous' ones from the closest of his comrades, could have been one way of initiating such an experimentation into socialist modes of democratic discourse. Whether it would have led to an institutionalised form of pluralism, socialist in content but distinct from the practice in capitalist societies, cannot be answered by backward extrapolation. What began in the Soviet Union around 1985-86 as Glasnost was not the realisation of the initial conditions of socialist democracy. The absence of any idea of, or effort at, realising socialist democracy has generated the need to come to terms with more elementary forms of democracy associated with enforced inequalities, threats to social existence and exploitative scarcity.

Abolishing Factions and Soviets

Instead of a search for democratic practices and instituting pluralist sources of debate, to digress into history here, the 10th Congress of the Communist Party of the Soviet Union (CPSU) in 1921 took two disastrous decisions. It abolished what it called the "factions". This led to a clamp down on all expressions of ideological differences and debate around these, as used to be the practice in that party. Eventually, in the name of factions, all ideological differences were repressed and those who refused to toe the line were eliminated. This process led to the astonishing situation where an overwhelming number of individuals who were members of the CPSU politburo at the time of the Russian Revolution, were labelled class enemies and imperialist agents. This same 10th Congress of the CPSU went on to abolish the Soviets. The Soviets were the one site where every issue was thoroughly debated by workers, peasants and soldiers before arriving at some decision. They were the vibrant grass root sites of democracy and of great importance in mobilising people for revolutionary actions. Here was an institution from where a democratic institutional structure—socialist in character—could have been built. It must be remembered that both these decisions were taken after the worker-peasant alliance had won the civil war. The argument of necessity cannot be invoked here. If these two institutions of ideological contestations and democratic debates could be assets during the civil war, it cannot be argued that these would be threats in the building of a socialist society. We ought to remember that the erstwhile Soviet Union was not a Cuba; it was a huge multinational country of continental dimensions. Lenin, and others, have a lot to explain for these actions which has left a legacy of authoritarian practices and despotic rule, not only in the Soviet Union, but in all other socialist societies; and subsequently authoritarian practices in all CPs anywhere in the world.

The absence of democracy had a further cascading effect in creating a feeling of implicit coercion within society. While I do not subscribe to the thesis that the Soviet Union had become a class society, nonetheless, social stratification had led to the emergence of a distinct, stable structure of elites, comprising the nomenklatura, technical experts, intelligentsia and sections of the middle classes. Despite a rise in real income, income distribution had also been moving in favour of these elites. In the absence of democratic space to agitate for income equalisation, for demanding changes in the composition of wage goods and durables and for improvement in working conditions, the feeling of coercion as an implicit feature of social existence had become widespread. One way of ascertaining this is by backward extrapolation from what had happened when political space for discussions and debates became available under Glasnost—these led not to a struggle for socialist democracy, but for the repudiation of the socialist system. It is clear now that people are not prepared to entertain any kind of a return to communist rule, the experience of it having been so bitter for persons as individuals.

Historical Culpability

To uncritically blame Glasnost for all that happened is to shut one's eyes to historical culpability. What Gorbachev was trying to revive in the first phase (I am emphasising the "first phase" because Gorbachev systematically blundered later on) of Glasnost was the early revolutionary history of dealing with the deeper levels of bourgeois theory with due seriousness, of accepting the complexity of one's own and others' theoretical positions, which was first ignored and then denied by Stalin. Gorbachev was repeatedly, again in the first phase, going back to Lenin, and not to Marx because it was Leninist practice which was revoked by Stalin. Hence, the relationship between Lenin, and what followed him, becomes important for socialist practice today, for every Communist Party, unless it has, successfully in practice, renounced certain legacies from Stalinist practice.

To come back to the issue at hand, a conceptualised practice, recognising higher forms of liberal democratic practice, could perhaps become the basis of creating sustained discursive networks for building an enduring, popularly derived, socialist consciousness as a bulwark against bourgeois ideas, rather than by their suppression. These absences, I suspect, have been the prime cause of dissipating the possibilities for the growth of socialist consciousness. The biggest casualty has been the possibility of the emergence of a distinct practice of socialist democracy. The absence of any picture of socialist democracy has generated the need today to come to terms with demands for simpler forms of democracy associated with the framework of liberal-democracy. As an aside, do such demands become, ipso facto, "bourgeois"? This will require a detour into the widely-held "Marxist" notions about liberal-democracy. I will withhold this inquiry for the time being and instead go into something near and immediate.

Lack of Theory

The CPS in India, including the Communist Party of India (Marxist) (CPI(M)), have, by default, accepted democracy as prevalent in India and therefore the framework of rights as given in the Constitution of India. But this has come about in a rather ad hoc manner, *without a moment of theoretical reflection*. This came about with the experience of "Emergency" with its disastrous consequences for the working class movement and popular struggles. It looks ad hoc because even in the early 1970s, the CPI(M) leader E.M.S. Namboodiripad, the foremost theoretician of communist practice in India, was talking of throwing the Indian Constitution 'lock, stock, and barrel' into the Indian Ocean. 'Emergency' can only be the basis for accepting 'bourgeois' democracy as a pragmatic need. No more. 'Emergency' showed to the communists the central importance of civil rights and their absence, as a source of brutality. In the understanding that then emerged, communists of all hues learnt that they cannot treat rights *instrumentally*, as was the case in practice, and that there is something of immense significance in civil rights, in and of itself. This led to an understanding, although vague, that, in any democracy under bourgeois conditions, there is more than merely the power of the ruling classes. If the daily life of people has to be protected from abuse, then the question of governmental power has to be attended to, here and now. This is the site of civil rights, of securing immunities to people in relations to the exercise of state power, however one may characterise its nature. All this was a gain in practice and programmatic conception.

Given this, the CPs have still not theorised the question of democracy nor is there a hint towards this in any document or debates. Unless a theoretical justification is systematically built up, practice will remain ad hoc. This has not happened thus far, nor does it appear likely to happen any time soon. It is not likely to happen, if only the official party publications are authorised to do so as these are not properly equipped, intellectually, for such a theoretical undertaking. A protracted debate at all levels of Marxist thinking, in and outside the parties, is required. The CPs have to forgo many of the practices of democratic centralism for this kind of a debate to come about. Let me focus on certain legacies from the Communist Party's history of understanding democracy and as well to the history of democracy itself.

Parliamentary Democracy: A Sham?

Let us look at an anomaly. Having accepted the historical

significance of civil and political rights, how does the communist understanding position itself in relation to the historical Leninist assertion that *parliamentary democracy and its rights are a sham.* Lenin may well have repeated what Marx had observed in the mid-19th century. In the context in which Marx made that observation, he was right in doing so but when Lenin repeats that, at a very different historical juncture, it becomes *a*-historical. When Marx asserted that the rights talked of in parliamentary democracy are a sham, he, as the representative of the working class movement, found that the bourgeois state had denied political rights to the workers, when liberal spokesmen kept declaring these rights to be universal. This glaring inconsistency between the declaration and the actual condition of denial of political rights to workers is what prompts Marx to say so.

Since that time the workers through protracted struggles and huge sacrifices have won the rights to form trade unions, to exercise universal franchise, to go on strike and form pickets, to contest elections, form their political parties and much more. For Lenin to repeat what Marx did, when conditions had so radically changed, is a negation of the heritage of the history of the working class struggles to wrest rights for themselves in face of the fierce resistance from the ruling classes. If we accept what Lenin is saying, in effect, it means that the great struggles of the workers and the victories they wrested from the ruling classes (and thus radically altered how state power is exercised through governmental agencies, including, in relation to them) are of no consequence. What seems surprising today is that Lenin, and the movement he was heading, did not acknowledge or even recognise that something so momentous has happened because of the working class struggles themselves.

The Lockean discourse of rights—the historical foundation of rights in liberal democracy—was *disordered* from about the middle of the 19th century with the working classes winning right after right. A whole new schedule of rights came about and became engrained. This was a working class gain secured through long and sustained struggles against the class rule of the bourgeoisie and was therefore, simultaneously, a shrinking of the prerogatives of the bourgeoisie. In a similar fashion, the present schedule of rights is again being disordered by women's movements and feminism, struggles for ecological and environmental protection and so on. New rights and entitlements are being added. A reconfiguration is underway in which, not only is something new being added, but much which was the prerogative of men is being shed. A century ago if a woman were to say, by looking at the rights schedule, that they are a sham, she would be right. But today were she to say so, it would be a historical misjudgment.

To equate the state of a theory today with its inaugural moment, is to collapse essence into origin. This is a serious methodological fallacy which many in the popular movements are, unfortunately, prone to. Marxists ought to be more sensitive to the fact that what comes to be, keeps changing. This is what the sense of being dialectical is.

Value of Political Emancipation

Moreover, Marx's comment was, as noted above, highly contextual and not dismissive of—call it bourgeois or liberal—democracy. Marx made an elaborate distinction between political emancipation and human (or social) emancipation. Political emancipation is nothing but *maximally* a regime of entrenched rights and the institutional buttressing of those rights so as to make them secure in practice. That is why in both in *The Jewish Question* and in the *Critique of Hegel's Philosophy of Rights: An Introduction*, Marx singles out England and France as successful instances of political emancipation, whereas Germany is referred to in a disparaging, reproachful manner for trying to achieve in philosophy what ought to be an actual condition of life in society, that is not a resolution of problem in thought but in actuality. To Marx, the resolution of problems in thought, as against concrete reality, is also idealism.

Marx had placed a high value on existing democracy, especially freedom of speech and expression, despite finding it *highly restrictive* from the point of humanity's emancipation from exploitation and alienation or for the recovery of the fullness of human potential. Bourgeois democracy cannot but be restrictive as, in the prevailing relations of production, labour power becomes a commodity and therefore things which human beings produce, the commodity form, comes to dominate over them instead of they having control over it. The abolition of the commodity form is a necessary condition for human emancipation; humanity being the measure of itself, neither the commodity nor God will do, as in the old renaissance wisdom. Marx therefore was clear that it is only by abolishing the rule of property that the *pre-conditions* for social emancipation can be achieved.

It is here, in a deeper theoretical sense, one may call liberal democracy a "sham". If we at all use this word, in what sense can we call it a sham? Marx, in the *Communist Manifesto,* had called the state an agency of class (bourgeois) dictatorship. Most communists accept this and, in an ultimate sense, they ought to. To get to the meaning of this formulation let us first treat it as a *proposition* and then try to reformulate it, a little hermeneutically.

Horizon of Probabilities

For Marx, the state is, over and above everything else, the *site for the reproduction of the relations of production* and thus facilitates capital accumulation. The various forms of governments that get formed within the capitalist state have great autonomy, though of varying degrees, to do things differently under changing conditions, under democratic or other pressures. This is an empirical fact which is observed every day. Precisely for this reason, we look at them as responsive to societal pressures. The greater a government is alert to popular egalitarian demands, the more democratic it is viewed to be. And there is no error involved at any level of understanding in viewing it so.

The problem however is of a different kind, outside the realm of empirical observation. The government, under the most democratic of liberal dispensations with the greatest degree of autonomy, cannot, is not allowed to, change the relations of production. In other words, the capitalist nature of production has to be sustained, whatever the degrees of welfare provisions conceded, without, of course, causing the "crises of accumulation". This is a *non-empirical given* and has led to social democracy, a welcome development under bourgeois conditions, though of a very vacillating nature.

This non-empirical given conditions the *probabilities* of the world within which we live and make choices. These choices are genuine and real, yet *limited* by the given condition, that of the range of probabilities the world offers us. All of it has serious implications for what we cherish as our agency. It is true that capitalism, for the first time in history, created the pre-conditions for the emergence of *agency*, and in a two-fold way. In one way, it made it possible for a large number of people to be autonomous, self re-making persons with a sense of moral responsibility—the well placed literati. In another way, more significantly, it created another class of people—the workers—who could not live without struggling and agitating for a world which becomes more liveable. This twofold development gave rise to a subjectivity which strived for fulfilment and therefore, the quest (a future project) becomes as much a part of our identity as are the roots.

But all this is possible within, what I have called above, the probabilities of the world. These probabilities are reductive of what can be done or desired by the *agent*. They allow a free play to subjective utilities but not to a quest to live in an economic order that overcomes capitalism. Agency thus becomes an intersection of subjective utilities and probabilities of the world; beyond this is the world of great difficulty, verging on impossibility, within any given liberal dispensation of democracy.

It appears that Lenin did not mean this when he referred to parliamentary democracy as a sham, because the context nowhere indicated this. On the other hand, when Marx calls liberal democracy a dictatorship of the bourgeoisie, all of this theory is clearly implicit.

Conclusions

I have gone into all this to argue that communists appear to be existing with a contradictory amalgam of received wisdom. That may be all right in itself, but the problem arises when they do not realise this condition. That is what was meant when it was stated earlier that the change in the CPs' positions about civil and political rights, and much else, has been without a "moment of theoretical reflection". From out of this contradictory amalgam, the communists choose what suits them in a given situation in an ad hoc manner. There is no exception to this, from the general secretary of the party, to its central committee or chief minister or an activist reacting contradictorily to different situations.

To get out of this situation, the CPs have to reflect on the complexity of the theoretical inheritance from Marx onwards, that has been lost in subsequent ideological sophistry. And, therefore, the legacy of the communist movement needs to be re-examined, with the useful to be recovered and the dated to be shed. Otherwise the debates, and practice, in the working class movement on the question of democracy, and much else, will continue to remain impoverished.

Democratic centralism, as an overarching, infallible principle will not allow this to happen. It will privilege the leaders above democracy and reduce the cadre into, albeit involuntarily, time servers and the communist movements into stagnant bodies watching history pass by.

21

On Democratic Centralism

Prakash Karat

In the recent period, along with a number of critical discussions on the electoral setback suffered by the CPI (M) and the Left in the 2009 Lok Sabha elections, there have been some questions raised about the practice of democratic centralism as the organisational principle of the Communist Party. Such critiques have come from persons who are intellectuals associated with the Left or the CPI (M).

Since such views are being voiced by comrades and persons who are not hostile to the Party, or, consider themselves as belonging to the Left, we should address the issues raised by them and respond. This is all the more necessary since the CPI (M) considers the issue of democratic centralism to be a basic and vital one for a party of the working class.

Instead of dealing with each of the critiques separately, we are categorising below the various objections and criticisms made. Though, it must be stated that it is not necessary that each of them hold all the views expressed by the others. But the common refrain is that democratic centralism should not serve as the organisational principle of the Communist Party or that it should be modified.

What are the points made in these critiques? They can be summed up as follows:

1. Democratic centralism is characterised as a Party

organisational structure fashioned by Lenin to meet the specific conditions of Tsarist autocracy which was an authoritarian and repressive regime. Hence, its emphasis on centralisation, creating a core of professional revolutionaries and secrecy. Thus democratic centralism is unsuitable for other societies and conditions and particularly where bourgeois democracy holds sway.

2. Democratic centralism is accused of creating a hierarchical, centralised structure which stifles democracy and democratic functioning. The writ of the Polit Bureau and Central Committee runs. The party members and cadres are to carry out the directives of the Central Committee. Contrary or dissenting views have no place to be heard or considered.
3. Democratic centralism is also held responsible for stifling creative thinking and development of Marxist theory. The top bodies of the party set out theory and it becomes a closed system which precludes any fresh thinking or absorbing new developments. Democratic centralism is suited to a structure where theory is interpreted by the leading bodies and it is carried out by the ranks. Theoretical discussions outside the approved framework is frowned upon, or worse seen as 'indiscipline'.
4. A party based on democratic centralism enables the party leadership to disregard the opinion of the party as a whole. This creates a barrier between the people and the Party. It prevents correction of a wrong position in time due to barrier in communication.
5. As far as the CPI (M) is concerned, democratic centralism in practice has been distorted with centralisation and commandism in West Bengal with no heed paid to views from below. On a general plane, it is asserted that a mass revolutionary party cannot be built with the Leninist form of organisation. Wrong tactical line being formulated can also be attributed to the wrong organisational practice.

I

The principle of democratic centralism has always been attacked by social democrats and non-Marxist leftists ever since the Bolshevik Party adopted it and when it was extended by the Communist International to all Communist parties in its third Congress in 1921.

When Lenin expounded and developed Marxist theory beyond what was set out by Marx and Engels, among his key contributions were the theory of imperialism, the role of the peoples of the colonial and semi-colonial countries in the world revolutionary movement and the concept of a revolutionary organisation.

At the heart of the issue is not just the organisational structure of the Party, but the basic role of a Communist Party. For social democratic parties, whose perspective is to work within the capitalist system itself, the need for a revolutionary organisation does not arise. Hence democratic centralism is anathema to them. For a Communist Party which works to overthrow capitalism and in India the bourgeois-landlord order, and replace it eventually with socialism, Party organisation has to be one which is equipped to wage the political, ideological and organisational struggle against the powerful state and the dominant ruling classes. Such a Party organisation cannot be only geared to fight elections in a parliamentary democratic system, however stable and long-lasting it is, or to be engaged only in exercising and using the democratic rights and institutions available within the framework of the hegemony of a bourgeois state.

The key issue would be whether the party is equipped to organise and lead the working class and the revolutionary mass movement? Lenin's conception of the Party was to build an organisation which could prepare and develop such a revolutionary mass movement. For this he stressed the importance of recruiting the advanced sections of the working class into the Party who can be made politically conscious and hence constitute the vanguard. Such an organisation is steeled through class struggle and mass movements and is able to function in all conditions—of legality, semi-legality and illegality. The exigencies of class politics require an organisation which is able to change the forms of struggle according to the prevailing situation. This requires a centralised party. Democratic centralism is best suited as the organisational principle for a party based on Marxism and class struggle. Class struggle is a collective act. Democratic centralism promotes collective decision-making and collective activity; it allows for freedom of thought and unity in action.

For collective functioning to be effective, it requires going beyond the democratic method of decision-making by majority opinion to bind the entire collective into implementing that decision. It is only democratic centralism which requires the minority to abide by the majority and the individual to submit to the will of the collective. The debates between the Bolsheviks and the Mensheviks in the Russian Social Democratic Party clarified some of the essential features of a revolutionary party and its organisation. Outside Russia, some of the prominent Marxist leaders like Karl Kautsky and Rosa Luxemburg criticised the Leninist idea of party organisation. For Kautsky, organisation was a precondition for revolutionary action. Rosa Luxemburg held that organisation is a product of the revolutionary mass movement. For Lenin, the Party and its organisation were both a precondition and a result of the revolutionary mass movement. As Lukács brilliantly summed up the Leninist concept, *the Party is both the producer and the product of the revolutionary mass movement.*[1] For Lenin, the Party is an organisation which prepares for the revolution; such an organisation has to be equipped to deal with all eventualities including the attack by the class enemies both on the political and organisational plane. Such an organisation has to have the strictest party discipline. It is only such a discipline which will enable the party to adjust to changed situations and to have the flexibility to change the forms of struggle.

To view democratic centralism divorced from a party adhering to Marxism and the class struggle will lead to a distorted understanding of this vital principle of party organisation.

II

What are the arguments against democratic centralism?

1. Specific to Russian Conditions

One of the main arguments of the critics of democratic centralism has been the specificity of this organisational practice for the Russian revolutionary movement. It was developed in Russia during the revolutionary struggle against Tsarism. The Bolshevik Party facing repression and exile needed an organisation which could work in these illegal conditions. It got consolidated after the revolution as the counterrevolutionary forces tried to suppress the revolutionary regime and it was backed by imperialist intervention. It was adopted by other Communist Parties. Can an organisational principle which served Russian conditions be adopted for parties working in different situations and conditions?

But can it then be said that it was Russia-specific and cannot be applied to other countries and other situations where Communist Parties work? Prabir Purkayastha says:

> The specific form of the Party came after the Bolshevik revolution when factions were banned. It could be argued that this was a specific form of the party necessitated by a revolutionary state besieged by all great powers in the fledgling socialist state. *The party evolving a command and control structure* of democratic centralism is a consequence of this situation and not a general principle. To carry forward this structure to all conditions and situations that was an exigency of a specific time and place does have implications for the Left movement today.
>
> That having been said, it is important that the Left re-examines the issue of democratic centralism. While the command and control structures has helped the CPI (M) to survive the disintegration that has overtaken many of the powerful Communist Parties that existed elsewhere, its problems are all too real, the major one being that the opinion of the Party as a whole can be disregarded by the Party leadership. This can lead to a dissonance between the masses and the leaders and also create barriers between the people and the Party. At times when the Party needs a course correction, democratic centralism can carry on with a wrong position for longer due to this barrier in communications.[2]

While it is true that democratic centralism was evolved by the Russian Social Democratic Labour Party and Lenin played the instrumental role in fleshing out the concept, the fact is that organisational forms and practices are integrally linked to the revolutionary character of the Party. It is not the Russian Party alone which faced attack and it was not the Russian Revolution alone which was sought to be suppressed by foreign intervention. Every revolution in the 20th century underwent the same process of repression, counterrevolution/civil war and foreign intervention. If Russia had the Tsarist repression, the Chinese communists faced the brutal repression of the Kuomintang; if Russia faced civil war, so did China, Cuba and other countries. Foreign intervention took place in China, Vietnam, Korea and Cuba. Even the peaceful and democratic assumption to government through elections in Chile saw its brutal displacement by a military coup.

Apart from the Chinese, Vietnamese and Korean revolutions, the Cuban Revolution is an example. Here the revolutionary takeover was not led by the Communist Party. But after the revolutionary forces were consolidated into the Cuban Communist Party after the overthrow of the old order, the party organised itself on the lines of democratic centralism.

There is as yet no instance of any revolution or advance to socialism where the party or organisation leading the process has not been organised on the lines of democratic centralism.

In Venezuela, where there was a revolutionary process, Chavez found it necessary to transform his 'movement' into a Party. That Party is not run on democratic centralism but it runs with a centralism which is centred on the personality of Chavez himself. How far this process can be taken forward without a Centralised Party remains to be seen.

Why have all the Parties that led revolutionary movement embraced democratic centralism? This is because no revolution is allowed to advance democratically and peacefully. Every revolution has to face attacks by imperialism and the class enemies. Without democratic centralism, the Party is disarmed and cannot be a revolutionary organisation. The important point Lenin made of the Party acting as a centralised force against the powers of the modern centralised state applies even now and to all countries. In fact, it has become more essential, given the highly advanced and mobile force that imperialism can marshal against any revolutionary force.

It is not only direct military intervention that has to be met, every revolution that takes place under a globally dominant imperialist system will be a revolution under siege. There will not be any time in the foreseeable future where socialism is going to flower under a peaceful and benevolently democratic atmosphere. As Fidel Castro quoting Lenin once said: "No revolution is worth its name, if it cannot defend itself." Democratic centralism is an essential armour of that defence.

The other corollary point made is that democratic centralism is suited for Parties in a revolutionary situation. Lenin had forged democratic centralism in the period of the actuality of the revolution. How can that principle be applied in countries where there is parliamentary democracy, legality and bourgeois decreed democratic rights?

It is not counterrevolutionary violence alone that has to countered. The Party has to move with a single purpose politically. It has to preserve and protect its ideological basis. The bourgeois state and the ruling classes are constantly trying to disrupt the political-ideological cohesion of the Party and to deflect it to reformist class collaboration. The war of ideas and the ideological struggle cannot be conducted effectively by a Party which abandons democratic centralism. Without democratic centralism, the Party would get converted into a discussion forum or a debating society.

Many Communist Parties have operated in a non-revolutionary situation in the second half of the 20th century. The situation has become more so in the first decade of the 21st century. But many of the these parties have survived because they adhered to democratic centralism. Whatever the ideological political weaknesses or mistakes, democratic centralism has kept them alive with potential as a revolutionary party. Whereas those parties which abandoned democratic centralism either ceased to be Communist Parties or disintegrated. The classic example is the Italian Communist Party, the biggest party outside the socialist countries till the early 1980s. But much before the collapse of the Soviet Union, it began the journey to liquidation by first giving up democratic centralism and culminating in giving up Marxism (or scientific socialism).

Even for a Communist Party with some popular base, functioning in a multi-party parliamentary democratic system, the attacks and pressures on the party are continuous and relentless. These come in the form of ideological and political attacks and efforts to disorganise and weaken the Party. Even in a peaceful time, the class struggle leads to a constant attack, as the Party is fighting against the ruling class policies. This is the experience of the CPI (M) too. While the political and ideological terrain of struggle is primary, they cannot be conducted effectively without an organisation which can counter the multifaceted attempts to disorganise it. Without democratic centralism, there can be only a social democratic party—not a revolutionary one.

Democratic centralism is equated with a "command and control structure". This is then extended to claim that "the opinion of the Party as a whole" can be disregarded by the Party leadership. Does centralism mean command and control? Is it proper to negate centralism on the grounds that it fosters a command and control structure? For a politically conscious Party member, centralism embodies the collective will and purpose, and not commandism. It is the exercise of both centralism and inner-Party democracy that constitutes democratic centralism. The CPI (M) Constitution has a whole section (Article XIII) on the principles of democratic centralism and how it should work in the Party. Of relevance to the discussion, here are the clauses (c) and (d):

> (c) All Party committees shall periodically report their work to the Party organisation immediately below and all lower committees shall likewise report to their immediate higher committee; (d) All Party committees, particularly the leading Party committees, shall pay constant heed to the opinions and criticism of the lower Party organisations and the rank-and-file Party members.

The CPI (M) constitution provides for "free and frank discussion within the Party unit on all questions affecting the Party, its policy and work", but it does not permit factional groups or factionalism within the Party. Purkayastha thinks this was a specific step taken due to the exigencies of the situation in Russia after the revolution. Actually, the forming of factions with a Communist Party would destroy the integrity of the Party organisation and disable its will to collective action. One has only to remember that in the last days of the CPSU, under the Gorbachevian leadership, factions were permitted and this contributed to hastening the disintegration of the Soviet Party.

It is not possible for a Party leadership to disregard the opinion of the 'Party as a whole'. Contrary to that, it is only when there is no democratic centralism, or a gross violation of it, that such a thing can happen. How is the opinion of the Party expressed but through the views put forward by the Party committees at all levels? If a majority of the state committees give a different opinion, can the Central Committee disregard their views in our Party? Or, can the Polit Bureau disregard the views of the majority in the Central Committee?

2. Stifles Inner-Party Democracy

The second argument is that democratic centralism, as an organisational principle, inherently leads to centralism and ends up curtailing democracy; that the rule that lower committees should accept the decision of the higher committee leads to lopsidedness and over-centralisation. This stifles democratic expression of views and suppresses dissent.

This is a more substantive criticism. Especially in view of the experience of many Communist Parties both ruling and non-ruling. Leading bodies such as the Polit Bureau, Central Committee or State Committees can exercise untrammelled rights by selectively invoking those provisions of democratic centralism which give them the last word. Bureaucratic centralism or over-centralism can be cited in many instances when inner-Party democracy and the principles of democratic centralism are violated. But democratic centralism should be seen comprehensively, not just as something which embodies the centralising principle.

Taken together the set of principles which embody democratic centralism make it more democratic in practice than many Parties which practice, in theory, democracy only. It is important to see not just the form but the content of the democracy practiced by Parties.

The Leninist concept of Party organisation does not regiment or exclude vigorous inner-Party debates and discussions on both theory and practice. What it offers is the widest scope for debate and discussions while demanding the unity of action on a centralised political line. As Lenin put it:

> In the heat of the battle, when the proletarian army is straining every nerve, any criticism whatsoever cannot be permitted in its ranks. But before the call for action is issued, there should be the broadest and freest discussion and appraisal of the resolution, of its arguments and its various propositions.[3]

Democratic centralism is not a set of rigid dogmas. The actual norms and set of rules for the exercise of democratic centralism will find varying expressions in the Parties of different countries and in different stages of the development of the same Party. The other thing to remember is that democracy and centralism cannot be set within a fixed ratio for all times. It will depend on the concrete circumstances in each country, on the political situation, on the strength of the Party, the political level of its Party members and the confidence that the ranks have on the leadership.

Trotsky, who disagreed with Lenin on many issues, defending the principles of democratic centralism stated:

> When the problem is political action, centralism subordinates democracy to itself. Democracy again asserts its rights when the party feels the need to examine critically its own actions. The equilibrium between democracy and centralism establishes itself in the actual struggle, at moments it is violated and then again reestablished.

Similarly, democracy is practiced, before the conference when the political line is being formulated. Centralism comes in when the line is being implemented.

The CPI (M) has sought to learn from the experience of the

Communist Parties, especially those which successfully led revolutions. Some of these Parties fell prey to violating the principles of democratic centralism. The cult of a leader and the extreme centralism built around him, led to the abandonment of inner-Party democracy.

The CPI (M) was not affected by this deviation at any time in its history. The collective functioning of the leadership and the leading bodies has prevented such a deviation. It is for our Party to decide to practice democratic centralism as a party of the working class. This will not hinder broader Left consolidation. Just as we cannot compel any other Left party to follow democratic centralism, so also no other Left force can object to our internal organisational principle.

Even when we have a multi-party system in the period of transition to socialism and thereafter, it will be necessary for the Communist Party to adhere to democratic centralism. In fact, this will be a key instrument which will help the Party to compete effectively against other currents and forces to win over more sections of the working people.

As far as Ashok Mitra is concerned, he does not reject democratic centralism *per se*.[4] He criticises its practice in the CPI (M) in West Bengal where, according to him, "there is an excess of centralism with not even a wee bit of democracy". This led to the Party getting cut off from the people.

On earlier occasions, Ashok Mitra had strongly criticised the CPI (M) and the Left Front government's policy of industrialisation and the land acquisition measures. According to him, the implementation of neoliberal policies was responsible for the Party's alienation from the people.

Even if this assumption is taken to be true, then it is not the distorted practice of democratic centralism and over centralism which is to blame. In fact, Ashok Mitra has said elsewhere that it is the dedicated and disciplined cadres of the CPI (M) who constitute the backbone of the movement in West Bengal. The setback suffered in West Bengal has its causes in the political, organisational and governmental plane. The Party's review of the Lok Sabha elections have pinpointed the reasons and the shortcomings. But the excess of centralism is not the real cause.

3. Theory and Praxis Under Democratic Centralism

Prabhat Patnaik has criticised the use of democratic centralism on the following basis. Theory has been seen as a closed system. The prevailing view has been that Marxist theory developed by Marx, Engels and Lenin is to be adapted and interpreted only.

Contrary to this, Marxist theory can develop only if it is open and engages with non-Marxist mainstream theoretical developments. Theory is the preserve of the leadership and its application is for the ranks. This is the pattern fostered by, or, suited to democratic centralism.

> Free scientific discussion is like oxygen for a revolutionary party; without such discussion it cannot survive. But such free discussion in turn requires not just complete intellectual freedom, but also the existence of a multiplicity of opinions (which in turn entails a multiplicity of political parties) and a redefinition of the concept of 'democratic centralism' as the organising principle of a revolutionary party.[5]

Patnaik is right in pointing out that theory is not a closed system which only needs interpretation and application. Marxist theory has to constantly grow and update itself, for which it needs to be open and engage with new ideas, opposing ideologies and new circumstances. He is also right that there has been a dogmatic understanding of theory in the past.

But to link this flawed understanding of theory with the principles of democratic centralism is not correct. The failure to discuss theoretical issues and for creatively developing theory lies in the dogmatic understanding of theory being a 'closed system' as Patnaik himself points out and the cause of it cannot be ascribed to democratic centralism. There can be debates on theory and theoretical explorations within the framework of democratic centralism.

As Lukács pointed out, organisation is a form of mediation between theory and practice.[6] While different theoretical interpretations and views can be aired and argued, when it comes to practice, it has to assume an organisational form. It is here that the consequences of theory get clarified and tested.

While disparate theoretical views can be there in discussions, when it comes to action through organisation, there has to be a conclusion and direction to act upon. Whether a theory is correct, or a political-tactical decision right, can be judged by experience and the circumstances in which such a line of action was decided. Democratic centralism does not impede or reject such reviews and learning from one's practice. In fact, it provides the framework to do so in a manner by which the Party maintains its political coherence, its ideological continuity and tactical flexibility.

While a whole range of theory needs free discussion and constant reexamination, this cannot be extended to areas where a political line or conclusion is drawn after a discussion. There can be no 'multiplicity of opinions' when the Party has to act on the basis of its decisions and line. The question of discipline arises not for suppressing theoretical discussions but for ensuring that the Party acts with a single purpose.

4. Social Democratic Trends Result in Challenging Democratic Centralism

The link between the trend towards reformist politics of the social democratic variety and the necessity to abandon democratic centralism is well established. This is explicitly seen in Javeed Alam's attack on democratic centralism.[7] His endorsement of liberal democracy, his unbalanced view of the working class gains under bourgeois democracy and his incorrect exposition of Lenin's views on bourgeois democracy are all symptoms of a moving away from the Marxist standpoint. Taking off from a correct point about the rights wrested by the organised working class movement in the late 19th and the first half of the 20th century, Alam goes overboard in declaring that "A whole new schedule of rights (for the working class) came about and became engrained." He also characterises the gains secured by the working class as "simultaneously a shrinking of the prerogatives of the bourgeoisie."

Alam completely ignores the erosion of these gains of the working class and the dismantling of their 'engrained' rights that took place under the neoliberal dispensation of the 1980s in Britain and the US and then spread to the whole of Europe. Even the right to strike and collective bargaining were eroded. The only right under liberal democracy which endures is the right to vote, under adult franchise.

Alam exaggerates the emancipatory content of democracy under capitalism and underplays its class nature. Liberal democracy posits democratic and equal rights for citizens and then proceeds to limit and negate this by separating it from the economic sphere. Democracy has to subserve the market and capital and this assumes a formal character.

Javeed Alam disagrees with the political positions of the CPI (M). He has bemoaned the fact that the CPI (M) leadership had not found the wisdom to join bourgeois-led governments at the Centre in the past and attribute such wrong political understanding and tactics to the iron hand and blind discipline imposed by democratic centralism on the Party!

Such a wrong type of criticism is made by others too. If a tactical line is considered wrong, it is then attributed to the functioning of democratic centralism, or its distorted way of working. For instance, if the political step taken to withdraw support to the UPA government in July 2008 was a mistake, then it is attributed to the undemocratic command system in vogue. Similarly, the electoral setback in West Bengal is blamed on the bureaucratic leadership which is cut off from the views of the rank and file.

The CPI (M), within the framework of democratic centralism, has vigorous inner-Party discussions and debates on tactics and policy matters. For instance, in 1996, on the question of joining the Government at the Centre both the majority and minority views were thoroughly discussed in the Central Committee. The decision was further reviewed in the 16th Party Congress and the issue clinched. This is the method of a Communist Party. Those who disagree with the political and ideological positions cannot claim that it is democratic centralism that is responsible for decisions they do not like. They are chary of accepting the principle that the minority should accept the majority decision and implement it. But to deduce from this, that democratic centralism stifles criticism and dissenting views is unwarranted.

To Sum Up

Democratic centralism should not be seen as a set of dogmas regarding organisation. The following facts regarding democratic centralism should be kept in mind:

1. For a party which sets out a strategy for a revolution and bases its tactics on such a revolutionary strategy, the principle of democratic centralism is essential for its organisation.
2. Wrong ideological understanding and incorrect strategy and tactics can adversely affect the organisation. Eventually, the political-ideological deviations and wrong trends can erode the practice of democratic centralism itself.
3. Democratic centralism is the organisational principle for a Party based on the Marxist outlook. But there cannot be one single formula of democratic centralism for all times and all parties. They will vary according to conditions in which parties are working and the practice may vary during different periods of a single party.
4. There can be no fixed ratio of centralism and democracy in democratic centralism. When the party is formulating its policies, at the time of conferences, etc., there will be democracy in action, free discussions within the party forums. Once a call for action is given, the aspect of centralism will predominate. When the Party subjects its actions to self-critical review, democracy will assert itself again.
5. The practice of democratic centralism is not determined by formal principles and rules. It depends on the ideological political level of the Party members, the concrete conditions and political situation in a country, the authority of the leadership and the experience gained in building the organisation through struggles and tackling inner-Party contradictions.

III

Experience in India

The practice of democratic centralism in the Party has gone through a number of stages. In the early stages, the fledgling Communist Party saw itself as part of the contingent of the Communist International. The approach was that on matters of theory and political line, the CI word was final. This is the attitude which lingered on in the united Communist Party, where the views of the CPSU were given weightage. This was an approach which stunted the development of theory and working out correct strategy and tactics. In the second stage, after independence, problems of revisionism and sectarianism had their impact on the organisational plane. But by and large, the practice of inner Party democracy was not negated.

After the formation of the CPI (M), there was a critical review of the organisational practice in the united Party. The document 'Tasks on Party Organisation' was an outcome of this and provided the basis for building and running the organisation of the Party. A pertinent point made by the document was that revisionism attacked the principle of democratic centralism: "Democratic Centralism, the highest principle and the kernel of a Marxist-Leninist party was subjected to furious assaults and seriously undermined."

How has the practice of democratic centralism shaped up in our Party? Is it a mechanical copying of how democratic centralism was practised by the Russian party or any other party?

In the Salkia Plenum, the CPI (M) called for the development of a mass Revolutionary Party. This has to be built up on the basis of the principles of democratic centralism. Without democratic centralism, only a mass party can exist. Despite the shortcomings and limitations in the proper exercise of democratic centralism, it is these principles embodied in the Party Constitution, which has enabled the Party committees to develop the mass base of the Party and recruit tens of thousands of Party members who are willing to work under the discipline of the Party. No other party in India can claim to have as extensive discussions and inner-Party democracy as the CPI (M). This has been possible not in spite of democratic centralism but because of it being exercised.

The CPI (M) is working in a parliamentary democracy ever since its inception. It is not only in parliament and legislatures, it is running states governments and also works extensively in local bodies in some states. The practice of democratic centralism has taken this experience into account. How to guide thousands of Party members in these institutions and local self-governments has been encompassed within the broad framework of democratic centralism.

The Party is working in vastly varied conditions in the various states. On the basis of a centralised political line, there is a considerable amount of autonomy for the state committees to work out concrete tactics. Democratic centralism does not mean uniformity in tactics in developing the mass movements and the mass organisations.

The Party is in touch with the people not only through mass organisations but is accountable to them through its representatives in elected bodies at various levels. It is not possible to work in these forums only with a centralised line. It is by the democratic involvement of the Party cadres and members that mass politics and the work in these multifarious bodies can be conducted.

Correctives Applied

The CPI (M) reviewed the experience of the exercise of democratic centralism after the collapse of the Soviet Union. In the 14th Congress of the Party in 1992, the distortions in democratic centralism practised in the Soviet Union and some of the other socialist countries were noted. Overcentralisation, bureaucratism and the lack of inner-Party democracy prevailed.

One of the mistakes made at the level of theory and practice was the application of the principle of democratic centralism to the State structure of the Soviet Union. Democratic centralism became the guiding principle for the Soviet State and not just of the Communist Party. This was one of the factors which deformed socialist democracy.

The CPI (M) took up some corrective measures. Some of them are as follows:

(i) Democratic centralism is the organising principle of the Party and cannot be applied to the state. In the Programme adopted by the CPI (M) in 1964 it was stated that the People's Democratic State would be based on the principle of democratic centralism. In the updating of the Programme in 2000, this was dropped.

(ii) In order to strengthen inner-Party democracy, certain steps were taken. It was decided that higher committees should not propose the name of the secretary of the next lower committee at the time of the conference. Panels for new committees were already being prepared by the concerned outgoing committees.

(iii) Ensure election by secret ballot, if there is a contest.

(iv) The Central Control Commission should be elected directly by the Party Congress and not be a commission of the Central Committee. The Constitution was amended for this purpose.

(v) To ensure democratic functioning of the mass organisations, all elected posts/committees should not be decided by the concerned Party committee.

In this connection, it should be pointed out that Javeed Alam has wrongly depicted the procedures for election to Party committees. He has stated that panels of members are proposed by the higher committees to the lower bodies. This is not so. The panel is prepared by the outgoing committee at the conference and not by the higher committee. He further states that elections are by show of hands. This is also incorrect. If there are any names proposed outside the panel and there is a contest, there has to be an election by secret ballot. If there are no alternative names to the panel proposed, then voting is by show of hands. Here delegates can vote against or abstain.

The proper exercise of democratic centralism depends crucially on the political-ideological level of the Party members. Paucity at this level can result in limiting democratic involvement in discussions and policy making. The other violations of democratic centralism exist because of organisational problems like factionalism, lack of collective functioning, wrong methods of leadership at various levels, etc. Correcting and eliminating such trends is part of the struggle to build the Party on correct political organisational lines. The rectification campaign now being undertaken in the Party is dealing with the issues related to strengthening democratic centralism and correcting the violations of this principle.

Functioning in a multiparty system under parliamentary democracy, the CPI (M) functions on the basis of democratic centralism because it is based on the revolutionary perspective that people's democracy will be a higher form of democracy than bourgeois democracy. That can be accomplished only by putting an end to the bourgeois-landlord rule.

If democratic centralism is violated and not practiced properly by the CPI (M), then its advance as a party leading the working class and working people towards social transformation gets thwarted. It is thus incumbent on the Party to seriously eliminate all distortions and malfunctioning of democratic centralism within the Party.

Lenin had remarked that politics cannot be mechanically separated from organisation. The critics of democratic centralism and those asking the CPI (M) to do away with democratic centralism are wittingly or unwittingly asking for a change in the Party's basic character and strategy. For the CPI (M), the choice is stark: no mass revolutionary party without democratic centralism. The struggle the Party has to constantly engage in is to inculcate the true essence and spirit of democratic centralism within the entire Party.

REFERENCES

1. Georg Lukács, *Lenin: A Study of His Writing and Thought* (New Delhi: New Left Books, 1970).
2. Prabir Purkayastha, 'The 2009 Elections and the Challenges from the Left', *The Journal*, Vol. I, August 15, 2010, Centre for Policy Analysis.
3. V. I. Lenin, *Collected Works*, Vol. 10, p. 381.
4. AM, 'The State of the CPI (M) in West Bengal', *Economic & Political Weekly*, July 25, 2009.

5. Prabhat Patnaik, 'Re-Envisioning Socialism', *Economic & Political Weekly*, November 3, 2007.
6. Georg Lukács, *History and Class Consciousness* (London: Merlin Press, 1971).
7. Javeed Alam, 'Can Democratic Centralism Be Conducive to Democracy?', *Economic & Political Weekly*, September 19, 2009.

22

In Defence of Leninism

Murzban Jal

Written against the background of the recent critiques of democratic centralism and the crisis of mainstream Left politics, this chapter argues for a defence of Leninism based on Marx's theory of the proletariat as "species being". By claiming that Lenin had internalised Hegelian dialectics as "the algebra of the revolution", the chapter views Leninism as the sublation *(Aufhebung)* of centralism to mass politics, where organisation and the masses cease to exist as binary halves, but have been synthesised as what Marx calls "the union of free individuals".[1] It encounters two terrains: (1) Marx's revolutionary humanism, and (2) dialectics that views concepts and ideas in the matrix of contradictions and conflicts and thus in permanent-revolutionary transitions. It consequently argues that Leninism has to be seen in the light of Lenin's encounters in the *Philosophical Notebooks*, rather than in a dogmatic and fetishised understanding of democratic centralism that began with the Stalinist counter-revolution.

The Centre and the Counterfeit

One begins with a kind of irony and revolutionary cynicism in remembering Lenin with his own words: "None of the Marxists understood Marx!"[2] One then moves from the page of irony to history itself: to 1917 and the overthrow of the Tsar and then

Kerensky, the cessation of the Imperialist War and the ushering of Bread, Freedom and Peace. 1917 was what Herbert Marcuse once called the "radical act"[3]. The radical act can never be forgotten.

In April 1917, just after the Tsar was swept away from power and a few months before the October Revolution, Lenin talked of a revolutionary seizure of power based on the initiative of the "people from below".[4] "The source of power is not a law enacted by parliament", so Lenin said, instead, one has the "direct rule of the people". The Republic of Soviets of Workers', Agricultural Labourers' and Peasants' Deputies is formed which abolishes the police, army and the bureaucracy.[5] Lenin thus recognises two distinct forms of power: the bourgeois "centralised power" and the "direct initiative of the people from below".[6]

In contrast to these historical facts and the historical reading of Lenin, it is not so much the factual Lenin that appears on the scene of history, but the *conjured Lenin,* the Lenin that Stalin and the global reactionaries had continuously projected as the authentic Lenin. In these discourses of *spurious Leninism,* Lenin is supposed to have incorporated the politics of a rigid and elitist centralised organisation that was opposed to the masses. That Lenin was abstracted from concrete conditions and "hypostatised" as a sort of a fetish by both the Stalinists and the Western imperialists has largely been forgotten. This forgetfulness of the concrete Lenin has led to the emergence of the ultra bureaucratic regimes in "so-called socialist" countries.

There are four concrete sites in which we argue out our defence of Leninism:

(1) The Karl Kautsky formulation of the relation between the intellectual and the masses that appears on two pages of Lenin's magnum opus *What is To Be Done?;*

(2) The almost conscious ignorance of the primacy of theory that Lenin had advocated, thus forgetting Lenin's dictum: "without revolutionary theory there can be no revolutionary movement";

(3) The confusion between Leninism and Stalinism and post-Stalinist politics, and thus the consequent confusion

between the Bolshevik Revolution and the Stalinist counterrevolution; and

(4) The lack of mass line, the abandonment of internationalism and the forgetfulness of the thesis of permanent revolution.

Since we are restricting our chapter on the Indian Left with the problem raised by Javeed Alam followed by Prabhat Patnaik, Prabir Purkayastha and Ashok Mitra, with a rebuttal given by Prakash Karat,[7] we will keep this Indian scene in mind. And since there is stagnation in the mainstream Indian Left movement with the political elite (mainly with the Parliamentary Leftists) largely alienated from the people, it is almost inevitable that Lenin's formulation of the revolutionary party comes into criticism. Now it is well known that there can be various responses to what roughly one can call "revolutionary Leninism". One could be the Luxemburg line, or the Trotsky one, Anton Pannekoek, Raya Dunayevskaya, the anarcho-sydicalists, the "socialists with human faces", etc. We will keep these different lines in mind when we are arguing out a defence of Leninism.

The first issue is of historical genealogy—one cannot reduce the problems of the Indian Left to the Leninist concept of the Revolutionary Party. The problems, at least of authoritarianism, have their genesis in Stalinism (socialism in one country, bureaucratic dictatorship of the anti-Bolshevik elites and the theory of socialist commodity production). Second, one has to note the difference between "democratic centralism" (which has for Lenin meant the dialectical interaction between the party and the masses, where the party is sublated and superseded at a higher level of existence *(aufgehoben)*, where the party becomes the masses and the masses become the party) and "bureaucratic centralism" (which appeared with the defeat of the European revolutions in the early 1920s and the triumph of the Soviet Thermidor led by Stalin, Bukharin and Zinoviev). One has thus to theorise in concrete history. Keeping these points in mind we note that there are two problems which contemporary Left politics is heir to: (1) the shoddy reading of *What is to be Done?*

and elevating the then issue of centralism into a doctrinal world view devoid of historical and dialectical meaning, and (2) the Stalinist counterrevolution (not yet systematically theorised by the Indian Left movement) which deliberately used Lenin's terminology to the service of Soviet state capitalism. Two further problems emerged: (1) that Karl Kautsky (remember he is along with Bernstein, the "father" of revisionism — it is he who introduces the binary: intellectuals/masses and the consequent problems of centralism) appears as Lenin, and (2) the Stalinist counterrevolution and the doctrine of state capitalism appear as the goal of Left politics.

Theoretical Roots of Centralism

In order to understand the theoretical roots of centralism one need not put the blame on Lenin, but primarily to go to Kautsky's formulation of the two classes (the bourgeois intellectual and the masses) which Lenin uses in his *What is to be Done?*. It must be noted from the outset that this form of reasoning emerges in the philosophy of Immanuel Kant and forms the corpus of un-dialectical thinking. According to this pre-dialectical formulation:

(1) "Socialism and class struggle arise side by side and not one out of the other, each arises in different conditions".
(2) The proletariat is unable to create socialist consciousness by itself. It is the bourgeois intellectual who creates socialist consciousness.
(3) Socialist consciousness come "from without" *(von aussen Hineingetragenes)*, it cannot arise spontaneously *(urwüchsig)*[8].

One could say that if one reads this formulation in abstraction, then the masses that make the revolution are absent from the picture of revolution.

It is also clear that this text of elite, ultra-centralism was nowhere near Marx's understanding of the proletariat achieving revolutionary consciousness from the understanding of its own situation. We shall argue that it was also absent from Lenin's formulation. As we insist Lenin's idea of centralism was a concept in transition and sublation and was thus merely one point (besides a host of other counterpoints) in the dialectics of revolution. It is then we shall be able to understand the important distinction between the "authentic Leninist party" and the "Kautsky-Stalinist party[9]". What we in the Indian Left movement have inherited is less of Leninism and more of Kautsky-Stalinism. It is a great burden and a spectre of the past that continuously haunts us.

Now, one knows that for Marx (contra Kautsky), the history of modem socialism is not a *Märchen* (to borrow a term from the *Manifesto),* a "nursery tale"[10], constructed by bourgeois intellectuals. After all, as Marx once famously said, "the educator himself needs education."[11] And clearly as one has seen from the dominant history of "so-called socialism" (a more polite way of calling Stalinism), the educator is above all criticism and most certainly one who needs no education. The history of 20th century "so-called socialism" becomes the history of the dictatorships of the uneducated educators. At the core of this peculiar dictatorship stands the politics of democratic centralism. Let us thus have a look at this peculiar character.

We begin the critique of democratic centralism inherited from the days of the Second International. One must note that for Marx and Engels centralism stood for authoritarianism and the destruction of the freedom of the individual[12]. It also ought to be noted that for Marx's *Capital,* centralisation is the culminating moment of capital accumulation and that this logic of monopoly capitalism is totally in variance with communism and mass democracy. And third one must note that the politics of fraternal *equaliberty* (equality, liberty and fraternity are operationalised as dialectical unities) stands at the base of Revolutionary Marxism. Last, and one will have to stress over and over again, that the socialist project ended and the doctrine of state capitalism appear as the goal of "so-called socialism" by 1928 with the complete control of Stalin and his school of falsification and the destruction of Bolshevism with the murder of the Old Bolsheviks in the late 1930s by the Right Mensheviks led by Andrei Vyshinsky. One cannot in any way take the Stalinist model to be imitated anywhere. In the critique of centralism and the search for authentic communist democracy, one must note these points.

We thus agree with Alam's thesis that the concept of democratic centralism is not an inalienable concept of Marxism, just as the ideas of classless society and non-exploitative modes of production are the essential attributes of Marxism. Yet it is also imperative to understand that this idea of centralism was not merely a contingent idea (one cannot wish it away), absolutely unnecessary to Marxism, but *a theory that appears and disappears both at the same time.* Two of Marx's concepts will guide this politics of appearance and disappearance; dissolution *(Auflösung)* and sublation (*Aufhebung*). Democratic centralism then is dissolved and sublated—that it involves a "lifting up" in which both preservation and cancellation takes place where reality reaches a higher level of existence. The politics of *Aufhebung* involves this dialectic of preservation-cancellation where revolutionary discourses reach a distinct higher phase. Remove this dialectical structure from Leninism and centralism collapses into a formal structure that is easily taken over by counterrevolutionary forces.

Now it is imperative to understand that democratic centralism was also used by revolutionaries like Trotsky. One cannot impose a formal opposition: Lenin vs. Trotsky, or Lenin vs. Luxemburg, thus making the claim that Trotsky and Luxemburg (contra Lenin) were emancipated from the "dogma" of centralism. Consider 'Trotsky: "The inner regime of the Bolshevik Party was characterised by democratic centralism. The combination of these two concepts", so Trotsky continued:

> democracy and centralism, is not in the least contradictory. The party took watchful care not only that its boundaries should be strictly defined, but also those of entered these boundaries should enjoy the actual right to define the direction of the party policy. Freedom of criticism and intellectual struggle was an irrevocable content of the party democracy.[13]

Also consider Luxemburg who argued way back in 1912 that the time had come "when the Party will need a leadership that is aggressive, pitiless and visionary" and not a party that has grown "shabbier and shabbier, more cowardly, more besotted with parliamentary cretinism."[14]

But there is also a distinct critique of both Lenin and Trotsky from thinkers like Raya Dunayevskaya who postulated a theory of revolutionary organisation based more on the young Marx's theory of alienation than on the politics of the vanguard party. In this critique of vanguardism the claim is that the Jacobin theory of revolution "from the above" was a theory borrowed more from the Kant repertoire, and has nothing to do with Marxist dialectics. It must also be noted that the followers of Dunayevskaya have recently started a Marxist Humanist International that is based on post-Leninist, post-Trotskyite politics of the vanguard party.

And if one takes up Marx's idea of the international revolution in ferment, from *A Contribution to the Critique of Hegel's Philosophy of Right. Introduction* and *On the Jewish Question* to *Capital* one will note the absolute divergence between Marx's formulation of the proletariat as the subject of history and that of the politics of *mere centralism.* But I would not stop with the critique of centralism as inherently authoritarian. Thus one does not merely say: *smash centralism, but smash the state* itself.[15] Remember Marx: *the smashing of the state is the prelude for every communist revolution.*[16] Also remember what Marx called the tragedy of all previous revolutions: *they perfected the state machinery, instead of smashing it.*[17] We started with the critique of centralism, by claiming it to be a counterfeit. We have gone to the essence of Marx's philosophy: remove all fetishes, thus remove the fetish of commodity production, but do not forget to remove the fetish of the state. Lenin's irony rings out again: *have the Marxists understood Marx?*

We are consequently reading Lenin in the storm and stress of the young revolutionary movement in Europe as well as the formation of a distinct revolutionary theory that would guide the proletarian movement away from revisionism led by Bernstein in Germany and the legal Marxists and the Menshiviks in Russia. This distinct move away from revisionism is not to succumb to the fetishism of capital accumulation and parliamentary democracy and to understand international revolution as the aesthetics of insurrection. Leninism is now understood as a necessary smashing of the state, not merely the bourgeois state, but the *state as state.* Communism, one must insist cannot borrow from the ideological bank of the bourgeoisie. One does not say: "The bourgeois state is bad, but the communist state is good. One says that there can be no communist state". Marx's "union *(Verein)* of free individuals"[18] replaces the state. Humanism replaces the reification and dehumanisation of class societies. And when Marxism appears as humanism and historicism one understands that "production by freely associated people"[19] can take place only through the *aesthetics of insurrection.* This is what the aesthetics of insurrection looks like:

> The content of the revolution is the destruction of the instruments of power of the state and their dislodgement *(Auflösung)* with the aid of the power of the proletariat...: The struggle ceases only when, as the end result of it, the state organisation is completely destroyed.[20]

It seems that one has gone a long way in understanding the Leninist critique of authoritarianism. Do not critique merely centralism, but critique the state itself. Centralism is merely one part of the state. But let us firstly understand that there is a problem in centralism, just as there is a problem of the state in post-Marx Marxism. After all, Luxemburg had pointed out long before Stalin came onto the scene, that Lenin's formulation was one of "pitiless centralism" and "conspiratorial centralism", where the elites of the central committee will be the "only thinking element in the party", while all the other social classes "would be its executive limbs".[21] That this model of centralism is uncannily similar to the metaphor of the Hindu god in the *Rg Veda*, where the Brahmans as the ideologists of Hindu centralism are located in the head of god, while all the other castes are the limbs, ought not to be surprising at all. It also ought not to be surprising that in the Communist Parties in India, the Brahmans have not left their seat of ideological hegemony. Even less surprising is the fact that revolution has not occurred in India. What is ironical is that what is absolutely alien to Marxism becomes a part of Left practice. Bourgeois centralism, caste elitism, the lethargy of the elites, etc, are not merely parts of the Left movement. They have become its essence. The masses are spontaneously communist. The party elites have become spontaneously bourgeois.

And since the boundaries of capitalism (the bourgeoisie and the proletariat) are replicated in Left politics (the central committee and the masses) one says following Étienne Balibar that one is living in the "extreme borders of cruelty".

> But here we must realise that, in many cases, we are at the extreme borders of cruelty. And I hope it is not a mere play of words if I say that we also encounter the question of *borders* in general: social and territorial borders are privileged places where codified violence borders on cruelty...[22]

Instead of abolishing these borders one recreates them. Why is this so? It is so because Marxism as the philosophy of dialectical and historical materialism has forgotten its very essence. It has forgotten to keep the masses at the core of its philosophy. One has to recall Louis Althusser who argued that Marxism has to be understood as a "theoretical anti-humanism". But what happens next is that "theoretical anti-humanism" becomes "practical anti-humanism". The unintended consequence has been the reification and distortion of political Marxism into a form of a-humanism (if not a peculiar type of anti-humanism itself) where the party supposed to be the incarnation of historical "truth" becomes not so much undemocratic, but messianic. Messiahs as we well know have not left a legacy of democracy. In contrast to this messianic philosophy, it is necessary to see Lenin as the practitioner of what Mikhail Bakhtin called "dialogical discourse" determined by revolutionary praxis. 1917 emerges from this dialogical praxis. It then becomes the *radical act. One has to reclaim this space of radicalism.*

Leninism and the Problem of Centralism

It is keeping these points in mind that we turn to the thesis of Leninism and the problem of centralism. If we earlier talked of boundaries and borders between the political committees and the mere masses —an "air-tight partition" is what Luxemburg calls it[23]—then it must be noted that Lenin immediately talked of the transcendence of this gap, a gap created not by the communist movement, but by class societies. The unbridgeable abyss within the communist movement was the creation of Stalinism that bathed the Bolsheviks in their own blood. One must note that this abyss in the era of the anti-Bolshevik counterrevolution would turn out to be the mimesis of the black hole of alienation that the young Marx had talked of in the *Economic and Philosophic Manuscripts of 1844*, an estranged abyss that would collapse with the demise of the Stalinist dictatorships and then get born again with the Yeltsin-Putin dictatorships. So what is the logical and historical conclusion of centralism: that "the expropriators are expropriated".[24] Its end and death is inscribed in its very beginning.

Our argument is historical, not dogmatic, nor scholastic. It is dialectical. It traces the contradictory lanes and by-lanes of history. *Dialectical and historical-humanist materialism* thus is the guiding methodology. Our argument will thus be in contradistinction with the legal Marxists, the liberals, the advocates of parliamentary socialism, the autonomists, etc. In fact, as we shall see, the Leninist dictum: to *treat insurrection as art* will be a logical outcome of the young Marx's idea of *communism as humanism and naturalism*.

The space that we inherit is contradictory. It is the American Marxist-Humanists who have repeatedly said, following Raya Dunayevskaya, that Lenin in his penning of *What is to be Done?* had not yet read Hegel. Lenin's own cynical irony—"none of the Marxists have understood Marx!"—hangs thus over his head. After all one must remember that in the dialectical understanding of history, the cunning character of history, what Hegel once called "the cunning of reason" (*die List der Vernunft*) is the governing factor, where the *government of the cunning* would destroy world revolutions.

Keeping this in mind, we turn back onto the problems of political stagnation in the Left movement. I will insist that authoritarianism and non-democracy (Alam's thesis) are based not so much on dogmatic clinging to old ideas, as much as it is with the abandonment of mass line and the attachment to two anti-Marxist fetishes: (1) the fetish of "socialist" commodity production, and (2) the fetish of the state where the borders between the party and the masses form the essence of the 'Left' fetish worshippers. That the caste factor is also the dictating factor and that the Indian Left has not taken caste as an essential factor of the Asiatic mode of production headed by the Oriental Despot ought not to be forgotten.

It must be noted however that there are two points concretely bound together in this critique—that of democratic centralism as being: (1) a complex term with overdeterminate and multiple meanings, differently used by Lenin, Luxemburg, and Trotsky, and (2) the politics of democratic centralism being inherently contradictory and problematic, thus by its very nomenclature, making it merely democratic in words and authoritarian in deeds. This type of Faustian, almost schizophrenic dualism, entails a very destructive politics based on boundaries between the privileged members of the central committee and the mere masses. One must state that these boundaries lie at the heart of not only capitalism, but to all class societies. The tragedy is that one did not recognise that the bourgeois intellectual privileged first by Kautsky, then institutionalised by Stalin, was nothing but the return of not only Kantianism but primarily the return of the Platonic doctrine of the philosopher-kings. The philosopher-king (as the born-again Oriental Despot), who stands above all classes and class struggle itself, as we all know, would be Stalin. Stalin did not merely mummify the body of Lenin and keep it for public display. He mummified the politics of Leninism. It is here that one asks: "From where does this politics of boundaries (primarily a class-based problem that emerged best in the political philosophy of Plato) emerge in Marxism? How does Platonism disguise itself as Marxism? And how does one tear the mask of the philosopher Plato and see the face of the gravedigger of the Bolshevik Revolution, Stalin himself?" But most importantly one asks: "How does one creatively understand Marxism in the 21st century without being burdened by the Stalinist counterrevolutionary past?"

One very apparent answer is to point out that the politics

of 20th century Marxism were being formulated in semi-feudal, monarchical Russia that was devoid of basic democratic norms, common to bourgeois democracies. But one can ask: "Are the conditions in India, not to forget Pakistan, Iran, Turkey, Iraq, US, etc, conducive to an 'open' leftist organisation where a natural evolution from capitalism to socialism is possible?" Or should one say that the Leninist organisation trained in underground work is essentially important for countries where the state has declared revolutionary politics *the single biggest internal threat*?

Since we are highlighting the philosophical underpinnings of the thesis of democratic centralism, one must point out that the proletarian revolution is possible only if the rigours of the philosophical contours of Marxism are understood, especially the *transition from Kant to Hegel*. So what is so specific to Classical German Philosophy? It is humanism and dialectics. And what do we learn from dialectical humanism? We learn that the centre negates itself, not to create a periphery, but to create the masses that are in permanent revolt.

As one knows (so often repeated by the founders of modern socialism), Classical German Philosophy has an heir: the modern-day proletariat. The dialectics of Hegel, Goethe and Feuerbach are realised as the international proletarian revolution. And those who are aware of the rigour of Classical German Philosophy, would recognise that there are two distinct terrains in it—that of the understanding (*Verstand*) and that of reason (*Vernunft*), that of capitalist alienation and the humanist transcendence of alienation, that of the centre and that of the masses, that of formal democracy and that of mass democracy and human freedom. Marx takes the side of the latter. Reason is intrinsically related to mass democracy, whilst the former as technological reason (the "reason" not to know, most certainly not to liberate, but to calculate and control) is incapable, as Lenin once put it, "of embracing the truth."[25] As we shall see, the politics of democratic centralism is located at this technological site of calculation and control that is totally blind to truth and human emancipation.

Now what one needs to do is to concretise the new site that

the young Marx continuously emphasised on: the site of "species being" (*Gattungswesen*). Species being is different from the sites of both civil society and the state. It is directly related to what Marx calls "*human* society."[26] Concretisation of the politics of species being implies understanding humanity in fraternal solidarity that is in rebellion against class societies. In this rebellion, socialisation of the means of production, the abolishing of private property and the appropriation of *humanity as humanity* are understood as the culminating moments of this idea. The philosophy of species being is the Leninist "direct initiative of the people from below."[27] Now what one has to understand is that humanity as species being critiques both the politics-in-command of "so-called socialism" as well as the entire political discourse of parliamentary democracy, not to forget the bourgeoisie's favourite child: fascism. Politics-in-command, parliamentary democracy and fascism stand at the calculating site of technological reason. All of them are devoid of humanity and reason.

But then one insists that Marx was after all not merely against centralised authority (or authority of any kind). As we just said he was against the state itself. The state (as abstract universality and the epitome of human exploitation) is defined as an estrangement of social activity that realises itself as an "illusory community" divorced from real people and real human interests.[28] It is illusory because "the modern state itself disregards real humanity or satisfies the whole of humanity only in imagination."[29] There can be nothing called a "free state" or a "people's state."[30] Anti-humanism is written on its banners.

And if one states that the state is an anti-humanist illusion and weapon against the masses, one also states that it is one which now resides in the misty world of the phantasmagoria, where humanity has lost its human essence. One must read Lenin's statement of liberalism as "sham" in this terrain of the anti-humanist phantasmagoria where the state as the counterfeit does its ghost march all over the world. Let us see why Revolutionary Marxism has disdain for this sham. Let us also see why one does not accept, what Lukács once called, "English Parliamentarism as an alternative ideal". We shall soon see that the sham character of liberalism lies in the fact that Monsieur Capital claims to be Madame Liberty and the counterfeit state claims to be the advocate of global liberty. We shall now have to state that liberalism is not merely sham, but also psychotic, just as the state in general is a sham and a counterfeit. Let us thus turn to the couch of psychoanalysis and examine Monsieur Liberal turned psychotic who marches with his deadly infantry with the flag of liberty placed on his bourgeois cannons.

Liberalism as Phantasmagoria, the State as Sham

We have already noted that there is a new site discovered by Marx—that of humanity that is free from commodity production, classes and the state. We have also noted that both the politics-in-command of so-called socialism and liberalism that have emerged from commodity production are wrong. Marx transcends this binary (politics-in-command/liberalism) to reach an entirely new terrain, the terrain of *the union of free people.*

We shall have to explain that the solution to Stalinism is not liberalism—for as we shall show: liberalism is caught in the fetishism of commodity production and monopoly capitalism. Since Marx's critique of political economy—the estranged *economic base* (of capital accumulation and the extraction of monopoly profits) *determines the distorted and reified superstructure*—is the explanation for liberalism, we shall go into this critique of monopoly capitalism and see how behind liberalism stands monopoly capitalism. Liberalism is different from Marxist libertarianism. Liberalism is the philosophy of the "Free-trader Vulgaris" where Mr Moneybags in search for the world market sees an apparent 'free' world of the good European and North American nations as against the *unfree* worlds of Asia, South America and Africa. The earlier truth of liberalism was the First Imperialist War, just as the present truths of liberalism are Gaza, Guantanamo Bay, Iraq and Afghanistan. Liberalism claims to present a world of liberty, equality and fraternity, but presents instead to the world its infantry, cavalry and artillery.

There are two premises to understand liberalism as sham:

(1) the geopolitics of the North Bloc imperialist nations (led by the USA) with its apparitions of the so-called "freedoms". The liberal has forgotten the freedom of the Palestine people and the Zionist-racist occupation, the destruction of Iraq, Afghanistan, Pakistan, etc—one can here recall Lenin calling the liberals "civilised hyenas...whetting their teeth" on Asia[31] and the reality of the unhindered exploitation of global labour power and natural resources, and (2) the philosophical critique of the ontology of the commodity that concretely unravels the nature of the apparitions of liberal freedoms. Freedom, as we shall see, is *abstract freedom*, just as equality and liberty are *abstract in nature* determined by *abstract labour* of the commodity principle. But one must point out that liberalism is not fascism. One should not fall in the old Stalinist error of equating Social Democracy with fascism (for Stalin it was worse than fascism). For abstract freedom is better than the communal-fascist pogroms of annihilation of entire populations. The most firm and solid ground for the critique of liberalism is not a politics of some contingent type but the philosophical critique of the ontology of the phantom commodity that Marx outlines in the very first pages of *Capital*. Thus one must note that one needs solid foundations for the Leninist critique of liberalism than to be obsessed with messianic and anarchist ideologies. Thus it must be noted that if liberalism is a sham, then the anti-liberal messiah is a bigger sham.

One does agree with the concrete Leninist critique of liberalism. But we now reframe it as: *liberalism is a fetish, to be precise a phantasmagoria; and the state is a sham*. It must be noted that one is claiming it to be a sham (better still a fantasy), specifically from the activist Bolshevik point of view of the union of free people. It is true that one is confronted by different types of bourgeois states. One cannot collapse liberalism into fascism. Liberalism it is true is a great step ahead of the earlier feudal subjugation of human rights or the present totalitarian fascist military juntas. It is also true that within liberal regimes the working classes can struggle for their rights. There is no doubt about that. Liberalism can think, it can philosophise. Fascism cannot think, nor can it philosophise. But Marxism is not liberalism. It is libertarianism. Liberalism keeps its infantry and artillery with it. Libertarianism abolishes all infantries and artilleries. On its banners is inscribed its ode to liberty. Nothing not even the greatest counterrevolutionary crisis against International Communism can erase this inscription from its banners.

And that is why it is imperative to imbibe the teachings of the European Enlightenment and not to substitute the philosophies of the European Renaissance with Stalinist messianism. Marxist humanism, after all, cannot be realised in the gulags. And that is why it is important to define Marxism as libertarianism. And it is this Marxist libertarianism that would attract millions and millions of workers, peasants, poets and philosophers to the communist movement. And when these millions would enter the scene of history then the mask of the centralist would fall off to reveal the face of the Oriental Despot.

But why do we say that liberalism is a shamanic fantasy? What is the philosophical motif for saying so? Why do we say that the "magical and necromantic commodity" (this is Marx's term) determines (*besitimmte*) the entire political and ideological superstructure of capitalism? For this we shall turn to *Capital* where we see two distinct 'free' worlds: the 'free' world of capitalism and the *free* world of communism. In *Capital* when Marx is mentioning the constellation of the base and the superstructure determined in every resort by certain forms of illusions, he also says that he intends to find the causal mechanisms of being plagued by these fantasies. Here we note how *capital flows are always accompanied by psychotic flows*. For capitalism involves the *loss of material reality*—in the negation of use values and the positing of value and exchange value[32]—as its basis, whilst psychosis involves *a complete disconnect from reality*.[33] Both capitalism and psychosis have lost all track of human reality. Thus the liberal who promises liberty is like the Physiocrat who claims that rent grows from the soil.

We thus learn that the inherent structure of capital flows is not only based on human alienation, but also a certain type of insanity. One thus turns to these *foundations* (capital-psychosis) by turning to the *base* of the commodity, what Marx calls the

Gemeinsame—literally the "common something" between commodities, or the essence of capitalism itself.[34] And when Marx starts his archaeological exploration of capitalism, he finds that the commodity has a "magical" and "enigmatical character",[35] where one has "put out of sight" the concrete character of the social world.[36] Now Monsieur Capital who claims to be a liberal "changes its features, hair, and many other things besides",[37] involves a necromantic type of transfiguration where he dissolves his bodily form and acquires a fictitious mental form. The spectre that Marx talks of—not the spectre of communism—but the spectre of capitalism is this Monsieur Capital who like the theologians, mystics and saints has lost his body and with the newly acquired mind is wandering all over the world for its daily prey. Dr Jekyll and Mr Hyde have become Dr Capital and Mr Liberty. At any time the good liberal doctor Jekyll will turn into the monster Hyde.

And that is why one needs to talk of the essence of capitalism, the essence that Marx discovers in the opening pages of *Capital*. What one finds is that this essence of capitalism is "ghostly objectivity" (*gespenstige Gegenständlichkeit*),[38] or as the Aveling-Moore translation goes an "unsubstantial reality."[39] Capitalism has negated not only use values and concrete labour. It has negated all humanity. We are plagued not merely by fantasies, but haunted by abstractions and ghosts. And for Marx the *essential ghost* of capitalism is liberalism with abstract labour as its essence and abstract rights as its appearance, where one stops at the factory gates, closes one's eyes to global exploitation and departs into the paradise of "the innate rights of man" where "alone rule Freedom, Equality, Property and Bentham."[40] After all, as everyone knows, bourgeois liberty is the liberty to choose one's exploiter. And that is why one is claiming that one needs firm foundations in order to critique liberalism, this firm and rigorous ground being the critique of the commodity form itself.

Liberal Democracy as 'Sham'

So what do we get? We get the essence of the capitalist mode of production comprising the abstract ("abstract labour" or "human labour in general"). We also get the essence of the bourgeois state as comprising the abstract (abstract rights). If thus bourgeois democracy talks of rights, it is rights in the abstract. Bourgeois society thus has abstract labour and abstract rights as its essence. Its conception of humanity is itself abstract, because it has abstracted humanity from its discourse. That is why liberalism is always accompanied by its infantry, artillery and cavalry. And that is why the liberals are not always shy to call on their fascist cousins when occasion demands. Liberalism shows off its statue of liberty. Marxism shows that liberty has been turned into a statue.

Lenin's statement of liberal democracy as "sham" is seen in this perspective. If abstract rights are inscribed in the constitution—as the rights of the citizen, for instance the discourse of "we the people"—what happens is the triumph of the logic of abstractions. The phantasmagoria thus triumphs leaving the class structure of capitalism permanently veiled. But if this form of political and legal abstraction is victorious, then combined with it is the power of another abstraction: "the power of money."[41] Politics has now become "the serf of financial power."[42]

Like in commodity production, likewise in parliamentary politics, *value exchange takes place between equivalents* (exchange between two commodities at the level of economics, between the Congress and the Bharatiya Janata Party at the level of politics) *and unequivalents* (unequal exchange between capital and wage labour at the level of economics, and between the political elites and the masses at the level of politics). This forms the core of the argument that liberalism is *necessarily* a "sham". After all, equality in liberal democracy is necessarily the equality between commodity owners, which at the depth structure, is a relation of inequality (the ownership of capital and the ownership of labour power). *Bourgeois equality is necessarily real inequality.*

That is why one claims that parliamentary democracy has (to borrow Žižek's phrase) a "pathological imbalance" between rights and duties.[43] This imbalance is seen in the perspective of the ontology of the commodity, where the masses become the "peculiar commodity" (to borrow Marx's expression of labour power) that produces a political surplus through its own exploitation. Parliamentary democracy finds itself in an ironical situation. It is a surplus (following the logic of surplus value), an excess (Bataille) and a supplementation (Derrida). But behind this surplus is "unpaid labour" and the "lack" (economic underdevelopment) registered at the level of the masses.

Parliamentary democracy is thus a signification of a "lack" (almost mimicking a Freudian castration anxiety) where the masses, in their supposed inclusion, are actually excluded. Like Stalinism, liberalism too becomes a "source of totalitarianism and a dogmatic attachment to the official word", for as said: "An excessive commitment to Good may itself become the greatest Evil."[44]

What then is the practical significance of this thesis? It implies that one cannot operate on the site handed down to us by capitalism. One cannot operate with the phantom commodity or the counterfeit state. One does not operate on the terrains of civil society (the favourite hunting ground of the non-governmental organisations), nor the state (the temptations of not only the Stalinists, but also the Trotskyites, as also advocates of the South American Left). Instead one looks into *human society* and into the open space (*Öffenlichkeit*) of the international multitude. It is here that we find the *real ground of class struggles* as against the *"sham" of the abstract phantasmagoria*. It is at this site that we relate the Leninist idea of liberalism as "sham" with Engels' "false consciousness" and Lukács' "reification of consciousness".

But there is a larger issue that needs to be grasped, namely that the politics of state power is to be avoided. What does this mean? Refrain from active politics? By no means! It means to negate the politics of the state, for one understands the state as a "duplicate", almost an opiate world of religion, a sort of an "imaginary world" appearing as the "holy family" of class societies.[45] *We call this process of duplication, a creation of a counterfeit*. The state is thus a counterfeit, a psychoanalytic "doubling" where this duplicate-double-counterfeit appears as a substitute for real people. One relates this process with Freud's analysis of the double that divides the self and creates a neurotic "recurrence of the same thing —the repetition of the same features...the same crimes...."[46] Yet Marx's understanding of the state is a *reverse psychoanalysis*. For Freud the "double" is the father appearing as the tormenting criminal; for Marx's understanding: *the state is the criminal that appears as the father figure*. The chief function of the state is to transform the pain of class societies into pleasure. That is why Marx insisted on the principle of the *Aufhebung des Staats*: transcend the state by transcending the horizons of class societies themselves.[47]

1917 is the permanent sign of this transcendence. But then the law of history seems to be that alongside revolutionaries march not only the masses, artists and philosophers, but also the counterrevolutionaries, priests and fascists. Unfortunately an ex-priest claimed to be a man of the masses, a poet and a philosopher. But when the mask slipped to show the real face of the counterrevolutionary it was too late. Bolshevism was destroyed. But then another law of history is seen operating, the *law of historical repetitions*. Stalin went and Yeltsin and Putin came. Politics-in-command went and liberal democracy came.

We are told by an upstart of Yankee imperialism (Francis Fukuyama) that liberal democracy, as the miraculous end of history has been achieved. Since we have also been told by the Indian state that the whole of India loves Yankee imperialism; we are somehow compelled to go back to the liberals. We go back to the beginnings of the 20th century. Besides the European liberals and the finance capitalists, we see Lenin, Luxemburg and Trotsky, besides millions of artists of the international revolution. We find thus that history repeats itself, not twice, but thrice: the first time as tragedy (1928), the second time as farce (1991) and the third time as joy.

It seems that we may just be living in the age of joy.

REFERENCES

1. Karl Marx, *Capital*, Vol. I (Moscow: Progress Publishers, 1983), p. 82.
2. V.I. Lenin, *Philosophical Notebooks, Collected Works* Vol. 38 (Moscow: Progress Publishers, 1980), p. 180.

3. Herbert Marcuse, 'Phenomenology of Historical Materialism', in *Telos*, 4, Fall (1969).
4. V.I. Lenin, 'The Dual Power,' in *V.I. Lenin, Selected Works in Three Volumes*, Vol. 2 (Moscow: Progress Publisher, 1977) pp. 34-5.
5. V.I. Lenin, 'The Task of the Proletariat in the Present Revolution,' in Ibid., p. 31.
6. V.I. Lenin, 'The Dual Power,' in Ibid., p. 34.
7. See Chapters, 19, 20 and 21 for Patnaik's, Alam's and Karat's views on democratic politics.
8. V.I. Lenin, *What is to be Done?* (Moscow: Progress Publishers, 1978), p. 40.
9. Slavoj Žižek, 'Postface: Georg, Lukács as the Philosopher of Leninism,' in Georg Lukács, *A Defence of History and Class Consciousness* (London: Verso, 2000), p. 170.
10. Karl Marx and Frederick Engels, 'Manifesto of the Communist Party', in *Marx. Engels. Selected Works* (Moscow: Progress Publishers, 1975), p. 35.
11. Karl Marx, 'Theses on Feuerbach', in Ibid., p. 28.
12. See Karl Marx, 'The Question of Centralism Itself and with Regard to Supplement to No. 137 of the *Rheinische Zeitung*', in *Marx. Engels. Collected Works*, Vol. I (Moscow: Progress Publishers, 1975) p. 182. Also see Engels, 'Centralism and Freedom', in *Marx. Engels. Collected Work*, Vol. 2 (Moscow: Progress Publisher, 1975), pp. 355-7.
13. Leon Trotsky, *The Revolution Betrayed: What is the Soviet Union and Where is it Going?* (Delhi: Aakar Books, 2006), p. 103.
14. Rosa Luxemburg, 'Letter to Franz Mehring, April 19, 1912', in Stephen Eric Bronner (ed.), *The Letters of Rosa Luxemburg* (New Jersey: Humanities Press, 1993), p. 149.
15. Karl Marx, 'To L. Kugelmann in Hanover, London, April 12, 1871', in *Marx. Engels. Selected Works* (Moscow: Progress Publishers, 1975), p. 670.
16. Ibid.
17. Karl Marx, 'The Eighteenth Brumaire of Louis Bonaparte', in Ibid., p. 169.
18. Karl Marx, *Capital*, Vol. I, p. 83.
19. Ibid., p. 84.
20. V.I.Lenin, 'State and Revolution', in *Lenin. Selected Works* (Progress Publishers, 1975), p. 342.
21. Rosa Luxemburg, 'Leninism or Marxism?' in *The Russian Revolution and Leninism or Marxism* (Michigan: The University of Michigan Press, 1961), pp. 84, 85, 87.

22. Étienne Barlibar, *Politics and the Other Scence* (London: Verso, 2002), p. 138.
23. Rosa Luxemburg, op. cit., p. 89.
24. Karl Marx, *Capital*, Vol. I, p. 715.
25. V.I. Lenin, *Philosophical Notebooks*, p. 93.
26. Karl Marx, 'Theses on Feuerbach', p. 30.
27. V.I. Lenin, 'The Dual Power', p. 34.
28. Karl Marx and Frederick Engels, *The German Ideology* (Moscow: Progress Publishers, 1976), pp. 51-4.
29. Ibid.
30. Karl Marx, 'Critique of the Gotha Programme', in *Marx. Engels. Selected Works* (Moscow: Progress Publishers, 1975), p. 326-7.
31. V.I. Lenin, 'The Historical Destiny of Karl Marx', in *Lenin. Selected Works*, p. 19.
32. Karl Marx, *Capital*, Vol. I, p. 45.
33. Sigmund Freud, 'Neurosis and Psychosis' and 'The Loss of Reality in Neurosis and Psychosis', in *The Penguin Freud Library*, Vol. 10,. *On Psycho-pathology* (London: Penguin Books, 1993).
34. Karl Marx, *Capital*, Vol. I, p. 45.
35. Ibid., p. 63.
36. Ibid., p. 46.
37. Ibid., p. 58.
38. Karl Marx, *Das Kapital*, Erster Band (Berlin: Dietz Verlag, 1981), p. 52.
39. Karl Marx, *Capital*, Vol. I, p. 46.
40. Karl Marx, *Capital*, Vol. I, p. 172.
41. Karl Marx, 'On the Jewish Question', in *Marx. Engels. Collected Works*, Vol. 3 (Moscow:Progress Publishers, 1975), p. 171.
42. Ibid.
43. Slavoj Žižek, *The Sublime Object of Ideology* (London: Verso, 1989), p. 21.
44. Ibid., p. 27.
45. Karl Marx, 'Theses on Feuerbach', p. 29.
46. Sigmund Freud, 'The Uncanny', in *The Penguin Freud Library, Vol. 14, Art and Literature* (London: Penguin Books, 1985), p. 356.
47. Karl Marx, 'Nationalökonomie und Philosophie (1844)' in *Die Frühschriften* (Stuttgar: Alfred Kröner Verlag, 1964), p. 235.

23

Revolutionary Movements in a Post-Marxian Era

Sumanta Banerjee

The key to revolutionary change in today's world lies beyond the traditional Marxist conceptual framework or the leadership of Marxist political parties. In India, four broad areas of protests constitute the major components of a new revolutionary strategy in the post-Marxian era – (i) movements by forest dwellers against both the state machinery and predatory commercial forces; (ii) protests by villagers against the establishment of industrial estates, big dams and nuclear plants that threaten to oust them from their lands and homes, and endanger the environment; (iii) civil society campaigns against corruption and crime; and (iv) secessionist struggles on the issue of self-determination in the North-East and Kashmir. How will a new generation of post-Marxian revolutionary theoreticians and practitioners invigorate these movements with a progressive ideological core and a comprehensive coordinated programme of socialist change?

To start in a lighter vein, let me recall this joke about a drunk, who is moving on all fours, on a road. He is searching for something under a lamp post. When asked by a passer-by, he tells him that he is looking for his keys. "Where did you lose your keys", the passer-by asks him. He replies: "Over there", pointing out into the darkness. The passer-by asks him: "But, if you've lost the keys over there, why are you looking for them here under the lamp post?" The drunken man answers: "Because the light is so much better here under the lamp post".

Sometimes I wonder whether we are behaving like the drunk in trying to find the key for the revolutionary transformation of our society under one single political lamp post—while the key may lie elsewhere beyond the circle of light shed by that lamp post. We perhaps believe that what is sought can be found only under the old lamp post of the traditional Marxist classics. That lamp post does indeed continue to shed light on many hidden corners of the capitalist mode of production and its present nefarious form of neoliberal globalisation. Marx was prescient in his acute analysis of the basic laws of global capitalist development, and therefore he remains relevant for those fighting to change that inequitable global order. His tools of analysis have been refined or modified by various schools of modern political scientists and sociologists in their attempts to examine different segments of society. But is the old Marxist lamplight wide enough to illuminate all the corners of the vast outer darkness of our present socio-economic order? Should we not increase the power of the Marxist bulb, to be able to incorporate the various upsurges of resistance against the neoliberal order of globalisation even in the heart of the West and against the United States' (US) global militarist ambitions in different parts of the third world, and discover the signs of a future revolutionary transformation of our society in the present outbursts of protests in different parts of India?

In other words, the key to revolutionary change in today's world lies beyond the "sacred" circle of the old Marxist gaslit lamp post. Outside the traditional Marxist conceptual framework, or the leadership of Marxist political parties, there are several new theoretical challenges and innovative forms of protest that are breaking out, and which need to be faced by Marxist ideologues and practitioners. Hitherto ignored social and political grievances of underprivileged and invisible sections of society (like demands of aboriginal people, ethnic and linguistic minorities, gender rights of women) are bursting out in sparks of resistance and lighting up the obscure corners of the vast darkness that lie outside the Marxist lamplight. I will come to specific instances in India in a while.

Opposed to this there has developed a parallel stream of fortune hunters among the upper and middle classes—who act as a buffer zone between the state and its business tycoon allies and multinational industrial patrons on the one hand, and the disgruntled masses on the other. This is the new generation of executives in multinational corporations, employees in the information technology sector, and a host of middlemen like contractors in the booming construction business, as well as professionals like academics, medical practitioners and others in the tertiary sector who have gained from the privatisation of their occupations in the neoliberal era of globalisation. This new generation of middle classes are ensconced under a curtain—which can be described as the "brass curtain". Like the "iron curtain" that was stitched by the US cold war tailors around the Soviet Union, China, Cuba and other socialist states in the 20th century, to insulate their socialist experiments from the rest of the world by military intervention and trade embargoes, today again the same US-led corporatocracy is embroidering a new curtain—the garish, glitzy "brass curtain" of crass privatisation and brash consumerism to protect its employees within a cocoon.

Middle Class as the 'Vanguard'?

The corruption of these newly educated sections of the middle classes brings me to another problem being faced today by Marxist practitioners—the ability or the desirability of the present middle class intellectuals to act as the "vanguard" (in the Leninist sense) in the struggle for socialist transformation. The power of the capitalist global order to seduce these influential members of the professional classes to its fold has robbed the Marxist movement of an enlightened intelligentsia from these classes which in the past had always invigorated it with fresh theoretical insights. The communist movement today, whether in India or abroad, lacks leaders possessing the intellectual calibre and practical experience of those of the past who could reconstruct their theoretical understanding of Marxism in accordance with their national needs in changing circumstances—whether Togliatti in Italy, Maurice Thorez in

France, Mao in China, Ho Chi Minh in Vietnam, or P.C. Joshi in India, who could animate a small communist party in the 1940s with a wide scale programme of leading peasants' movements and working class strikes, organisation of relief for the victims of the 1943 Bengal famine and 1946 communal riots, and building up of a rich cultural venue (in the shape of the Indian People's Theatre Association and the Progressive Writers' Association) that brought together some of the best talents from the contemporary Indian scene of arts, music, theatre and literature.

In parenthesis, let me in this connection touch upon briefly the problematic of the "vanguardist" role of the party—in the paradigm of revolutionary strategy. In Russia in the past, the urban educated middle class intelligentsia formed the leadership of the Bolshevik Revolution. In China, the Maoist concept of leadership was based on rural-based communist organic intellectuals mainly from the peasantry. But both these forms of party hegemony, in the Soviet Union first and China later, led to the bureaucratisation of the communist movement (which provoked Mao to launch the Cultural Revolution to "bombard" the party headquarters in China, but which sadly enough ended up in violent chaos and factional fights within the Chinese Communist Party).

Against this backdrop of the tragic historical experience of a single party hegemony in the socialist movement and post-revolutionary societies in the 20th century, participants in the present movements and agitations for socialist change in the 21st century often propose another alternative that suggests the doing away of the party altogether—harking back to the anarchist vision of a socialist movement based on (pure) spontaneous popular protests rejecting control by any political party or centre. The World Social Forum through its various congregations (including one in Hyderabad in 2003) has brought together these various voices of protest in a pluralistic ambience. These voices await synchronisation and gradation from "bilambit" to "drut" in the "raga" of Indian revolutionary transformation. This needs a new generation of creative and innovative artistes—both ideologues and practitioners—who can both bring about the revolution and create the post-revolutionary society.

There are tensions between these non-party movements and the political parties which want to intervene. A typical example is the adivasi peasants' uprising against police atrocities in Lalgarh in West Bengal sometime ago, that was hijacked by the Communist Party of India (Maoist) (CPI(Maoist)) in its attempt to orient the uprising towards the tactics of guerrilla warfare as a part of its strategy of agrarian revolution to capture state power. The Maoists there (led by Koteshwar Rao, known as Kishenji, an ideologue and tactician from Andhra Pradesh), in their amoral opportunist device, backed Mamata Banerjee's Trinamool Congress, deployed their armed squads in her favour to eliminate their rivals in the ruling CPI(Marxist), campaigned for her in the elections, and paved the way for her coming to power. Once she won the elections with their help, Mamata got rid of her Maoist comprador, by allowing the security forces to kill Kishenji (who was the most vociferous champion of Mamata Banerjee in his TV interviews on the eve of the elections). The Maoist party's "vanguardist" role in Lalgarh thus proved to be a total disaster, and also exposed the naïve political judgment of the Maoist leadership.

In contrast with these ideologically committed, well-meaning but politically confused, and militarily ill-equipped middle class leaders of the Maoist movement, who face death in false encounters in the jungles of Chhattisgarh or Jharkhand, a new generation of middle class professionals is emerging in the India's tertiary sector. Employed in Indian and multinational corporate houses and the IT sector, they are protected by the flashy "brass curtain" of the neoliberal global order. But like the "iron curtain" of the past, this curtain is also vulnerable to fissures, as evident from the huge wave of protests that began over the past year, from among this section of the salaried petty bourgeoisie in Greece in Western Europe and Egypt in West Asia—and can soon reach the shores of the Indian middle class.

Marxian and Post-Marxian Politics

When we take into account these changing contours of anti-state protest—both among the wider masses and the privileged classes—we feel the need to enlarge the circle of the light from the Marxist lamp post to cover these various segments in the hitherto neglected vast space of complex class relationships, and the complicated forms of manifestation that they are assuming. But before taking up the specific cases of anti-state movements in India that need to be incorporated in a Marxist programme of socialist transition, let me briefly dwell upon the historical context of the political position from which Marxists are grappling with this challenge today.

To put it in a broader perspective, the protests—whether the social movements, peasants' uprisings and working class strikes in India, or the Occupy Wall Street agitations in the US and Europe, or the Arab Spring in West Asia—are taking place in a post-Marxian political scene. This is not to suggest that there is a fragmentation of the ideological core of socialism that has sustained Marxian and post-Marxian politics. I am trying to highlight two factors that are changing the terrain of the struggle: (i) the changes in the economy brought about by a new technology ushered in by the neoliberal global order that has changed the composition of both the industrial working class and the professional middle classes, on the one hand; and (ii) the growing self-assertion by hitherto ignored oppressed communities and sections of the population, which are being marginalised by the impact of this neoliberal economic order, on the other. These complex developments need to be factored in by Marxist ideologues and practitioners who are involved in bringing about a socialist transformation.

It is these changes that call for post-Marxian strategy of revolutionary transformation. By using the term post-Marxian, I mean a period characterised by several important traits that signify both continuation as well as departure from the original programme and prognosis made by Karl Marx in the 19th century. It also implies the end of one phase of Marxist experimentation with revolutions and socialist reconstruction in Russia and China.

Marx's paradigm of revolution was marked by certain important preconditions—one, the movement was required to be led by the industrial proletariat of the contemporary advanced capitalist states of the west; two, in order to carry out the strategy of overthrowing the capitalist state and capturing power, the tactics that were to be adopted were primarily city-based insurrections (the model available to and appreciated by Marx, being the Paris Commune that took place during his lifetime); three, the post-revolutionary state that was to be installed was designated as a form of "dictatorship of the proletariat", as a transitional phase towards the development of a communist society; four, once the proletariat captured power in Europe, it would lead to the emancipation of the people of the colonies in Asia, Africa and America (of Engels to Kautsky, 12 September 1882: "...the countries inhabited by a native population which are simply subjugated, India, Algiers, the Dutch, Portuguese and Spanish possessions, must be taken over for the time being by the (European) proletariat and led as rapidly as possible towards independence").

All these preconditions of the traditional Marxist paradigm had faced challenges in the course of the revolutionary movements and post-revolutionary construction of socialist states in both Europe and elsewhere during the last 100 years or more. The outbreak of the 1917 Bolshevik Revolution in a backward capitalist state, followed by seven decades of experiments in socialist reconstruction there, and the communist revolution and post-revolutionary turmoil (e.g. Cultural Revolution in China), defied the trajectory of change that was designed by Marx. They gave rise to new problems that had escaped the attention of Marx and Engels—like issues of human rights, demands of nationalities, ethnic identity, environmental concerns and feminist self-assertion. To give one instance—the post-Marxian ideologues and practitioners are today facing a new challenge in the Arab world. Various layers of complex socio-economic and religious interrelationships are propelling different types of agitations there—ranging from acts of terrorism by the conservative religious Taliban and Al Qaida outfits in Afghanistan, Pakistan, and countries in West Asia and Africa on the one hand, to movements by secular groups in Tunisia, Egypt, Turkey and other parts of the Arab world on the other.

There is a need for an extremely nuanced Marxist approach to these various types of popular upsurges. Marxists also need to acknowledge that the pro-Left secular regimes (cf Baathist) in countries like Iraq under Sadaam Hussain, Libya under Gaddafi, Syria under Assad, had failed their people during the last decades. Like their socialist counterparts in the Soviet Union and East Europe, they had also notched up atrocious records of corruption and repression of democratic opposition—which aroused mass discontent. Although secular and pro-poor in some of their reforms, they carried on the feudal legacy of dynastic succession of the Arab sheikhs, by promoting their sons or nephews (cf the progeny of Sadaam and Gaddafi). This is not peculiar to the Arab world. Even the communist ruling party in North Korea has not been able to rid itself of this feudal habit of dynastic succession. In the Arab world, in the absence of an alternative left leadership to oppose the corrupt and repressive ruling Baathist and other secular regimes, the people flocked to the Islamist fundamentalist eagles which swooped down to occupy the vacuum of political opposition.

A post-Marxian strategy of revolutionary transformation therefore should also take into account these failures of past socialist regimes, the roots of corruption and state terror that led to their fall. Yet, there is a continuity which flows from the Marxist analysis of capitalist development. We are rediscovering Marx's relevance today when, under the neoliberal order of globalisation, a reorganisation of the international division of labour is taking place which, as Marx pointed out in *Capital*, Vol. I, is "suited to the requirements of the chief centres of modern industry" (which are in this case the US-dominated Western economic powers, that are setting up special economic zones, call centres, etc, in India and other countries which form the peripheries to the "chief centres").

Further, our present-day critique of the global environmental threat again harks back to Marx's warning that such an ecological crisis was bound to happen because of the capitalist economic system. At the end of Chapter XV of *Capital*, 'Machinery and Modern Industry', Marx wrote: "...all progress in capitalistic agriculture is a progress in the art, not only of robbing the labourer, but of robbing the soil; all progress in increasing the fertility of the soil for a given time, is a progress towards ruining the lasting sources of that fertility." Are we not observing today the saturation of the fertility of the soil in Punjab, Haryana and other areas due to the excessive and indiscriminate use of chemical fertilisers and pesticides in the race for progress in growth? Marx ended the chapter with the following words: "Capitalist production, therefore, develops technology, and the combining together of various processes into a social whole, only by sapping the original sources of all wealth—the soil and the labourer".

To put it in simplistic terms therefore, Marx could get under the skin of the capitalist mode of production, and predict its future course—which capitalism as an economic system has generally followed. But his critique was limited by the conditions of the historical period in which he was writing—a period when capitalism in Europe was taking on a ruthlessly aggressive posture, concentrating on primitive accumulation of capital, exploitation of resources from its colonies, and pauperisation of its own industrial proletariat.

The tactics that Marx and Engels suggested for overthrowing this inequitable and oppressive capitalist structure was a revolutionary insurrection by the urban industrial proletariat of Europe. The immediate model was the Paris Commune. Both of them dismissed the possibilities of national minorities or the rural poor in the colonies as becoming decisive forces in the revolutionary transformation.

In fact, in 1848, Engels defended the French campaign against Bedouins in Algeria in the following words: "The struggle of the Bedouins was a hopeless one... And if we may regret that the liberty of the Bedouins of the desert has been destroyed, we must not forget that these same Bedouins were a nation of robbers..." (*Northern Star*, 22 January 1848).

But towards the end of their revolutionary careers, Marx and Engels possibly toyed with the idea of giving the benefit of doubt to the parliamentary politics of the bourgeois system to bring about the radical change that they had envisaged. Engels writing in March 1895 in his Introduction to his friend's classic work—*The Class Struggles in France*—analysed the changes since the 1848-50 period in these words:

> With ...successful utilisation of universal suffrage... an entirely new method of proletarian struggle came into operation, and this method quickly developed further...the conditions of the struggle had essentially changed. Rebellion in the old style, street fighting with barricades, which decided the issue everywhere up to 1848, was to a considerable extent obsolete...the conditions since 1848 have become far more unfavourable for civilian fighters and far more favourable for the military. In future, street fighting can therefore be victorious only if this disadvantageous situation is compensated by other factors.

Engels then claimed with confidence: "We, the 'revolutionists', the 'overthrowers'—we are thriving far better on legal methods than on illegal methods and overthrow". This was refuted by history, as is well known by future developments in Europe. The capitalist rulers could hijack the democratic right of universal suffrage to their advantage by buying off a section of the working class—who became the "labour aristocracy" as described by latter-day Marxists. The capitalist system could also incorporate into the vast tertiary sector of its economy large sections of the middle classes. Engels had placed hope in these sections when he wrote in his 1895 article: "...by the end of the century we shall conquer the greater part of the middle strata of society, petty bourgeois, and ...grow into decisive power..." His dream was soon to be shattered.

Thus, while the Marxian critique of capitalism in its basic analysis still remains relevant, the Marxian programme of socialist transformation—either through armed insurrections or through universal franchise—has suffered vicissitudes. In the last century, in Russia, China, Vietnam and Cuba the tactics of armed revolution succeeded in the capturing of power by the communists—but with mixed outcome as far as the goal of socialist transformation is concerned. The parallel alternative of attempting the transformation through universal franchise has also been tried out by Marxist political parties in Europe (at one time conceptualised as euro-communism—which failed to take off).

An Alternative Global Marxist Strategy

In the present phase of capitalism, where the system has been able to consolidate its monopoly over the global economy (with the collapse of the alternative socialist system in the Soviet Union, and the incorporation of the so-called communist state of China into that economy), Marxian ideologues and practitioners have to fashion a new set of strategy and tactics on an international scale to challenge that global monopoly. It cannot and should not be a replication of attempts to consolidate revolutionary forces that we witnessed in the 1930s under the hegemony of a single communist party (that was based in the Soviet Union) in the name of the Comintern or the Cominform in the 1940s. There cannot be a repetition of a similar hegemony that was attempted by the Chinese Communist Party in the 1960-70 period when its theoretician Lin Piao sought to impose on communist fighters in Third World countries, the tactics of encirclement of cities by villages—tactics that proved a disaster.

The alternative global Marxist strategy therefore has to be more nuanced to be sensitive to the various types of popular protests and rebellions in different parts of the world and select, incorporate or reject them according to its ideological principles. Surely the Marxists cannot support the orthodox religious and terrorist Al Qaida—just because it is killing US soldiers!

There is a need to refashion the Tricontinental strategy that was envisaged by Che Guevara in the 1960s. Che dreamed of more and more Vietnams to defeat US imperialism. That is not possible today. But his basic concept of creating and expanding more and more centres of movements against US expansionism still remains valid. Such movements are taking place in different parts of the world—in different forms, whether armed or non-violent, whether the Zapatista insurrection in Mexico or the parliamentary experiments in Venezuela and Bolivia.

India as a Site for Post-Marxian Experiments

But it is in India, more importantly, where the two alternatives within the Marxian framework of change have coexisted with various degrees of success and failure for several decades. Here for the first time, communists could get elected to a state legislature (in Kerala in 1957) to be able to form a government—but to be dismissed as soon as they introduced land reforms and changes in the educational sector that threatened vested interests. Since then, it had been a long struggle for parliamentary communists to inch their way to form governments in states and operate within the limited constraints of a centrally ruled structure, but make use of the constitutional powers to bring about certain socio-economic reforms within that structure. We have to acknowledge that the Indian Constitution, notwithstanding the mendacity of the Indian state, still offers opportunities to communists to implement these reforms. For more than three decades, from 1977 to 2011, the communists ruled at a stretch in West Bengal, enjoying enough rights to bring about institutional changes to meet the basic needs of the people like healthcare, housing, education, and to introduce a governance free from corruption and criminality. But, sad to say, the communists in power in West Bengal, after the initial period of limited land reforms and efforts to involve people in decision-making at the grass-roots level (through the panchayati system and similar popular mechanisms), failed to solve these basic requirements of the citizens in their quotidian existence. They soon sank into the slimy mire of corruption and crime in the area of daily governance, and degenerated into agents of the neoliberal global order in the area of economic reforms (cf Singur, Nandigram, Lalgarh).

Similar to the pattern followed by the communist rulers in the Soviet Union and East European countries in the period preceding their downfall, and in China today, in West Bengal also a bureaucratic hierarchy developed in the CPI(M)'s organisation, where power and privilege from the top echelons of the party flowed to the apparatchiks at the bottom, who maintained the party's control and influence over the people through a judicious mixture of distribution of largesse and terror. The terror tactics which was predominantly resorted to by the CPI(M) during the latter days of the Left Front rule in West Bengal (in Singur, Nandigram) spelt the rout of the CPI(M) in the 2011 elections. Like the Soviet and East European party bureaucrats and party-patronised privileged elite, who had to pay the price for their terrorisation, corruption and arrogance, and lost power at the end of the 1980s, the West Bengal CPI(M) leaders and their protégées are now biting the dust.

I think it is necessary to locate this degradation of the CPI(M) in West Bengal in the wider context of the historical record of moral degeneration of communists in power in general. Critics from the Maoist camp of the alternative strategy of armed struggle, in a simplistic manner, attribute this degradation to the bourgeois parliamentary system, which they feel, is bound to corrupt communists whenever they join it. But how can the Maoists gloss over the corruption of the communist rulers who came to power through armed struggles and were given a chance to build an egalitarian society under a communist revolutionary system? Whether in Stalin's Russia or Mao's China, they acquired notoriety for amassing wealth and terrorising their own people. There seems to be a continuity in the institutionalisation of coercion and terror in governance by communist rulers from the Soviet Union in the 1930s to Kampuchea under Pol Pot in the 1970s. On a mini-scale, we discover the same symptoms in the policies and practices of the Left Front government in West Bengal during the final decades of its regime—in a violent manner it tried to suppress popular protests in Singur, Nandigram and Lalgarh against its industrial projects that threatened the livelihood and homes of the local villagers.

The basic questions that I am raising are—what social or political enzyme in our past programme of building socialism could have distorted an idealist revolutionary Stalin into a cynical brute, or brought about the mutation of a young sensitive Marxist like Pol Pot into a ruthless reprobate? How could communists make such a violent departure from the fundamental Marxist humanitarian premise of respecting the rights of individuals and enhancing their capacity to develop as perfect human beings? The roots of Marxism are embedded in the basic proposition that Karl Marx made in his *Economic and Philosophic Manuscripts of 1844*: "...the complete return of man to himself as a social (i.e. human) being—a return accomplished consciously and embracing the entire wealth of previous development".

In the post-Marxian strategy of revolution, there is an urgent need to restore this Marxian premise of respecting and encouraging the right of the individual to full development of his/her creative capacities. The communist-led governments in the past provided the basic material amenities to their people, and educated and trained them to the level from where they could serve the economic and political interests of the state. But beyond that level, they forbade them to think, or to question the state's policies. Questioning the status quo, which is the basis of human progress, was suppressed in socialist states. Yet, Marx in his theoretical pursuits and political praxis followed the famous dictum—*'De omnibus dubitandum'* (doubt everything). The post-Marxian revolutionaries, both in the course of their ongoing struggles and in the territories where they have come to power, have to respect and restore the democratic rights of both the participants in their struggles, and the citizens who live in these territories. To hark back to Che Guevara's dream, communists in power, while bringing in an equitable socio-economic order, should also shape new human beings who are capable of developing their individuality.

The Present Situation in India

In the light of the above mentioned historical experiences of the communist movement in the past and the changes that are taking place in the post-Marxian era, let me come to the possibilities of revolutionary transformation of the current popular movements in India. I identify four broad areas of such protests in the present Indian context—(i) movements by forest dwellers and tribal people mainly in the hill areas against both the state machinery of oppressive functionaries (like forest guards), and predatory commercial forces that threaten their livelihoods (ranging from the peaceful Chipko movement opposing destruction of forests in the western Himalayas to the violent Maoist-led resistance in the forests of Chhattisgarh, Jharkhand and neighbouring areas against the encroachment by corporate houses to displace them from their homelands to make way for industrial development); (ii) protests by villagers in the plains against the establishment of industrial estates, installation of big dams and nuclear plants among others that threaten to oust them from their lands and homes, and endanger the environment; (iii) civil society campaigns by people like Anna Hazare, and citizens' groups like "Wada Na Todo", or those monitoring elections, which voice the grievances of common citizens against wide-spread corruption and crime in the political system and society in general; lastly, (iv) the most controversial area that challenges Marxist ideologues and practitioners in India—the secessionist struggles on the issue of self-determination by various dissatisfied ethnic and regional communities in the North-Eastern states of Nagaland, Manipur, Assam, and in the North-Western state of Kashmir. They range from armed insurrections to peaceful mass demonstrations in the streets, which reflect the popular feeling that they have had a raw deal by remaining within the Indian Union.

It is these different explosions of protest breaking out in various corners of India that constitute major components of a new revolutionary strategy in the post-Marxian era. They need to be dovetailed with the traditional Marxist proposition of a worker-peasant alliance as the main propelling force for a revolutionary change. Such a proposition implies that a joint struggle by the industrial working class and the rural peasantry alone can be decisive in bringing about the change. But in a country like India, with diverse sociocultural communities, uneven levels of economic development and political consciousness, and fragmentations within the working and peasant classes, Marxist practitioners have to both honestly comprehend this reality and be patient enough to sensitise these various sections of a vast disgruntled population to the political ideology of socialism, and convince them to participate in a multi-level revolutionary endeavour with flexible tactics to move towards a socialist transformation of Indian society.

Relating to the Present Struggles

Yet, each of the movements mentioned above has its own complexities with which Marxist ideologues and political parties often feel ill at ease. For instance, as for the first category—the struggles of forest dwellers and tribal population—should

Marxists regard them as pre-capitalist forms of protest against the introduction of technology, like the Luddite rebellion in the early days of industrialisation, primitive forms of protest, which following past historical pattern, are likely to disappear against the inevitable progress of industrialisation? Or, should they be recognised in the third world context, as assertions of a strong traditional sense of sociocultural identity reinforced by protests against the modern industrial corporatocracy's encroachment on their territory? How can Marxists synchronise their voices with those of the industrial working class? Besides, different groups in these movements have different approaches to social change. Some, like non-governmental organisations, want to strengthen the role of local forest dwellers and tribal people in decision-making within the present structure, and make the prevailing capitalist system more humane. Some like the Maoists want to destroy the structure and strengthen the antagonistic movement against capitalism by leading these tribal populations in an armed struggle in confrontation with the state.

The Maoists in their areas of control in Chhattisgarh, Jharkhand, Malkangiri and other pockets of resistance, have often succeeded in carrying out land reforms, and meeting the basic needs of the local villagers. But the encirclement of their pockets by the state's security forces has led to the elimination of most of their top leadership (Azad, Kishenji and others, killed in false encounters), large-scale arrests of members of their central committee, and increasing surrender of their cadres. In the absence of any effective political guidance from the central leadership, most of the Maoist guerrilla squads are fast turning into roaming gangs of extortionists and criminals in areas like Jharkhand. This again suggests the failure of the leadership in educating the Maoist ranks in the basic ideology of Marxian socialism and humanism. Like their parliamentary counterpart —the CPI(M)—the Maoists are also facing a political crisis and a challenge to their moral credibility. In the light of their experiences of armed struggle during the last three decades or so, the Maoist leaders have to be self-critical, ask themselves whether the tactics of a protracted armed struggle (that was viable in China from the 1920s till the 1940s) can be replicated in 21st century India, and reformulate their programme for a radical change.

Let us take the second type of movements—those against big dams and industrial projects, prompted by concerns of local villagers about threats to their livelihood and environment (cf the Narmada Bachao Andolan). Do the Marxist parties have a plan to incorporate their demands in their overall strategy of a socialist transformation in India? To come to the third category of protests, how should Marxists relate to the Anna Hazare type campaigns which take up burning social issues, but stop only at demanding the reforming of the present structure of governance without challenging the basic capitalist system that gives birth to corruption and crime? How can Marxist parties take up these quotidian problems of the citizens, try to help them in overcoming the myriad problems that they face—and in the course, politicise them to make them aware of the need for breaking down the present political structure to replace it with a socialist system? To recall Marx again—"The communists fight for the attainment of the immediate aims, for the momentary interests of the working class; but in the movement of the present, they also represent and take care of the future of the movement" (*Communist Manifesto*, 1848). In other words, the present revolutionary strategy has to be linked to the future post-revolutionary stage of reconstruction.

But more challenging for Marxists is the fourth area of protests—the secessionist movements. Most of the centres of these secessionist struggles happen to be situated in territories which border countries with which India is in a rather hostile relationship—China in the North-East, and Pakistan in the North-West. As a result, a perpetually paranoid Indian state administration had always responded to demands for autonomy by these ethnic and regional communities by denigrating them as foreign-inspired and suppressing them by military means. Indian Marxist parties—whether the parliamentary communists or the armed CPI(Maoist)—have always betrayed an ambiguous attitude towards these movements in their theorisation about nationalities. In their tactics, they have often betrayed a certain expediency—sometimes dismissing the secessionist movements from the statist point of view of protecting the Indian nation's territorial integrity (e.g., by the parliamentary communist parties), sometimes by batting for them to fight the Indian state (e.g., the Indian Maoists' support to the United Liberation Front of Assam (ULFA) and Islamist terrorist groups, their logic being "my enemy's enemy is my friend". So, any stick is good enough to beat the Indian state!).

The ambiguity and expediency in the policies of the Indian Marxists towards the nationalities can be traced back to the conflict among Marxist ideologues on the question of the right of self-determination of nationalities right from the days of the first socialist state in the Soviet Union. As early as 1917, Rosa Luxemburg questioned the wisdom of the new Soviet state's grant of that right to every nationality (within the erstwhile Tsarist-ruled territory of the Russian empire) without taking into account the feudal and fascist character of the leaders of these local nationalities who could come to power by taking advantage of the right of self-determination (cf *The Russian Revolution*, 1917-18). On the issue of self-determination of nationalities, today also the Marxists face a dilemma. While agreeing on the principle of the right of self-determination, should they allow it to be usurped by chauvinist ethno-nationalist groups like the Liberation Tigers of Tamil Eelam in Sri Lanka, ULFA in Assam, or religious fanatic terrorist organisations like the Hizbul in Kashmir? Drifting with the current of self-determination, should the Marxists (particularly the Maoists) be passive witnesses to the future occupation of Kashmir by a Taliban-type mullacracy imposing coercive shariat laws on women among others?

Humanising Strategy and Tactics

It would be both naïve and dangerous for Marxists to celebrate all forms of resistance, just because they are anti-US. Washington's neo-imperialist adventures in Afghanistan and West Asia have provoked popular anger, opening up space for many different forms of resistance. In the absence of any secular and democratic leadership, this space is being dominated by fanatic religious militant groups like the Al Qaida, and an equally dogmatic religious regime like Iran.

But to come back to the various types of anti-state movements in India—both violent and non-violent, secular and religious—the majority of their participants remain dispersed, each group tightly ensconced within the shell of their respective concerns. They need to coalesce into a single movement. And it is here where a new generation of post-Marxian revolutionary theoreticians and practitioners can invigorate them with a progressive ideological core and a comprehensive coordinated programme of socialist change. There can be debates over the methods of bringing about that change—whether through parliamentary reforms or armed struggle, or a combination of both (as experimented with in Nepal and some countries in South America). As in the past, when Indian Marxist parties drew inspiration from the Soviet Union and China as models of socialist states, at present, among Marxist circles in India (like the CPI(M) in particular), there is a lot of curiosity and expectations about the socialist experiments being carried out in Latin America. Cuba, particularly, during the last several decades, has braved US sanctions and has succeeded in bringing about basic socio-economic reforms that have improved the health and educational standards of its people. Venezuela under Chavez has shown impressive social gains for its people, and has even inspired the concept of a Bolivarian Alternative for the Americas (ALBA) as a pivotal force to bring about a radical change in Latin America.

But, while raising my fist in a red salute to these experiments in socialism, I also want to keep my fingers crossed. Let us not be carried away by the immediate socio-economic successes of these regimes. There are problems like allegations about the suppression of dissident intellectuals in Cuba. In Venezuela, there were complaints about a coterie growing around the late Chavez (known as Chavismo) who were reaping profits and enjoying privileges. Is there going to be a repetition of the same pattern of bureaucratisation and corruption of the political system as happened in the Soviet Union and China in the past?

Basically, it boils down to the problem of humanising the

strategy and tactics of revolutionary change, and democratising the post-revolutionary reconstruction of society. Let us not reduce the problem to a simplistic debate over parliamentary or non-parliamentary methods, or tactics of violence or non-violence—an either/or approach towards the transformation of our society in a socialist direction. On this particular debate, let me end by quoting Rosa Luxemburg:

> Legislative reform and revolution are not different methods of historic development that can be picked out at pleasure from the counter of history, just as one chooses hot or cold sausages. Legislative reform and revolution are different factors in the development of class society. They condition and complement each other, and are at the same time reciprocally exclusive, as are the north and south poles, the bourgeoisie and the proletariat (*Social Reform or Revolution*, 1900).

24

The Importance of Democracy in Socialism

Arup Baisya

The French and Russian revolutions have left an indelible mark on the contending ideologies of capitalism and socialism in an epochal sense. But in both the cases, capitalism not only survived but also extended its material and ideological sphere of influence. The fall of "really existing socialism" necessitates wide-ranging interactions and debates for evolving a conceptual framework beyond those of the traditional Marxist parties. The infallibility of the central committees of a communist parties was premised on their being considered the supreme faculty guiding and teaching the masses instead of relying on the masses to learn. This dogmatic approach does not allow us to go beyond the "sacred" circle of the old Marxist gaslit lamp post. But the popular upsurges against the neoliberal order of the globalisation of capital are compelling practising communists who consider Marxism as the philosophy of praxis, to develop new conceptual frameworks.

Dwelling on the various aspects of this new conceptual framework, Sumanta Banerjee in the previous chapter asserts that questioning the status quo, which is the basis of human progress, was suppressed in the socialist states and raises the basic question—what social or political aspect of our past programme of building socialism could have led to such distortions. While underlining the mistakes in building socialism in Russia or China, and dwelling on the question of leadership and trying to incorporate the new form of popular upsurges in the Marxist conceptual frame- work, the author has not gone to the extent of presenting a new approach to resolve the existing dichotomy.

Limits of Vanguardism

The vanguardist party (in the Leninist sense) and its single-party hegemony in post-revolutionary societies of the 20th century created a situation favourable for it to enjoy the privilege of seeing the people and society without being seen, and thus transform the people into the object and subject of power. This conception of the role of the party also contributed to leading the mainstream Indian Left parties into parliamentary cretinism or crass militarism. That the form of struggle (parliamentary or armed) should not be the basic tenet that determines whether the movement is revolutionary or not becomes crystal clear from Marx's position that the simple exercise of the social power that has accumulated or is accumulating in the hands of labour is in and by itself a revolutionary act.

From the perspective of Marx, it can be said that during this epochal structural crisis of capitalism, the ideology of consumerism gets radically questioned from a socialist perspective built on economic emancipation of the working class. The ruling ideology is structurally determined to misrepresent narrow self-interest as the general interest of society and at times of major crisis, this claim of "general interest" gets exposed as empty rhetoric.

All those who try to articulate the interest of the subordinate classes should not only set out from the premise that there is an alternative, but also define the condition of bringing about that alternative. That is why the socialist project cannot remain content with the negativity of the political revolution, but must strive for the intrinsically positive social revolution in the course of which the associated individual can "change from top to bottom the condition of their industrial and political existence, and consequently their whole manner of being". And this is why we must insist, with Rosa Luxemburg, that:

> socialism will not be established by any government, however admirably socialist. Socialism must be created by the masses, must be made by every proletarian. So the party emerging from below with the understanding that people are transformed as they struggle for justice and dignity, and can spearhead the practice of revolutionary democracy which is vital for the life of the party as well as the masses for developing the 'revolutionary mass consciousness'.

The huge protests that began since 2011 year from among sections of the salaried petit bourgeoisie in Greece in Europe and in Egypt in West Asia can soon reach Indian shores in the new generation of middle class professionals that is emerging in its tertiary sector. The revolt of this class may, at best, be the ideological core of a mass revolutionary upsurge. But the organisational question for destroying the existing system with a view to simultaneously construct a new one cannot be resolved, especially in a predominantly peasant country like India, until and unless those activities are given priority which can build new social relations based upon the consciousness of the unity of the people, albeit a unity, as described by Marx, based upon the recognition of difference.

Identity and Difference

This premise of unity based upon recognition of difference and the premise that puts humans—not machines (productive forces) or the State ahead of everything will guide us to formulate the Marxist programme of socialist transformation. This will also guide us to formulate the programme for a revolutionary change incorporating the broad areas of the current popular movements.

We can learn lessons from the experiences of secessionist movement on the most vexed issue of self-determination in the Eastern region. The Communist Party of Bangladesh has the common understanding and organisational legacy with the Communist Party of undivided India's Bengal. Correctly judging the popular mood, the East Pakistan Communist Party had held some internal discussion on the demand for an independent East Pakistan and it was generally agreed that it was a legitimate demand. The aspiration of the rising Bengali middle class had a progressive role to play in opposition to the *jotedar* and the mahajan, who were in alliance with the ruling class of West Pakistan, to maintain the status quo and thus the workers and peasants' movement was contingent to this movement for self-determination. Following the Indo-China war and the split of the Communist Party, both factions formulated their policy on self-determination on whether the policy and role of the Pakistan state in international politics served the interest of the Soviet Union or of China. Thus a statist outlook became the yardstick for interpreting a popular movement.

From a similar mechanical viewpoint of judging a movement with the yardstick of armed struggle, the Indian Maoists extended their support to the United Liberation Front of Assam (ULFA). But judging from the people's point of view, it would not have been difficult to see that the ULFA's secessionist struggle has a structural pull towards converting the struggle for Assamese self-determinism into aggressive chauvinism. Assam being a multi-identity state has diverse identity aspirations and assertions with inherent contradictions developed from multitudinous interests overlapping each other. So if this complex issue of identity aspirations is not resolved through the principle of democracy and federalism with a view to building greater unity, the unqualified support to the secessionist movement will lead to a cul-de-sac.

Further, the armed struggle itself may become a tool for the ruling class to strengthen their grip on state power. The trend of the traditional Marxists to judge a phenomenon from the extraneous partisan factors of increasing their parliamentary or military might instead of focusing the content of democracy and people's initiative, jeopardise the interest of revolutionary change. So, when the Assam unit of the CPI (M) was supporting the Bodo chauvinist demand (Bodos are minority in the territory they demanded), the West Bengal unit of the same party was opposing the Jharkhandi-Adivasi cultural aspiration in Lalgarh and Jangalmahal, denying the legitimacy of the Kamtapuri identity and strongly opposing the Gorkha demands, all to uphold the indivisibility of Bengal.

It is true that the industrialisation and modernisation of the marginalised Third World countries, which began with the notion of "catching up" with the developed countries and the emergence of new information technology and the service sector in the present phase of neoliberal globalisation, have given birth to a modern working class as well as a professional middle class in countries like India. It is also true that after a long phase of identity-based movements and the dalit and backward class assertion in India, a new upper middle class—ready to be co-opted within the ruling clique— has emerged from within. Also, workers and peasants' movements in the vast countryside and peripheral regions are even now contingent on the diverse identity movements.

In conclusion, it needs to be emphasised unequivocally that the question of freedom and democracy are central to the formulation of a Marxist strategy, both for revolution and for building socialism. That is why, in the text of the *Communist Manifesto* Marx and Engels give equal importance to these two goals—"to raise the proletariat to the position of the ruling class" and "to win the battle of democracy".

25

Leninism as Radical 'Desireology'

Murzban Jal

This chapter is an inquiry in the political philosophy of Lenin with special emphasis on the understanding of Bolshevism in the contemporary era of late imperialism in permanent crises. In contrast to orthodox Marxism which has hitherto understood Marxism as state socialist and ideological, this chapter understands Revolutionary Marxism as anti-state and ideology as the discourse of what Marx called the "spectral person" and consequently nothing but a theory of spectres. It contrasts the old problematic of state socialism and ideology with another problematic that it calls "desireology", a new discipline that firstly emphasises the importance of understanding Hegel—the philosopher par excellence of the European Enlightenment and the French Revolution—and then transforms this understanding in the theories of the Leninist party and the revolutionary dictatorship of the proletariat. On begins with two quotes, the first from Marx, the second from Lenin. Consider first Marx:

> To be radical is to grasp the root of the matter. But for humanity the root is humanity itself.[1]

Consider then Lenin:

> So long as the state exists there is no freedom, where there is freedom there is no state.[2]

Revolutionary Humanism and the Proletariat

Clara Zetkin, writing on Lenin, talked of three deplorable characters for Lenin. They are the monk, Don Juan and the philistine. According to Zetkin's recollection of Lenin, one must "be neither a monk, nor Don Juan, but not anything in between either, like a German philistine."[3] And yet, it seems that these deplorable characters have not only not left the scene of politics; on the contrary, it is the monk, Don Juan and the philistine who while representing the revisionist characters of the 19th and early 20th centuries' social reformists—Ferdinand Lassalle, Eduard Bernstein and Karl Kautsky—claim to speak in the name of revolution. With the heralding of this triumvirate, Marxism would become ventriloquist in character and essence. It would want (what Robespierre once called) a *Revolution without a Revolution*. Instead of being on the barricades of historical materialism, one found oneself sitting in Parliament arguing about nuclear deals and capitalist scams with the liberals, neocons and fascists. One forgot what Lenin had said in 1915: "Much has been left in the world that must be destroyed by fire and iron".

One also forgets what Lenin said in 1917 of parliamentary democracy as the "talk shops" of "political prostitution" and that social democracy had forgotten that parliamentarism has necessarily to be abolished for a higher type of democracy.[4] This higher form is, as Lenin informs us, "primitive democracy."[5] One recalls here Marx's celebration of the archaic.[6] One thus has to be primitive in order to be the most modern of all modems. One also has to be archaic in order to have a *Revolution with a Revolution*.

Two important questions emerge: (1) "Why is it that these three deplorable and pretentious characters continue their tragicomic ghost-walk such that history seems to be appearing more in tragic and farcical forms than in the form of revolutionary joy?" (2) "Why can we not break the continuum of the tragicomic structure of history so as to exorcise these reformist spectres and thus be able to have a clear-cut revolutionary programme suitable for world revolution in the 21st century?" There could be a number of reasons for this, reasons that go well beyond current times and beyond the scene of Indian politics. Firstly, following a certain type of peculiar logic that Žižek recently outlined where the "Event"— the term is Alain Badiou's—(post-1917, especially after the defeat of the Hungarian and German revolutions in 1918) was lost which pushed the agenda of world revolution into the back stage of history.[7] Secondly, the "Event" was fossilised by the "event managers" where the "managers of the revolution" (meaning the NEP men after Lenin's death in 1924) took over from the revolutionaries and became the "managers of state capitalism". After all "the problems of the revolution", as Lenin said in *State* and *Revolution,* "hardly concerned them". (But the managers were not only the Stalinists. They were also the American New Dealers, Italian and German fascists, Iranian mullahs, Pakistani generals and Indian democrats.) And thirdly, instead of having the *Real of the Revolution* (to borrow from the Lacanian problematic), one had the *Imaginary of the Revolution,* or, to be precise, the *Ghost of the Revolution.* Since 1924 the very "Idea of communism" to borrow the Leninist-Žižekean term[8]—was transfigured. We yet live in the world of transfiguration.

The tragicomic idea of history has a very rigorously defined structure—the structure of being haunted by the past of "old politics"—the structure of the old politics of liberalism, transfigured communism and fascism. One has debates more on the politics of multiparty democracy and its binary: authoritarianism, than on mass politics. ·What happens is a peculiar type of political distortion that does not remain merely on the political plain. It penetrates into every area of the human lifeworld. This distortion—that Lukács had immortalised as the reification of consciousness and a feeling of helplessness and known since Freud as the feeling of dread and terror, or simply the feeling of the uncanny *(das Unheimlich)*—remains the dominant part of class history even today. The leitmotiv of this chapter is to go to the roots of this distortion and the dominance of the uncanny type of tragicomic history and consequently to treat the question of revolution not as economism and parliamentarism, but as cultural and aesthetical education determined by the critique of political economy. It recalls Marx's dictum: to produce according to "the laws of beauty."[9] It is then that one understands the Leninist politics of treating insurrection as art. Revolutionary politics becomes a dramaturgy—a theatre of the "Real". It keeps, what Žižek calls, "the sublime feeling of enthusiasm" at its basis.[10]

One has to state that besides the Young Bolsheviks (from Mavelich to Meyerhold), it was Lukács who had pointed out this cultural-revolutionary politics following the German humanist tradition, followed by Karl and Hedda Korsch in the 1930s, where politics was not understood merely as state power, nor was aesthetics only about dealing with the questions of "art" and the "beautiful". Instead this new politics is the synthesis of art and politics (as revolutionary humanism) and thus is the study in the relation between revolution and human sensibilities. Marxism becomes the "science of revolutionising knowledge and thus revolutionising human sensibilities themselves." As the new politics of cultural and aesthetic education—thus the politics of insurrection as art—Marxism turns to a fundamental issue: on how mass humanism as new humanism is possible as the revolutionary dictatorship of the proletariat.

It takes two terrains hitherto disconnected—the young Marx's theory of alienation (not known to Lenin, the *Economic and Philosophic Manuscripts* of *1844* were discovered by David Ryazanov after Lenin's death) and Lenin's party of aesthetical insurrection—to reformulate the theory and praxis of revolution as the spontaneous activity of the masses. In contrast to the spurious Leninists who debunk spontaneity, we understand spontaneity as authentic human praxis[11] Lenin, one must note, embraced spontaneity not only in the *Philosophical Notebooks*[12], but also in *What is to be Done?*[13] We read Lenin therefore as the philosopher of spontaneity.

Revolutionary Proletarian Dictatorship

Since we shall be concentrating on the idea of the revolutionary dictatorship of the proletariat—the revolutionary dictatorship of spontaneous mass democracy as radical desireology—we must firstly state that two philosophical sites are immediately bound to it—the sites of humanism and mass democracy and that of Hegelian dialectic of contradiction, negation, negation of negation, dissolution *(Auflösung)* and transcendence *(Aufhebung)*. What we learn from these two sites is that governed by the dialectic of historicism and humanism, the dictorship of the proletariat is actualised as *anti-state,* an anti-state which is the transcendence *(Aufhebung)* of the state and the dissolution *(Auflösung)* of *all* dictatorships and *all* classes. Hegel's dictum: to understand *truth as a process* is inserted in the Marxist theory of transition. So what new we understand from this dialectical-humanist formulation is that the revolutionary dictatorship of the proletariat is the negation and dissolution of all dictatorships because it is the negation of all classes.

By keeping Marx's theory of the transcendence of the state[14] as central to this chaper, we must stress that the very emergence of the idea of the revolutionary proletarian dictatorship has to appear as anti-state based itself on the mass politics of new humanism. This new theory transcends the old theory of an intermediary stage mediating between socialism (the so-called lower stage of communism) and communism proper. In this sense Leninism in the 21st century transcends Lenin himself, for it was he who did not erase the two stages in his *State and Revolution.* Circumstances compelled him to agree with the two stages. Circumstances now force us to erase them. By claiming that there are two stages of communism—the lower stage, where the child or the infant communist still has the birth marks of the notorious capitalist parent stamped on its unfortunate forehead and the higher stage where the terror of the parent is simply forgotten—and that in the lower stage the infant communist can take the state apparatus and imitate the neurotic and violent parent is simply not tenable. One thus directly challenges the two stages theory in the 21st century. It is Žižek who recently said that socialism is not any more a stage in the history of communism—"the infamous 'lower phase' of communism"—it is the "true competitor, the greatest threat to it."[15]

And if this is indeed so—that Marxism does not compete with only capitalism, but also with socialism—how can one develop a systematic science of Marxism relevant for the 21st century? One must note here that post-Marx, Marxism (at least since Plekhanov, some will say since Engels) has borrowed more from the alien problematic of 19th century positivism and theories of evolution where spurious historicism was born whereby dialectics became more of a combination of mechanism and sophistry. That the Second International became a bearer of this mechanical sophistry is well known. That the burden of this sophistry lies yet on our unfortunate heads is not so well known.

After all, it is not only the Stalinist counterrevolution that "parasited" on this rendering of Marxism. It was Gramsci who had said that a schizophrenic sort of combination entered leftist discourse which was half theological, half mechanical-materialist, where Marxism of the Second International with its theory of the march-past of the iron laws of history was made to look like "impassioned finalism which appears in the role of the 'substitute' for the Predestination or Providence of confessional religions."[16] There are two problems: one that Marxist theory was wrongly formulated under the auspices of the positivist sciences, where Marxism was made to mimic the bourgeois binary: political passivity and the discourses of "iron laws independent of human will and consciousness". Stalin canonises this formulation, but despite the de-Stalinist programmes, neither these "iron laws" disappear, nor the politics of passivity. After all, as Gramsci once stated, these iron laws that run their course with the force of their mystical "inevitabilities"—inscribed in the classical discourse of the Menshevik "inevitable revolution"—were in actuality "the clothing worn by real and active will when in a weak position."[17]

In contrast to this formulation of spurious historicism we are going back to Marx's original repertoire and discovering the new continent of knowledge by stating that Marxism is human natural science, or simply the natural science of humanity[18] wherein one understands what Lukács once called "the actuality of the revolution."[19] Not only are the problems of spontaneity, vanguardism, the place of the communist will, revolutionary violence, parliamentarism vs. insurgency, the withering of the state, etc., to be understood in this problematic of human natural science—a science that understands how the masses gripped with radical theory become the weapons

(*Waffen*) and force (*Gewalte*) of the humanisation of history by ending once and for all the history of class societies —but also the various understandings of Leninism from the Old Bolshevik critique of Miasnikov to Lukács, Dunayevskaya, Althusser, Lefebvre, Kevin Anderson, Carrere d'Encausse, Žižek and Simon Pirani. The weapons and revolutionary force that Marx first highlighted in his critique of Hegel[20]—recalling his famous phrase: force is the midwife of every old society pregnant with a new one[21]—now enters the scene of world revolutions as the weapons of mass struggle and New Humanism.

On Lenin's Laughter

I noted in my chapter on the defence of Leninism that with the collapse of the Soviet Union and the evangelic announcement of the "end of history", not only were the liberals and neocons seen on the scene of world politics, but also to the great dismay of the liberals and neocons, one also saw Marx, Lenin, Trotsky, Luxemburg and millions of poets and fighters of revolution. We saw that history was to repeat itself culminating not in farce, but in revolutionary joy. We turn to this joyous moment.

We thus move to 1908. We are with Lenin and Gorky in Capri. The 1905 revolution is crushed by the forces of the Tsar. Gorky wants to discuss philosophy with Lenin and he responds with laughter. A section of the Bolshevik leadership led by Lunacharsky, Bognadov and Bazarov has taken an extreme left turn politically (they want to boycott all types of politics), but a right turn philosophically (they are influenced by the rather bizarre theory of "matter has disappeared"). They claim to be Bolsheviks but have become empiro-critics. 'They are seized by to borrow Lenin's expression) an infantile disorder. Gorky wants Lenin to have a discussion on philosophy with them. Lenin breaks into laughter. He says that he would love to meet Gorky. But a philosophical discussion? Lenin thinks not. Nevertheless, he himself goes into philosophy. His conclusion: philosophy is not only a lost path, but it is the falsest of false paths *(der Holzweg der Holzwege)*.[22]

One here recalls Marx's statement of philosophy as a neurotic return *(Wiederherstellung)* of theology and simply fit to be overthrown.[23] Philosophy is thus a lost path, especially the philosophy that has turned its back onto Hegel and the concerns of the French Revolution as the phenomenology of history as human freedom. Not only is philosophy the lost path, but now the philosopher is understood as the lost person, because philosophy has forgotten its very basic question: "What is free humanity?" Philosophy shuts its eyes to what Hegel called "the fanaticism of freedom" and thus becomes the philosophy of the academicians. There is no use in involving oneself with what Lenin called "graduated flunkeys" with their "torturous idealism" whose sole aim is to prove the stupidity of materialist philosophers.[24]

Thus Lenin's laughter. After all, why discuss philosophy when the state is unleashing all its repressive terror on the masses? Why waste time with discussions on lost paths and lost people? Yet it is important to remember, as Marx had once reminded us, one cannot turn our backs to philosophy by "muttering a few trite and angry phrases about it."[25] One has to understand this lost path (or to borrow from Marx's lexicon), one has to understand these *estranged paths*, these paths of false consciousness and even falser realities, paths that lead us nowhere. And for that one needs a new discipline, a philosophy of negation, which is the "negation *(Negation)* of philosophy" itself.[26] Now what Marx proposes as a philosophy of revolution, an authentic philosophy of praxis, is something that has to emerge from the storm and stress of the proletarian movement where philosophy is transcended *(aufheben)* by making it a reality *(verwirklichen)*. Thus one transcends philosophy by making it a reality, just as one makes it a reality by transcending it.[27]

This transcendence *(Aufhebung)*, supersession and overcoming of philosophy, "abolishes eternal truths; ...abolishes all religion, and all morality, instead of constituting them on a new basis."[28] One thus has "the most radical rupture with traditional ideas."[29] The old idolatry of words perishes. Consequently this new theory is not a return to traditional philosophising, but is the birth of a new philosophical science, a unified knowledge in the form of dialectical and historical-humanist praxis.[30] It seems that for Lunacharsky and company, the Marxist programme of revolution was totally misunderstood.

Lunacharsky disagreed with what he thought was Engels' metaphysical materialism. But he did not engage Hegel's *Science of Logic*, or Marx's *Capital*. He did not merely skip Hegel, but also Marx. He, of course, forgot what Marx's idea of praxis meant, especially the Marxist reading of a different practice of philosophy. In 'discovering' the idealist philosophy of Mach, he actually went back to Berkeley. This little lesson from Lunacharsky is relevant today. For just as he misunderstood the dialectic and retreated into pre-Marxist philosophy, our contemporary parliamentary leftists too misunderstand dialectical materialism and the dictatorship of the proletariat as the self-activity of the working classes, only to retreat into the bourgeois binary: liberalism/the politics of single-party dictatorships.

Two very dialectical concepts come in Marx's theoretical revolution: *Aufhebung* or transcendence-sublation through a "lifting up" of philosophy at a higher historicist and humanist level; and *Verwirklichung* or realisation of this historicist and humanist transcendence of philosophy, not only as the philosophy of revolutionary praxis, but as revolutionary praxis itself. Marxist theory thus becomes a force and weapon that has gripped the masses. Lenin's laughter is seen in this perspective, a perspective that he insists is found not with the academic philosophers, but with the revolutionary insurrectionist proletariat.

Now this theme of radical philosophy—a different practice of philosophy, philosophy as insurrection—is well known, but the epistemic dynamics of negation, transcendence and realisation—aspects that made not only the Bolshevik Party, and the Soviets, but also the 1917 Revolution—are almost not thought within the Marxist movement in India. Althusser, for instance, thought it to be a useless question. Marx, for him, was yet infatuated with his youthful longing for Hegelian dialectics. It was only Karl Korsch who in his *Marxism and Philosophy* raised this very important Marxist question of (what is translated as) "the abolition of philosophy", but closely tied to the abolition of the political state itself.[31] Translations, one must note, are almost always notorious for misrepresentations. In Althusser's *For Marx* we hear of the "suppression of philosophy"[32] where *Aufhebung* is said to be a "sly concept"[33] fit to be totally discarded from Marxism. But *Aufhebung* (as we note contra Althusser) is not suppression. Marx was no Stalinist who wanted to suppress philosophy. Nor did he (now turning to Korsch) want to abolish it. One will have to read the *Aufhebung* of philosophy in a different perspective.

Let us start with our first proposal: Marxism is philosophical. To understand the idea of the revolutionary proletarian dictatorship one has to understand this philosophy. But this philosophy is different from all hitherto existing philosophies. Marx opens a new continent of knowledge: dialectical and historical-humanist materialism with the mechanism of alienation-reification-fetishism embodied in the very womb of class histories. The history of class struggles is at the same time the history of human alienation and the struggle against it. The second proposal: the opening of the new continent of knowledge has a small history of its own—the histories of the ancient Greek philosophers, the European Enlightenment and the French Revolution, the critique of political economy, Hegel's philosophy and the radical philosophies of the non-Western world.

Keeping this very complex mechanism that is unevenly structured at the back of our minds, we proceed to the most important question of the nature of Marxist philosophy. For Marx, philosophy has to become worldly, just as the world has to become philosophical.[34] And how does this happen? It happens when the human mind liberated "turns into practical energy" and thus "turns against the reality of the world" itself.[35] There is now a "practice of philosophy", a practice that is basically theoretical.[36] The revolutionary programme of the *realisation of philosophy* has a "double-edged demand": to turn against the bourgeois world and also to turn against hitherto existing philosophy itself.[37]

With this double-edged demand we go back to Marx's human natural science as a different practice of philosophy and thus repose the classical philosophical question: "What is humanity?" as "What is communism and how is it actualised?" At least for Lenin, Gorky's offer for philosophical dialogue is practically empty. Gorky is a humanist, his novels deal with the human condition. But his "philosophical offer" contains no humanity in it. For instance, the theme of "matter has disappeared" (raised by the empiro-critics) seems to be a cloak for the main issue: "the revolution is at an ebb". Not only has matter disappeared for the 'Left' Bolsheviks, God now has appeared. The 'Left' Bolsheviks have become "God builders". For Lenin they are not serious with the rigours of Marxist theory. His aphorism: "without revolutionary theory there can be no revolution"[38] starts haunting us once again.

Revolution as Cultural Practice

And so the transformation of theory, a theory that is most modern and best equipped in dealing with the contemporary scenario, becomes the leitmotiv of revolutionary Marxism. One therefore transforms theory in order to transform society. But there is another transformation that is extremely necessary (usually ignored by mainstream Marxism): the transformation of human nature itself. It was Sweezy in *Post-Revolutionary Society* who reminded us of this extremely important point.[39] The revolutionary party that is the school for the revolutionising of human sensibilities also becomes the school for transforming human nature—from the bourgeois nature (of the ownership of private property, of controlling people and destroying humanity and the natural environment) to human nature as *real human nature* (and not the "nature" of owners of property).

The latter nature is the nature that emerges from the alienation of humanity, whilst there is an "authentic" human nature, or what Marx calls "essential nature", a human nature that is defined as human morality, human activity and human enjoyment.[40] For Marx then: "Human nature is the true community of humanity"[41] where the demand is now about the "Rights of Humanity."[42] These rights, for Marx, can never be fulfilled by the state, but by a "state" that is no longer the political state that is independent of humanity, but by the anti-state which is the "state of human nature."[43] One moves now from the realm of the political state (governed by the managers of bourgeoisdom) to the state of humanity, to the masses and thus to authenticity itself. Marxist authenticity is to live without classes and the state.

And since we put the theory of revolutions on a new footing, a revolution that seizes humanity by its roots, we say that this theme of the transformation of human nature becomes an essential theme for Revolutionary Marxism. And this is so because Marx puts his theory of international revolution on firm philosophical foundations. Marx's internationalism is not a contingent idea, an idea that is tied down to certain phases of history, where a Stalin could say that capitalism in the age of liberalism could have an international character, but in the period of imperialism (governed by Stalin's imaginary "uneven law") one had to become a nationalist and sing "long live socialism in one country!"

Let us look at Marx's necessary theme of internationalism based on the principles of humanism. For Marx, there is indeed something called a "universal human nature"[44] where one states that truth is not partisan, but what is true is "true for all humanity, not what is true for some people."[45] Thus, for Marx, communist truth does "not recognise the boundaries of political geography."[46] It is not bound to "the illusory horizon of a particular world or national outlook", but to "the true horizon of the human mind."[47] And that is why we say that Marxist politics of the anti-state is essentially philosophical where one finds a "philosophical people (who) can find their corresponding practice only in socialism",[48] wherein emerges "humanity's true community", the community of human nature.[49]

Being forgetful of this philosophical communism, communism as humanism and naturalism, one returns back to the tragic character of history where Marxism appears in its unphilosophical form—in the form of instrumental-managerial reason (one recalls here Adorno's "administrative reason")—a reason that is devoid of not only philosophical reason, but reason altogether. Instead of this instrumental Stalinist Platocracy, one puts the masses at centre stage that calls for the "positive transcendence (*Aufhebung*) of private property" combined with the "appropriation for and by humanity of the human essence (*das menschliche Wesen*) and of human life (itself)."[50] And thus if one asks: "what is the importance of Leninism in the 21st century?", one will say that one has to treat the role of the party as what Korsch once called, "human sensuous activity, as praxis."[51]

Objectivity thus is not merely "brute matter" as Sartre once thought it to be, or the Menshevik-Stalinist "objective" laws of history as the Left yet imagines it to be. It does not comprise of mere "facts", but it primarily includes the subject within its ambit. It thus has within it the idea of the revolutionary proletariat. Thus as there can be no objectivity without humanity, there can be no objective politics without the proletariat. Dialectical materialism now redefines objectivity as humanity's being and becoming-in-the-world defined by labour and insurrection. Not only do humanity and labour get to be parts of objectivity, but also the praxis of revolution as insurrection. Objectivity is thus not the contemplative objectivity of the Second International (which our parliamentary Left blindly mimics). Instead objectivity is defined as insurrection; in fact objectivity is to be considered as the aesthetics of insurrection. Radical aesthetics becomes an essential part of objectivity. In this way the Leninist party enters the scene of objectivity.

One insists here that this transfiguration of revolutionary politics into fetishised objectivity and thus into passivism and social democracy is not merely a problem of a certain type of politics. It is not merely a problem of tactics and strategies, but a problem of theory as theory. Thus when it is recently said that there is "an implicit theoretical ambiguity at its core", i.e. at the core of left-wing politics in contemporary India[52], the claim is correct. This claim is now linked to those posed by Korsch[53] in the 1920s followed by those by Dunayevskaya[54] and Kevin Anderson.[55] One recalls Lenin again: without revolutionary theory, there can be no revolutionary movement. Those who think that the narrative of revolution is inscribed merely in the womb of the crises of capitalism such that the revolution would somehow happen "inevitably" are simply wrong.

Revolution is the real explosion of human freedom as a beautiful moment of universal solidarity. The party of insurrection then is the party of this beautiful moment.

Marx's Species Being and the Leninist Party

So what does the Leninist do in this realisation of the beautiful moment? The Leninist hears the voices of the masses. It does not fear the revolution as Stalin, Zinoviev and Kamenev did in April 1917, nor like the Mensheviks turn their backs to the question of the revolutionary seizure of power, nor does it goof up as the Tudeh party did in Iran in 1979. Instead one recalls the early Marx's idea of the proletariat as species being and then true to its dialectical character joins the individual with the social, a joining that one calls following the terminology of Hegel: the concrete universal. The communist party becomes the party of this concrete universal where "real individuals"[56] linked to the ideas of class struggle and the appropriation of the human essence remain at the base of revolutionary politics.

There are three terms in this historicist and humanist reading of the concrete universal: the individual (the individual person), the particular (the specific class) and the universal (society and history). The role of the Leninist party is to join these three elements. So what happens when one has joined these elements? This joining brings forth the site of species being —the site of anti-state politics—into the site of revolution. In this revolutionary site of humanity realising itself as species being, humanity's individual and species-life (*Gattungsleben*) are synthesised.[57] Just as Marx had pointed out that: "We must avoid postulating 'society' again as an abstraction *vis-à-vis* the individual. The individual *is the social being.....*"[58]; so too we must avoid postulating the revolutionary party as an abstraction vis-à-vis the individual. After all "humanity's individual and species-life are not *different*", to recall Marx again, "however much—and this is inevitable—the mode of existence (*Daseinweise*) of the individual is a more *particular* or more general mode of life of the species, or the life of the species is a more *particular* or more *general* individual life."[59]

The Leninist party becomes the embodiment of this species character of humanity. But then it has to break old barriers—not only the barrier of the state, but also the barrier of the ideological. The party as species being is no longer "ideological". Instead it becomes "desireological", where revolutionary consciousness as self-consciousness (i.e. conscious of its own potentialities as well as consciousness of the world) becomes the "state of desire in general."[60] To raise the level of mass consciousness to the level of insurrection as art is the part played by the science of Radical Desireology.

But one has to note that this species character of the communist lifeworld is not realised in an abstract way, in the way of abstract universals loyal to Badiou's fidelity to the Event. There is no abstract Event, but "many zigzags on this road",[61] zigzags that do not pose questions in the abstract, thus do not pose only the question of proletarian emancipation, independent of the questions of gender, caste and oppressed nationalities. This species character of communism is inclusive. Since it takes "all the classes"[62] into its fold, it is essentially humanist. There is no "uniquely unique" standpoint understood only by the revolutionaries. The revolution is universal and yet carries a partisan character to it. Though "all the people" ought to be involved in the revolutionary struggle, some outright deny it, some stay at a cynical distance ("Really will the revolution make any difference?") and some insist on being happy in the unhappy home of alienation, or happy in what Žižek calls "the Kantian celebration of the sublime effect of passive observation."[63]

The party thus with its many zigzags has to confront this alienation that turns human beings into bourgeois cynics. To confront this alienation it produces what Brecht called the "alienation effect" and what is known since Fredric Jameson as the "dialectical shock". Taking this shock element with it, the party breaks the stranglehold of the "terrible sublime" of bourgeois passivity by becoming the embodiment of the species character of humanity. It has to keep the idea of human freedom as the beautiful moment of universal solidarity as central to revolutionary politics.

Ideology: Disembodiment and the Repressed Unconscious

We now come to the central concern of this essay with a rather startling claim that Revolutionary Marxism is not an ideology and can never be so. Why is this so? What are one's reasons for claiming that ideology is not only false consciousness and the instrumental irrational of the capitalist class, but some sort of terrible nightmare where Freud's good old repressed unconscious is replayed as the "terrible sublime" that suppresses revolutionary praxis? Now we know that the masses are not merely confronted with the Repressive State Apparatus of capitalism (the police, army, RSS bombers, Iranian mullahs, the CIA, etc), they are also confronted by the Ideological State Apparatus. In this apparatus (one ought to say: "neurotic apparatus"), political ideology in the age of late capitalism does not take an explicit propagandist form, but appears more subtly as cultural signs and depoliticised forms as represented in the culture industry. Now we also know since Adorno how this culture industry works—via the monopolistic control of the media—whereby politics functions in a rather "innocent" way, taking depoliticised forms of class neutrality. The old ideologists were the popes and the Stalinists. The new ideologists are Robert Murdoch and Robert Gates, BBC and CNN. What we see is that behind the "Idea" of this very ideological media industry is finance capital. And seeing Gates around, accompanied by the Iranian mullahs, the Zionists, Hamas and the RSS, one will see that behind bourgeois ideology is not only finance capital, but also the military arms complex. Ideology in the age of late imperialism is best manifested as the ideology of bourgeois violence. Freud's psychotic patient becomes the best ideologist.

What one does now is to understand the discipline of ideology, not in its classical rendering from Destut de Tracy to Ralf Mannheim as the 'rational' theory of ideas—thus the explication of the theories of liberalism, socialism, fascism, etc—but the one that ruptures this theory of "ideas" with the humanist, classbased critique of the ideological superstructure.

The critique of ideology then becomes an extension of the critique of religion. Ideology (like religion) is then understood as nothing but an inverted consciousness of an inverted world. Its chief function is veiling social relations of production. This, as we all well know, is the intervention of the Frankfurt School. But what happens is that in this inverted and distorted consciousness, the moment of the sublime occurs (the sublime that blocks the *Real* of the revolution), whereby the ideologist involves himself in a fantasy comprised of "world shattering phrases", a fantasy that has broken all connections with reality,[64] somehow miming both the metamorphosis of commodities and Freud's reading of the psychotic who is totally disconnected from reality.

Ideology is not only commodity fetishism and psychosis, but is "commoditised psychosis", and as commoditised psychosis is also the worst form of dogmatism since it "by no means examines its general premises."[65] Like the ancient gods who took life-devouring forms of their own, ideology (of any sort, whether papal, fascist, Stalinist, or CNN-BBC inspired neoliberalist) takes this same form of phantasmagorical independence from societal relations of production. And just as the ancient gods erased humanity, so too is the case with ideology. Ideology interpellates people as objects. In ideology people lose their humanity and chase "apparitions", "spectres" and "whimsies."[66] Ideology is then nothing but "idealist humbug."[67] The true ideologist, as *The German Ideology* notes, is Don Quixote. He is the evangelist par excellence and appears as the apostle and saint of years long gone by, as Stalin of years not long gone by, and now as Bush and Hillary Clinton, not to forget Obama—Žižek's "Bush with a human face",[68]—accompanied by Mickey Mouse and Superman, the present messiahs of Yankee imperialism. But then what is Marx's anti-ideological, materialist solution? It is to remain on the "real ground of history", to disbelieve the evangelic tales of the apparitions (thus to disbelieve in liberalism: the master ideology of our times) and to assert that it is "not criticism but revolution (that) is the driving force of history."[69] The difference between the ideologist (even when he imagines he is producing a "true consciousness") and the revolutionary is that the former "wants to produce a correct consciousness about an existing fact; whereas for the real communist it is the question of overthrowing the existing state of things."[70]

Since we are claiming that ideology is necessarily predicated on commodity production, we must note that the process of alienation-metamorphosis-disembodiment is at work where the categories of use value, value and exchange value correspond to the Lacanian categories of the Real, Imaginary and the Symbolic. Ideology is thus:

(1) the *Imaginary* and the *Symbolic* with the denial of the *Real* as its necessary base, similar to the metamorphosis of commodities, where capitalism erases both use values and humanity to posit value, exchange value and the occult-like process of capital accumulation, and

(2) a "projected lack" and the site of denial, where this projection of human alienation becomes a machine (like value and exchange value) that controls humanity. The basic structure of ideology is constituted in the binary: lack/surplus, i e, lack (both economic and cultural lacks) at the level of the masses and surplus at the level of the bourgeoisie. As the alienated lack it takes the form of the repressed unconscious.

It is thus important to point out that the basic structure of ideology is similar to the one of the phantom commodity, just as it is important to state that it is this ghostly objectivity that governs both the phantom commodity and ideology as psychosis. Ideology becomes thus the duplicate world similar to the mist-enveloped world of religion. It is also akin to the schizophrenic "doubling effect" that Freud pointed out in *The Uncanny*. And because ideology mimics the phenomenological process of commodity production, and since it mimics the core structure of abstract labour, its essential structure becomes this ghostly abstract.

One can write anything on the pages of this ghostly abstract. The fascists can justify their Auschwitzs and Gujarats; the liberals their Kashmirs, Gazas and Guantanamo Bays. And since ideology emerges from the ghostly abstract of commodity production and then mimics this ghost, it takes the form of a spurious humanisation and false democracy. The true ideologist is the true ghost, and the true ghost is the false human and false democrat. What we learn is this spurious humanisation, this false democracy, is actually only the return of mythology and theology in modern utopian dress. So what do we learn from this? We learn that humanity purged mythology and theology only to embrace it once again. Freud's eternal recurrence of the neurotic becomes Marx's perpetual recurrence of the ideologist. Once upon a time the shamanistic priest ruled with the rites of mythology and theology. Now the same shamanistic priest has returned with a new set of rites and new sets of messianic promises.

In contrast to the realm of the "ideological" (and the fixation with "ideas"—recall how Marx in *The German Ideology* claims that humanity was fixated with the "idea" of gravity and with the removal of this idea he believed he would not drown)—let us learn to exorcise and humanise ideas. One must also learn how to encounter the unconscious. Consequently one should cease being obsessed with "consciousness" and "ideologies". Instead one goes into the triple critiques of alienation, political economy and the unconscious. The first thing that one encounters in this triple critique is the dominant definition of ideology that emerges in *Capital*: "We are not aware of this, nevertheless we do it" (*Sie wissen das nicht, aber sie tun es*).[71] The communist is faced with this politics of the unconscious. The communist now has become a psychoanalyst.

But then we do not simply have the politics of the unconscious. We also have a new definition of ideology: "they know it, yet they do it!"[72] It is both these contexts that have to be dealt with. We have to deal with the unconscious (the first definition from Marx) as well as with a type of what we know after Žižek as an "enlightened false consciousness" or simply a petty bourgeois cynicism.[73] Lenin's important 1902 intervention comes in: understand the spontaneity of the masses and engage in the politics of the human essence. That is why the Leninist insists: keep humanity and its concerns as the basis of Left politics and stop talking nonsense of the "laws" of history. After all, one must recognise: there are no inevitabilities in history, most certainly no inevitable communist revolution. It is now a matter of radical desiring. Let us from now on desire the communist revolution.

Revolutionary Desire

One moves from the politics of the unconscious to the revolutionary site of desire. Leninism is all about revolutionary desire. When he insisted in *What is to be Done?* on the role of the professional revolutionary he implied the art of desiring. This art is primarily a solution to bourgeois cynicism and to the spectacle of late imperialism in permanent crisis. One is not dealing anymore with "consciousness". One is now in the midst of desire. Thus one is not interested anymore in changing "consciousness". The left-wing ideologist who intends to "teach" the worker about his own situation is nothing but the bourgeois educator who remains perpetually bourgeois.

So instead of ideas and ideologies one puts "the real, corporeal *human being*" with its "real objective *essential powers* (*wirklichen gegenständlichen Wesenkräfte*)[74] at the centre of revolutionary politics. Marx's will to revolutionary power now enters the scene of revolution. Instead of ideologies we have the natural powers (*naturlichen Kräften*) and vital powers (*Lebenskräften*)"[75], or simply "human essential powers" (*menschlichen Wesenkrafte*)[76] of the proletariat on this new scene of revolution. The theme of consciousness is now transcended for a theory of human essential powers.

And since the "ontological essence of human passion (*Leidenschaft*) coming into being"[77] is now our focus, we say that the revolutionary party is also the party of passion. As passion it immediately confronts both capital accumulation and the state. In contrast to hitherto existing left discourse—whether Stalin, Trotsky or Mao inspired—our theme of the immediate abolishing of the state remains central to our reading of Leninism. For it is the state (as the organising committee of the passionless bourgeoisie) that thwarts the passions of the revolution.

From State as Sham to the State as Defecation

We once stated that the state is a sham. Now we recall Freud and claim that the state is defecation. Strictly Freud is talking of money and not the state as defecation when he mentions the "connections between the complexes of interest in money and defecation" and the "money complex" emerging thereon.[78] But money is not only dirty and filthy.[79] It is literally "the faeces of hell."[80]

Now no Marxist can have objection to this Freudian intervention. What we are doing is transforming the theory of money as defection into the theory of state as the faeces of psychotic hell. Let us have a look at the relation between gold and excrement. Now we know from Freud that gold that the devil gave to his paramour turned into excrement after he departed.[81] We are keeping these above stated points in mind (both money and the state as shit) with special regards to the abolishing of commodity production, money and the state immediately at the dawn of the revolution. It is from this juncture with Marx's "free association of moral human beings"[82]—the free humanity that refuses to "be educated from above"[83]—that one is able to turn to Lenin's "people from below". In the 1936 letter to Benjamin, Adorno wrote that the proletariat is credited with an "achievement, which according to Lenin, it can be achieved only through a theory introduced by intellectuals as dialectical subjects."[84] That the proletariat is able to realise itself not in a messianic way led by the infallible General Secretary, but in a well-thought-out way led by the insurrectionist masses in the abolishing of capitalism and all classes is fundamental for Marx's politics of human freedom.

After all, one very well knows that Marxism is essentially the discourse of human freedom. Since we know that the public space of species being displaces the politics of the state we cease being bewitched by the various types of state-politics. We also cease being bewitched by the so-called "democracy" that American imperialism throws at the whole world. Of course, Marxism is democratic, but this democracy is not an institutional democracy of the liberal variety that deals with the institutions of the legislative, judiciary, etc, whilst conveniently forgetting classes and humanity. It is here that one must note that not only is "democracy" a historical phenomena, but is also an overdetermined term. Therefore one must point out that there are five forms of democracy that Marxism recognises:

(1) the revolutionary type that Marx decoded in his reading of the Russian commune (*Obschina*) and other pre-capitalist social formations based on common land (*ager publicus*), a democracy that leap frogs the capitalist mode of production and its liberal superstructure,
(2) the classical type that emerged with the Greek polis,
(3) the liberal type as enunciated by John Locke,
(4) the Rousseau and Robespierre types, and
(5) the Marxist form of democracy as the realisation of *humanity as humanity* and the universal citizen.

In this case singling only the bourgeois type of democracy determined by corporate capitalism makes bourgeois democracy itself a fetish for sale in the global market. One forgets that the term is itself of class origins. In this sense, as Lenin states, democracy is itself ambiguous with multiple meanings. "Democracy", so Lenin states, is thus no ideal, but itself a "*state* which recognises the subordination of the minority to the majority, i.e. an organisation for the systematic use of *force* by one class against another, by one section of the population against another."[85] In contrast to this state of affairs, the politics of species being as the politics of the "union of free people"[86], creates an entire "new generation", as Lenin recalls Engels, reared in new, free, social conditions which will be able to discard the entire lumber of the state—of any state, including the democratic-republican state.[87]

And so we re-read the idea of the state with all its contradictions leading to an explosion—and explosion of human freedom that leads us to the double ideas of communism as humanism and naturalism (*Economic and Philosophic Manuscripts of 1844*) and the revolutionary dictatorship of the proletariat (*Critique of the Gotha Programme*), a "dictatorship" that does not reinstate any form of dictatorship, but that which dissolves all types of dictatorships. The proletariat dissolves itself when it abolishes capitalism and smashes the state. Consequently the dictatorship of the proletariat dissolves all dictatorships. It is literally (to borrow Hegel's term) the non-being (*Nichts*) of the state. Hegel's negation becomes the Leninist anti-state. Because the dictatorship of the proletariat goes through the process of dissolution and transcendence, it is realised only as the anti-state. To stick to Lenin's dialectical remarks it is a state which is not a state, a machine which is not a machine.[88] As the Soviets of Workers' and Soldiers' Deputies, Lenin's "crowd of civilised people" displaces the state machine altogether.[89] The need for government consequently disappears.[90] One forgets the old language of administrative reason and learns a very different type of language:

> We would therefore propose to replace the state everywhere by *Gemeinwesen*, a good old German word which can very well convey the meaning of the French word commune.[91]

One has to insist that the commune "was no longer a state in the proper sense of the word."[92] Now what we get is a distinct relation between Marx's communist polis as *Gattungswesen* (species being) and Engels's *Gemeinwesen.* Both indicate the spaces of the "commons" that the proletariat consciously creates by seizing the means of production from the bourgeoisie and distributing it according to the principle of "each according to one's abilities to each according to one's labour, needs and enjoyment". And that is why one insists that Lenin's "proletarian state" is strictly anti-state. The proletariat in realising its very essence becomes immediately humanist, humanist in the very scientific sense that the human is opposed to things and spectres (commodity, money, capital and the state). This new state of affairs is the state of authenticity, the state of humanity as humanity, recalling the young Marx's conception of the state of the "Rights of Humanity" which is simply the state of human nature itself.[93] And just as the real human community is not the community of commodity owners, it has to be understood that this real human community is the community of human nature.[94]

From this new language that we have learnt, it must be emphasised that one cannot operate with the worn-out language of "old politics". One needs to transcend this language of the liberals and the orthodox leftists, by questioning the debates of multiparty vs. single party political systems. In this sense not only is the language of "so-called socialism" questioned, but one also questions the critical Marxist texts like Lukács' *The Process of Democratisation.* One has to emphasise this point because even certain types of critical Marxists forget that the state (whether liberal or authoritarian) as defecation intervenes only when the masses "could not represent themselves", to borrow Marx's celebrated phrase, in order that "they must be represented."[95] Both the orthodox and the critical Marxists forget that this representation (i. e, the state as representing the "people") is a duplicate and counterfeit representation. One has to state that the state (whether liberal or authoritarian) is the psychotic criminal appearing as the father figure, and thus becomes the above stated defecation: dirty "matter in the wrong place"[96], only when the masses are dominated by the alienation inherent in capitalism and the reification consciously created by bourgeois democracy.

And so if capitalism creates alienation, and if the state produces this psychotic filth, the Leninist party is involved in a different type of production: (1) of communist consciousness and revolutionary desire, and (2) the consequently alteration of people (*Veränderung des Menschen*), a process that is necessary (*nötig*) and directly related to the question of human needs.[97] Necessity (the necessity of communism) is understood as a "living life", not the blind, anarchic and fatalistic conceptions of necessity practised by the parliamentary leftists, most certainly not the necessity that is born from what Lenin calls, "the lifeless bones of a skeleton."[98] Necessity becomes a radical contingency and a radical need bound to human freedom.

We learn from Marx that this search for freedom is the driving force of revolutions and that the manifestos of freedom have to continuously written and rewritten. Meanwhile one sees instead of substituting the state with the union of free people and instead of abolishing the parliament with free humanity, the three deplorable characters—the monk, Don Juan and the philistine—marching back onto the scene of left politics in India.

And here one does not hear the discourses on imperialism, wars and the human condition, not even on the idealist type of philosophy that Gorky wanted with Lenin. With the march-past of these three deplorable characters one hears only silence.

Meanwhile Lenin's laughter is heard once again. Are the comrades listening?

REFERENCES

1. Karl Marx, 'A Contribution to the Critique of Hegel's Philosophy of Right. Introduction' in *Marx. Engels. Collected Works*, Vol. 3 (Moscow: Progress Publishers, 1975).
2. V.I. Lenin, 'State and Revolution' in *Lenin. Selected Works* (Moscow: Progress Publishers, 1977).
3. Clara Zetkin, 'My Recollections of Lenin', in V.I. Lenin, *On the Emancipation of Women* (Moscow: Progress Publishers, 1985).
4. V.I. Lenin, 'State and Revolution', in *Lenin. Selected Works* (Moscow: Progress Publishers, 1977), pp. 293-7.
5. Ibid., p. 292.
6. Karl Marx, 'First Draft of the Reply to V.I. Zasulich's Letter, 1881,' in *Marx. Engels. Selected Works in Three Volumes* (Moscow: Progress Publishers, 1977), p. 154.
7. Slavoj Žižek, *First Time as Tragedy, Then as Farce* (New Delhi: Navayana, 2009). pp. 75, 92, 95, 127.
8. V.I. Lenin, 'The Proletariat Revolution and the Renegade Kausky', in *V.I. Lenin. Selected Works in Three Volumes*, Vol. 3 (Moscow Progress Publishers, 1977), p. 69; Slavoj Žižek op.cit., p. 125.
9. Karl Marx, *Economic and Philosophic Manuscripts of 1844* (Moscow: Progress Publishers, 1982), p. 69.
10. Slavoj Žižek, *The Ticklish Subject* (London: Virso, 1990), p. 139.
11. Karl Marx, *Economic and Philosophic Manuscripts of 1844*, pp. 66, 84.
12. V.I. Lenin, *Philosophical Notebooks. Collected Works*, Vol. 38 (Moscow: Progress Publishers, 1980), p. 141.
13. V.I. Lenin, *What is to be Done?* (Moscow: Progress Publishers, 1978), p. 53.
14. Karl Marx, 'Nationalökanomie und Philosophie (1844)', in *Die Frühschriften* (Berlin: Alfred Kröner Verlag, 1964), p. 235.
15. Slavoj Žižek, *First Time as Tragedy, Then as Farce*, p. 96..
16. Antonio Gramsci, *Selection from the Prison Notebooks* edited and translated by Quinton Hoare and Geoffrey Nowell Smith (New York: International Publishers, 1987), p. 336.

17. Ibid., p. 337.
18. Karl Marx, *Economic and Philosophic Manuscriptes of 1844*, p. 99.
19. Georg Lukács, *Lenin, A Study of the Unity of his Thought*, trans, Nicholas Jacobs (Cambridge: The MIT Press, 1974), pp. 9-13.
20. Karl Marx, 'A Contribution of the Critique of Hegel's Philosophy of Right. Introduction', in *Marx. Engels. Collected Works*, Vol. 3 (Moscow: Progress Publishers, 1975), p. 182.
21. Karl Marx, *Capital*, Vol. I (Moscow: Progress Publishers, 1983), p. 703.
22. V.I. Lenin, *Materialism and Empiro-Criticism* (Moscow: Progress Publishers, 1975), p. 320.
23. Karl Marx, *Economic and Philosophic Manuscripts of 1844*, p. 127.
24. V.I. Lenin, op.cit., p. 320.
25. Karl Marx, 'A Contribution to the Critique of Hegel's Philosophy of Right. Introduction', p. 180.
26. Ibid.
27. Ibid., p. 181.
28. Karl Marx and Fredrick Engels, 'Manifesto of the Communist Party', in *Marx. Engels. Selected Works* (Moscow: Progress Publishers, 1977), p. 58.
29. Ibid.
30. Karl Marx, *Economic and Philosophic Manuscripts*, p. 98; Karl Marx and Frederick Engels, 'Theses on Feuerbach', in *Marx. Engels. Selected Works*, p. 34.
31. Karl Korsch, *Marxism and Philosophy*, trans. Fred Holliday (New York: Monthly Review Press, 1970), p. 52.
32. Louis Althusser, *For Marx*, trans. Ben Brewster (London: Allen Lane, 1969), p. 45.
33. Ibid., p. 82.
34. Karl Marx, 'Difference between the Democritean and Epicurean Philosophy of Nature', In *Marx. Engels. Collected Works*, Vol. 1 (Moscow: Progress Publishers, 1975), p. 85.
35. Ibid.
36. Ibid.
37. Ibid., p. 86.
38. V.I. Lenin, *What is to be Done?*, p. 25.
39. Paul Sweezy, *Post-Revolutionary Society* (Kharagpur: Cornerstone Publications, 2000), pp. 42-3.
40. Karl Marx, 'Critical Marginal Notes on an Article by a Prussian', in *Marx. Engels. Collected Works*, Vol. 3 (Moscow: Progress Publishers, 1975), pp. 204-25.
41. Ibid., p. 204.
42. Karl Marx, 'The Leading Article in No. 179 of the *Kölnische Zeitung*',

in *Marx. Engels. Collected Works*, Vol. I (Moscow: Progress Publishers, 1975), p. 199.

43. Ibid.
44. Ibid., p. 191.
45. Ibid.
46. Ibid., p. 192.
47. Ibid.
48. Karl Marx, 'Critical Marginal Notes on an Article by a Prussian', p. 202.
49. Ibid., p. 205.
50. Karl Marx, *Economic and Philosophic Manuscripts of 1844*, p. 94.
51. Karl Korsch, 'Leninism and the Comintern', in Douglas Kellner (ed.), *Karl Korsch: Revolutionary Theory* (London: University of Texas Press, 1977), p. 152.
52. See the chapter 'The Crises of the Left' by Prabhat Patnaik.
53. Karl Korsch, *Marxism and Philosophy*, pp. 53-6; 'The Crises of Marxism' in *Karl Korsch: Revolutionary Theory*.
54. Raya Dunayesskaya, *Rosa Luxemburg, Women's Liberation and Marx's Philosophy of Revolution* (Urbana and Chicago: University of Illinors Press, 1991); *The Power of Negativity: Selected Writings on the Dialictic of Hegel and Marx*, ed., Peter Hudis and Kevin Anderson (Maryland: Lexington Books, 2002).
55. Kevin Anderson, *Lenin, Hegel and Western Marxism, A Critical Study* (Urbana and Chicago: University of Illonois Press, 1995).
56. Karl Marx and Frederick Engels, *The German Ideology*, pp. 36-7.
57. Karl Marx, *Economic and Philosophic Manuscripts of 1844*, p. 93.
58. Ibid.
59. Ibid.
60. G.W.F. Hegel, *The Phenomenology of Mind*, trans. J.B. Baillie (London: George Allen & Unwin, 1966), pp. 220, 225.
61. V.I. Lenin, 'Eighth Congress of the RCP(B), March 18-23, 1919', in *Lenin. Selected Works in Three Volumes* (Moscow: Progress Publishers, 1977), p. 119.
62. V.I. Lenin, *What is to be Done?*, pp. 69, 79, 81, 82, 85-7, 96, 125-6, 172.
63. Slavoj Žižek, *The Ticklish Subject*, p. 140.
64. Karl Marx and Frederick Engels, *The German Ideology*, p. 36.
65. Ibid., p. 34.
66. Ibid., p. 61.
67. Ibid.
68. Slavoj Žižek, *First as Tragedy, Then as Farce*, p. 107.
69. Karl Marx and Frederick Engels, op.cit., p. 61.
70. Ibid., p. 65.

71. Karl Marx, *Das Kapital*, Erster Band (Berlin: Dutz Verlag, 1981), p. 88.
72. Slavoj Žižek, *The Sublime Object of Ideology* (London: Verso, 1989), p. 29.
73. Ibid.
74. Karl Marx, *Economic and Philosophic Manuscripts of 1844*, pp. 135-6.
75. Ibid., p. 136.
76. Ibid., pp. 96, 111, 136.
77. Ibid., p. 120.
78. Sigmund Freud, 'Character and Anal Eroticism'; in *The Penguin Freud Library, Vol. 7. On Sexuality* (London: Penguin Books, 1991), p. 213.
79. Ibid.
80. Ibid.
81. Ibid.
82. Karl Marx, 'The Leading Article in No. 179 of the *Kölnische Zeitung*', pp. 192-3.
83. Ibid., p. 193.
84. Theodor Adorno, 'To Walter Berjamin, London, March 18, 1936', in Fredric Jameson (ed.), *Aesthetics and Politics* (London: New Left Books, 1977), p. 122.
85. V.I. Lenin, 'State and Revolution', p. 320.
86. Karl Marx, *Capital*, Vol. I, p. 82.
87. V.I. Lenin, op.cit.
88. Ibid., p. 326.
89. Ibid.
90. Ibid., p. 334.
91. Frederick Engels, 'To Bebel, March 18-25, 1875', in *Marx. Engels. Selected Works*, p. 335.
92. Ibid.
93. Karl Marx, 'The Leading Article in No. 179 of the *Kölnische Zeitung*'; p. 199.
94. Karl Marx, 'Critical Marginal Notes on an Article by a Prussian,' p. 205.
95. Karl Marx, 'The Eighteenth Brumaire of Louis Bonaparte', in *Marx. Engels. Selected Works*, p. 171.
96. Sigmund Freud, op.cit., p. 213.
97. Karl Marx and Frederick Engels, *The German Ideology*, p. 60; Karl Marx, *Economic and Philosophic Manuscripts of 1844*, p. 90.
98. V.I. Lenin, *Philosophical Notebookes*, p. 89.

26

Theological Marxism

Arun Patnaik

As I read Murzban Jal's 'Leninism as Radical' 'Desireology', I am reminded of Hal Draper's remarks on Marxists who usually forget that the standards of scrutiny they apply in judging liberalism and capitalism ought to be applied to Marx's own ideas. Draper, being a Marxist himself, implies how Marxists offer a split methodological discourse and advises us instead to follow Paul Sweezy's uniform methodological guideline. Sweezy argued that just as Marxism tries to distinguish between the essence and non-essence of liberal philosophies, so also non-Marxists may follow the same methodological criterion while dealing with Marx. By implication, what Sweezy recommends for non-Marxists must apply to Marxists while evaluating Marx's own ideas. Marxism must not indulge in self-love and must not claim that Marx is always right. Marxism must subordinate itself to world history as well as specific history or what Lenin calls "the concrete analysis of the concrete situation". Historical materialism today must move beyond Marx. That is indeed the spirit of the adjective: historical. Otherwise, it would not remain historical or materialistic as I shall show below.

If Murzban Jal or the Communist Parties were to identify themselves with the spirit of Marx's method, not simply parrot his slogans or concepts (such as "the task, however, is to change the world" or theory of transcendence of the state, etc), then they ought to be doing the following things as advised by Marx in the above passage.

First, try to identify with real struggles of people. Second, never advise people to cease their struggles or call such struggles foolish just because they do not match with a pre-existing set of principles. Never ask struggles to "kneel down" before the communists in a doctrinaire way. Third, communists should not lay claim to any "true slogan of struggle", for the real struggles of real people and their principles are true starting points for a Marxist. Fourth, the communist must not collapse into a romantic rebel but must carry out a criticism of popular struggles, if necessary. But any such criticism must not lead a communist to throw popular struggles overboard. However, communists followed the last principle rather than the first three principles of Marx. Communists are out to teach the world, without ever learning from it or identifying with its struggles. As a result, the world today refuses to learn from them.

Teach and Learn

Instead of asking communists to kneel down before the world, Jal asks them to bow down before Marx, whereas poor Marx asks his comrades not to impose themselves on the world and moreover urged them to learn from it, while teaching the world. Jal offers us a critique of communists in terms of their theological belief in Marx: Marx is always right. His advice to our comrades is contrary to Marx's own advice to his own comrades. Nowhere does Jal talk about the crisis of communism in terms of its refusal to identify with people's struggles against capitalism in many forms and organisations other than those already identified by communists themselves. This is a more serious problem in communist circles: a doctrinaire attitude as Marx characterises it. The communists' imposition of what they think is the "true slogan of struggle" on people's struggles is a major problem not even identified by Jal's philosophical sophistry. Similarly, he does not tell us that the communists ought to learn from people's struggles rather than look up to Marx or Lenin.

Jal misses Marx's methodological advice to his comrades that they must have a dialectical relation with the world at any point of time and as a result of this, he falls for Marx's slogans and principles and produces a theological reading. Jal does not advise comrades that they ought to discover the world's own principles in people's struggles rather than parrot Marx's own discoveries in the 19th century. As Louis Althusser noted, there are many new movements like women's movements and ecology movements in our times. We can add to the growing list: national movements, Dalit movements, adivasi movements, anti-nuclear movements and anti-displacement movements. In the neoliberal era, such movements tend to grow. It necessarily involves the transcendence (affirmation, negation and overcoming) of Marx's principles as outlined by him more than a century ago. Paul Sweezy's advice to non-Marxists must be carried out by Marxists themselves with respect to Marx. So a question needs to be asked: What is the essence of Marx that needs to be distinguished from the non-essence from the point of view of present-day struggles? People's struggles are the foci of Marx's "new materialism" or what Engels calls historical materialism. This method needs to be applied to Marx's critique of political economy. Without this procedure, any reading—pro-Marx or anti-Marx—would remain trapped within a Biblical spirit. A true communist must act like Marx rather than imitate him. He/she ought to *identify, learn, never impose,* and *educate* people's struggles for a better world.

Marx's 'Deficits'

What constituent in Marx's critique of political economy must be transcended in the 21st century? There are quite a lot of deficits in Marx. His theory of the state is very weak. This needs to be improved upon. His simplistic theory of withering away of institutions (including the family/state) cannot be rehashed as Jal proposes. Today, people's struggles focus on the transformation of the state rather than its abrupt or gradual abolition (=withering away). The central feature of all movements is to reconstruct the nature of the state, expand its networks, promote autonomy of subaltern classes or communities, work for the expansion of their autonomy and so on which the neoliberal state dreads to offer. Withering away of the state is not even a daydream option as was, no doubt, the case in the 19th century. A rethinking of the old Marxian principles is necessary today.

Marx's dualities in conceiving civil society need a relook. Sometimes, he confuses civil society with a general society. Sometimes, he flattens it with capitalist economy, a point well made by Gramsci in disagreement with Marx. His theory of property-based exploitation needs to be expanded to incorporate non-property-based oppression/suppression as Foucault and Gramsci point out. His definition of class in terms of ownership of the means of production needs to be expanded to add "control over the distribution of the surplus" as Cem Somel highlights. His simplistic conception of division of labour that we can do whatever we desire to do from morning to post-dinner needs to be relooked at as pointed out by many Marx sympathisers. As stated by S. Timpanaro, his conception of praxis as progressive, optimistic and transcendental needs to be re-examined. There could be room for pessimism in human nature. Certain painful material realities like death, natural disasters, animalist desires of human beings, etc, cannot be transcended. A socialist praxis must aim to engage with these aspects rather than wish them away or suppress them. By not recognising these aspects, Marx's praxis retains idealistic residues. Therefore, there are limits to transcendental praxis. Similarly, Marx's attitude towards human rights is slippery, even though he talks about "rights of humanity" as stated by Jal. It is not clear if such rights of humanity, in communist society, may arise against the state or civil society or nature. There is thus no theory of human rights possible in Marx, as the state, civil society and antagonism with nature wither away in the communist phase of history. Thus, a Marxist theory of human rights today is very opportunistic. Marxism does not believe in human rights and yet the human rights movement is a cover for Marxist expansionism, a point made by K. Balagopal very forcefully.

Last but not the least, let us not forget Marx's hostile/condescending attitudes towards all his contemporaries, like, for example, his view of J.S. Mill's liberal socialism. While his attitude towards past thinkers is dialectical (critical appreciation), he did not adopt such a position when he critiqued his contemporaries. Communists share the same attitude towards anything other than themselves, leading thus to a greater fragmentation of the communist movement once they notice a communist dissident. Communists display a very illiberal attitude towards inner party democracy or inter-party democracy. This has pushed them to an irrelevant corner of history. But this illiberalism is inherited from Marx and Lenin. If the communist movement has to be relevant today, it must rethink all this and must remain open to a sympathetic critique rather than latch on to a "tailist" sympathiser who may only have a corrupting influence over the social movements.

A 21st Century Marx

We cannot give up Marx today nor can we own him fully. As we live in new times and new contexts, we need to transcend the limits set by him. We must pose the old questions raised by Marx's "mode of production" perspective, new materialism, dialectical thinking, and so on; however, we must ask such questions in a new format. We may also discover new insights in his works about domestic labour as part social and part natural but an initial form of the division of labour. We may learn new insights from his penchant critique of capitalism for destroying nature and animal freedom, not just human freedom. Marxism-Leninism blinded us for a long time in the above matters. However, we must ask new questions too, those not raised by Marx. Also, we must not hesitate to overcome the illiberal barriers created by Marx for his failure to live up to the expectations of his own dialectical and materialist theory as discussed above. For, we acutely realise his deficits now comparison with the 19th century context. As Marx said, every generation can only ask those questions that it can seek to solve. May be our generation is better placed to ask these questions today. I am afraid, by suppressing all these insights or questions on Marx offered by many Marxists or socialist sympathisers today, Jal reinforces a theological attitude among comrades, even though he is rightly critical of them for their parliamentary cretinism or adventurism.

27

Anti-Marxism as Putrefied Theology

Murzban Jal

For the last two decades ever since the collapse of Stalinist state capitalism in Eastern Europe and with the heralding of Western capitalism characterised by the works of Fukuyama and the celebration of messianic capitalism, there has also been euphoria by certain intellectuals that Marxism is dead. Arun Patnaik follows this line of thought, one that is also reminiscent of the language of the cold war intellectuals. His claim that one must move beyond Marx, possibly to the discourses of Foucault, also suggests a subtle censorship, since he does not suggest that Foucault was the same scholar who celebrated Ayatollah Khomeini's coming to power. One must also mention his suggestion that Marx was a sort of fanatic was also claimed by E.H. Carr, who as we know, kept his historical scholarship for the service to the British Empire. And, that it was J. Edgar Hoover (the founder of the Federal Bureau of Investigation and the hunter of communists in the US) who also used the same paradigm of operation. It is not my case that Marx and Marxism ought not to go under the hammer of ruthless criticism. It is my case that a sort of censorship operates in the type of criticism. This chapter seeks to uncover the censorship mechanism. One knows that it was Freud in his *Interpretation of Dreams* who used this understanding of censorship mechanism to uncover the latent content of the unconscious. Let us try to see the latent content of Patnaik's criticism of Marxism.

One however begins with some sort of irony. While there has been resurrection of Lenin studies in the Western world (especially by Žižek, Lars Lih and Paul le Blanc) there has also been an almost impasse in the studies on Leninism in India. What we know as "Leninism" is what Charu Mazumdar in his anarchist rejection of the Established Left imprinted on the imagination of the Radical Left. Or a softer version of "Leninism" is what the CPI(M) proclaimed in subtitles to differentiate itself from the then pro-Congress CPI. Our understanding of Leninism is totally distinct from these two versions. It of course has nothing to do with Stalin's manipulation of Lenin's ideas. It deals with the historical evolution of Lenin's thought, keeping in mind Marx's theory of alienation and class struggle and the transcendence of both these. It is here that Lenin's theory of party comes in.

Marx's Supposed Deficits

We begin with the criticism of Marx offered by Patnaik. Recall the old criticism which chastised Marx as a fanatic who wanted to change the world with brutal force. Recall that it was not only the voice of J. Edgar Hoover and the anti-communist faction of the Culture Industry that spoke these words, but also that of the scholar E.H. Carr. Remember how Carr, the scholar par excellence, the historian who wrote volumes on the Russian Revolution, had titled his biography on Marx *Karl Marx: A Study in Fanaticism* (1934). Now we see the new critic, the critic as liberal, ecologist, anti-nuclear activist, feminist, nationalist, besides a whole lot of things never ever imagined. What does this new critic say? The new critic says that, since capitalism has changed since the days of Marx, Marxism is outdated. And what is the innermost detail that he has understood? He has understood that by "historical" (in the term "historical materialism") is meant that one "must move beyond Marx."

We also learn that there is a "spirit" of Marxism. And this spirit whispers in the ears of the new critic, "move beyond Marx!" Once upon a time Hamlet confronted the spirit of his dead father. Now the new critic confronts directly the spirit of Marx. The new critic then quotes Draper, Sweezy and Althusser, all out of context, to prove how one must move beyond Marx.

We will see how these great insights are achieved, not after reading the Marxist classics, but after listening to the spirit of Marx. Patnaik has direct access to Marx's spirit. We see that after conversing with Marx's spirit, followed by the chasing away of this very same spirit, the arrival of another spirit, the spirit of Lenin. Marx's spirit asked the new critic to move beyond him. Now Lenin's spirit says: have "concrete analysis for concrete conditions". And what do these concrete conditions say? They say that one cannot talk of changing the world or transcending the state. One cannot transcend the state, but one must transcend Marx. For purposes of authenticity, our critic says that of all the people Sweezy is supposed to have said that. If Althusser is supposed to have whispered in the new critic's ears that one must be a feminist and ecologist, then Sweezy is supposed to have said that one must transcend Marx. If we learn these principles from our critic, the communists will be able to come out from the "Biblical spirit" that they are caught up in.

So let us exorcise the evil Biblical spirit and see what our feminist, ecologist, nationalist, has to say about the deficits of Marx. There are, so we read, "quite a lot of deficits in Marx". "His theory of the state is very weak". Marx was very "simplistic". He talked of the withering of the state which must be defended at all cost. Instead Patnaik (after understanding what the term "historical" in "historical materialism" means) says that one must "reconstruct the nature of the state, expand its networks...". What does this mean? Expand the networks of the state, the state that is above all classes that works for the fictitious public good? Again what can it really mean? Expand the networks of the armed forces in Kashmir and the north-east, expand the network of the Salwa Judum, expand the secret NATO forces working in South Asia?

Besides Marx's alleged faulty theory of the "withering away of the state" (Marx never said it, Engels did) we are now told that the relation between the state and civil society was also faulty. Marx did not know what civil society meant. He "sometimes confuses civil society with general society. Sometimes", so we hear, "he flattens it with capitalist economy, a point well made by Gramsci in disagreement with Marx."

Marx should not have flattened civil society. Maybe because he did it Anna Hazare is out to overthrow the Indian state. Marx flattened civil society. Anna Hazare flattens the Indian state.

Besides not understanding both civil society and the state, Marx also had a "simplistic conception of division of labour that we can do whatever we desire to do from morning to post-dinner." What! How dare one simplify division of labour? And how dare one desire to do whatever from morning to post-dinner? Besides studying desires from morning to post-dinner, our liberal has found more deficits. Marx did not understand "pessimism in human nature." He did not study "painful material realities like death, natural disasters, animalistic desires of human beings (which) cannot be transcended."

We learnt earlier that the state cannot be transcended. Now we learn that pessimism, natural disasters and animalistic desires cannot be transcended. But wait again! Patnaik does not like desires from morning to post-dinner, desires the theologian Marx promoted. What is the essence of the new discipline discovered by Patnaik, the new discipline called "Theological Marxism"? The essence of Theological Marxism is that it sees Marx as promoting animalistic desires. Maybe the main problem with Marx's theory of the state and civil society is that there is too much pessimism, natural disasters and animalistic desires. We cannot transcend the state, because we cannot transcend the state of animals! We can put this in syllogistic form:

> Animals have states (the state of animalistic desire).
> Human beings are animals.
> Therefore they too necessarily have a state that cannot be transcended or which cannot "wither away".

We go further. "By not recognising these aspects, Marx's praxis retains idealistic residues. Therefore there are limits to transcendental praxis." What do we learn from this? We learn that Marx's praxis was transcendental because he wanted to transcend the state and flatten civil society, but not transcend "animalistic desires" which he advocated from morning to night and beyond. And because Marx studied this beyond, he was both transcendental and a theologian. And besides being a transcendental theologian, Marx was also against human rights. Yes, so our liberal claims, Marx did talk of "rights of humanity", but he did not understand whether they "arise against civil society, the state or nature." "Thus, a Marxist theory of human rights is very opportunistic. Marx did not believe in human rights and yet the human rights movement is a cover for Marxist expansionism." We knew that Marx was illiberal, a transcendental theologian. Now we learn that he was an opportunist and imperialist expansionist.

Marx's Purported 'Illiberalism'

After learning of all these deficits we learn how hostile/ condescending he was to his contemporaries like J.S. Mill. And because Marx was hostile with everyone (especially with Mill) the "communists share the same attitude towards anything other than themselves, leading thus to a greater fragmentation of the communist movement once they notice a communist dissident." And because Marx did not like Mill, he did not like liberalism: "Communists display a very illiberal attitude towards inner party democracy or inter-party democracy." "This illiberalism is inherited from Marx to Lenin...Marxism-Leninism blinded us for a long time in the above matters."

To articulate Patnaik's criticism of Marxism let us digress to Carr's version of Marx to understand how Patnaik repeats all the old points. Now it is well known that Carr was not only the celebrated "historian" who wrote volumes on the Bolshevik Revolution, but also wrote Marx's biography in the times of the Stalinist counterrevolution. Carr, like both the Stalinists and the critics of Marxism, did not distinguish Marxism and the revolutionary legacy (that went from Marx and Engels to Plekhanov, Lenin, Luxemburg and Trotsky, to Gramsci and Lukács) from Stalinism. What appears in Carr's biography is Marx appearing as a "genius of destruction."[1] We are also told that Marx was not a great philosopher, economist, nor a leader of people, or had any love for humanity.[2] Yet Carr considered himself "a better Marxist than the Marxists themselves."[3] Patnaik is caught up in the same tradition. He wants to be a liberal and does not know what to do with Marx. He cannot totally disown him. He wants to be a liberal and does not want to face the consequences of liberalism. After all, Gaza and Guantanamo Bay, Afghanistan and Iraq, are projects of liberalism. They are not fascist ones. It is this confusion that haunts the liberal.

Yet the critic of Marx follows the same tradition that Western liberalism and Stalinism institutionalised, namely the continuity between Marx and the Stalinist counterrevolution. Remember that Stalin's coming to power was over the dead bodies of not only Trotsky, Bukharin, Zinoveiv, Kamanev, Rykov, but the entire Bolshevik central committee at the time of the 1917 revolution, not to forget countless Marxist revolutionaries. Stalin killed more Marxists than any other counterrevolutionary. Patnaik forgets this. He forgets that I talked of the shadow of this counterrevolution hovering over us even now. He forgets that I talked of Marxism as dialectical and historical-humanist materialism, and not the fatalistic and bland version of "historical materialism" where anything, and everything can be fitted in: from Stalin to Fukuyama. He forgets that I mention Marxism as "human natural science", where this humanity, the humanity of the here and the now, defines history in general and revolution in particular. He also forgets that I have said that it is this humanity and this human natural science that defines the understanding of the problems of spontaneity, vanguardism, the place of the communist will, the problems of parliamentary politics, etc.

For a Marxist Libertarianism

He forgets that I am talking of philosophy (to be specific, Marxist philosophy), that philosophy has a definite rigour, and that philosophical arguments cannot be substituted by anti-communist rhetoric. He forgets that I talked of the masses as recovering their human essence. He forgets that it is in this *radical recovery* that the same humanised masses become the weapons (*Waffen*) and force (*Gewalte*) of democratic movements. He refuses to talk of the various renderings of Leninism from Trotsky and Lukács to Kevin Anderson and Žižek that I mentioned in my chapter. His ideological horizons are determined by Stalin's manipulation of Leninism and liberal cold war rhetoric. And since he forgets what Revolutionary Marxism as New Humanism means, we will have to remind him. We remind him by recalling Fromm's reading of the revolutionary legacy that Western liberalism has so far manipulated:

> The general habit of considering Stalinism and present-day Communism as identical with, or, at least a continuation of revolutionary Marxism has also led to an increasing misunderstanding of the personalities of great revolutionary figures: Marx, Engels, Lenin and Trotsky. Just as their theories are seen as related to those of Stalin and Khrushchev, the picture of the "revolutionary fanatic" is applied to them as it is applied to the vengeful killer Stalin, and to the opportunistic conservative Khrushchev. This distortion is a real loss for the present and the future. In whatever way one may disagree with Marx, Engels, Lenin, Trotsky, there can be no doubt that as persons they represent a flowering of Western humanity.[4]

While there is the distortion of Marxism (mostly by the Stalinists), it is imperative to argue for a Marxist-libertarianism, where political freedom and human rights are placed at the centre of Marxism. That is why I talk of Marxism as anti-state and Marxist politics based on the idea of communism as humanism and naturalism (a form of "direct communism") and Lenin's praxis of insurrection as art. And that is why we insist that we offer another perspective for radical politics that transcends both liberalism as well as the politics offered by the organised left led by the CPI(M). But then we also offer an alternative that is distinct from the politics of the Trotskyists and the Maoists too.

REFERENCES

1. E.H. Carr, *Karl Marx: A Study in Fanaticism* (London: J.M.Dent & Sons, 1934), p. 301.
2. Ibid., p. 300.
3. Ibid., p. VII.
4. Erich Fromm, 'Trotsky Diary in Exile', in *Science & Society*, Vol. 66, No. 2, Summer, 2002, pp. 271-72

28

An Act of Transgression

Arun Patnaik

I appreciate Murzban Jal's rejoinder ('Anti-Marxism as Putrefied Theology') to my response ('Theological Marxism') to his ('Leninism as Radical 'Desireology') on two counts, apart from setting a trend of healthy academic debate. First, he criticises me for what I know rather than what I do not know. This is the best part of his critique. Second, I also admire his critique as he has not greeted my response with a conspiracy of silence, usually seen in left-wing circles in India. But Jal accuses me for forgetting so many insights that are in his chapter. He forgets to note that I ended my response by appreciating Jal's attempt to criticise what he metaphorically calls "the monk, Don Juan and the philistine", in a veiled reference to three forms of Stalinism represented by the Communist Party of India (CPI), the Communist Party of India (Marxist) (CPI (M)) and the Communist Party of India (Marxist-Leninist Liberation) (CPI(ML)) organisations, respectively. Due to a paucity of "discussion space", I could not develop his ideas further. It remains so, for a potential critique of Indian Stalinism has not been developed by Jal; himself.

Transgression

I notice he tries to transcend liberal cold war psychology in his rejoinder but returns to it. I will give one illustration to support my argument. He criticises me for carrying the cold war psychology of liberals against Marx, forgetting altogether that I appreciate Marx's breakthrough for his mode of production perspective, rational dialectical method, praxis-oriented history/theory and sexual division of labour preceding class division of labour, an insight lost to us for long due to our obsession with "the monk or Don Juan or the philistine". He forgets to note that my criticism of Marx is informed by many developments within communist, socialist and ecological movements after Marx rather than pre-Marx liberalism. But, more importantly, he argues as if "you are not with Marx, you are against Marx". I need not repeat here that I am not with Marx for several reasons. Yet, I would like to reiterate Hal Draper's argument which has been ignored by Jal: echoing Sweezy, just as comrades dialectically examine non-Marxists, so also non-Marxists should examine Marx's contributions dialectically. But Draper adds the following: the followers of Marx should adopt a dialectical critique of Marx as well. Thus, instead of transcending cold war liberal psychology which is incidentally Leninist phraseology as well, Jal returns to adopt the same against the critiques of the trio: "the monk, Don Juan and the philistine". Sudipta Kaviraj elsewhere calls such tendency as transgression rather than transcendence.

Transgression takes place if a critic or an actor (like Bankim's Kamalakanta, for Kaviraj) intends to transcend an object/subject but returns to it in several forms without even knowing that such a strategy may smack of double standards in theory/practice. Such a transgressive moment is usually devoid of immanent criticism.

For, an author following a transgressive method does not tell us any internal strength or weaknesses of a theory or practice. Jal's critique does that. He does not tell us if there are any useful insights in my response which Jal may have to absorb and advise comrades to follow the same. That is why, following Kaviraj, I would like to call his critique an act of transgression. He intends to transcend, but fails to do so. His dialectical language is a mere mantra.

Therefore, I think Jal's chapter reinforces a theological spirit among the comrades in India: "Marx is always right". That is indeed a cause for deep worry as he seems to be an independent minded Marxist. I would not be surprised if our comrades refer to Jal's rejoinder as an exemplar of my anti-Marxism. Here, he adopts the dialectical ritual usually followed by the Indian Left. In the dialectic reasoning that Jal merely talks, there is no space for anti-Marxism or pro-Marxism phraseology. If you take either/or positions in dialectics, then you use dialectics as a ritual or mantra. Following dialectics, I would like to submit what Hal Draper says: do not reject Marx outright and do not accept Marx blindly. That is what Marx follows in the case of his predecessors, not contemporaries like J.S. Mill, a point made by Gerry Cohen. We need to adopt the same dialectical stance, while discussing his contributions as well. D.D. Kosambi made a similar point against Indian Leninism: it has substituted Marx's method for his formulations and it relies on his formulations as a mantra to browbeat enemies (i.e. OM which stands for "official Marxists" including independent Marxists like the Royists).

Towards an Expansive State

Last but not least, I would like to avoid a misunderstanding. I concede that Jal's polemic against my idea of expansion of the state is probably warranted as I offer no clarification in my defence. However, I would like to ask a question that Jal conveniently ignores: why in the neoliberal era, do political movements not talk about the "withering away of the state"? Does the old slogan of the communist movement have any potency for a new political movement challenging the neoliberal paradigm? I offer a "Yes answer", provided we understand the sense of Lenin before Leninism or Gramsci. The state withers away by expanding itself: the state, due to pressure from below, must expand so much that it overcomes/transcends its dual characteristics of both standing apart from and against civil society, as argued by Marx. This may happen, as Gramsci shows, only when the subaltern societies are absorbed within new civil society. For, the old civil society aided by the state excludes the subaltern societies. Also, this may happen when the state too is absorbed or what Gramsci calls the return of the state to the domain within civil society by expanding the latter. As and when the state becomes an expansive state (i.e. the state ++), the extreme state (state qua state) withers away. Both domination and separation of the state from civil/subaltern society need to be challenged by movements from below. That is what the new problematic of withering away of the state means. This is not same as the anti-state position which is popular among anarchists/Marxist radicals who would like to abolish state power abruptly (Bakunin) or gradually (Engels).

For, the new problematic of the withering away of the state assumes that the state may still retain its speciality of functions, but it does not stand in separation from civil society in order to dominate civil society on the one hand, and subaltern society on the other. Both Lenin and Gramsci thus expand Marx's ideas. So I submit that the expansion of the state must be viewed from the point of civil society and subaltern societies rather than from the point of the state itself. This is one of the original contributions (or revisions which Jal may not like to know) of Lenin before Leninism and Gramsci after Leninism. I reject the Leninist phraseology but accept Lenin predating the birth of Leninism for which Lenin himself is partly responsible. There is no point in simply passing the buck to Stalin and company. But this may involve another round of debate.

29

The Left in Decline

Prabhat Patnaik

Empiricisation or the pursuit of a political praxis that is uninformed by the project of transcending capitalism was ultimately responsible for the defeat of the CPI(M) in West Bengal. It is this empiricisation that is far more worrying than the election defeat itself. In a period when many have abandoned the concept of imperialism, the CPI(M) remains steadfast in its adherence to this concept; as long as the concept and the project remain valid, the historical relevance of the party remains unimpaired. But if the party does not arrest the process of empiricisation it has been experiencing and finally ends up accepting the hegemony of bourgeois theory, then it will get supplanted by some other communist formation subscribing to a theoretical position similar to what it has today.

It is ironical that the very process that has brought about the decline of the CPI(M) is being suggested by many as the panacea for its revival. I shall call this process which has caused the decline, a process of "empiricisation", by which I mean the pursuit of a political praxis that is uninformed by the project of transcending capitalism. Of course the ripening of a revolutionary situation occurs only sporadically. For long stretches of time therefore the political praxis to be pursued appears mundane and pedestrian, and constitutes what B.T. Ranadive used to call "the small change of politics". But even "the small change of politics" for a Communist Party must be informed by the project of transcending capitalism, and when this does not occur we have only "the small change of politics" per se, i.e. empiricisation. This process of empiricisation, which is ultimately responsible also for the election defeat in West Bengal, is far more worrying for any Left sympathiser than the election defeat itself, for an election defeat may well get reversed the next time around, but it is much more difficult to reverse a process of empiricisation. Since a necessary condition for a reversal of empiricisation is an awareness of its occurring, I shall concern myself here with a discussion of this process. This may also help to prevent further *deliberate* empiricisation in a desperate bid for rejuvenation.

1

What distinguishes a Communist Party is not that it does not "soil its hands" with mundane, empirical, everyday politics (that would be barren ultra-Leftism), but that its process of engagement even with politics at this level is imbricated by its project of transcending capitalism, informed by a consciousness of what Lukacs (1924) had called "the actuality of the revolution".[1] To be animated by the "actuality of the revolution" does not mean to believe that the revolution is around the corner; it only means that the engagement with the "small change of politics" is on the basis of a theory that spans the entire distance between *quotidienne* politics and the project of transcending capitalism. If this theory linking the "here and now" to the overall project of transcendence is absent from the praxis engaged in "here and now", then we have a process of empiricisation of the movement.

Four Tendencies Arising from Empiricisation

Such empiricisation in the context of our polity gives rise to at least four kinds of tendencies: first, it gives rise to the range of "sins" attributed to the party by its opponents, and even mentioned in the self-critical documents of the party itself as afflicting it at various levels, such as careerism, "satrapism", bureaucratism, and bossism at the local level. Second, it gives rise to a tendency to "adjust" to given situations to prevent losses, instead of carrying it forward as a part of revolutionary praxis. This in turn entails a process of alienation of the party from the "basic classes" that it is supposed to struggle for, viz. the workers, peasants, agricultural labourers, and the rural poor. The "party's interests" are seen in isolation from, and as being distinct from, the interests of the basic classes, and for the defence of the "party's interests" immediate, "here and now" measures are thought of and resorted to, which may well diverge from the interests of the basic classes. Third, empiricisation leads to a shrinking of the distance between the communist party and the other political formations.

All this has been visible for some time now, including especially in West Bengal where the alienation of the CPI(M) from the basic classes (especially the peasantry) led to its electoral defeat after 34 years of Left Front rule. But the fourth feature of empiricisation, a basic one, is that it tends to produce further empiricisation, giving rise to a dialectic. And if the process is allowed to continue unchecked, then it leads *eventually* to the party's being hegemonised by the ideology of capitalism, to its rejection of the concept of imperialism which underlay the original split in the Second International and the very formation of the communist movement, and to a virtual disappearance of the difference between the communists and other political formations. At that point, even if the communists (or whatever other name they choose to call themselves by, at that date) win elections and form governments on their own, it makes little substantive difference either to the project of transcendence of capitalism or even to the conditions of the basic classes.

Two caveats are in order here. First, the CPI(M), though launched on this process of empiricisation, is still far from any such dire scenario. Its empiricisation therefore must not be overstressed. The very fact that it pulled out its support from the United Progressive Alliance (UPA) government on the Indo-US Nuclear Deal, even though such pulling out damaged its "party interests" in an immediate sense, and evoked criticism even from its self-confessed well-wishers like Amartya Sen, shows paradoxically the degree to which it still remains free of empiricisation. The point is not whether it handled the entire episode of the nuclear deal well; it certainly did not. But the point is that on an issue which it perceived as being linked to imperialist hegemony over the country, it did not put any "party interest" above what it saw as the class interests of the "basic classes". This fact underscores the extent of its freedom from empiricisation. Likewise the fact that at this very moment, thousands of only cadres in West Bengal are facing the most severe repression for the "sin" of *remaining committed* to the cause that the party stands for, underscores the vitality of the party. The fact that this vitality has not been snapped as yet by going too far down the road of empiricisation.

Second, this process of empiricisation is, if anything, even more pronounced in the case of the other segments of the Left, especially those who claim to be to the left of the CPI(M). Some of them have even gone to the extent of joining the "anti-corruption" movement of Anna Hazare which epistemologically substitutes itself for "the people" (and does not just theoretically argue for positions which it perceives to be in the people's interests), without any mandate from the latter; and claims superiority over the body which does actually have, under the terms of the Constitution, mandate from the people, namely Parliament; and thereby undermines the democratic order to push to the forefront a "chosen few". (The Maoists no doubt are a separate category; but, chasing a will-o'-the-wisp in the jungles of central India, they have taken themselves, paradoxically, out of any mainstream anti-imperialist revolutionary project.)

2

The question that naturally arises is: why did such empiricisation occur in the ranks of the Left, and in particular of the CPI(M)? Some would argue that this is an inevitable outcome of parliamentary politics, but that is a complete non sequitur. Revolutionary politics, as Lenin always emphasised, thrives best when the revolutionary forces have complete freedom of operation, which is why bourgeois formations are forever trying to roll back the freedom of operation, that comes with parliamentary democracy, for the political formations that speak for "basic classes". The role of the Left therefore, far from shunning parliamentary democracy, must be both to participate in its institutions and to struggle for a deepening of their democratic content. This has been so much a part of Marxist understanding that no less a revolutionary than Rosa Luxemburg had actually wanted her party to participate in the parliamentary elections in Germany, and had not been in favour of the Spartacist uprising (though Karl Liebknecht had been); but she had been outvoted and had consequently led the uprising along with Liebknecht, in the course of which both were murdered.

To see empiricisation as the inevitable outcome of participating in parliamentary politics not only lacks theoretical validity, but represents a form of fetishism. Karl Marx in *Capital* had talked of "commodity fetishism", where social relations were perceived as relations between things, and the origin of surplus value was located in some mystical properties of the things constituting means of production. Here we have a situation where mystical powers are being attributed to parliamentary institutions *per* se.

Revisionist Theoretical Understanding

One obvious cause for such empiricisation that Marxist theory has always emphasised is of course the development of a revisionist theoretical understanding. The material basis of such a development has also been much discussed in Marxist literature, and has been typically located in the fact that a section of the working class becomes a beneficiary of the fruits of imperialist exploitation.

In Margarethe Von Trotta's 1986 film *Rosa Luxemburg* there is a telling scene that captures the tendency towards empiricisation. The entire social democratic leadership of Germany is sitting around a lunch table and Karl Kautsky tells Rosa Luxemburg, who was then engaged, along with Clara

Zelkin and Franz Mehring, in a struggle to uphold the revolutionary tradition of the party: "Rosa, Why don't you involve yourself more in the women's question?" The unspoken part of Kautsky's question obviously is: "Why do you bother about issues of imperialism and revolution?" We have here a double empiricisation: the "women's question" is sought to be empiricisd by being detached from the overall revolutionary movement, and an outstanding revolutionary is being asked to submerge herself in something that is so detached from the revolutionary movement.

But when there is no obvious change in the theoretical understanding of a party, and no obvious material basis, of the sort emphasised by Lenin and others (viz. the improved material condition of a section of the "basic classes" made possible through the "super-exploitation" of others), that could be adduced as causing such a change in theoretical understanding, then the phenomenon of empiricisation still remains to be explained. One circumstance that does induce such empiricisation is when the popular movement reaches a plateau, when it stagnates. Stagnation gives rise to the apprehension that there may be a slideback; to prevent such a slideback all sorts of temporary expedients are resorted to which mark the beginning of empiricisation, but such empiricisation contributes further to the stagnation of the movement, causing further resort to empiricisation, and thereby setting up, as mentioned earlier, a dialectic of empiricisation.

Such a dialectic is illustrated by a story about Czechoslovakia in 1968. During the "Prague Spring", when Alexander Dubcek's group was having discussions with the representatives of the Soviet Union (prior to Dubcek's removal by the Soviets), they pointed out that "Prague Spring" should not be blighted since it would have a remarkable impact on the Left movement in Western Europe. To this the Soviet representatives' reply was: "Don't talk nonsense, there is no possibility of any expansion of the Left in Western Europe!".'[2] Dubcek's removal certainly eliminated any residual possibility of an expansion of the Left in Western Europe. The process of empiricisation in the Soviet Union was itself a response to the stagnation of the Left in Western Europe, and it consisted in consolidating its hold on whatever it controlled in Eastern Europe without "risking" any "Prague Springs". But this served precisely to reinforce further the stagnation of the Left in Western Europe.

CPI(M)'s Situation

The CPI(M) has been in a somewhat similar situation. Its strength has remained confined to just a few regions of the country. In these regions too the base it has was created through struggles undertaken during the 1930s and the 1940s, and though there has been a subsequent expansion of this base (otherwise it would not have got the massive electoral support it did in the three states it ruled), that expansion has also reached a plateau. Its primary response to this stagnation has been to consolidate, the way it sees best, what it already has; and this fact itself has contributed to its stagnation. For instance, its attempt to pursue "industrialisation" in West Bengal in a bid to consolidate itself there by preventing possible middle class alienation from it, which it sees as essential in a context where the party is not growing elsewhere, has actually also stood in the way of the party's growth elsewhere. Its capacity to take up peasant struggles against land alienation, which is the principal issue of struggle all over the country at present, has been hamstrung by its loss of credibility because of incidents like Singur.

But while stagnation may tend to induce empiricisation, both stagnation and empiricisation cannot be dissociated from the broader international context within which the CPI(M) has had to operate. The collapse of the Soviet Union has dealt a massive blow to the socialist project; and even though the CPI(M), as a disciplined party, has not suffered in terms of an erosion in its ranks, the damage to the core of its inner convictions is undeniable. The natural tendency has been to repose faith in China despite all misgivings about the trajectory it is following; and the remarkable economic "success" of China has bolstered such faith. In the process, however, the party which once had the courage to take on ideologically both the

Soviet Union and China, because, respectively, of their Right and Left deviations, has been remarkably reticent in expressing any reservations *in public* (notwithstanding pervasive private reservations) about China's development *from a socialist perspective.* What is more, China's apparent "success" has created a *tendency* within the party for accepting economic policies, such as providing incentives to corporate capital in states where it is in power, which would have been anathema some years ago. *Indeed, within the overall context of the collapse of the Soviet Union, the most potent factor behind the empiricisation of the party has been the influence of the Chinese example.*

3

There has been an additional factor at work as well. And this relates to the fact that in communist literature, the question "what after land reforms?" has not received as satisfactory an answer as it requires. Lenin's classic formulation in *Two Tactics of Social Democracy* which had been written in the Russian context but had provided the theoretical foundation for communist practice in the 20th century in countries, where the bourgeoisie arrived late on the historical scene, ran as follows:

> The proletariat must carry the democratic revolution to completion, allying to itself the mass of the peasantry in order to crush the autocracy's resistance by force and paralyse the bourgeoisie's instability. The proletariat must accomplish the socialist revolution, allying to itself the mass of the semi-proletarian elements of the population, so as to crush the bourgeoisie's resistance by force and paralyse the instability of the peasantry and the petty bourgeoisie.

While the first part of the statement was clearly understood and implemented by Third World communist revolutionary movements, the transition from the first to the second, when it should occur, what should be the correlation of class forces to be aimed at, what in particular should be the attitude of the socialist revolution to the peasantry, remained vexed questions. From the episode of collectivisation in the Soviet Union (even if one accepts that there was no alternative to it at the time because of kulak resistance) to the Great Leap Forward in China (even if one believes that the problem with the Great Leap was not that it was conceptually wrong but that its timing turned out to be unfortunate), this second stage of the transition is where problems have arisen, derailing, in each instance, the entire socialist project.

What after Agrarian Reforms?

If this problem, of how do we follow up the initial breakthrough by way of carrying forward the democratic revolution through agrarian reforms, has vexed the communist revolutionary project, it has by no means been absent even in cases like India where the Left has led state governments within an overall bourgeois order. Since the proletariat proper, consisting of production workers in the modern sector of the economy, has typically been too small in such states, the slogan of industrialisation, even on the basis of reliance on large private corporate capital, has tended to gather momentum, and this in turn has given rise, at the conceptual level, to a "stage theory": let us follow up land reforms by developing capitalism first, and at the next stage we shall think of socialism.

A stage theory, however, is a direct theoretical expression of the process of empiricisation. This may appear odd at first sight: many would even consider the Marxist theory of history itself to be an example of "stage theory". But this is erroneous, since Marxism does not just describe "stages" or divide history into different stages corresponding to different modes of production but seeks to explain the dynamics of history, the transition, if at all, from one stage to another.[2]

More pertinently, it may be thought that the project of building capitalism does after all link the "here and now" to the revolution, since it is sustained by a perception of the revolution. But this is wrong: the building of capitalism requires a suppression of the basic classes, while the transcendence of capitalism requires an activation of the basic classes. The presumption behind a stage theory approach, if it is adopted by the communists therefore, is that at some point the very same party which presides over the suppression of the basic classes will suddenly and mysteriously start doing the exact opposite, and that the basic classes will follow it in either case, which is absurd. The party that presides over the building of capitalism will end up being no different from standard bourgeois parties; notwithstanding its lip service to the revolution therefore, building capitalism, like what any other bourgeois party tries to do, is an instance of empiricisation.

Forces Pushing Empiricisation

It follows that there are powerful forces in the current situation that push the Left towards empiricisation. The Left has to resist this push; it has to overcome empiricisation if the socialist project is to be carried forward. It must not only carry out struggles on the burning issues of the day wherever it can, undeterred by the empiricisation-dictated tactics of defending Left-led state governments whom such struggles may embarrass or threaten, but it must, even while running such state governments, ensure to the best of its ability that new ways are always innovated to advance the interests of the basic classes, to improve their material conditions so that their capacity to resist increases. All this is not easy, but the Left has to come to terms with this problem; and I believe, based on my reading of the Kerala LDF experience, that it is possible for the Left to come to terms with it.

4

What it must *not* do, however, is to pay heed to the friendly advice that is emanating from many quarters that it should get further empiricised in order to improve its position. There are two kinds of suggestions that have typically been advanced. The first states that the Left should become "social-democratic", by which presumably is meant a dropping of its concept of imperialism, and hence by inference, an acceptance of the view that a humane society, which does not oppress other countries and peoples, is compatible with capitalism. This first suggestion amounts in short to asking the Left to abandon its entire transformational project.

Abandon the Basic Classes?

Now, if imperialism as a category did not *actually* exist, and was a mere figment of the Left's imagination, the adherence to which was preventing the Left from fighting for the interests of the basic classes, then this advice would make eminent sense. But such advice is offered, not on the basis of any argument that imperialism does not exist, but on the grounds that the Left would "grow" if it abandoned such baggage. This is nothing else but empiricisation: it amounts to saying that to serve its own "party interests" the Left should abandon the interests of the basic classes it is supposed to represent, who are everywhere getting squeezed by the neoliberal policies imposed by international finance capital which constitutes the core of contemporary imperialism. This would amount in short to a self-obliterating act on the part of the Left *as Left*, no matter what electoral dividends it brings in its wake.

The second suggestion talks of an Indian Left outside of the large communist parties, which together with progressive civil society groups that are taking up particular local issues in various parts of the country, can constitute an "Indian New Left" that can carry forward popular movements. Some versions of it visualise the inclusion of communists other than the CPI(M) in such a coalition; others may be "generous" enough to include even the CPI(M) provided it drops some of its specific characteristics. Now, a common feature of virtually all such groups that are supposed to constitute the core of the so-called "Indian New Left" is that they do not accept the category of *imperialism*. They may recognise and be opposed to specific "imperialist" acts like the invasion of Iraq and Afghanistan, or the bombing of Libya, but they do not see imperialism as a structural characteristic of capitalism.

The *practical necessity* for the transcendence of capitalism has been argued over the last hundred years on the basis of this structural characteristic of capitalism. A theoretical abandonment of this concept, for which, I repeat, no argument has been advanced, is tantamount to an abandonment of the project of transcending capitalism. It entails being incorporated within the system, fighting no doubt on behalf of the people on specific issues, but leaving its overall structure intact. *It amounts, even in theory, to fighting merely for reforms within capitalism, and not for socialism.*

Question of Capitalism vs Socialism

It may of course be thought that socialism is a pie in the sky, while fighting for reforms is a concrete means for improving the conditions of the people. For instance a movement for the advancement of the Dalits, or for improving the condition of women can achieve much, without necessarily getting embroiled in questions of capitalism versus socialism. But this is an erroneous impression. Any improvement in the condition of rural women or any decisive blow against the caste system requires a breaking up of the old pre-capitalist "community". Capitalism historically had done precisely that in its metropolitan base and the socialist project entailed the coming into being of a new "community" that is voluntarily entered into and is based on the position of individuals, uprooted from their original habitats, in the new production process that comes into being. But capitalism in our country, notwithstanding its apparently vigorous development, is failing precisely to break the old "community" because of its incapacity to absorb the individuals uprooted from their traditional habitats into a new proletariat, thanks to the phenomenon of "jobless growth". This is the reason high growth rates coexist with khap panchayats; and as long as institutions like khap panchayats exist, the fetters upon the social advance of dalits or women will remain strong, which is why capitalism versus socialism remains as vital a question today as it ever was.[5]

Everybody, of course, is free to choose his or her political praxis and some may choose to be reformists without any project of transcending capitalism. But this, according to Marxist theory is erroneous praxis, not because one is ordained to desire socialism, but because no amount of fight for reforms can possibly make capitalism into a humane society, *a proposition whose invalidity to my mind has not yet been established.*

In a period when large numbers of people have abandoned the concept of imperialism, from "paid hirelings" of finance capital, to many Western Marxists, to "official" spokesmen in China, to even Third World intellectuals in countries like India, who willy-nilly are dazzled by the so-called high growth rates that have brought palpable benefits to the middle class, the

CPI(M) remains steadfast in its adherence to this concept and hence to the entire project of transcendence, intellectually built around it by Lenin and others. As long as the concept and the project remain valid, the historical relevance of the CPI(M) remains unimpaired. And if perchance the party does not arrest the process of empiricisation it has been experiencing, and finally ends up accepting the hegemony of bourgeois theory, then it will get supplanted by some other communist formation subscribing to a theoretical position similar to what it has today. But no coalition of *reformist* forces, no matter how well-meaning and serious, can possibly *replace* the communists as defenders of the interests of the basic classes. All this however does not preclude their working together on common issues.

REFERENCES

1. This was narrated by an exiled member of Dubcek's team at a meeting of the Tawney Group (of Left faculty members) in Cambridge, UK, in the early 1970s where I had been present.
2. For a critique of stage theory from a Marxist perspective, see the review of W.W. Rostow's book *The Stages of Economic Growth* by Baran and Hobsbawm (1961).
3. For an elaboration of this argument see my 'Globalisation and Social Progress', in *Social Scientist*, January–February, 2011.

30

'The Left in Decline': A Historical Perspective

Arup Baisya

In extending the argument of Prabhat Patnaik on the question of the decline of the Left (read CPI(M) and CPI), Hiren Gohain claims (see Chapter 33) that one fails to understand "why the familiar and clearer term 'revisionism' should not be used" instead of "empiricisation". In a brief discussion on Prabhat Patnaik's article, he wrote "the looming conclusion is that it has botched its parliamentary role allowing bourgeois forces to gain the upper hand..." He further remarks:

> Participation in parliamentary democracy has also meant seeking and holding power in the states. That has meant acceptance of central policies to some extent, acquiescence in the anti-people role of the police, and compromises with the bureaucracy. True, there has been some degree of power-sharing at lower levels, and the panchayats had a more popular character. But there too the party became an instrument of domination rather than service to the people. Lastly it succumbed to the capitalist paradigm of development with it present mantra of private sector-led ....largely jobless growth, and was hustled into adoption of anti-people policies, robbing the masses of their right to land, water and other natural resources.

He concludes by saying how otherwise one does explain the party's "alienation from the basic classes" without considering the change of class character of the party.

It is a good sign that critical arguments on Left rule in Indian states are pouring out from within the pro-Left (especially pro-CPI(M)) intellectual quarters after the fall of Left Front in West Bengal. But the argument needs to be extended further, and a brainstorming exercise should be undertaken on the question of "Left resurgence" based on the experience of not only Left rule in some parts of India but also on the worldwide experience of building socialism. Why should the CPI(M) not be considered a ruling class party? The answer to this question and that of the transformation of the official Indian Left requires one to delve into the history of Stalinism, the Comintern[1], and the communist movement in India.

Toeing the Stalinist Line

From such a perspective, we can broadly underline the turn of the events when the Indian communist movement, the legacy of which is borne by the CPI(M), sided with the forces of reaction. When Stalinist forced collectivisation of the peasantry had shattered the worker-peasant alliance and reversed the trend from socialism to bourgeois nation-building, pursuing military intervention in the name of exporting socialism, Soviet Russia was transformed into a social-imperialist power. The CPI(M) emulated the Russian path as the model for building socialism. The Leninist party in the Soviet Russia, which was well-entrenched amongst the working class as well as the radical intelligentsia, achieved the alliance with the peasantry through radical land reform. But radical land reform realised the Russian peasants' age-old dream of becoming landowners. The market forces thus released ended up producing growing differences within the peasantry. The Stalinist way of solving this problem did not advance the building of socialism. But parties like the CPI and the CPI(M), so infatuated with socialism in Russia, did not even notice that Maoist China had successfully addressed the "peasant question" through agrarian revolution instead of forced collectivisation and throttling the dissenting voices within the party. They toed the Russian line and served the Russian national goal of global expansion in the guise of "exporting communism" till the complete collapse of Soviet system and disintegration of Soviet Russia. Then these parties started to cite the success story of the Chinese model of "market socialism" when it became clear that the capitalist roaders gradually took control of the helm of affairs after the Cultural Revolution came to an unsuccessful end.

At the formative stage, most of the leaders and organisers of the Bengal Left came from that section of young men and women who flaunted the extreme nationalist views of the independence movement and engaged themselves in the extremist path of annihilating British magistrates and police officers with bombs and pistols. The political prisoners who were languishing in jail and had been converted to Marxism were released from jail for supporting the British war effort. Those who joined the Communist Party of India remained outside the jail during the Quit India Movement in 1942 and faced the people's hatred for betraying the cause of independence. However, the relentless and selfless service to famine-stricken people in the Bengal famine gave the communist leaders some credence.

The post-independence Left party in Bengal started further expanding its base due to the Left leanings of the refugee upper-caste, educated section who were sentimentally involved with the Hindu refugees in West Bengal. Most of these upper-caste youths came from Kulin zamindar families who earned their notoriety by being ruthless and oppressive vis-à-vis their Muslim and lower caste tenants in East Bengal. So those communist leaders were not organically linked with the working class who are predominantly comprised of the most oppressed castes and communities. But the displaced people had no other option but to embrace the Left who fought for their rights. The worldwide turbulent situation of the 1960s, the extension of support to the working class struggle, the resurgence of cultural and literary activities, and the participation of the Left in the food movement gave it overwhelming support from the Bengali masses. With this popular base, party apparatchiks emerged from above the working class and came to power in Bengal with a reformist agenda.

Comintern Hegemony

During the pre-independence, anti-imperialist struggle, the Indian Left—toeing the line of the Comintern—failed to emerge as a mass Communist Party and build a mass organisation based on the worker-peasant alliance. After the death of Lenin, and especially during the period of 1935-43, the Comintern became the instrument of Soviet foreign policy. When the revolutionary wave subsided and the hope for the revolution in Western Europe faded away, the national interest of the Soviet Union gradually started coming to the fore. The changing policy directives of the Indian Left were in keeping with the vicissitudes of the Comintern's character. In 1922, the demand for a comprehensive 'Programme of National Liberation and Reconstruction' in the name of CPI was raised at the Gaya Session of the Congress that received a message of solidarity from Comintern. Against the background of peasant repression in Chauri Chaura and the growing militancy of the peasantry, an Indian Left Manifesto, commonly known as Manilal Doctor's Manifesto, proposed the idea of a Labour and Kisan Party of India and advocated the abolition of the standing army, arming of the masses and the organisation of militias with a view to radicalise political life. This document, subsequently revised in various phases, had the following features, according to G. Adhikari: (1) it was an attempt to formulate a complete economic and political programme for national independence; (2) it urged the formation of a legal Left-wing mass party inside the Congress; and (3) it emphasised the idea of forming workers' and peasants' mass organisations in defence of their class demands.

After the 1931 Calcutta session, the Indian Communists, instead of pursuing Lenin's theses on the colonial question, adopted the colonial theses of the Comintern's sixth congress and emphasised the control of the party leadership over the workers and peasants from above rather than the process of raising mass-consciousness and building a mass Communist Party whose members are organically linked with the struggling masses. The expulsion of the nationalist leadership from the league against imperialism also underlined the communist leadership's endeavour to ensure the monolithic character of the mass organisation. The Indian communists also imbibed the idea of one-party rule in a post-revolutionary society from the practice of the Communist Party of the Soviet Union and the influence of the Comintern. Competition with parties representing the interests of other classes to win over the masses creates the space for a democratic environment which is necessary for the healthy interaction of diverse opinion within and outside the party. This acts as an important countervailing factor to save the party from plunging into the quagmire of ultra-centralism and inertia of moribund party life.

The foreign policy of Soviet Russia that advanced its own national interests blurred the distinction between fascism and bourgeois democracy; the united front strategy had gradually been abandoned after the death of Lenin. The concept of democratic centralism drifted in favour of centralism sans democracy, and those who differed with this new strategy were considered as rivals who were eliminated. The organisational arm-twisting and manoeuvring of the monolithic Russian Communist Party constricted the space within the Comintern for democratic debate of member revolutionaries, especially after the sixth congress.

The German invasion of the Soviet Union that changed the balance of forces was viewed by the Indian communists as transforming the character of the conflict—from imperialist war to people's war. The Indian communists toed the formulation of the Comintern and, in doing so, they even abandoned the line of "conditional support" to the British and opposed the August movement launched by Indian National Congress.

During Lenin's time, the Comintern had a democratic character. In line with Lenin's theses on the colonial question, the Berlin group of Indian revolutionaries Maulana Barkatullah, Virendranath Chattopadhyaya, Bhupendranath Dutta emphasised not only the unity of the anti-imperialist forces in India, but also the specificities of Indian society like the caste question. But the present-day major Left parties like the CPI and the CPI(M) bear the organisational and theoretical tradition of the Comintern of the post-Lenin period.

Party of the Ruling Class

So the major Indian Left parties mechanically toeing the post-Lenin Soviet line transformed themselves into regimented parties maintaining their relation with the basic classes through a command structure. The release of initiative of the rural poor due to the land reform implemented by the Left Front in West Bengal was arrested after the incorporation of the new middle classes within party command structure. The party refrained from empowering the rural poor and the working class by furthering the agrarian reform process and by allowing active participation in the panchayati raj system through the Gram Sansad mechanism. By silencing the voice of the rural poor who could have been a potent force for modern agriculture, cooperative farming and for development of indigenous industries, the Left Front plunged into crisis. The vibrant rural life that resulted from the implementation of Operation Barga was subsequently throttled by the CPI(M)'s control of all spheres of public life through its command structure and control of the administration. This situation led them to follow the neoliberal development path.

West Bengal sprang a major surprise when, two years into liberalisation, in September 1994, Jyoti Basu announced his government's new industrial policy in the assembly. "We are all for new technology and investment in selective spheres where they help our economy and which are of mutual interest. We have the state sector, the private sector and also the joint sector. All these have a role to play", said the chief minister. In pursuing this new policy of the Left, Basu exercised caution; Buddhadeb stomped. The latter even wanted the CPI(M) to back the Pension Fund Regulatory Development Authority Bill in Parliament. "Team Buddha" was so engrossed with the success story of the neoliberal drive that his government not only invited notorious companies like Dow Chemicals, but was also planning to invite Wal-Mart to take hold of the retail market. The central CPI(M) leaders with their characteristic double speak always backed the neoliberal policy of the Left Front in West Bengal. The major left parties like CPI(M) are ideologically and organisationally plunged deep into parliamentary cretinism and perhaps lost the will to revive the path of working class struggle. So there is no reason not to consider the present-day major Left parties like the CPI(M) as parties of the ruling class.

REFERENCE

1. For the period 1920-42, we draw on Sobhanlal Datta Gupta's *Comintern and the Destiny of Communism in India, 1919-1943* (Kolkata: Seribaan, 2006).

31

For a Left Resurgence

Dipankar Bhattacharya

The drubbing received by the Communist Party of India (Marxist) [CPI(M)] and the Left Front in the elections to the West Bengal state assembly in 2011 has triggered widespread speculation about the future of the Left in India. Quite predictably, one can hear a loud celebratory noise in the dominant "mainstream" media which treats the CPI(M)'s Bengal debacle as the beginning of the end of the Left in India. This shrill cry is remarkably reminiscent of the "end of history" triumphalism in the American media in the wake of the collapse of the Soviet Union. But after a decade of war and quite a few years of stubborn recession, the discourse in the United States itself has now shifted to the whisper of a possible advent of an American Autumn. Undoubtedly, the "end-of-the-Left" ideological campaign in India will also find itself equally out of sync with the developing climate of popular unrest against corruption and corporate loot.

Even as we reject the roars of bourgeois triumphalism, and the ruling class wisdom that advises Indian communists to reinvent themselves as social-democrats wedded to the idea of making capitalism more humane while abandoning the idea of transcending capitalism, we must however also acknowledge the genuine concerns in Left and democratic circles about the future of the Left and the need for a necessary realignment of

Left forces for a rejuvenation of the Left movement. In this context, a welcome debate seems to be shaping up, beginning with Sumanta Banerjee's insightful account of the recent transfer of power in West Bengal from the CPI(M) to the Trinamool Congress (TMC). Banerjee sees little prospect of a course correction in the CPI(M) and stresses the need for the rise of a new Indian Left through closer cooperation and realignment among the non-CPI(M) Left.

Patnaik has quite categorically argued that the CPI(M) is suffering from a deep-seated malady of" empiricisation", a delinking of practice from the spirit and vision of transcending capitalism, which has the potential to derail the party completely from the trajectory of Left politics. He however believes that the CPI(M) still has the ideological wherewithal to overcome the degenerative dialectic of "empiricisation" and in case it fails to do that, it can only be supplanted by a communist formation whose theoretical positions are akin to those of the CPI(M).

In a brief response to Prabhat Patnaik, Hiren Gohain has taken the debate deeper into the CPI(M)'s very approach to parliamentary democracy (See chapter 33). Gohain holds that a non-revolutionary approach to Parliament leading to a steady assimilation to the attitudes of the ruling classes and fatal weakening of extra-parliamentary initiatives and imagination has caused the CPI(M)'s growing alienation from the basic classes. The divergence of the party's own interest from the interests of the basic classes has led to brutal suppression of popular protests as witnessed in Singur and Nandigram and it cannot just be brushed aside as a mere case of "empiricisation".

Before we proceed with this discussion, let us take a look at the CPI(M)'s own official review of the West Bengal poll outcome. The review acknowledges that the party has suffered a major defeat, identifies a host of reasons and promises "a more elaborate review...to examine whether the Left Front government did enough to implement alternative policies to the neoliberal framework". But for all practical purposes, the review would like us to believe that the defeat is essentially attributable to a conspiracy by the ruling classes and imperialism to dethrone the CPI(M) because of its opposition to neoliberal policies and the Indo-US nuclear deal, and the popular aspiration for change resulted from just a fatigue among the people because of the prolonged duration of the CPI (M) rule.

Patnaik's account is clearly at considerable variance from the CPI(M)'s official narrative. He argues that the CPI(M) has essentially had to pay a price for taking it upon itself to build capitalism while abdicating the guiding vision of transcending capitalism. Patnaik talks of the CPI(M) abandoning the basic classes while the CPI(M) review blames the TMC for driving a wedge between the party and sections of the peasantry by invoking the land acquisition issue. But both Patnaik and the CPI(M) underplay the real gravity of the Bengal debacle, and obscure, if not altogether ignore, the core internal reasons. They thus fail to stress the urgent lessons for any real recovery.

Land and Liberty

For any objective observer of West Bengal developments, there can be no denying the fact that 2011 marked a total reversal of 1977. In 1977, the CPI(M) had come to power riding on a popular quest for restoration of democracy in Emergency-eclipsed West Bengal. By the lale 1960s the CPI(M) had already emerged as the main organisational beneficiary of the gains of decades of communist-led popular struggles in Bengal, but 1977 provided the defining moment, and the CPI(M) went on lo consolidate its position through panchayati raj and Operation Barga. If land and liberty were thus the twin planks that had created a big base for the CPI(M) in the early years of Left Front rule, the same were the core issues for the people in 2011 as well. A widespread quest for liberation from the stifling domination of the CPI(M)-led government apparatus and a growing unrest among large sections of the peasantry and the rural poor over land and livelihood led to the CPI(M)'s ignominious exit in 2011.

It is this context which must be the real cause of concern for all well-wishers of the Left. The Right has returned to power in Bengal by capitalising on the ruling Left's loss of credibility and legitimacy vis-a-vis the basic classes and the core agenda of democracy, land and rural welfare. While Mamata Banerjee enhanced and consolidated her mass appeal with the slogan of

Ma-Mati-Manush (mother, land and humanity) the CPI(M) in Bengal came to be bracketed with brutal massacres, special economic zones (SEZs) and Tata Nano! There can be no real introspection without squarely addressing this crux of the problem. And it is not only for the CPI(M) leadership to introspect, but the pro-CPI(M) intellectuals who discredited themselves by trying to defend the indefensible CPI(M) role in Singur and Nandigram should also do some soul-searching.

It is well known that the dominant opinion in the CPI(M)'s Bengal leadership refuses to admit and discuss, let alone rectify, this real problem and instead looks for scapegoats in the CPI(M)'s acts of omission and commission at the Centre. If the CPI(M) Central Committee's refusal to let Jyoti Basu become the prime minister of a Congress-backed ragtag United Front government in 1996 was considered the first "historic blunder", the 2008 withdrawal of support to United Progressive Alliance —I (UP—I) government is being treated as the second. The presumption is that it is this act of withdrawal which facilitated the renewed unity between the Congress and the TMC thereby sealing the CPI(M)'s electoral fate in West Bengal.

Nothing could be farther from the truth than this wishful and bankrupt line of thinking. The TMC and the Congress would have anyway come together in West Bengal and, as the Kolkata corporation elections showed, even if the Congress had stayed aloof, it could have hardly stopped the TMC surge in the state. But the CPI(M) lacks the will to resolve this debate and the result is a review which seeks to project the party's debacle in West Bengal as an anti-imperialist martyrdom of sorts. This is how the CPI(M) would like to avoid any real critical scrutiny of the developments in West Bengal as well as its role at the Centre.

To set the record straight, for most part of UPA-I's tenure, the CPI(M)) did effectively collaborate with the government. The SEZ Act 2005 was allowed to be passed unopposed—Prakash Karat made a candid confession in the course of a discussion with students of Jawaharlal Nehru University that the CPI(M) had failed to assess the issue from the point of view of the peasantry, looking at it more from a trade union angle. It is another matter that even from the point of view of working class struggles in SEZs, the Act deserved to be opposed no less categorically. Even on the issue of Indo-US nuclear deal, the withdrawal of support eventually came over a rather procedural wrangling with the government by which time the Indo-US strategic partnership had already gathered enough momentum.

CPI(M)'s Anti-Imperialism

Prabhat Patnaik often refers to Lenin's thesis on imperialism and cites anti-imperialism as the decisive communist credential of the CPI(M). The biggest merit of Lenin's thesis was his identification of imperialism as a structural development of capitalism itself. He showed us how war and aggressive external intervention by imperialist powers was not just a foreign policy question— and certainly not an aberration arising from a failure of diplomacy, but rooted in the intrinsic expansionary urge of capital. Going by the Leninist definition of imperialism, it should be clear that anti-imperialism in India today cannot therefore be limited only to challenging the Indo-US nuclear deal and strategic partnership—it must challenge the whole gamut of neoliberal policies that are promoting corporate loot and ravaging all our resources.

How has the CPI(M) fared on this real test of anti-imperialism? While lauding the CPI(M)'s stand on the nuclear deal, Patnaik is compelled to admit that the CPI(M)) in West Bengal was busy building capitalism on the neoliberal plank. When a party does this in its strongest bastion, its opposition to the same policies elsewhere naturally lacks sincerity or substance. And now thanks to WikiLeaks' disclosure of American embassy cables from India, we know very well how senior CPI(M) leaders maintained close links with American officials in India even as the party was publicly decrying India's nuclear deal and strategic partnership with the United States.

Mere theoretical recognition of imperialism was never enough for Lenin. Under Lenin's leadership, communists the world over demarcated themselves from reformists and social-democrats by evolving and following a whole set of revolutionary tactical principles guided by and catering to a revolutionary strategic vision. This revolutionary praxis achieved its greatest success in the victorious socialist revolution in Russia, but it was meant for communists working in a wide variety of conditions—from the bourgeois parliamentary republics of Europe and America to the colonies and semi-colonies in Asia, Africa and Latin America.

Central to the demarcation between communists and social-democrats was the question of intervention in parliamentary politics and utilisation of electoral victories. In contrast to the social-democratic thesis of participation in bourgeois governments and sharing of power with the bourgeoisie, communists resolved to use any power won in elections at local or provincial levels (outright communist victory in elections to the highest level of bourgeois state power was clearly considered highly unlikely) for the advancement of class struggle and as part and parcel of an overall revolutionary opposition to the central authority.

The CPI(M) had moved away from this communist policy quite early on in the course of its protracted parliamentary journey. Against the backdrop of the inspiring victory of the CPI(M) and its Left Front partners in 1977, the slogan that had captured the imagination of Left ranks was none other than *"bam front sarkar sangramer hatiyar"* (Left Front government is a weapon of struggle). But it did not take the CPI(M) long to realise that such a slogan would not be tenable with the imperatives of a stable government. Thus the slogan was soon effectively withdrawn and replaced by *"bamfront sarkar unnayaner hatiyar"* (Left Front government is an instrument of "development", experienced by the people mostly as bulldozer of development). In the wake of Singur, Nandigram and Lalgarh, a good majority of people in West Bengal saw it degenerate further as *"utpiraner hatiyar"* (instrument of repression).

If only Patnaik bothered to look beyond the question of a sheer theoretical recognition of the danger of imperialism into the realm of strategy and tactics of a communist party, he would have noticed how the CPI(M) had abandoned the communist attitude to the question of power in a bourgeois state to opt for a social-democratic framework of relief and reform through power-sharing. The updated CPI(M) programme of 2000 made a provision for the party's participation in central government as a junior partner—a major departure from the famous Para 112 of the party's 1964 programme which had distinguished the party from the CPI all through the 1960s and 1970s right up to the 1996-98 period when the majority of the CPI(M) Central Committee refused to let Jyoti Basu become the prime minister of a Congress-backed United Front government even as two CPI leaders accepted ministerial positions.

Parliamentary Cretinism

Patnaik does not see any link between the CPI(M)'s model of intervention in parliamentary politics and the trajectory of "empiricisation". Instead Patnaik accuses those who see a link between the two of being victims of what he calls parliamentary fetishism. Now this is quite interesting. Marx had taken on commodity fetishism to deepen the study of capital—starting from the commodity-crowded surface of capitalism he had taken the reader to the core question of production and appropriation of surplus value. But in its lead of taking us beyond Parliament to unravel the class nature of the state and explore the means of stronger proletarian intervention in bourgeois politics, Patnaik employs the term parliamentary fetishism only against those who advocate a boycott of parliament and others who stay away from the political process. Conspicuously absent is any critical gaze at all at those who deliberately invoke parliament to limit the people's political initiative and imagination, and who habitually always put the aura and privilege of parliament above the rights and struggles of the people.

He seems to be completely oblivious of the fact that while fighting against "boycottists" and Left adventurists, Lenin always held that the communist movement faced a much bigger danger from parliamentary cretinism. In his response to Prabhat Patnaik, Hiren Gohain (See chapter 33) has quite rightly highlighted the CPI(M)'s failure in combining parliamentary work and extra- parliamentary struggles, even contrasting it to the imagination and vigour (albeit of the reactionary type) displayed by the Right in their multifarious extra-parliamentary initiatives and programmes.

In fact, Patnaik's own argument regarding the ongoing popular agitation against corruption presents a glaring example of parliamentary fetishism. It is one thing to critique the framework or provisions of the Jan Lokpal Bill or the limited agenda and way of functioning of what has come to be known as "Team Anna" but to project the whole thing as a threat to democracy or parliament is clearly missing the wood for the trees. One understands the desperation of discredited bourgeois leaders to try and hide behind the parliamentary shield, but why should the forces of social transformation be afraid of an awakened people?

Should communists keep aloof from the growing anti-corruption awakening among the people in the name of defending parliament and saving democracy from "mobocracy" or should communists welcome the people's anger and try and direct it against the whole regime of corporate loot and denial of people's rights?

The way ahead for the Left clearly lies through a radical realignment of Left forces on the basis of united struggle. After two decades of domination of neoliberal policies, almost all sections of the people are up in arms against the disastrous consequences of this policy regime. Fundamental questions regarding the nature of economy and polity are being discussed and debated quite widely. While the Right will definitely try to use this climate to its own advantage and liberals will only limit themselves to shallow and superficial reforms, the Left must seize this opportunity to deepen and widen the struggles and lead them on to their logical conclusions. The more the Left gets integrated with the developing resistance of various sections of the people, the more will be the momentum generated for a resurgence of the Left. And that alone can be the true resolution of the debate over the "decline" of the Left.

32

The Avoidable Tragedy of the Left in India

Pranab Bardhan

In the two and a half decades since the collapse of the Soviet Union, the Left in India has not renewed itself. In the context of the electoral debacle in West Bengal and the defeat in Kerala, this chapter revisits the issue and asks, what future now for the Left in the country? The Left certainly has a role to play in India but to be able to do so it needs to pay attention to the many general issues that currently afflict it.

Almost exactly two and and a half decades ago, around the time of the fall of the Soviet Union, I wrote a piece in the *Economic & Political Weekly* on the avoidable of tragedy of the Left in India. I wish I could say that the Left has been wiser in the intervening period. I used to think that once the gerontocracy at the helm of the Left parties moved on, the younger leadership would be more innovative and imaginative. Unfortunately, some of the younger leaders who have since been at the helm have turned out to be even more unthinking, dogmatic, and dense. With "democratic centralism", which is mumbo-jumbo for tyrannical control by the leadership, the Left parties have also disabled themselves from easy course correction. Even though I am writing this after the Left debacle in West Bengal, and the marginal defeat in Kerala, in this article I will mostly talk about the general issues afflicting the Left, some of which, if paid serious attention to, can still restore the legitimacy of what I believe to be a necessary role the Left can and should play in India.

Self-deception

I am always struck by the amazing capacity of the Left parties for self-deception in the face of a crisis, avoidance of the hard realities and resort to cliches and solace from sacred texts. In the context of a fast-changing world, their policy pronouncements continue to be obsolete formulae-driven and marked by chanting of catechisms: Market bad, State good; public sector good, private bad; leftist unions even when they act in reactionary, anti-poor and high-handed ways have to be defended; in foreign policy, America bad, China, Russia good (even when the latter countries now display rampant oligarchic, crony capitalism), even the theocratic-authoritarian regime in Iran has to be supported because it fights the evil American empire, and so on.

In West Bengal the resounding defeat of the Left Front, even with its history of considerable achievements in organising popular participation in meaningful land reform and rural decentralisation, is not just due to the peasant disaffection with its recent efforts at land acquisition, but more due to widely and intensely resented all-pervasive and oppressive party control of all aspects of local life. If you want a public hospital bed for your seriously ill family member, you have to be a supplicant with the local party boss; if you want to start a small business or be a street vendor you have to pay protection money to the party dada; if you want to ply a taxi or an autorickshaw you have to pay a tribute to the local party union; if you want a school-teacher's job you have to be approved by the "local committee" and pay them an appropriate amount; your children are to go to schools where the union activist teacher is often absent, compelling you to pay good money in sending them to his private coaching classes; if you want to build a house you have to employ party-approved construction workers and buy higher-priced or inferior-quality building materials from party-approved suppliers; if you want to buy land, you have to go through the party-connected "promoter", etc.

All-Powerful Party

In the name of Marxism the long-ruling party essentially became the all-powerful local mafia. Of course, in true godfather-style they will often help you in emergencies, if you show your loyalty. This way of operating a party is not unique to West Bengal, the Shiv Sena does it all the time, but they do not add insult to injury by spouting revolutionary or anti-imperialist rhetoric, or chanting *lal salam* even as they fleece or intimidate you, while the police nearby show studied indifference.

The party leaders have a habitual way of explaining electoral defeats by saying that their cadres have "lost touch with the people"; the common people often wish they did.

Leninist Legacy

The overriding principle of supremacy of party control is a poisonous Leninist legacy, and its degeneration into local tyranny is a sad but inevitable consequence. The Leninist principle is often invoked for the sake of discipline. Apart from the Rashtriya Swayamsevak Sangh (RSS), the Communist Party of India (Marxist) [CPI(M)] used to be the most disciplined political organisation in the country. No more. While the tightness of control over dissenting opinion at the top continues, it has now become flabby and unruly below, and in many local areas run by extortionists over whom the top leadership has very little control hopefully, after the party's defeat in West Bengal and the subsequent end of police protection, the thugs will now look for greener pastures, and there is a chance now for the CPI(M) to cleanse itself.

In the all-India context the Left is now mainly effective as a lobby for public sector employees, and it occasionally flexes its muscles by calling bandhs (on a suitable Monday or Friday), which paralyse city life, give babus a long weekend, while starving the poor informal workers who depend for their daily livelihood on casual wage work or street vending. The image of the Left in the minds of the vast numbers of the poor is that of the union organiser for the corrupt or callous public employees whom they have to face as the potential recipients of the paltry delivery of basic social and administrative services.

Failure in Basic Services

In the history of communist countries while governments have miserably failed in many aspects of the economy, at least in basic health and educational services they have often done a much better job than in non-communist countries at the same income level (China, Vietnam, Cuba are obvious examples). But this does not apply to West Bengal. The party organisation was solidly based on unionised school-teachers, health workers, clerks and other public employees—and they used their union clout to default in the delivery of public services. The coddled bureaucracy was allowed to be lackadaisical, files moved much slower than in secretariats of many other states, and the culture of union-protected impunity for public employees (including the police) thrived. The appointments and promotions in colleges and universities, directly orchestrated from the party office in Alimuddin Street and screened for party loyalty, decimated Bengal's long—enjoyed advantage in academic, intellectual and professional pursuits.

Informal Sector Bypassed

A major failure of the Left in India is in not being able to organise, except in localised pockets, the overwhelming majority of workers who are informal, often self-employed. The modes of organising these workers would have to be quite different: as home is often the workplace rather than concentrated centres like factory or office, wage or job security is not the main issue, welfare benefits and general economic security may be the more important ones, citizen rights may be more salient than worker rights, etc. Non-left non-government organisations with a citizen rights-based approach or Gandhian organisations (the most well-known of which is SEWA, organising a trade union of self-employed women) have often been more successful in this area. There needs to be a major reorientation in Left thinking on labour issues in this direction. In general Left thinking in India slurs over the contradictions within the labour movement (particularly between formal and informal workers·) and the special organisational exigencies of the latter.

On land issues also the Left parties, which used to be at the forefront of movements, have largely run out of steam. First of all, on land distribution or tenurial security rights, the Left parties in both Kerala and West Bengal have found out in their bitter experience that peasants once having received those rights do not feel particularly obliged to continue to vote for the parties that originally won those rights for them. In politics gratitude for past once-for-all beneficial actions soon wears out. Second, particularly in West Bengal, over time small and middle farmer families have come to capture the rural leadership in the local party, and this has led to some weakening of the cause of agitating for the wage demands of landless workers; it is no coincidence that the wage rise of the latter hurts those farmers who hire labour.

Third, in densely populated parts of India the land-man ratio is declining fast, pushing a large part of the land below the minimum viable cultivable unit. So earlier radical slogans like "land to the tiller" do not resonate as much. The Left should be active in organising some form of joint management in cultivation of tiny plots, particularly in matters of water, energy, knowledge of new agronomic practices and land nutrient inputs, and in marketing. But it is hardly active in these matters. The history of the cooperative movement in agriculture is dismal in India. Cooperatives, when they exist, more often than not have degenerated into moribund bureaucratic entities or front organisations for milking stale subsidies, or occasionally captured by the rich and powerful (as in the case of sugar cooperatives of Maharashtra). The successful cases of cooperative organisations like the Gujarat Cooperative Mille Marketing Federation (Amul) have very little to do with the Left. Yet the importance of cooperative marketing will loom larger as Indian agriculture shifts from traditional grain to high-valued produce (like fruits, vegetables, livestock and dairy products). Lack of progress on this front will only bring about the dominance of large retail companies (with enough resources to invest in cold storage and transportation) and contract fanning, which the Left in India often reflexively opposes (though the Chinese Party has gone for them in a big way).

Fourth, as the productivity per person declines in agriculture and as its share in GDP gets very small, the overwhelming proportion of even farmers' children (there is survey evidence for this) want to get out of agriculture. Yet the transfer of land to other more productive uses has given rise to politically explosive protests in different parts of India. In the case of Nandigrarm and Singur the attempts at land acquisition for industrial use has been resented by the people, partly because (a) the Left Front government (following largely the obsolete colonial law) offered inadequate compensation; (b) unnecessarily and clumsily used force; (c) the battle (at least in Nandigrarm) was less about land acquisition (the state government announced quite early in the process that no land will be acquired there) and more about turf warfare between CPI(M) and Trinamool goons—the Left government did little to control the gangland warfare; and (d) the long-term Left neglect of the backward state of education made many peasants concerned that their children will not be qualified to get any jobs in the new factories.

The Left now should not draw the wrong lessons from their electoral defeat, as some in the CPI(M) are already urging. Even after the bitter experience of the recent past, farmers may give up land voluntarily if they are offered a substantial share in the surplus that will be generated from the alternative use of land (say in the form of a steady annuity income, rather than cash that tends to get frittered away), if local participatory and deliberative processes are used to inform and involve them, if the annuity flow is administered by a credibly independent and efficient organisation, and if enough arrangements for skill formation and vocational training for farmers' children are made.

Dispossession and Displacement

Some within the CPI(M), and many to the left of the CPI(M) are understandably preoccupied with the general issue of dispossession and displacement effects of industrial and commercial development, particularly on the lives of the poor.

Many of the abuses they point out are indeed egregious. There are difficult issues and trade-offs involved here. I can only make a plea for some balance between the need for economic development that creates productive jobs and enhances social surplus (which can potentially be redistributed) on the one hand, and on the other the need for minimising (and adequately compensating for) the dislocation by means of a process in which the local stakeholders can be full participants. The use of land and minerals by profit-seeking companies for non-traditional higher-productivity activities is in some ways historically indispensable (as Marx would have recognised) if we want any change in the miserable way of life that the peasants and adivasis have endured for centuries—as the Marxist economist Emmanuel once wrote, the horrors of capitalism fade in comparison with the horrors of pre-capitalism. There is too much romanticising of the traditional life among some otherwise well-intentioned activists (both of the Gandhian and far-left persuasion) and too little interest in assessing the complex trade-offs involved. On the other hand, in the current dispensation the surplus generated in the process of development in these areas is grossly inequitably distributed, much of it grabbed by the corporate oligarchy, real estate tycoons, the mining mafia, and their political patrons and collaborators. We have to find a balanced, equitable, and sustainable way of dividing the surplus and minimising the loss (both private and social, including environmental). In this the democratic Left (as opposed to the misguided and violent extreme Left) can play a valuable role in espousing the cause of the deprived, increasing their awareness and information, catalysing their organisations and acting as watchdogs against the abuses of state violence and corporate power.

Associational Life

One important difference between Kerala and West Bengal is the much richer associational life in Kerala's society, with a long history of literacy and solidarity movements for low caste emancipation, people's science movements, civic organisations (including those related to churches) and, of course, a strong set of Left-led organisations of landless workers and small peasants. Civil society is much weaker in West Bengal, in spite of strong unions of clerks, schoolteachers and peasants (industrial unions are weak and demoralised in a string of declining sunset industries). Associational life has been largely hijacked by the party, explicitly discouraging the growth of non-party civic organisations in its shadow. There are some lower caste associations (like those of the "matua" group, which the party in its desperation before the elections tried to appease, too late), but unlike in other states they have been marginal to the bhadralok-led politics. While bhadraloks presided in the upper echelons of the party, the lower level operatives used the party dominance to arm themselves and create their little mafia fiefdoms, which thrived with the neutered police looking away. In the absence of robust civic organisations, the local-level politics quickly fell into a vortex of violence. The Trinamool Congress fought an uphill battle with its own squads of goons, and finally won with the headwind of accumulated popular disgust at the tyranny of party control and peasant anxiety about their land. But decentralisation which is supposed to have been a success in West Bengal should have provided a local-democratic arena for resolving conflicts and a check to the violence. While panchayats in West Bengal have not been captured by the landed oligarchy (as in many other states) largely on account of the prior land reform, and some of the welfare benefit programmes did reach sections of the poor, local governments are weak in terms of finance which mostly comes from above and local elections are fought not so much on local issues but more on state-level partisan issues. Benefits often went to sections of the poor who were in a clientelistic relationship with the ruling party. So the panchayats became just one more arena for bitter partisan battles, usually around the allocation of the scanty doles from above, from state-supported or centrally-sponsored schemes. Kerala panchayats have been given a lot more finance by the state government, decentralised planning is more participatory, and in some districts there is even a record of municipal governments running business enterprises (in collaboration with local private business and voluntary organisations)—something practically non-existent in West Bengal.

On Market Reform

Finally, the Left parties have to give up on their blatant hypocrisy on market reform. The reform policies pursued in Delhi are routinely described as "neoliberal", supposedly adopted under imperialist and World Bank influence, while basically similar policies are followed in Kolkata, Agartala or Thiruvananthapuram. Just as many decades back, after long and acrimonious debates, the Communist Parties in India reconciled to working under "bourgeois democracy", they have to reconcile themselves to the market principle. These are both about competition, one in the polity, and the other in the economy. Markets have a large number of well-recognised problems: market "failures" in resource allocation on account of externalities and imperfect information, inequalities that markets tend to facilitate, the instability, unemployment, and the economic and cultural dislocation that they often bring about, etc. But there are ways of mitigating these negative effects. The alternative to markets is often worse. The history of socialist countries has shown us repeatedly how without competition among producers and a mechanism for exit of chronically inefficient firms, no economy can attain or retain its vigour and dynamism. Political or bureaucratic allocation of resources and control of prices often lead to corruption, black markets and stagnation. The inequality in wealth in socialist countries is between the privileged members of the party oligarchy (and their accomplices) and the rest, and unemployment takes the form of low-productivity "disguised unemployment". Barring utopian projects on the drawing board of many wishful thinkers, no one has yet shown us in practice a consistently and durably viable and technologically dynamic economy for a large enough country that has been run on traditional socialist lines of controls and state monopoly. The socialist economies of Eastern Europe and Russia collapsed largely on their own endogenous systemic weakness. Common people in capitalist South Korea are immeasurably better off than in socialist near-starvation North Korea (which started off with an initial industrial advantage over the South). For three decades now China has deliberately attempted following a comprehensive policy of state-guided capitalism (adapting the models in South Korea, Taiwan, Singapore, and earlier Japan for their own circumstances) and has succeeded famously. In many respects Chinese policy has been much more "neoliberal" than Indian. Vietnam is following policies similar to China.

Possible Priorities

I think the Left should concentrate on leading popular struggles against capitalist excesses and injustices (rampant inequality and the consequent capture of political processes, displacement of poor people, macroeconomic instability—most recently due to short-sighted recklessness of unregulated financial markets abroad, and environmental degradation). The required systemic modifications and regulations will not make the capitalists happy, but through democratic pressures one can work out a bargaining arrangement in which the social justice objectives are vigorously pursued, but the incentives for production and surplus generation are not hurt too much; and state and community-level coordination mechanisms are used to cope with various kinds of coordination failures in the economy without substantially giving up on the important coordinating and disciplining functions of the market. Such a bargaining equilibrium may or may not be called "social democracy"—a term which raises suspicion in many on the Left, while many on the liberal side smell too much socialism in it. Forgetting about the well-known European examples, even among developing countries, in Latin America a small country, Costa Rica, has a thriving democracy with a superb system of welfare benefits for the masses; in a large country, Brazil, under the Workers' Party the erstwhile high inequality is going down (their index of income inequality is now about the same as in China), and education and health services have advanced a great deal and they are aiming at a form of social democracy, without giving up on the capitalist features of production. The Indian situation is, of course, different, but there are many international examples now to learn from (particularly in regulations and in provision of social services) and adapt to our circumstances.

Even within India, a non-Left state like Tamil Nadu has advanced in the last three decades much more than West Bengal under the Left, both in industrialisation and in delivery of social services. Kerala, of course, has been on top in terms of social services for many decades, both under Left and non-Left rule, but its production system has not been dynamic enough, and it is more of a remittance economy. In general, the Left has to think hard why it is now only a regional party, and why even in its regions of strength it is getting weaker.

When Marx in his last years was learning about Russian data and special conditions, he was quite open to changing his long-held ideas formed from his study of West European history (as he explicitly indicated to some of his correspondents), much to the consternation of some of his faithful followers. Sticking to old dogmas in the face of changing reality and new information is definitely un-Marxian.

33

Decline of the Left: A Critical Comment

Hiren Gohain

Empiricisation

Though one might quibble about the term "empiricisation" that Prabhat Patnaik introduces in his discussion of the decline of the Left in India, one recognises the fatal trend denoted by it. It covers such tendencies as bureaucratism and bossism, the propensity to "adjust" to given situations instead of attempting to transform them through revolutionary praxis leading to a hiatus between the "party's interests" and those of the basic masses, gradual assimilation of the party to bourgeois parties in character, and virtual abandonment of the concept of imperialism during a period of world history when it has assumed a menacing all-engulfing form. The influence of the Chinese example at the time when the Left parties reached a plateau after securing partial land reform is cited as one of the major reasons for their straying from the revolutionary path. If such is the overall picture, one fails to understand why the familiar and clearer term "revisionism" should not be used. And once that term is applied, there would be an inexorable need for more severe and searching course-correction.

Actually the four tendencies are closely interrelated and they proceed from the same source, an abdication of revolutionary responsibility. This explains not only the absence or scarcity of theoretical engagement with the party's experience at different stages of the class-struggle (the Left Front's experience of holding power at the level of states, had never been summed up theoretically in a sharp, illuminating manner, but only described with tired clichés), but also the practical compromises with exigencies of bourgeois politics, like courting the support of certain communal forces and helping in propping up short-lived coalitions at the centre. Such exercises drew the attention of the party/ies away from the urgent work of organising and educating the masses at the grass-roots through struggle.

One has no quarrel with the proposition that the Left must make use of the opportunities for organising and educating the masses provided by parliamentary democracy. But it is quite another thing if the Left gradually sinks into the morass of parliamentary politics in the name of defending democracy from authoritarianism of various sorts. For it must be acknowledged clearly that the parliamentary democracy prevailing in India has a rather shallow and fragile basis.

Participation in Parliamentary Democracy

As Marx pointed out in his *Critique of the Gotha Programme* (Section I), "Right can never be higher than the economic structure of society and its cultural development conditioned thereby". Now the socio-economic and political formation of contemporary India does not appear to be the same as that of the mature capitalist West. In collusion with imperialism and native capitalism powerful feudal remnants still dominate large parts of the countryside with the help of a bureaucracy and police with a feudal mindset. Only a small section of the people is entitled to civil liberties. Large sections of the population are held in a social and political stranglehold where these rights mean nothing to them. One does not see the Left engaged in a struggle along with these wretched victims of systemic oppression for acquisition of those rights. Rather it is assorted non-governmental organisations (NGOs) that form no unified bloc and are ideologically heterogeneous, who seem to be in the forefront of such struggles. The Left fights for such rights in parliamentary fora and legislatures, cushioned from the actual circumstances and stresses of struggle on the ground. Rights to assemble and organise at the ground level are suppressed not only by the police and private armies of rich landlords in many parts of the country, but also by traditional feudal authority.

Practical assimilation to the attitudes of ruling-classes was seen at its worst in suppression of popular protests at Singur and Nandigram. There "party interest" definitely has overcome the interest of basic classes. Can one call it mere "empiricisation" and leave it at that?

The role of the Left in Parliament also has not come up to expectations. It has from time to time offered a reasoned criticism of the government's policies and taken a stand against anti-people policies and legislation, but with little effect. Its role in Parliament has not awakened the masses to the harm inflicted on them by the class-interest of the government, or aroused resistance against it. Even in the matter of defending the hard-won rights of labour against the neo-liberal joint offensive of the government and private capital, they have not shown much success. Thus the customary justification for participation in parliamentary democracy does not ring true in this case.

Deep-rooted Malady?

How does one explain this failure? Only tactical errors or some other deep-rooted malady? Even the praiseworthy adamant stand against the nuclear deal with the United States did not click with the masses. On the all-important issue of the price rise, the Left has not been able to convey to the masses its interpretation of the phenomenon by combining parliamentary with extra-parliamentary struggles. The fight against corruption has benefited the Rightist forces even more. The looming conclusion is that it has botched its parliamentary role allowing bourgeois forces to gain the upper hand. Can it be called a consequence of empiricisation? Or is it something more?

Participation in parliamentary democracy has also meant seeking and holding power in the states. That has meant acceptance of central policies to some extent, acquiescence in the anti-people role of the police, and compromises with the bureaucracy. True, there has been some degree of power-sharing at lower levels, and the panchayats had a more popular character. But there too the party became an instrument of domination rather than service to the people.

Finally, it succumbed to the capitalist paradigm of development with its present mantra of private sector-led and export-oriented and largely jobless growth, and was hustled into adoption of anti-people policies, robbing the masses of their right to land, water and other natural resources

The frenzy of elections often leading to bloody feuds among different sections of the masses undermining their democratic unity, and the lure of power, have seriously weakened the Left's extra-parliamentary initiatives and programmes, reducing them to lifeless rituals. Rightists have shown more imagination (of the reactionary type) and vigour in such work. The unconscious tendency to lean on the (bourgeois) state as a source of positive power for the good of the masses has sapped the Left of its energy to work independently at the grassroot level. At this very moment rampant neoliberal policies are disrupting and upsetting workers' lives with rising prices, a food crisis and unemployment. Vast numbers of people are being proletarianised and they are being brutally exploited through contractual employment. Yet they are not being organised into a militant force, and are rather herded into dispersed NGOs like islands in a sea of misery. They have become prey to superstition, religious mania and machinations of a hundred odd new-fangled cults.

I hope that the above incomplete account has shown how a particular non-revolutionary approach to parliamentary democracy in India today has led to both ideological dilution and practical impotence. This trend has encouraged both a slackening of guard and large-scale infiltration of opportunist middle class elements into party ranks. Patnaik does not believe that there has been a change in the class character of the party to explain the empiricisation. But how otherwise does one explain its "alienation from the basic classes"?

34

On the Left in Decline

Kripa Shankar

If overwhelming evidence shows that the CPI(M) has abandoned the project of "transcending capitalism" then Prabhat Patnaik ('The Left in Decline') should come to the logical conclusion that the CPI(M) is no different from any standard bourgeois party.

The communist movement in India has been characterised by its loyalty to the Soviet Union. Like a religious faith, it accepted any directive as the last wisdom to be followed without any argument or demur. When the Soviet Union was in alliance with the United Kingdom, the Communist Party of India (CPI) opposed the Quit India Movement at the behest of the Soviet Union and got alienated from the people. After the Second World War, when the Soviet Union found that the imperialist countries were conspiring against it, in a desperate response, in 1948, it directed the CPI to make a final assault on the government to overthrow it through armed struggle. But the Soviet Union soon realised that governments in newly independent countries like India were not lackeys of imperialism. They wanted to develop their countries and were anxious to befriend the Soviet Union with this end in view. The Soviet Union now took a U-turn and directed the CPI in 1950—through an editorial in *For a Lasting Peace and People's Democracy* which was the central organ of the then international communist movement—to form a united front with the national bourgeoisie which was in power but was facing imperial machinations with the connivance of the comprador bourgeoisie. It gave this line a theoretical justification by arguing that the bourgeoisie in such countries is divided between a nationalist and a comprador section. The latter was aligned with imperialism. Hence the task of the CPI was to ally with the national bourgeoisie to thwart the designs of imperialists.

It was a watershed for the CPI. Now it would collaborate with the government of the national bourgeoisie. There was now no agenda to fight the government except in words. The party would be looking for every opportunity to join the government if the occasion so arose. The focus was to increase its representation in the state assemblies and Parliament by electoral manoeuvring. Regional bourgeois parties had come up because they wanted greater space and opposed the central government. The CPI went into coalition with regional parties and formed the government in some of the states in 1967 but with no programme. This signified the beginning of degeneration. It behaved like any other bourgeois party. Indira Gandhi appeared to be friendlier to the Soviet Union and now the directive was to support the former in a more upright manner. CPI supported the Emergency although CPI (Marxist) (CPI(M)) opposed it but also denounced the JP movement.

Transcending Capitalism?

The CPI(M) ruled West Bengal uninterruptedly for more than three decades. Where is the evidence that it stands for transcending capitalism? Despite a high concentration in land it did not go in for acquiring the land of the richest farmers even at the market price and get it distributed among the landless. On the other hand, it was very keen to get agricultural land acquired for the monopoly houses and multinational corporations. The budgetary expenditure on agriculture and all allied activities, including minor irrigation, did not form even 3% of the total expenditure and was all along lower than the police budget. It was not prepared to provide cheap bank loans to the poor through interest subsidy so that they could make some investment in small remunerative activities like rearing small cattle, poultry, fisheries, etc. It could run massive rural employment generation activities like constructing rural roads, irrigation sources, storages, etc, but there were no funds after paying interest charges and expenditure on administration. The government was not prepared to tax the richer segments and resorted to reckless borrowings making it the largest indebted state on a per capita basis. It had a lower tax-state GDP ratio than many other states. Interest payments accounted for more than one-third of the state revenue. It was lukewarm in devolving power and funds to panchayats and municipalities "to enable them to function as institutions of self-government" as enjoined by the 73rd and 74th amendments of the Constitution. It could have opened a new chapter in rural reconstruction where people could take their destiny in their own hands but refrained from doing so. Rural areas could have pulsated with a new life and vigour, But all this was anathema to the government.

Prabhat Patnaik asserts that the CPI(M) has a project of transcending capitalism and is opposed to the neoliberal policies imposed by international finance capital Then why invite the same for creating hubs of super profits? The Salim group was cajoled. Tata Motors was invited to set up a car factory in Singur and not a powerhouse which the people need. Was firing on unarmed farmers by police in Nandigram in which 14 persons were killed a part of the fight that CPI(M) was waging against neoliberalism? PP asserts that the CPI(M) is wedded to the project of transcending capitalism because whatever reforms may be undertaken, capitalism cannot provide a humane society. There can be no disagreement about the latter part of the statement but the assertion that the CPI(M) is wedded to transcending capitalism is nowhere in evidence if we go by what the CPI(M) had done while in office.

Patnaik cites the example of CPI(M) withdrawing support to the United Progressive Alliance (UPA) government on the issue of the Indo-US nuclear deal. Then why the frantic effort to form a Third Front with parties like Samajwadi Party, Janata Dal, Bahujan Samaj Party, All India Anna Dravida Munnetra Kazhagam (AIADMK), Telugu Desam, etc, which are no better than Congress insofar as their support to neoliberal policies is concerned? The bigger question is that knowing full well that the UPA was pursuing neoliberal policies at the behest of international capital, why was the CPI(M) supporting it from the very beginning? It appears that it was keener to come to office through a Third Front which again would follow the same neoliberal policies because of its class composition. CPI(M) was doing the same in West Bengal and Kerala.

Patnaik is gung-ho about the parliamentary path little realising its infirmities in a country like India where money and muscle power matter most. One-third of the members of parliament have criminal records and with each election their proportion is rising. All the bourgeois parties are patronising criminals as they can intimidate voters. Glorification of the parliamentary path to the conclusion of mass mobilisation, mass upheaval and upsurge has also much to do with the degeneration and decadence of the CPI(M) and other so-called Left parties. Patnaik is also unwilling to learn anything from Anna Hazare's episode which shows that people are prepared to come to the streets if genuine issues of the masses are addressed. Significantly it has also shown that people have lost faith in political parties because all the major parties that have been in office for some time have followed the same policies that benefit the elite.

Stooge of the Bourgeoisie?

Long ago Lenin said that the party should learn from the people. Why did the people consider the CPI(M) and the Left Front irrelevant? It is because they see it as not much different from any other bourgeois party. This is their life experience; the demagogy that the CPI(M) stands for transcending capitalism stands exposed. Patnaik rightly claims that if a communist party abandons the concept of transcending capitalism and instead "presides over the building of capitalism (it) will end up being no different from standard bourgeois parties, notwithstanding its lip service to the revolution". If overwhelming evidence shows that the CPI(M) has abandoned the project of transcending capitalism then Patnaik should come to the logical conclusion that the CPI(M) is no different from any standard bourgeois party. In that case he should give a call for a new communist party which will be consistent in its opposition to the capitalist path and will depend on mass mobilisation and mass upsurge to dethrone the ruling bourgeoisie rather than forming a united front with it and thereby end as a stooge of the bourgeoisie.

35

On Understanding the Decline of the Established Indian Left

Murzban Jal

The inability of the Indian Left to construct a project of the transcendence of capitalism (the central thesis of Prabhat Patnaik) has to be understood as constituted within a crisis of world Marxism that began with the crystallisation of the Stalinist counterrevolution which paraded state capitalism as authentic socialism. This chapter is on reading the misunderstanding of the fundamentals of Marx's scientific discovery by the Established Left in India, especially on the transient characters of commodity production, value and the state; and that communism transcends commodity production and abolishes the state immediately after the revolution. As the Established Indian Left took the non-Marxist model of commodity production governed by an alleged "socialist" state, it was destined to be destroyed by the inner contradictions of state capitalism. To project a transcendence of capitalism one needs to project a world that is devoid of commodities, money and the state. It is this task that the Left in India in alliance with international communism must concentrate on.

Locating the Crisis of the Indian Left

We begin our critique of the Established Left in India by recalling our earlier critique of the Parliamentary Left in 'Leninism as

Radical Desireology' for using the readymade state apparatus for socialist purposes, as well as articulating the thesis of the state as not merely a sham, but in Freudian terms in articulating it as defecation. In this chapter we understand not only the state in this psychoanalytic problematic, but the entire capitalist mode of production, dominated by the production of commodities. With this Freudo-Marxist articulation we see how this defecation and human waste have become fetishes to be revered by neoliberal society. That the bourgeoisie reveres this waste should not surprise anyone. But the fact that the Left in India does so becomes the source of our critique. We begin by turning from this articulating of revering waste to a metaphor borrowed from Slavoj Žižek. In contrast to the replies to Patnaik by Gohain, Lahiri Bhattacharya, and Baisya, our discussion focuses on the theoretical apparatus of Revolutionary Marxism and what Marx's discovery of the new continent of knowledge as the discovery of a post-commodity society implies.

Žižek, in discussing the *burakumin*, the caste of untouchables in Japan, talks of a character in Sue Summi's novel *The River with No Bridge*, how as a child she witnessed a relative who scratched the toilet used by the emperor to preserve a piece of shit as a sacred relic, simply to honour the emperor.[1] The metaphor of the preservation of human waste of the elites by the oppressed subaltern classes is not only a metaphor for a certain type of bourgeois politics. It is in actuality what one calls after Hegel, the *Wesen* (the essence) and *Begriff* (the concept) of bourgeois politics. Two concepts emerge from this metaphorical reading of human enslavement: (1) bourgeois politics as the epitome of this human waste that becomes a fetish to be worshipped,. and (2) on social and political hierarchies and the fetish worship of the elites in the age of late capitalism. It is around this argument that I begin the discussion on the crisis of the Left. A certain type of Freudo-Marxism will guide my argument. The state and the commodity principle realised as the politics of state capitalism will be the waste-cum-fetishes that devours the Indian Left movement.

Our response to Prabhat Patnaik on the decline of the Left is based on a deep structured argument. We agree with Patnaik that the Established Left is governed by a form of "empiricisation" where the programme of communism as the transcendence of capitalism is totally forgotten for a form of state-capitalist social engineering. But, as we shall see, the project of transcending capitalism can never be formulated if a rigorous critique of the old socialist principles (keeping commodity production intact within the socialist order) is not undertaken.

In contrast to a mere socialist sociology which is largely promoted by the Indian Left, this chapter shall talk of theory, to be precise of Marxist theory. We shall talk of how Marxist theory ought to be present at all times in the political programme and praxis of the Left. We shall talk of the politics of the particular and the general and, in this sense, talk of the philosophy of the particular and the general. In this sense, we will not limit ourselves to how bourgeois politics is dominated by the Washington Consensus that imposes the neoliberal agenda of finance capitalism on India. We will not talk of privatisation, globalisation of capital, special economic zones, nuclear deals, etc, in isolation. We will talk of these in relation to the general idea of capitalism and commodity production and relate these to the philosophy of the fetish character of commodities. We will not merely talk of what one may call the "Indian question", but what Alain Badiou calls after Lenin "the question of the dictatorship of the proletariat in general"[2]. To talk of the transcendence of capitalism implies mentioning these. It implies talking of the double fetishes of commodity production and parliamentary democracy and how these fetishes create illusions and fantasies. But it also implies talking of the not too fashionable politics that Lenin insisted on. To talk of the transcendence of capitalism would necessarily imply the mentioning of the not so fashionable Lenin.

This chapter in agreeing with Patnaik on the transcendence of capitalism is consequently based on the general character of Marxism, thus based on the necessity of the transcendence of the horizons of both commodity production and the state as such. We start with our basic proposition: since almost all shades of the Indian Left move within the horizon of "market socialism" keeping the instruments of the state and the commodity principle intact, we are compelled to say that the central idea of the crisis of the Left emerges when one forgets this double fetish characters (the state and commodity production) that now parasite on the Left movement. And since the Indian Left (most notably the Communist Party of India (Marxist)) has never articulated a post-commodity society, they can never imagine a post-capitalist society. In this sense one can chide them that it is not Marx's *Capital* that serves as a model, but Stalin's *Economic Problems of Socialism in the USSR* and Mao's *Critique of Soviet Economics* that institutionalised state capitalism in the Left movement.

And since Patnaik mentions the transcendence of capitalism without talking of the commodity principle and the phenomenology of commodities in *Capital*, we are bound to quote Lukács' historical statement: "the problem of the commodity must not be considered in isolation or even regarded as the central problem in economics, but as the central, structural problem of capitalist society in all its aspects".[3] Keeping the problem of the commodity as central to our contemporary imagination, will see how a philosophical analysis of the commodity is able to articulate the concerns highlighted by Patnaik. Let us first see how by keeping the problem of the phantom commodity as the central problem of capitalism one is able to put forth the solution to the crisis within the Left movement.

Philosophical Foundations of the Problem

We first redefine the classical historical materialist theorem: the economic base determines the political and ideological superstructure with a new dictum: the fetishised commoditised economic base of neoliberal finance capitalism determines an illusory political superstructure. Understanding how the illusions dictated by the commoditised base has seeped into both the national imagination as well as the imaginary of Left politics, we recall two important texts which come in when one is analysing the contemporary crisis of the left: Stuart Hall's *Illuminations: Walter Benjamin, Essays and Reflections* and Kevin Anderson's *Lenin, Hegel, and Western Marxism: A Critical Study.*

Whilst according to Hall, the crisis of the Left emerges from the inability to apprehend the character of the age and to develop a moral-political critique of the specific epoch of capitalism, for Anderson, the root of the problem is the inability to understand the mechanism of the Hegelian dialectic that lies at the root of Marx's revolutionary critique of capitalism. We are in a sense caught up in the pre-dialectical site. In this same sense we are caught up in the pre-revolutionary site. We imagine ourselves to be revolutionaries, whilst in actuality we use the methodology of the bourgeoisie.

Our response to Patnaik's chapter 'The Left in Decline' (whilst agreeing with the spirit of it) however goes deeper, i.e. goes into the philosophical foundations of the problem: the problem of the commodity and the state, and that the Left in India has never looked beyond these avenues. Along with these two problems this chapter questions the unilinear view of history, the view that emerged in Stalinist Russia which stated that history is governed by so-called "iron laws" that dictate the march-past of history from primitive communism to slave society, feudalism and capitalism, finally culminating in socialism. Lastly, unlike the mainstream Left that keeps the question of caste only as a peripheral issue, this chapter (in the second part) puts the caste question central to the question of the Indian revolution.

Our response is a Marxist philosophical response. We agree that the horizons of capitalism have to be transcended. But we claim that this transcendence is possible if we transcend the parameters of thinking of not only the Stalinists and the Maoists, but also those of the Trotskyists and the present South American Left. The central focus in this chapter is on Marx's double critiques of commodity production and the state as representations of human alienation. Keeping his problematic of alienation, we are saying that the state does not have to be viewed only as a "committee of the bourgeoisie". Instead we need to relate this bourgeois committee with the idea of the state as the imaginary form of human alienation. In this dialogue with Patnaik we will emphasise on these two crucially important humanist points of Marx. We will also see that the Left that is in decline did not take Marx's radical humanist critiques of the commodity and the state. Instead it made a strange kitsch-like combination of Soviet type of political economy and liberal theories of the state, thus incorporating the old Proudhonist theories of socialist commodity production (institutionalised by Stalin and Mao) into the terrain of parliamentary politics. Little did they know that both these are essentially elitist and anti-Marxist. The decline of the Left is thus viewed in the moving away from the ideas of Marx. The decline is thus much more deep rooted than otherwise thought.

On Revolutionary Dialectics

Let us reflect on the decline of the left in what Kevin Anderson has recently said:

> Certainly none of the major Marxist thinkers of the twentieth century who were also leaders of the parties—not only Leon Trotsky, Luxemburg, Karl Kautsky, or Mao Zedong—with the sole exception of Gramsci (and even then those writings were locked away in prison or in party archives for many years afterward), had made that "return" to the Hegelian dialectic that Marx called "the source of all dialectic". Nor did any of the younger layer of Bolshevik theoreticians, such as Bukharin or Yevgeny Preobrazhensky, make such a move.[4]

This reflection articulates the theoretical roots of the decline of the Left, a decline that was since the mid-1920s rooted in a false socialist problematic, a falsity that took the Left away from not only Marx, but from Hegelian dialectics to the old formal logical problematic of Aristotle. Yet one must state that informed Marxists in the last century did emphasise on the Hegelian reading of Marxism. This Hegelian reading did not encompass merely Lukács, Gramsci and Karl Korsch, but a few years before the trio entered the scene of revolutionary history, it was Lenin in 1914 who put the Hegelian dialectic at the basis of Bolshevik praxis. The Hegelian dialectic did not merely encompass the questions of trade unions, the national question, on the question of the revolutionary International and mass struggle against capitalism and imperialism (especially against the imperialist war), but was also the basis that solved the questions of insurrection and the seizure of power. There is something specific about the Hegelian dialectic that required Lenin breaking free from the entire continent of scientific reasoning that began with Aristotle and closed with Kant. Lenin in this sense broke out from the old logical framework. But the global Left by and large ignored Lenin's Hegelian intervention. They forgot that to understand revolution one has to understand insurrection as art. And to understand these one has to understand dialectics. In this sense nowhere does Patnaik mention the theoretical and logical roots of the problem of the decline of the Left.

Now we all know that the paradigm of formal scientific reasoning (from Aristotle to Kant) is different from the dialectical one (Hegel, Marx, Lenin). We knew that Gramsci, Lukács and Ilyenkov talked of it, that Zeleny wrote about it, not to forget Raya Dunayevskaya. And yet political praxis in India is largely untouched by this Hegelian logic. That it retreats not only to Kant, but also to Aristotle should not be a surprise. And this retreating into Kant and Aristotle is not merely a retreat into predialectical logical thinking, but also a retreat into pre-Marxist politics. We do not think about the idea of the masses in ferment. We do not think about insurrection. Thinking in terms of Kant we think of parliamentary democracy, of morality and goodness, of eternal peace and such abstract metaphysical ideas. We have forgotten: if one does not think dialectically, one cannot think Marxistically. One cannot think (what Lenin said in the *Philosophical Notebooks*) of self-movement (*Selbsbewegung*) and negativity, of historical motion that moves through leaps and bounds. One thinks instead of parliamentary cretinism and anarchist adventurism.

What we are claiming following Anderson's claim is that a severe crisis has set into Marxism—a crisis that was essentially theoretical and which cannot be reduced to the polemics that characterised the politics of Stalinism, Trotskyism and Maoism. The crisis is objective. As the Left are armed with theories from Aristotle to Kant and from Stalin to Mao, there is a fundamental failure of the Left to grasp the radical character of what Benjamin called the "time of the Now".[5] The crisis also lies in the fact that we are perpetually bound by the epistemological and ideological horizons set by capitalism. The solution too has to be objective, an objectivity that has to transcend the fetishism of false objectivity: of reified (or false) objectivism. One has to transcend the horizons of bourgeois thinking.

On Marx's New Physics

With the transcendence of the horizons of bourgeois thinking and the framing of the idea of revolutionary time, the "time of the Now", we make our first claim: within the discipline of historical materialism, the sub-idea of *historical physics* emerges. We now have the idea of time. We thus claim that Marx's scientific discovery—the discovery of the continent of history—also constitutes the idea of revolutionary time, a time zone that is entirely distinct from bourgeois time. We thus claim that one cannot confuse these two distinct time zones: historical time as spiral time and reified time as circular time. To understand the present epoch, to fathom the peculiarities of this age, one needs to differentiate historical time from reified time, and consequently understand the "time of the Now".

And what do we learn from this? We learn that the crisis of the Left—here one means the international left from Stalin to Mao and from Trotsky to Hugo Chavez—is constituted within the matrix of reified time or to be precise phantom time, in Benjamin's phrase, of "empty, homogeneous time",[6] time that cannot "blow open the continuum of history".[7] And why is this so? It is so because the time zone that we are constituted in is the time of abstract time, the time of commodity production. We are under the eternal spell of commodity production. We think within its horizons. We breathe its air. We could not transcend commodity production. We of course cannot transcend capitalism. We live thus in what Patnaik in 'The Left in Decline' calls the "mundane and the pedestrian" where we have only the "small change in politics". A bill is passed. Another is not. Someone fasts. Someone does not. Someone comes on TV. Someone does not. Some go to jail. Some do not. Some join the Greenpeace, some join Human Rights Watch. We not only live the life of this small change in politics, but we are bewildered by what Dunayevskaya calls after Trotsky, "the small coin of concrete questions", the small coin that leads us away from Revolutionary Marxism.[8] Not only do these small coins fit in our bourgeois pockets, they fill our heads.

Now what happens is that reified and mundane time (or non-spiral, non-historical time), which is also Benjamin's empty, homogeneous time becomes Freud's neurotic time: the time of the eternal recurrence of capital accumulation: M-C-M^1. And since we know that M (money) is an idealist signifier reappearing in augmented form (M^1) and is also the mode of appearance of the ghost called "value",[9] we talk of this process of capital accumulation: M-C-M^1 as the march-past of the ghost. Just as Marx had said in *The German Ideology* that philosophy as dreamt by the idealist philosophers is nothing but the "history of ghosts"; so too one talks of the history of capital accumulation as the historical march-past of the ghost. We thus have two formulations: (1) time within the capitalist mode of production is reified time, circular or neurotic time, and (2) it is also ghostly time. What happens is that revolutionary movements are necessarily defeated in this zone. And if the revolution takes place that does not abolish commodity production and the state then: "The old filthy business would necessarily be restored".[10] The filthy business, started in 1928, was realised in 1991. In 2011, we yet hold this filthy business dear to us. We simply want to work with the same filthy tools. We want to be the burakumin, waiting for the emperor to perform his natural duties.

Now what happens is that in this reified-defeatist zone is that history, or radical history, cannot be rendered possible. What we live in is spurious history, neurotic history, or simply phantom history. We once learnt that capital is a barrier to capital. Now we forget this very important lesson and think only within the parameters of Monsieur Capital's dictates. This is the first terrain in which we locate why and how the Left has declined. It is the ontological terrain. The Left declines because it operates in the reified, non-historical time zone. It operates with reified-defeatist tools. Keeping this very important point in mind, especially on the idea of commodity production as determining the neurotic time of the eternal recurrence of capitalism, we go into the problem of the decline of the Left and what the crisis of the Left indicates. Our claim is that a particular reification of consciousness emerges with commodity production and this reification does not merely penetrate into the general ideological superstructure, or only into minds of social scientists. It also grips the minds of the Left. We call this reification of consciousness, a mimesis: mimesis of commodity production and consequently the mimesis of phantom time. We are all plagued by the phantom commodity. Our ideological horizons are determined by it. Not only did Stalin and Mao err by creating a fallacious category of "socialist commodity production", but the same error occurred with Trotsky, not to forget Preobrazhensky and Bukharin.

And it is in this space of mimesis of the phantom commodity that we claim that Patnaik's articulation on the decline of the Left is a welcome sign in the Indian Left movement. What Patnaik calls "empiricisation" we call "mimesis of the phantom commodity". The fetish-like attachment and bewilderment towards parliamentary politics will be seen as this mimesis of the phantom commodity. And by focusing on an empiricisation of political praxis, i.e. on the mimesis of the phantom commodity combined with the phantom parliament, the Left parties find themselves in a position that is no different from other bourgeois parties. And by putting the project of the transcendence of capitalism as the essential project of Marxism, Patnaik has in a certain way started a debate on how one defines the status of revolutionary praxis. Yet, as I shall argue out, the question though posed, relapses into a form of empiricisation itself if one works within the parameters of the Indian Left, because the Organised Left in India shall not be able to conceive of the project of the transcendence of capitalism. By "Organised Left" I mean not only the parties of the Left Front led by the CPI(M), but also the Maoists and other "left of CPI(M)" parties and groups.

The Nature of Marxist Science

My response to Patnaik is on the nature of Marxist science that Marx first raised in the *Economic and Philosophic Manuscripts of*

1844 and has in no way to be reduced to a polemic. The questions posed are important and need a scientific response. As we shall soon see, there are two important scientific revolutions to be taken into consideration: the first started by Hegel and best represented in his *Phenomenology of Mind* and the *Science of Logic*; and the second revolution that begins with Marx's *Economic and Philosophic Manuscripts of 1844* where he points to the construction of a human natural science.[11] We, of course, had heard of dialectical and historical materialism. But we seem to be oblivious to Marx's original human natural science. And what is the fundamental aspect of this New Science? The fundamental aspect is that it raises the very important humanist and communist question: "What is free humanity?" by differentiating the sites of humanity (or classless societies) from the phantom site of commodity producing class societies. That this line of demarcation is so fundamental to Marx seems again to escape one's critical imagination. That is why one needs to state that the Left is stuck with the ideas of old socialism— what Marx called "*crude* communism"—which is nothing but the "manifestation of the vileness of private property, which wants to set itself up as the positive community system".[12] The Left seems to have forgotten that their brand of old socialism is perpetually "affected by private property, i.e. by the estrangement of humanity".[13] Since the Indian Left has within its political cranium, the mechanism of crude communism as the governance of private property and human alienation, the seeds of its decline are to be found within its own fallacious theoretical problematic.

But the Left is not merely caught up with the ideas of old socialism. It is caught up with the old bourgeois logic of reification, where subject and predicate, civil society and state, the real and ideal are inverted, and privilege almost of a theological type is granted to the idealised Indian state with the even more idealised Indian Parliament. That the Indian liberals and the conservatives love the state should not shock anyone. But why does the Left do so? In order to understand the Indian Left's succumbing to this state logic one will have to move to Marx's critical epistemology in the *Theses on Feuerbach* where he differentiates the sites of the worlds of object (along with political passivity and contemplation, one would add: "parliamentary democracy as a form of political passivity") from "human sensuous activity" or simply as "revolutionary practical- critical activity".[14]

Now it must be noted that this is not merely a question restricted to a materialist psychology, but in fact remains the core for the production of the critique of capitalist political economy and bourgeois politics (especially parliamentary politics). In order to understand the epistemic mechanism of political passivity (the core component that defines the declining factors of the Left, and thus in order to understand the core factor of parliamentary politics), it must be noted that Marx in the very first page of *Capital* identifies the phantom commodity as a dehumanised thing: Marx's words are *Gegenstand, Ding, Sache,*[15] and as we very well know, the thing too loses its material form and becomes a ghost.[16] What happens is that the commodity as the dreaded thing and ghost converts real human beings into mere "personifications" and "embodiments" of these ghostly class interests.[17] One could therefore add that not only does capitalism in its real practice give privilege to capital and profit over people, but also its political practice—here one means parliamentarism —depreciate people. The Left parties in India use this same reified logic of the domination of the object world over people. That "bossism" "satrapism" and "careerism" rule the roost in the Left parties should not thus shock anyone. And keeping this difference between the world of objects, along with its ghosts (not only capital and the parliament, but also the Communist Party) and the world of humanity (the former is the world where only reified activity is possible, whilst in the latter revolutionary praxis is its leitmotiv), it is imperative to state that Marx states that capitalism favours the rule of the thing and ghost, as the rule of capital and profit. The privileging of profits over people is found not only in the ideological cranium and practice of neoliberalism. It is the essence of the commodity principle, a principle that the praxis of the Left has not been able to transcend.

The world of capitalism is thus necessarily anti-humanist.

It does not deal with people. People are only accidental and incidental to it. In exact opposition, communism breaks off immediately with commodity production and the entire political logic of the state, not merely with this or that state, but with the state as such. And since Left politics has kept the idea of commodity production within the ambit of its ideological parameters (with the institutionalisation of the incorrect idea of "socialist commodity production" and the "politics of command" by Stalin and Mao), the crisis that it would eventually suffer from is both necessary and obvious. One did not need a Singur, a Tata, or a Mamata Banerjee to explode the revisionist politics of the Organised Left. It did not need an explosion that came "from the outside". It was an implosion that emerged from within.

The Left saw through the ideological spectacles of not Marx or Engels. Instead it saw through the commoditised, authoritarian and counterrevolutionary visions of Stalin. And thus one could say: the project of transcending of capitalism could never have been an order for the parliamentary Left. Their model of transcending capitalism was the transcendence of Anglo-American capitalism, of the transcendence of the West European and North American types, but not of capitalism as capitalism.

Marx and Engels' Vision of Socialism

Note in contrast to the Stalinist, Trotskyist and Maoist visions what Marx and Engels had to say. We take *Capital*, *Critique of the Gotha Programme* and *Anti-Dühring* to understand the essential difference between Marx's vision and that of the so-called "socialist experiments" that the Left loves mimicking. Note that the Left has never taken these very important issues. For Marx when the "union of free people" carries on its work with means of production held in common, "the labour-power of all the different individuals is consciously applied as the combine labour-power of the community".[18] Unlike capitalism that is built on the inherent split between personal and social labour (thus not only letting value and money intervene to fill this wide abyss, but also the state), in communism "the total product...is directly social product".[19] Social relations are consequently not reified, not built on class domination. They are "simple and intelligible".[20] They need neither value, nor the state to intervene. Further, unlike the Left's idea of the socialist market, for Marx, in communism (here it is the first stage) neither do the producers exchange their products, neither does labour appear here as the value of these products.[21] For individual labour no longer exists in an indirect fashion but directly as a component part of the total labour.[22] Since Marx's communism is moneyless, one receives "a certificate from society that he has furnished such and such an amount of labour (after deducting his labour for the common funds), and with this certificate he draws from the social stock of means of consumption as much as costs the same amount of labour. The same amount of labour which he has given to society in one form he receives in another".[23]

Look again at Engels and note how this formulation is radically different from the old socialist version of transfigured socialist political economy: "From the moment when society enters into possession of the means of production and uses them in direct association for production, the labour of each individual, however varied its specifically useful character may be, becomes at the start and directly social labour".[24] When Engels says that with "the quantity of social labour contained in a product need not then be established in a roundabout way",[25] he meant that value (and exchange value and money as modes of manifestation of value) need not intervene. Society can simply calculate how many hours of labour are contained in a product of labour. Consequently "society will not assign values to products".[26] And "people will manage everything very simply, without the intervention of much-vaunted 'value'."[27] A very important question is posed: Would the Indian Left ever agree with this very Marxist formulation?

What happened to the post-Marx vision of socialism is concentration of the idea of the "just" (consequently Platonic) distribution of wealth, erasing the ideas of the mode of production and class struggles from revolutionary discourse. Look again at Engels and one will find how far the Left in India with its economism and trade unionism, and along with these the propagation of the politics of "a fair day's wages for a fair day's work", is from the revolutionary idea of the "abolition of the wages system altogether".[28] One would then have to ask: "Did the Organised Left in India *ever* propagate the ideas of the abolition of the wages system? After all have not the Left trade unions, not only the Centre of Indian Trade Unions and the All India Trade Union Congress, but also the ones that went under the generic term "Marxist-Leninist", *only* indulge in economism and the struggle for higher wages, and thus indulge in the maintenance of the system of the capitalist slave wages system?"

Thus to Patnaik who wants a radical critique of capitalism, we can only say: if one wants to critique capitalism, one will first have to go to the cell form itself, thus go into Marx's critique of commodity production, such that not only the high capitalism of the Yanks and the Brits, but also Soviet and Chinese capitalism, as also the capitalism of the Third World variety undergo a radical critique. In this radical critique not only will we have a critique of the revisionist politics of economism, but also a critique of parliamentary fetishism.

On Combating the Prohibition Against Thinking

The problem, to recall Žižek again, is that "all this occurs against the background of a fundamental *Denkverbot*, a prohibition against thinking. Today's liberal-democratic hegemony", so Žižek continues, "is sustained by a kind of unwritten *Denkverbot* similar to the infamous *Berufsverbot* in Germany of the late sixties".[29] Not only does the capitalist culture industry render unnecessary the process of radical thinking, but also parliamentary democracy has this Žižekean "prohibition against thinking". And to recall Žižek once more, "one of the sure signs of capitalism's ideological triumph today was the disappearance of the very term 'capitalism' and the dangerous temptation of the anti-globalisation movements to transform a critique of capitalism ('which ought to be centred on economic mechanisms, forms of work participation and profit extraction, and so on') into a critique of imperialism".[30]

If one looks carefully one will find a close connection

between the world that prohibits thinking and the "roundabout" world that exists in what Engels called "oblique and meaningless ways".[31] This close connection between thoughtlessness and meaninglessness becomes even more clear when one sees how the CPI(M) mimes Mahmoud Ahmadinejad and the Aryan mullahs' war against satanic imperialism—imperialism that is said to be devoid of capitalism. After all one knows that the world of capitalism is what Žižek calls after Habermas, *Undurchsichtlichkeit*, the new opacity.[32]

However one has to state that it is not merely neoliberal ideology that prohibits thinking. It is also the Established Left which has joined hands in this prohibition of critical thinking. It is in this space where we see how the model of state capitalism and its authoritarian types of "social-capitalism" (determined by commodity production, value, money and "socialist" capital accumulation) has become the model of the Organised Left in India. At the most the Left can make claims to be Proudhonists, or Utopian Socialists—Utopians who are incorruptible, Utopians who can join the stable of liberalism, Utopians who want what Stalin called "a special kind of commodity production"[33]—but most certainly a great wall separates them from the ideas of Marx. And that is why one needs to say that the project of the transcendence of capitalism that has been put in the backburner in the Indian Left movement distinctly since the last two decades—when the Stalinist "special kind of commodity production" collapsed—has its roots sunk much deeper. If 1928 led to the "special kind" of socialism, a socialism that mimicked state capitalism led by the Platonic managers of this "special" commodity, the collapse of the Soviet Union converted the Left in India into bricoleur and tinker-men of capitalism. In this context one must recall the old CPI(M) statement: "There is no alternative to capitalism". Thus any attempt to talk of an alternative model of social history, forget talking of the transcendence of capitalism, is a sheer impossibility. The problem is not merely of tactics or strategy. It is theoretical: the inability to understand dialectical and revolutionary materialism, the inability to go into the deep structure of capitalism and thus the inability to comprehend bourgeois economics. Marx's great discovery: the discovery of the continent of history remains lost once again. One reads now what Patnaik calls "the party's being hegemonised by the ideology of capitalism" in a deeper structure of Marx's original critique of political economy. To Patnaik's question, we respond: the party was always hegemonised by the ideology of capitalism. Earlier it was the Soviet model of state capitalism. Now it is the free-for-all barbaric model of neoliberalism, where in the Trojan horse gifted to India by the World Bank and the International Monetary Fund one sees the Yankee occupants playing chess with the comrade satraps.

To avoid the Trojan horse, what the New Revolutionary Left will have to learn is how to manage "everything very simply, without the intervention of much-vaunted 'value' ",[34] to see that production no longer "goes on behind the backs of the producers" or in a "roundabout way".[35] It is clear that the Left in India does not have Marx's model of communist society—an international society that is devoid of commodities, money, classes, the state and nations. Consequently it relapses into Platonic models of state capitalism regulated by the "Idea" of the incorruptible politicians. Its sole reason to exist is that the Communist Parties are not communal, casteist and corrupt, unlike all bourgeois parties. But its material base is capitalist through and through. Its empiricisation is mimicking Platonic state capitalist models. Consequently the decline of the Left has to be understood as similar to the decline of the Platonic "Idea" and the emergence of the Yankee barbarian neoliberal model.

Since the model of the Left is state capitalism with a "just" mode of distribution, we need to contrast Marx and Engels' visions of communism as post-commodity, post-state and post-nation societies, with the Stalinist revisionist model of "socialist" (rather bureaucratic-Platonic) commodity production. To counter Marx's ideas, a terrible revisionism in ideas was necessary, a counterrevolution in the realm of the social sciences that was carried out by Stalin. Trotsky himself is to blame. In *Philosophy and Revolution*, Dunayevskaya claimed that Trotsky refused to accept Stalin as a counterrevolutionary mole kept in the Bolshevik party by Tsarist agents.[36] That Trotsky ignored

Lenin's advice to remove Stalin from the post of General Secretary also ought to be noted. The counterrevolution in the realm of ideas has to be seen in parallel to the massacre of the Old Bolsheviks by Stalin.

Stalin's Counterrevolution in the Realm of Ideas

According to Stalin's counterrevolution in the realm of ideas, one must "disregard certain other concepts taken from Marx's *Capital*... (like) "surplus" product, "necessary" and "surplus" product, "necessary" and "surplus" time... (For) it is strange, to say the least, to use these concepts now."[37] One also does not talk of internationalism, for socialism has already been accomplished "in our country".[38] One also disregards Marx and Engels' formulation of the impossibility of communism in one country. Instead one bows down to Stalin's "new idea" of national-socialism. One therefore has to talk of the possibility of Stalin's "socialism in one country", maybe extend this formula and talk of "socialism in one state". The internationalist formulation that Marx and Engels insisted on was said by Stalin to be an "old formula".[38] So what did Stalin do? He "put an end to this incongruity between old concepts and the new state of affairs in our socialist country, by replacing the old concepts with the new ones that correspond to the new situation".[39]

Let us see the new things that Stalin did. He took the magical and necromantic commodity, this "queer thing, abounding in metaphysical subtleties and theological niceties",[40] and claimed to have tamed this fetishised monster into "a necessary and very useful element".[41] Marx had talked of value as "dead substance"[42] and "a live monster that is fruitful and multiplies".[43] Yet for Stalin (along with Mao) this principle of death is very necessary and useful. Marx had insisted on the fetish character of commodities. He also said that society would not be able to control value, but value would devour society. Stalin exorcised this monster and then said: "our commodity production radically differs from commodity production under capitalism".[44] In direct opposition to Marx, for whom value has "a personification with its own will and interest",[45] as also has a "soul of its own";[46] for Stalin, value (namely, the dead monster with its own soul) "is not a bad thing".[47] Stalin extolled the vanguard of Platonic socialism, namely, what he himself called "our business executives", to let value "influence production". Value—which appeared in Western Europe as Monsieur Capital (the liberal monster)—reappeared again as Generalissimo Stalin (the post-liberal angel) in the Soviet Union. That value is not only the core component of capitalist societies, but has also nestled in the hearts of the comrades is the tragic part of recent history. With the Stalinist revisionist tools that the Left has in hand, its history can be written both as tragic history as well as the history of its permanent decline.

And because the Left extols Stalinist capitalism and Stalin's general methodology of understanding Marxism as a "science" that studies laws "independent of the will of man"[48] whereby one "may discover these laws, get to know them, study them, reckon with them in his activities and utilise them in the interests of society, but he cannot change or abolish them".[49] Marx's general precept of changing the world goes consciously repressed. For the Indian Parliamentary Left, one must interpret the world in various ways, but never change it. And when Stalin's counterrevolution in the realm of ideas is transformed into practice, one can only find decline.

The Politics of "General Human Emancipation"

So how does one struggle against this trend? I said earlier in 'Leninism as Radical Descreology' that one necessarily has to move to a new space, the space of the "commons" that Engels had called *Gemeinwesen*. I also said that this commons involves the critique of the state, especially the critique of parliamentary democracy. Let us see how one can use this new space and see how human emancipation is possible. Let us also see how the Indian Left could never pose this question, but like the liberal bourgeoisie would at the most talk of political emancipation.

The term "universal human emancipation" is picked up from Marx's *A Contribution to the Critique of Hegel's Philosophy of Right: Introduction*. As it is necessary to formulate a radical politics of the union of free people that is market free and state free (an idea that the Left in India seems totally to be ignorant of), one is reformulating Marx's principles of classless and nationless communism. In this early essay—a theme that he first outlined a little before in his *On the Jewish Question*—he talks of two types of emancipations, the first is this human emancipation and the other is political emancipation. According to Marx the type of political emancipation is a spurious type of emancipation. What political emancipation does is not liberate people. It, on the contrary, emancipates the state from religion and other unnecessary admixtures. And that is why one has to learn to differentiate the idea of "universal human emancipation" that gives way to "revolutionary energy and intellectual self-confidence" which itself leads to "universal self-liberation"; and the "partial, *merely*, political revolution".[50]

Political emancipation is necessarily idealist. Despite it being structured in the site of the secular world, it is structured like religion. It claims to give freedom, while bondage is written on its banners. It is contradictory and confused in nature: "The limits of political emancipation are immediately apparent for the fact that the state can liberate itself from a restriction without humanity being *truly free* of it, that the state can be a *free state* without humanity being *free humanity...*"[51]. For Marx, not only is the state idealist and theological, it appears as a messiah, to be precise as Christ, "the intermediary between one human and another human's freedom. Just as Christ is the theological intermediary to whom humanity transfers all his divinity, all his *religious constraint*", so the state is the messianic intermediary to whom humanity transfers all his non-divinity and all his *human unconstraint*.[52]

So what do we learn from this? We learn that the state is not only the managing committee of the bourgeoisie and the engine of class despotism. We learn that this despot appearing as the messiah compels humanity to "transfer all his human constraints" on the messianic bourgeois committee.[53] What one needs to do is to develop a rigorous Marxist theory of the state from the early Marx's theory of alienation and stop being obsessed with the functionalist theories of the state that claim that every society needs a state: the feudal lords needed one, the capitalists need one; consequently the communist will also require a state. To my mind not only has the Left in India ignored Marx's writings in this "young" or "early" period, thus ignored works from Marx's 1843 *Critique of Hegel's Philosophy of the State* to *On the Jewish Question* and the *Economic and Philosophic Manuscripts of 1844*, but also ignored Lenin's *State and Revolution* and consequently built its political theories on non-revolutionary foundations. Now it is well known that the CPI(M) has not only the best and most radical intellectuals and it has at no time been bereft of theory, unlike a certain type of Radical Left who were most happy to read Mao's *On Contradiction*, supplemented by party pamphlets penned by Charu Mazumdar and Chandra Pulla Reddy.

So who would take up Marx's concerns of alienated humanity, relate this with his theory of class struggle and then develop and actualise this theory in practice, namely, that the state is the representation of both class tyranny as well as of alienated humanity? How should one make this theory of the state *alive* to people, such that they know that their emancipation —that includes Ranadive's "the small change in politics" that Patnaik recalls—is directly linked to the smashing of the state? Every small change in politics has to be linked with the concerns of alienated humanity as well as with the programmes of class struggle and of the smashing of the state. We have already noted before that the state is not to be understood as a rational organisation, but a counterfeit and a sort of defecation. That this counterfeit and defecation have *necessarily* to be smashed could then be said to be a self-evident statement.

Let us look at the young Marx's humanist theory of the state. We have seen that the state is both a counterfeit and defecation. But also as "the perfect political state (the state) is, by its nature, humanity's *species-life*".[54] What happens is that as species-life, politics of the bourgeois variety (i.e. politics of the state), reduces life to a form of a counterfeit—or simply, a false and filthy life. Since we are articulating that not only is parliamentary politics false (but that the entire politics of the state is a fraud) one must note the alienated and schizophrenic condition that the politics of the state leads us to. We must also be wary of the Organised

Left's attempt to tame this counterfeit-filth combine. Let us note the genealogy of the state and relate this with the dynamics of civil society.

We see that the bourgeois breast has two souls: the soul of the state where humanity is said to be a social being, and the soul of civil society which is the realm of the egoistical individual. Humanity leads a "double life", a Mephistophelian life in heaven and a Faustian life on earth. One here recalls Freud's notion of "doubling" from where the feeling emerges of a complete breakdown of the human personality followed by the emergence of dread and psychosis.[55] In this schizophrenic double-life, the individual lives in "the *political community*, as a *community being*, and in civil society, where he is active as a *private individual*, regards other men as a means, degrades himself into a means, and becomes the plaything of alien powers".[56] In both the realms (of state and civil society), humanity is necessarily an *illusory being*. In the state he is an illusory social being, an "imaginary member of a fictitious sovereignty, divested of his real individual life and filled with an unreal universality".[57] As member of the now declared royal civil society (after the media sponsored messianic fast-onto-mystical-death) he imagines himself to be a "profane being", even a "real individual", while in actuality is merely an "illusory phenomenon".[58]

Why Embrace Falsity?

The immediate question that comes up is: if the state is the spurious site of false universality—a condensation of human alienation—and thus is itself a form of false consciousness that produces a false practice, then why have the comrades embraced this falsity? Why does the CPI(M) function within the fractured domains of civil society and the state, knowing well that this dichotomy is a type of social and political schizophrenia that actively represses radical praxis? To my mind it is because they have perfected best the logic of the French Revolution and along with it have understood the very important text of *The Rights of Man and the Citizen*. But they have been able to understand these in the context of Marx's critique of alienation and the state where what Marx calls "the splitting of humanity"[59] remains its tour de force. That the fact that the state—not this or that state, not the liberal or the fascist state, but the "state as such"[60]—is to be recognised as the "unreality and the imaginary form" of human alienation[61] is yet to be understood. And because these two unfortunate and split souls of the *egoistic individual* and the *abstract citizen*[62] dwell within the even more unfortunate breast of not only the Indian liberal and the fascist, but also our national leftist, one has to tell them: "*political emancipation* by itself is not *human* emancipation".[63] Political theory, especially the left-of-centre type of political theory talks of the state, talks of political emancipation, but an emancipation that is woven round pre-Marxist theories. As they cannot talk of human emancipation, as they cannot *smash the fetish of the state*, one can only say that "it is the *sophistry of the political state* itself[64] which enslaves their political imagination.

Recall recent talks of how parliament is sovereign. Recall that people become predicates to this sovereign. Recall that this sovereign, as the Modern Prince, is completely alienated from people. Recall then that all other forms of political revolutions—New Democratic—or whatever jargon one wants to blab out, is necessarily built on the theory of the alienated Modern Prince. The idealism of the state was carried out in Europe by liberalism. In India it is the Left that can truly perfect this "idealism of the state",[65] where the biblical heaven is realised in its mythical national-socialism. Francis Fukuyama wanted liberalism to govern the world. This is not the tragedy. The tragedy is that it is the Indian Left which has become the bearer of liberalism. The Old Liberals, as we well know, are sitting in the Pentagon busy searching for new nations to destroy, after blowing out Afghanistan and Iraq.

Our critique is however historical and structural. Today imperialism functions in what is called the space of "humanitarian interventionism". But humanitarian imperialism is not something contingent to the present age. It belongs to the deep structure of bourgeois democracy where:

> Democracy is a contradiction in itself, an untruth, nothing but hypocrisy at the bottom. Political liberty is sham liberty, the worst

> form of slavery...The contradiction must come out... (in the form of) real equality... (in the form of) communism.[66]

We yet live in the age of this "sham liberty" where one cannot discover that the real roots of bourgeois democracy lie in the social contract between capital and labour. Yet sham liberty cannot be overcome in what Marx calls "crude and thoughtless communism",[67] most certainly not in Stalinism, nor in the born-again messianic forms of political theology that are propagated by organisations like the Hezbollah. The Organised Left cannot see the historicity of democracy and what the meaning of "democracy in contradiction" means. Because they stick to the spaces of Old Physics, especially to civil society and the state, and because they are enslaved by this patronising Nehruvian state, they cannot allow the contradictions of democracy to play out their historical role. And that is why the Parliamentary Left led by the CPI(M) either declares this Nehruvian state as the "Holiest of the Holy" and also has fascination for anti-communist organisations like the Hezbollah. Since the Aristotelian method is the only one available to them, since Hegel is totally out from the bounds of their reasoning, their beloved either/or method compels them to choose between Yankee imperialism and the Hezbollah, just as they are torn between the Congress and the Bharatiya Janata Party in actuality while murmuring curses at both of them.

Another Frankensteinian Monster

We have seen the fallacy of socialism that is built on the principles of the commodity and the state. We saw how they became Frankenstein-like monsters, to borrow Marx's phrase "independent beings endowed with life".[68] We have also seen that the Left in India has embraced these Frankenstein-like beings. We now move to another Frankensteinian monster that the Left has not been able to conceptualise: the caste system and how caste is inexorably linked to modern classes, political power and ideological hegemony. If one has said that the transcendence of capitalism needs the transcendence of the commodity principle and the state, one now says that it necessarily requires the transition of the caste system and its entire ideological superstructure. Though Patnaik had once talked of caste and the Asiatic mode of production (with reference to E.M.S. Namboodiripad) to be considered for Marxist reasoning, his articulation on the decline of the Indian Left does not once refer to caste. Neither have those who have responded to him done so. Patnaik's "basic classes" are then simply meaningless. In contrast to this form of reasoning, it is Kevin Anderson who has articulated another dimension to Marxism which includes the following:

(1) How the revolutionary subjectivity of African-Americans was a driving force in American society.
(2) How racism had held back the development of a labour movement in the industrial northern states of the US.
(3) How race had distorted the consciousness of the poor whites of the South.
(4) How slavery and capitalism were intertwined.
(5) How the struggle against slavery and racism in America is an international cause for the emancipation of labour.

Now link Anderson's reading of race and put the word caste. Put the Dalit in place of Anderson's reading of the African-Americans. Replace caste in each of the above five formulations and one gets a different perspective of Indian society, especially a different perspective of the Indian proletariat. Caste would turn out to be (to borrow Gunder Frank's phrase from a different context): *the underdevelopment of development*. The revolution against caste and its entire superstructure that was perfected by what we call the "Indian Fanonists" (after Frantz Fanon), Phule, Periyar and Ambedkar, was tragically ignored by the Mainstream Left.

To understand the decline of the Indian Left is to understand that the Stalinist, Trotskyist and Maoist baggage did not allow any space for a Marxist reading of non-Western societies. It meant that not only does one read Marx's essays of the 1850s in a different light, but one also reads his *Ethnological Notebook*, a text almost unknown to the Indian left. The "basic classes" that Patnaik seeks emerge from a womb that is different from the European one that saw the transition from feudalism to capitalism. And since feudalism was absent from India, the Indian Left was left chasing European ghosts. Attention thus has to turn to the historical materialist genealogy of the basic classes. But then one does not merely challenge the manifestos written by the Stalinists and the Maoists. One also challenges the theories formulated by R.S. Sharma and Irfan Habib who mistakenly imposed the European ideas of feudalism and capitalism onto India.

And finally since the Indian Left has never talked of Marx's idea of "the human essence" (*das menschliche Wesen*) and not understood that communism is nothing but the recovery of this human essence that has been destroyed by the caste-class system, they could not understand the subaltern humanist theory of casteless and classless society. Caste is not a mere pre-capitalist remnant that will automatically wither away. It is the Frankensteinian soul of "modern" India and an active agent of global capital accumulation. Marx's smashing of the state now synthesises with the radical subaltern smashing of the prison of caste and the superstructural iron cage that holds the caste system together. It is in this perspective of not only the prison house of caste, but the prison house of Hinduism, that one understands Ambedkar's theme of the "annihilation of caste".

Will the comrades be ready for this?

REFERENCES

1. Slavoj Žižek, *The Ticklish Subject: The Absent Centre of Political Ontology* (London: Verso, 2000), p. 189.
2. Alain Badiou, 'One Divide Itself into Two', in Slavoj Žižek, et al., *Lenin Reloaded: Towards a Politics of Truth* (Durham: Duke University Press, 2007), p.8.
3. Georg Lukács, *History and Class Consciousness*, trans. Rodney Livingstone (London: Merlin Press, 1983), p. 83.
4. Kevin Anderson, *Lenin, Hegel and Western Marxism: A Critical Study* (Urbana and Chicago: University of Illinois Press, 1995), p. 6.
5. Walter Benjamin, 'Theses on the Philosophy of History' in *Illuminations*, Trans. Harry Zohn (Glasgow: Fontana/Collins, 1979), p. 265.
6. Ibid., pp. 263, 266.

7. Ibid., p. 263.
8. Raya Dunayeveskaya, *Philosophy and Revolution—From Hegel to Sartre, and from Marx to Mao* (New Jersey: Humanities Press, 1982), p. XVIII.
9. Karl Marx, *Das Kapital*, Erster Band (Berlin: Dietz Verlag, 1981), p. 52.
10. Karl Marx and Frederick Engels, *The German Ideology* (Moscow: Progress Publishers, 1976), p. 54.
11. Karl Marx, *Economic and Phlosophic Manuscripts of 1844* (Moscow: Progress Publishers, 1982), p. 99.
12. Ibid., p. 90.
13. Ibid.
14. Karl Marx, 'Theses on Feuerbach', in *Marx. Engels. Selected Works* (Moscow: Progress Publishers, 1975), p. 28.
15. Karl Marx, *Das Kapital,* p. 49.
16. Ibid.
17. Karl Marx, *Capital,* Vol. I (Moscow: Progress Publishers, 1983), p. 21.
18. Ibid.
19. Ibid., p. 83.
20. Ibid.
21. Karl Marx, 'Critique of the Gotha Programme', in *Marx. Engels. Selected Works*, p. 319.
22. Ibid.
23. Ibid.
24. Frederick Engels, *Anti-Dühring: Herr Eugen Dühring's Revolution in Science* (Moscow: Progress Publishers, 1978), p. 374.
25. Ibid.
26. Ibid.
27. Ibid., pp. 374-75.
28. Frederick Engels, 'Trade Unions', in *The Wages System. Articles from the Labour Standard* (Moscow: Progress Publishers, 1984), p. 16.
29. Slavoj Žižek, 'A Plea for Leninist Intolerance', in *Critical Inquiry*, Winter, 2002.
30. Ibid.
31. Frederick Engels, *Anti-Dühring*, p. 375.
32. Slavoj Žižek, op. cit.
33. J.V. Stalin, 'Economic Problems of Socialism in the USSR', in J.V. Stalin, *Selected Writings* (Calcutta: National Book Agency, 1976), p. 299.
34. Frederick Engels, op. cit., p. 375.

35. Karl Marx, *Capital,* Vol. I., pp. 52, 57.
36. Raya Dunayaveskaya, *Philosophy and Revolution*, p. 318, n.1.
37. J.V. Stalin, op. cit., p. 300.
38. J.V. Stalin, 'Reply to the Discussion' in J.V. Stalin, *On the Opposition* (Peking: Foreign Languages Press, 1975), p. 448.
39. J.V. Stalin, 'Economic, Problems of Socialism in the USSR', p. 300.
40. Karl Marx, *Capital,* Vol. I., p. 76.
41. J.V. Stalin, op. cit., p. 299.
42. Karl Marx, op. cit., p. 189.
43. Ibid.
44. J.V. Stalin, op. cit., p. 299.
45. Karl Marx, *Capital,* Vol. I, p. 453.
46. Ibid.
47. J.V. Stalin, op. cit., p. 301.
48. Ibid., p. 288.
49. Ibid., pp. 288-289.
50. Karl Marx, 'A Contribution to the Critique of Hegel's Philosophy of Right. Introduction', in *Karl Marx. Early Writings,* trans. Rodney Livingstone and Gregor Benton (New York: Vintage Books, 1975), pp. 253-54.
51. Karl Marx, 'On the Jewish Question', in Ibid., p. 218.
52. Ibid., p. 219.
53. Ibid.
54. Ibid., p. 220.
55. Sigmund Freud, 'The Uncanny', in *The Penguin Freud Library, Vol. 14, Art and Literature* (London: Penguin Books, 1990), pp. 356-58.
56. Karl Marx, op. cit.
57. Ibid.
58. Ibid.
59. Ibid.
60. Ibid., p. 222.
61. Ibid., p. 216.
62. Ibid., p. 234.
63. Ibid., p. 226.
64. Ibid., p. 220.
65. Ibid., p. 233.
66. Frederick Engels, 'The Condition of England I, The Eighteenth Century' in *Marx. Engels. Collected Works*, Vol. 3 (Moscow: Progress Publishers, 1975).
67. Karl Marx, *Economic and Philosophic Manuscripts of 1844*, p. 88.
68. Karl Marx, *Capital*, p. 77.

36

'Good' Economics but 'Not so Good' Politics

Arun Patnaik

After reading Prabhat Patnaik's response to his critics, I am reminded of Lenin's expression: "good scientist but bad philosopher" from Lenin's work on "Empirio-criticism". What Lenin says about "empirio-criticism" is applicable to what Patnaik calls "empiricisation" of the Communist Parties (henceforth CP). First let me say where I agree with him. I agree that unlike the years of anti-colonial regimes during 1950s to 1980s, neoliberal capitalism is aligned with ruling classes in each country. There is greater consensus in the capitalist camps globally. I also agree with him the need to innovate an "unprecedented command over theory" in order to counter its hegemony. I also see merit his argument in what Prakash Karat recently calls for "socialism in a new format". In a veiled reference, Patnaik hints that "unprecedented theory" may create conditions of unity, without which forces of resistance today remain deeply fragmented. Only through a united counter-hegemony front, it is possible for subaltern societies to resist a hegemonic bloc. Unlike the usual left-wing rhetoric that blames globalisation leading to the collapse of socialist states, Prabhat Patnaik argues that socialist states collapsed due to their internal contradictions also. Where I agree with his contentions, I simultaneously disagree.

Prabhat forgets to add the lessons from Lenin's empirio-criticism: learn from the strength of enemies without which the CPs cannot construct an unprecedented theory, let alone build a *united* force of counter-hegemony. Without the CPs in fray, counter-hegemony may persist under the non-CP leadership and cannot be eliminated by a hegemonic bloc altogether, a point where the author rightly agrees with Hiren Gohain. Both admit and also recognise that there are many forms of counter-hegemony led by the non-party organisations. But both fail to notice that the CPs must learn from these initiatives, in order to be able to develop a new unprecedented theory to unite them. Please remember that these are non-party left-wing friends, to use Lenin's expression. To push Lenin's argument further: what about learning from the strength of enemies? This question is not even addressed by Patnaik. For Lenin clearly says, a point misunderstood by Western Marxism, Marxism cannot progress a step forward, unless it learns from its combative opponent: positivism. This is indeed one of the principles of dialectical reasoning. When the CPs refuse to learn from the strength of allies, how will then they learn from the combating enemies who are fiercely united today than ever before? A good economic analysis may turn out to be a weak political analysis if these questions are *not* asked and answered.

Learning from People and Non-Party Left: Prananath's Path

Prabhat Patnaik is right in recalling his father's experience in the Quit India Movement. Prananath Patnaik was jailed for several years during the period despite his CP was opposed to the movement. Similarly, during the national emergency (1975-77), many CPI cadres in Rourkela were arrested, despite their party siding with the emergency rule. Such heroic examples are always there in the long party traditions. However, I would like to recall the role of his father popularly known as Prananath babu in building CP in Odisha. It is necessary for his son and followers to learn from his principles further to craft "an unprecedented theory". His father never forgot Lenin's principles as above. Recounting this, a socialist leader L.N. Behera from Rourkela told me in 1989 that "if Prananath babu were alive when I joined socialist movement in my young age, I would have probably joined the CPI". Why? For, he used to advise his comrades to learn from masses and non-party Left. I do not know if Prananath believed in Lenin's principle of learning from the strength of enemies. Most probably he did. I am happy to note that in Odisha once upon a time, there walked a comrade who could be easily compared with the philosophical instincts of Lenin and Gramsci. If we take Prananath's advice to his comrades seriously, the CP must learn from a large variety of experiences from outside the CP. Therefore, I would like throw back Prabhat's words: Is the CP prepared to develop "epistemological exteriority" on the basis of lessons from all those who are seen as "epistemological exterior" by the party? Is he, to put it simply, prepared to learn lessons from Anna Hazare and many such "messianic personalities", standing as epistemic exteriors of the CP? That is the key question to debate today, if we want to revive "socialism in a new format". Otherwise, the search for "unprecedented theory" would always elude the CPs. I ask methodological questions rather than do "a concrete analysis of concrete situations", as no good theory can ever be developed without significant methodological foundations. I do not see that Patnaik and his friendly critics posit such questions in this debate on the decline of the Left. To put bluntly in the language used by Lenin, Gramsci and Prananath, the CPs gradually declined across the world due to their inner failure to learn from: (a) masses; (b) non-party Left; and (c) the strength of enemies. This is how Prananath would have most probably answered the problem posed by his own son, a fellow comrade.

Inversion of Cause-Effect Relationship

There is still another reason why I say good economics may not be followed by a 'not-so- good' politics. Following Eric Wright's political class struggle approach, I submit that neoliberalism emerged as a global ideology and politics *due to* the declining/ stagnating Left world over. Patnaik on the other hand argues, "globalisation of capital necessarily weakens the working class in every country". Patnaik inverts the cause-effect relationship.

But more importantly, if Patnaik admits what I claim, he would then have to inquire into the weaknesses of political forms of class struggle predating the birth of neoliberal times. True, Patnaik recognises the collapse of socialist states due to their internal crisis. But he forgets to add that the nature of Marxism developed world over had (still has) global nature rather than confined within the history of post-revolutionary states. It is important to recognise that these weaknesses of CPs globally led to the decline/stagnation of working class struggle. These weaknesses include among others blind sectarianism, fratricidal wars, vilification and killing of dissents since 1928, "Peidmontese tendency" (a phrase used by Gramsci: monopoly over leadership) growing in CPs (on national/international issues), dominating attitude in national-popular questions leading to many fragmentations, co-sharing the cold war psychology of the Right since the 1950s (those who are not with Marx are against Marx), the stagnation of productive forces since 1960s under iron curtains in actually existing socialist countries, the suppression of dialectics of difference within CPs and outside, the emergence of Marxism as a supra-historical ideology, a point well anticipated by Marx in his letter to Vera Zasulich, and so on. These factors no less contributed to the decline of the Left globally which in turn led to the rise of 'globalisation' since "the collapse of the Berlin Wall" in 1989. The weaknesses of A feed into the rise of non-A. Instead of subjecting the Left under a razor-sharp critique, Prabhat Patnaik conceals bad politics of the CPs the world over, which no less helped the cause of bad economics of contemporary capitalism. There are still a few positive and negative elements in Patnaik's thesis. However, these methodological questions are more important for the moment.

37

Trajectories of Fascism: Extreme-Right Movements in India and Elsewhere

Jairus Banaji

The term "theories of fascism" was the trademark for the kind of discussion that went on in strictly Marxist circles, in Germany and elsewhere, in the 1960s and early 70s. It was a major part of the revival of Left theory that characterised the radicalism of the 60s. In some ways the highpoint of this current of discussion came with the publication by Wolfgang Abendroth, in 1967, of a collection of Marxist texts that included essays by Otto Bauer, Arthur Rosenberg and August Thalheimer. These writings span the period from 1930 to 1938. Bauer, who was Austrian, identified the nationalism of the intelligentsia as a major cementing force in the ideology of fascism.[1] Rosenberg too assigned central importance to ideology and to the intelligentsia, seeing the latter as a key social base of the fascist movement, but unlike Bauer he saw the mass element in fascism as its distinctive feature. Thus, unlike almost all other left-wing writers of the period, he underlines the mobilising force of anti-semitism, the power of this and other ideologies, especially nationalism, to feed into the construction of a fascist mass base.[2] The terrible fact that we have to face up to and learn from is that the great majority of the German people accepted the Nazi regime at least passively. I'll come back to this in a moment. The other important element in Rosenberg's analysis, which was by far the best to be developed by the Left in the 1930s, was the connivance or active complicity of the existing state authorities in condoning fascist violence, turning a blind eye to illegal activities such as conspiracies and political murders and repeated assaults on the Left. The police establishment and the judiciary played the main roles here in implicitly buttressing the fascist movements. In Italy the *squadristi* or fascist squads which first emerged in the rural areas of northern Italy and Toscana to suppress sharecroppers and other workers could operate with total impunity *because* the government authorities stood by and simply allowed them to do so. In Germany the courts played an especially important role in being soft on right-wing violence. As Franz Neumann notes in his great book *Behemoth,* "At the centre of the counterrevolution [he means against the Weimar Republic] stood the judiciary". A third and final element that emerges from Rosenberg's analysis is what he calls the fascists' "peculiar tactic" of using stormtroopers. In fact, a plethora of paramilitary organisations emerged across the political spectrum and more even than the stormtroopers it was the paramilitarisation of wider nationalist circles in Germany and their use of targeted political assassinations that truly reflected the extra-parliamentary Right's resolute opposition to the new democracy.[3] Given that some 350 government politicians were assassinated by the nationalist terror groups, this backlash had the features of an armed insurrection against Weimar democracy but played out in slow motion and unevenly. I say "wider nationalist circles" because on one estimate over 1 million German males belonged to the various paramilitary formations in the summer of 1919.[4] That is a staggering number. The culture of militarism that led into the war carried over into the Weimar Republic in the shape of this organised element, the so-called Volunteer Associations of which the most famous was the Freikorps. What I'm going to do in the main part of this lecture is return to some of these themes after suggesting a theoretical framework for dealing with them. We know that the violence of the Right often takes the form of pogroms but what are pogroms? Or to put this another way, how are pogroms intelligible in any theory that rejects positivism? In the final part I'll look at the way fascism works in the context of Indian democracy, and then draw out the distinctiveness of India's fascist movement by comparing it with the German case.

Now the "theories of fascism" strand of the literature on fascism had more or less run dry by the mid-1970s, and the field was rapidly swamped by a burgeoning academic literature that became both more specialised and humongously massive in the scale on which books and articles began to appear. One offshoot of this explosion of the more purely academic work on fascism was that new themes were developed. Of these probably the most important was the literature on the Nazi genocide, supplemented by extensive new research on the persecution of marginalised social groups such as women, youth and sexual minorities, and on the murderous policies of "eugenic cleansing".[5] This had such an impact on the field that it forced the more thinking elements of the Left to reconsider classic Marxist accounts of fascism, as Enzo Traverso did in his brilliant little book which was subtitled *Marxism After Auschwitz*. Did conventional Marxist explanations that prioritised the class base of fascism or the economic forces at work behind its emergence have any real sense of the kind of rupture that the concentration camps came to signify?

Let me start with one aspect of this broader issue. In his book *Une culpabilité ordinaire?* Edouard Husson writes, "As for the so-called "ordinary Germans", it's plausible to argue that while not all of them participated in the massacres, all of them *have* to be held politically responsible for supporting the *Führer* who made the genocide possible—all, that is, except those who were politically opposed to Nazism."[6] Husson is saying that the mass of ordinary Germans were responsible for the crimes of Nazism insofar as they bore political liability for installing the regime. The distinctions implied here are those that Karl Jaspers laid out in his famous lecture *Die Schuldfrage*.[7] Indeed, Jaspers argued that the notion of "collective guilt" was only ever valid in the specific sense of political liability, but he also made it clear that he thought that "those who went right on with their activities as if nothing had happened" were indeed morally guilty as well. He wrote, "I, who cannot act otherwise than as an individual, am morally responsible for all my deeds, including the execution of political and military orders. It is never simply true that "orders are orders"."[8] So how do we deal with this potentially huge mass of morally impervious individuals who, as Jaspers says, "went right on with their activities as if nothing had happened?" They were not hard-core Nazis but they were crucial to the success of Nazism all the same.

To take this further, Sheehan writes that what the Nazis required of the bulk of the population was "compliance, not conviction".[9] In Germany in the 1930s there was the overtly Nazi element, the direct perpetrators (both the Nazi leadership and Party organisations as well as "large sections of the German non-Nazi élites in the army, industry and bureaucracy"),[10] and on the other side the bulk of the civilian population (ethnic Germans and Poles) who went along with the regime. The precise German term for the latter is *Mitläufer*. They were, it is said in the literature, morally indifferent to the fate of the regime's victims. But this characterisation, which comes from Ian Kershaw, doesn't seem even vaguely satisfying. Two holocaust historians Kulka and Rodrigue settle for the term "passive complicity" as a stronger description of the role of the *Mitläufer*. Again, what does it mean to be passively complicit in the criminality of a regime, whether it's a fascist government or any other? What explanation or even sort of explanation is there for what Browning calls a "widespread receptivity to mass murder" when speaking of Germans under Nazism?[11] No form of positivism is going to be able to match the kind of explanation we need. And that in part is why the horror of the holocaust confronts us as a sort of brute facticity, the sense of sheer intellectual defeat that Tim Mason expressed when he wrote, "I have always remained emotionally, and thus intellectually, paralysed in front of what the Nazis actually did and what their victims suffered. The enormity of these actions and these sufferings both demanded description and analysis, and at the same time totally defied them. I could neither face the facts of genocide, nor walk away from them and study a less demanding subject."[12]

So let's start with passive complicity. The only theoretical text I'm aware of that helps to make sense of this notion, to make it intelligible, is the massive enterprise Sartre undertook in the two volumes of his *Critique of Dialectical Reason*. The *Critique* was written at the end of the 1950s, against the background of a savage war of repression in Algeria. Algeria figures in the *Critique* as Sartre's prime example of why exploitation has to be inseparable from oppression, as he puts it. Colonial regimes encapsulate a perpetual circularity between those moments, between practices of extermination, plunder and violence, and the inert functioning of the economic system itself with its seeming institutional autonomy and its institutionalised racism. The initial violence of the colonisers renews itself throughout the history of the regime and the struggle between classes under colonialism is neither purely comparable to the molecular order nor simply praxis through and through, but an interlacing of these moments or forms of intelligibility.[13]

However, the really interesting aspect of the way the French war in Algeria shaped the arguments of the *Critique* would almost certainly have remained permanently opaque to us if Simone de Beauvoir had not documented precisely how that background influenced both her and Sartre at the time. In *Force of Circumstance* she writes, "I am an intellectual, I take words and the truth to be of value; every day I had to undergo an endlessly repeated onslaught of lies spewed from every mouth...What did appal me was to see the vast majority of the French people turn chauvinist and to realise the depth of their racist attitude. Bost and Jacques Lanzmann...told me how the police treated the neighbourhood Algerians; there were searches, raids, and manhunts every day; they beat them up, and overturned the vendors' carts in the open-air market. No one made any protest, far from it. It was even worse, because, whether I wanted to be or not, I was an accomplice of these people I couldn't bear to be in the same street with..."[14] And later she writes, "This hypocrisy, this indifference, this country, my own self, were no longer bearable to me. All those people in the streets, in open agreement or battered into a stupid submission—they were all murderers, all guilty. Myself as well." And she adds at the end of a powerful passage "Sartre protected himself by working furiously at his *Critique de la raison dialectique.*"[15]

What is striking here is her sense of sheer powerlessness in the face of the humongous propaganda that accompanies and justifies every war of repression (the French in Algeria, the US in Vietnam, the Indians in Kashmir and parts of the North East). And de Beauvoir confesses to a sense of complicity in the crimes committed by the French in Algeria, by what her government was doing in the name (of course) of "all" French people, in 1957 and 1958. Now this sense of complicity resonates through large parts of the *Critique* as the powerlessness of a specific kind of human multiplicity that Sartre calls the "series" or "serialities". Their impotence is experienced and lived in the face of the non-series, that is, the organised groups, especially those that make up the state, the state being for Sartre an ensemble of organised groups of the kind he calls institutions. So where do classes fit in this schema? Classes for Sartre are not unified subjects capable of some common class-wide action, as a certain voluntarism imagines, but "shifting ensembles of groups and series",[16] hence simultaneously organised and unorganised, with a perpetual circularity between groups and series, that is, no guarantee that class-groups will not dissolve into seriality (into pure dispersion, the state of having no organised existence) or for that matter re-emerge from it in future.

The group for Sartre is the negation of seriality, it emerges as a transcendence of the state of pure impotence and dispersion that characterises the vast mass of any society. Overall it is seriality that defines the larger swathe of any class in the sense that even within the bourgeoisie it is only a minority that is sufficiently organised (formed into groups of one kind or another) to have the power to control and dominate the rest of society, that is, to dominate the serialities of its own and of other classes. The state of being part of a dispersed molecular mass defined by a reciprocity of solitudes, determined only by otherness, by what others are doing and feeling, unified solely from the outside, by some external object (unified with these people here by the bus we are waiting for; unified with this mass here that has come to Jantar Mantar to see Hazare fasting or descended on Ayodhya to demolish a mosque) is what Sartre means by seriality.

As for the relationship between groups and series, two are especially interesting. The essential point about the series is that it is inert, it can do nothing, engage in no action of its own, yet have many things done to it. It follows that the state "can never be regarded as the product or expression of the totality of social individuals or even the majority of them, since this majority is serial anyway and could not express its needs and demands without liquidating itself as a series so as to become a large group."[17] From this Sartre concludes that "the idea of a diffuse popular sovereignty becoming embodied in a sovereign is a mystification. There is no such thing as diffuse sovereignty." Serialities "do not have the power or nature either to consent to or to resist the State."[18] Our acceptance of the state's power is simply our interiorisation of the powerlessness to refuse it.[19] As a serialised mass the vast mass of any population has "no means of either contesting or establishing legitimacy" for a given state.

A second more sinister relationship. Groups are constantly working series or working on them as the worked matter of their common praxis. This is most obvious in the action of the mass media which essentially addresses vast series of serialities most of which are indefinite and completely powerless in the face of the powerful groups that control and dominate the media. The most important action of groups on series is the kind Sartre calls "other direction" or "directed seriality". Other-direction is a term borrowed from David Riesman's book *The Lonely Crowd* and it brings us squarely to the issue of fascism. Political propaganda works on the same principle as advertising, that is, of generating an illusion of what Sartre calls "totalised seriality."[20] The series can do nothing, it is dispersed and inert, but the magic of advertising lies in the group's ability to "exploit seriality by pushing it to an extreme so that recurrence itself will produce synthetic results."[21] This sentence, obscure as it sounds, comes in a section that will end by discussing anti-semitism and pogroms. By "recurrence" Sartre means the perpetual flight that characterises the milieu of the Other (collective objects like markets, inflation, public opinion, and ideology, where serial action is both indeterminate and circular). The form of conditioning contained in the work of organised groups on series is one where the means used is to "manipulate the practico-inert field to produce serial reactions that are retotalised at the level of the common undertaking, that is to say, reshaped and forged like inorganic matter. And the means to this means is to constitute the serial as a false totality for everyone."[22] "Recurrence, controlled from outside as a determination projected from everyone, through Others, into the false totality of a common field, and, in reality, into pure reflexive flight" is what Sartre says he means by other-direction.[23] In politics the advertiser's phantom unity of consumers fixated on the illusion of a totalised seriality (as if the unity of a flight was a real unity) finds its precise counterpart in mass mobilisations based on the manipulation of series and seriality. Manipulated seriality is the heart of fascist politics. Here in India the techniques of other-direction take a panopoly of forms from sustained communal propaganda to communal mass mobilisations. If the mass element in fascism is its distinctive feature, even more distinctive is the way this mass is put together, constructed and mobilised, through what Sartre calls the "systematic other-direction of the racism of the Other, that is to say, in terms of the continuous action of a group on a series."[24]

The pogrom then is a special case of this "systematic other-direction", one in which the group "intends to act on the series so as to extract a total action from it *in alterity itself*."[25] The directing group is careful "not to occasion what might be called organised action within inert gatherings." "The real problem at this level is to extract organic actions from the masses" without disrupting their status as a dispersed molecular mass, as seriality.[26] So Sartre describes the pogrom as "the passive activity of a directed seriality",[27] an analysis where the term "passive" only underscores the point that command responsibility is the crucial factor in mass communal violence, since the individuals involved in dispersive acts of violence are the inert instruments of a sovereign or directing group. Thus for Sartre the passive complicity that sustains the mass base of fascism is a serial complicity, a "serial responsibility", as he calls it,[28] and it makes no difference, in principle, whether the individuals of the series have engaged in atrocities as part of an orchestrated wave of pogroms or simply approved that violence "in a serial dimension", as he puts it.[29] In both instances, what is involved for him is "impotence and an inert identification with the criminal", an identity in alterity which makes all of them responsible.[30]

In *The Origins of Totalitarianism* Hannah Arendt writes that "totalitarian movements use and abuse democratic freedoms in order to abolish them."[31] But in Italy and Germany the fascist movements emerged less to use/abuse democratic freedoms than to reverse the process of democratisation that flowed from the post-war crisis and create movements for the overthrow of still precarious emerging democracies. The distinctive feature of India's fascism is that it has had to grow in a society where the mass of the population remains committed to democracy and no agenda for the overthrow of democracy can ever be affirmed overtly in those terms. Thus Arendt's characterisation of fascist movements using/abusing democratic freedoms to abolish them is, paradoxically, more true of India than it ever was of Europe.

In India fascist tendencies are currently at work in two forms, one direct, the other more insidious. The more direct form consists chiefly in the mobilisation of a communal mass base which fluctuates in intensity but is clearly seen by the RSS as the organic strategy, and the one most directly linked to its ideology of extreme nationalism. That ideology was not a product of the RSS specifically, since the Hindu Mahasabha played an equally seminal role in forging its main elements. I'm referring of course to the fanatically extreme nationalism that was embodied in different ways in Savarkar and Golwalkar and encapsulated India's version of a fascist utopia ethnically cleansed or purged of its 'alien' elements. Everyone knows that both propagandists were deeply influenced by the Nazi extermination of the Jews and took that as their model for the way Muslims would have to be dealt with, in principle anyway. But mass communalism and sustained communal propaganda have been supplemented by more insidious subversions of democracy that combine the elements of a war of position with a war of movement. Thus progressive control of the media by the extreme Right which includes the mainstreaming of the extreme Right by the media, so that overtly communal elements are repeatedly projected as normal and innocuous (note the repeated presence of hard-core RSS elements on the prime time talk shows of channels like NDTV and CNN-IBN) and the BJP's earlier relentless parliamentary agitations when the secular UPA was in power, consciously calculated to induce a breakdown in the functioning of parliament and project that as the bungling of a corrupt and ineffectual government, both have the character of a war of position, that is, a protracted war of attrition against India's democracy that legitimises fascist politics and creates a dispersed revulsion against "the parliamentary system." A vital part of this trench warfare has been a widespread infiltration of the state apparatuses, a molecular penetration of the police, the bureaucracy and the intelligence agencies, which creates a state within the state, and one that is barely camouflaged when investigations into the criminal activity of the RSS underground (into the RSS cadre who have drifted into groups like Abhinav Bharat) are sabotaged by the state itself, or when the police are overtly implicated in communal carnages such as the explosion of violence led by the Shiv Sena in Bombay in January 1993. The war of movement on the other hand takes the form of a strategy of tension, a term invented by the Italian Left to characterise the spate of bombings and assassinations perpetrated by neo-fascist terrorist groups in the late 1960s and 70s (from 1969 to 1980). Many were false flag bombings that were blamed on extra-parliamentary left-wing organisations, the way the RSS bombings are blamed on Muslims. About the Piazza Fontana bombing of December 1969 which was initially blamed on the anarchists, the neo-fascist activist Vincenzo Vinciguerra stated, "The December 1969 explosion was supposed to be the detonator which would have convinced the political and military authorities to declare a state of emergency." The Bologna railway bombing of August 1980 was one of the most horrific in this series of neo-fascist terror strikes, killing 85 people and injuring some 200. In *Godse's Children* Subhash Gatade has shown how the investigations into similar attacks in India have progressively revealed a unified or coordinated network of conspirators, all implicated with the RSS, with Indore as a key centre of this underground.[32] That the RSS outsources the strategy of tension and publicly disowns it is of course mere subterfuge, not vastly more credible than its disowning of Godse himself.

Although fascist nostalgia is not a major characteristic of the extreme Right in Europe today, and a sort of electoral fascism is more widespread (appeals to racism and xenophobia to mobilise electoral support),[33] the Sangh Parivar is in some ways a purer version of the political culture of a more traditional fascism. The pogroms in India have far exceeded in scale anything that Germany saw in Weimar or the Nazi period (short of the mass extermination of the Jews when the Nazis finally turned to the 'final solution'). The culture of communalism is also at least as widespread in India as anti-semitism ever was in Germany, especially after the war. In republican Germany only one region, Bavaria, acted as "a cauldron of radical Right insurgency",[34] the crucial base that allowed Hitler and the Nazis to survive when there was a general retreat of the nationalist Right in the mid-1920s. In India, by contrast, RSS-controlled governments have been in power in different regions at different times (even before 2014) and Gujarat in the past ten years has been a microcosm of what the rest of India would look like if fascism ever took over completely. What the RSS has never had and always seemed to discourage was a leadership cult. With the repeated acclamations of Modi as the most successful prime minister this seems to be changing now, for it is the first time this political sector has found a figurehead around whom to build a Führer cult. Kershaw points out that the Hitler cult was the "crucial adhesive" of the Nazi movement, its "integrating mechanism". Hitler was, as he says, "the sole, indispensable force of integration in a movement that retained the potential to tear itself apart."[35] This cannot be said of the Sangh Parivar, since Modi's rise to what *he* would like to see as absolute mastery and the abject submission of everyone else grates with a political tradition of collective control divested of any fanatical cult of one individual. Since electoral fascism is a major part of their strategy, however, they may well be willing to make tactical concessions in this direction, unleashing a dynamic that no one can foresee at the moment. Finally, whereas German capital was split in its political allegiances, and Thyssen was wholly exceptional in joining the Nazi party whereas "the more liberal faction of industry continued to support the Chancellor Brüning" (this in 1932),[36] in India by contrast the last few years have seen a spate of well-publicised bear hugs between our captains of industry and Modi, in a display of feigned servility that shows that industrial capital at least is ready for fascism if large and overwhelming sectors of the Indian people most likely are not.

As you know, the Supreme Court was forced to intervene to transfer cases out of Gujarat. In the Best Bakery case Justice V.N. Khare even stated he had no confidence in the Gujarat government. He was quoted as saying, "I have no faith left in the prosecution and the Gujarat government." There could scarcely be a more scathing indictment of the brazen subversion of the justice system that soon came to characterise the whole way in which the Gujarat government manipulated the machinery of the law, fabricated or suppressed evidence, eliminated potential witnesses, and even concocted a whole series of encounter killings to create the impression that the Chief Minister's life was constantly under threat (when Modi was the Chief Minister of Gujarat) from potential assassins. Internal assassinations such as those of Haren Pandya or Sunil Joshi have been one of the cruder ways in which the right-wing seeks to evade legal scrutiny. The spinelessness of the judiciary and its overt or covert sympathies with the extreme Right was a major part of the story of the success of German fascism. We have not reached that state of judicial disintegration yet, and luckily we still have a Supreme Court that is beyond the direct reach of regimes immersed in criminality, even if its Special Investigation Teams can be subverted.

More insidious, however, is the inert grip of ideology. Much of the drive behind the emergence of a more repressive, authoritarian state in India is fuelled by a muscular nationalism that is now characteristic, in serial inert ways, of a large section of the urban middle classes, the media, the intelligentsia and capital. The Left has simply refused to campaign against this deluded form of patriotism which, because it imagines India as a global power, would rather have crores of rupees spent on defense and the nuclear industry than on constructing a viable public health system or affordable homes for the mass of people or even programmes to eradicate malnutrition. It is this nationalism, the pure self-delusion of a country that imagines it can be a major capitalist power on the back of mass deprivation and overt oppression, that has the potential for military conflict, a peculiarly destructive one when combined with that "continuous invocation of a threatening "other"" that Sumit and Tanika Sarkar ascribed to the new organised Hindutva of the 1990s.[37] The slogan "India First" rearticulates Golwalkar's mystical nationalism, the hyperorganicism of the nation as some sort of super-individual, as an animate being, but it does so in the idiom of big-power chauvinism, of the race for global hegemony, against the looming background of a potentially huge military-industrial complex that domestic capital is starting to whet its appetite for. For Golwalkar nationalism meant the dissolution of the individual in a larger whole. Gandhi therefore accurately described the RSS as a "communal body with a totalitarian outlook." Today those ideas have re-emerged in more sanitised and potentially more destructive ways. But where is the opposition to them? Where is the political culture that says, "Fascism shall not pass"?

REFERENCES

1. See Otto Bauer, 'Fascism', in Tom Bottomore and Patrick Goode, eds., *Austro-Marxism* (Oxford, 1978), pp. 167–86.
2. See Arthur Rosenberg, 'Fascism as a Mass Movement', *Historical Materialism*, 20.1 (2012), pp. 144–89.

3. R.G.L. Waite, *Vanguard of Nazism: The Free Corps Movement in Postwar Germany 1918–1923* (Cambridge, Mass., 1952).
4. Waite, *Vanguard of Nazism*, p. 39.
5. For example, Jane Caplan, 'The Historiography of National Socialism', in Michael Bentley, ed., *Routledge Companion to Historiography* (London, 1997).
6. Edouard Husson, *Une culpabilité ordinaire?Hitler, les Allemands et la Shoah* (Paris, 1997) p. 138.
7. Translated as Karl Jaspers, *The Question of German Guilt*, tr. E.B. Ashton (Westport, Conn., 1948).
8. Jaspers, *Question of German Guilt*, p. 25.
9. James Sheehan, 'National Socialism and German Society: Reflections on Recent Research', *Theory and Society*, 13 (1984), pp. 866–7.
10. Ian Kershaw, *The Nazi Dictatorship: Problems and Perspectives of Interpretation* (London, 2000), p. 103.
11. For these references (Browning, Kershaw, etc.) see my introduction to Rosenberg in *Historical Materialism*, 20.1 (2012), pp. 133ff.
12. Tim Mason, *Social Policy in the Third Reich: The Working Class and the 'National Community'*, tr. J. Broadwin, ed. Jane Caplan (Oxford, 1983), p. 282.
13. Jean-Paul Sartre, *Critique of Dialectical Reason, Volume One*, tr. Alan Sheridan-Smith (London, 1976), pp. 716ff.
14. Simone de Beauvoir, *Force of Circumstance*, tr. Richard Howard (Penguin Books, 1968) pp. 378, 381.
15. De Beauvoir, *Force of Circumstance*, pp. 396–7.
16. Sartre, *Critique*, p. 638.
17. Sartre, *Critique*, pp. 635–6.
18. Sartre, *Critique*, p. 636.
19. R. D. Laing and D. G. Cooper, *Reason and Violence: A Decade of Sartre's Philosophy* (London, 1971), p. 162.
20. Sartre, *Critique*, p. 644.
21. Sartre, *Critique*, p. 643.
22. Sartre, *Critique*, pp. 649–50.
23. Sartre, *Critique*, p. 650.
24. Sartre, *Critique*, p. 652.
25. Sartre, *Critique*, p. 644.
26. Sartre, *Critique*, p. 654.
27. Sartre, *Critique*, p. 653.
28. Sartre, *Critique*, p. 654.
29. Sartre, *Critique*, p. 757.

30. Sartre, *Critique*, p. 761. "After 1848…[French] employers were a curious historical product of the massacres for which they were collectively responsible without actually having committed them", p. 767.
31. Hannah Arendt, *The Origins of Totalitarianism* (New York, 1985) p. 312.
32. Subhash Gatade, *Godse's Children: Hindutva Terror in India* (New Delhi, 2011).
33. The best recent study is David Art, *Inside the Radical Right: The Development of Anti-Immigrant Politics in Western Europe* (Cambridge, 2011).
34. Ian Kershaw, *Hitler 1889–1936: Hubris* (London, 2001) p. 212.
35. Kershaw, *Hitler*, pp. 260, 267.
36. Dick Geary, 'Employers, Workers and the Collapse of Weimar', in Ian Kershaw, ed., *Weimar: Why Did German Democracy Fail?* (London, 1990), p. 104.
37. Tapan Basu and others, *Khaki Shorts and Saffron Flags* (New Delhi, 1993), p. 113.

Bibliography

Anweiler, Oskar, *Die Ratebewegung in Russland* (Leiden: E.J. Brill, 1958).

Arakelyan, Vazgen, *Privatisation as a Means to Property Redistribution in Republic of Armenia and in the Russian Federation* (academic dissertation, University of Tampere, Finland, 2005).

Bettelheim, Charles, *Class Struggles in the USSR* (New York and London: Monthly Review Press, 1976).

Bhagwati, Jagdish, *In Defence of Globalisation* (New York: Oxford University Press, 2004).

Bobbio, N., 'Gramsci and the Concept of Civil Society': *Civil Society and the State*, John Keane, ed. 73-100 (London: Verso, 1988).

Böhm-Bawerk Eugen von, *Karl Marx and the Close of His System* (edited by Paul M. Sweezy) (Philadelphia: Orion Editions, 1949).

Borkenau, Franz, *World Communism* (Ann Arbor: University of Michigan, 1962).

Boron, Atilio A., *Imperio & Imperialismo: Una lectura crítica de Michael Hardt y Antonio Negri* (5th ed) (*Empire & Imperialism: A Critical Reading of Michael Hardt and Antonio Negri*) (Buenos Aires: CLASCO, 2004).

Bremmer, Ian and C. Welt, 'Armenia's New Autocrats', *Journal of Democracy*, Vol. 8, No. 3, (1997), pp. 77-91.

Bush, Josh, "Why Is Russia's Productivity So Low?", *Bloomberg Businessweek* (2009), http://www. businessweek.com/ globalbiz/content/may2009/ gb2009058_530398.htm. Viewed on June 9, 2010.

Buttigieg, J.A. 1995. 'Gramsci on Civil Society', *Boundary* 2 22: 3, 1-32.

Buttigieg, J.A. 2004. 'Power, Consent and Gramsci', *Streaming MP3, International Gramsci Society*, (http://www.italnet.nd.edu/ gramsci/audio-video/).

Carr, E.H., *The Bolshevik Revolution* I (London: Macmillan, 1960).

Cohen, G.A., 'Marxism after the Collapse of the Soviet Union', *Journal of Ethics*, 3, (1999). Conquest, George Robert A., *The Great Terror: A Reassessment* (Oxford: Oxford University Press, 1990).

Crossman, Richard, (ed.) *The God That Failed* (New York: Columbia University Press, 2001).

Curti, Merle, *Human Nature in American Thought: A History* (Madison: University of Wisconsin Press, 1980).

Daniels, Robert V., 'Political Processes and Generational Change' in Archie Brown (ed.), *Political Leadership in the Soviet Union* (London: The MacMillan Press, 1989).

Daniels, Robert, *The Conscience of the Revolution.* (Cambridge: Harvard University Press, 1960).

Djilas, Milovan, *The New Class: An Analysis of the Communist System* (London: Thames & Hudson, 1957). Eyal, Gil, I Szelényi and E. Townsley, *Making Capitalism without Capitalists: Class Formation and Elite Struggle in Post-Communist Central Europe* (London: Verso, 2001).

Femia, J., 'Civil Society and the Marxist Tradition', *Civil Society: History and Possibilities,* eds. S. Kaviraj and S. Khilnani, 131-146 (Delhi: Cambridge University Press, 2002).

Ferro, Marc, *Des soviets au communism bureaucratique* (Paris: Gallimard, 1980).

Foster, J.B., 'Marx and the Environment', *In Defence of History: Marxism and Postmodern Agenda,* eds. E.M. Wood and J.B. Foster, 149-162 (New York: M R Press and Delhi: Aaakar Books, 1997, 2006).

Francese, J., 'Thoughts on Gramsci's Need. To Do Something 'Für ewig'', *Rethinking Marxism,* 21:1, 54 -66, 2009.

Friedman, Milton, *Capitalism and Freedom* (Chicago: The University of Chicago Press, 2002).

Fukuyama, Francis, 'The End of History?', *The National Interest,* Vol. 16, Summer (1989).

Getzler, Israel, *Kronstadt (1917-21), The Fate of a Soviet Democracy* (Cambridge: Cambridge University Press, 1983).

Gould, Stephen J., *The Mismeasure of Man* (New York: W.W. Norton, 1996).

Gramsci, A., *The Selections from Prison Notebooks,* New York: (International Publishers, 1971).

Green, M. 2002. 'Gramsci Cannot Speak: Presentation and Interpretations of Gramsci's Concept of the Subaltern'. *Rethinking Marxism* (14:3, 2002).

Habib, I., *The Agrarian System of Mughal India* (Bombay: Oxford University Publications, 1963).

Hardt, Michael and A. Negri, *Empire* (Cambridge, Massachusetts and London: Harvard University Press, 2000).

Hayek, Friedrich A., *The Road to Serfdom* (Chicago: The University of Chicago Press, 2007).

Heilbroner, Robert, 'The Triumph of Capitalism', *The New Yorker*, January 23, (1989).

Hoffman, David, *The Oligarchs: Wealth and Power in the New Russia*, (Perseus, 2002).

Hofstadter, Richard, *Social Darwinism in American Thought* (Revised Edition) (Boston: The Beacon Press, 1955).

Kagarlitsky, Boris, *Russia under Yeltsin and Putin* (London: Pluto, 2002).

Kaviraj, Sudipta, 'Perestroika: Reflections on the Theory of Power', *Social Scientist*, Vol. 17, No. 7/8, July-August, (1989).

Keane, J. (ed.), 1988b. *Civil Society and the State*. London: Verso.

Keane, J. 1988a. *Democracy and Civil Society*. London: Verso.

Kolakowski, Leszek, *Main Currents of Marxism: Its Rise, Growth, and Dissolution*, Vol. 2 (Oxford: Clarendon Press, 1978).

Lakatos, Imré, *The Methodology of Scientific Research Programmes: Philosophical Papers*, Vol. 1 (Cambridge: Cambridge University Press, 1978).

Lorenz, Richard, *Sozialgeschichte der Sowjet-union I (1917-45)* (Frankfurt a. Main: Suhrkampf, 1976).

Marcuse, Herbert, *Soviet Marxism: A Critical Analysis* (New York: Columbia University Press, 1958).

Marx, K., and Engels, F. 1976. *The German Ideology*. 1847. Moscow: Progress Publishers.

Marx, K., *Pre-Capitalist Economic Formations*, edited with an Introduction by E.J. Hobsbawm (London: Lawrence and Wishart, 1964).

Marx, Karl and F. Engels, *Manifesto of the Communist Party*, in *Marx Engels Collected Works*, Vol. 6 (London: Lawrence & Wishart, 1976).

Marx, Karl and Friedrich Engels, *Die Deutsche Ideologic*, in MEW (Berlin: Dietz, 1973).

Marx, Karl and Friedrich Engels, *Manifest der kommmunistischen Partei* (Frankfurt a. Main: Fischer Taschenbuch, 1979).

Marx, Karl, *Critique of the Gotha Programme*, in *Marx Engels Collected Works*, Vol. 24 (London: Lawrence & Wishart, 1989).

Marx, Karl, *Das Kapital I*, in *Marx-Engels Gesamtausgabe* (MEGA 11/6) (Berlin: Dietz, 1987).

Marx, Karl, *Konspekt von Bakunins Buch 'Statichkeit und Anarchie'* in *Marx-Engels Werke* (MEW) 18 (Berlin: Dietz, 1973).

Marx, Karl, *Misere de la philosophie*, in *Oeuvres: Economic* I (Paris: Gallimard, 1965).

Melkonian, Markar, 'The Karabagh Movement: A Balance Sheet' in Levon Chorbajian (ed.), *The Making of Nagorno-Karabagh: From Secession to Republic* (Basingstoke, UK/New York: Palgrave, 2001). A revised version is available at www.marxist.com/correspondence/karabagh_ movement 500.html.

Melkonian, Markar, *Marxism: A Post-Cold War Primer* (Boulder: Westview, 1996).

Menger, Carl, *Principles of Economics* (New York: New York University Press, 1981).

Miliband, R. 1983, 'State', *A Dictionary of Marxist Thought*, eds. Tom Bottomore and others, 464 - 468. Oxford: Blackwell.

Mouffe, C. and Laclau, E., *Hegemony and Socialist Strategy: Towards a Radical Democratic Politics* (London: Verso, 1985).

Mouffe, C. and Laclau, E. 1999. 'In Interview.' Ed. Ian Angus. Institute of Humanities, Simon Fraser University. (http://www.knowtv.com/primetime/conflicting/mouffe.html)

Myrdal, G., *Objectivity in Social Research*. London (Gerald Duckworth & Co., 1969).

Namboodiripad, E.M.S., "The Indian National Question: Need for Deeper Study", *Social Scientist*, December, (1982), No. 115.

Namboodiripad, E.M.S., "The Relevance of Lenin's 'Imperialism" to the Current World Situation" in Prabhat Patnaik ed. *Lenin and Imperialism* (Delhi: Orient Longman, 1986).

Namboodiripad, E.M.S., Adi Shankara and His Philosophy: A Marxist View, *Social Scientist*, January-February (1989), No.188-189.

Namboodiripad, E.M.S., *Kerala: Society and Politics* (New Delhi: National Book Centre, 1984).

Namboodiripad, E.M.S., *Selected Writings*, Volume 1 (Bombay: National Book Agency, 1982).

Namboodiripad, E.M.S., *The National Question in Kerala* (Bombay, 1952).

Nozick, Robert, *Anarchy, State, and Utopia* (New York: Basic Books, 1977).

Patnaik, A.K. 1988. 'Gramsci's Concept of Commonsense', *Economic and Political Weekly*, 23, 5: PE 2 – PE 10. (http://www.jstor.org/stable/4378042)

Peregalli, Arturo, *Stalinismo* (Genova: Graphos, 1993).

Pinker, Steven, *The Blank Slate: The Modern Denial of Human Nature* (New York: Penguin, 2002).

Popper, Karl, *The Open Society and Its Enemies* (Princeton: Princeton University Press, 1971).

Popper, Karl, *The Poverty of Historicism* (London and New York: Routledge, 2002).

Rabinowitch, A., *The Bolsheviks in Power* (Bloomington: Indiana University Press, 2007).

Resnick, Stephen A. and R.D. Wolff, 'Class Contradictions and the Collapse of the Soviet Union' in Daniel Egan and L.A. Chorbajian (ed.), *Power: A Critical Reader* (Upper Saddle River, NJ: Prentice Hall, 2005). Reprinted from: Resnick. and Wolff, *Class Theory and History* (London and New York: Routledge, 2002).

Rosenberg, W., 'Russian Labour and Bolshevik Power' in D. Kaiser (ed.), *The Workers' Revolution in Russia 1917* (Cambridge: Cambridge University Press, 1987).

Sarian, Armand, 'Economic Challenges Faced by the New Armenian State', *Demokratizatsiya*, Spring (2006). Look Smart Find Articles, http:// findarticles.com/p/articles/mi_qa3996/is_200604/ ai_n17174529/pg _1. Viewed on 15 June 2007.

Sartre, J.P., *Search for a Method* (New York: Vintage Books, 1963).

Sassoon, Anne S., 'Civil Society', *A Dictionary of Marxist Thought*, eds. Tom Bottomore and others, 72-74 (Oxford: Blackwell, 1983).

Satter, David, *Darkness at Dawn: The Rise of the Russian Criminal State* (New Haven and London: Yale University Press, 2003).

Segerstråle, Ullica, *Defenders of the Truth: The Socio-biology Debate* (Oxford and New York: Oxford University Press, 2000).

Serge, Victor, *Memoires d'un Revolutionnaire* (Paris: Laffont, 2001).

Sweezy, Paul, *Post-Revolutionary Society* (New York: Monthly Review Press, 1980).

Taylor, C., *Hegel* (Cambridge: Cambridge University Press, 1975).

Trotsky, Leon, *The Revolution Betrayed: What Is the Soviet Union and Where Is It Going?* (New York: Pathfinder Press, 1972).

White, Stephen, *Communism and Its Collapse: The Making of the Contemporary World* (London and New York: Routledge, 2001).

Wilson, Edward O., *On Human Nature* (Cambridge, MA and London: Harvard University Press, 2004).

World Bank, 'Unleashing Prosperity: Productivity Growth in Eastern Europe and the Former Soviet Union' (2008), http://sitere sources.worldbank.org/ ECAEXT/Resources/publica, viewed on June 9, 2010.

Notes on Contributors

Javeed Alam former Chairman of Indian Council of Social Science Research, New Delhi. He authored *Who Wants Democracy?* and *India: Living with Modernity.*

Arup Baisya is a social activist and writer based in Silchar, Assam.

Jairus Banaji is an international Marxist scholar and the author of many books among them are *Agrarian Change in Late Antiquity, Theory as History* and *Exploring the Economy of Late Antiquity.*

Sumanta Banerjee is a political commentator and a prolific writer who has authored books on colonialism, crime, urbanization and revolution. His main works are *In the Wake of Naxalbari* and *India's Simmering Revolution*

Pranab Bardhan is Professor Emeritus of Economics at the University of California, Berkeley. He has conducted theoretical and field research on rural institutions in developing countries, on the political economy of development policies and on international trade and globalization. He is the author of many books among them are *Land, Labour and Rural Poverty, Essays in Development Economics, The Political Economy of Development in India, Market Socialism: The Current Debate and Awakening Giants, Feet of Clay Assessing the Economic Rise of China and India.*

Dipankar Bhattacharya is General Secretary of the Communist Party of India (Marxist-Leninist) Liberation.

Prasenjit Bose is an economist and radical activist. He has a PhD in Economics from Centre for Economic Studies and Planning, Jawaharlal Nehru University, New Delhi. He is a regular contributor in debates on economics and public policy.

Kunal Chattopadhyay is Professor of Comparative Literature at the Jadavpur University, Kolkata and Editor of *Radical Socialist.* He is the author of *Marxism of Leon Trotsky.*

Paresh Chattopadhyay teaches political economy at the Department of Sociology, University of Quebec at Montreal. He is the author of *The Marxian Concept of Capital and the Soviet Experience* and *Marx's Associated Mode of Production: A Critique of Marxism.*

Bernard D'Mello is a member of the editorial staff of the *Economic &*

Political Weekly, Mumbai. He has authored *What is Maoism and Other Essays*.

Hiren Gohain is an Assamese literary and social critique. He is the author *of Tradition & Paradise Lost: A Heretical View, Assam: A Burning Question, On the Present Movement in Assam* and *Nature and Art in Shakespeare: An Essay on Hamlet*.

Murzban Jal is Professor and Director at the Centre for Educational Studies, Indian Institute of Education, Pune and author of *The Seductions of Karl Marx, Zoroastrianism: from Antiquity to the Modern Period* (ed.), *The New Militants, Why We Are Not Hindus* and *What Ails Indian Muslims* (ed. with Zaheer Ali).

Prakash Karat is former General Secretary of Communist Party of India (Marxist).

Himanshu Kumar is a Gandhian human rights activist.

Soma Marik is Associate Professor of History, RKSM Vivekananda Vidya Bhavan, Kolkata. She is an activist in Nari Nirjatan Pratirodh Mancha (Forum Against Oppression of Women, Kolkata) and the network Maitree.

Markar Melkonian teaches philosophy at California State University, Northridge. He is the author of *Marxism: A Post Cold War Primer* and *Richard Rorty's Politics: Liberalism at the End of the American Century*.

Arun Patnaik is Professor at Department of Political Science, University of Hyderabad, Hyderabad. He is a Gramsci scholar.

Prabhat Patnaik is Professor Emeritus at the Centre for Economic Studies and Planning, School of Social Sciences, Jawaharlal Nehru University, New Delhi. He is the author of many books among them are *Whatever happened to Imperialism and Other Essays, Re-envisioning Socialism* and *A Theory of Imperialism* (with Utsa Patnaik).

Kripa Shankar was professor at G.B. Pant Social Science Institute, Allahabad.

Cem Somel is an economist at Abant Izzet Baysal University, Bolu, Turkey.

Achin Vanaik was formerly with the Department of Political Science, Delhi University. He is the author of many books among them are *Masks of Empire, Communalism Contested: Religion, Modernity and Secularization, The Rise of Hindu Authoritarianism: Secular Claims, Communal Realities, Globalization and South Asia: Multidimensional Perspectives* and *The Painful Transition: Bourgeois Democracy in India*.